MW00356380

The Elgar Companion to
Austrian Economics

The Elgar Companions

The Elgar Companion to Institutional and Evolutionary Economics
Edited by Geoffrey M. Hodgson, Warren J. Samuels and Marc R. Tool

The Elgar Companion to Radical Political Economy
Edited by Philip Arestis and Malcolm Sawyer

The Elgar Companion to Classical Economics
Edited by Heinz D. Kurz and Neri Salvadori

The Elgar Companion to Austrian Economics

Edited by

Peter J. Boettke
Manhattan College
Riverdale, USA

Edward Elgar
Cheltenham, UK • Northampton, MA, USA

© Peter J. Boettke 1994

All rights reserved. No part of this publication may be reproduced, stored in a
retrieval system or transmitted in any form or by any means, electronic, mechanical
or photocopying, recording, or otherwise without the prior permission of the publisher.

Published by
Edward Elgar Publishing Limited
Glensanda House
Montpellier Parade
Cheltenham
Glos GL50 1UA
UK

Edward Elgar Publishing, Inc.
136 West Street
Suite 202
Northampton
Massachusetts 01060
USA

Paperback edition 1998

This book has been printed on demand to keep the title in print.

British Library Cataloguing in Publication Data
Elgar Companion to Austrian Economics
  I. Boettke, Peter J.
  330.15

Library of Congress Cataloguing in Publication Data
The Elgar companion to Austrian economics/edited by Peter J.
  Boettke
        p.   cm.
    1. Austrian school of economists.   I. Boettke, Peter J.
  HB98.E43   1994
  330.15'7—dc20   93–42453
                                                                       CIP

ISBN   1 85278 581 0 (cased)
        1 85898 776 8 (paperback)

Contents

PART II   FIELDS OF RESEARCH

PART III   APPLIED ECONOMICS AND PUBLIC POLICY

A   Political philosophy

B   Public policy economics

PART IV   HISTORY OF THOUGHT AND ALTERNATIVE SCHOOLS AND APPROACHES

A   Classic debates

PART V   CONCLUSION

Acknowledgements

I would like to thank Edward Elgar for initiating the project. Warren Samuels's vote of confidence in my ability to organize such a project at such an early stage in my professional career is gratefully appreciated. Warren's devotion to critical scholarship in economics and social theory, his openness to ideas and approaches different from his own, and his warm personality have provided a great example of how to live and learn in this academic business. Mario Rizzo and Don Lavoie saw the importance of organizing a volume such as this and encouraged me to undertake the project.

The Austrian Economics Program at New York University provided an ideal environment for embarking on the collection. Israel Kirzner and Mario Rizzo provided critical input and support throughout. Financial assistance from the Sarah Scaife Foundation for general support of the Austrian Program is gratefully acknowledged. In addition I would like to thank Sean Keenan, Gilberto Salgado, Charles Steele and Steve Sullivan for helpful research assistance on the project.

The bulk of the project was completed while I was a 1992–3 National Fellow at the Hoover Institution on War, Revolution and Peace at Stanford University. Dr Thomas Henriksen, the director of the National Fellows Program, and Ms Wendy Minkin, the administrator of the program, provide the fellows with a wonderful environment within which to work and learn. Ms Jennifer Medveckis provided helpful research and organizational assistance. Financial support for the 1992–3 academic year from Hoover and from the Earhart Foundation is gratefully acknowledged.

I should thank all those who contributed to the volume. As with any project of this size, not all those invited to contribute agreed to do so, but I was quite fortunate in the overwhelming positive response I did receive from scholars scattered throughout the world. I also received input from many of the contributors concerning potential additional topics to be covered in the volume and potential contributors to be contacted. I am grateful for the suggestions and time these individuals provided. Any remaining gaps or errors in organization are my responsibility. A special word of thanks must go to Ms Julie Leppard of Edward Elgar Publishing Limited who supervised the technical production of the manuscript.

My wife, Rosemary, and our two sons, Matthew and Stephen, provide the foundation for my life and work, and I greatly appreciate their patience and loving support.

Finally, I would like to thank my teachers in Austrian economics. At Grove City College, Hans Sennholz introduced me to the writings of Mises and Hayek, and changed my career aspirations. At George Mason University, Don Lavoie refined my understanding of Austrian Economics and acted as my mentor and friend throughout graduate school. At New York University, Israel Kirzner has deepened my understanding of Austrian economics and serves as a role model of careful and rigorous scholarship. I am grateful to these three gentlemen for all they have taught me.

Contributors

Mark Addleson, Program on Social and Organizational Learning, George Mason University, Fairfax.

Gary M. Anderson, Department of Economics, California State University, Northridge.

Charles W. Baird, Department of Economics and the Smith Center, California State University, Hayward.

Robert J. Batemarco, Department of Business and Economics, Marymount College, Tarrytown, NY and the Foundation for Economic Education, Irvington, NY.

Don Bellante, Department of Economics, University of South Florida, Tampa.

Bruce L. Benson, Department of Economics, Florida State University, Tallahassee.

Walter Block, Department of Economics, College of the Holy Cross, Worcester, Massachusetts.

Peter J. Boettke, Department of Economics, New York University.

Samuel Bostaph, Department of Economics, University of Dallas, Irving.

Donald J. Boudreaux, Department of Legal Studies, Clemson University, South Carolina.

William N. Butos, Department of Economics, Trinity College, Hartford.

Alejandro A. Chafuen, president, Atlas Economic Research Foundation, Fairfax.

Gregory B. Christainsen, Department of Economics, California State University, Hayward.

Roy E. Cordato, Lundy-Fetterman School of Business, Campbell University, North Carolina.

Robin Cowan, Department of Economics, University of Western Ontario, London.

Tyler Cowen, Department of Economics, George Mason University, Fairfax.

Thomas J. DiLorenzo, Department of Economics, Loyola University, Baltimore.

James A. Dorn, Department of Economics, Towson State University.

Kevin Dowd, School of Financial Studies and Law, Sheffield Hallam University.

John B. Egger, Department of Economics, Towson State University.

Jerome Ellig, Program on Social and Organizational Learning, George Mason University, Fairfax.

Ulrich Fehl, Department of Economics, Philipps-Universität, Marburg, Germany.

Robert Hébert, Department of Economics, Auburn University.

Paul Heyne, Department of Economics, University of Washington, Seattle.

Jack High, Graduate School of Business, Harvard University, Boston.

Friedrich Hinterberger, Division for Eco-Restructuring, Wuppertal Institute for Climate, Environment and Energy, Liebig University, Germany.

Kevin D. Hoover, Department of Economics, University of California, Davis.

Steven Horwitz, Department of Economics, St Lawrence University, Canton.

Sanford Ikeda, Department of Economics, State University of New York, Purchase.

Anthony de Jasay, independent scholar, Palvel, France.

Sean Keenan, Department of Economics, New York University.

Wolfgang Kerber, economist, Walter Eucken Institut, Freiburg, Germany.

Israel M. Kirzner, Department of Economics, New York University.

Arjo Klamer, Art and Cultural Sciences, Erasmus University, Rotterdam, The Netherlands, and Department of Economics, George Washington University, Washington, DC.

Peter G. Klein, Department of Economics, University of California, Berkeley.

Roger G. Koppl, Department of Economics and Finance, Fairleigh Dickinson University, Madison.

Randall S. Kroszner, Graduate School of Business, University of Chicago.

Richard Langlois, Department of Economics, University of Connecticut, Storrs.

Don Lavoie, Program on Social and Organizational Learning, George Mason University, Fairfax.

Peter Lewin, Department of Economics, University of Dallas, Irving.

Fiona C. Maclachlan, Department of Economics, Manhattan College, Riverdale.

G.B. Madison, Department of Philosophy, McMaster University, Hamilton, Canada.

E.C. Pasour, Department of Agricultural and Resource Economics, North Carolina State University, Raleigh.

David L. Prychitko, Department of Economics, State University of New York, Oswego.

Ralph Raico, Department of History, SUNY College, Buffalo.

W. Duncan Reekie, Department of Business Economics, University of the Witwatersrand, Johannesburg, South Africa.

Mario J. Rizzo, Department of Economics, New York University.

Peter Rosner, Institut für Wirtschaftswissenschaften, University of Vienna, Austria.

Charles K. Rowley, Department of Economics, George Mason University, Fairfax.

Malcolm Rutherford, Department of Economics, University of Victoria, Canada.

Joseph T. Salerno, Department of Economics, Pace University, New York.

Andrew Schotter, Department of Economics, New York University.

Kurt Schuler, independent scholar, Arlington, Virginia.

Mark Skousen, Department of Economics, Rollins College, Winter Park.

Barry Smith, Department of Philosophy, SUNY, Buffalo.

Charles N. Steele, Department of Economics, New York University.

Erich W. Streissler, Department of Economics, University of Vienna, Austria.

M.E. Streit, Max-Plank-Institut zur Erforschung von Wirtschaftssystemen, Jena, Germany.

P.D.F. Strydom, economist, Sankorp Ltd, Sandton, South Africa.

Esteban F. Thomsen, economist, Techint, Buenos Aires, Argentina.

Mark Thornton, Department of Economics, Auburn University.

Viktor Vanberg, Center for Study of Public Choice, George Mason University, Fairfax.

Karen I. Vaughn, Department of Economics, George Mason University, Fairfax.

Richard E. Wagner, Department of Economics and Center for Study of Public Choice, George Mason University, Fairfax.

Deborah Walker, Department of Economics, Loyola University, New Orleans.

Ulrich Witt, Department of Economics, Albert-Ludwigs Universität, Freiburg, Germany.

Leland B. Yeager, Department of Economics, Auburn University.

Zenon Zygmont, Department of Economics, Reed College, Portland.

1 Introduction

Peter J. Boettke

The Austrian school of economics is not monolithic. There are various strands and subcultures within the contemporary Austrian school. There are, for example, those who think of Austrian economics as a branch of mainstream neoclassical economics, there are those who see the school as representative of a radical alternative to the mainstream, and there are those who see the school mainly within a broader program of social theory. Moreover, this divergence of opinion is not a recent phenomenon. The tension between the different interpretations of the Austrian school can be felt throughout its history.

Carl Menger's *Principles of Economics*, when published in 1871, was a challenge to both classical political economy and the German historical school. Most historians of economics reserve a place for Menger alongside Leon Walras and William Stanley Jevons as one of the co-founders of the marginalist revolution and the birth of neoclassical economics. All three sought to provide a general theory of economic action based on marginalist principles of individual decision making. Menger, though, sought to distance himself from both Walras's and Jevons's analytical approach, and not simply on grounds of product differentiation in the textbook market. Menger's criticisms were substantive and argued that the mathematical approach to understanding human decision making simply could not get at the essence of economic phenomena which the marginalist revolution in his hands was attempting to unmask. Menger represented an alternative not only to classical political economy and German historicism, but also to the emerging theory of neoclassicism.

The next generation of Austrian economists, Eugen von Böhm-Bawerk and Friedrich von Wieser, did not view themselves as radical alternatives, but rather contributors, to the mainstream of neoclassicism. And to a large extent this self-image was justified. Vienna became a leading center for economic thought in the period from 1880 up to the 1930s. Austrian contributions to basic choice theory (such as ordinal marginal utility theory and the concept of opportunity cost), capital and interest theory, monetary theory and business cycle theory, market theory and development were incorporated into the mainstream body of economic thought throughout the world. By the 1930s it could be, and was, legitimately argued that all that was important in the Austrian literature was embodied within neoclassicism. Yet there remained something radically different about Austrian economics: (1) it was not mathematical, (2) it was often philosophical, (3) the dynamic nature of economic activity took center stage, and (4) it dealt with social and political issues beyond market exchange and production. The Austrians were quintessential members of the mainstream of economic thought, but their methodological position and analytical approach in monetary theory, capital theory and even basic price theory forced them into increasing confrontations with the mainstream of English language economics.

The tension within Austrian economics and its relationship to neoclassicism can be seen quite clearly in Ludwig von Mises's classic work, *Human Action: A Treatise on Economics*, published in English in 1949. Mises's book was at one and the same time an embodiment of orthodox economics and a radical tome in political economy. Here Mises offered an alternative way to do economics and social science from the received wisdom of his day on a methodological and analytical front. But Mises also referred throughout *Human Action* to the teachings of 'modern economics' and placed himself within the mainstream camp against the unorthodox teachings of Keynesians, welfare state interventionists and radical socialists. This tension, it should be stressed, was not due to a delusional fantasy on Mises's part, but inherent within the various strands of Austrian economics and their relationship to developments in neoclassical economics.

Additional indirect evidence for this position comes from an examination of the reception of the major personalities in the economics profession who were trained in the Austrian tradition at the University of Vienna under either Böhm-Bawerk or Wieser or attended the Mises seminar on economic theory. The list of names would include such prominent figures within twentieth-century economic thought as Joseph Schumpeter, Friedrich Hayek, Gottfried Haberler, Fritz Machlup, Oskar Morgenstern, Lionel Robbins and others. Individuals like Schumpeter, Haberler, Machlup, Morgenstern and Robbins would carve out their own unique place within economics for their theoretical nuances (due in large part to Austrian themes of imperfect knowledge, dynamic market processes, the importance of time and methodology), but they were still viewed by most other economists, and most importantly by themselves, as mainstream neoclassical economists. Mises and Hayek, on the other hand, would be increasingly viewed as part of an alternative approach to economic theory, and their work was viewed as part of a broader project to revitalize classical liberal social theory.

The modern revival of interest in the Austrian school, and specifically the work of the major figures who orchestrated that resurgence in the 1970s, Israel Kirzner, Murray Rothbard and Ludwig Lachmann, continued to reflect this tension. Part of this can be attributed to the intellectual temperament of the individuals in question. Kirzner, for example, concentrated his work on providing neoclassical economics with the missing theory of economic processes. The Austrian theory of entrepreneurship, according to Kirzner, provided the disequilibrium foundations of equilibrium economics that were required to complete the neoclassical project of explicating the operating principles of the price system. On the other hand, Lachmann sought allies among heterodox critics of mainstream economics and, in particular, the subjectivist critics of the resurgence of late classical formalism as represented in the equilibrium preoccupation of modern economics. The extension of subjectivism from values to expectations, Lachmann argued, would complete the revolution in economic theorizing begun by Menger in the 1870s. Notice that both Kirzner and Lachmann were critical of equilibrium economics, but they differed on scientific strategy and the meaning of the implications of their criticism. Rothbard pushed for an even more radical approach than either Kirzner or Lachmann. The Rothbardian system challenged the logical status of mainstream economics on its own grounds. Mainstream utility theory, market structure theory, public goods theory, monetary theory and welfare economics were all found to possess logical flaws which demanded reconstruction from an Austrian perspective. In addition, Rothbard explicitly sought to construct an interdisciplinary social theory with the purpose of advancing radical liberalism. A unified science of liberty was to be constructed by Rothbard and his followers.

Emphasizing the intellectual temperament of these scholars in their choice of strategy to advance Austrian economics masks the real substantive issues involved. Kirzner, Lachmann and Rothbard can legitimately claim that their research program was Austrian and not a deviation from the tradition. The work of Mises and Hayek, for example, reflects a mix of all three stratagems throughout their career. Technical economics, philosophical radicalism and a passionate commitment to liberalism are weaved together throughout the finest contributions in the Austrian literature. Contemporary Austrian economists are still in the process of grappling with these issues. Debates within and between the various factions continue over such fundamental issues as the extension of subjectivism, the use of equilibrium models, the nature of human choice, the methodological foundations of the human sciences, the role of political theory and the relationship of ethical argumentation to economic science.

Despite the heterogeneity of opinion within the Austrian school on these and other issues, there exist common characteristics of the work done in this tradition that justify the label of a 'school' of thought. The basic set of questions Austrians raise, and the approach to answering those questions, reflect *the* Austrian approach. In this tradition, the task of economics is twofold: first, the economist must render economic phenomena intelligible in terms of purposive human action; second, the economist must trace the unintended consequences of those actions. In order to accomplish these tasks, Austrians believe that three basic methodological tenets should be adhered to: (1) methodological individualism, (2) methodological subjectivism, and (3) theoretical attention should be on processes rather than equilibrium states. From Menger on this has been the unifying task and method of approach of the Austrian school of economics.

This *Companion to Austrian Economics* was organized in a manner intended to highlight the common ground between all the branches of Austrian economics while demonstrating the breadth and diversity of the school. The idea was to create an encyclopedia of the key concepts relating to the concerns traditionally associated with Austrian economics written by scholars from around the world. In the invitation process, no effort was made to impose a particular view of Austrian economics on the project, but rather to respect the various views that make up contemporary Austrian economics. In fact, many of the authors would not even consider themselves 'Austrian', but their work demonstrates a basic similarity and interest in questions which have historically been associated with the Austrian school.

Parts I to III were organized to reflect a general Austrian methodological point about the levels of economic science. From Menger on, Austrians have argued that there are three distinct levels of discourse within economics. There is *pure theory*, which generates timeless and universal principles of human action. This represents the hard core of Austrian theory. This hard core, however, has been 'defended' on various philosophical grounds throughout the history of Austrian economics, from essentialism to neo-Kantian apriorism, to phenomenological reflection, to contemporary hermeneutics. The second level of analysis is *applied theory*, in which the general principles of pure theory are worked out within different institutional environments and social contexts. That individuals have ends and utilize means to obtain those ends is incontrovertible, but the nature and consequences of purposive human action are institutionally contingent and contextual. The third level of economic research is *history and public policy*. At this level, the principles derived from pure theory and applied theory are employed to aid interpretation of concrete historical phenomena or contemporary issues in public policy.

The rationale for theory in Austrian economics since Menger's *Principles* has always been to aid the act of interpretation. In other words, the sole purpose of theory was to provide a framework which would enable researchers to improve historical understanding. Public policy economics, from this perspective, is an example of contemporary economic history. It is important to stress, however, that in the Austrian tradition history and empirical data cannot be employed unambiguously to falsify a theory. Rather, data represents facts which must be organized and interpreted through a theoretical framework. Since all facts are theory-laden, appeals to the data cannot constitute a final arbiter in disputes. The appeal to objective data is a non-starter because the data are incapable of speaking for themselves. The meaning of the data is what is in question. Historical interpretation illustrates the power of the theoretical framework adopted.

Refutation of any theory is an exercise in logic and scholarship. A theory which has been demonstrated to be logically flawed, ignorant of basic facts, uninformed about the empirical magnitude of events and lacking in perspective can be rejected. Realism matters within the Austrian tradition. Theoretical exercises, therefore, strive to be both logically coherent and relevant to the everyday world within which individuals live. Economic theory constitutes a 'story' of the way individuals behave within different contexts. Historical research constitutes an examination and a 'fitting' of the facts to tell a coherent and relevant story. The assessment of different historical interpretations is the outcome of a process which enlists the community of scholars in a free and open dialogue. Science is not a solipsistic exercise characterized by certain methods or procedures, but rather a set of values shared concerning the importance of logic, the use of acceptable evidence and rules of behavior amongst scholars. Within a certain institutional infrastructure, the scientific process, like the market process, generates progress in knowledge out of the seemingly anarchistic competition between individual researchers that is far greater than that of any single participant. There simply is no process outside the 'free market for ideas' that can be relied on to generate the progress of knowledge. No method or procedure can take the place of the open dialogue of questioning and answering.

Many individuals have misinterpreted the Austrian methodological argument concerning theory and history. It is often asserted that Austrians disregard empirical research, but, as has just been argued, this is a misreading of the Austrian tradition. Instead, developing a sensibility towards empirical information and the writing of better history is the goal of theoretical research within the Austrian tradition. What Austrians have repeatedly stressed, however, is that interpretation is a product of theory choice and, therefore, the significant debates in the social sciences are theoretical debates.

Part IV introduces the classic theoretical debates in the history of Austrian economics. In addition, various predecessors of the Austrian school and contemporary alternative schools and approaches are discussed.

Each entry in the *Companion* is followed by a list of references which can serve as further reading on each topic. It was intended that the entries should serve simultaneously to introduce students to the Austrian school and be able to serve as an important research tool for scholars working within the Austrian tradition. There was an almost inexhaustible array of topics that could be covered. As mentioned above, Austrian economists have made contributions to technical economics, methodology of the social sciences, political theory, political science, and so on. Some omissions are evident in the final product, as is some repetition. It is hoped that these flaws are not serious enough to hinder the teaching function and research impact of the project.

One final note. It was decided early on to eliminate biographical entries. This was for two reasons: first, informative biographies exist elsewhere and the interested reader can find the relevant sources; and second, it was thought desirable to discount personalities and focus attention on the questions and conceptualizations of the Austrian school. It is true that Austrian economics is the economics of Menger, Mises and Hayek, for example, but it is much more than that. Contemporary Austrian economics is a live and growing body of literature that raises important questions for economic and social organization. Every school of thought has its major figures, but the important factor for continued relevance of any school is the power of its basic ideas.

PART I

METHODOLOGY AND THEORETICAL CONCEPTS IN AUSTRIAN ECONOMICS

A Methodological principles

2 Methodological individualism

Gregory B. Christainsen

The practice of viewing social wholes (such as national economies) as the product of individual actions has been a feature of the Austrian school of economics since its inception. This 'methodological individualism', as it was eventually called, was endorsed by Carl Menger as early as the preface of his *Grundsätze der Volkwirthschaftslehre*, published in 1871.

The methodology to be followed in the social sciences is seen by Austrians as a fundamental field of study, something to be pursued rigorously before work in various subdisciplines is undertaken. In Menger's time, this focus provoked a debate with the thinkers of the German historical school. During the 1930s, this focus led Hayek to question not only the conclusions of Keynesian analysis, but the intellectual foundation of the entire Keynesian approach. And today, questions of methodology have been raised anew as scholars try to unravel the complexities of cultural evolution.

Menger's only other book-length work, *Untersuchungen über die Methode der Socialwissenschaften und der politischen Ökonomie insbesondere* (1883), was devoted exclusively to the question of how one should approach the study of social phenomena. The passage below provides a good summary of his essential position:

> the phenomena of 'national economy' are by no means direct expressions of the life of a nation as such or direct results of an 'economic nation'. They are, rather, the *results* of all the innumerable individual economic efforts in the nation, and they therefore are not to be brought within the scope of our theoretical understanding from the point of view of the above fiction. Rather the phenomena of 'national economy', just as they present themselves to us in reality as results of individual economic efforts, must also be theoretically interpreted in this light.

Menger's position was adopted to varying degrees by later members of the Austrian school, but as was true of other key features of Austrian economics – for example, subjectivism – methodological individualism was ultimately rejected by influential players in the development of economic thought.

The split between the Austrians and other economists regarding methodology was best illustrated by the discussions of business cycle theory during the 1920s and 1930s. Before the First World War, Keynes had reviewed Ludwig von Mises's book, *Theorie des Geldes und der Umlaufsmittel* (1912), but because of Keynes's limited knowledge of German, the book did not make much of an impression on him. Mises had attempted to put forward a business cycle theory that was firmly grounded in the incentives facing individual decision makers.

In the 1920s, however, Keynes's discussions of the gold standard were conducted almost entirely in terms of aggregate concepts, in apparent disregard of their respective microstructures. That is, he spoke of the relationship between the money supply, the aggregate level of prices and the aggregate level of nominal wages. He paid almost no attention to *relative* prices and wages. This disregard for the microeconomic issues involved was especially evident after the arrival of F.A. Hayek in London in 1931. Hayek's *Prices and Production* (1931) took the economists of Britain by storm. Its strong appeal lay in its effort to employ methodological individualism so as to integrate the theory of money with the rest of microeconomic theory. Said Hayek:

> If ... monetary theory still attempts to establish causal relations between aggregates or general averages, this means that monetary theory lags behind the development of economics in general. In fact, neither aggregates nor averages do act upon one another, and it will never be possible to establish necessary connections of cause and effect between them as we can between individual phenomena, individual prices, etc.

In opposition to Hayek's insistence on an individualistic (microeconomic) approach was Keynes's collectivistic ('macroeconomic') approach. This fundamental difference in outlook was the source not only of theoretical disagreements, but of disputes about the usefulness of statistical analysis in the social sciences. The most important theoretical disagreements concerned the relationship between total consumption and total investment and the relationship between the aggregate demand for final goods and services and total employment. Keynes argued that an increased demand for consumer goods will reliably lead to an increase in investment. There may indeed be many instances where this relationship holds, but Hayek argued that, particularly in the neighborhood of full employment, there are plausible sets of microeconomic conditions, for example if the costs of employing capital goods are rising relative to wage rates, under which increased consumption might cause a *decrease* in investment.

With respect to the relationship between aggregate demand and total employment, Hayek presented a detailed microeconomic analysis that ended up echoing Mill's dictum that 'demand for commodities is not demand for labor'. What ultimately matters, according to Hayek, is the relationships between supply and demand in all of the different product and input markets. These relationships depend, in turn, on the entire structure of product and input prices and the substitutability of inputs across industries. If there were general unemployment, for example, and increased product demand was felt only in particular sectors in which there were not idle resources, the increased demand might lead only to increases in prices in these sectors and not to an across-the-board increase in employment (especially if labor were not very substitutable across sectors).

More recently, of course, the 'macroeconomic' literature on the Phillips curve has argued that increases in aggregate demand are likely to produce increases in total employment only if they produce increases in product prices that exceed what people had anticipated. The misunderstanding of the nature of the Phillips curve by Keynesian analysts was perhaps the most spectacular example of the misuse of statistical analysis by prominent economists. Phillips's original presentation did indeed suggest that there was a reliable inverse relationship between (the rate of) aggregate unemployment and (the rate of change of) the aggregate nominal wage rate. Without a detailed understanding of the respective microstructures of these aggregates, however, statistical analysis was bound to lead to the conclusion that increases in aggregate demand that brought about 'just a little more wage and price inflation' were desirable in order to reduce the misery of high unemployment. In this fashion Keynesian economics contributed to the emergence of 'stagflation', because it turned out that the increased demand could lead to inflation, but offered no long-term solution to labor market discoordination.

The practice of methodological individualism should thus make us pause before accepting the projections of econometric models. The main point is that econometric models assume an underlying structure of individual actions and, if the nature of individual relationships changes, the projections of the model will prove unreliable. In *Prices and Production*, Hayek commented that even the quantity theory of money – the view that 'the' money supply determines the aggregate price level – must be questioned as being collectivistic, and he eventually decided to probe more deeply into issues in the philosophy of science rather than continue his quarrels with economists who talked on a completely different plane from himself. In his 'Personal Recollections of Keynes and the "Keynesian Revolution"' (1978), Hayek emphasized that his displeasure with Keynes's *General Theory* (1936) was primarily methodological: 'my disagreement with that book did not refer so much to any detail of the analysis as to the general approach followed in the whole work. The real issue was the validity of what we now call macroanalysis.' Hayek eventually devoted an entire book, *The Counter-Revolution of Science* (1952), to questions of methodology.

Note that, at the time of Hayek's cash with Keynes, the Econometric Society was being formed, and Hayek was deeply involved in the debate over socialism. Many of those affiliated with the Econometric Society were part of a larger intellectual movement that held that a greater use of statistical analysis offered the prospect of efficient social planning that could help to foster a more humane and just world. The social sciences would thereby become both more 'scientific' and more 'social'. Keynes's theories, and the associated call for active government management of economic affairs, fit in nicely with many of these ideas.

Hayek feared, however, that extensive social planning based on a misguided use of statistics would not only result in colossal misallocations of resources, but lead to a politicization of society and a probable loss of individual liberty as well. It should therefore not have been a surprise when, on the occasion of the awarding of his Nobel Prize in economics, Hayek again stressed the importance of an individualistic approach to the social sciences.

In his Nobel memorial lecture (1974) Hayek argued that there is a fundamental difference between most of the subject matter of the social sciences and the subject matter of the natural sciences. This difference rules out most attempts to use the empirical methods of the latter in the study of the former. In both cases meaningful theories must, in principle, be empirically testable, but Hayek argued that the phenomena of the social sciences are such that empirical testing is often practically impossible because the characteristics of all the individuals whose actions generate the overall order under study are just too complex to capture with statistics. These characteristics include subtle circumstances of time and place, subconscious dispositions and habits. If the analyst nevertheless goes on to treat only what is measurable as important, and then tries to establish causal relationships among measurable entities, his explanations of social phenomena are likely to be seriously deficient. The measurement and use of aggregate variables in macroeconomics is a case in point.

None of the leading Austrian economists was oblivious to the possible usefulness of statistical analysis within a limited sphere. Menger believed that common experience provided evidence of various types of individual actions that were likely to occur, and even some knowledge of the probabilities that certain typical situations will arise. What Hayek has called 'pattern predictions' – qualitative judgements based on 'if–then' statements as opposed to quantitative predictions of specific events – may then be possible. Specific predictions cannot be reliably made because they would require the analyst to have complete information about every single individual taking part in the process under study.

In the same vein, a sports commentator may be able to form a plausible theory of the factors that make for a successful team, but he will be unable to forecast with regularity the precise results to be expected in particular contests. The idea that any group of people, especially people subject to political pressures, is competent to forecast 'how far real GNP may fall below its potential' and to determine 'aggregate spending multipliers and corrective changes in fiscal policy' is viewed by Austrians as preposterous. In *The Fatal Conceit* (1988) Hayek did say that statistical studies of the connections between aggregate entities 'may sometimes, I concede, indicate some *vague* possibilities, but they certainly do not explain the processes involved in generating them'. In other words, there are again complex and non-stationary microstructures of individual actions that underlie these aggregate entities; the relationships among aggregates will only be stable insofar as these microstructures are *not* changing during the period under study.

The most common objection to the practice of methodological individualism is that individuals do not exist as mere atoms. They inhabit families, communities and nations that help to shape their respective outlooks on life. The essential culture that they inhabit may have existed long before today's individuals were born, and it may continue long after they are gone. Of what use, then, is a theory of individual action (that is, microeconomics or 'praxeology') that abstracts from this culture? Ludwig von Mises (1949) provided this reply, with reference to praxeology:

> Most of a man's daily behavior is simply routine ... He does many things because he was trained in his childhood to do them, because other people behave in the same way, and because it is customary in his environment. He acquires habits, he develops automatic reactions. But he indulges in these habits only because he welcomes their effects. As soon as he discovers that the pursuit of the habitual way may hinder the attainment of ends considered as more desirable, he changes his attitude ... Indulgence in a routine which possibly could be changed is action.
>
> Praxeology is not concerned with the changing content of acting, but with its pure form and its categorical structure. The study of the accidental and environmental features of human action is the task of history.

And surely Mises could have added that history itself consists of individual actions.

At the end of his life, Hayek had started to analyse the processes by which cultures evolve. In this effort he claimed to be true to the principles of methodological individualism. He often spoke of the natural selection of cultures, however, and his discussions sometimes invoked the biological concept of 'group' selection. To some commentators, this meant that Hayek had deviated from an individualistic approach. Hayek himself argued that, whether biological selection operates at the level of the individual organism, or, rather, with reference to a whole species, is an unresolved scientific question. He also said that his view of cultural evolution did not depend on the resolution of this issue in the field of biology.

At the end of the twentieth century, then, the integration of the pure theory of individual action with the evolution of cultures remains a controversial subject both inside and outside the Austrian school.

See also:
Chapter 10: Ideal type methodology in economics; Chapter 11: Praxeology; Chapter 9: Causation and genetic causation in economic theory

Bibliography
Hayek, F.A. (1931), *Prices and Production*, London: Routledge & Sons.
Hayek, F.A. (1952), *The Counter-Revolution of Science*, Glencoe, IL: Free Press.
Hayek, F.A. (1974), 'The Pretence of Knowledge', published (1978) in *New Studies in Philosophy, Politics, Economics and the History of Ideas*, Chicago: University of Chicago Press.
Hayek, F.A. (1978), 'Personal Recollections of Keynes and the "Keynesian Revolution"', in *New Studies in Philosophy, Politics, Economics and the History of Ideas*, Chicago: University of Chicago Press.
Hayek, F.A. (1988), *The Fatal Conceit: The Errors of Socialism*, ed. W.W. Bartley, III, Chicago: University of Chicago Press.
Keynes, J.M. (1936), *The General Theory of Employment, Interest and Money*, New York: Macmillan.
Menger, C. (1871), *Grundsätze der Volkwirthschaftslehre*, translated (1950) as *Principles of Economics*, ed. J. Dingwall and B.F. Hoselitz; reprinted, New York: New York University Press, 1981.
Menger, C. (1883), *Untersuchungen über die Methode der Socialwissenschaften und der politischen Ökonomie insbesondere*, translated (1963) as *Problems of Economics and Sociology*, ed. L. Schneider, Urbana: University of Illinois Press.
Mises, L. von (1912), *Theorie des Geldes und der Umlaufsmittel*, translated (1980) as *Theory of Money and Credit*, Indianapolis: Liberty Classics.
Mises, L. von (1949), *Human Action, A Treatise on Economics*, New Haven: Yale University Press.

3 Subjectivism

Steven Horwitz

Although the Austrian school does share some core methodological concepts with most other economists (for example, methodological individualism broadly understood), the fundamental tenet that distinguishes Austrians from neoclassicism is their belief in subjectivism. It is from subjectivism that so many uniquely Austrian insights flow. As Hayek (1952, p. 52) argued 40 years ago, all of the major advances in economics over the preceding 100 years were steps in the further progression of the subjectivist perspective. He points specifically to the work of Mises as the most consistent of these applications and argues that all of Mises's core theoretical conclusions can be traced back to their subjectivist underpinnings. It is equally true that all of the major new insights and refinements of Austrian economics (though not economics generally) in the 40 years since Hayek wrote are also the result of the consistent pursuit of subjectivism.

For Austrians, subjectivism is more than just an economic methodology, it is an entire approach to the study of human action. The human sciences (including economics) study the interaction between humans and things, or humans and humans. In particular, the theoretical human sciences attempt to explain the unintended and unforeseen patterns of results that evolve from these human interactions. Within economics, this approach leads very naturally into the Austrian emphasis on spontaneous order, where the emergence of institutions and other orderly patterns of behavior are explained as the unintended social resultant of actions driven by the subjective perceptions of individuals (Hayek, 1973, chapter 2).

Consequently, the economist offering a theoretical explanation of human interaction and institutions must start with the subjective meaning that individuals attach to their actions. As Hayek (1952, pp. 44, 53) puts it, 'So far as human actions are concerned the things *are* what the acting people think they are ... [and] unless we can understand what the acting people mean by their actions any attempt to explain them ... is bound to fail.' This is the fundamental subjectivist point: social scientific explanations must start with the subjective mental states of the actors being studied. This requires that social scientists take seriously the roles of context and interpretation and recognize that it is the subjective perceptions of actors that drive their actions, not the objective reality that might underlie the situation. Subjectivism argues that we will be unable to attach meaning to human action if we attempt to describe it in terms that make no references to human perceptions and plans. Austrians argue that without references to meaning our understanding of the social world is of a meager and unsatisfactory kind.

In many ways it is only natural that Austrians adopt a full-blown subjectivist perspective, in that it was Carl Menger who founded the Austrian school on the basis of the subjective theory of economic value. Rather than adopt the labor theory of value of some of his predecessors, Menger (1981, p. 146, emphasis in original) argued that 'value is entirely subjective in nature. ... Goods always have value *to* certain economizing individuals and this value is also *determined* only by these individuals.' This enabled Menger to reorient economics away from a study of the behavior of businessmen and the creation and division of wealth, to a more comprehensive science of human action. In particular, Menger created a theory of price formation that began with the subjective preferences of participants on both sides of the market. This is in contrast to approaches that recognize subjectivity on the demand side, but see the supply side in terms of objectifiable production or opportunity costs.

Unfortunately, as Mises (1933, pp. 172ff) notes, Menger did not pursue this subjectivism consistently enough. Menger tried to distinguish between 'real' and 'imaginary' wants, based on whether individuals correctly understood a good's objective ability to satisfy a want. The next step forward in the subjectivist paradigm was to recognize that the subjectivity of value depended on a further subjectivity, namely knowledge. An explanation of market phenomena need not make judgements about the accuracy of actors' knowledge. All that was necessary for an explanation of, for example, an actor's willingness to pay a certain price, was the subjective *perception* of the actor. Although one might realize ex post that the good purchased was not what one thought it was, this is irrelevant for the explanation of price. The actor's mental state at the moment of choice is where explanations of price formation and market processes begin.

James Buchanan (1969) later argued that subjectivism needs to be thoroughly applied on the cost side of the market as well. For Buchanan, and most Austrians, all costs are seen as subjective opportunity costs. While neoclassicism surely recognizes the notion of opportunity cost, it normally does so by objectivizing it into forgone revenues. Buchanan's point was that opportunity costs are ultimately foregone *expected utility*, from either purchases not make or the cash equivalent of sales not made. Because cost was forgone and never actually experienced, it could never be objectively known. Even the chooser does not know what she forgoes precisely because she forgoes it. What informs choice, argued Buchanan, is our expectation of what each option might bring us. Consistent with the other work of Austrians (see below), we cannot know the expectations of others, especially when they are not realized. All choices are therefore rooted in balancing subjective opportunity costs.

Many of Buchanan's ideas on cost grew out of the burgeoning subjectivism in London in the 1930s, especially in the work of Hayek. For Hayek and other Austrians of the day, subjectivism, especially referring to knowledge, was at the root of a number of important issues in economic theory and political economy. Subjectivism explains Hayek's position in the two most important intellectual debates among economists of the 1930s – the rise of Keynesianism and the socialist calculation debate. In both cases, Hayek argued that his opponents misunderstood the subjectivist message, especially concerning the role of equilibrium in economic theory. In the debate with Keynes, Hayek argued that macroeconomic aggregates are inappropriate guides for policy as the relationships that comprise them are ultimately grounded in the subjective perceptions of market actors. As a result, macroeconomic theories that attempted to establish causality between aggregates were problematic. This was especially true for Keynes because of the absence of a theory of capital in *The General Theory*. As Hayek (1941) and Lachmann (1956) have argued, the capital structure is fundamental to the market process, and capital is an essentially subjective phenomenon, as what counts as capital is determined by the plans of resource owners. The same objective good may be capital for one person but not for another. Aggregate notions of saving and investment overlook these issues.

In the calculation debate, Hayek's neoclassical opponents argued that a socialist planning board is theoretically just as able to discover equilibrium prices as is a market and is thus equally able to allocate resources rationally. This argument hinged on the view that the board would have the data of the market 'given' to it, in much the way that one takes knowledge as given in the theory of perfect competition. Hayek saw this as a confusion over the nature of knowledge and the notion of it being 'given'. The 'givenness' of knowledge, for Hayek, was just a restatement of subjectivism, in that it meant that the observing economist had to start any explanation of economic processes with the perceptions of market actors. It did not mean that the economist knew everything that the actors knew, as has become the norm in neoclassical theory.

This latter view of 'givenness' enabled planners to assume they could acquire the knowledge needed to find equilibrium prices. Hayek's subjectivist view suggested that such knowledge not only *was* not known by observers, but *could* not be so known. When one recognizes that much of the knowledge relevant to economic coordination is subjective 'knowledge of the particular circumstances of time and place' (Hayek, 1948, p. 80), then it becomes impossible to imagine it marshalled in one mind or group of minds. The whole raison d'être of the market, for Hayek, was that it enabled the use of subjective knowledge through intersubjective signals such as prices and profits. These phenomena are the unintended outcomes of the interplay between the subjective perceptions of suppliers and demanders. Precisely because they rejected these subjectivist underpinnings, the neoclassical defenders of planning misunderstood the nature of market processes. Markets are better seen as process for the creation, discovery and use of knowledge that originates in the subjective mental states of individuals.

These Hayekian arguments provided the platform for the recent revival of Austrian subjectivism as well as other subjectivist-influenced schools of thought such as the Post Keynesians and followers of the late G.L.S. Shackle. Since the Austrian revival in the mid-1970s, the major development in subjectivist thinking. The first has been Ludwig Lachmann's work on the relationship between expectations and equilibrium. Lachmann has argued that, once the creative and imaginative nature of choice and its implied variety of reactions to market changes is recognized, how can Austrians feel assured that market processes tend toward equilibrium? The 'kaleidic' view of markets in Lachmann's work, called 'radical subjectivism' because of its rejection of any tendency towards equilibrium, is the next logical step in the subjectivist paradigm. Whereas Hayek moved Austrians from subjective value to subjective knowledge, Lachmann has taken the next step to subjective expectations.

The subjectivism of Austrian economics can be compared to the objectivism of more neoclassical approaches. At a general level, Austrians have not been guilty of what Mirowski (1989) calls 'physics envy'. Much of neoclassical economics has been patterned on the way physics approaches its subject matter. The problem, from a subjectivist perspective, is that human beings are not atoms or billiard balls. The deterministic utility maximization equations of general equilibrium theory deny any scope for the 'subject'. Agents do not make real choices, they exercise no imagination and their maxima are simply functional implications of objective data. Although this might accurately describe the path a billiard ball takes over a frictionless surface, to a subjectivist it does not describe real, historical human action.

This general equilibrium approach to economics has found its most logical extension in rational expectations models. In such models the fundamental mental phenomena that interest subjectivists are ignored. By assuming that agents will make use of all relevant available information in forming their expectations, the theorist once again eliminates any real 'subject'. Expectations are defined independent of the context, ability or individuality of market actors. For Austrian subjectivism, the main fact to be explained in economics is how actors with *different* expectations and knowledge are able to coordinate their behavior despite such differences and despite the anonymity inherent in markets. The notion of a movement from the individualized knowledge of actors to the coordination of the market-place is ruled out ex hypothesi when one uses rational expectations models. The progressive objectivization of neoclassicism all the way to expectations drives an even deeper wedge between it and Austrian economics, which has progressively *subj*ectivized the same path.

Similar subjectivist insights fuel Austrian criticisms of other macroeconomic approaches. Even without the assumption of rational expectations, Keynesian and monetarist macroeconomic models that attempt to derive functional relationships between statistical aggregates also fail to account for the importance of the subject on two levels. First, the aggregates themselves are likely to be meaningless to the subjective decision-making patterns of individuals. Individual decisions to buy and sell are not made according to the consumer price index (CPI) or aggregate investment (although some financial decisions might be). Thus the relationships between such aggregates are merely statistical and are difficult to explain in terms of specific human choices. Second, viewing the macroeconomy as a set of aggregate relationships obscures the underlying individual actions that comprise the economy. For example, monetarist models that hypothesize a direct relationship between an increase in the money supply and the price level rightly point out that inflation is always a monetary phenomenon. However, stopping there ignores the transmission process and its effects on individual prices. From a subjectivist perspective, the interesting question is how changes in the supply of money affect the decisions of individuals. Given that money supply increases occur at specific times and places, how the individuals who receive them react will be crucial to explaining the macroeconomic patterns that result. Subjectivists are interested in these individual reactions and are thus able to note the relative price effects of inflation that result and see how these price changes lead to recognizable patterns of behavior (as in the Austrian theory of the trade cycle). By focusing only on aggregates and not taking the role of the subject seriously enough, mainstream approaches miss the full story.

It can be briefly noted that Austrians argue that some non-mainstream approaches also suffer from insufficient subjectivism. Neo-Ricardian approaches (such as Sraffa's) which are concerned with the distribution of wealth between various factors of production or which focus on input coefficient matrices are attempting to objectivize what are essentially subjectively driven phenomena. Some forms of institutionalism, to the extent that they divorce the emergence and power of institutions from their bases in the subjective perceptions of individual actors, can also be seen as lacking important subjectivist insights.

For Austrian economics, subjectivism virtually defines the way it views economics and in so doing demarcates its approach from most others in economics. Many of the uniquely Austrian perspectives on economic phenomena, as well as the path by which they have developed, are simply the consistent application of subjectivism and its emphasis on the individual's active, perceiving, interpreting mind as the beginning, but not the end, of economic understanding.

See also:
Chapter 22: The Austrian theory of price; Chapter 2: Methodological individualism; Chapter 11: Praxeology

Bibliography
Buchanan, James (1969), *Cost and Choice*, Chicago: University of Chicago Press.
Hayek, F.A. (1941), *The Pure Theory of Capital*, Chicago: University of Chicago Press.
Hayek, F.A. (1948), *Individualism and Economic Order*, Chicago: University of Chicago Press.
Hayek, F.A. (1952), *The Counter-Revolution of Science*, Indianapolis: Liberty Press.
Hayek, F.A. (1973), *Law, Legislation, and Liberty*, vol. 1, Chicago: University of Chicago Press.
Lachmann, Ludwig M. (1956), *Capital and Its Structure*, Kansas City: Sheed Andrews & McMeel.
Lachmann, Ludwig M. (1977), *Capital, Expectations and the Market Process*, ed. Walter Grinder, Kansas City: Sheed Andrews & McMeel.
Menger, Carl (1981), *Principles of Economics*, New York: New York University Press.
Mirowski, Philip (1989), *More Heat than Light*, Cambridge: Cambridge University Press.
Mises, Ludwig von (1933), *Epistemological Problems of Economics*, New York: New York University Press.

4   Market process

Sanford Ikeda

Perhaps the greatest challenge for someone trained in standard neoclassical economics who seeks to discover the meaning of Austrian market process theory lies in acknowledging the existence of 'radical ignorance'. To be radically ignorant differs from being ignorant by choice, or 'rationally ignorant', because the former reflects an actor's utter unawareness of some aspect of the world germane to choice. For instance, we can say that someone who has not read *The Wealth of Nations* is rationally ignorant if, given full knowledge of the value of the book to him as well as the time and effort needed to read it, he has decided that the costs of reading it outweigh the benefits. Alternatively, he may be unaware of the book's very existence or any benefit that might accrue to him from reading it. The latter case, in which he is not ignorant by choice, is an example of radical ignorance. Furthermore, if he does become aware of *The Wealth of Nations*, it cannot result from a deliberate decision to do so on his part, since this would presuppose his prior awareness of the costs and benefits of becoming aware, which would raise the question of the source of this prior awareness, and so on. To avoid an infinite regress, it is necessary at some point to interpret the perception of costs and benefits as an act of discovery, regarding information about which the actor had no prior awareness.

Similarly, market exchanges may not take place owing to high information costs, or because actors are completely unaware of the existence of double coincidences of wants regardless of whether information costs are low or even non-existent. In the first case, leaving a trade unconsummated is consistent with equilibrium: since actors are informed of all relevant constraints, alternatives and values, they have no cause to regret their decision (for it is actually implicit in the structure of the problem) and therefore have no incentive to alter the status quo. In the second case, actors will have unwittingly overlooked a profitable exchange, and without prior knowledge of the error's existence their awareness of it will follow, if it does at all, not a calculated choice but an act of creative discovery. In the light of their discovery, actors would then have an incentive to alter their plans.

The fact of profit and loss is central to the market process. Unexploited profit opportunities generate losses, while discovered error creates profit. Kirzner (1973) has used the term 'entrepreneurship' to describe that aspect of human action which is alert to opportunities to make profits or avoid losses.

(Non-economists are usually surprised to find the concept of entrepreneurship absent from the core of modern neoclassical theory and the role of profit and loss correspondingly marginalized.) In the context of the market process, *entrepreneurship* essentially consists of alertness to instances in which, owing to the presence of radical ignorance, resources (broadly defined) are under- or overvalued relative to their other uses. While the incentive to act entrepreneurially lies in the desire to better one's subjective condition, the social function of entrepreneurship, its normative character, involves the uncovering of inconsistencies and errors, with respect to the underlying preferences of actors in the market, generated by radical ignorance.

Also driving the process of error revelation is the heightened profit awareness on the part of other actors that tends to follow an entrepreneurial discovery in a line of activity, which promotes the emergence of a rivalrous, spontaneous, profit-seeking process. However, because this rivalry could take forms harmful to the general welfare, social institutions serve to define and encourage acceptable behavior (or to censure unacceptable behavior) within a market order. These institutions include laws governing property ownership, exchange and the peaceful settlement of disputes, as well as the rules and customs that give context and meaning to these laws, direct their application and foster their evolution. In addition, institutions such as money and credit, the price system, banks, insurance and the firm may also have emerged, simplifying trade and advancing the coordination of plans. Indeed, these institutions, viewed collectively, constitute what we commonly understand by 'the market'.

In summary, the 'market process' is a spontaneous order sustained by an institutional framework in which private property and free exchange predominate, and which emerges from the largely independent purposes of individual actors who plan in the face of partial ignorance and unanticipated change.

Normative market process theory
From the point of view of market process theory, the usefulness of an equilibrium-based, normative construct such as Pareto optimality, long the centerpiece of neoclassical welfare economics, is severely limited as a normative criterion. Its chief weakness has little to do with the traditional criticisms that have been levelled against it (for example, those of Kaldor, Hicks, Scitovsky and Arrow). Indeed, most of its alternatives share the same limitation as the Pareto criterion, namely an exclusive focus on situations in which radical ignorance is absent and agents possess all relevant information. They fail to recognize what modern market process theorists refer to as the 'knowledge problem', wherein decision makers find themselves radically ignorant of relevant information dispersed among different individuals across the mar-

ket. The impossibility of complete knowledge on the part of an actor about the current and future states of the world renders moot the question of whether an actual change produces a Pareto improvement.

Equilibrium-based criteria are necessarily concerned principally with end states, in which all equilibrating adjustments have played themselves out and entrepreneurial activity has ceased. In contrast, a process-based normative criterion would be concerned less with the degree to which actual conditions on the market deviate from an ideal end state, and focuses instead on whether conditions exist on the market (for example, the market institutions mentioned earlier) that facilitate the discovery of market-based errors. (We will not discuss the important question of the normative value, if any, of coordination in the other social processes, such as the political process.) Such a criterion would ultimately refer to the underlying preferences of consumers, yet it would be indifferent to the efficiency of *current* resource allocation per se.

Competition and monopoly in the market process

In market process theory, the necessary and sufficient condition for competition is free entry, the sole requirement of which is the absence of a monopoly over an input essential to a line of production. (For an alternative Austrian view of monopoly, see Rothbard, 1970.) Absent resource monopoly, entrepreneurs are vulnerable to competitive entry so long as an exploitable profit opportunity exists in their line of production. This is because entrepreneurship – simple alertness to profit opportunities in contrast to deliberate search for information – requires no resource and is therefore a costless activity. The costlessness of entrepreneurial profit seeking renders the market process, as we have seen, inherently rivalrous and competitive. Is this process equilibrating? This is not the place to address the issue of whether equilibrium is an appropriate tool for the social sciences. However, even if the competitive market process might be seen as equilibrating in some sense – since it tends systematically to reward the entrepreneurial perception of error – one cannot gain from this any assurance that the catallaxy or even a particular market will actually attain or even near an equilibrium. As before, if plan coordination has a normative value, at best one might promote those social institutions that aid in the discovery of error.

As mentioned, entry is discouraged (that is, the opportunity for profitable entry is denied) where an entrepreneur–producer monopolizes an essential input. Hence, even though the market process is, taken as whole, a rivalrously competitive one (this is modified somewhat, below), it is possible for resources in particular lines of production to be underutilized with respect to consumer preferences (in order to generate monopoly rents) compared to the level of use that would obtain were ownership divided among more than one independent resource owner. Because of the lack of a profit incentive, entry that would tend to adjust the underutilization when ownership is divided will not be forthcoming. Thus, even though entrepreneurial discovery is costless, monopoly and monopoly power may yet exist.

In the market process paradigm, however, competition and monopoly are not polar opposites as in neoclassical theory. Instead they coexist, and do so in a manner radically unlike that described in the standard models of imperfect or monopolistic competition: they are both phenomena of non-equilibrium and are not synthesized into a hybrid equilibrium construct. Indeed, monopoly and monopoly power that serve to guard entrepreneurial rewards for innovation or other discoveries that promote social cooperation are elements of competition understood as a dynamic process. Moreover, so long as there is no monopoly over such inputs as scientific or artistic genius, a successful monopolist earning monopoly rents (which are entrepreneurial profits viewed from the time period before the act of entrepreneurial monopolization) will attract rival innovators who will tend over time to erode a monopolist's position. And since the entrepreneurship needed to market innovations is costless, it is immune from monopolization.

Should a single owner or collective gain economic ownership over an ever greater share of market resources, what is the effect on the competitiveness of the system as a whole? We know from the socialist calculation debate that, under monopoly ownership of all resources and complete central planning, competition in the market ceases altogether. This seems to suggest not only that the competitive process and complete system-wide monopoly are incompatible, but that increasing monopolization of resources, beyond some point, begins to degrade the competitive process. On the one hand, monopoly in a single line of production may lessen competition in the entire system to a slight degree, by reducing the likelihood of discovery in areas complementary to that line (since in certain circumstances the monopolist may be the only actor with an entrepreneurial incentive to make such discoveries); while, on the other hand, it may boost competition by protecting entrepreneurial profits long enough to ensure sufficient compensation to innovators, so that *on net* such monopolies promote the market process. Quite possibly, however, at some point before the system has become totally collectivized, monopolization may become on net harmful to the market process.

Examples of 'Process' in neoclassical economics

References to economic 'processes' are fairly common in the standard literature. How do these relate to the concept of process outlined here? While a complete examination of the literature would be impracticable, it might be helpful to examine briefly some representative examples from this literature and contrast them with Austrian market process theory. (For a more complete discussion, see Ikeda, 1990, 1992.)

Economists often call 'dynamic' those models that either treat as change-able what is commonly regarded as parametric in a mathematical function or perhaps embody change in the structure of the function itself. These are contrasted with static models in which variables, constraints and functions are unchanging or given exogenously. Most capital growth models would be an example of dynamic models of this kind. To the extent, however, that these constructs merely describe equilibrium paths of change, for example, so-called 'dynamic equilibrium' models, they do not fit the definition of 'process' in the sense intended here. Market process analysis accommodates unanticipated change and in so doing embraces non-equilibrium phenomena. While dynamic equilibrium models do embody change of a sort, it is fully anticipated (with certainty or probabilistically) leaving no scope for radical ignorance, entrepreneurial discovery and all that these entail.

Information theory might seem to be another likely area in which to find genuine market processes described. Briefly, in most models residing in the 'search' component of information theory, agents are assumed to possess perfect probabilistic knowledge of various courses of action; that is, they are able to list all possible states of the world and attach to each a probability of its occurrence. Given this information, agents search for ever better outcomes until expected costs and benefits are equated at the margin according to the usual optimality rule. In this approach, information is treated as a commod-ity, and agents fall short of omniscience only because it is too costly – they remain 'optimally' or 'rationally' ignorant. In contrast, one cannot simply pay to remove radical ignorance because, being radically ignorant, one would not know that there was anything to buy. Without radical ignorance no genuine market process is possible.

So far the 'signalling' or 'informational efficiency' branch of information theory has also failed to capture the critical idea of radical ignorance. An important aspect of this approach is the role it attributes to prices, a role that goes beyond their merely reflecting relative scarcities to that of actually serving as means to communicate information (for example, product quality) or as sources from which asymmetrically held information can be inferred so as to facilitate the coordination of individual plans. Moreover, these 'knowl-edge surrogates' can sometimes direct agents to act in ways that frustrate plan coordination or result in equilibria that are suboptimal or non-existent, as in Ackerloff's famous 'lemons' example. This, however, is quite different from analysing non-equilibrium *processes*, about which market process theory is concerned. While the basis of the informational efficiency approach is so-called 'asymmetric information', the starting-point of market process theory is radical ignorance (see Thomsen, 1992).

The concept of 'rivalry' is now quite common in the theory of games and oligopoly. Generally speaking, the models in this literature describe the outcomes of interactions among agents who possess various strategies and expectations about the strategies and expectations of their opponents. By and large, however, these models also fall short of describing market processes in two ways. First, it is usually assumed that agents at the outset are fully aware of all possible players, strategies and pay-offs, leaving no scope for entrepreneurial discovery. Second, these models share the chief aim of standard neoclassical theory, namely to examine the equilibrium outcomes and the conditions under which an equilibrium is or is not likely to obtain.

In some neoclassical analyses of the 'stability' of general equilibrium systems, it is sometimes possible to find scope for entrepreneurial activity and genuine market processes. This is especially true of the work of Fisher (1983). Stability analysis qualifies as market process analysis to the extent that it is concerned primarily with understanding the forces that promote or hinder equilibration, and to the extent that agents are assumed initially not to possess complete information about the optimal equilibrating path, and where a learning procedure for removing radical ignorance takes place. Most approaches to stability analysis, however, are regrettably ad hoc.

Summary
To summarize our discussion of the character of the market process, let us now contrast its salient features with those of a market equilibrium. A market equilibrium, whatever its structure, has the following properties:

1.   There is complete coordination (mutually reinforcing expectations) among the plans of individual agents, where these plans are also consistent with underlying preferences, technology and resources.
2.   Behavior is 'rational' in that, *ceteris paribus*, given all relevant information, agents maximize utility by choosing the least-cost means to satisfy their given preferences.
3.   All change is predictable, ruling out the possibility of genuine error, regret and surprise.
4.   Economic profits and losses, being inconsistent with equilibrium, are non-existent or fleeting.
5.   Equilibrium prices prevail, ensuring consistency of plans among individuals and with the underlying data.
6.   Given transactions costs, the market allocates resources to their most highly valued uses.

The contrasting traits of a market process are as follows:
1.   Plans of at least some actors conflict and are inconsistent with the underlying data, though partial coordination preserves a degree of coherence in the market.

2. Action is 'purposeful' in that actors seek to improve their perceived state of the world, though they are aware of less than all of the available means to do so.
3. Their knowledge of relevant data being incomplete, actors experience error, unpredictable change, regret and surprise.
4. Persistent and recurring economic profits and losses are essential.
5. Non-equilibrium prices exist, reflect discoordination, but signal opportunities for profitable plan adjustment.
6. The presence of error causes inefficient resource allocation, which the market process tends to correct.

(Note: Austrians frequently use the term 'market' in the broad sense. Market theory in standard economics, for example, usually refers to the analysis of the behavior and performance of particular market structures, while for Austrian market process theorists it could also mean the theory of the 'catallaxy', that is, the social order based on private property and voluntary exchange.)

From this comparison and the previous discussion the reader can appreciate the critical importance of radical ignorance and the coordinating tendency of rivalrous entrepreneurial discovery for the Austrian theory of the market process.

See also:
Chapter 15: Entrepreneurship; Chapter 14: Competition; Chapter 21: Profit and loss; Chapter 23: Non-price rivalry

Bibliography
Fisher, Franklin M. (1983), *Disequilibrium Foundations of Equilibrium Economics*, Cambridge: Cambridge University Press.
Ikeda, Sandford (1990), 'Market-Process Theory and "Dynamic" Theories of the Market', *Southern Economic Journal*, **57**, (1).
Ikeda, Sanford (1992), 'L'analyse du processus de marché dans l'organisation industrielle: Kirzner, la contestabilité et Demsetz', *Journal des Economistes et des Etudes Humaines*, **2**, (4).
Kirzner, Israel M. (1973), *Competition and Entrepreneurship*, Chicago: University of Chicago Press.
Kirzner, Israel M. (1992), *The Meaning of the Market Process: Essays in the Development of Modern Austrian Economics*, London: Routledge.
Rothbard, Murray N. (1970), *Man, Economy, and State: A Treatise on Economic Principles*, Los Angeles: Nash.
Thomsen, Esteban F. (1992), *Prices and Knowledge: A Market-Process Perspective*, London: Routledge.

B   Philosophical background

5 Aristotelianism, apriorism, essentialism

Barry Smith

It is customary to draw a distinction in the history of science between a broadly 'Galilean' and a broadly 'Aristotelian' approach to methodology (see, for example, Lewin, 1930/31). The proponent of the former sees science as a matter of the formulation and testing of hypotheses of a quantitative sort. Such hypotheses, conjoined with the results of observations of present events, allow the theorist to predict specific future events in specific ways, and can thereby be seen as amounting to an *explanation* of the phenomena in question. The proponent of the latter, Aristotelian methodology, in contrast, sees science not in terms of prediction and explanation but rather as a descriptive enterprise, a matter of qualitative laws governing the connections between certain essences or categories. Such laws may in addition be seen as having the peculiar property that they can be known a priori, which is to say, without the application of special methods of experiment and induction.

The Aristotelian methodology was for a long time regarded as having been entirely superseded, so that all modern scientific disciplines came to be seen as tending inevitably towards the status of the exact physical sciences. More recently, however, it has been recognized that there are a number of scientific domains, especially in the sphere of the human sciences, where the Aristotelian methodology is still appropriate and indeed necessary. This is increasingly true, for example, in the spheres of linguistics and anthropology and in other cognitive sciences. For at least a hundred years, however, the standard-bearer of the Aristotelian methodology has been the school of Austrian economics, and it is the 'Aristotelianism' of the Austrians that we shall seek to set out more precisely in what follows.

The doctrine of Austrian Aristotelianism can be said to embrace the following theses:

1. *The world exists, independently of our thinking and reasoning.* This world embraces both material and mental aspects (and perhaps other *sui generis* dimensions, for example of law and culture). And while we might shape the world and contribute to it through our thoughts and actions, detached and objective theorizing about the world in all its aspects is nonetheless possible.

2. *There are in the world certain simple 'essences' or 'natures' or 'elements', as well as laws, structures or connections governing these.* All such laws are *strictly universal*, both in the sense that they do not change histori-

33

cally and in the sense that they are capable of being instantiated, if appropriate conditions are satisfied, at all times and in all cultures. Propositions expressing universal connections amongst essences are called by Menger 'exact laws'. Such laws may be either static or dynamic – they may concern either the coexistence or the succession of instances of the corresponding simple essences or natures. It is exact laws, as Menger sees it, which constitute a scientific theory in the strict sense. The general laws of essence of which such a theory would consist are subject to no exceptions. In this respect they are comparable, say, to the necessary laws of geometry or mechanics, and they are contrasted with the mere statements of fact and the inductive hypotheses of 'Galilean' science (see Menger, 1985, p. 59).

3. *We can know what the world is like, at least in its broad outlines, both via common sense and via scientific method.* Thus Austrian Aristotelianism embraces not only commonsense realism but also scientific realism, though Aristotle himself ran these two positions together in ways no longer possible today. The commonsense realism of Menger (as of all Austrian economists) is seen in his treatment of agents, actions, beliefs, desires and so on. In regard to these sorts of entity there is no opposition between reality as it appears to common sense and reality as revealed to scientific theory. Menger's (or the Austrian economists') scientific realism, on the other hand, is revealed in the treatment of phenomena such as spontaneous orders and 'invisible hand' processes, where common sense diverges from the structures disclosed by theory.

4. *We can know what this world is like, at least in principle, from the detached perspective of an ideal scientific observer.* Thus in the social sciences in particular there is no suggestion that only those who are part of a given culture or form of life can grasp this culture or form of life theoretically. The general structures of reality are not merely capable of being exemplified, in principle, in different times and cultures; like the basic laws of geometry or logic they also enjoy an intrinsic intelligibility which makes them capable of being grasped, again in principle and with differing degrees of difficulty, by knowing subjects of widely differing sorts and from widely differing backgrounds. Indeed, because the essences and essential structures are intelligible, the corresponding laws are capable of being grasped by the scientific theorist in principle on the basis of a single instance.

5. *The simple essences or natures pertaining to the various different segments or levels of reality constitute an alphabet of structural parts.* These can be combined in different ways, both statically and dynamically (according to coexistence and according to order of succession). Theoretical research, for Menger, 'seeks to ascertain the *simplest elements* of everything real, elements which must be thought of as strictly typical just because they are the simplest' (1985, p. 60). Scientific theory results, then, at least in part, when

means are found for mapping or picturing the composition of such simple and prototypical constituents into larger wholes. Such composition is not simply a matter of heaping or gluing together. It is a matter of certain entities or features or properties of entities arising in reflection of the existence of special sorts of combinations of other sorts of entities. Thus for example a *good* exists as such only if certain quite determinate preconditions are simultaneously satisfied (see Menger, 1981, p. 52).

6.   *The theory of value is to be built up exclusively on 'subjective' foundations, which is to say exclusively on the basis of the corresponding mental acts and states of human subjects.* Value for Menger – in stark contrast to, for example, Marx – is to be accounted for exclusively in terms of the satisfaction of human needs and wants. Economic value, in particular, is seen as being derivative of the valuing acts of ultimate consumers. The different representatives of the philosophical school of value theory in Austria, too (above all Franz Brentano, Alexius Meinong, Christian von Ehrenfels and Oskar Kraus) accepted different forms of subjectivism as here defined. Thus all of them shared with Menger the view that value exists only in the nexus of human valuing acts (see Smith, 1990a; Grassl and Smith, 1986).

7.   *There are no 'social wholes' or 'social organisms'.* Austrian Aristotelians hereby embrace a doctrine of *ontological* individualism, which implies also a concomitant *methodological* individualism, according to which all talk of nations, classes, firms, and so on is to be treated by the social theorist as an, in principle, eliminable shorthand for talk of individuals. That it is not entirely inappropriate to conceive individualism in either sense as 'Aristotelian' is seen for example in Aristotle's own treatment of knowledge and science in terms of the mental acts, states and powers of individual human subjects.

It is thesis 3, above all, which establishes the line between the Aristotelian doctrine and that of Kant (for whom there looms behind the world we know an inaccessible world of 'things in themselves'). Theses 1 and 3 mark off Austrian Aristotelianism from all idealist doctrines of the sort which embrace the view that the world of experience or of scientific inquiry is somehow created or constituted by the individual subject or by the linguistic community or scientific theory, or what one will. Theses 2 and 4 distinguish the doctrine from all sorts of historicism, as also from hermeneuticist relativism and other modern fancies. Most importantly, however, the doctrine is distinguished via thesis 3 from the Galilean (positivistic, empiricistic) methodology which rests on the assumption that the ultimate atoms of reality (1) enjoy only quantitative properties and (2) are associated together in ways which are both accidental and unintelligible. All intelligible structures and all necessities are, from this perspective, merely the spurious reflection of thought constructions introduced by man.

Austrian Aristotelianism as formulated above is in large part a doctrine of ontology: it tells us what the world is like. The question of apriorism, on the other hand, is strictly epistemological: it relates exclusively to the sort of account one gives of the conditions under which knowledge is acquired.

Defenders of apriorism share the assumption that we are capable of acquiring knowledge of a special sort, called 'a priori knowledge', via non-inductive means. They differ, however, in their accounts of where such knowledge comes from. Two broad families of apriorist views have to be distinguished in this regard. On the one hand are what we might call *impositionist* views. These hold that a priori knowledge is possible as a result of the fact that the content of such knowledge reflects merely certain forms or structures that have been imposed or inscribed upon the world by the knowing subject. Knowledge, according to such views, is never directly of reality itself; rather, it reflects the 'logical structures of the mind' and penetrates to reality only as formed, shaped or modelled by a mind or theory.

On the other hand are *reflectionist* views, which hold that we can have a priori knowledge of what exists, independently of all impositions or inscriptions of the mind, as a result of the fact that certain structures in the world enjoy some degree of intelligibility in their own right. The knowing subject and the objects of knowledge are for the reflectionist to some degree *pretuned* to each other. Direct a priori knowledge of reality itself is therefore possible – knowledge of the sort that is involved, for example, when we recognize the validity of a proof in logic or geometry (where it is difficult to defend the view that the character of validity would be somehow imposed upon the objects in question by the epistemic subject).

The impositionist view finds its classical expression in the work of Hume (in his treatment of causality), in Kant and in the logical positivists. The reflectionist view, on the other hand, finds its classical expression in Aristotle; it was developed further by successive waves of scholastics extending far into the modern era and brought to perfection by Brentano and his successors, above all by Adolf Reinach and other realist phenomenologists in the early years of this century (see Mulligan, 1987).

For the Austrian economists, some at least of the propositions of economics are a priori in the sense that the corresponding structures enjoy an intrinsic simplicity and intelligibility which makes them capable of being grasped by the economic theorist – in principle – in a single instance (see Menger, 1985, p. 60 on the 'rule of cognition for the investigation of theoretical truth'). Note, however, that the fact that such structures are intelligible need not by any means imply that our knowledge of them is in any sense infallible or incorrigible, nor that it need in every case be easy to obtain or to order into the form of a rigorous theory. Indeed, much confusion in the literature on Austrian methodology has arisen because the alien moment of incorrigibility, together with connotations of special mental processes of 'insight' or 'intuition', have come to be attached to the aprioristic thesis in a way which has made the latter seem eccentric and unscientific.

Still greater confusion has arisen, however, as a result of the no less pervasive assumption that all talk of the a priori must of necessity imply an impositionist or Kantian framework. (This confusion was embraced, inter alia, by Mises: see Smith, 1990b.) The apriorism lying in the background of Menger's thinking, however, is quite clearly reflectionist. Menger believes that there are a priori categories ('essences' or 'natures') in reality and that a priori propositions reflect structures or connections among such essences which exist autonomously in the sense that they are not the result of any shaping or forming of reality on the part of the experiencing subject. The impositionist apriorist, in contrast, insists that a priori categories must be creatures of the mind. He, therefore, may hold that the issue as to which sorts of economic structures exist is a matter for more or less arbitrary legislation by the economic theorist, or a matter of the 'conceptual spectacles' of the economic agent. No grain of such ideas is to be found in Menger, who is quite clearly working against the background of an assumption to the effect that the universals of economic reality are not created or imposed in any sense, but are discovered through our theoretical efforts.

See also:
Chapter 3: Subjectivism; Chapter 9: Causation and genetic causation in economic theory; Chapter 6: Phenomenology and economics; Chapter 10: Ideal type methodology in economics

Bibliography
Grassl, W. and B. Smith (eds) (1986), *Austrian Economics: Historical and Philosophical Background*, London/Sydney: Croom Helm; New York: New York University Press.
Johansson, I. (1989), *Ontological Investigations: An Inquiry into the Categories of Nature, Man and Society*, London: Routledge.
Lewin, K. (1930/31), 'Der Übergang von der aristotelischen zur galileischen Dankweise in Biologie und Psychologie', *Erkenntnis*, **1**, 421–60.
Menger, Carl (1981), *Principles of Economics*, New York/London: New York University Press.
Menger, Carl (1985), *Investigations into the Method of the Social Sciences with special reference to Economics*, New York/London: New York University Press.
Mulligan, K. (ed.) (1987), *Speech Act and Sachverhalt. Reinach and the Foundations of Realist Phenomenology*, Dordrecht/Boston/Lancaster: Martinus Nijhoff.
Rothbard, Murray N. (1957), 'In Defense of "Extreme Apriorism"', *Southern Economic Journal*, **23**, 315–20.
Smith, B. (1990a), 'On the Austrianness of Austrian Economics', *Critical Review*, **4**, 212–38.
Smith, B. (1990b), 'Aristotle, Menger, Mises: A Categorial Ontology for Economics', *History of Political Economy*, annual supplement to **22**, 263–88.

6   Phenomenology and economics

G.B. Madison

In recent years a number of scholars have begun to take increasing note of the affinities that exist between Austrian economics and that philosophical movement known as 'phenomenology'. Phenomenology originated at the turn of the century in the work of Edmund Husserl (1859–1938), was subsequently developed in an 'existential' direction by, among others, Martin Heidegger (1889–1976) and Maurice Merleau-Ponty (1907–61) ('existential phenomenology') and is currently represented by what is generally known as 'philosophical' or 'phenomenological hermeneutics', the leading exponents of which are Hans-Georg Gadamer (b. 1900) and Paul Ricoeur (b. 1913). In this entry the term 'phenomenology' will be used in a wide sense, to refer to all three of the phases of the movement just mentioned. We will seek to explore not the historical connections between phenomenology and Austrian economics (an interesting topic in its own right) but the philosophical or theoretical affinities linking together the two disciplines. These affinities are numerous, and they go deep.

Like all the sciences, both human and natural, economics contains an implicit philosophy, that is, a view of what 'reality' consists in (in modern times the predominant, Cartesian, view was that 'reality' is essentially nothing more than matter-in-motion) and, correlatively, a view of the nature and function of human understanding (the object of which is 'reality' – moderns have generally viewed the 'mind' as, in the words of Richard Rorty, a simple 'mirror of nature'). This philosophy is often merely presupposed and inarticulate, but it nonetheless informs even the most 'empirical' of scientific research, often with unfortunate results, if the philosophy in question is inappropriate to the object domain of the science in question. Phenomenologists maintain that the philosophy traditionally appealed to by mainstream, neoclassical economics – positivism – is totally inappropriate to its proper object, economic activity on the part of existing human beings. A similar critique has been made by economists themselves (for example, Frank H. Knight, earlier in the century, and, more recently, by a student of Knight's, James Buchanan). F.A. Hayek was particularly outspoken in this regard. In *The Counter-Revolution of Science*, written in the 1940s, Hayek launched an all-out critique of what he called the 'physicalism' and 'scientism' infecting the discipline of economics and 'the slavish imitation' on the part of economics of 'the method and language of [physical] science'. Although he did not use the term (as yet non-existent), what Hayek was arguing for was the need for economics to make the 'interpretive' or 'hermeneutical turn' (see Madison, 1989). (In his '"What Is Truth" in Economics' (1940), Knight, cognizant of philosophical developments on the Continent, had pointed to the need for economics to reconceptualize itself as 'an interpretative study [*verstehende Wissenschaft*].') Pursuing lines of inquiry opened up by Hayek and others, Austrian economists have increasingly – and explicitly – looked to phenomenology (hermeneutics in particular) for a philosophy of science suitable to their own discipline.

A pioneer in this regard was Ludwig M. Lachmann who, as a visiting professor at New York University from 1975 to 1987, exerted a profound influence on a whole generation of younger Austrian economists, represented most notably by Don Lavoie and others trained at the Center for Study of Market Processes at George Mason University. What all of these economists have in common, and what distinguishes them from a great many of their professional colleagues, is, as Lachmann put it in calling for the formation of a 'Hermeneutics Club' at New York University, an intense concern for '*general* ideas'. Perhaps the most 'general' of ideas in this regard are those having to do with the phenomenological critique of *objectivism*.

From its beginnings in the work of Husserl, phenomenology has insisted that the 'objective' methods of the natural sciences are not appropriate to the human sciences. To attempt to model the human sciences on the natural sciences, as logical positivism sought to do, is to fall into the error of 'objectivism' or 'naturalism': human beings are not mere objects in the physicalistic or naturalistic sense of the term; they are *subjects* in their own right. From this it follows that the crucial question facing social scientists is one of *methodology*: what method is most appropriate to the human sciences, if the 'objective' approach of the natural sciences is for the most part not suitable in their case? Some of the most fruitful of exchanges between phenomenology and Austrian economics have been those focusing on this issue. As Lachmann noted, the study of the market process 'calls for treatment by a method inspired by the hermeneutical style, a method which defies the spirit of orthodox formalism' (1991, p. 145).

Economics and the human condition

Ever since the nineteenth century, economists, awed by the natural sciences, have sought to model their discipline on physics (the notion of 'equilibrium' constituting one of the chief instances of this 'slavish imitation of the method and language of science', in Hayek's words). In tandem with the critique of objectivism on the part of phenomenologists, Austrians have consistently protested against the continuing attempt on the part of neoclassical economists to reduce economics to a Newtonian mechanics of human affairs. Just as existential phenomenologists have maintained that the human subject is most primordially an *acting* subject, Austrians have argued that the proper object of economics is human action (compare Mises's *Human Action*) and that, in addition, to be properly understood human action calls for a different mode of analysis than that which is applicable to mere bodily or physical motion. In basic accord with the hermeneuticists, they have insisted that human or social reality cannot be understood adequately if methodological priority is not accorded to the categories of meaning and purpose (categories which are obviously inapplicable in the realm of natural reality). Economics must not be conceived of as an 'experimental' science in search of nomological–deductive law but as a hermeneutical science in search of meaning. The proper task of economics, as an interpretive discipline, is that of explicating (interpreting, bringing to reflexive awareness) the *meaningful patterns of action* that are themselves constitutive of that order of human activity referred to as 'economic' (just as the task of the interpretive anthropologist is to explicate the meaningful patterns of action that go to make up what is called a 'culture').

Another way of expressing the matter would be to say that the Austrian critique of 'the spirit of orthodox formalism' is at the same time a call for economics to turn its attention away from mathematical abstractions and to concentrate instead on *real* people in *real-life* situations. In issuing this call, Austrians are saying that the proper object of economics is what Husserl called the *lifeworld*, a notion which is perhaps Husserl's most enduring contribution to twentieth-century continental thought. Husserl advanced his notion of the lifeworld in the course of his critique of modern, Galilean or mathematical physics, the distinctive feature of which is that (in contrast to pre-modern science) it deliberately and methodically turns its back on the real world of human experience, the lifeworld, substituting for it a world of idealized abstractions. The 'objectivities' of modern science, Husserl argued, are 'nothing more than a garb of ideas thrown over the world of immediate intuition and experience, the lifeworld'. Modern science deals not with realities (in any directly meaningful sense) but with formalistic idealizations. This is as true of modern physics as it is (or was subsequently to be) of modern economics. Notions such as *homo economicus* (for example, 'rational expectations') and 'equilibrium' are nothing more than a 'garb of ideas' concealing the lifeworld experience of real, flesh-and-blood agents.

Eschewing scientistic abstractions, Austrian economics seeks to focus its attention not on 'rational expectations' or 'equilibrium' but on such real-world phenomena as uncertainty and the catallactic order (in the Hayekean sense of the term). In instances such as these one can detect a profound affinity between phenomenology and Austrian economics in regard to *substantive* issues (in addition to the methodological affinities mentioned above). The Austrian and phenomenological view of the human condition (traditionally referred to as human 'nature') are convergent to a remarkable degree. Before Heidegger and Merleau-Ponty, Gadamer and Ricoeur, no philosophy had taken seriously the fact that human existence is essentially finite. Existential and hermeneutical phenomenology is, from one point of view, nothing other than a systematic attempt to draw all the philosophical consequences which stem from the undeniable fact of human finitude. Austrian economics, it could likewise be said, is nothing other than a systematic attempt to draw all the economic consequences which stem from the finitude of human knowing (compare the Mises–Hayek contribution to the 'socialist calculation debate') and human acting (see the work of Israel Kirzner on entrepreneurship).

For phenomenology human existence is essentially temporal and is, moreover, future-oriented. All action is intentional or purposive; unlike natural being, human reality is never fully understandable in terms merely of what it actually is but, as Heidegger pointed out, only in terms of the *non*-existent future into which it is constantly projecting itself. Humans act *in order to* bring into being a state of affairs which would not exist, or probably would not exist, unless they acted (a point insisted upon by Mises). This is another way of saying that the future is inherently indeterminate and uncertain (unlike the future of physical systems, as understood by classical physics – the model for neoclassical economics – which is in principle fully determinable or 'predictable'). This is another way of saying that human action (such as entrepreneurship) is *creative* (and not merely adaptive, as scientism would have it). And this in turn means that all human action involves genuine risk and is a way of coping with ignorance and uncertainty.

It is notable that all of these basic phenomenological themes are central precepts of Austrian economics, ones which serve to set it apart from the scientism rampant in mainstream, neoclassical economics. Austrian economics is nothing other than an attempt to conceptualize, along implicitly phenomenological lines, the basic characteristics of human agency that are not conceptualizable within the naturalistic and atemporal universe of discourse that neoclassical economists have adopted in their attempt to make of economics an 'exact' science like physics. This rejection of scientistic exactitude (what Lewis White Beck once referred to as the Natural Science Ideal) on the part of Austrian economics should not, however, as many of its critics nevertheless allege, be interpreted as an abandonment of disciplinary *rigor*; as Husserl ever insisted, a discipline can be 'rigorous' without necessarily having to be 'exact' (compare in this regard Hayek's remarks on 'pattern predictions' in his Nobel lecture, 'The Pretence of Knowledge'). On the basics of the human condition, phenomenology and Austrian economics are thus in fundamental and substantial agreement, and this agreement is reflected in many other areas – for instance, in their views on the nature and scope of human understanding.

Economics and human understanding

Phenomenology is most properly characterized as a form of *meaning-analysis* (Heidegger's 'existential analytic', for instance, set forth in his *Being and Time*, was an attempt to disclose the basic meaning-structures of human existence). Phenomenologists customarily make a distinction between 'explanation' and 'explication' and they maintain that 'explanation', that is mechanistic, cause-and-effect accounts of states of affairs, is a totally inappropriate method when, as in the social sciences, we are seeking to understand what is specifically human about human reality. Human reality is characteristically and essentially meaningful, and meaning can never be grasped by cause-and-effect explanation. (To 'explain' something is to give an account of it in terms of other *things* called 'causes', but meaning is not a 'thing' and thus is not a caused 'effect'.) The only way in which meaning can be apprehended is by means of 'explication', that is interpretation (*ex-plicatio, aus-legung*). This is why phenomenology is so strenuously opposed to 'objectivism' in the human sciences. (Philosophy is itself, it may be noted, a human science, in the most basic sense of the term, since, as Montaigne pointed out, its one and only object is human reality itself.) Meanings are not things or objects in the objectivistic sense of the term; they do not exist 'in themselves', neither in the world, naturalistically understood, nor in some intelligible heaven. They exist only in relation to human *subjects*, and they are to be understood as the result of the *projects* (as Heidegger would say) in terms of which these subjects define or constitute themselves.

It is to be noted that phenomenology is equally opposed to all forms of *subjectivism*, that is, all attempts to account for meanings solely in terms of the *conscious* intentions of acting subjects. This was the reason for Husserl's early attack on 'psychologism', the attempt (as in nineteenth-century British empiricism) to 'explain' meanings in terms of the psychological workings of the human 'mind'. Meanings do indeed have a kind of 'objective' existence – precisely insofar as they are *not* reducible to mere psychology and do not exist merely 'in' subjective consciousnesses. Indeed, the core feature in the development of the phenomenological movement, from Heidegger to present-day hermeneutics, has been the attempt on the part of phenomenologists to break out of the traditional 'philosophy of consciousness', to abandon, in other words, all forms of 'subjectivism'. This is why phenomenology is so thoroughly concerned with the phenomenon of intersubjectivity: meanings are 'objective' precisely to the degree that they are intersubjective, existing not in individual 'minds' but, so to speak, outside them, in-between individual subjects, embodied in social and institutionalized practices. The notion of meaning, phenomenology insists, must be 'desubjectivized' or 'depsychologized'.

It might seem that here phenomenology and Austrian economics part company, in that the latter has traditionally opposed itself to mainline, neoclassical economics by defining itself as a form of 'subjectivism'. This is not at all the case, however. Consider, for instance, the subjective theory of value first articulated in 1871 by Carl Menger. In opposition to traditional economic thinking, from the Middle Ages up to and through Marx's labor theory of value (and the corresponding notion of use value), Austrian economics maintains that 'value' is not something objective, in the objectivistic sense of the term, but can only be understood in terms of the valuing (or evaluating) activity of individual *subjects*. The parallel with phenomenology is obvious here: values are a form of meaning, and meaning, phenomenology maintains, must be understood in terms of human subjects, *for whom* this meaning exists. For Menger, values were the expression of preferences on the part of individual subjects, of the satisfaction they *expect* to derive from the incremental use of various goods (compare in this regard his quite phenomenological views on the relation between higher order or capital goods and lower order or consumer goods). As Lachmann has observed, Menger's formulation of the 'marginalist revolution' (as opposed to that of Jevons and Walras) represents an 'interpretive turn' in basic economic theory (see Lachmann, 1990).

In his application of the subjective theory of value to interest rates, Mises developed these phenomenological themes even further. Like Husserl, Mises understood time, the key element in interest, not in empirical or objectivistic terms but as a *dimension of human action*, in terms of *time-consciousness*. Also, what is important for economic understanding is not Böhm-Bawerk's notion of the 'average period of production' which, Mises said, is 'an empty concept' but the time-preference of individuals; economic phenomena must be understood in terms of *forward-looking* decisions on the part of individual producers and consumers. All of this is thoroughly and profoundly phenomenological. From its beginnings time has constituted one of, if not the, key concept of phenomenology – from Husserl's early work on time-consciousness, through Heidegger's definition of human existence in terms of temporality (the future being, for Heidegger, the basic dimension of human temporality), to hermeneutics' insistence on the thoroughgoing temporal or historical nature of human understanding itself. In all these instances, phenomenology, like Austrian economics, has sought to view time both non-objectivistically and as the core feature of human being and acting.

The important thing to note in this regard is that the Austrian 'subjective theory of value' has nothing 'subjectivistic' about it and is, indeed, as 'anti-subjectivistic', in the phenomenological sense of the term, as is phenomenology itself. This is perhaps nowhere more apparent than in the work of Hayek. The proper object of an interpretive economics, Hayek maintained, is that societal order or 'whole' called an 'economy' (or, more correctly, a 'catallaxy'). This order of human praxis is, as Merleau-Ponty might have said, one of embodied meanings, spontaneous meanings which are not the result of a 'universal constituting consciousness'. Merleau-Ponty's discussion in his *Phenomenology of Perception* of the relation between the 'lived body' (*le corps propre*) and the perceived or phenomenological world and his notion of 'incarnate' knowledge (very similar to Polanyi's notion of 'tacit' knowledge) could serve, in fact, in terms of the most basic structures of human existence, as a philosophical underpinning to the Mises–Hayek thesis regarding the role of dispersed or contextualized knowledge, so central to Austrian economics. Just as for Merleau-Ponty, so likewise for Hayek, these 'tacit' or 'practical' meanings – the proper object of an interpretive economics – are not to be understood 'rationalistically', that is, in terms merely of the conscious intentions of individual economic agents, as the deliberate product of individual 'minds'. (Hayek's long-standing critique of 'rationalism' is paralleled by the critique, central to phenomenology, of both rationalism and technologism.) As Hayek ever insisted, economic 'meanings' are to be understood as the result of human *action* (whence the 'subjectivism' of Austrian economics); they are not, however, to be viewed simply as the result of human *design* (that is, 'subjectivistically'). What makes of economics a social science is that it is concerned with the social consequences of economic agency on the part of individual human beings, and what makes these consequences 'social' is that they are largely the *unintended* consequences of action on the part of a myriad of individual human agents. As Paul Ricoeur would say, just as what makes a text a text is that it breaks free from the psychological intentions of its author and develops a life of its own (the meaning of a text, hermeneutics maintains, is not to be equated with the intentions of its author), likewise human action gives rise to unintended consequences (Ricoeur refers to this as the 'autonomization of human action') and it is this that constitutes the *social* dimension of action.

The view of human understanding implicit in Austrian economics and explicitly thematized by phenomenological hermeneutics is one which effects a decisive break with the long tradition of Western logocentrism, a tradition which has continued unabated in mainline economic theory. One of the prime characteristics of logocentric thinking is that it thinks always in terms of end states to be achieved (compare Aristotle's view – still appealed to by some today – of a thing's nature as the teleological end at which it aims). This is to say that this form of thinking always subordinates *process* to *stasis*. If Austrian economists have increasingly rejected as irrelevant the notion of 'equilibrium' so sacrosanct to traditional economic theory, it is for methodological reasons, because it is a counterproductive way of attempting to understand market *processes*. (It should be noted that in the phrase 'market process' the emphasis falls on 'process'; the notion of '*the* market' is a logocentric notion corresponding to nothing in the human lifeworld; it is as abstract an idealization as Walras's omniscient and atemporal 'auctioneer'.) A new generation of Austrians have looked to Gadamer's notion of 'conversation', a form not of instrumental but of communicative rationality or understanding, as a model for conceptualizing market processes. (The market according to this view is a kind of conversation conducted in the 'language of prices'.) Just as, for Gadamer, a genuine conversation is a form of 'play' (or 'game', *Spiel*), characterized by a continuing to-and-fro movement under the sway of no pre-ordained goal, so likewise are the processes of a genuinely free market. The market or catallactic order, Hayek himself has said, is best viewed as a kind of *game* in which specific outcomes are never guaranteed but which can generally be counted upon to expand the opportunity horizons – what Gadamer would call 'truth' – of an ever greater number of people (a non-zero-sum game). For both hermeneutics and Austrian economics, truth, meaning and value are not end states finally to be arrived at but are of the nature of an open-ended, never-ending and infinitely complex *process* (so complex, in fact, that no designer, however omniscient in theory, could ever control its outcome).

Individuals and institutions
As mentioned in the preceding section, in its attempt to break out of the traditional 'philosophy of consciousness', phenomenology has emphasized the phenomenon of *intersubjectivity*. Phenomenology has sought to reconceptualize the very notion of subjectivity, thoroughly rejecting in the process the atomistic individualism so pervasive in modern thought in general, and in empiricism in particular. (As Merleau-Ponty insisted, subjectivity is essentially an *inter*subjectivity.) Much the same could be said of Austrian economics. Again, this is nowhere more evident than in the work of Hayek. Although Hayek took over the term 'methodological individualism' to designate his own position, this position was anything but 'individualistic' (see Madison, 1990a); that is, Hayek never attempted to account for social 'wholes' in terms of atomistic, pre-given and self-contained individuals (the celebrated 'Robinson Crusoes' of traditional economics). In *The Counter-Revolution of Science*, Hayek in fact said that he somewhat regretted having adopted the term 'individualism', a term, he said, 'which has been so abused and so misunderstood'. For Hayek the human being is *essentially* social (a true *zoon politikon*). What has often not been sufficiently recognized is that Hayek's work is unique in that it is a rare attempt to conceive of the 'social' in properly social, that is non-individualistic, terms, in terms of the *logic* proper to it – contrasting in this regard with both the (reductionistic) atomism of neoclassical economics and Marx's 'collectivism' (Marx, too, thought in individualistic terms, the only difference being that for him society was one great individual, one immense Robinson Crusoe). In its way of attempting to

conceptualize the 'social', Austrian economics is in profound agreement with hermeneutics.

Hayek was not only an economist; he was also a social scientist in the widest sense of the term. One of the main focuses of phenomenological hermeneutics has always been the philosophy of the human sciences, and this is one area in which one can expect a great deal more collaboration between Austrians and hermeneuticists. The task in this regard would be to build on Hayek's insights in such a way as to work out a fully developed theory of the *logic* of social orders, such as that of a democratic polity or a market economy.

Another area of overlap calling for greater collaborative effort is that of general political economy. Hermeneutics not only embodies a general theory of human understanding, it also entails a specific *political* theory (see Madison, 1994) and, as Don Lavoie has remarked, this theory is one which best fits the market process. Unlike mainstream neoclassical economics, which customarily seeks to present itself as a form of 'value-free' science, Austrian economics is anything but value-free when it comes to politics. (One has only to think of the work of Mises and Hayek.) The point to be noted in this regard is that the political theory implicit in Austrian economics is identical with the one which follows from hermeneutics.

Like Hayek, Paul Ricoeur has insisted that in the final analysis it is only *individuals* who do things, since 'society' is not an 'agent'. However, like Hayek as well, Ricoeur (and hermeneutics in general) insists that individuals are truly empowered to do things – and, indeed can be 'individuals' in, as Hayek would say, the 'true' sense of the term – only within the context of appropriate *institutional* ('societal') frameworks (cf. Hayek's insistence on the need for general systems of rules or laws). The institutions which alone make free economic agency possible are those of the liberal state (the 'rule of law'). A great deal of work remains to be done on 'institutional' questions, in particular on those having to do with the political economy of democratic capitalism. This is one area where cooperation between Austrians and phenomenologists promises to be extremely fruitful. One of the central tasks in this regard is that of reformulating the kind of classical liberalism that is entailed by both Austrian economics and hermeneutics in a suitably *postmodern* fashion, in such a way as to make it relevant to the global civilization and economy now coming into being.

Hermeneutical theory and economic practice

Unlike many of their more positivistic colleagues, Austrian economists realize full well the overriding importance of, as Lachmann would say, '*general* ideas', that is, philosophy. As Mises once remarked: 'The history of mankind is the history of ideas. For it is ideas, theories and doctrines that guide human action, determine the ultimate ends men aim at and the choice of the means employed for the attainment of these ends. ... It is ideas that make history, not the "material productive forces", those nebulous and mystical schemata of the materialist conception of history' (1981, p. 518). Ideas do have consequences, and theory can make a difference. This is especially true of hermeneutical theory, which is entirely oriented to practice (see Madison, 1991b). In looking to phenomenology Austrians are not wasting their time in idle 'philosophical speculation'. As Donald McCloskey has long maintained in his work on the rhetoric of economics, economists need to achieve a greater reflective awareness of the theoretical underpinnings of their own discursive practices; this, he insists, can help to make them better economists. Phenomenology and, more specifically, hermeneutics seek only to provide practicing economists with a number of useful theoretical tools in their continuing attempt to conceptualize, in a genuinely appropriate manner, the economic lifeworld of real-life human beings.

See also:
Chapter 5: Aristotelianism, apriorism, essentialism; Chapter 3: Subjectivism; Chapter 8: The interpretive turn

Bibliography
Knight, Frank H. (1940), '"What is Truth" in Economics', *Journal of Political Economy*, LXVIII, (1), February, reprinted in Idem., *On the History and Method of Economics*, Chicago: University of Chicago Press, 1956.
Lachmann, Ludwig M. (1991), 'Austrian Economics: A Hermeneutic Approach', in Don Lavoie (ed.), *Economics and Hermeneutics*, London: Routledge.
Madison, G.B. (1986), *The Logic of Liberty*, Westport, Conn.: Greenwood.
Madison, G.B. (1988), *The Hermeneutics of Postmodernity: Figures and Themes*, Bloomington: Indiana University Press.
Madison, G.B. (1989), 'Hayek and the Interpretive Turn', *Critical Review*, 3, (2), Spring.
Madison, G.B. (1990a), 'How Individualistic is Methodological Individualism?', *Critical Review*, 4, (1 & 2), Winter–Spring.
Madison, G.B. (1990b), 'Between Theory and Practice: Hayek on the Logic of Cultural Dynamics', *Cultural Dynamics*, 3, (1).
Madison, G.B. (1991a), 'Getting Beyond Objectivism: The Philosophical Hermeneutics of Gadamer and Ricoeur', in Don Lavoie (ed.), *Economics and Hermeneutics*, London: Routledge.
Madison, G.B. (1991b), 'The Practice of Theory, The Theory of Practice', *Critical Review*, 5, (2), Spring.
Madison, G.B. (1994), 'Hermeneutical Liberalism', in M. Brumlik and H. Brunkhorst (eds), *Gemeinschaft und Gerechtigkeit*, Frankfurt: Fisher Taschenbuch.
Mises, Ludwig von (1949), Human Action: A Treatise on Economics, New Haven: Yale University Press.
Mises, Ludwig von (1981), *Socialism*, Indianapolis: Liberty Classics.

7 Formalism in twentieth-century economics

Arjo Klamer

Formalism, strictly taken, is the practice or doctrine of representing a phenomenon in systems consisting of well-defined elements in logically explicit relationships. In economics the prime example of formalism is the axiomatized general equilibrium model of Kenneth Arrow and Gerard Debreu (1954). Such a model represents economic reality in the form of formal relationships among well-defined agents, commodities and prices.

Formalism is a contested practice in economics. Austrians, among others, have resisted it with the argument that dynamic market processes and human subjectivity cannot be reduced to a system of formal relationships. Yet in the mainstream of academic economics the voices of opposition are weak. The neoclassical tradition, which has defined the mainstream throughout the twentieth century, implies the methodological standpoint that economics be a science and that therefore economists, as scientists, seek formalist representations of economic phenomenon just as natural scientists do for natural phenomena. In actuality, however, only a small subset of neoclassical practice measures up to the formalism of an Arrow–Debreu general equilibrium model. After a further characterization of formalism *vis-à-vis* alternative approaches, this entry will sketch the general context in which formalism came about and traces its emergence in economics.

Formalism characterized

If a formalist approach appears to be natural when natural phenomena are the subject of inquiry, empirical and historical approaches tend to be perceived as congenital to the study of social and economic phenomena. When the problem is, say, economic growth, or the lack thereof, the overriding inclination is to track the history of a particular economy, gain an understanding of concrete institutions such as the laws of the land, the organizations and the values of its people and compose from all the material an account of the economic growth in that country, possibly with a few numerical tables and graphs thrown in for good order.

In contrast, the formalist approach starts with the formulation of simplifying assumptions which enable the construction of the 'underlying' structure of a generic economy. In neoclassical economics the simplifying assumptions are behavioral (for example, 'n rational agents have the following objective functions and face the following constraints') and situational in the sense that they define the characteristics of the generic economy (for example, perfectly competitive commodities markets and fixed technology). The latter assumptions include the *ceteris paribus* conditions; that is, conditions that are assumed to be constant. In later stages of the inquiry the investigator may relax the *ceteris paribus* assumptions (allowing technology to be a variable, for example).

For those who are enamoured of the historical and empirical approaches, formalist representations are overly abstract and the assumptions that enable their construction unrealistic. For formalists their approach characterizes the scientific approach. Formalists such as Gerard Debreu argue that science requires the articulation of a rigorous model which is as general as possible, parsimonious in its assumptions and explicit in that all constitutive elements are spelled out and well-defined. To them all these requirements are met in the formalistic approach, with alternative approaches producing loosely articuled, fuzzy, local and historical knowledge about the economy. Apart from its alleged scientific qualities, formalism has an esthetical appeal for many an economist.

The objective of a purely formalist approach is the construction of a fully axiomatized system. The development of such a system first requires the identification of so-called 'primitive concepts', that is, the concepts that are the basic building-blocks of the system. Each one of these primitive concepts is specified as a mathematical object. For example, the Arrow–Debreu model is built on, among others, the concept of the action of an agent which is defined as a point in commodity space. Once relationships among the primitive concepts are postulated, the analytical problem is the determination of the solution, or equilibrium, of the system. In the typical economic model the relationships are between prices and quantities, and the equilibrium solution is defined as the prices at which the plans of buyers and sellers of commodities are consistent. By definition the system is in disequilibrium when the plans of agents are inconsistent (as when at a given price quantity demanded exceeds quantity supplied).

A formal representation of the economic system resembles the grammar of a language. Like grammar, a formal general equilibrium system represents the basic economic structure. As Debreu (1984) notes, the form of the system is separated from its content. The primitive concepts can be given novel interpretations which transform the meanings of the formal system and render it applicable to new situations. *Pace* McCloskey (1983), we do well thinking of a general equilibrium system as an analogy, or extended metaphor, of the economy. Of course the economy is not actually a formal general equilibrium model, but formalists consider it useful and pertinent to think about the economy 'in terms of a general equilibrium model'. Thinking about one (unknown) thing in terms of another (known) thing, is thinking metaphorically. The development of the metaphor ('the economy is a system of markets') into a well-articulated model transforms the metaphor into an analogy. Investigators are then allowed to explore the characteristics of the analogy. Because a formal model of the economy is an extended metaphor, it can never be claimed to be literally true. The general equilibrium model provides a manner of speaking and thinking about the economy. The effectiveness and pertinence of this manner of thinking is a matter of judgement. As already said, Austrian economists are among those who have persistently criticized the formalist approach for being inappropriate in a study of human processes.

Formalism in economics can take many different forms. The formalisms which we have discussed thus far concern the axiomatic models of the economy and are most general and most abstract among the formalisms. They permit the investigator to ask the most general questions, such as: 'Does a system of competitive markets have a solution?' and 'What are the welfare properties of that solution?' The larger body of economic theoretical constructions are watered-down formalisms. Most economic models are incompletely specified, with ill-defined primitive concepts and crude assumptions. They are designed to address specific phenomena and issues – say the US car market, or the determinants of economic growth – and can be articulated in such a way that they can be put to empirical tests.

As a matter of fact, empirical testing in economics usually requires the specification of the topic under investigation in terms of a mathematical model, that is, a formalism. The inclusion of randomly distributed error terms permits the application of (formal) econometric techniques in order to test the model against the data. Accordingly, the formalist approach is intricately connected with empiricism in economics as it is reflected in the econometric program. Recent methodological investigations, however, have indicated that the original ideal of the verification, or if not that the falsification, of the formal models by means of econometric techniques can probably never be met in reality. Many judgements are needed in the transformation of the model in such a form that it can be tested, as well as in the econometrics itself, and each of those judgements is a source of potential doubt. In view of the uncertainties, econometric tests can provide support to hypotheses that are derived from formal models; they cannot, however, verify or falsify the hypotheses in any definite sense.

A brief history of formalism in economics
Form, and with it formalism, is a contested concept which has fed many a philosophical discussion. One question is, for example, whether form is inherent in nature, and thus to be discerned by humans, or whether form is conceptual and exists in our mind. Plato is to be connected with the first position, Kant with the second. It is understandable that formalism became

most pronounced in mathematics. In that context it stands for the position that mathematical forms, that is numbers, sequences of numbers and logical operators, are existing in themselves and hence are 'meaningless' (compare Debreu's position that the form of a system is separate from its economic content). The modern mind also had no great difficulties accepting formalism as an approach in the study of nature. In their search for the deep secrets of nature, natural scientists did well casting their intuitions and findings in rigorous mathematical forms. Less obvious has been the adoption of formalist representations in the study of the social, including the economical.

Controversies on the appropriateness of a formalist approach in economics tend to reflect conflicting conceptions of the social and the nature of the studies of the social. Compare Adam Smith and David Ricardo. Adam Smith, the so-called father of modern economics, evoked in the *Wealth of Nations* the image of a system of markets analogous to a celestial system with self-interest as the counterpart to gravitation, the force that holds the system together. He does not, however, present a formal model, not even to the discerning modern eye. Ricardo did not present an explicit formal model either, but his analysis was sufficiently systematic to enable the translation into one. This difference is telling: whereas Smith was interested above all in moral questions – how individuals and governments should act in commercial society – Ricardo sought to conceptualize and analyse economic processes. It is a difference between social thought, in Smith's case, and social science, in Ricardo's case (see Bergner, 1981).

The scientific investigation of the social is a relatively recent phenomenon. A prerequisite proved to be this distinction of thought for the sake of knowing how to act from the investigation of human action for knowledge sake or, in other words, the distinction between practical and theoretical knowledge. The social had to be conceived as a subject for inquiry, just as nature was.

The story begins around the year 1619 in 'a room heated by an enclosed stove where [René Descartes] had complete leisure to meditate on [his] own thoughts'. After eliminating everything, he knew he was left with the only knowledge he could be certain of: *Cogito ergo sum*. From this axiom he built up a system of thought which includes the conceptualization of the human body as a machine. Moving from Descartes' pathbreaking thought to a full-fledged analysis of the social proved to be difficult and required a few centuries. Only in the eighteenth century did it become common to think of the economy as a 'thing' and humans as objects which could be investigated in the way natural things and objects were. In the nineteenth century the historical and empirical approaches prevailed. The economy was read in the same way that Darwin read nature; that is, as a system with a history. With the successes of physics, however, students of the economy became increasingly captured by the idea of an invariant structure that underlies (changing) appearances. The idea of the invariant in the economy set the stage for formalism. Physicists had set the example by representing the invariant in Nature by formal systems. Economists followed their lead (see Mirowski, 1989). Among the pioneers of formalism in economics were Sir William Petty (1623–87), Daniel Bernouilli (1700–82), David Ricardo (1772–1823), Augustin Cournot (1801–77), William Stanley Jevons (1835–82) and Leon Walras (1834–1910).

However, the formalists were a minority among economists well into the twentieth century. Mathematical representations became common in the academic journals only after 1935 (Mirowski, 1991). Axiomatic models, which are the purest formalist representations, caught on around that time with the work of, among others, John von Neumann, Kenneth Arrow and Gerard Debreu. The major challenge for formalists has been the determination of the solution of formal economic systems; that is, the existence of a unique equilibrium (see Weintraub, 1983). From Leon Walras to John Hicks it was believed that a solution would exist when the number of equations exceeded or equalled the number of unknowns. John von Neumann and Shizou Kakutani provided around 1940, independently of each other, a more refined existence proof using Brouwer's fixed point theorem from topology. Recent investigations have thrown the very possibility of a unique equilibrium solution into doubt. Especially when agents are allowed to develop strategies in response to the actions of other agents – the main premise of so-called 'game theory' – multiple solutions occur. In that case the system is undetermined.

Formalism and modernism
The formalist approach in economics resonates with modernism, the dominant cultural movement in the twentieth century. Around the turn of the century the move across the intellectual and artistic landscapes was away from the human subject and the classical tradition towards abstract and formal representation. Classical architecture, with its domes and pillars, was being replaced by sleek, functional and rectangular constructions. In painting the Cubists formally rearranged reality on their canvas, whereas painters such as Piet Mondrian and Vassily Kandinsky embraced formalism as the way to express the deeper, or higher, realities of life. In philosophy logical analysis displaced the discursive approaches of the great German and British philosophers.

Economists were actually quite late in making the modernist move towards the abstract and the search for formalist representations, following suit only after 1935 or so. After about 1960, faith in modernism began to waver (Harvey, 1989). With his *Structure of Scientific Revolutions* (1962) Thomas Kuhn stirred doubts about the possibility of certain scientific knowledge. These doubts stimulated the critics of formalism in economics. Formalism, however, continues to be, if not the dominant practice, the dominant ideal in academic economics. The question is, however, whether this vestige of modernism can survive very long, given the doubt that formalist representations will provide certain knowledge about the economy, including knowledge that enables us to effectuate desired economic outcomes.

If the arts and other intellectual disciplines are a good example, economists may expect an unraveling of the current hegemonic position of the formalist approach as the ideal in their discipline, and the beginning of a time in which many different approaches will coexist, including historical, institutional and interpretive approaches.

See also:
Chapter 5: Aristotelianism, apriorism, essentialism; Chapter 11: Praxeology; Chapter 2: Methodological individualism

Bibliography
Arrow, Kenneth and Gerard Debreu (1954), 'Existence of an Equilibrium for a Competitive Economy', *Econometrica*, July, 265–90.
Bergner, Jeffrey T. (1981), *The Origin of Formalism in Social Science*, Chicago: University of Chicago Press.
Debreu, Gerard (1984), 'Economic Theory in the Mathematical Mode', *American Economic Review*, **74**, 267–78.
Harvey, David (1989), *The Condition of Postmodernity*, Oxford: Basil Blackwell.
McCloskey, Donald N. (1983), 'The Rhetoric of Economics', *Journal of Economic Literature*, **XXI**, (2), June.
Mirowski, Philip (1989), *More Heat than Light*, New York: Cambridge University Press.
Mirowski, Philip (1991), 'The When, the How, and the Why of Mathematical Expression in the History of Economic Analysis', *The Journal of Economic Perspectives*, Winter, 145–57.
Weintraub, E. Roy (1983), 'On the Existence of a Competitive Equilibrium: 1930–1954', *Journal of Economic Literature*, **21**, March, 1–39.

8 The interpretive turn
Don Lavoie

Under the influence of Ludwig M. Lachmann, several Austrian scholars, including Boettke, Ebeling, Horwitz, Lavoie, Madison, Prychitko and Rector, have begun to challenge the traditional Austrian school from the standpoint of hermeneutical philosophy. Scholarship throughout the humanities and sciences has been undergoing a profound transformation in its understanding of knowledge. This 'interpretive turn', as Richard Rorty termed it, represents in many ways the resurgence of an earlier tradition of hermeneutical resistance to positivism, the *verstehen* (understanding) tradition, of which the old Austrian school was a part. This once powerful current of continental thought – including, for example, Wilhelm Dilthey in philosophy, Max Weber in sociology and Ludwig von Mises in economics – had been marginalized by the rise of positivism. Many of the themes raised by the old tradition have now come back to the center of scholarship once again. In some ways the interpretive turn is simply a vindication of the traditional Austrian positions against positivist neoclassical philosophical attitudes.

The interpretive turn going on in the larger scholarly community today, though, is not merely a 'return', a restoration of the older hermeneutics tradition. It represents the culmination of a confrontation of the hermeneutics tradition with Edmund Husserl's phenomenology, resulting in a transformation of both of the philosophical schools. The notion of understanding articulated by the likes of Dilthey and Weber has been subjected to rather sharp internal criticism by subsequent, more phenomenological contributors to the hermeneutics tradition, such as Alfred Schütz, Martin Heidegger, Hans-Georg Gadamer and Paul Ricoeur.

This development is especially significant for students of Mises, whose views of economic theory and history were *separately* shaped by, respectively, phenomenology and hermeneutics, when they were completely distinct traditions. The interpretive Austrians believe that traditional Austrianism, like mainstream economics, has over-dichotomized economic theory and history from one another. They are arguing that the combined philosophical perspective now called phenomenological hermeneutics is just what the school needs to overcome its own formalism and reconnect theory and history to one another. They contend that the school needs to take its own interpretive turn.

What is hermeneutics?

Despite its unfamiliar name and terminology, hermeneutics is a very practical philosophy. It aims at understanding the process of understanding itself, at disclosing the domain of meaning. It is a philosophy that is not based on abstract speculation, but on practical experiences with exegesis, the challenges of reading difficult texts. It explores the many complex things that go on, for example, when we read a sentence or a book. It refers essentially to the way in which, in the sciences, the arts, history and everyday life, we manage to come to an understanding of other people's actions and words. It is especially helpful in its illumination of the notion of the lifeworld, the everyday world within which ends and means are given significance (see Dreyfus, 1991; Gadamer, 1989).

The hermeneutical Austrians' challenge has been primarily aimed at mainstream neoclassical economics, which they charge with the vice of formalism, but the challenge has implications for the 'mainstream' of the Austrian tradition as well. Formalism is the artificial severing of economic theory construction from application, in effect the separation of theory from contact with the lifeworld, with everyday reality as we know it. In neoclassicism it takes the form of mathematicization, but formalism has its Austrian variants as well.

The interpretive Austrians' challenge to traditional Austrian methodology is a bold and controversial critique of all of the school's usual methodological self-descriptions. Criticizing Austrian methodology is made especially difficult by the fact that the school's methodological self-descriptions have been far more divergent than its actual practices, so divergent in fact that, from a methodological perspective, Menger, Mises and Hayek hardly seem even to be members of the same school. The hermeneutical Austrians contend that none of the Austrians' usual methodological positions, from Aristotelianism to Kantianism, to Neo-Kantianism, to Popperianism, adequately captures the virtues of their own substantive economics, and that contemporary hermeneutics does.

Hermeneutics is a radical philosophy with fundamental implications for the way we think about science, meaning, intentionality, language, culture, tradition, value and other significant matters. Space will not permit going into the whole range of implications the philosophy has for economics and the theory of human action. We confine our attention here to just two criticisms, the critique of atomism and of objectivism, and direct them at only one of the traditional Austrian methodological positions, that of Mises. It is hoped that the two specific critiques will illuminate the larger problem of formalism, which has been plaguing economics in general.

The overall hermeneutical challenge to traditional Austrian economics can be summarized by referring to what this handbook calls the three 'core methodological tenets' of the school, subjectivism, methodological individualism and market process, and seeing how they each look from the standpoint of hermeneutics. Of course, everything depends here on exactly how the tenets are interpreted. The hermeneutical Austrians endorse each of the tenets, but only when each is interpreted in a particular way.

Subjectivism is the principle that comes from Menger's critique of classical economics' objective theory of value. Goods need to be understood as 'having value', not in the sense that they may have mass or color, but in the sense that value is attributed to them by evaluating subjects. Since Menger's time the principle has been widened to refer to the need to render one's explanations of economic processes in terms that relate them to their meaning in the purposeful actions of human beings. An interpretive approach to subjectivism is one that stresses the importance of *meaning* in this sense (Lavoie, 1991b). *Methodological individualism* is the principle that it is only individuals who have purposes and who act. It is a critique of the naive holism which attributes goals to institutions, or nations, or races, without attempting to relate these social wholes to the purposes of their constituent individuals. An interpretive orientation to methodological individualism sees it as insisting that we make our explanations *choice-theoretic*, that we trace events back to the meaningful human purposes that drive them (Madison, 1991). In economics *market process* stands for what is really a more fundamental category which applies not only to markets, but to all sorts of institutions: *spontaneous order*. It is the principle that the social manifestation of meaningful action is that of an evolving system which exhibits systematic, but generally unintended, consequences. It is under this rubric that Austrians place their objections to equilibrium theorizing, and their concern for the importance of a non-spatialized notion of time. An interpretive orientation to spontaneous order is one that stresses the path dependency of evolutionary systems, and thus the importance of *history* (for example, O'Driscoll and Rizzo, 1985; Parsons, 1991).

The three tenets can be understood to be inseparable aspects of one integrated activity, the doing of economics. Doing economics in an Austrian way is tracing systemic (spontaneous order) patterns of events to the (subjectively) meaningful purposes of (individual) human actors. It applies theoretical ideas, value theory, capital theory and entrepreneurship, to its interpretation of the flow of unintended consequences from intended purposes. If this is what the tenets mean, they are unobjectionable from a hermeneutical point of view.

But Austrian economics drags into its traditional interpretation of the principles two aspects that need not be read into them and which will be labeled *atomism* and *objectivism*. For the school to take its own interpretive turn it will need to overcome its tendency towards atomism, which mistakenly locates the domain of meaning in isolated individual minds, and objectivism, which over-dichotomizes theory from history, and scientific from everyday understanding.

Atomistic subjectivism

Subjectivism is often expressed by Austrians in mentalistic terms. Subjective tastes are 'in the mind' of the actor; subjective cost is the next most valued option the actor had in mind at the moment of choice. Empirically understanding the cost of an action would thus appear to involve some kind of mysterious mind-reading process. Taken seriously, this principle would seem to condemn any empirical work as inherently crippled. It is fundamentally incapable of getting access to what the principle of subjectivism asserts is the most important driver of economic change, the subjective realm.

This idea of subjectivism is a throwback to Cartesian philosophy, and to its problem of Other Minds. It is mired in the metaphysical view that all I can be certain of is what is self-evident to my own mind and that, in order to interact with others, I need to take it on faith that other minds are constituted like mine. It was in partial rebellion against this whole way of thinking that Husserl developed phenomenology. He elaborated the idea that the basis of all knowledge is the intersubjective lifeworld, and not the subjective individual mind. Alfred Schütz began to correct for this element in the *verstehen* tradition by confronting Weber's theory of understanding with Husserl's work. If subjectivism is taken to signal the concern for the domain of meaning, then radicalizing subjectivism ought to mean moving away from the Cartesian model of the isolated individual mind, and towards the notion of intersubjectivity and language. This move might permit more Austrians to realize that to be a radical subjectivist does not mean to forsake empirical work. There is no need for Austrians to read other people's minds or invent time machines in order to do economic history. Meaning is not inaccessibly buried in the private recesses of isolated minds; it is publicly available in all sorts of readable texts.

The tendency to understand subjectivism in mentalistic terms is reinforced by the interpretation of methodological individualism which goes beyond the critique of naive holism and tries to privilege the analysis of the isolated, individual actor over the analysis of social institutions and processes. This is manifest in the habit Austrians have continued from their predecessors in economics of building their (supposedly general) analysis of action *first* in a conceptual experiment based on the Robinson Crusoe context, and *then* introducing the analysis of action in markets as a special case of isolated action. Austrians often interpret methodological individualism to mean that before we can say anything about social interaction – such as market exchange – we need a solid general theory of action, and that the way to construct a general theory of action is to remove the complication of social interaction, and first clarify the simpler case of isolated man, directly facing nature.

All of this looks rather dubious from an interpretive perspective. To be sure, society is composed of individuals, but just as surely individuals are composed of society. The claim that the action of an isolated actor is fundamentally simpler than social action is not convincing. Social complications are not so easily removed as by merely staging a hypothetical shipwreck. The Crusoe of the novel thinks in socially constituted categories; he is unquestionably the product of the British culture of his day, and this is not an imperfection of the story that economic theory can remove. Getting rid of social complications means getting rid of meaningful action itself. Real human action is carried out in a linguistically constituted world (Dreyfus, 1991). Ends and means are only meaningful in terms of the relevance domain of culturally embedded actors. Action is social at its very roots, in the very ability to formulate plans.

Thus Crusoe economics is either deceptive or incoherent. If Crusoe has a culture he is able to engage in purposeful behavior, but society is being slipped in through the back door, and the whole conceptual experiment loses its point. If he does not have a culture he is an idiot, incapable of formulating the sorts of complex plans, making fish net and so forth, which economists like to tell stories about.

The hermeneutical critique of atomistic Austrianism argues that what is valid in the principle of methodological individualism is already implicit in a properly interpreted subjectivism. Methodological individualism is a healthy, but perhaps redundant, principle to the extent that it makes the claim that explanations of action should refer to the subjectively perceived constraints and incentives faced by individual actors. It does not need to be accompanied by the privileging of Crusoe conceptual experiments (Lavoie, 1991a). The interpretive approach questions the use of the Crusoe model as its basic framework for the analysis of action in general, but it may still be desirable to set out a general analysis of action-as-such, as a basis for considering the distinct kinds of actions one associates with markets. The general analysis of action should not, however, be developed in an asocial context. Pre-market linguistic interaction is a more appropriate framework for the analysis of action in general. Markets could be studied as a special kind of discourse, as an extension of linguistic interaction (Horwitz, 1992).

But challenging atomism is not all that the interpretive turn involves for the Austrian school. Even when one understands that meaning is an intersubjective rather than a subjective phenomenon, as did Schütz, there remains another danger in traditional Austrianism, the danger of objectivism.

An objective science of subjective phenomena

Some Austrians like to think of themselves as involved in an objective study of subjective phenomena. They, the scientists, supply a value-free logic of the implications of the subjective, value-laden preferences of the actors under investigation. The scientist, including the economic theorist, discovers *objective* truths that are detached from his own biographical situation, whereas the everyday actor in the economy forms *subjective* judgements about future conditions. Mises saw entrepreneurial judgement as a kind of historical understanding, applied to the future instead of the past. The mysteries of *verstehen* infect the cognitive work of everyday life as inevitably as they infect historical cognition, for Mises, but economic theory formation was supposed to be different. It, like all science, was supposed to be immune from the mysteries of *verstehen*. It was a matter of pure, aprioristic reasoning, an application of Husserlian phenomenology to economics.

Both sides of this formula, 'an objective science of subjective phenomena', are misleading, and taken together they are dangerous. Science, whether social or natural, is not objective in the sense of being ahistorical and perspectiveless, nor is the subject matter of the human sciences subjective in the sense of being arbitrary. The effect of objectivistic attitudes is not so much to make empirical work impossible as to make it unappealing, unable to attain the status of genuinely scientific research.

There is a peculiar tension in traditional Austrianism between its tenet of subjectivism, understood as the focus on intersubjective meaning, and its also fundamental tenet of spontaneous order. What subjective meaning seems to emphasize, intentions, is precisely what spontaneous order de-emphasizes. Spontaneous order explanations are attempts to give an account of evolutionary processes, whereas meaning appears to be an issue of recovering something fixed, the original intent, and so seems not to involve anything like explanation. Such hermeneutical writers as Schütz, basing their work on Husserl, leave one wondering exactly how to relate the level of meaning to the level of causal spontaneous order analysis. But according to post-Heideggerian hermeneutics, meaning turns out to not really be strictly about the recovery of original intentions at all. Understanding is itself rendered as a dynamic process.

The interpretive critique of Austrian atomism argues that what it is we are 'getting at' when we understand is not the private contents of individual heads, but public discourses that are readily accessible. The interpretive critique of Austrian objectivism focuses on the 'getting at' process itself, and argues that understanding is not a merely reproductive, but rather a creative, productive process. Hermeneutics argues that economics (and science in general) does not supply us with an objective reproduction of economic reality as it is in itself, it creatively produces an interpretation from a particular perspective. As Gadamer (1989, pp. 296–7) puts the point, 'Not just occasionally but always, the meaning of a text surpasses its author.' We 'understand in a different way,' he says, 'if we understand at all.' Gadamer's account of understanding presents it as a spontaneous order process, and his overall philosophy provides an ontology of such processes (Lavoie, 1990).

At the time when Mises was drawing from the interpretive philosophy of his day, historical understanding appeared to be a matter of subjective, personal judgement, to an extent that scientific research was thought not to be. How can one scientifically recover the original intentions of an actor? The fear of reducing economic science to a mere matter of interpretation, to the mysterious domain of trying to understand Other Minds, seemed to condemn any field tainted with *verstehen* to second class status in the sciences. To defend the scientific status of economics, Mises and other Austrians were forced to dichotomize economic theory from history. *Verstehen* was endorsed for history, but ruled out of bounds in economic theory, so that its metaphysical complications would be able to contaminate only the empirical side of the human sciences. The theoretical side was to be based not on understanding but on abstract, logical 'conception'. This was conceived by Mises in the manner of Husserl's phenomenology, as a matter of hypothetically bracketing off some aspects of reality in order to bring into relief other aspects. But just as Husserl's philosophy came to be a corrective to Dilthey's, so Dilthey's came to correct Husserl's. Phenomenology after the work of Heidegger abandoned the notion of phenomenological bracketing as an acultural, purely logical operation, and recognized the rootedness of concepts in intersubjective understanding. Theory no less than history involves *verstehen*. The way we undertake conceptual experiments like phenomenological bracketing is historically and culturally situated. But all this need not be taken as a threat to the scientific status of economics. All science, Husserl was saying, is only possible on the basis of the intersubjective. Subjectivism, at least as reinterpreted to mean intersubjectivism, does not imply arbitrariness.

If the sort of understanding taking place among scientists is something different in kind from that taking place among agents in the economy, then the connection between science and everyday life may become problematic. Austrians like to remark that scientists are human actors too, so that if economics is the general science of action it should apply to scientists' actions too. But they seem to have felt the need to put science on a categorically different footing from the lifeworld in order to secure its objectivity. Fifty years ago scholars who failed to make such claims for science were not taken seriously. Today scholars who are still making such claims for science are the ones who risk being dismissed out of hand.

Hermeneutical Austrian economics

The hermeneutical critiques of traditional Austrian economics summarized here involve expanding its central tenet, subjectivism, and then essentially absorbing each of the other two tenets into this expanded subjectivism (Figure 1). The critique of atomism absorbs methodological individualism and subjectivism into one principle, intersubjective understanding. The critique of objectivism absorbs spontaneous order into its notion of understanding as well. Intersubjective understanding is itself a spontaneous order process.

Atomistic	Objectivistic	Hermeneutical
Austrianism	Austrianism	Austrianism

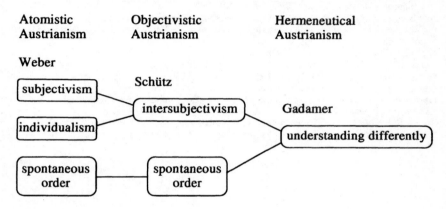

Figure 1

Thus the effect of the interpretive turn can be seen as a radicalization of subjectivism, transforming it from being just one among several distinct and somewhat divergent methodological tenets into being the single integrative concept which underlies the whole methodology of the Austrian school.

See also:
Chapter 6: Phenomenology and economics

Bibliography
Boettke, Peter J. (1990), 'Interpretive Reasoning and the Study of Social Life', *Methodus*, **2**, (2), December, 35–45.

Dreyfus, Hubert L. (1991), *Being-in-the-World: A Commentary on Heidegger's Being and Time, Division I*, Cambridge, Mass.: MIT Press.

Ebeling, Richard M. (1986), 'Toward a Hermeneutical Economics: Expectations, Prices and the Role of Interpretation in a Theory of the Market Process', in I. Kirzner (ed.), *Subjectivism, Intelligibility, and Economic Understanding: Essays in Honor of Ludwig M. Lachmann on his Eightieth Birthday*, New York: New York University Press.

Gadamer, Hans-Georg [1960] (1989), *Truth and Method*, revised translation by J. Weinsheimer and D. Marshall, New York: Crossroad.

Horwitz, Steven (1992), 'Monetary Exchange as an Extra-Linguistic Social Communication Process', *Review of Social Economy*.

Lachmann, Ludwig M. (1971), *The Legacy of Max Weber*, Berkeley: Glendessary Press.
Lachmann, Ludwig M. (1991), 'Austrian Economics: a Hermeneutic Approach', in Don Lavoie
    (ed.), *Economics and Hermeneutics*, London: Routledge.
Lavoie, Don (1990), 'Understanding Differently: Hermeneutics and the Spontaneous Order of
    Communicative Processes', *History of Political Economy*, annual supplement to vol. 22, pp.
    359–77.
Lavoie, Don (1991a), 'The Discovery and Interpretation of Profit Opportunities: Culture and
    the Kirznerian Entrepreneur', in Brigitte Berger (ed.), *The Culture of Entrepreneurship*, San
    Francisco: Institute for Contemporary Studies.
Lavoie, Don (1991b), 'The Progress of Subjectivism', in Mark Blaug and Neil de Marchi (eds),
    *Appraising Modern Economics: Studies in the Methodology of Scientific Research Pro-
    grammes*, Aldershot: Edward Elgar, pp. 470–86.
Madison, G.B. (1991), 'Getting Beyond Objectivism: The Philosophical Hermeneutics of
    Gadamer and Ricoeur', in Don Lavoie (ed.), *Economics and Hermeneutics*, London: Routledge,
    pp. 34–58.
O'Driscoll, Gerald P., Jr. and M.J. Rizzo (1985), *The Economics of Time and Ignorance*, New
    York: Columbia University Press.
Parsons, Stephen D. (1991), 'Time, Expectations, and Subjectivism: Prolegomena to a Dy-
    namic Economics', *Cambridge Journal of Economics*, **15**, 405–23.
Prychitko, David L. (1990), 'Toward an Interpretive Economics: Some Hermeneutic Issues',
    Methodus, **2**, December, 69–71.
Rector, Ralph A. (1991), 'The Economics of Rationality and the Rationality of Economics', in
    Don Lavoie (ed.), *Economics and Hermeneutics*, London: Routledge.

9 Causation and genetic causation in economic theory

Robin Cowan

Over the course of the history of economic thought, causation has, at various times, been associated with different ideas – logical implication, functional dependence, predictive capacity and genetic connection, to name a few.[1] Early in the twentieth century, causal analysis ceased to be central to economics as attention was captured by the marginal revolution and equilibrium analysis. Towards the end of the century, causal analysis has begun to reappear in some areas of economic inquiry, as interest in path-dependence, non-linear dynamics and evolutionary systems has grown. Throughout the century, however, Austrian economics retained a causal view at the center of its research program. In its view of causation, similarly to the view that has begun to reappear elsewhere in economics, the notion of generation is central. Within economics, this view has been developed, largely by Austrian economists, and has found the name genetic causation.

Central to the idea of genetic causation are three things. The first has to do with purposiveness. Economic agents have purposes and act on them. A fundamental principle of modern economics is that agents have goals and desires, or ends, and seek efficient means to attain those ends. Thus a basic feature of causation in economics concerns the causes of action, namely the desires and beliefs of the agents. The second aspect of genetic causation is that overall market outcomes are causally related to individual actions. Market outcomes are thus causally reducible to the desires and beliefs of agents. The final aspect of causation is the genetic nature of a causal process. A cause is not simply something that always precedes its effect. Causes must be understood as initiating a *process* the outcome of which is the effect.

The methodological idea that understanding a phenomenon involves ideas about causation, and in particular genetic causal processes, must be contrasted with a methodological view still common in neoclassical economics, namely that understanding a phenomenon involves finding a model such that the properties of equilibrium can be derived from underlying parameters. On this latter view there is no place for causation in economics.

Causes are events that generate other events, called effects. But an event is necessarily a change in the pre-existing state of affairs, so if there is no change in a system, then ipso facto, there are no events, and thus there can be no causation. In economics, when considering causation and causal analysis, a change must be defined as 'any divergence of the actual from the expected development, irrespective of whether it means a "change" in some absolute sense' (Hayek, 1948, p. 40). When an economic system is in equilibrium, agents' expectations are fulfilled and their plans are successfully carried out, so agents never encounter situations that would lead them to change their beliefs. At the foundation of changes in economic data are human actions, the causes of which are changes in beliefs and desires. The equilibrium method, by focusing exclusively on situations in which beliefs do not change, in an important sense eliminates change, and therefore causation, from the analysis. Indeed, to put the matter more strongly, the aim of the equilibrium approach is to find the level of analysis at which no change occurs – the standard response to a putative disequilibrium in which agents make mistakes or encounter events that appear (to the analyst) to force them to change their beliefs is to show that by including a formerly ignored market (often the market for information) or by redescribing a good (often in terms of a lottery) the phenomenon is made an equilibrium after all, and agents are not in fact changing their beliefs (see, for example, Hahn, 1984). But if there is no change there are no events, and thus neither causes nor effects.

On this view, insofar as there are changes or causes, they are external to the system being modeled. The system, as it were, only responds to shocks from the outside. When all causes are external to the model they are, by definition, outside the realm of economics. Outcomes are determined entirely by economic primitives such as endowments and, until recently, technology and institutions. A change in any of these primitives may cause a change in the equilibrium, but 'such changes are just exogenous shocks, whose consequences, but not causes, are open to economic investigation' (Hausman, 1990, p. 172). In contrast to the equilibrium method, the genetic causal approach sees causation in economics in two ways: as it relates to individual decision making and as it relates to market processes. The former refers to the cause of a particular decision or action, while the latter refers to the sequence of decisions that cause overall market outcomes. While these two levels are clearly related, the connection between them is very complex (not least because of the fact that many consequences of actions are unintended) and has not yet been thoroughly explored. (See below.)

Genetic causal analysis of individual decision making emphasizes the role of motives and desires as causes of human action. Böhm-Bawerk, Weber, Sombart and Keynes all shared the view that there was a causal relation between ends and means. All of these thinkers, though using different vocabulary, believed that the cause of an action was that which the agent hoped to achieve by that action. On this view the cause of economic actions and change lies in the beliefs and desires of the agents, and to understand an economic decision involves understanding the connection (in the agent's mind) between the action (means) and the effect the agent desired to produce (end). None of these thinkers would have subscribed to the view that all determinants of an equilibrium were equally causes because, to use Böhm-Bawerk's terms, the end gives the means its importance, and not vice versa. As a simple example, producers' goods come into being for the sake of consumers' goods, not the reverse. (Max Weber (1992) used and developed this line of thought as the foundation of *verstehende* social science.) Werner Sombart (1930) pressed this view further. For him, to explain a complex social phenomenon was to trace it back to the motives that led to the actions that produced it. In contrast to Böhm-Bawerk (1959) who stressed individual motives, however, Sombart often laid emphasis on collective motives.

Classical analysis of competition centred on a genetic causal view of the market process, because its conception of competition was one of rivalrous behaviour, rather than of a particular type of equilibrium. In order to increase market share, and so profits, sellers would undercut their rivals. Similarly, buyers would attempt to outbid others trying to buy the same good. Rivalrous motives are thus essential to understanding this process. On an aggregated level, the center of the classical inter-market process was capital movement, which was a response to changes in the relative rates of profits in different industries. Whenever market prices (determined by supply and demand) deviate from natural prices (determined by the cost of production), the profit rate in the affected industry deviates from the profit rate in the lead sector, agriculture. Capital allocation is determined by the competition for it – in industries in which the market price exceeds the natural price capital users are able to bid up the price of capital. Thus capital flows to these sectors until the market price returns to its natural level. These underlying causal processes justified viewing the state of equilibrium as a center of gravity towards which the system, continually in motion, was always moving.

The beginnings of the move away from causal analysis might be seen in Ricardo and Cournot, both of whom put aside the immediate effects of changes in the economy and concentrated on the end result of the competitive process. This is in contrast to Malthus, who was more concerned with the immediate effects of specific changes. The Cournot–Ricardo approach came to dominate the later formalization of the theory of (perfect) competition. Böhm-Bawerk, while concerned about causation in value theory, was content with the identification of causes in the motives of individual agents, but was not concerned with giving a detailed account of the process whereby these motives produced market outcomes. Thus he did not develop causal ideas at the level of the market. In contrast, the classical economists examined causal processes operating in the market, but tended not to attempt any explicit development of causes at the level of the individual. In his concept 'genetic causal equilibrium', Hans Mayer (1932) sought to bring these two levels of causation together in one analytical framework, also seeking to integrate this causal analysis with the Ricardian concern for the 'permanent state of things'.

Mayer's concern was with the causal path towards an equilibrium, and the sequence of decisions taken by agents along that path. These decisions would reflect the fact that along any path (whether towards an equilibrium or away from it), agents' beliefs are changing as they encounter unexpected events and frustrations. As an individual learns more about his environment, he is better able to allocate his resources, and so moves closer and closer to an equilibrium position. Mayer wanted to explain how this 'permanent state' could be generated by a transient process. By his own admission he did not get very far, and a general theory of the path continues to elude economists in this tradition. Lachmann (1986), however, has made an explicit attempt to go beyond Mayer.

Friedrich Hayek (1948), following Mayer, saw the central issue as being to show how a state of equilibrium is, or can be, reached from a state of disequilibrium. Hayek's approach to this problem was very much in the genetic causal tradition. He saw the market as a process of acquisition and transmission of knowledge. On this view, equilibrium is defined in terms of agents' beliefs in the sense that equilibrium obtains when the plans of agents are mutually compatible. When all agents can carry out their plans, no agent has reason to revise his beliefs about the world (since all of the predictions made in the formation of the plan have been realized) and a steady state obtains. But when some plans are frustrated, there must be agents whose predictions were incorrect, and so who will revise their beliefs (about the external world and about what others are planning to do) and subsequently their plans. In this way, the causal market process consists in the acquisition and dissemination of knowledge: agents learn both about the external objective world and about what other agents are planning to do, and through their actions communicate this knowledge to other agents. These changes in beliefs continue until all plans are compatible, that is, until there is an underlying compatibility or equilibrium of beliefs.

As the idea of genetic causation has evolved from the work of Böhm-Bawerk, through Mayer down to the present day, several characteristics have come to be seen as central to the concept. They can be divided into two groups: those following from the belief in the purposiveness of agents, and those associated with the idea of genetic connection.

Purposiveness

Economic agents have ends – to maximize utility or to maximize profits – and they endeavor to adopt means that will achieve these ends. In an important sense economics is a science about action. Recent work in action theory has convinced philosophers of the role of *desires* and *beliefs* as the causes of actions[2] (see Davidson, 1968). A causal explanation of an action demands consideration of what the agent was trying to achieve and what he believed the facts were. This insight has been extended from short-lived, individual actions to longer-term plans – desires and beliefs cause agents to form plans aimed at satisfying their desires, and the series of actions undertaken in fulfilling those plans have their own causal repercussions (see Bratman, 1987).

A cause is a real mental event or change

Desires and beliefs are causes of plans and of actions. An agent forms a plan based on his current desires and beliefs and, if these do not change, he carries out that plan. A cause, then, can produce a sequence of actions, each of which is part of the plan. It is important to note, though, that, without *changes* in beliefs or desires, an action cannot originate. A desire *comes into being* and the agent acts for the sake of satisfying it. If the act is successful the desire is extinguished, at least for a time. When the execution of a plan involves many actions and takes place over an extended period, it can appear that a *state* of desire causes an action. Two considerations argue that this is not the case. First, while the continued existence of the motivating desire may be necessary to the performance of all of the actions in an extended plan (suggesting that this state of desire is a cause of the actions) it cannot be seen as an originating cause. The continuing desire does not *generate* the actions, though it does, in a sense, allow them to take place, in the way that air allows a match to light when struck. The *initial* appearance of the desire is the originating cause, and the working out of the plan is the process that connects the many actions to the originating cause. The second consideration is the distinction between a simple static condition (an agent likes apples) and the continual recurrence of an event (an agent gets hungry every day). Static analysis of essentially dynamic problems tends to collapse the latter into the former. Thus, strictly speaking, only changes in desires and beliefs can be originating causes of actions.

Within the genetic causal approach, the goal is to understand the economic system as a causal process, so genetic causal explanations must treat causes, namely desires and beliefs, as real, not simply as instrumental, entities. If desires and beliefs *are* real, then ignoring, for example, the informational and computational limits of agents cannot lead to understanding the phenomenon in terms of its causes. The desires and beliefs implicit in an analysis that admits of no restrictions on agents' mental abilities are not the real causes of individual decisions.

There can be no backwards causation
Since economic change originates in changes of desires and beliefs of economic agents, a later event cannot be the cause of an earlier action. Changes in the world that engender actions must be apprehended by the individual. Only current desires and current beliefs (even if they refer to future time periods) can influence actions, so backwards causation, at least in economics, is ruled out. Discussion of perfect foresight equilibria sometimes elides this point. When everything that is expected is always realized, the role of the beliefs, and therefore the expectations, of the agent tends to be lost. But it remains the case that it is the expected or imagined utility that motivates or causes action.

A cause need not be necessary or sufficient for its effect
Throughout the history of philosophical analysis of causation there have been attempts to understand causation as a set of necessary and/or sufficient conditions for the occurrence of an effect. Recently, however, this view of causation has been rejected as not capturing essential elements (for example, Miller, 1987). That necessity and sufficiency are not enough to characterize causation as it is understood in economics seems correct. The same action may be an appropriate response to a multitude of desire–belief combinations and, conversely, several different actions may be appropriate responses to a particular desire–belief combination. In other words, a particular effect can be caused in several different ways, and a particular cause can have alternative effects. The first assertion needs no elaboration. The second follows from the fact that many different actions may be appropriate responses to a particular situation and, it should be noted, necessarily introduces some indeterminacy into economic analysis. The tradition of modeling economic phenomena in ways such that there is a unique equilibrium has difficulty with this view: as a result, models with multiple equilibria are becoming more common.[3]

Genetic connection
A causal explanation is more than a simple list of causes and their effects. It must include explication of the process that links the desires of agents to the generated market outcomes. Were all desires immediately satisfied, and all beliefs immediately validated, the need for a genetic connection would be replaced by a need simply to demonstrate the consistency of the desire–belief combination and the resulting market outcome. The passage of time between cause and effect, as actions are played out in the market, implies that the process can, in principle at least, be elucidated. The process between initial desires and beliefs and the final outcome consists of three stages: the formation of plans, consistent with beliefs, aimed at satisfying desires; the discov-

ery of errors in beliefs when plan implementation is unsuccessful; and revision in response to the errors (see Bode, 1943).

A cause must be external to its effect

Because an effect is the result of a process which flows from a cause, an effect and its cause(s) must be distinct. They must at the very least, be separated by the process that generates one from the other. An event or state cannot be (part of) its own cause, so it cannot be the case that an equilibrium exists prior to (or contemporaneously with) the actions that bring it about. To be sure, the correct anticipation of an equilibrium may be a cause of the equilibrium, but this is not to say that equilibrium is self-caused.

This observation points to an important feature of economic action. If processes start out of equilibrium, agents will not necessarily try to charge the equilibrium price (or more generally engage in equilibrium behavior). The behavioral assumption that agents maximize profits implies that they will try to charge the profit-maximizing price, whatever it may be at the time they are setting prices. It is easy to show that, when agents charge profit-maximizing prices, the process in which trades are made, and beliefs and prices revised, is central to determining which equilibrium price emerges. Equilibrium prices and quantities in this case are not determined solely by preferences and initial endowments of the agents, as is implied by simple equilibrium analysis (see Fisher, 1983). The problem is then to find the conditions under which the cause (charging the profit-maximizing price) generates a process that ends in a state in which agents' plans are fulfilled, and are therefore not revised, that is to say, an equilibrium.

A cause bears an asymmetric relation to its effect

A fundamental feature of a causal relation is that it is not symmetric: a cause generates its effect; an effect does not generate its cause. This asymmetry is a direct result of the nature of purposive behaviour: 'It is the end that lends the means its importance, not vice versa' (Böhm-Bawerk, 1959, p. 111). A second source of the asymmetry in genetic causation lies in the genetic connection between actions and market consequences. Though prices may influence the nature of transactions, it is transactions that produce or generate prices, not vice versa.

An absence of asymmetry can often be seen in models where capital accumulation is treated with a differential equation, so that future capital levels are determined by the present level of capital. Differential equations simply describe covariation, though, so they can in principle be read to explain present capital levels as determined by future capital. This lack of asymmetry between cause and effect alerts us to the fact that a causal explanation requires more than an accurate depiction of the way two variables move together.

A genetic connection is a process in time and not a series of states
That a process is more than a series of states was elaborated by Henri Bergson (1975), who pointed out that an arrow does not get from one point to another simply by being in different places at different points in time – it must move. Putting several stationary states together into a sequence does not constitute movement; a process is an indivisible whole. In any true process, then, there must be an inner principle of change. Any observed phase along the process must contain the seeds of the next phase. A process exhibits an inherent link among past, present and future.

The link among the periods for economic agents is the fact that they make and execute plans based on their expectations of the future, all the while revising and modifying both expectations and plans in the light of new information: 'Plans are made [now] for the attainment of certain aims ... and ... they are based on individual expectations concerning future conditions, expectations which in turn are influenced by individual interpretation of past events' (Lindahl, 1939, p. 36). When an agent is unable to carry out his plan, or if the plan yields unexpected results, the plan will typically be modified. Exactly how the plan is revised depends on what the agent expects the future to be like. Since interpretation of the past and forming expectations about the future are intimately related, plan revision is dynamically continuous.

The dynamic continuity of genetic connections implies that there is a temporal aspect to genetic causation: 'The idea of causality ... is inseparable from the idea of time. A process of change involves a beginning and a becoming, and these are only conceivable as processes in time' (Menger, 1981). Because of the inherent limitations in agents' abilities to apprehend and process information, learning is a process that takes time. While frustration in the implementation of a plan may happen 'now', the individual may not be able to correct all of his errors right away. Furthermore, though bygones may be bygones, the past places conditions on the optimal response to new information. Decisions made about the design of technology, though learned to have been incorrect, will typically influence the way an agent responds to the suboptimality of that technology. The correct response to the information that the technology is badly designed may be to modify it (to a non-optimal but better design) rather than to discard it and acquire new, optimally designed technology. This implies that a genetic connection is not an instantaneous relation but a temporally coherent process of gradual error correction and plan revision.

The use of genetic causation in economic explanation is an attempt to grapple with the realities of desires and beliefs, of change, and of the adjustment path. It requires an acknowledgement that an attempt to understand dynamic processes in a detailed way may be extremely ambitious. Because of the complexity of data encountered on the path, and because of the constraints on agents' abilities to apprehend and process information, it is likely that the best that research in this spirit shall ever be able to do is to explain the general *pattern* of adjustment responses and hence of the ultimate equilibrium (should one occur).

Notes

1. This entry draws heavily on Cowan and Rizzo (1991).
2. Desires, as discussed in action theory, are closer to Samuelson's concept of revealed preference or simply to goals than to the idea of subjective tastes.
3. Especially in game theory, industrial organization and macroeconomics models in which there are many equilibrium outcomes for a given set of data have proliferated. Historically, a common response to the multiple equilibrium phenomenon is to redefine the equilibrium concept in order to reduce the number. This is the route taken in the refinements literature in game theory. It is not clear a priori that the number of equilibria should be reduced, but a very strong argument for eliminating one or some of the possible equilibria is a causal one, namely that the agents in the model could not engage in a process that would produce that equilibrium.

See also:

Chapter 2: Methodological individualism; Chapter 5: Aristotelianism, apriorism, essentialism; Chapter 11: Praxeology

Bibliography

Bergson, H. (1975), *Creative Evolution*, trans. Arthur Mitchell, Westport, Conn.: Greenwood Press.
Bode, K. (1943), 'Plan analysis and Process analysis', *American Economic Review*, **33**, 348–54.
Böhm-Bawerk, Eugen von (1959), 'On the Value of Producers' Goods and the Relationship Between Value and Costs, trans. H.F. Sennholz, in 'Further Essays on Capital and Interest', *Capital and Interest*, vol. III, South Holland, IL: Libertarian Press, pp. 97–115.
Bratman, M. (1987), *Intention, Plans and Practical Reason*, Cambridge, Mass.: Harvard University Press.
Cowan, R. and M.J. Rizzo (1991), 'The Genetic-Causal Moment in Economic Theory', C.V. Starr Center for Applied Economics Working Paper, RR#91–13.
Davidson, D. (1968), 'Actions, Reasons and Causes', in A.R. White (ed.), *The Philosophy of Action*, Oxford: Oxford University Press.
Fisher, F.M. (1983), *Disequilibrium Foundations of Equilibrium Economics*, Cambridge: Cambridge University Press.
Hahn, F. (1984), 'On the Notion of Equilibrium in Economics', in *Equilibrium and Macroeconomics*, Cambridge, Mass.: MIT Press, pp. 43–71.
Hausman, D. (1990), 'Supply and Demand Explanations and Their *Ceteris Paribus* Clauses', *Review of Political Economy*, **2**, (2), 168–87.
Hayek, F.A. (1948), *Individualism and Economic Order*, Chicago: Chicago University Press, pp. 33–56.
Lachmann, L. (1986), *The Market and an Economic Process*, Oxford: Basil Blackwell.
Lindahl, E. (1939), *Studies in the Theory of Money and Capital*, London: George Allen & Unwin.
Mayer, H. (1932), 'Der Erkenntniswert der funktionellen Preistheorie', in *Die Wirtschaftstheorie der Gegenwart*, vol. II, Vienna: Julius Springer.
Menger, Carl (1981), *Principles of Economics*, trans. J. Dingwall and B.F. Hoselitz, New York: New York University Press.
Miller, R.W. (1987), *Fact and Method*, Princeton: Princeton University Press.
Sombart, W. (1930), *Die drei Nationalökonomien: Geschichte und System der Lehre von der Wirtschaft*, Munich: Dunker & Humbolt.
Weber, Max. (1922), *Gesammelte Aufsätze zur Wissenschaftslehre*, Tübingen: J.C.B. Mohr.

10 Ideal type methodology in economics
Roger G. Koppl

The term 'ideal type' is used to describe a variety of abstractions used by social scientists. An ideal type is ideal because it is an imaginary construction, an *idea* in the mind of a scientist. It is a type because it is the idea of some class or *type* of entity. Thus an ideal type is just how we like to think of something for scientific purposes. While we might thus call any theoretical construct an 'ideal type', economists today apply the term more narrowly. As the term is typically used by Austrian economists, an ideal type is an 'intelligible' representation of an action or an actor. A representation is intelligible if it identifies the subjective meaning of the action as it appears to the actor. Ideal types of persons are 'personal ideal types'. Ideal types of action are 'course-of-action' types'.

Reference to subjective meanings brings to the analysis of social phenomena the 'understanding' or *verstehen* common to both Austrian economics and interpretive sociology. It also raises the question of the status or nature of the 'understanding' social scientists are supposed to have of these subjective meanings. In some discussions the understanding of subjective meanings is achieved through a special faculty of intuition that allows us to obtain knowledge by 'entering into' the lifestream of other persons. This idea seems to be Romantic at root and based on an exaggerated Cartesian dualism according to which quite different epistemological principles apply to mental and physical phenomena. Following Alfred Schutz (1967) and Fritz Machlup (1978), many Austrian economists reject this position. According to them, the subjective meanings an analyst 'understands' to be present are conjectured; they are imputed by him to the actors and not somehow 'extracted' from the phenomena being explained. On this view, economists who use the method of ideal types should be willing to consider competing conjectures about what subjective meanings are both operative and important in different contexts. Empirical evidence, whether or not numerical, should be considered in weighing competing conjectures.

The subjective meanings social scientists impute to the ideal types of their models are ordinary conjectures about matters of fact, not lived experiences in all their fullness. They are therefore more or less empty of particulars. They are abstract representations of certain aspects of the thought processes of individuals who may themselves be imaginary, as in the case of counterfactual arguments. They are 'constructs of the second order', as Schutz has put it. These constructs of the second order are just how we like to think of subjective meanings for scientific purposes.

Because the explanatory purposes of the social scientist are different from the purposes of the actors in his model, economists often wish to represent the subjective meanings of their actors in ways the actors themselves would not recognize. It may thus be true, on the one hand, that business enterprises generally seek profits and respond appropriately to changes in relative prices even though, on the other hand, the officers of these same enterprises would deny that they equate marginal costs and marginal revenue. When considering competing conjectures about subjective meanings, economists should distinguish between the motives, expectations, propensities and so on being imputed to the actors and the semantic structures chosen to represent those subjective meanings. Failure to do so can result in bogus falsifications of theory and needlessly confused debate.

The semantic structures with which economists represent subjective meanings make up an important group of conventions that have evolved over the history of the discipline. As conventions, they contain an element of arbitrariness; other semantic structures could have served the same scientific purposes. Thus something like the Duheme–Quine thesis applies to the social sciences. But the causal relations of interpretive social science are more than abbreviated descriptions of observable regularities. They are representations of externally existing phenomena. One may ask if a model has identified the 'true' causes of the phenomena being explained. In this sense, social scientists can strive for a kind of 'realism' widely regarded as unattainable in the physical sciences.

Following Dilthey, some writers have claimed that arguments depending on a reference to subjective meanings are necessarily 'particular' to some more or less precise historical context. According to this line of reasoning, social scientists may hope to 'understand' historical phenomena, but they cannot construct 'general' propositions. In other words, subjectivism is anti-theoretical. Alfred Schutz and Fritz Machlup have shown that the 'understanding' of interpretive sociology is not, in fact, anti-theoretical. They have shown that the 'generality' of an argument depends, among other things, upon the 'anonymity' of the personal ideal types it uses. Arguments relying on highly anonymous ideal types may have the reliability and broad applicability necessary to label them 'theoretical'. In other words, subjectivist economics can identify law-like regularities in society. The anonymity of a personal ideal type is the degree to which it is empty of particular content. An ideal type of the Connecticut Yankee of the 1830s contains lots of particulars about his beliefs, abilities, knowledge and preferences. We know a lot about his style of life. The ideal type of a postman contains far fewer particulars; it is highly anonymous. The ideal type of 'acting man', Ludwig von Mises' *homo agens*, is completely devoid of particulars. It is anyone considered as an actor. *Homo agens* is the perfectly anonymous ideal type.

Propositions assuming personal ideal types of low anonymity are less reliable than those assuming personal ideal types of high anonymity. Machlup used three economic propositions to illustrate this linkage between reliability and anonymity.

> Statement (1): 'If, because of an abundant crop, the output of wheat is much increased, the price of wheat will fall.'

> Statement (2): 'If, because of increased wage-rates and decreased interest rates, capital becomes relatively cheaper than labor, new labor-saving devices will be invented.'

> Statement (3): 'If, because of heavy withdrawals of foreign deposits, the banks are in danger of insolvency, the Central Bank Authorities will extend the necessary credit.' (1978, p. 64)

Statement (3) is probably true in most applications: our knowledge of the incentives of central bankers leads us to expect the sort of actions predicted in the statement. But central bankers are individuals who may act out of character or in contradiction to their material incentives. As Machlup noted, it makes a great deal of difference whether the central bank gets its advice from Keynes or from Hayek. The personal ideal types presumed in statement (3) are not highly anonymous and for that reason the statement can be applied with only a modest degree of confidence.

Statement (2) is also likely to hold in most applications. The statement assumes quite anonymous ideal types who may be relied upon to respond to their incentives. We may be sure that in the assumed conditions entrepreneurs and engineers will try to find ways to save labor. But the statement makes the further presumption that some persons will succeed in finding new devices that economize on labor. This relatively specific assumption about the 'mind-contents' of the personal ideal types presumed in the statement may not always correspond to the facts of experience. Thus, while statement (2) is more reliable than statement (3), it may not always lead to correct expectations.

Statement (1) is highly reliable. It is difficulty to imagine what idiosyncrasies of behavior among wheat farmers or commodity traders could prevent an abundant crop from depressing wheat prices. The personal ideal types presumed in the statement are all highly anonymous. We need to know very little about the participants in the markets to be sure that the predicted result will indeed hold. We need to know only such things as that wheat farmers prefer more profits to less. As an empirical proposition, statement (1) is not 'apodictically certain'. But it is a highly reliable guide to our expectations.

Machlup's three exemplary propositions show us that the degree of anonymity of the personal ideal types of a model influences the degree to which we may rely upon the conclusions of the model to guide our expectations. Economic propositions presuming only highly anonymous personal ideal types may be highly reliable guides to economic expectations. Economic propositions presuming personal ideal types of very low anonymity cannot be reliably applied to any but, perhaps, a small number of phenomena. This analysis of the role of anonymity shows us that what makes a proposition of interpretive social science 'particular' in Dilthey's sense is not the reference to subjective meanings, but the specificity with which those subjective meanings are described. The use of anonymous ideal types allows us to refer to subjective meanings in propositions that are perfectly 'general' in their applicability. In other words, subjectivism is not anti-theoretical.

The two following comments support the claim that the analysis of anonymity we get from Schutz and Machlup illuminates both economic theory and economic phenomena. Austrian economists generally make relatively little use of the mathematical theory of games, and yet this theory was addressed initially to precisely the most characteristically 'Austrian' problems in economic theory. The reason for this apparent paradox is that the theory of games requires the analyst to use only highly anonymous ideal types. But, in the small-numbers contexts such as oligopoly to which game theory is frequently applied, the use of highly anonymous ideal types is inappropriate. In such contexts, the idiosyncrasies of the individual players matter and a satisfactory analysis often requires the use of rather non-anonymous ideal types. The requirement that all personal ideal types be highly anonymous restricts the applications subjectivist economists can make of game theory.

The theory of competitive markets presumes that no market participant has much power. All participants are subject to the discipline of profit and loss. This assumption warrants the use of only highly anonymous ideal types in the economist's model of competitive markets. When the assumptions of the economist's model of competition hold, markets exhibit the law-like regularities of his theory. But sometimes market participants have power. Some markets are oligopolistic, governments often trade or intervene in markets, and so on. When some participants have power, the market process is influenced by the actions of one or a few individuals who are more or less immune from the discipline of profit and loss. In such a market, the predictions of the standard theory of competitive markets are less reliable guides to expectations. No law-like regularity of the sort identified in 'neoclassical' models is likely to hold reliably when the presence of powerful market participants requires the analyst to use relatively non-anonymous ideal types. In this sense it may be said that the exercise of power makes markets less orderly (see Koppl and Langlois, 1993).

The use of ideal types is not unique to subjectivist economics. The 'rational maximizers' of 'neoclassical' economics, for example, are personal ideal types. Subjectivists, however, are generally willing to ask if the subjective meanings imputed to the personal ideal types of their models have an 'objective probability' of being operative in the social phenomena being explained. They are willing to apply criteria other than 'predictive power' to the appraisal of their personal ideal types. Subjectivists are willing to use personal ideal types of varying degrees of anonymity, depending on the problem being addressed. And they are willing to use both mathematical and non-mathematical representations of subjective meanings. Subjectivists today generally reject the sort of methodological restrictions on the use of personal ideal types that would prescribe or proscribe the use of one sort of ideal type, 'rational maximizers' for example. They do, however, prefer 'understandable' models (see the article on 'invisible hand' explanations in this volume) in which the subjective meanings imputed to the personal ideal types of the model are shown to be plausible and intelligible.

See also:
Chapter 5: Aristotelianism, apriorism, essentialism; Chapter 11: Praxeology; Chapter 6: Phenomenology and economics; Chapter 2: Methodological individualism

Bibliography
Dilthey, Wilhelm (1982), *Selected Writings*, Cambridge: Cambridge University Press.
Koppl, Roger and Richard N. Langlois (1993), 'When do Ideas Matter? A Study in the Natural Selection of Social Games', *Advances in Austrian Economics*, **1**, (1).
Machlup, Fritz (1978), *Methodology of Economics and Other Social Sciences*, New York: Academic Press.
Schutz, Alfred (1967), *The Phenomenology of the Social World*, trans. G. Walsh and F. Lehnert, Evanston, IL: Northwestern University Press.

11 Praxeology

David L. Prychitko

Modern economics calls itself the science of choice; it studies choices that inevitably flow from the fact of scarcity. In contemporary neoclassical theory, individuals are modeled as rational agents that maximize utility subject to constraint. The argument is familiar to any student of economics: maximization between two scarce goods occurs when an agent chooses a combination of goods such that the ratio of their marginal utilities equals the price ratio. In its generalized form, an 'action' of an agent is a point in R^L, the commodity space. All the assumptions behind the Lagrangian technique specify the terribly unrealistic conditions under which neoclassical utility maximization takes place.

The Austrian school, especially with Mises (1966), starts from a very different concept of choice, and consequently weaves a dramatically different 'foundation' for economic theory. Austrians have argued that economic theory is (or should be) a subset of 'praxeology' (after Alfred Espinas, the nineteenth-century French historian), which is the formal science (*logos*) of praxis, or human action. Ludwig von Mises has gone so far as to say that praxeology is the 'ultimate foundation of economic science' (Mises, 1978); Murray Rothbard considers praxeology to be 'the method of the social sciences' (Rothbard, 1979, part 2).

The praxeological a priori: the action axiom

Contemporary Austrians reject neoclassical choice and utility theory, which interprets individuals as atomistic and passive reactors, technically responding to objectively given means, ends and constraints. Instead, Austrians favor studying purposive, meaningful action: in this view, individuals adopt goals and consciously apply means to attain them. Praxeology is considered a general, or universal, theory of human action, and Austrian economics is considered its best developed subset.

The claim that individuals act, that they apply scarce means to attain goals, is taken to be the essence of human being. 'For man human action and its vicissitudes are the real thing', writes Mises. 'Action is the essence of his nature and existence, his means of preserving his life and raising himself above the level of animals and plants. However perishable and evanescent all human efforts may be, for man and for human science they are of primary importance' (Mises, 1966, pp. 18–19). Although both Austrian economics and neoclassical economics rest upon a notion of methodological individual-ism, there is clearly a praxis philosophy at work in Austrian economics that has no counterpart in mainstream theory. Moreover, Austrians have claimed that this insight into human being is more than simply an interpretive ap-proach to economics: it is considered to be a primordial truth.

Specifically, Mises claims that human action is an a priori truth, a univer-sally valid presupposition, an 'ultimate given'. For Mises, the truth behind the claim that humans act is not gained through experience – it is not a testable hypothesis – but rather it is known prior to experience, it is a phenomenon of consciousness. Mises asserts a neo-Kantian claim by arguing that the principle of human action necessarily flows from the human mind's 'logical categories':

> Human knowledge is conditioned by the structure of the human mind. If it chooses human action as the subject matter of its inquiries, it cannot mean anything else than the categories of action which are proper to the human mind and are its projection into the external world of becoming and change. All the theorems of praxeology refer only to these categories of action and are valid only in the orbit of their operation. (1966, p. 36; cf. 1978, chapter 1)

Not all Austrians agree. Opposed to Mises's appropriation of Kant, Rothbard argues that we become aware of the human action 'axiom' and other 'sub-sidiary axioms' through our experience in the world. He goes so far as to say that these axioms are 'radically empirical' (Rothbard, 1976, p. 24; 1979, pp. 35–6). Israel Kirzner, on the other hand, claims that human action is true through introspection (1976, p. 43).

Still, most Austrians agree that the action axiom is universally true, self-evident and therefore unchallengeable: to even question the claim that hu-mans act is to adopt an argument (a means) to demonstrate the claim's alleged falsehood (an end) and thus it is to engage in an action itself in order to refute the existence of action (Rothbard, 1976, p. 28). The claim of the ultimate self-evident truth of human action (whether defended on Kantian or other grounds) is the key to understanding the Euclidean nature of Austrian School praxeology and economics, for whatever is deduced from an abso-lutely true axiom is apodictically true, as long as the logic is correct. Hence, for Austrians, praxeology is not only a study of human action; praxeology establishes a value-free, universally valid theory deduced from the implica-tions of the action axiom.

Causality, time, uncertainty
Some examples are in order. If action consists of the goal-driven use of scarce means, the attempt to move oneself into a more satisfactory state of affairs (subjectively perceived), then action presupposes that the actor (rightly

or wrongly) expects that the means he or she employs can causally achieve the ends. (I drink water when I'm thirsty, for instance.) Whether that particular causal assumption is true or not will be learned by experience (water tends to cure my thirst, wine doesn't). Nevertheless, inherent in any notion of human action is the 'category' (Mises), or subjective anticipation, of cause and effect.

Moreover, this means–ends rationality presupposes that individuals can imagine a future that is different from the present (I'm thirsty now, but I expect that my thirst will be quenched after drinking some water). Action thus embodies a forward-looking character, which implies the presence of time and uncertainty. To act is to embark upon change, to create, to make a difference, to substitute one state of affairs for (it is hoped) a better state of affairs. Change, of course, takes place over time. And to be conscious of time, and willing to act, implies uncertainty. If a being enjoyed full and perfect knowledge (or its probabilistic counterparts), it would not have to act, but instead would react to its environment in a pre-programmed manner. The type of uncertainty humans face cannot be reduced to given probability distributions (which neoclassical economists mislabel 'uncertainty' when it is, to recall Frank Knight's useful distinction, mere 'risk').

Perhaps here we can understand better Austrian criticisms of neoclassical economics: general equilibrium theory has developed an abstract model to an abstract question: can a decentralized economy converge into a general economic equilibrium? Yes, provided that, among other things, individual agents behave atomistically, while enjoying full and complete information, facing perfect certainty, reacting in formal, logical time. The thrust of neoclassical theory has been to establish the economic characteristics of general equilibrium. This is far from the realm of Austrian praxeology, which explains tendencies towards general equilibrium by reference to individual human actions.

Theory and history: the status of praxeological laws

The praxeological criticism of neoclassical theory goes further. Standard theory employs a variety of admittedly unrealistic, 'operational' assumptions that depend upon an 'as if' defense: every first-year student who actually understands the first chapter of their microeconomics textbook learns that individual agents do not 'really' make choices by referring to their indifference maps or topological analysis. Nobody 'really' does what the next 20 chapters of the book illustrate. The models are only 'as if' depictions. The predictability of the theory is what matters, not the realism of its assumptions. Following a Popperian positivism, the hypotheses of standard economics are supposed to be falsifiable, and only tentatively considered true if supported by empirical data. In this way, predictability is the goal of neoclassical economics, and econometrics is supposed to serve as the technique by which to test theory's predictive power.

According to praxeological rhetoric, the core of praxeological 'laws' is deduced from the action axiom; such as the law of diminishing marginal utility, the law of demand and the law of supply. Even the notion of diminishing marginal returns is considered an a priori true law, deduced from the action axiom. Having been derived through logical deduction from an absolutely true premise, there is no need to 'test' praxeological laws with econometrics, nor would they be refined by mathematical economics: their truth is already implied by the fact that humans act (Mises, 1966, pp. 55–6, 350–57; cf. Rizzo, 1978). Of course, other 'subsidiary' axioms may be gleaned from historical experience (for example, the notion of the disutility of labor, and the presence of a general medium of exchange, are broadly empirical and are not necessarily deduced from first principles); nevertheless, the epistemological status of Austrian economics is unchanged when applied to a world where the disutility of labor exists, or where money is present, provided these auxiliary assumptions are present. Moreover, praxeological laws are christened *wertfrei*, or value-free, totally independent of the ethics, values or any other biases of the theoretician.

Perhaps the rhetorical thrust of praxeology is best summed with Mises's statement:

> The theorems attained by correct praxeological reasoning are not only perfectly certain and incontestable, like the correct mathematical theorems. They refer, moreover, with the full rigidity of their apodictic certainty and incontestability to the reality of action as it appears in life and history. Praxeology conveys exact and precise knowledge of real things. (Mises, 1966, p. 39).

This is a far cry from mainstream positivism. Praxeology is considered necessary to understand history – praxeology allows the historian to clarify and systematically interpret empirical reality – but the data of history bear no impact on the core of a priori praxeological principles. At best, historical experience 'merely directs our curiosity toward certain problems and diverts it away from other problems' (Mises, 1966, p. 65).

Beyond apodictic and apoplectic certainty: praxeological pragmatics

But is it persuasive? If praxeology does what neoclassical economics cannot do – provide apodictically certain knowledge of social reality – why is not everyone an Austrian school praxeologist? After all, would any scientist in her right mind wilfully jettison absolute truth if it stared her in the face (or if it could be bought from Laissez Faire Books)? There are, undoubtedly, several possible answers to this question. By way of conclusion, I wish to raise four criticisms that may help explain the failure of Austrian praxeology to gain more than a handful of supporters, as well as point towards a more useful recasting of praxeology.

First, there are other praxeologies (usually spelled 'praxiology'), associated with the efforts of Eugen Slutsky, Oskar Lange, Tadeusz Kotarbinski and a number of contemporary Polish and East European scholars (see Auspitz *et al.*, 1992) that Austrians have paid little attention to (Rothbard, 1971, notwithstanding), but which may illustrate strengths, as well as limits, to the Austrian conception. Moreover, Austrians may have something to learn by exploring the recent and explosive literature in praxis philosophy – the panoply of analytic and interpretive accounts of human action stretching from Marx's radical anthropology to the ontological claims behind Gadamer's hermeneutics (see, for example, Bernstein, 1971; Ricoeur, 1991). Perhaps a richer, if not more problematic, notion of rationality and action is in order.

Second, the epistemological status of praxeological laws and their relationship to history is questionable in the light of contemporary philosophies of science and epistemology. While Mises was correct to argue, during the decades of high positivism, that empirical facts of the human sciences are theory-laden, that historical data are dependent upon theoretical presuppositions, his claim that praxeological theory is itself 'out of time' (Mises, 1966, p. 99), a product of logical mental categories, something strictly separable from history, must now be dismissed as outdated, if not absurd. It simply does not square with the last three decades of research into the history, nature and philosophy of science.

Third, Austrian praxeology has failed to answer the apparently innocent, but troubling, Caldwell Question: how does one choose between *rival* systems of thought that also claim to be deduced from absolutely true axioms? (Caldwell, 1984). The foundations of Austrian school praxeology may tremble when faced with a rival apodictic system (as Hollis and Nell's purported to be), for now the praxeologist faces a *choice* between two perhaps contradicting, but allegedly apodictically certain theories. *Now* what are the criteria for theory choice? Are those criteria grounded upon an ultimate foundation, too? How can such a conflict be resolved if each side claims absolute truth?

Fourth, praxeology has become dogma among its most ardent defenders. This should be no surprise in the light of my last statement. A scientist that claims he beholds timeless, absolute truth embodied by an irrefutable system of thought, no matter how sincere his beliefs may be, is a scientist who effectively closes himself off from discourse. The claim of 'apodictic certainty' tends to break down into a kicking, stomping, unreasonable and apoplectic certainty in the face of criticism. In fact, it is but a small step (or logical deduction, as it were) to conclude that those who do not fully embrace the praxeological system are either morally suspect (that is, they really do recognize the truth within praxeological thought, but refuse to endorse it) or nihilist (that is, they reject logic and the primordial fact of human action), or just plain stupid. Apodictic certainty creates closure and disables scientific discourse. It goes without saying that this approach to the community of social scientists leaves praxeology with little evolutionary potential and may merely attract those who are predisposed to dogmatic thought or its ideology.

Having raised these criticisms, however, I do not think that Austrian economic theory must be dismissed. To the contrary, I believe Austrian economists have many important insights, and the human sciences would be worse without them. Focusing upon humans as actors, as opposed to the purely rational reactors of standard economics, grappling with questions of time, subjective perception, expectations and radical uncertainty, and interpreting social systems as the product of largely unintended consequences is clearly a defensible research program which can open doors between Austrian economists and Post Keynesian, institutionalist and radical political economists, as well as other, hitherto largely ignored scholars in history, ethnography, anthropology, psychology and sociology. By abandoning praxeology's epistemological pretenses, by which I mean the rhetorical claims of 'ultimate foundations' and 'apodictic certainty' and all that they imply, and adopting a pragmatic, as opposed to apodictic, justification of a science of human action, Austrian School economists might gain a more sympathetic hearing. Now whether this approach would still be considered 'Austrian economics' or even 'praxeology', is difficult to say. It would, nevertheless, be an improvement.

See also:
Chapter 2: Methodological individualism; Chapter 3: Subjectivism; Chapter 7: Formalism in twentieth-century economics; Chapter 5: Aristotelianism, apriorism, essentialism

Bibliography
Auspitz, J. Lee, Wojciech W. Gasparski, Marek K. Mlicki and Szaniawski Klemens (eds) (1992), *Praxiologies and the Philosophy of Economics: the International Annual of Practical Philosophy and Methodology, Volume I*, London: Transaction Publishers.
Bernstein, Richard J. (1971), *Praxis and Action: Contemporary Philosophies of Human Activity*, Philadelphia: University of Pennsylvania Press.
Caldwell, Bruce (1984), 'Praxeology and its Critics: An Appraisal', *History of Political Economy*, (fall).
Kirzner, Israel M. (1976), 'On the Method of Austrian Economics', in Edwin G. Dolan (ed.), *The Foundations of Modern Austrian Economics*, Kansas City: Sheed and Ward.
Mises, Ludwig von [1949] (1966), *Human Action: A Treatise on Economics*, New York: Laissez Faire Books.
Mises, Ludwig von [1962] (1978), *The Ultimate Foundation of Economic Science: An Essay on Method*, Kansas City: Sheed Andrews & McMeel.
Ricoeur, Paul (1991), *From Text to Action: Essays in Hermeneutics, II*, Evanston, IL: Northwestern University Press.
Rizzo, Mario J. (1978), 'Praxeology and Econometrics: A Critique of Positivist Economics', in Louis M. Spadaro (ed.), *New Directions in Austrian Economics*, Kansas City: Sheed Andrews & McMeel.

Rothbard, Murray N. (1971), 'Lange, Mises, and Praxeology: The Retreat from Marxism', in *Toward Liberty, Volume II: Essays in Honor of Ludwig von Mises on the occasion of his 90th birthday*, Menlo Park, CA: Institute for Humane Studies.

Rothbard, Murray N. (1976), 'Praxeology: The Methodology of Austrian Economics?', in Edwin G. Dolan (ed.), *The Foundations of Modern Austrian Economics*, Kansas City: Sheed and Ward.

Rothbard, Murray N. (1979), *Individualism and the Philosophy of the Social Sciences*, San Francisco: Cato Institute.

C Concepts and principles in economic theory

12 Marginal utility

Jack High

Marginal utility formed the bedrock upon which economists erected a new theory of social action. Within the space of two generations, between 1871 and 1912, all of economic theory's heavy beams – consumer choice, factor pricing, output decisions, the determination of interest rates and the value of money – were recast and reframed in the light of valuation at the margin. Although modification has continued to the present, the general principles of economics remain as they stood in 1912, the year in which Ludwig von Mises's *Theory of Money and Credit* applied marginal utility to the value of money. Except for Adam Smith's 'invisible hand' – or its modern equivalent, equilibrium – marginal utility is perhaps the most revolutionary idea in the history of economics.

Like other seminal ideas – such as calculus in mathematics and evolution in biology – marginal utility was discovered independently and simultaneously by more than one person. William Stanley Jevons in England, Leon Walras in France and Carl Menger in Austria all developed the idea, and used it to effect, in pathbreaking treatises. Jevons's *Theory of Political Economy*, Walras's *Elements of Pure Economics*, and Menger's *Principles of Economics* appeared within three years of one another, between 1871 and 1874.

Statements of marginal utility had appeared earlier. William Lloyd (1833) in Britain and Hermann Gossen (1854) in Germany defined marginal utility and explained its connection to price. Both were ignored. So, initially, was Jevons. In 1862, he presented a paper on marginal utility to the British Association for the Advancement of Science, who received it, said Jevons, 'without a word of interest or belief'. Not until the treatises of the 1870s did marginal utility exert a noticeable influence, and then it turned economics on its head.

The theory that was so thoroughly reworked was the English classical school of Adam Smith and David Ricardo. This school imputed the price of a good to the amount of labor that went into its production. 'If among a nation of hunters,' wrote Smith, 'it usually costs twice the labour to kill a beaver which it does to kill a deer, one beaver should naturally exchange for or be worth two deer. It is natural that what is usually the produce of two days' or two hours' labour, should be worth double of what is usually the produce of one day's or one hour's labour' (1976, p. 53) There were obvious exceptions to this principle. Land commanded a price even if no labor went into its production, and non-reproducible goods, such as Rembrandt paintings, exchanged at prices that had little to do with the amount of labor that it took to produce them. Despite the large number of goods that lay outside its purview, however, the labor theory of value was the basic principle of price determination.

Marginal utility theory reversed cause and effect. The Mercedes-Benz automobile does not command a high price because much labor went into producing it. On the contrary: it is because a Mercedes commands a high price that so many engineers and craftsman can be paid to produce it. According to marginal utility theory, the prices of consumers' goods determine the prices of labor, and of land and capital as well. Although the direction of causation in marginal theory seems sensible, it leaves unanswered a vexing question: what determines the prices of consumers' goods? This question had confounded the classical economists and other social philosophers for a long time.

At first blush, it seems as if there ought to be a direct connection between the utility of a consumer's good and its price. If we, as consumers, find that a good is highly valuable to our purposes, then we ought to be willing to pay a high price for it. Correspondingly, if we find that a good is only marginally serviceable, then we ought not to pay much for it. However, this seemingly plausible relationship between use value and exchange value was contradicted by observation. 'Nothing is more useful than water, but it will purchase scarce any thing,' said Adam Smith. 'A diamond, on the contrary, has scarce any value in use; but a very great quantity of other goods may frequently be had in exchange for it' (Smith, 1976, p. 33).

Marginal utility theory resolved the water–diamond paradox and revealed a sensible relationship between use value and exchange value. Water, while essential to human life, is so abundant that we use it, not only to drink and to bathe, but also to mop our floors, sprinkle our lawns and wash our cars. If our supply of water were diminished, we would not deprive ourselves of the drinking water so vital to health; rather, we would wash our cars or scrub our porches less often. It is this least important or marginal use that determines the value of water to us. Because the marginal use value of water is low, the price we are willing to pay for it is correspondingly low. Conversely, diamonds are scarce relative to our desire for them. For many of us, our only purchase of a diamond is to express our enduring love for the most important person in our lives. The price we are willing to pay for such service is correspondingly high. If diamonds were as plentiful as cut glass, so that their sparkle commonly adorned ash trays and dog leashes, their use value would be low and so, too, would their price.

The principle of marginal utility gained wide acceptance by economists in the late nineteenth and early twentieth centuries. In Britain, the pioneer Jevons, along with Philip Wicksteed, Francis Edgeworth, William Smart and

Alfred Marshall, effectively expounded the doctrine. In the USA, Simon Newcomb, Irving Fisher, J.B. Clark and Frank Fetter exerted a wide influence. On the continent, Walras and his followers, especially Vilfredo Pareto, and Menger and his followers, especially Eugen Böhm-Bawerk and Friedrich Wieser, made a persuasive case for marginal utility theory.

While Menger and the Austrians held marginal utility theory in common with all economists, their treatment of the idea, and of theory generally, was sufficiently different from the others for it eventually to form a distinct line of thought. From the beginning, Jevons, Walras and their followers worked with a continuous utility function, $U(x)$, where U denotes the amount of utility, and x the quantity, of an economic good. Marginal utility was defined as the first derivative, dU/dx, of the total utility function. The Austrians, by contrast, focused on discrete, discontinuous value scales. The consumer has a set of ends, denoted abstractly by the ordered set $\{e_1, e_2, e_3, \ldots e_n\}$, that can be attained only with the use of economic goods. If the consumer has only one unit of a good, x_1, she will use it to attain her most important end, which we designate as e_1. If she has a second unit, x_2, she will use it to attain her next most important end, e_2, and so on. The marginal utility of x is the importance that the consumer places on a unit of x. This importance is imputed to the good from the least-valuable end attained. For example, if the consumer has three units of x, the marginal utility is the importance the consumer attaches to e_3 because that is the end she would forgo were she to lose a unit of x. The value scale enables us to define marginal utility without assuming the existence of a continuously differentiable utility function. In fact, the total utility function may be dispensed with altogether.

The notion of opportunity cost appears in the Austrian theory in a way that it does not in other theories. Consider our consumer again, this time with one unit of x, which can be used to attain e_1 or e_2 or e_3, up to e_n. In choosing to attain e_1, the consumer forgoes attaining e_2 through e_n. The most highly valued of these forgone ends, e_2, is the opportunity cost of attaining e_1; e_2 is the end that would have been attained had x not been used to attain e_1.

Another difference of the Austrian construction is its derivation of the law of diminishing marginal utility. Jevons postulated that the total utility function increased at a decreasing rate, so that marginal utility decreased as the supply of good increased. This assumption was justified on psychological grounds; we delight more in our first bite of ice cream than our second. In the Austrian treatment of utility theory, diminishing marginal utility theory follows from the value scale. As the consumer gets additional units of x, she applies them to attain successively less important ends. Consequently, the marginal utility of x diminishes as the supply increases. The marginal utility of x_3 is less than that of x_2 because the consumer places less importance on e_3 than on e_2.

Corresponding to the law of diminishing marginal utility, there is also a law of increasing cost, which is nothing more than diminishing utility considered from another angle. If our consumer has on hand ten units of x, and gives up one of the units, the opportunity cost will be e_{10}, because that will be the end she forgoes by losing a unit of x. If she gives up a second unit of x, the cost will be higher, because she will forgo attaining a more important end, e_9. If she gives up a third unit, the cost will be yet higher, e_8, and so on. This is ultimately the reason that, as more of a good is supplied to the market, its cost will increase. The law of diminishing marginal utility implies the law of increasing cost.

Perhaps the most notable difference of Austrian utility theory was its treatment of measurability. The derivation of marginal utility from a total utility function required that utility be measurable, like weight or distance. Although economists such as Jevons realized that they could not yet measure utility, they assumed that it was in principle measurable, and that we would someday have the instruments necessary to carry out the task. Although Austrian economists, especially Wieser and Böhm-Bawerk, sometimes spoke as if utility were measurable, Menger's theory did not rely on measurability. In the Austrian scheme, the definition of marginal utility, and the principle of diminishing marginal utility, required only that ends and means could be sorted by rank. In technical phraseology, Austrian theory was ordinal rather than cardinal.

In the 1930s, at the persuasive instigation of John Hicks and R.G.D. Allen, economists replaced marginal utility theory with indifference curve theory, primarily because of the mistaken notion that indifference curves did not require utility to be cardinally measurable, whereas marginal utility did. Hicks and Allen directed their arguments against marginal utility theory as developed by Jevons and Marshall. They ignored the work of Menger, Ludwig Mises, Oskar Morgenstern and other economists in the Austrian tradition, who had long argued that measurability was untenable and unnecessary for utility theory. The marginal utility baby was thrown out with the cardinal measurement bath water because Hicks and Allen were unaware of Austrian advances in utility theory.

The Hicks–Allen development of utility theory has been especially unfortunate for teaching economics. Marginal utility is useful in conveying to students the fundamentals of the discipline. Even today, principles textbooks frequently introduce students to economics using marginal utility. Nearly as frequently, marginal utility theory is accompanied by the assumption that utility is measurable. A unit of utility is often denoted as a utili. Such an assumption impresses the thoughtful student as fanciful, a charge to which economic theory is prone anyway. A healthy dose of ordinal ranking would imbue utility theory with a realism that it badly needs.

Utility theory in the Austrian tradition has been the object of very little research in the postwar period. Mises gave a brief statement of it in *Human Action* (1949). Murray Rothbard provided an able and much needed elaboration in *Man, Economy, and State* (1962) and J. Huston McCulloch took some promising steps in 'The Austrian Theory of Marginal Use and of Ordinal Marginal Utility', published in 1977. Both in its practical form, as exemplified by the work of Rothbard, and in its more formal manifestation, as exemplified by the work of McCulloch, the theory of marginal utility is overdue for restatement and advance. Economic theory would benefit considerably from a more sensibly based utility theory.

See also:
Chapter 3: Subjectivism; Chapter 22: The Austrian theory of price; Chapter 20: Supply and demand

Bibliography
Black, R.D. Collinson (1970), 'Introduction' to W.S. Jevons, *Theory of Political Economy*, Harmondsworth: Penguin Books.
High, Jack and Howard Bloch (1989), 'On the History of Ordinal Utility Theory: 1900–1932', *History of Political Economy*, **21**, spring.
Jaffee, William (1976), 'Menger, Jevons, and Walras Dehomogenized', *Economic Inquiry*, December.
Jevons, William Stanley [1871] (1970), *The Theory of Political Economy*, Harmondsworth: Penguin Books.
Kauder, Emil (1965), *A History of Marginal Utility Theory*, Princeton: Princeton University Press.
McCulloch, J. Huston (1977), 'The Austrian Theory of Marginal Use and of Ordinal Marginal Utility', *Zeitschrift für Nationalökonomie*, 37.
Menger, Carl [1871] (1976), *Principles of Economics*, New York: New York University Press.
Mises, Ludwig (1949), *Human Action*, New Haven: Yale University Press.
Rothbard, Murray (1956), 'Toward a Reconstruction of Utility and Welfare Economics', in Mary Sennholz (ed.), *On Freedom and Free Enterprise*, Princeton: Van Nostrand.
Rothbard, Murray (1962), *Man, Economy and State*, Princeton: Van Nostrand.
Schumpeter, Joseph (1954), *History of Economic Analysis*, Oxford: Oxford University Press.
Smith, Adam [1776] (1976), *An Inquiry into the Nature and Causes of the Wealth of Nations*, Chicago: University of Chicago Press.
Walras, Leon (1874), *Elements of Pure Economics*, translated by William Jaffee, Fairfield, NJ: Augustus M. Kelley Publishers, 1977.

13 Cost

Mario J. Rizzo

The doctrine of the subjectivity of costs is clearly tied to that aspect of economics which seeks to understand the causes of and obstacles to choice rather than its consequences. Since these causes are the desires and beliefs of individuals (see Cowan's entry on causation), they are found among the contents of the human mind. The distinction between causes and consequences is obscured by the assumption of perfect foresight characteristic of the fundamental neoclassical economic theory. It is still further obscured by the compression of time into a single period *à la* Walras and Pareto. Not only are all intended consequences (causes) realized under perfect foresight, but they are *instantaneously* realized in the single-period formulation.

The Austrian view of cost is that it is a subjective, forward-looking and ephemeral phenomenon tied inextricably to the moment of choice. This is in sharp contrast to the traditionally objectivist conceptions that are found in the major textbooks, even at the graduate level. Observe that Henderson and Quandt (1980, p. 74) treat costs simply as money outlays made by the firm under perfect competition. McCloskey (1982, p. 10), on the other hand, rejects the direct-outlay view but focuses on alternative output producible by the given employment of factors. Geometrically, this is portrayed as the slope of the budget line. In the famous Smithian example, one hour's labor can produce either one beaver or two deer. So the cost of beaver is deer, and the cost of deer is beaver. In either of the above cases, cost is an objective thing – a sum of money in the first case or an animal in the second. The objectivity displayed here is plausible only in perfectly competitive equilibrium where the trade-off is certain and the same for all traders. There is no question of any important subjectivity in these conceptualizations.

The early Austrians, particularly Friedrich von Wieser (1893), wrote ambiguously about cost being the 'value' of the alternative product. Whether they meant subjective value or market value was often unclear. It is clear, however, that they were *interpreted* as meaning market value. To that extent, the early Austrian view is only partially subjectivist. It is subjectivist insofar as market values are determined by marginal utilities, but it is objectivist because these values are set in markets and can be objectively measured in the form of a money price. In more recent years, Ludwig von Mises (1949, p. 97) wrote of costs as 'equal to the value attached to the satisfaction which one must forego in order to attain the end aimed at'. Unfortunately, this is not adequate as a strict definition because it leaves too much of a critical nature unsaid. The ambiguity present in the work of the early Austrians is still here. Does Mises mean market value or personal subjective value? Equally important, the uncertain, forward-looking quality of costs is absent. Costs must refer, not to what *has been* given up, but to what the agent *expects* to give up if a certain course of action is followed. Thus we ought to define costs in the following way: the cost of adopting a course of action is the expected want satisfaction that is perceived to be sacrificed by forgoing the next most highly-valued course of action.

The process of determining costs is another aspect of the process of determining value. Consider that an individual has a rank ordering of prospective want satisfactions. Each of these satisfactions is causally related to a particular course of action. The individual will value, that is, rank order, these courses of action in accordance with the satisfactions they are expected to produce. In establishing this value scale the individual is valuing expected want satisfaction *A* most highly, *B* the next most highly, and so on. So if only one course of action can be chosen (owing to limited means) the individual will choose the course that results in *A* at the expense of the course that results in *B*. Just as determining which alternative is chosen involves valuation, so determining which is rejected involves the same overall process of valuation.

The static conception of valuation entails a view of costs as given or 'out there' simply to be computed in the determination of choice. Nevertheless, cost, like value, must be discovered (Thirlby, 1973a, p. 140; Kirzner, 1973, pp. 32–7): that is, in both cases, the agent must discover which courses of action lead to which results in terms of want satisfaction. The discovering of costs is a part of the general entrepreneurial view of economics obscured by equilibrium analysis.

In order to appreciate fully the meaning of subjectivism in the theory of costs, it would be useful to state some of its primary theoretical implications. These were stated by James M. Buchanan (1968, p. 43) roughly as follows:

1. Cost exists only in the mind of the decision maker.
2. Cost is forward-looking, based on anticipations.
3. Cost can never be realized (or, in some sense, achieved).
4. Cost can never be measured by an outside observer (nor ever really by the individual himself – how can want satisfaction be measured?).
5. Cost can be dated only at the moment of choice.
6. Cost must be borne exclusively by the decision maker.

The reader should note that most, perhaps even all, of the above are obscured in competitive equilibrium. Although costs still exist only in the decision maker's mind, the presence of perfect knowledge means that there is never any uncertainty about them. Secondly, the forward-looking quality of costs lacks real meaning when past, present and future are the same. Furthermore, while costs still cannot be realized, agents in perfect competition have perfect hypothetical knowledge. They know what *would have been* the case if an alternative course of action had been chosen. Additionally, the impossibility of measuring costs loses some of its force when a money 'equivalent' is measurable. Finally, the existence of cost only at the moment of choice is now uninteresting, since the moment of choice and the moment of consequences are collapsed into each other in a one-period Walrasian model.

The subjectivism of costs is most clearly distinguished from the conventional view in the theory of the firm. Here matters are not in principle different from the characteristics described above. In practice, however, they appear somewhat different because of a simplifying assumption. Traditionally, we assume that the firm (or its decision maker) simply wishes to maximize net revenue. We do not inquire about any other goals or the want satisfactions the firm owners seek in their capacity as consumers. We put to the back of our minds the fact that utility is the ultimate motive. If we imagine the firm outside of long-run equilibrium, then cost is the 'entrepreneur's *own valuation* of a course of action he rejects. And because, as a first approximation, money revenue is regarded as the entrepreneur's single aim, this outcome would be an alternative money revenue' (Thirlby, 1973c, p. 277, emphasis added).

Let us now examine Buchanan's implications of the subjectivity of costs in the context of the theory of the firm. First, cost exists only in the mind of the entrepreneur–decision maker. It is not the consumer's or anyone else's valuation of the displaced course of action that can be considered an obstacle to the decision taken. Furthermore, cost is not an outlay by the firm but, in disequilibrium, the alternative perceived profit opportunity. Second, cost is based on anticipation. In the theory of the firm Keynes's idea of 'user cost' is a clear reflection of this: 'User cost is the reduction in the value of ... equipment due to using it as compared with not using it [now] and preserving it to be used later' (1936, p. 70). Third, cost is never realized. The decision maker never knows for sure whether he has covered costs. Remember that to cover costs is the same as maximizing revenue. Can we ever be sure that we have maximized revenue? Obviously not. Fourth, cost cannot be measured by an outside observer. As Thirlby reminds us, 'reckoning [cost] is dependent for what it is upon the unique knowledge and attitude (towards uncertainty or risk) of the unique and uniquely situated individual who calculates it' (1973c, p. 281). This places a limit on economic regulation. Suppose a public utility regulator wanted to ensure that the firm operated at the point where total costs equal total revenue. He could not do this simply by announcing the

appropriate rule. He would have to become the firm's entrepreneur and estimate the relevant costs. Fifth, cost exists only at the moment of choice. This
means that costs are incurred only during the firm's planning stage. Furthermore, there are no costs during the equilibrium implementation of a plan, or
what Thirlby calls 'production under standing orders' (1973b, p. 175).

We have in the course of this entry referred to three value notions of cost.
Consider, explicitly: (1) the entrepreneur's own valuation of the course of
action he rejects; that is, his estimate of the alternative money revenue,
including profits (Thirlby's formulation); (2) the market value of the entrepreneur's resources themselves; that is, the outlays on the factors of production (the Henderson–Quandt definition); and (3) the consumers' valuations of
the displaced product (the standard interpretation of Wieser). In competitive
equilibrium the *measures* of all three converge (although they remain distinct
conceptually). The entrepreneur's own estimate of alternative money revenue
will equal his outlays on the factors of production. This is because the prices
of the factors are determined by the market values of alternative product, and
are equal to them in equilibrium. Furthermore, the outlays on the factors of
production will equal the consumers' valuations of displaced product because there are zero profits in equilibrium.

The discussion above about the convergence of various cost measures
should not mislead the reader into thinking that the subjectivity of costs is
absent in competitive equilibrium. Nevertheless, much of what is *interesting*
and *useful* about the subjectivity of costs manifests itself in disequilibrium.
To the extent that we are interested in economic processes or economic
'dynamics', the subjectivity of the entrepreneur–agent's estimates of cost
cannot be ignored.

See also:
Chapter 3: Subjectivism; Chapter 2: Methodological individualism; Chapter 12: Marginal utility; Chapter 4: Market process; Chapter 21: Profit and loss

Bibliography
Buchanan, J. (1969), *Cost and Choice*, Chicago: Markham.
Henderson, J. and R. Quandt (1980), *Microeconomic Theory: A Mathematical Approach*, New
   York: McGraw-Hill.
Keynes, J. (1936), *The General Theory of Employment, Interest and Money*, London: Macmillan.
Kirzner, I. (1973), *Competition and Entrepreneurship*, Chicago: University of Chicago Press.
McCloskey, D. (1982), *The Applied Theory of Price*, New York: Macmillan.
Mises, L. von (1949), *Human Action*, New Haven: Yale University Press.
Thirlby, G. [1946] (1973a), 'The Subjective Theory of Value and Accounting "Cost"', in J.
   Buchanan and G. Thirlby (eds), *LSE Essays on Cost*, London: Weidenfeld & Nicolson.
Thirlby, G. [1946] (1973b), 'The Ruler', in J. Buchanan and G. Thirlby (eds), *LSE Essays on
   Cost*, London: Weidenfeld & Nicolson.
Thirlby, G. [1960] (1973c), 'Economists' Cost Rules and Equilibrium Theory', in J. Buchanan
   and G. Thirlby (eds), *LSE Essays on Cost*, London: Weidenfeld & Nicolson.
Wieser, F. von (1893), *Natural Value*, ed. W. Smart, London: Macmillan.

14 Competition

Mark Addleson

Multiple meanings of competition

The meaning of competition is relatively unambiguous. If asked what they understand by competition, the chairman of a large corporation, the owner of the neighborhood supermarket and your neighbor who is a sports fan are likely to give views that are somewhat similar, no doubt providing their own interpretations of the verb 'to compete'.

Competition defines a particular type of relationship between two or more people or between groups of people. Although competition takes different forms – from, say, rival armies engaged in pitched battle, to chess opponents quietly contemplating each other's moves and assessing their possible options – there are certain common elements in all competitive situations. Competition has a broadly similar meaning to all of us: rivalry; the quest for a common goal; the process of selecting or ranking participants on the basis of their performance in terms of criteria on which the participants have agreed, or to which they subscribe; the desire to get ahead of, or to outdistance, other people, teams or groups. Perhaps the essential element in competition is that competitors, in whatever situation competition occurs, recognize one another as opponents or as rivals.

While it is possible to observe people playing chess or baseball, or fighting, or buying (at an auction), or selling (second-hand motor cars), in most cases it is not possible to observe competition. Instead, as 'observers', we have an empathetic understanding (*Verstehen*) that people in different contexts are rivals who are attempting to steal a march on one another. We interpret certain social situations as instances of competition or of competitive conduct. All these arguments apply *mutatis mutandis* to the types of competition that are found in business life: competition for more senior positions in the company, competition among companies for market share, or competition between salesmen to 'reach target' by the end of the month.

The meaning of competition is unambiguous, or relatively so, as long as economists stay out of the picture. Examine the economist's definition of the term, as used both in scholarly writings and to underpin economic policy, and two considerations emerge. What the economist understands by competition bears little, if any, resemblance to the idea of a rivalry between people; and he has a number of concepts of competition, each of them quite different. These points are not new. Hayek's (1948) is a lucid early exposition of such ideas and McNulty (1968) states this position with conviction, also explaining why it matters that economists' definitions of competition differ from the meaning of competition that is in general use. Why do economists employ concepts of competition that differ radically from the generally accepted meaning of the term? It is also important to establish how and why these meanings differ among three schools of economic thought – classical, neoclassical and Austrian. Can any lay claim to a better, or more satisfactory, concept of competition? What criteria determine whether a concept of competition is satisfactory; and, what is the foundation of a satisfactory theory of competition?

Economics needs a theory of the competitive conduct of businesses and of businessmen because the theory is used to draw conclusions about markets and market economies, about how they work and how well they work. At least from the time of Adam Smith it has been recognized that competition features prominently in such explanations. Even though economists continually redefine the meaning of the term to suit their purposes, the competition that matters is the competition amongst individuals and businesses that underlies market activity. In addition, economists seek to advise on the formulation of policy which, depending on the circumstances, aims either to promote or to restrain competition – again, competition associated with doing business. For good reason, there is, today, notable dissatisfaction with the types of policies that most industrialized countries possess to regulate competition (see Armentano, 1986). A satisfactory theory of competition, then, is one that provides insight into the nature of competitive conduct serving to explain what competition (as rivalry) among businesses means, what forms it takes, and to clarify the implications of competitive conduct. Unless the theory does these things it also fails to provide an adequate foundation for the formulation of economic policy on competition.

Why the meanings of competition differ

The concept of competition is a central notion in the writings of classical, neoclassical and Austrian economists and apparently all have been interested in the competition that characterizes business and market activities. So the question is, why the proliferation of different meanings? Explaining the economists' meanings of competition requires a taxonomy, not a definition; and a taxonomy needs a framework. The following is a framework which may help to answer the question.

Thanks to a rekindling of interest in methodology, economists are at home with the idea of regarding theories as different 'languages' (see Coddington, 1972). Because each theory serves to constrain and to focus the economist's attention, economists working with different languages – say, that of classical as opposed to Austrian theory – actually pose and attempt to answer different questions. The variety of meanings of competition associated with different schools reflects the varied interests of scholars, interests shaped by the languages which they employ. Recognizing the existence of different languages is the first step in clarifying the different meanings of competition. The appropriateness of a particular concept of competition depends on what questions we wish to answer and whether the theory, or language, is suited to its purpose.

The second step, which also sheds some light on the suitability of these notions, is the recognition that there is a common denominator in the languages of these schools. All three direct attention to the economy as a *system*; meaning that either the whole economy, or a part of it, is conceived as something that exists 'out there', as an integrated, self-contained entity or as a bounded structure. And the theorist's chief concern is how the system functions: how, and how well, the different elements of the system fit together, and what sort of result the interaction of the different elements produces. With regard to the latter, neoclassical theorists focus on the existence and stability of equilibrium, Austrians on the equilibrating and disequilibrating forces in the market process.

Though the nature of the entity differs from theory to theory, the idea of a system and its 'outcome' is common to the schools and it shapes the meaning of competition that each employs. It is also the major obstacle to a satisfactory theory of competition. The view of the economy as a system, manifested in different concepts of equilibrium and, for Austrians, in a market process, represents a particular conception of the scheme of things. It is in marked contrast to the individual's or businessman's understanding or interpretation of events to which the commonly used concept of competition applies.

When Austrians, or their neoclassical or classical counterparts, refer to competition, the notion applies to forces which influence either the direction and adjustment of a system, or the interrelationship between elements as these affect the system as a whole. As opposed to a particular type of relationship among people or among firms, competition is something which 'drives' the system (either the market or the economy). The ability to incorporate the former concept into economic theory, and to explore its implications, depends on being able to jettison the 'system view' – for competitive interrelationships are obliterated in this formulation of economic problems – and to develop a conceptual framework that embraces interpretive understanding (*Verstehen*), the basis on which individuals recognize that others are competitors and understand the nature of the rivalry.

Three different notions of competition

Classical theorists conceive of an economic system as having a centre of gravitation and of the prices of commodities at all times as gravitating towards the 'natural' price – their long-run equilibrium values. The classical notion of competition is commensurate with this conception of an economy (Eatwell, 1980). Competition is a set of forces – impersonal and abstract – which are associated with the movement of actual prices towards their natural levels. In this scheme, individuals and their relationships with one another are irrelevant. What matters is the system and its 'laws of motion'. Competition as rivalry or a type of action simply has no counterpart in the language of classical economics, which deals with determining forces and does not accommodate the interpretation of human conduct. At the same time, it should be noted that the classical scheme entirely glosses over questions of where these competitive forces operate, since the language omits reference to specific businesses or to particular markets. The latter are vague abstractions which do not have a 'real' existence. The same considerations apply both to how competitive forces operate and when they work – how long it takes for the forces to establish themselves.

Neoclassical theorists, of both partial- and general-equilibrium persuasions, conceive of their system (either the market or the economy as a whole) as having a number of separate, but interrelated, parts. Their interests lie in the *structure* of the system, in whether and how the parts are coordinated; in whether they fit together to form a coherent whole; in what is necessary to ensure that agents' 'decisions' are coordinated; and in the conditions that are satisfied when coordination is attained. Not surprisingly, the concepts of competition that underlie neoclassical theory, such as perfect and imperfect competition, define competition as a state of affairs which determines whether the coordination occurs and whether the results are satisfactory or less than optimal. Shackle (1972) explains the importance of perfect competition, as a substitute for the device of recontracting or of the Walrasian auctioneer, in ensuring the coordination of agents' decisions.

The language of neoclassical theory requires a different conception of competition from that associated with classical theory. The neoclassicist's conception of the economy and economic problems, however, also precludes the interpretation of social interrelationships – which is the basis for understanding competition – and it omits any explanation of how and where competition (as rivalry) occurs. The arena of competition, the market, treated as a structure or system with clearly defined boundaries, is a formal entity that has no actual counterpart as far as the businessman is concerned.

The Austrian notion of competition (see Hayek, 1948; Kirzner, 1973; O'Driscoll and Rizzo, 1985) arises out of two themes of Austrian theory: the task of explaining the unintended consequences of human conduct (Hayek,

1948) and that of relating economic phenomena to the plans and knowledge that give rise to them. The first of these has much in common with the object of neoclassical theory in exploring the *coordination* of agents' decisions, and in their analysis of competition Austrians pose questions about coordination (and 'discoordination') (see Kirzner, 1973; O'Driscoll and Rizzo, 1985, chapter 6). Austrian subjectivism involves the recognition that knowledge, expectations and plans exist 'behind' human action so, not surprisingly, the Austrian notion of competition highlights the extent of the coordination of knowledge and plans. Forces of coordination are interrupted, or overtaken, by discoordinating forces, and competition is synonymous with a continuing market process (Lachmann, 1986).

This brief account of the meaning of competition within three important conceptual frameworks offers an explanation of why the meanings differ between theories. It is said that the Austrian notion of a competitive *process* is superior to the neoclassical conception of competition as a *situation*. But in none of these schemes is the treatment of the rivalrous, *intersubjective* nature of competition satisfactory. The reason is that all are constructed around the idea of a system (reflecting equilibrating and disequilibrating forces). When the theorist defines the problems of economics as pertaining to the operation of a system, he adopts a standpoint (and language) which obscures the nature of and meaning of competitive conduct. The language of equilibrium or of the market process does not furnish the tools to study the individual's, or manager's, perceptions of his relationships with other people or firms.

Competition from a hermeneutical standpoint
Questions that need to be answered, but which a 'system view' obscures, include: what are competitive activities; who competes with whom; on what basis, or by what means, do businesses compete? A hermeneutical approach to economic problems is likely to facilitate this quest because its rationale is to expose the individual's understanding (*Verstehen*) of the conduct of others. Austrian economists, including Hayek, Lachmann and some of the current generation of Austrian theorists, have hinted at, or have actually suggested, the need for Austrian theory to take a hermeneutical turn. Providing a satisfactory theory of competition is a strong justification for doing so.

What can an interpretive approach reveal about the meaning of competition? Firms compete in many ways. One of these is through the products or the services they sell in order to attract customers and to improve the position of the business. It has been suggested (Addleson, 1984) that this type of competition be interpreted as the attempt by the business to provide an *offer* to potential buyers which they will regard as better, or more attractive, than other offers from which they might choose. But, who are the potential buyers? What are the other offers? What is it about the offer that makes it more or less attractive? On what basis do firms compete and why are some more, but others less, successful? What is the 'field' of competition? When and why do competitors use the marketing tools of price and distribution channels? To what extent does technology or access to subsidized finance secure a competitive edge? What is the basis for competition in the service sector? In answering these questions it will be necessary to differentiate between firms and between industries. What is the appropriate basis for classifying businesses? These are important questions both in terms of the intellectual aim of producing a satisfying explanation of competition and in respect of economic policy.

Competition has nothing whatsoever to do with 'market structures', so competition and monopoly are not extremes on a continuum. It is inconceivable that a monopolist, defined as a single seller of a particular product – if one can be found in a particular area – has no competition, either actual or potential, to influence its activities. The conventional view, which rests upon a concern that the system produce a satisfactory outcome, is that barriers to competition are bad. Yet it is often in the nature of rivalry that each of the rivals erects barriers *in order to compete*, trying to ensure his own success. Competition means preventing others from being successful. Though some businesses do not compete directly, those that do seek to get ahead of their rivals. Whether they accomplish this through pricing policy, by innovation, or by lobbying for protection, competing businesses want their rivals to fail, or to be less successful than they are.

Austrian economics, in highlighting the incompatibility of competitors' plans, begins the task of understanding these considerations; but, a substantial reconstruction of its methodology is required in order to make additional progress. The relevance of these issues is enormous and is reflected in, say, developments in the personal computer industry (Apple and IBM, Japan versus America) and in the problems of competition that confront businesses in an integrated Europe. These examples emphasize the need for a suitable framework for exploring the meaning of competition.

See also:
Chapter 4: Market process; Chapter 15: Entrepreneurship; Chapter 21: Profit and loss; Chapter 23: Non-price rivalry

Bibliography
Addleson, M. (1984), 'General Equilibrium and "Competition": On Competition as Strategy', *South African Journal of Economics*, **52**, (2), 156–71.
Armentano, D.T. (1986), *Antitrust Policy: The Case for Repeal*, Washington: Cato Institute.
Coddington, A. (1972), 'Positive Economics', *Canadian Journal of Economics*, **5**, (1), February, 1–15.
Eatwell, J. (1980), 'Competition', in I. Bradley and M. Howard (eds), *Classical and Marxian Political Economy*, London: Macmillan.

Hayek, F.A. (1948), *Individualism and Economic Order*, Chicago: University of Chicago Press.
Kirzner, I.M. (1973), *Competition and Entrepreneurship*, Chicago: University of Chicago Press.
Lachmann, L.M. (1986), *The Market as an Economic Process*, Oxford: Basil Blackwell.
McNulty, P.J. (1968), 'Economic theory and the meaning of competition', *Quarterly Journal of Economics*, **82**, November, 639–56.
O'Driscoll, G.P., Jr. and M.J. Rizzo (1985), *The Economics of Time and Ignorance*, Oxford: Basil Blackwell.
Shackle, G.L.S. (1972), *Epistemics and Economics: A Critique of Economic Doctrines*, Cambridge: Cambridge University Press.

15 Entrepreneurship

Israel M. Kirzner

A solid case can be made for the claim that entrepreneurship has, throughout
the history of the Austrian school, been among its central theoretical constructs. In their history of the variety of ways of understanding the essence of
entrepreneurship, Hébert and Link (1988, p. 64) refer to the three 'distinct
viewpoints' in early neoclassical economics (the 'Austrian, French and British'). They remark that, 'of the three, the Austrian approach proved most
fertile for advancing the theory of the entrepreneur'. In a paper exploring
aspects of the history of entrepreneurial theory, Dolores Tremewan Martin
(1979, p. 271) observes that 'much of the modern economic analysis ... is
devoid of any serious consideration of the role of the entrepreneur ...', but
adds in a footnote that 'the primary exceptions to this general trend in the
literature are found in the writings of the "modern Austrian economists"'.

In the following pages we will briefly examine some highlights in the
history of Austrian theories of entrepreneurship; canvass some contemporary
disagreements among Austrians in regard to entrepreneurship; and seek to
explain why it was that the Austrians, rather than other schools of marginalist
economics, came to assign such importance to the entrepreneurial role.

The entrepreneur in the earlier Austrian tradition

It is well known that it was only in the course of the marginalist revolution
that economists came to recognize an analytically distinct role for the entrepreneur. In classical economics – or at least in its dominant British version –
there was simply no distinct entrepreneurial function. It was the capitalist
upon whom, it appears, the economists implicitly relied to assure fulfilment
of the tasks we generally consider to be entrepreneurial. The profit share of
income earned by the capitalist, in classical economics, corresponded mainly
in fact to what neoclassical economics was to identify as interest on capital.
For the classical economists there was no pure entrepreneurial profit, because
for them there was no pure entrepreneurial role. It was in the course of the
neoclassical development of the theory of the market that economists came to
recognize the importance of the function played by the entrepreneur who
acquires all the resource services – including those of capital – in order to
produce the product to be sold to consumers. During the 1880s and 1890s
there emerged a small flood of articles dealing with this entrepreneurial role.
It was at this time that the American theorists, J.B. Clark and Frederick B.

Hawley, developed their separate theories of pure profit (upon the elements of which Frank Knight was later to build his own more nuanced theory). It was soon after this period that the Austrian J.A. Schumpeter introduced his own theory of the entrepreneur, laying the foundation for his characteristic way of seeing and understanding the capitalist process.

The Austrians were prominent participants in this discovery of entrepreneurship. Carl Menger had already, in his 1871 *Grundsätze*, paid some significant attention, at least, to the entrepreneurial function. In characteristic subjectivist fashion, indeed, Menger (1950, p. 160) emphasized the element of information and the act of will involved in this entrepreneurial function (although, unlike Schumpeter and later Austrians, he saw the exercise of this function as merely a special kind of labor service). During the 1880s his teaching apparently inspired two of his students, Mataja and Gross, each to write his dissertation on the entrepreneurial role. There has been some disagreement among historians of thought concerning the influence exercised by Menger upon subsequent Austrian developments in the theory of entrepreneurship. Streissler (1972, pp. 432f) has maintained that Schumpeter built his own theory of entrepreneurial innovation largely on Menger's foundations. This seems to contrast sharply with Knight's typically dismissive assessment of the influence of Menger's contribution in this respect. (See also Martin, 1979; Kirzner, 1979, chapter 4, for discussions of Menger's concept of the entrepreneur in the context of the subsequent Schumpeterian and Knightian views.) Be this as it may, there seems little ground to doubt that Schumpeter's own emphasis on the entrepreneur was rooted, not in his well-known admiration for Walrasian general equilibrium theory, but in the subjectivist, Austrian legacy he imbibed from Böhm-Bawerk's seminars.

An assessment by the historian of thought of the state of entrepreneurial theory in the economics of 1914 would recognize the importance of the Austrian contributions, but would certainly not pronounce entrepreneurial theory to be exclusively or even predominantly the province of the Austrians. The bulk of the prewar literature on entrepreneurship and on entrepreneurial profit was certainly contributed by economists of other schools. Yet general mainstream interest in this branch of economic theory was to decline sharply following the war. Knight's work would of course represent a magisterial contribution to the identification of the entrepreneurial role and to the understanding of pure entrepreneurial profit. It offered a crystal-clear articulation of the distinction between the utterly certain Walrasian world of perfectly competitive equilibrium and the real world of radical, inescapable uncertainty. But the progress of mainstream neoclassical economics in the succeeding half-century was virtually to ignore the implications of this distinction. Even among Knight's own disciples microeconomics came to mean, in the second half of of the twentieth century, the theory of markets in complete competitive equilibrium, with no possibility of pure profit, and none of the uncertainty which calls forth the special characteristics of the Knightian entrepreneur. It was during this period that understanding of the entrepreneurial role became, if only by default, more or less an exclusively Austrian concern. It was in the economics of Ludwig von Mises that this was most obvious.

Entrepreneurship in mid-twentieth-century Austrian economics

What Mises contributed to the theory of entrepreneurship may not be immediately obvious to the superficial reader of his works. Although the index to his *Human Action* (1949) demonstrates the importance of the entrepreneur for Misesian economics, a reader may be excused for concluding that what Mises had to say about the entrepreneur was not exactly pathbreaking. The nuances which separate the Misesian entrepreneur from the Schumpeterian or the Knightian might well appear to be only of marginal significance, but the truth is that it is indeed the role which Mises assigns to the entrepreneur which sets Misesian economics so decisively apart from mainstream mid-twentieth century economics. And the modest revival of the Austrian approach during the past two decades must be seen as recognition of the valuable character of precisely this aspect of the Misesian system.

What sets the Misesian system apart from mainstream neoclassical economics is the Misesian portrayal of *the market as an entrepreneurially driven process:*

> The operation of [the factor] market is actuated and kept in motion by the exertion of the promoting entrepreneurs, eager to profit from the differences in the market prices of the factors of production and the expected prices of the products ... The activities of the entrepreneurs are the element that would bring about the unrealizable state of the evenly rotating economy if no further changes were to occur... The competition between the entrepreneurs...reflects in the external world the conflict which the inexorable scarcity of the factors of production brings about in the soul of each consumer. It makes effective the subsumed decisions of the consumers as to what purpose the nonspecific factors should be used for and to what extent the specific factors of production should be used. (1949, pp. 331, 335)

It was in the course of the famed inter-war debate on the possibility of economic calculation under socialism that Mises's entrepreneurial view of the market process came to be crystallized and subsequently clearly articulated. As Lavoie has emphasized, it was appreciation for the entrepreneurial character of the market process which enabled the Austrians to see the fallacy of quasi-market 'solutions' (such as those of Lange and Lerner) to the calculation problem. This writer has argued that Hayek's important contributions to the calculation debate, although couched in terms of utilization of knowledge rather than in terms of entrepreneurial discovery, ultimately reflect, at least implicitly, a similar understanding of the market process.

In fact the novelty of the Misesian perception of the market as a continuing process of entrepreneurial competition is mute evidence of the drastic decline, in mid-twentieth-century mainstream economic thought, of awareness of the entrepreneurial role. As Baumol has observed, the entrepreneur had virtually disappeared from the theoretical literature. And it was indeed the Misesian emphasis on the entrepreneurial role which inspired subsequent Austrian interest in the theory of entrepreneurship.

The Misesian entrepreneur further explored
Much of this subsequent Austrian interest has been reflected in the present writer's work seeking to articulate more definitively the essential characteristics of the Misesian entrepreneur, and to demonstrate how central these characteristics must be for an understanding of the competitive process. As one writer has put it, the 'leitmotif' of this work has been that 'the exploitation of the gains from trade will not take place automatically. To achieve the advantages of co-ordination through exchange requires first that these potential gains are noticed. The entrepreneurial role is to be "alert" to as yet unexploited gains from trade' (Ricketts, 1992, p. 67).

Mainstream economics has of course always assumed that exploitation of gains from trade *will* take place automatically, as soon as the gains exceed the relevant costs. This assumes that all opportunities for winning pure gain are instantly perceived and exploited. It follows that the market outcomes, at any given instant, must necessarily be understood as embodying the fulfilment of the most exacting conditions for equilibrium. Each economic agent in the market must, at each instant, therefore be assumed *not* to be grasping for pure profit (since all such opportunities for pure profit have *already* been grasped and eliminated). This has forced mainstream microeconomics into a straitjacket in which all decisions being made at each instant are, somehow, automatically fully coordinated ('pre-reconciled') with every other decision being made in the system. This has restricted modern microeconomics to strictly defined states of equilibrium. This has, in turn, had the consequence that the notion of *competition* has had to mean, not any process during which competing market participants struggle to get ahead of one another, but a state of affairs in which any such struggle is both unnecessary and inconceivable.

By liberating economics from the assumption that all opportunities for pure gain have already been captured, this Misesian-inspired perspective on markets permits us to see market processes as ones in which such opportunities – hitherto overlooked – come to be perceived and exploited. This has opened up an entirely fresh dimension for economic activity, a dimension necessarily missing from an equilibrium-bound microeconomics. This new dimension is that of entrepreneurial *alertness* and entrepreneurial discovery. Whereas traditional economics has operated in a framework in which outcomes can be attributed to either (or a mix of) (a) deliberate maximizing choice, or (b) pure luck, this entrepreneurial perspective draws our attention to a third possible (and, in general, necessary) source for observed outcomes. This third source is *discovery*, in which unfocused, unspecified, purposefulness – a generalized intentness upon noticing the useful opportunities that may be present within one's field of vision – in fact yields discovered opportunities (which may then be subsequently exploited in maximizing choice fashion). Such discovery cannot itself be characterized as rational, maximizing choice (in the way in which deliberate cost-conscious *search* activity has been treated in the theory of information literature) because, prior to the moment of discovery, the potential discoverer is perceived not to have any specific search objective or search procedure in mind and is (therefore) not seen as weighing the likely benefits of a successful find against the costs of necessary search. (In fact his discovery may consist in *realizing* that he *has* before him a promising opportunity for profitable search.) Nor can a discovered opportunity be entirely attributed to pure luck. Although, to be sure, the objective existence of the opportunity itself (prior to its discovery but at a point in space and time likely to result in discovery) may (disregarding the philosophical reservations one may have concerning the 'existence' of an unperceived opportunity) be seen as entirely a matter of luck, its discovery must, at least in part, be attributed to the alertness of the discoverer.

The notion of entrepreneurship as the alertness necessary for the discovery of opportunities has had important implications for the positive understanding of market processes, and for ethical judgements concerning the moral status of market outcomes. The positive theory of the competitive market process has come, in this line of modern Austrian economics, to mean the sequence of market trades and acts of production which can be attributed to the succession of entrepreneurial discoveries generated by disequilibrium conditions. To compete means, in this framework, to perceive an opportunity to serve the market better (than it is currently being served by one's competitors). This view of the function of the entrepreneur has been central to the modern Austrian appreciation of free markets, and to its understanding of the perils of interventionist public policies.

These Austrian insights concerning the role of entrepreneurial discovery have also revealed the *discovered* character of pure entrepreneurial profit. This has permitted an ethical view of the possible justice of such profit in a manner not open to mainstream economics (for which pure profit is likely to appear to have been enjoyed by the entrepreneur strictly as a matter of his good luck). This insight has been explored in Kirzner (1989).

Entrepreneurship: some contemporary Austrian debates

Although the central features of Misesian entrepreneurship are, by and large, accepted within modern Austrian economics, certain features emphasized in this writer's expositions of it (as outlined in the preceding section) have been challenged during recent years by a number of Austrian economists, as well as by others. (One line of modern Austrian work, *not* dealt with in this section, is that identified with the late Ludwig Lachmann. That work has sharply questioned the equilibrative character of entrepreneurship which is central to the Misesian view.) We may group these debates around two related themes.

Creativity

The 'alertness' view of entrepreneurship appears to separate entrepreneurship from any genuinely creative activity. To be alert to an opportunity would appear not to include anything except noticing that which is *already* fully developed, merely waiting to be grasped. A number of modern Austrians have been unhappy with such implications. See also Ricketts (1992).

Uncertainty

The 'alertness' view of entrepreneurship has been understood by its critics effectively to abstract from uncertainty. To define entrepreneurship in terms of *seeing* opportunities, it is held by the critics, seems to identify it exclusively with success: to define it in terms apparently impervious to the very possibility of entrepreneurial loss. Yet surely such possibility of loss cannot be separated from the exercise of entrepreneurship. As soon as entrepreneurship is extended from simultaneous arbitrage to intertemporal arbitrage, uncertainty inevitably enters the picture. All this has suggested to the critics that the essence of entrepreneurship be sought in such qualities as *imagination* (White, 1976) or *judgement* (High, 1982).

In his more recent writings the present writer has attempted to meet some of these criticisms. He has of course agreed that uncertainty is inseparable from the entrepreneurial function in the context of ongoing time; so that it is indeed the case that the futurity of entrepreneurial activity must entail both judgement and imagination. Entrepreneurial alertness, in regard to opportunities the profitability of which lies in the future, cannot be exercised without imagination of that which does not yet exist, and without judgement concerning which of today's active forces is likely, in the course of time, to dominate the others. To concur warmly in these valid and important observations is not, however, to retreat from the insight that the essence of all entrepreneurial action is the perception of opportunities − offering profit in the present, the near future, or the distant future. To recognize that alertness in a world of uncertainty may call for good judgement and lively imagination does not, surely, affect the centrality of the insight that entrepreneurship refers, not to the deliberate exploitation of perceived opportunities, but to the alert perception of opportunities available for exploitation.

Rather similar considerations relate to the criticisms which see the emphasis on alertness as being blind to the role of creativity in the entrepreneurial role. Surely, such criticisms run, what the entrepreneur does, in so many cases, is not so much to perceive a given opportunity as to imaginatively *create* that which nobody had hitherto dreamed of. To such criticisms it seems appropriate to respond that, while the opportunity to be discovered is often indeed the opportunity to be created, this truth should not obscure the more fundamental insight regarding entrepreneurship. This insight is simply that for any entrepreneurial discovery creativity is never enough: it is necessary *to recognize* one's own creativity. In other words, an essential ingredient in each successful creative innovation is its innovator's vision of what he can creatively accomplish.

The point in these responses to the critics is that, while the entrepreneur operates under uncertainty, and therefore displays imagination, judgement and creativity, his role is not so much the *shouldering* of uncertainty as it is his ability *to shoulder uncertainty aside* through recognizing opportunities in which imagination, judgement and creativity can successfully manifest themselves.

Austrian economics and the entrepreneurial role
The centrality of the entrepreneur in Austrian economics, virtually since its inception in 1871, appears to be no accident. If one accepts *subjectivism* as being the unifying thread which has characterized the Austrian economic tradition throughout its history, then the centrality of entrepreneurship seems eminently understandable. Mainstream economics, with a lesser emphasis on subjectivism, has been prone to presuming that the mere objective presence of the possibility for gains from trade is sufficient to ensure their exploitation. Economic agents are presumed to maximize in terms of the opportunities which exist, without any concern regarding any possible gap between the opportunities which exist and the opportunities which are perceived to exist. Market prices are interpreted as the outcomes consistent with a state of the world in which all market participants are maximizing in respect of the opportunities objectively inherent in the actions of all their fellow participants. There is no need, in such an analytical scheme, for any role specifically geared to ensuring that the opportunities perceived in fact tend to correspond to what is objectively available. There is no need for any role specifically geared to explaining any process through which market outcomes might tend to come to express actual (as against possibly erroneously perceived) mutual possibilities – since no possibility of such a gap is entertained.

It is in a consciously subjectivist mode of analysis, such as that of the Austrian tradition, in which the possibility is taken seriously that agents may be seeking to maximize within erroneously perceived frameworks, that scope for entrepreneurship can easily come to be recognized. Within such a tradition an emphasis upon knowledge and ignorance, imagination and discovery has indeed emerged naturally and organically. Despite the changes over time in Austrian entrepreneurial constructs, and despite contemporary Austrian marginal disagreements concerning the essential entrepreneurial functions, it seems reasonable to attribute the perennial Austrian interest in the entrepreneur to the tradition's consistent subjectivist thrust.

See also:
Chapter 4: Market process; Chapter 14: Competition; Chapter 21: Profit and loss; Chapter 23: Non-price rivalry

Bibliography

Hébert, Robert F. and Albert N. Link (1988), *The Entrepreneur: Mainstream Views and Radical Critiques*, 2nd edn, New York: Praeger.

High, Jack (1982), 'Alertness and Judgment: Comment on Kirzner', in Israel M. Kirzner (ed.), *Method, Process and Austrian Economics, Essays in Honor of Ludwig von Mises*, Lexington: D.C. Heath.

Kirzner, Israel M. (1979), *Perception, Opportunity and Profit, Studies in the Theory of Entrepreneurship*, Chicago: University of Chicago Press.

Kirzner, Israel M. (1989), *Discovery, Capitalism, and Distributive Justice*, Oxford: Basil Blackwell.

Martin, Dolores Tremewan (1979), 'Alternative Views of Mengerian Entrepreneurship', *History of Political Economy*, **11**, (2), summer, 271–85.

Menger, Carl (1950), *Principles of Economics*, translated and edited by J. Dingwall and Bert F. Hoselitz, Glencoe IL: Free Press.

Mises, Ludwig von (1949), *Human Action*, New Haven: Yale University Press.

Ricketts, Martin (1992), 'Kirzner's Theory of Entrepreneurship – A Critique', in Bruce J. Caldwell and Stephan Böhm (eds), *Austrian Economics: Tensions and New Directions*, Boston: Kluwer Academic.

Streissler, Erich (1972), 'To What Extent Was the Austrian School Marginalist?', *History of Political Economy*, **4**, fall.

White, Lawrence H. (1976), 'Entrepreneurship, Imagination and the Question of Equilibration', ms., published in Stephen C. Littlechild, *Austrian Economics*, vol. III, Aldershot: Edward Elgar, 1990, pp. 87–104.

16 Time in economics

Mario J. Rizzo

The dynamic conception of time, that is, the subjective perception of the passage of time, is today, in this author's view, the uniquely Austrian perspective on time. In the first half of the twentieth century, Austrians were among the very few economists who took time, in the sense of a planning period, seriously in their theoretical work. And today it may still be the case that Austrians are more consistent or thoroughgoing in applying the idea of a planning period in various parts of economic theory (as in the theory of costs). Nevertheless, this is no longer sufficiently distinct from what other economists do, so that time in this sense cannot be a significant distinguishing feature of Austrian economics. While the idea of a planning period has now been fruitfully utilized by economists of many schools, there is a distinction between the passage of time during the process of planning and the temporal periods in the plan itself that is very important and generally unrecognized. As we shall see later, the process of planning takes place in time as lived (the dynamic view of time) while the contents of the plan itself are in a spatialized and intellectualized time (the static view of time)

The dynamic conception of time was formulated, in the modern era, by the philosophical traditions growing out of the works of Henri Bergson and Edmund Husserl. Bergson dominated the intellectual climate in Europe during the first two or three decades of the twentieth century. Husserl's influence, although less dramatic, was very important in subsequent years and ultimately more long-lasting. While it may not be possible to trace specific intellectual influences through footnotes or explicit adoption of terminology, it is abundantly clear that the Bergsonian conceptualization of time rationalizes and lends coherence to the somewhat disjointed observations on the importance of time in much of the Austrian literature on economic processes. More importantly, it is only Bergson's work that clarifies what is implicit in the Austrian contribution and what successfully differentiates it from neoclassical dynamics. Without Bergson's insights into the limitations of mechanical models and his strictures about the reality of time and of change, it is difficult to see Austrian economics as any more than a footnote to neoclassical economics.

As intimated above, the dynamic conception of time is an outgrowth of the traditional Austrian focus on the plan as the center of economic analysis. It is an easy step to go from the static plan to the plan as affected by the activity of planning. In a completed plan the actor has statically allocated time to different acts (or vice versa). There is no substantive difference between the allocation of acts over time and the allocation (by, say, a manager) of the acts of a number of individuals across space. This is the spatialized or container view of time: time is an empty, homogeneous container that can be made as small or as large as is convenient. It can, if the analyst chooses, be filled with either exogenous or endogenous events, just as space can be filled with objects. Fundamentally, time in this sense does nothing; it completely lacks any causal efficacy. Dynamic or Bergsonian time, on the other hand, involves the growth of knowledge as individuals plan or revise their plans. Time as experienced is time as learning from experience or, to put it another way, temporal experience *is* learning. As we shall see in greater detail later, this accounts for Ludwig Lachmann's celebrated statement: 'As soon as we permit time to elapse we must permit knowledge to change' (1959, p. 73).

The crucial distinctions between the static and dynamic conceptions of time lie in memory and anticipation. The static universe of Newtonian mechanics is one without either memory or anticipation. Each moment is isolated from its predecessor or successor in much the same way as points on a line are radically separate from one another. The equations that describe motion in such a world are unaffected by either the past or the future. In fact the concepts of past and future lose much of their meaning here. From the configuration of initial conditions existing in the present and the (timeless) equations of motion, the physicist can equally well predict a future state of the universe or retrodict a past state. Nothing in the universe would be different if the past and future states were replaced by states in different locations. The past, present and future could be laid out simultaneously without any substantive changes in the mathematics of the Newtonian system. The physicist would, in principle, be in a position like that of Laplace's famous demon:

> An intellect which at any given instant knew all the forces acting in nature, and the position of all things of which the world consists – would embrace in the same formula the motions of the greatest bodies in the universe and those of the slightest atoms; nothing would be uncertain for it, and the future, like the past would be present to its eyes. (Laplace, 1886, p. vi)[1]

Time as lived, time as experienced, is inextricably linked to memory of the past and anticipation of the future. In the terminology of Husserl (1964) an experience is a triadic relationship: retention or immediate memory, primal sensation, and protention or immediate expectation. (The idea of primal sensation is merely a limiting notion between retention and protention.) Of these three aspects of an experience, memory, at least for Bergson, was primary. It is from memory that our anticipations are drawn, or perhaps more accurately, shaped. This 'shaping' is not a rigid determination but a plastic control, a focus or a filtering out of the unimportant and a selection of the important. The linking together of the remembered past, present and anticipated future in this way has been called 'dynamic continuity' (Čapek, 1971, pp. 90–91).

Paradoxically, it is the very continuity of time in the Bergsonian perspective that is responsible for the continuous production of novelty. The passage of time is a flow of novel experiences insofar as the present *is unlike the past* or, more precisely, unlike our memory of it. On the other hand, the world of pure matter, that is, the world of Newtonian mechanics, is one absolutely devoid of novelty because each moment in time is isolated and unconnected with what has gone before and what will happen later. There can be no novelty when a moment is solitary; novelty exists by reference to another time. Hence novelty implies dynamic continuity. Less obviously, the reverse is also true. Dynamic continuity implies novelty.[2] Consider the following, admittedly extreme example[3] and its generalization, given by Bergson:

> Let us take the most stable of internal states, the visual perception of a motionless external object. The object may remain the same, I may look at it from the same side, at the same angle, in the same light; nevertheless the vision I now have of it differs from that which I have just had, even if only because the one is an instant older than the other. My memory is there, which conveys something of the past into the present. My mental state, as it advances on the road of time, is continually swelling with the duration which it accumulates: it goes on increasing – rolling upon itself, as a snow ball on the snow. (1975, p. 4)

> From this survival of the past it follows that consciousness cannot go through the same state twice. The circumstances may still be the same, but they will act no longer on the same person, since they find him at a new moment of his history. Our personality, which is being built up at each instant with its accumulated experience, *changes without ceasing* ... That is why our duration is irreversible. (Ibid., pp. 5–6, emphasis added)

The 'survival' of the past, that is, memory, ensures that the individual is never the same at successive phases of his history. Each moment in the flow of time must be novel relative to this changing consciousness. Thus 'the opposition between the novelty of the present and the persistence of the past is only apparent' (Čapek, 1971, p. 127).

Suppose an individual implements an intention according to a plan. The making of that plan was based, in part, on the individual's anticipation of the future consequences of the relevant courses of action. To a certain extent, even if everything happens as expected, there will still be novelty in the actual occurrence.[4] This novelty is fundamentally due to the sometimes subtle changes in the individual's standpoint as his knowledge grows through the swelling of memory. Moreover, projections of the future contain gaps or 'empty horizons which will be filled in merely by the materialization of the anticipated event' (Schutz, 1962, p. 69). This is because the individual makes predictions with respect to the typical features of an event – those held in common with other, often past, events – and not with respect to the unique (or Bergsonian time-dependent) features (O'Driscoll and Rizzo, 1985, pp. 76–9). The filling in of these unique features consists, by definition, of the unexpected. These unexpected experiences, to be sure, may not be relevant for the individual's current purposes. Even if they are, it may not be possible to develop a better plan. So, while novelty is an inevitable feature of time as lived (real time, Bergsonian time), the practical significance of that novelty varies with circumstances. In principle, however, change and novelty are the norm. The irrelevance of change for practical purposes is something that must be demonstrated in the context and not simply assumed.

The importance of the dynamic conception of time for economic theory can be presented under three overlapping headings: dynamic continuity, heterogeneity and causal efficacy.[5]

Dynamic continuity
The link between periods must be subjective or, more exactly, it must be in the form of a change in knowledge growing out of earlier experience. This means that as time elapses the perspective of the individual changes. Thus the idea of an equilibrium coexisting with time-consciousness is either a literal contradiction or a crude approximation. The growth of knowledge will disrupt individual plans (normally in heterogeneous ways) and thus is incompatible with most conventional concepts of equilibrium.[6] In a world of Bergsonian time, equilibrium is continually destroyed or, better yet, never actually achieved as individuals face a continual flow of novelty. This means, as Frank Hahn told us more than 40 years ago, that the 'experience of the first situation must always enter as a new parameter in the second situation' (1952, p. 805).

Heterogeneity
Each phase of time as lived is differentiated from its predecessor and its successor. This contrasts sharply with homogeneous points on a line, the spatial analogy characteristic of the static conception of time. These points, dimensionless and hence durationless, are homogeneous except for their location. The heterogeneity of Bergsonian time, on the other hand, implies, first, temporal irreversibility and, second, the intrinsic uncertainty of all economic life. Temporal irreversibility can be illustrated by Alfred Marshall's long-period industry supply curve. Marshall conceived of this curve as downward-sloping because, as the scale of an industry increased, firms would discover new, cheaper techniques of production initially appropriate only to the larger output. But as these new techniques are refined at the higher level

of output, costs would drop even further. Thus the new technique might become more efficient than the old at lower levels of output as well. This suggests that the long-period supply curve is irreversible. If industry output were to fall back to a previous level, costs would not so return. The acquisition of knowledge at the higher output level cannot be unlearned.

The intrinsic uncertainty of the future rests on the flow of novelty that is part of the passage of time. Consider, in turn, the prediction of an event and the event itself, each the same in every objective way. The abstract prediction will be different from the *experience* of the event because memory in the latter case has been 'swollen' by anticipation (as in Bergson's snowball analogy). In an interesting example of what it means to 'learn', Hahn illustrates the change in knowledge that may occur in the transition from prediction to actual experience:

> Suppose that at t the agent has assigned probabilities to the two events that it will and will not rain in Cambridge at $t + 1$. At $t + 1$ he will know which has been true. ... An example of learning in my sense would occur if at $t + 1$, having observed rain, the probability he attaches to rain in Cambridge at $t + 2$ differs from that which he attached to that event at t conditional on rain at $t + 1$. (1984, p. 55)

The change in mental state at $t + 1$ generated by the individual's prior (probabilistic) prediction may lead to a change in the way the still farther future is viewed (that is, a change in the assigned probabilities) and hence a change in actions. The individual experiencing a predicted event is not in the same mental state as the individual making the prediction precisely because the predicted event follows upon the prediction. Consequently, prediction is always subjectively inadequate and hence uncertainty is, *in a strict sense*, ineradicable.

In other circumstances, the event may actually be changed by the individual's prediction. Oligopolists, for example, charge a price that depends, in part, on what other firms are (perceived to be) planning to charge. Thus an oligopolist's prediction of what others will do may change his own behavior and thus the behavior of these other firms. A similar example can be found in Keynes's famous analogy of the stock exchange with a beauty contest. In this contest the object is to predict what others will find to be the prettiest or handsomest face. The prediction of predictions in the beauty contest is the same, Keynes believed, as the prediction of predictions of prices that drives the asset markets. A change in predictions here can change the actual result.

Causal efficacy

In his discussion of the static or Newtonian conception of time, Bergson remarked that 'time is here deprived of efficacy, and if it *does* nothing, it *is* nothing' (1975, pp. 14–15). The mere elapse of time, in the static sense, does not produce physical changes, whether they are observable or not. Time can pass without anything happening. As we saw above, time is effectively obliterated in a mechanical system's equations of motion. The function of the subscript '*t*' is no different from the function of a location subscript in these differential equations. More importantly, the dynamic relationships do not depend on '*t*'. The laws of the universe are timeless.

If, on the other hand, we inhabit a universe of real time, then time itself is causally efficacious. To put matters less abstractly, the growth of knowledge, which is generated by the passage of time, is the primary causal factor in social systems. Austrians, in their characterization of markets, have therefore been correct to place great emphasis on changes in knowledge as the source of motion in market processes (Kirzner, 1973). Obviously, the growth of knowledge is not simply an event in an individual's mind but involves the transmission or communication of knowledge across many individuals.

Concluding remarks

The dynamic conception of time is not an arbitrary 'add-on' to the body of Austrian thought. First, as we have seen, it arises out of a shift in emphasis from the static plan to the process of planning itself. Attention to the process of planning is a natural outgrowth of Austrian concern with disequilibrium and hence with revision of plans. The process of revising plans, as well as making plans in the first place, takes place in time as lived.

We are now in a position to understand the connection between Austrian economics and the dynamic conception of time in a second, very profound way. No one doubts that subjectivism has been a critical element in the development of Austrian economics. This subjectivism, when applied to time, produces 'time-consciousness'. Time-consciousness implies differentiation among the past, present and future. There can be no such differentiation without novelty. What would enable us to distinguish, in a temporally *homogeneous* world, one time period from another? Clearly, nothing. Novelty, however, can exist only by reference to a differentiated past – a past that exists in memory. Thus time-consciousness implies both novelty and dynamic continuity. These two pillars of the dynamic conception of time – Bergson's conception – are implied by the very subjectivism long advanced by the Austrian school.

Notes

1. Translated by Milič Čapek (1961, p. 122).
2. 'The pastness of the previous moment is impossible without the novelty of the present' (Čapek, 1971, p. 128). If there were no novelty of the present, what would differentiate past and present? The very existence of time-consciousness requires novelty.
3. The force of the extreme example is that if the argument is true in this case, it is true, *a fortiori*, in less extreme cases.

4. 'No matter how I try to imagine in detail what is going to happen to me, still how inadequate, how abstract and stilted is the thing I have imagined in comparison to what actually happens! ... For example, I am to be present at a gathering; I know what people I shall find there, around what table, in what order, to discuss what problem. But let them come, be seated and chat as I expected, let them say what I was sure they would say: the whole gives me an impression at once novel and unique... Gone is the image I had conceived of it, a mere prearrangeable juxtaposition of things already known!' (Bergson, 1965, p. 91).
5. The characteristics of Bergson's concept of time are summarized in Čapek (1971, pp. 90–91). For a discussion of the importance of both the Bergsonian and static conceptions of time in economics, see O'Driscoll and Rizzo (1985, pp. 52–70).
6. But see O'Driscoll and Rizzo (1985, pp. 71–91) and Loasby (1991).

See also:
Chapter 3: Subjectivism; Chapter 18: Marginal productivity

Bibliography
Bergson, Henri, [1946] (1965), 'The Possible and the Real', in *An Introduction to Metaphysics: The Creative Mind*, translated by Mabelle L. Andison, Totowa, NJ: Littlefield, Adams, & Co, pp. 91–106.
Bergson, Henri [1911] (1975), *Creative Evolution*, translated by Arthur Mitchell, Westport, Conn.: Greenwood Press.
Čapek, Milič (1961), (1971), *The Philosophical Impact of Contemporary Physics*, New York: Van Nostrand.
Čapek, Milič (1971), *Bergson and Modern Physics*, Dordrecht, Holland: D. Reidel.
Hahn, Frank H. (1952), 'Expectations and Equilibrium', *Economic Journal*, 62, 802–19.
Hahn, Frank H. [1972] (1984), 'On the Notion of Equilibrium in Economics', in *Equilibrium and Macroeconomics*, Cambridge, Mass: MIT Press, pp. 43–71.
Husserl, Edmund (1964), *The Phenomenology of Internal Time-Consciousness*, lectures from 1905, translated by James S. Churchill, Bloomington, Ind.: Indiana University Press.
Kirzner, Israel M. (1973), *Competition and Entrepreneurship*, Chicago: University of Chicago Press.
Lachmann, Ludwig M. (1959), 'Professor Shackle and the Economic Significance of Time', *Metroeconomica*, 11, 64–73.
Laplace, Pierre Simon, marquis de (1886), *Introduction à la Théorie Analytique des Probabilités*, in *Oeuvres Complètes*, Paris: Gauthier-Villars.
Loasby, Brian J. (1991), *Equilibrium and Evolution*, Manchester: University of Manchester Press.
O'Driscoll, Gerald P. Jr. and Mario J. Rizzo (1985), *The Economics of Time and Ignorance*, Oxford: Basil Blackwell.
Schutz, Alfred (1962), 'Choosing Among Projects and Action', in *Collected Papers: The Problem of Social Reality*, The Hague: Martinus Nijhoff, vol. I, pp. 67–96.

17 Risk and uncertainty

Richard Langlois

The concepts of risk and uncertainty are fundamental to what distinguishes modern Austrian economics from other approaches. Nonetheless, these concepts are often as misunderstood within and around the boundaries of the Austrian camp as they are elsewhere in the profession. In the end, what is distinctive about Austrian and related understandings of risk and uncertainty is an emphasis on what we will call *structural uncertainty*; that is, a lack of complete knowledge on the part of the economic agent about the very structure of the economic problem that agent faces. This emphasis stands in contrast to the neoclassical focus on *parametric uncertainty*; that is, a lack of complete knowledge ex ante about the values that specific variables within a given problem structure will take on ex post.

Risk, uncertainty and probability
One of the central tenets of the Austrian approach is methodological subjectivism, the position that economic analysis must make use of the subjective knowledge and preferences of the economic agent. For example, the subjective theory of value holds that value is not a property of goods themselves but arises in the appraisal of a good by a human mind. In probability theory, there is a somewhat analogous distinction between the subjective and objective theories of probability. In the latter, uncertainty is understood as a property of the world, in much the same sense that value is held to be a property of goods themselves in an objectivist theory of value. By contrast, the subjective theory of probability holds uncertainty to reflect a subjective and personal state of knowledge about the world. Despite the obvious analogies, however, the bulk of Austrian writers have not embraced the subjective theory of probability. The important exception, of course, is Oskar Morgenstern, who was one of the earliest and most important figures to apply subjective probability to decision making (von Neumann and Morgenstern, 1944). For the most part, the mainstream of the Austrian school and its fellow travellers have been right to reject subjective probability theory – or, at any rate, the uses to which this approach has been put, notably the expected-utility representation of decision making under uncertainty. At the same time, however, those rejecting subjective probability theory have often perpetrated confusions and misunderstandings of their own.

The objective theory of probability enters the ken of most students of economics in the guise of classical statistical inference. For example, one might seek to infer the true probability of drawing a red ball from an urn by sampling, that is, by picking a few balls. The true probability is understood to be the fraction of balls in the urn that are red – an objectively measurable property of the world. The immediate argument against this view of probability is its limited usefulness in the economic sphere. Most decisions economic agents must make are not repeatable experiments but are made once only. Launching a rocket is an event like drawing a ball from an urn; but it is not very meaningful to talk about the true underlying probability of a successful rocket launch in the same sense as a true underlying probability of drawing a red ball.

By defining uncertainty as a state of mind, not a state of the world, subjective probability theory makes the probability calculus applicable even to once-and-for-all events. The probability that the rocket will launch successfully becomes nothing more than an articulation of one's knowledge (however imperfect) about the launch. And situations of the balls-in-the-urn type become just special cases in which our knowledge has a particular structure – a discontinuity, in effect: we can gain some information easily by observing the objective frequency of balls in the urn, but we cannot learn more about which ball will emerge without some impossibly complex model of the physics of the drawing process. Because of this more general applicability, subjective probability theory quickly gained pre-eminence in the neoclassical theory of behavior under uncertainty, a revolution ushered in by Friedman and Savage (1948) and inspired by von Neumann and Morgenstern (1944). Although most neoclassical economists agree that subjective expected-utility theory is *the* neoclassical theory of behavior under uncertainty, one should note that most neoclassical modeling actually presumes *objective* probability, since equilibrium requires agents ultimately to agree upon or learn an underlying probability distribution that not only is intersubjectively shared but actually conforms to the objective stochastic structure of the economy.

Whether subjective or objective, however, uncertainty in neoclassical theory presupposes *certainty* about the structure of the world. Consider Kenneth Arrow's definition: 'Uncertainty means that we do not have a complete description of the world which we fully believe to be true. Instead, we consider the world to be in one or another of a range of states. Each state of the world is a description which is complete for all relevant purposes. Our uncertainty consists in not knowing which state is the true one' (Arrow, 1974, p. 33). As ordinary language suggests, however, one can take uncertainty to mean that one does not in fact know with certainty a listing of all possible states of the world. This uncertainty about the very structure of the world, not captured in neoclassical modeling and not well-suited to the probability calculus, is what I have called structural uncertainty and to which others have given names like 'partial ignorance' or 'radical uncertainty' (Langlois, 1984).

Thus we are left with a tripartite framework, as summarized in Figure 1. There is 'risk' or 'class probability', to which classical statistics is applicable. Subjective probability theory is also applicable to this kind of uncertainty, but in addition it also applies to other kinds of events so long as there is perfect knowledge about the structure of the decision problem, including a complete list of all possible states of the world. Finally, there is structural uncertainty, which refers to imperfect knowledge of the structure of the decision problem. Here the calculus of probability is less clearly applicable.

Parametric uncertainty		Structural uncertainty
Subjective probability		
Objective probability	'Case probability'	Structure of decision problem unknown
	Non-seriable events	Not all states of the world known
'Class probability'	But states of the	Novelty and
'Risk'	world known	entrepreneurship

Figure 1

Mises, Knight and Shackle

One unfortunate effect of the victory of subjective probability theory, however desirable in other respects, was that it obscured this distinction between structural and parametric uncertainty, a distinction that Austrian economists are now struggling to recognize and reassert. Part of the reason, however, is that this distinction was not always clear in earlier discussions of uncertainty.

Ludwig von Mises (1949), for example, distinguished between *class probability* and *case probability*. Frank Knight (1921), a figure who shared much with the Austrian school, made a similar and more famous distinction between situations of *risk* and situations of *uncertainty*. In circumstances of class probability or 'risk', the occurrence of a random event can be grouped in an actuarial way as an instance of a class of such events; the probability of that event can thus be determined as the relative frequency of occurrence of the event within the population. An example would be the probability of a house fire, calculated as the observed relative frequency of fires in houses of similar type. Situations of case probability or 'uncertainty', by contrast, involve one-of-a-kind events that cannot be identified as instances of a larger class. And it is in these unique, 'non-actuarial' situations that most economic decision making takes place.

It is not entirely clear whether Mises believed that one could talk about the 'probability' of occurrence of an instance of case probability. But he did think that the calculus of probability was applicable only to class probability, and he even went so far as to defend the classical objective formulation of probability theory – of which his brother Richard von Mises was a leading exponent – as 'the only logically satisfactory one' (Mises, 1949, p. 109). The situation in Knight's case is somewhat different. Contrary to popular myth, Knight understood perfectly well that the probability calculus was applicable to situations of uncertainty as well as to those of risk. The assignment of a probability to an event, for Knight, is an exercise in judgement. But Knight went beyond this truism of subjective probability theory to insist that judgement under uncertainty required two parts or stages: 'the formation of an estimate and the estimation of its value' (Knight, 1921, p. 227). The first of these is at least partly qualitative, a judgement about the structure of the decision problem itself and the appropriate categories of action (Langlois and Cosgel, 1993).

G.L.S. Shackle (1961) is another figure congenial to the Austrian school who has written extensively and poetically about the nature and role of uncertainty. Shackle views the future as fundamentally unknowable, and criticizes probability theory (as applied to decision making) for failing to take account of this fundamental ignorance. In many ways, Shackle's viewpoint is the one articulated above: the very construction of the probability calculus relies on certain knowledge of the structure of the world, whereas in reality agents do not have such knowledge and, in particular, are not capable of enumerating all possible contingencies or 'states of the world'. One of Shackle's most provocative suggestions has been to make the probability calculus more ignorant by substituting the system of 'potential surprise', whose variables differ from conventional probabilities largely in that they fail to sum to one.

Schumpeter and Kirzner

The possibility of structural uncertainty has implications for economic theory that have not yet been well explored, even by Austrians. For example, it may have implications for the economics of institutions (Langlois, 1986) and the economics of organization (Langlois, 1984). Perhaps the clearest example of the characteristic Austrian focus on structural uncertainty, however, is to be seen in the theory of entrepreneurship. In the work of both Schumpeter and Kirzner, the essence of entrepreneurship lies not in bearing risk (or even uncertainty) but in stepping outside existing cognitive frameworks. (As argued above, this was also more true of Knight than most suppose.) The Schumpeterian entrepreneur breaks the crust of convention, leading the means of production into new channels (Schumpeter, 1934). The Kirznerian entrepreneur is alert to previously unnoticed possibilities (Kirzner, 1973). As argued above, dealing with structural uncertainty by using judgement (as against 'bearing' uncertainty) is also more characteristic of the Knightian entrepreneur than is usually recognized. In all cases, the essence of entrepreneurship is to alter the existing framework of means and ends, to introduce novelty into the system. And in all cases, the agent's behavior is guided not by the calculus of expected utility but variously by intuition (Schumpeter), alertness (Kirzner) or judgement (Knight).

See also:
Chapter 25: Prices and knowledge; Chapter 15: Entrepreneurship; Chapter 14: Competition; Chapter 21: Profit and Loss

Bibliography
Arrow, Kenneth J. (1974), *The Limits of Organization*, New York: Norton.
Friedman, Milton and L.J. Savage (1948), 'The Utility Analysis of Choices Involving Risk', *Journal of Political Economy*, **55**, (4), August, 279.
Kirzner, Israel (1973), *Competition and Entrepreneurship*, Chicago: University of Chicago Press.
Knight, Frank H. (1921), *Risk, Uncertainty, and Profit*, Boston: Houghton Mifflin.
Langlois, Richard N. (1984), 'Internal Organization in a Dynamic Context: Some Theoretical Considerations', in M. Jussawalla and H. Ebenfield (eds), *Communication and Information Economics: New Perspectives*, Amsterdam: North-Holland, pp. 23–49.
Langlois, Richard N. (1986), 'Coherence and Flexibility: Social Institutions in a World of Radical Uncertainty', in Israel Kirzner (ed.), *Subjectivism, Intelligibility, and Economic Understanding: Essays in Honor of the Eightieth Birthday of Ludwig Lachmann*, New York: New York University Press, pp. 171–91.
Langlois, Richard N. and Metin M. Cosgel (1993), 'Frank Knight on Risk, Uncertainty, and the Firm: A New Interpretation', *Economic Inquiry*, **31**, July, 456–65.
Mises, Ludwig von (1949), *Human Action*, New Haven: Yale University Press.
Schumpeter, Joseph A. (1934), *The Theory of Economic Development*, Cambridge, Mass.: Harvard University Press.
Shackle, G.L.S. (1961), *Decision, Order and Time in Human Affairs*, Cambridge: Cambridge University Press.
von Neumann, John and Oskar Morgenstern (1944), *The Theory of Games and Economic Behavior*, Princeton: Princeton University Press.

18 Marginal productivity
Walter Block

There may, perhaps, be more important concepts in economics than marginal productivity, but if there are, there can be only a few of them. For marginal productivity is a core element in the analysis of so many crucial elements of the dismal science: wage determination, the return to capital, land rents, the distribution of the product, optimal size of the population, wealth, specialization, the division of labor and comparative advantage – the list goes on and on. Fortunately, given space limitations, there are very few disputes with regard to this issue between Austrians and their colleagues in the economics profession. One such concerns time discounting of marginal productivity (Block, 1990), the subject of our present analysis.

We are all familiar with the process of discounting the future. From the earliest courses in economics we are taught that money receivable right now is not the equivalent of money receivable one year hence; that money receivable one year from now is not equivalent to money which will fall into our clutches after a period of two years. And not just because inflation may erode part of the value, or because of the risk of never seeing the money. Even in a perfectly certain world of no inflation, where all accounts receivable were fully guaranteed, we would still value money more, the sooner we were to receive it. If this were not so, we could never act in the present (Mises, 1966, p. 484), for every action done now *could* have been done in the future. The fact that we choose to act in the present, when we could have waited, shows that we prefer the present; that we enjoy goods, the sooner, the better. But the future will present the same alternatives: action and non-action. *Future* action will thus *also* imply time preference for the present, paradoxically. By acting in the immediate future, instead of waiting for the even more distant future, we also show ourselves as present-oriented. The only way to illustrate a lack of preference for the present is never to act at all – a manifest impossibility for human beings.

But even no action at all will not logically imply time preference for the future over the present. No implications whatsoever in this regard follow from non-action.

One implication of the foregoing is that we discount money receivable in the future. This is done in accordance with the rate of interest. Simply put, we prefer a dollar today to a dollar tomorrow because we can always put our present dollar in the bank, collect the interest payment and have more than a dollar. Given a non-inflationary world and a guarantee that the bank will not renege, we are sure to have more in the next period. If the rate of interest is 10 per cent, then $1.00 today will be worth $1.10 at the end of one year. Alternatively, we can say that payments receivable in the future are *discounted* to obtain present discounted values. Thus $1.00 due at the end of one year is worth $0.90 today, for $0.90 is the amount of money that has to be put in the bank today for it to turn into $1.00 at the end of the year (ignoring rounding errors and compound interest). We can say, then, that $0.90 is the present discounted value of $1.00 receivable in one year.

All of this is elementary, and accepted by the entire economics profession. It would not be worth mentioning, but for the fact that virtually all economists refuse to *apply* the doctrine of discounting future income streams to the case of marginal productivity. Specifically, in the view of most economists, there is a tendency, on the market, for factor payments to equal the marginal value product (MVP) of the factors. Abstracting from questions of perfect or imperfect competition, this means, for example, that, in the view of the profession, wages will come to equal the value of the marginal product of labor (the marginal physical product of labor multiplied by the price at which the product can be sold).

In contrast, the Austrian school (Rothbard, 1962, pp. 406–9, 431–3) insists that what tends towards equality with wages is not MVP, but *discounted* MVP, or DMVP. There is no real point at issue when work on immediate consumption goods is considered. For example, the wage of the grocer's clerk, it is admitted by both sides, will tend to equal his MVP, because there is virtually no time that elapses between the labor and the consumption of the final good. Since there is no time under which the discounting process can work, DMVP reduces to MVP. The divergence between the Austrian and orthodox schools is reached in the cases where labor is added to the value of intermediate or higher order goods. Consider a year's labor on a process that will not reach the consumption stage for a number of years. Here, the Austrians insist that cognizance be taken of the time element; that, just as we all commonly discount values receivable only in the future, we not falter when it comes to applying this insight to discounting the value of labor imputed to products which will not be usable until some years have passed. The Austrians argue, in other words, that *all* values receivable in the future be discounted by the rate of interest, even the values of the marginal product of labor, or any other factor, when such value cannot be used in consumption until an elapse of time has taken place.

Why do the non-Austrian economists refuse to follow the Austrians on this seemingly straightforward application of the principle of discounting held by all? This is difficult to answer, since most economists completely ignore DMVP, concentrating on MVP instead. Therefore the few orthodox economists who even *mention* DMVP (rejecting it in favor of MVP) are of great interest. In the view of Sir John Hicks, (1963) DMVP and MVP are consistent with each other; they are, in effect, alternatives, and either can be reasonably chosen. In Professor Hicks's words (1963, pp. 17ff). 'This conception [DMVP] is intermediate between "net productivity" and "marginal productivity", as we have defined them; just as they are consistent with each other, since they describe the same phenomenon under slightly different assumptions, so "discounted marginal productivity" is consistent with them.' And what are these 'slightly different assumptions' that distinguish 'net' and 'marginal' productivity? Hicks answers: '"Net productivity" assumes the methods of production to be fixed; marginal productivity assumes them to be variable.' But this is puzzling, for it is nonsense to suppose that the methods of production are fixed. What makes these proceedings mysterious indeed is that no one knows this better than Professor Hicks himself, for in his very next sentence he tells us (1963, p. 14): 'In fact, there can be very little doubt that [the methods of production] nearly always are variable to some extent; and consequently the marginal productivity theory has a deeper significance than the [net productivity theory].' If this is so, it seems hard to conclude that 'net' and 'marginal' productivity theories are equivalent.

But what of our main point: are DMVP and MVP theories equivalent? What reason does Professor Hicks give in support of his view that these are consistent with each other? In point of fact, he gives *no* reason to support this conclusion. What he does say is that, if we make the highly artificial assumption that the period of production ('the length of time elapsing between the payment of labor and the sale of the product') is fixed, then, 'in order to maintain the condition of equality of selling price and cost of production, the cost of [any] additional circulating capital [equal to the wage paid multiplied by the period of production] must be deducted from the marginal product, i.e. the marginal product (estimated in this manner) must be "discounted" (Hicks, 1963, pp. 17ff). But this statement poses more problems than it answers. First, there is the question of exactly *what* is to be deducted from the MVP. In the Austrian view, the deduction is equivalent to discounting the MVP by the rate of interest. In Hicks's (1963, pp. 17ff) view, what is to be deducted from the MVP is nothing based on the interest rate, but rather, 'the cost of additional circulating capital ... [which comes about] ... when the amount of labour employed slightly increases'. Circulating capital, it will be remembered, is equal to 'the wages paid, multiplied by the length of time elapsing between the payment of labor and sale of the product'. Why this amount is selected, rather than any other, is never explained. Nor are we given any reason to believe that a discount, so constructed, is equivalent to the discount based on the market rate of interest. On the contrary, there is every reason to suppose that the two methods will give *different* results. In the Austrian view, the discounting period is between the time of the payment of labor and the *final* sale to the consumer. In the Hicksian vision, the relevant time, the period of production, is measured from payment of labor to the sale of the intermediate product. For Hicks, then, *any* sale will do, whether or not it is to the final consumer of the good.

For Austrians this matter is not at all arbitrary. The reason final consumption is insisted upon is that this alone is consistent with the essence of the whole process of production. The end, the goal, the final aim of production is *consumption*. It is not until the process has reached the consumption phase that it can be said to be completed in any meaningful sense. A worker's efforts have no value whatsoever if they are not eventually carried through to the consumption level. These efforts, then, must be discounted back to the present from the time that they come to fruition, that is, from the time that they become embodied in an item of final consumption. If this were not so, then the concept of DMVP would make no sense. For if every time a change in vertical integration of industry occurred, and there were greater or fewer stages of production between the worker's efforts and the final consumption stage, this would mean an increase or decrease in the number of sales that the good had to go through before it reached the consumer. But if this is so, it would imply a change in the 'length of time elapsing between the payment of labor and the sale of the product'. Thus, every time vertical integration increased, and more stages of production were created, this 'period of production' would decrease; if the period of production decreases, then, for Hicks, the circulating capital must fall, since circulating capital is the wage multiplied by the period of production. And if circulating capital falls, then the DMVP must rise, since DMVP equals MVP minus a decreasing circulating capital, and MVP stays the same. Alternatively, vertical disintegration would imply a decrease in DMVP. Thus, a purely *legal* phenomenon, the ownership and organization of business enterprise, would intimately affect a purely *economic* phenomenon, the DMVP, which is defined in terms of productivity and the interest rate, and not at all in terms of mere legalistic ownership and sale.

Hicks gives no reason for wanting to 'maintain the condition of equality of selling price and cost of production'. Indeed, the Austrian view would be the diametric opposite. Here, there is no assumption that, merely because businessmen invested in a product, and undertook certain expenses and costs, *therefore* the consumer will spend an amount of money necessary to make the process profitable. This could only occur if we assumed perfect knowledge and hence an evenly rotating economy, an experience denied to man on this side of the Garden of Eden.

Finally, and most importantly, this scenario of Hicks's is *not* an indication that DMVP and MVP theories are consistent with each other, as Hicks supposedly sets out to show. Rather, it is a *denial* of that claim. If we accept all the assumptions made, it is an *acceptance* of the DMVP view ('the marginal product must be "discounted"') and hence a *rejection* of the MVP theory, which denies that any such deduction must be made. We need not, of course, accept the fixity of the period of production; we can, with Hicks, in his very next paragraph, 'assume that the period of production is variable' (Hicks, 1963, p. 14). If we do, we will learn that 'the additional product created by additional labour under the circumstances (of variability of the period of production) is a true marginal product, which in equilibrium must equal the wage, without any discounting (Hicks, 1963, pp. 17ff). So we see Hicks in his true colors: a complete reversal of field, where the MVP theory is now to be accepted, fully, and the DMVP theory to be rejected: again, far from his stated view that they are equivalent.

Undaunted by this, in his most recent conclusion, professor Hicks completely reverses field once again: 'Such a modernized wage-fund [the DMVP theory, with the realistic assumption of a variable period of production] is perfectly consistent with marginal productivity [MVP]; and I have often been tempted to use it on a considerable scale in this book. But I have concluded that the advantages of such a treatment would not compensate for the obstacles it would probably place in the way of readers brought up on the English tradition' (Hicks, 1963, pp. 17–18). In other words, DMVP and MVP theory are once again fully compatible, but MVP theory is preferable on aesthetic grounds! What is to be done? We can conclude that MVP and DMVP theory are logically inconsistent, one denying the need for any discounting of MVP and the other insisting upon it.

Professor Earl Rolph (1951) also sees a possible reconciliation of the DMVP and the MVP theories. Defining the former as the view that '[factors] receive the discounted value of their marginal products', Professor Rolph sees the dispute as merely a verbal one: 'An examination of the context in which these two propositions appear in economic discussions reveals that the term "product" does not mean the same thing' (1951, p. 279). In the MVP view, '"product" refers to the *immediate* results of present valuable activities', while 'in contrast, the term "product" in the phrase "discounted value of marginal product" refers to some *remote* product' (emphasis added). Now this 'remote product', to the Austrian, is *consumption*, the be-all and end-all of production. True, if one is prepared to admit that any immediate results of an industrial process, such as a hole in the ground, in preparation for a new dwelling, that will not result in consumption goods for years to come, are *equivalent* to a final product, then one can agree with Professor Rolph that 'the only apparent difference between the two views is a choice of words to say virtually the same thing' (1951, p. 282).

The Austrians, however, are not willing to make such a facile equation. It is only in the evenly rotating economy, where full and perfect information of all future events is given to all market participants, that each and every immediate result of an industrial process in the higher orders of capital goods will be guaranteed to come to fruition, eventually, as a consumption good. In the real world, *not all* 'immediate results' of production will be so blessed. Many holes in the ground will remain just that – holes in the ground. Be the intentions of the entrepreneurs ever so well motivated, they will not all be filled up with houses.

Moreover, even if all intermediate efforts are crowned, eventually, with final consumption results, the equation of DMVP and MVP is still invalid. Even in this case there would be a *time element* differential to distinguish between them. The higher the order of production, the further removed, in time, from consumption. As Professor Rothbard (1962, p. 432) states:

> Every activity may have its immediate 'results', but they are not results that would command any monetary income from anyone if the owners of the factors themselves were joint owners of all they produced until the final consumption stage. In that case, it would be obvious that they do not get paid immediately; hence, their product is not immediate. The only reason that they *are* paid immediately (and even here there is not strict immediacy) on the market is that capitalists *advance* present goods in exchange for those *future* goods for which they expect a premium, or interest return. Thus, the owners of the factors are paid the *discounted* value of their marginal product.

It must be concluded, then, that an immediate result of a higher order production process is *not* equivalent to consumption; and that factors do *not* receive the undiscounted value of their immediate marginal products. Rather, factors tend, in the unhampered market, to receive the *discounted* value of what their marginal products are thought to be worth as potential, future consumption goods.

In the remainder of this entry we shall construct another objection to DMVP theory, and then try to show that it too fails to disprove the validity of DMVP. According to this objection, DMVP theory is satisfactory for the intertemporal level, but not on the intratemporal. Intertemporally, it makes sense for the value of a factor to be determined, in part, by how many years away from final consumption it lies. If factor A is to be used *now*, and factor B one year from now, then the price of B must be adjusted downward accordingly; B must sell for less then A. But suppose A and B are identical! If intratemporal equilibrium is to be attained, then identical factors must receive the same remuneration. B's price cannot then be adjusted downward by the discount, as DMVP theory would have it.

First, suppose that there are two equally skilled carpenters: Ike and Mike. They are exactly alike insofar as carpentry abilities are concerned. They each, therefore, have the same MVP. An entrepreneur, employing several other carpenters, will benefit (lose) by the exact same amount whether he hires (fires) Ike or Mike. His revenues will change by the same amount regardless of which carpenter he deals with. Under such assumptions, intratemporal equilibrium must require that Ike and Mike receive equal wages. If they do not, the familiar market forces will be set in motion to make sure they do. But suppose Ike takes a job in a consumption industry, where his work is practically simultaneous with consumption, and Mike finds employment in a higher-order production process, whose fruits will not be available for consumption for ten years. It would seem, according to DMVP theory, that Mike's wages would have to be heavily discounted, and hence much lower than Ike's. But if this is so, it is in violation of the intratemporal equilibrium that must exist, since we are dealing with equally productive workers, by assumption.

Consider, also, two identical 100 pound bags of coal. Intratemporal equilibrium demands that they receive the exact same price. But if one of them is used for heating a home right now, and the other used in the beginning step of a process which will not be completed for one year, then it would seem that this latter bag of coal will have to sell at a lower price, low enough to reflect the discount called for by the DMVP theory. The examples could be multiplied without limit (Böhm-Bawerk, 1959). Fish is used for immediate consumption – and also for salting and curing. Some wine is allowed to ferment for one year. But other wine, identical to the first at the outset, is allowed to ferment for longer periods of time. DMVP theory, it is contended, cannot be correct if it calls for different prices for the same identical good, service or factor. And yet, if this is not what would satisfy DMVP, it is hard to see what would.

The way to solve this paradox is to take this objection 'by the horns' and show it to be without merit. Accordingly, for the sake of argument, assume its analysis is correct: if the MVP of the bag of coal to be used up for consumption is $100, and the rate of interest is 5 per cent, then it follows ineluctably that the equilibrium DMVP of an identical bag of coal, to be used in a one year-long process, is $95, ignoring compounding complications. So the intertemporal or time market may be in equilibrium, but the spot coal market certainly cannot, for one bag of coal sells for $100 while another, identical to the first in every way, sells for $95. The only problem is, entrepreneurs at the higher level of production will not be able to buy any coal! Why should they be able to if they are only willing to pay $95 for something that coal owners are able to charge $100 for?

What must then happen? The entrepreneurs at the higher stage of production will have to abstain from all projects using coal that cannot attain a DMVP of at least $100, the alternative cost of coal. But at a 5 per cent interest rate, in order to reach a DMVP of $100, the MVP must be $105. In the words of Professor Rothbard (1962, p. 409):

The more remote the time of operation is from the time when the final product is completed, the greater must be the difference allowed for the annual interest income earned by the capitalists who advance present goods and thereby make possible the entire length of the production process. The *amount* of the discount from the MVP is greater here because the higher stage is more remote than the others from final consumption. Therefore, in order for investment to take place in the higher stages, their MVP has to be far higher than the MVP in the shorter processes.

Thus we see that this objection is without merit. The DMVPs must be equated, in the evenly rotating economy, in all areas of production, not the MVPs. Coal will have the same price (assuming equal quality) wherever it is used in the structure of production: for consumption goods or in long-term heavy industry. But the further away, in time, from consumption a process is, the higher will its MVP have to be to make its employment there profitable, and to result in a DMVP equivalent to the lower orders of production, and in consumption.

See also:
Chapter 37: Labor economics; Chapter 22: The Austrian theory of price

Bibliography
Block, Walter (1990), 'The DMVP–MVP Controversy: A Note', *Review of Austrian Economics*, **4**, 199–207.
Böhm-Bawerk, Eugen von (1959), *Capital and Interest*, vol. 2, South Holland, IL: Libertarian Press.
Hicks, John R. (1963), *The Theory of Wages*, 2nd edn, New York: St Martin's Press.
Mises, Ludwig von (1966), *Human Action*, 3rd edn, Chicago: Henry Regnery.
Rolph, Earl (1951), 'The Discounted Marginal Productivity Doctrine', in *Readings in the Theory of Income Distribution*, Homewood, IL: Richard D. Irwin.
Rothbard, Murray N. (1962), *Man, Economy and State*, New York: Van Nostrand.

19 Efficiency

Roy E. Cordato

Modern Austrian economists have always been critical of the concept of efficiency as a normative guide for economic analysis. The orthodox 'cost–benefit' approach to efficiency, which has its roots in Pigouvian welfare economics and the perfect competition model, is unacceptable from the perspective of Austrian methodology. Standard efficiency theory, particularly when used as a measure of 'social welfare' and a guide to public policy, necessarily invokes interpersonal utility comparisons, and completely abstracts from the dynamic considerations of market process analysis. Consequently, many if not most Austrian economists have rejected the use of efficiency as a policy guide in favor of some form of ethical criteria (see Egger, 1979). Until recently (Cordato, 1992a) the only significant exceptions have been Kirzner (1963) and Armentano (1982) who adopted Kirzner's approach in analysing antitrust policy.

Economy, catallaxy and efficiency

While Austrians have typically been most critical of orthodox efficiency analysis for ignoring subjective value theory and for its lack of attention to dynamic change and the imperfection of knowledge, these are symptoms of a more fundamental difference in 'world view'. This difference is captured in the distinction that has been made by Mises (1966, pp. 232–4) and Hayek (1976) (also see Buchanan, 1979) between 'economy' and 'catallaxy'. According to Hayek:

> An economy ... consists of a complex of activities by which a given set of means is allocated in accordance with a unitary plan among competing ends according to their relative importance. The market order serves no such single order of ends. What is commonly called a social or national economy is in this sense not a single economy but a network of many interlaced economies... The cosmos of the market neither is nor could be governed by a single scale of ends; it serves the multiplicity of separate and incommensurable ends of all its separate participants (1976, p. 108)

The orthodox, neoclassical approach misconstrues the social phenomenon that is being analysed. The concept of allocating 'society's' resources to their 'highest valued uses' only makes sense in the context of an economy with a single hierarchy of ends. But the defining characteristic of a society, particularly a free society, is that it is made up of separate individuals and groups with no overarching 'single order of ends' on which to rank alternative resource allocations. It is therefore impossible, indeed meaningless, to talk about 'social costs' or 'social benefits'. Envisioning society as an economy leads orthodox economists to adopt a flawed and ultimately irrelevant theory of efficiency.

The concept of 'economic' efficiency relates to the means–ends framework of individuals and organized groups, such as firms, unions or civic organizations, whose goals can be ranked on a single value scale. From the perspective of Austrian economics, it refers to the extent that the individual's means are consistent with the ends being pursued (see Kirzner, 1963). This is an information problem associated with the formulation and execution of plans. The efficiency of an individual's plans will depend on the accuracy of the information that an individual has with regards to the appropriateness of the means being used to the ends being pursued. It should be clear that to assume perfect knowledge in this context would be to assume away the economic efficiency problem entirely.

In order to assess the efficiency of a market or the catallaxy as a whole, an alternative concept, which might best be called 'catallactic' efficiency, needs to be applied. Since the ends of participants in the catallaxy cannot be compared in terms of their relative social value, methodologically speaking, catallactic efficiency must be what Hayek called 'ends independent' (1976, p. 36). In other words it must recognize the multiplicity of ends being pursued by market participants and accept those ends as given. As Kirzner has argued, 'efficiency for the social system means the efficiency with which it permits its individual members to achieve their several goals' (1963, p. 35). Theories of efficiency that invoke 'social utility functions' or social cost–benefit analysis as a guide to determining the relative efficiency of alternative resource allocations are ends-dependent. They implicitly make judgements concerning the relative importance to society of the ends being pursued by different market participants.

'Maximizing' catallactic efficiency
Catallactic efficiency must be assessed not in terms of alternative market outcomes but in terms of alternative institutional settings or 'comparative systems'. The relevant question for economists is this: what is the institutional setting that will maximize the extent to which the individual members of the catallaxy will be able 'to achieve their several goals'? Invoking the distinction between catallaxy and economy, catallactic efficiency will depend on the extent to which the institutional setting allows individuals to pursue and achieve economic efficiency. Given this, there are two properties that the efficient institutional setting must have. First, it must provide for access to

and use of the means necessary for the formulation of plans and the ultimate achievements of goals. Second, it must facilitate the discovery and use of information regarding the appropriateness of means to ends.

The first issue concerns the ability of actors to gain control of physical resources, which is essential for the formulation of all plans and the ultimate achievement of all goals. In order for an individual to achieve his goals he must be able to make plans with respect to the use of resources and be reasonably confident that, when the time comes to implement those plans, the resources will be available. This means that the efficient institutional setting must be based on clearly defined and enforced private property rights. An essential right that must be included in the overall bundle of property rights is the right to make contracts and freely exchange property titles. Free exchange is essential if individuals are to be able to acquire more appropriate means for the attainment of their ends. Indeed, every freely made exchange is an act of giving up less appropriate means for more appropriate means. The exchange process also allows individuals to pursue mutually incompatible goals in harmony. Both parties, at least ex ante, benefit from free exchange, regardless of the goals that the exchanging parties are pursuing.

The second issue, regarding the discovery, acquisition and use of information is also integrally linked to the ability to freely contract and make exchanges. In a social setting, the better people are able to identify advantageous exchange opportunities the better they will be able to make plans, acquire more appropriate means and pursue their goals more efficiently. Therefore knowledge of exchange opportunities is a crucial ingredient for catallactic efficiency. Such knowledge is conveyed through market prices that are the cumulative result of previously made exchanges. By considering the array of product and price offerings that confront him, the individual can discover those others whose plans most consistently mesh with his own. Movements in relative prices provide information concerning changes in resource scarcities, technology and the plans of others. Discrepancies between input prices and the prices that might possibly be obtained for the final product alert insightful entrepreneurs to exchange opportunities that are not being exploited. The potential profits move those entrepreneurs to facilitate those exchanges. Furthermore, through the competitive entrepreneurial process of facilitating and exploiting exchange opportunities, the incentive is created to generate additional information (that is, through advertising) that is not directly conveyed by prices. (In the orthodox view, based on the efficiency norm of perfect competition, advertising is associated with product differentiation and therefore inefficiency. From the perspective of catallactic efficiency, advertising is associated with the enhancement of knowledge of exchange opportunities and is therefore evidence of an efficient market process.)

With these concerns in mind, an institutional setting can be specified that might be described as 'maximizing' catallactic efficiency. That is, it is an institutional setting that would allow the pursuit of goals within the catallaxy to proceed as efficiently as possible. It should be recognized that our analysis is carried out within the context of the inherent imperfection of knowledge, where errors in applying means to ends are often made and plans must be readjusted. People are pursuing goals within an 'open ended' context of trial and error. The 'maximization' of catallactic efficiency does not refer to the achievement of any end state but to a setting that would allow for the generation of information that is as accurate as possible and that would provide incentives for people to recognize errors and adjust their plans accordingly.

The outlines of this institutional setting should have three characteristics (see Kirzner, 1963, p. 13; Cordato, 1992a, p. 66): all property titles should be privately held; property rights should be such that individuals are able to use their property as means to their own individually determined ends; and the use of property should be constrained such that people are not permitted to violate the similar property rights of others. This institutional setting, more than any other, would promote catallactic efficiency. Private property is the cornerstone. Without it individuals would be unable to carry out any meaningful planning process. This setting also abstracts from the ends that are being pursued, that is, it is 'ends-independent', by insuring that individuals will be able to pursue their highest valued goals as they perceive them. Thirdly, the only constraint – that people do not violate the similar rights of others – ensures that conflicts in plan formulation and implementation would be minimized.

This institutional setting will also maximize the extent to which the exchange process will facilitate the execution of plans and promulgate and disseminate accurate information. Within this context individuals would be free to make any mutually agreeable exchange and, within the broad constraint described, make any contract with any mutually agreeable stipulations. Therefore this institutional setting maximizes the extent to which individual preferences, expectations and perceptions of resource scarcities come to bear on the use of resources and hence on the exchanges that are made. The resulting prices will capture as much information concerning these variables as possible.

Aiding in the entire process of exchange formulation and execution, at both the individual and social exchange level, is the fact that this institutional setting minimizes uncertainty concerning legal rights and obligations, within the context of maximizing the pursuit of goals. The individual planning process is always forward-looking and involves the use of property at points in the future. To pursue plans efficiently, individuals need to be certain that their rights to make use of legitimately acquired property will be upheld. Certainty with respect to legal rights and obligations removes what could be an important source of error from the entire market process.

Conclusion: inefficiency and public policy

In the context of catallactic efficiency, where we are viewing market activities that are proceeding through time, inefficiency is a fact of life. This is because knowledge is never perfected. The entire process is one of *minimizing* error in a context where mistakes, to some extent, will always be made. Perfect efficiency, that is, perfect knowledge, is not only an unobtainable goal, it is not even a relevant benchmark for analysis.

Inefficiency should be of concern, from a normative public policy perspective, only when it is a result of deviations from or interferences with, the institutional setting described above. From a public policy perspective, this setting should be viewed as the 'ideal'. Markets will be more or less efficient (inefficient) to the extent that this institutional setting is approached. The role of policy analysis, then, is to ferret out flaws in the existing institutional arrangement; explain how those flaws result in particular efficiencies for individual and mutual plan formulation and the price system; and propose possible public policy solutions for moving the institutional setting towards the ideal.

Catallactic efficiency can be invoked in all of the areas that are typically addressed from a normative economics perspective. This author has drawn out the implications of catallactic efficiency for the theory of externalities and public policy in the areas of tort law (Cordato, 1992a and b) and environmental economics (Cordato, 1993). The analysis here also implies a theory of competition and monopoly and a unique mode of public policy analysis in the area of industrial organization and antitrust law (see Armentano, 1992). Other areas that are ripe for analysis from this perspective include public finance and the effects of alternative forms of taxation on catallactic efficiency and regulation.

See also:

Chapter 33: Comparative economic systems; Chapter 29: 'Invisible hand' explanations; Chapter 3: Subjectivism; Chapter 30: Spontaneous order; Chapter 24: The economics of information

Bibliography

Armentano, D.T. (1982), *Antitrust and Monopoly: Anatomy of a Policy Failure*, New York: Wiley & Sons.
Armentano, D.T. (1992), 'Property Rights, Efficiency, and Social Welfare', Foreword to Cordato, *Welfare Economics and Externalities in an Open Ended Universe: A Modern Austrian Perspective*, Boston/London: Kluwer Academic Publishers.
Buchanan, James (1979), 'What Should Economists Do?', in *What Should Economists Do?*, Indianapolis: Liberty Press.

Cordato, Roy E. (1992a), *Welfare Economics and Externalities in an Open Ended Universe: A Modern Austrian Perspective*, Boston/London: Kluwer Academic Publishers.

Cordato, Roy E. (1992b), 'Knowledge Problems and the Problem of Social Cost', *The Journal of the History of Economic Thought*, fall.

Cordato, Roy E. (1993), *Social Cost, Public Policy, and Freedom of Choice*, Washington, DC: Institute for Research on the Economics of Taxation.

Egger, John (1979), 'Efficiency is Not a Substitute for Ethics', in Mario J. Rizzo (ed.), *Time, Uncertainty, and Disequilibrium*, Lexington, Mass.: Lexington Books.

Hayek, F.A. (1976), *Law, Legislation, and Liberty*, vol. 2, Chicago: University of Chicago Press.

Kirzner, Israel (1963), *Market Theory and the Price System*, Princeton, NJ: Van Nostrand.

Mises, Ludwig von (1966), *Human Action*, Chicago: Contemporary Books.

20 Supply and demand

Paul Heyne

If economics is the science of exchanges, in the tradition of Adam Smith, then supply and demand analysis is the core of economics. How should supply and demand analysis be conducted if the goal is to explain the operation of what Smith called 'a commercial society', a society in which the division of labor has become so thoroughly established that everyone 'lives by exchanging, or becomes in some measure a merchant' (Smith, 1776, p. 37)?

Austrian economists have objected persistently in recent years to the preoccupation of contemporary economists with equilibrium states and the formal conditions for equilibrium, and their neglect of the processes generated by disequilibrium (Kirzner, 1980). Change and progress, along with almost everything else that is either puzzling or interesting about a commercial society, occur in response to disequilibrium situations. The contrasting ways in which contemporary economists engage in supply and demand analysis illustrate most of the matters at issue.

The equilibrium-obsessed approach to supply and demand assumes that a demand function and a supply function 'determine' a market-clearing price – the price at which the quantity people want to purchase is equal to the quantity people want to make available for purchase. If the quantity demanded is greater than the quantity supplied, the price will rise, causing the quantity demanded to decrease and the quantity supplied to increase, until the two quantities are equal. If the quantity supplied is greater than the quantity demanded, the price will fall to equate them. The analyst does not ask what decisions by real actors produce these changes in prices and quantities or how the decision makers obtain the information that prompts them to act as they do. Prices and quantities 'adjust themselves' to satisfy the conditions of 'equilibrium'.

Some versions of analysis in this mode introduce an auctioneer to bring about the equilibrium that the given demand and supply functions dictate; but the auctioneer is altogether imaginary. The auctioneer's presence in the analysis does nothing to illuminate the processes by which actual prices move towards market-clearing levels in the world of real exchanges or to suggest what will occur if these movements of prices and quantities are impeded. The auctioneer is a mere device that enables the analyst to proceed in disregard of the fact that no one knows the shape or position of actual demand and supply functions or the market-clearing prices with which they are consistent.

Actual processes of demanding, supplying and generating prices take place in a world of limited information where the pressing problem for market participants is not how to select the economical choice among given alternatives but rather how to locate alternatives and discover the terms on which they might be available. Once everything is known, the correct choice is a mere matter of logical or mathematical deduction. In a commercial society, however, everything is not known to any single actor or even any set of actors. The knowledge relevant to economic decisions is scattered among many people who characteristically do not realize that others are interested in the knowledge they possess, and who often do not even 'command' their own knowledge because it is tacit knowledge of which they have had no occasion to become consciously aware (Hayek, 1945).

The illusion that a modern economy could be centrally planned and directed was long sustained by the assumption that all knowledge relevant to economic decisions could be known to a single mind, a single coordinating intelligence. The equilibrium-obsessed approach to supply and demand analysis helped foster and maintain this illusion. Austrian economists insist that the acquisition and dissemination of knowledge is a fundamental problem in any commercial society, and that no explanation of the processes by which decisions are coordinated in such a society will be helpful if it assumes that all participants know everything that they need to know in order to make markets clear.

When the demand for a particular good suddenly and unexpectedly increases, what happens next? The Austrian economist has no standard answer and will be reluctant simply to say, 'The price rises.' What often occurs in such cases is that retail sellers find themselves running low on inventory, and so place larger orders with their suppliers who in turn place larger orders with their suppliers. At some point in this process more resources will ordinarily be demanded to expand production of the good for which consumer demand has increased. If larger quantities of these resources can be obtained without bidding up their price, the increase in consumer demand might well produce no change at all in the retail price. Consumers could instead find themselves faced with temporary shortages that take the form of waiting periods. The claim that sellers would profit from such a shortage by raising their prices and therefore would do so assumes without warrant that sellers know exactly what is going on and are, moreover, indifferent to such factors as the ill-will of valued customers that might result from a temporary price increase designed to exploit a temporary shortage.

Supply and demand is a process in which people pursue the diverse projects that interest them in substantial ignorance of the projects that happen to interest others. When property rights are reasonably clear and secure and participants are substantially free to exchange as they prefer, supply and demand tends to become a process of mutual accommodation. When a good becomes more scarce, the process will tend to produce a higher money price for the good insofar as sellers who recognize conditions of excess demand find it in their interest to ask a higher price. This higher price will in turn persuade demanders to economize on their use of the now scarcer good and persuade suppliers to shift more of their resources into the provision of the good.

When property rights are not clearly defined or are poorly protected, or when market participants are prevented by law, custom or social pressure from negotiating the terms of exchange that they find most satisfactory, the supply and demand process will tend to produce less mutual accommodation. It will more frequently generate costs for demanders that, unlike money prices, are not simultaneously benefits to suppliers. When, for example, the political authorities impose rent controls in response to an unanticipated increase in the demand for rental housing, the quantity of rental housing demanded will at first exceed the quantity supplied. With suppliers prevented by law from asking openly for higher money rents, some other component of the cost of acquiring rental space will inevitably rise. The quantity that demanders succeed in purchasing obviously cannot exceed the quantity supplied; some procedure will consequently evolve, with or without design, that allocates the available supply among those competing to acquire it. Frequently demanders will end up obtaining apartments by paying the legal maximum money price plus higher non-monetary costs, such as the costs of increased waiting and searching. Because these non-monetary costs provide no additional benefits to suppliers, the fact that they are rising will not ordinarily induce suppliers to discover and adopt procedures for more effectively satisfying the demands of consumers. In such circumstances, negative-sum games rather than positive-sum games will emerge from the processes of supply and demand (Cheung, 1974).

An economic analysis that largely assumes away the problem of acquiring and disseminating knowledge will give little attention to the social institutions that evolve to facilitate wealth-enhancing exchanges in a world of scarce knowledge. On the other hand, those who see the coordination of diverse projects in a situation of highly limited knowledge as the central problem of a commercial society are compelled to be students of institutions. They will recognize that the arrangement of satisfactory exchanges requires the acquisition of knowledge about the characteristics of both goods and people, and that innumerable institutions have evolved over time to reduce transaction costs by providing such information in a suitable form and a timely manner. The supply and demand process develops within the context of institutions that are themselves continuously evolving in response to that process. Economists who recognize this will be reluctant to take institutions for granted; they will more likely regard institutions as part of the social reality that needs to be explained and understood (North, 1990). Such institutions include even the 'rules of the game'. While the process of supply and demand presupposes the property rights of the demanders and suppliers, along with established customs, principles and laws, all these 'rules of the game' are themselves the continually evolving outcome of supply and demand processes. As such, they are an appropriate object for research by those who want to use the tools of supply and demand to enhance the understanding of commercial society (Barzel, 1989).

The characteristic Austrian emphasis on the continuing processes of supply and demand rather than on the end states they produce fits comfortably with the unwillingness of most Austrian economists to construct comparative assessments of end states. Economists frequently argue that various forms of market intervention by government, such as price controls, produce 'inefficient' results by preventing resources from moving to their most highly valued uses. The thoroughgoing subjectivism of the Austrian perspective provides no criterion for comparing the goods or satisfactions realized under one set of institutional arrangements with those realized under another set. Economists may legitimately argue that price controls prevent resources from moving to those uses that yield the highest *monetary* valuations; but monetary valuations cannot be equated with valuations because different people value money differently. The implication of all this is that the economist's legitimate contributions to policy discussion will largely be limited to discovering the rationale of observed practices and tracing out the probable consequences of alternative policy proposals (Coase, 1988). There is no logical termination point in any direction for this kind of analysis. When supply and demand analysts have finished predicting or explaining the consequences of a particular scheme of price controls, they can use the same tools to talk about what might be expected in a world without any such controls, or to examine the political exchanges that produced the price controls, or to spell out the probable consequences of some alternative political scheme for dealing with whatever pressures prompted the imposition of price controls in the first place.

Another point about the Austrian understanding of supply and demand merits special notice in the context of Anglo-American economics, where Alfred Marshall managed to popularize the notion that supply and demand represent two sets of independent factors that jointly determine prices. From the Marshallian perspective that dominates most textbook presentations, demand reflects tastes and preferences, the subjective aspect of the situation, and supply reflects costs of production, the objective aspect. This account of the matter cannot be accepted by anyone who subscribes to the opportunity cost theory, which asserts that the costs affecting decisions to supply are the value of forgone opportunities. Costs are not material facts dictated by physical reality but the outcome of social transactions. Costs are themselves the product of demand and supply, because the cost of producing any good will depend in part upon the demand for other goods that can be produced with the same resources. Marshall obscured this relationship with his doctrine of 'real costs', which he thought of as the 'efforts and sacrifices' of those whose exertions and abstinence provide respectively the labor and the capital for production (Marshall, 1890, pp. 338–9). Philip Wicksteed tried to straighten out the confusion in his presidential address to Section F of the British Association in 1913 (Wicksteed, 1914) but was not able to overcome what had by that time become the settled orthodoxy: a pair of scissors requires two blades to cut. In this misconception, supply and demand are the two independent blades that cut through the mysteries of price determination, and any attempt to explain supply by reference to subjective valuations is simply the opposite error to that of the classical economists who had tried to explain prices exclusively on the basis of costs.

The concepts of supply and demand provide a valuable pair of complementary tools because the factors that affect exchange transactions and resource allocation decisions can *usually* be *usefully* sorted into the two categories of those that influence supply and those that influence demand. The heuristic value of having two vises in which to hold our observations should not be allowed to obscure the fact that everything ultimately depends upon everything else.

See also:
Chapter 4: Market process; Chapter 22: The Austrian theory of price; Chapter 25: Prices and knowledge

Bibliography
Barzel, Yoram (1989), *Economic Analysis of Property Rights*, New York: Cambridge University Press.
Cheung, Steven N.S. (1974), 'A theory of price control', *Journal of Law and Economics*, **XVII**, (1).
Coase, R.H. (1988), 'The firm, the market, and the law', in *The Firm, the Market, and the Law*, Chicago: University of Chicago Press.
Hayek, Friedrich A. (1945), 'The use of knowledge in society', *American Economic Review*, **XXXV**, (4), reprinted in *Individualism and Economic Order*, Chicago: Henry Regnery Company, 1948.
Kirzner, Israel M. (1980), 'The "Austrian" perspective on the crisis', in *The Crisis in Economic Theory*, special issue, *The Public Interest*.
Marshall, Alfred (1890), *Principles of Economics*, 9th (variorum) edn, New York: Macmillan, 1961.
North, Douglass C. (1990), *Institutions, Institutional Change, and Economic Performance*, New York: Cambridge University Press.
Smith, Adam [1776] (1981), *An Inquiry into the Nature and Causes of the Wealth of Nations*, Indianapolis: Liberty Classics.

Wicksteed, Philip (1914), 'The scope and method of political economy', *Economic Journal*, **XXIV**, (1), reprinted in *The Common Sense of Political Economy and Selected Papers and Reviews on Economic Theory*, London: Routledge & Kegan Paul, 1933.

21 Profit and loss

Charles W. Baird

Inasmuch as economics is the study of the logical implications of human action, and the essence of human action is the substitution of a more satisfactory state of affairs for a less satisfactory one (Mises, 1949), profit and loss are at the core of economics. Human action and market processes cannot be understood without understanding profit and loss. In this entry I first explain what profit and loss are and are not. Next, I consider two social functions of profit and loss. Then I address the question of whether profit is deserved. Finally, I examine four additional misconceptions regarding profit.

What are profit and loss?

All human action takes place in a framework of ends and means. Each person purposively applies means in an attempt to achieve ends. When a person substitutes a more satisfactory state of affairs for a less satisfactory one, the former is the end and the sacrifice of the latter is the means. From the perspective of an individual, whether isolated or a market participant, profit is the difference (if positive) between the subjective value he attaches to the end achieved and the subjective value he attaches to the means that had to be expended to achieve the end. If this difference is negative (that is, if the value he attaches to the end achieved is less than the value he attaches to the means expended) the individual suffers a loss. Profit and loss, in this most basic sense, are not quantifiable on any objective scale. They are not, for example, measured in money.

Even at this basic level, profit and loss depend on uncertainty and the erroneous evaluations that emerge therefrom. According to Menger's Law, since the value that a person attaches to something depends on its perceived usefulness to him, he imputes the value of any end back to the means that are sufficient to achieve that end (Menger, 1871). Suppose that means M is sufficient to achieve end E. If an individual attaches a value to M that is less than the value he attaches to E it is because he is *unaware* that M can achieve E. With perfect knowledge such an erroneous evaluation of M would be impossible. The profit that is grasped by using M to achieve E is the difference between the value attached to E and the *erroneous* value attached to M. Before M can be deployed to achieve E, the individual must notice that such a possibility exists. The profit opportunity exists at that moment of entrepreneurial insight. Immediately thereafter, as the individual grasps the profit opportunity, the value he attaches to M will equal the value he attaches to E.

From the perspective of the market, profit is usually measured in terms of money, and it is associated with entrepreneurship in the context of business enterprise. Therein, an entrepreneur is a person who assembles all the resources physically necessary for the production of a good which he then resells to consumers. He does so because he perceives that the price for which he will be able to sell the good exceeds the sum of the prices he must pay to the resource owners from whom he secures the necessary inputs. Such a discrepancy between the final good price and the sum of the prices paid for the inputs necessary to produce the good is an erroneous evaluation of those inputs. It can happen only because of uncertainty. If market participants were aware of the full value of the inputs, the money value of the final product would have been imputed back to the set of necessary inputs, and there would be no profit opportunity.

The set of necessary inputs could also be overvalued. An entrepreneur who mistakenly thinks that the price for which he could sell a product is greater than the sum of the prices of all the necessary inputs will be disappointed. The perceived profit opportunity will, ex post, turn into a loss. Such an entrepreneurial error is usually due to an overestimate of the price for which the product may be sold. This causes the entrepreneur to impute too high a value to the necessary inputs. With the certainty that accompanies perfect knowledge, all inputs would be valued according to their most highly valued uses. But in the uncertain real world it is the role of the entrepreneur to discover opportunities to redirect resources from lower valued to higher valued uses. The role of profit is to 'switch on' entrepreneurial alertness to such opportunities and thus make their discovery possible (Kirzner, 1973).

The entrepreneur who first notices a profit opportunity grasps it by acquiring the undervalued inputs at their low prices, producing the product and selling it at the higher price that consumers are willing to pay. If his perception is correct he will make profit, and that will attract the attention of other entrepreneurs who will try to imitate his success. Competition among entrepreneurs to obtain undervalued resources will cause more and more resource owners to realize they can successfully ask higher prices for them. Competition among entrepreneurs to sell the final good will cause more and more consumers to realize that they can successfully offer lower bids for it. This competitive process grinds away at the erroneous market evaluations until, in equilibrium, they, and their concomitant profit, disappear.

The resources that are physically necessary for the production of a good (that is, the inputs in a neoclassical production) fall into three categories – land, labor and capital. Market participants who own these resources, as resource owners, do not receive profit therefrom. For example, capitalists are people who own physical and financial capital. Entrepreneurs, in assembling resources, hire or buy capital services from capitalists in exchange for a resource price called interest, just as they hire labor services for a resource price called a wage.

Entrepreneurs, *qua* entrepreneurs, are not owners of production function inputs. Their key attribute is alertness to discrepancies between resource prices and final goods prices. Their role is to notice that it would be profitable to convert resources into outputs through production. Profit comes from mental alertness to such opportunities, it does not come from capital (or labor or land). Nor does it come from technological knowledge of *how* to convert inputs into outputs. Such knowledge is part of the labor input. Entrepreneurial knowledge is awareness that it is profitable to produce the product; it is not knowledge of how to produce the product. Once the opportunity has been noticed and grasped there is nothing for entrepreneurs to do. The assembled resources are then sufficient for production. As this implies, entrepreneurship is not managing and coordinating an enterprise. The important functions of management and coordination are labor functions, not entrepreneurial functions. Profit, therefore, is not a reward for managing and coordinating an enterprise.

The fact that a person who is an entrepreneur may also be a resource owner obscures the nature of profit. An accountant defines enterprise profit as being gross receipts from sales minus total costs. Accounting profit is an ex post measurement of the performance of an enterprise. Suppose, as is often the case, that the person who assembles resources to grasp a hitherto unnoticed profit opportunity also runs the enterprise and is its principal investor. Such a person plays two separate roles – as a resource owner he supplies labor and capital, and as an entrepreneur he envisions and initiates the undertaking. The 'profit' that an accountant would calculate for this enterprise would be overstated. To get true ex post profit two deductions would have to be made. First, the entrepreneur must count as cost the highest amount he could earn elsewhere by selling his managerial labor services to other enterprises. That is an ordinary factor (input) payment, a cost of production, not profit. Second, the entrepreneur must count as cost the highest interest income he could earn if he invested his capital in alternative investments of like risk. That, too, is an ordinary factor payment, a cost of production, not profit. There is true ex post profit if and only if there is something left after *all* the bills have been paid, including the bills the entrepreneur owes to himself.

While an external observer can know whether or not an undertaking is profitable only after the fact, an entrepreneur is not a passive residual claimant. The entrepreneur notices what is to him a real profit opportunity, and he attempts to grasp it. He could be wrong, but for him the profit exists before all the bills are actually paid. The profit that motivates the entrepreneur is ex ante profit. The entrepreneurial vision is an active originating force that sets in motion the series of transactions that accountants evaluate after the fact. Alertness to hitherto unnoticed preferred possibilities is purposive human action. Profit is attributable to that alertness. It is not merely a lucky outcome in an uncertain environment (Kirzner, 1979).

Two social functions of profit and loss

One social function of profit and loss is to coordinate the diverse activities of all market participants. In a market economy each market participant formulates his own economic plans in the light of the circumstances he confronts by using the imperfect knowledge he has about market conditions and the intentions of others. His perception of prices he will have to bid to obtain what he wishes to buy, and prices he can successfully ask for what he wishes to sell, summarize those market conditions and intentions for him. When different buyers and different sellers base their plans on inconsistent expectations regarding bid and ask prices, their individual economic plans will be uncoordinated. Some buyers and sellers will not be able to carry out all their planned exchanges, and other buyers and sellers will not be able to carry out any of their planned exchanges. In a word, there will be disequilibrium (Hayek, 1945).

In disequilibrium, when market participants attempt to carry out their plans they will discover that their price expectations are wrong. Buyers (sellers) who thought they could buy (sell) at an unrealistically low (high) price, will have their expectations directly falsified. They will then attempt to discover the best terms they can, altering their plans accordingly. This striving for better terms is profit-seeking and loss-avoiding behavior. A buyer (seller) who pays (accepts) a higher (lower) price than another buyer (seller) pays (accepts) for the same good suffers loss relative to what he could have done if he had been aware of the better prices. A buyer (seller) who gets to buy (sell) for the lower (higher) price makes profit relative to the exchanges he would have been able to make if his exchange partners had been aware of the better prices. Again, inconsistent evaluations in the market are the source of the profits and losses. Buyer and seller alertness to such discrepancies and the profit-seeking, loss-avoiding actions that follow, together with the arbitrage activities of third parties who notice the discrepancies, eventually eliminate them.

Buyers (sellers) who are so pessimistic that they over- (under) estimate the bids (offers) they have to make to buy (sell) what they want and so plan not to buy (sell) any, will not have their expectations directly falsified because their decisions keep them out of the market. However, their profit-motivated alertness to what others are doing, and the alertness of others to the profit opportunities involved in bringing the pessimists into the market, can be relied on to correct the erroneous evaluations.

In equilibrium, all input and output prices are correctly perceived by all market participants. There are no price discrepancies and concomitant profit opportunities to be grasped by changing bids and offers. The uniformly perceived prices cause each market participant to make production and exchange plans that are consistent with the plans of all other market participants. But that is the *result* of the profit-seeking and loss-avoiding behavior of all market participants in situations of disequilibrium. Paradoxically, when profit-seeking and loss-avoiding actions have done their job there are no more profits to be sought and losses to be avoided.

Another social function of profit and loss is to promote consumer interests. An entrepreneur makes profit by redirecting resources away from those uses that are less highly valued towards those uses that are more highly valued by consumers. An entrepreneur whose actions result in loss does the opposite. Profit is evidence that consumers are receiving more value out of existing resources than before. Loss is evidence that consumers are receiving less value out of existing resources than before. Although entrepreneurs intend only to make profit and avoid loss, the unintended consequence of their actions is to improve consumer welfare. Profit seekers can do well for themselves only by doing good for others.

Are profits deserved?
Profit is thought by many to be a four-letter word. Profiteering is almost universally denigrated as an anti-social act. Karl Marx (1867), for example, taught that profit was the result of the exploitation of labor. Even many mainstream economists are uneasy about profit and struggle to justify it. J.B. Clark justified profit as a factor income. In equilibrium, each factor's price is a payment for its marginal contribution to output. A factor's price times the quantity of the factor used in production equals that factor's appropriate share of the total incomes generated by the enterprise in which the factors are employed. Similarly, as Clark would have it, profit is the income that the factor called entrepreneurship earns. Entrepreneurs provide coordinating services. There is an equilibrium profit per unit of entrepreneurship which, when multiplied by the quantity of entrepreneurship employed, equals the entrepreneur's appropriate share of total enterprise income.

But entrepreneurship, correctly understood, is not a factor of production like labor and capital. It is meaningless to talk about increasing or decreasing the quantity of entrepreneurship employed in a firm. Entrepreneurship is alertness to hitherto unnoticed profit opportunities. Either the profit opportunities are noticed or they are not. Marginal adjustments of entrepreneurship cannot be made. There is no marginal revenue product of entrepreneurship. In equilibrium, the job of the entrepreneur is over and profit is zero. Thus it is impossible to justify profit on the same grounds used to justify wages and interest. There can be equilibrium wages and interest, but 'equilibrium profit' is an oxymoron.

The most successful defense of profits is based on the observation that the entrepreneur discovers profit opportunities (Kirzner, 1989). Entrepreneurship is not a necessary input in the sense of a neoclassical production function, but, until someone notices that it would be profitable to assemble resources and undertake a program of production, there is no production. It may be technologically possible to produce fiber optic lines for telecommunications, but until some entrepreneur notices that to do so would be profitable and then undertakes to grasp that opportunity, the opportunity does not exist. The entrepreneur actually *creates* the profit opportunity by discovering it. It is a widely shared ethical intuition that one who, acting on his own without help from others or the resources they own, brings something into existence has a just entitlement to do it. The discovery of the profit opportunity requires no resources. It requires only alertness. Putting the discovery into action requires resources, and resource owners receive payment in accordance with the terms they agree to when their resources are hired by the entrepreneur. Profit is the result of the creative act of discovery that makes it possible for resource owners to receive their incomes.

Four additional misconceptions regarding profit

It is routine for financial analysts and journalists to calculate 'profit rates' by dividing ex post profit by the amount of capital invested in the firm. Even if the ex post profit is calculated correctly, this implies that the source of profit is capital. But, as we have seen above, the source of profit is not capital, it is the entrepreneur's alertness. Capital does not beget profit, alertness does. Since it is impossible, actually meaningless, to measure the quantity of alertness, it is impossible and meaningless to compute profit rates (Mises, 1951).

Politicians are fond of calling profits of which they disapprove 'windfall profits' and confiscating them through taxation. The most common definition of 'windfall profits' is gains that are due to sheer luck. If profit were due to sheer luck there would be no systematic tendency for the market process to eliminate disequilibrium. There would be winners and losers, but there would be no mechanism to rely on systematically to correct erroneous evaluations. True profit, on the other hand, is due to entrepreneurial alertness. While it is true that market participants may receive gains due to pure luck, it is impossible for third parties ever to separate 'windfall' gains from true entrepreneurial profit. Conceptually it may be true that pure windfalls can be confiscated without harm to the market process, but entrepreneurial profits cannot. Secure property rights to the profits obtained by entrepreneurial alertness are necessary to motivate that alertness. Without it the whole market process breaks down.

It is often asserted that cutting out middlemen can save costs because each middleman adds on his own profit margin to the actual resource costs he incurs. But in equilibrium a middleman's 'profit margin' is just a wage paid for the services the middleman supplies. If the middleman is a lower cost producer of those services than the person who would cut the middleman out, that person will end up with higher, not lower costs. In disequilibrium a middleman (acting as an entrepreneur) may receive a true profit. For example, consider simple arbitrage. An entrepreneur notices that someone is willing to sell something at a price that is significantly lower than the price that someone else is willing to pay for it. The seller and the buyer do not know of this opportunity. The entrepreneur has discovered it. The entrepreneur grasps the opportunity by buying low (at a price that includes all his transactions costs) from the first person and selling high to the second person. If this middleman is cut out there would be no exchange at all. No costs will have been saved because no costs at all would be incurred. The middleman's true profit, if any exists, will eventually be ground down to zero by imitators who will compete by offering buyers and sellers better terms.

Finally, it is routine for neoclassical economists to discuss 'profit maximization'. This discussion is typically carried on in the context of a given set of cost and revenue functions with respect to which the task is to find the rate of product output that makes profit as big as possible. But this cannot be profit maximization in the Austrian sense of profit. With specified cost and revenue functions all that separates the decision maker from the correct answer is mathematical manipulation of the equations. True profit is impossible in a context of certainty about costs and revenues. Moreover, the 'profit-maximizing' output rate is a flow that can continue indefinitely, but profit cannot continue indefinitely. It is inevitably ground down to zero by the competitive market process. At best, neoclassical 'profit maximization' refers to the calculations an entrepreneur would make after he had formulated specific perceptions of the cost and revenue functions. It says nothing about the role of entrepreneurial alertness in formulating those perceptions or the process by which erroneous perceptions are corrected.

See also:
Chapter 13: Cost; Chapter 2: Methodological individualism; Chapter 17: Risk and uncertainty; Chapter 15: Entrepreneurship

Bibliography
Clark, J.B. (1899), *The Distribution of Wealth*, New York/London: Macmillan.
Hayek, F.A. [1945] (1984), 'The Use of Knowledge in Society', in *Individualism and Economic Order*, Chicago: Henry Regnery Company.
Kirzner, I.M. (1973), *Capitalism and Entrepreneurship*, Chicago: University of Chicago Press.
Kirzner, I.M. (1979), 'Alertness, Luck and Entrepreneurial Profit', in *Perception, Opportunity, and Profit*, Chicago: University of Chicago Press.

Kirzner, I.M. (1989), *Discovery, Capitalism, and Distributive Justice*, New York/Oxford: Basil Blackwell.

Marx, Karl [1867] (1930), *Capital*, Vol. I, London: J.M. Dent & Sons.

Menger, C. [1871] (1976), *Principles of Economics*, New York/London: New York University Press.

Mises, L. von (1949), *Human Action*, New Haven: Yale University Press.

Mises, L. von [1951] (1962), 'Profit and Loss', in *Planning for Freedom*, South Holland, IL: Libertarian Press.

22 The Austrian theory of price

Jack High

Introduction

Prices are essential to the operation of markets. The prices that businesses ask for their products determine how much customers will buy. The prices offered for labor, land and capital goods determine both the allocation of resources among various uses and the distribution of income among society. Proper pricing is vital to a firm's profitability; pricing too high or too low can be fatal to an otherwise profitable business. Moreover, prices convey information; they signal the relative scarcity or abundance of many thousands of goods. It is unimaginable that a complex world economy could function without the work performed by prices (see Hayek, 1948).

Because of its primacy to markets, price formation has been a central concern of economists since the inception of their science. The labor theory of value as expounded by Adam Smith, David Ricardo and others attempted to explain why the prices of some goods are high and others are low. The inadequacies of the labor theory of value, and its replacement by marginal analysis, revolutionized the theory of price. Marginal analysis reversed causation between the prices of consumers' goods and producers' goods. In the labor theory, the value of labor determined the price of beaver; in the marginal theory, the prices of beaver pelts determine the wage of the trapper. The ultimate arbiter of wages and rents is the prices of consumers' goods and the prices of consumers' goods depend on the relative marginal utilities of the goods. If an additional unit of a good, such as diamonds, has a high value to the consumer, it commands a high price in the market; a good for which an additional unit has a low value to the consumer, such as water, commands a low price. Not only did marginal theory reverse the direction of causation, it brought the pricing of land, labor and capital goods under a single principle, now known as the marginal productivity principle.

The marginal revolution substantially improved the theory of price, but subsequent developments in economics unduly narrowed the scope of the theory. The increasing attention paid to competitive equilibrium, particularly in the post-Second World War period, relegated actual market prices, as opposed to their hypothetical counterparts in equilibrium, to a secondary place in economics. Economists could say a great deal about the way producers and consumers would react to given prices, but they could say very little about the way prices were formed and adjusted. This is most evident in general equilibrium theory.

Stability analysis

The existence proofs of a general equilibrium depend, inter alia, on producers and consumers maximizing their particular functions with respect to 'given' prices. 'Given', in this context, means that there is a single market price for each good, and that no one can change any price. Even if we accept, for the sake of argument, that given prices make sense for an equilibrium state, they create a problem for explaining how prices might adjust. If no one can change prices, how can they reach their equilibrium values?

General equilibrium got around this problem with the fictional device of an economy-wide auctioneer. This *deus ex machina* of economic theory called out a price for each good in the market, took buy and sell orders, calculated excess demand, and raised or lowered price according to whether excess demand was positive or negative. The primary question of price adjustment was whether prices would converge to their equilibrium values. This line of inquiry was known as stability analysis (see Arrow and Hahn, 1971, pp. 22, 322). Stability analysis had several pronounced shortcomings, the most notable of which was that price adjustment was not undertaken by buyers and sellers in the pursuit of their own self-interest. The fundamental motivating force of economic theory was absent from the theory of price formation. Stability analysis had an air of unreality about it; it seemed almost impossible to anchor the theory to the operations of actual markets (see High, 1990, pp. 23–6).

Search theory

Economic theory experienced a self-acknowledged 'crisis' in the 1970s. The crisis was precipitated by the appearance of 'stagflation', and the subsequent realization that macroeconomics was not integrated with microeconomics. General equilibrium theory was singled out for some heavy criticism, mainly because it ignored the problems of unemployed resources and inflation. One prominent economist even referred to general equilibrium theory as science fiction (see Clower, 1975).

Providing microeconomic foundations for macroeconomics became a prominent theoretical enterprise in the 1970s, and one of these foundations, search theory, looked like it might provide a more realistic theory of price adjustment. Search theory dropped the assumption of perfect competition. It allowed sellers to set their own prices, which would normally result in a price distribution for each good. Buyers would then search over the distribution in order to find more advantageous prices at which to trade. They would continue their search until the marginal costs and benefits of search were equal. Search theory had the advantages of allowing traders to set their prices and of incorporating self-interest into the search process (see Stigler, 1961; Alchian, 1970).

Nevertheless, search theory never really developed into a realistic explanation of price formation. The main obstacle to this seems to have been the postulate of a random distribution of prices over which agents searched. A random distribution was required in order for price searchers to calculate their marginal costs and benefits, but the kinds of knowledge required for randomness were inconsistent with the way in which markets provide information. Consider a worker searching over a group of employers for a higher wage offer. In order for the distribution of wages facing the worker to be random, she would have to know which wages were being offered, but she could not know which firm was offering which wage. Markets do not normally disperse information this way. Usually workers will learn of a wage offer and the company offering it at the same time, in which case the distribution of wages is not random (see High, 1983–4).

Austrian theory
Price adjustments in a market economy are set within a larger framework of institutions that have evolved over a long historical period. The most important of these institutions are money, monetary calculation, the division of labor and specialized traders. Menger first pointed out that an increasing division of labor and the evolution of money are mutually reinforcing developments in economic life. As more and more people specialize in production, it becomes increasingly difficult for each person to exchange what he has produced for what he wants to consume. Indirect exchange immediately helps to alleviate this problem, and ultimately leads to the acceptance of commonly accepted media of exchange, or money (Menger, 1892).

At the same time that economies develop the use of money, they also develop specialized markets for various goods. The same people who specialize in the production of, say, jewelry or clothing or foodstuffs will become specialists in exchanging these goods. They will establish trading posts and they will be alert to the prices at which these goods will exchange for money. The terms on which specialized producers will be willing to exchange depend on their past experience with market conditions for their products. Thus, from the beginning stages of markets, specialized knowledge of trading conditions is built into prices. Division of labor is accompanied by division of knowledge about supply and demand conditions in various markets. Already we can see how misleading it is to assume that a fictional auctioneer randomly calls out prices, or to assume that a price distribution is stable. These theoretical constructions ignore the experience and judgement that are built into market prices.

The emergence of money will facilitate a more minute and complex division of labor, for two reasons. First, money makes it much less costly to exchange specialized products. Second, money makes possible profit and loss calculations. Specialized producers can purchase raw materials and transform them into products that are exchanged for money. The amounts of money expended on production can be compared with the amounts of money received in revenues. Producers can calculate whether it has been advantageous for them to engage in their particular forms of production and marketing.

As specialized production becomes more minute and complex, so does the knowledge necessary to carry out exchange. Producers, or specialists whom the producers hire, will familiarize themselves, not only with market conditions on the revenue side of the ledger, but with market conditions on the cost side as well. In deciding how much to offer for additional material or workers, the producer will carefully estimate the prospective revenues from such purchases. Thus wage and price offers in resource markets also reflect the seasoned judgement and experience of specialized traders (Mises, 1949, pp. 207–20).

There are two other elements of the market process that contribute to the judgement and experience that go into price formation. The first is the profit motive. Profit and loss calculations not only make it possible for a producer to tell whether he is using resources to advantage, they also give him an incentive to do so. If he offers too much or too little to hire labor, or if he prices his product too high or too low, the producer forgoes potential profit or perhaps even suffers loss. The second element that contributes to sound judgement in pricing is the selection process of profit and loss. Those who are skilled at estimating which products to manufacture, which resources to use and which prices to offer will prosper; their firms will succeed and the sphere of their influence will widen. Those who are poorer judges will struggle and perhaps fail; their firms will not grow and their judgement will be restricted to a relatively narrow sphere. Thus those who have relatively greater ability to judge market conditions, and hence to form accurate price estimates, will have relatively more influence in markets (Mises, 1952, especially p. 123).

Within this context of market institutions, it is possible to isolate pricing decisions and to study how prices will change under various assumptions. For example, the economist can assume that all producers of the same product charge the same price, but that the price is below its market-clearing level. Under these circumstances, producers are likely to discover that they can increase profitability by raising price, thus moving it towards its market-clearing level. Or the economist can assume that different producers charge different prices, even for the same good, and examine the likely movement of prices in this situation. With price dispersion, the self-interest of traders will generally, but not always, move prices towards their market-clearing levels. For examples of this kind of analysis, see Rothbard (1962, pp. 112–18, 123–33); Kirzner (1963, chapter 7) and High (1990, pp. 134–67). For a rigorous mathematical examination of the conditions under which prices will definitely converge to an equilibrium, see Fisher (1983).

These kinds of exercises have analytical value. They are a definite improvement upon traditional stability analysis, where the assumption of perfect competition precludes traders from changing prices. In the Austrian analysis, price formation is endogenous to the market process; price movement is the result of self-interest. Austrian analysis is also an improvement on search theory; the assumptions about what traders know and can be expected to learn are much more realistic in Austrian theory. The analysis is not constrained by the postulate of a random distribution of prices. Finally, the Austrian theory of price adjustment shows how unlikely it is that market prices will be at their equilibrium levels. The assumptions that must hold in order to prove convergence are so stringent that only a fantastic leap of faith could bring us to believe that the market is usually in a state of general equilibrium. The theory of price adjustment is important in its own right: it is not a handmaiden to equilibrium theory. A cogent explanation of price adjustment is, in fact, the core of any realistic theory of the market as a process.

See also:
Chapter 25: Prices and knowledge; Chapter 20: Supply and demand; Chapter 4: Market process; Chapter 21: Profit and loss

Bibliography
Alchian, Armen A. (1970), 'Information Costs, Pricing, and Resource Unemployment', reprinted in Edmund S. Phelps (ed.), *Microeconomic Foundations of Employment and Inflation Theory*, New York: W.W. Norton.
Arrow, Kenneth and Frank Hahn (1971), *General Competitive Analysis*, San Francisco: Holden Day.
Clower, Robert (1975), 'Reflections on the Keynesian Perplex', *Zeitschrift für Nationalökonomie*, 35.
Fisher, Franklin (1983), *Disequilibrium Foundations of Equilibrium Economics*, Cambridge: Cambridge University Press.
Hayek, Friedrich von (1948), 'The Use of Knowledge in Society', reprinted in *Individualism and Economic Order*, Chicago: Henry Regnery.
High, Jack (1983–4), 'Knowledge, Maximizing and Conjecture: A Critical Analysis of Search Theory', *Journal of Post Keynesian Economics*, winter.
High, Jack (1990), *Maximizing, Action, and Market Adjustment*, Munich: Philosophia Verlag.
Kirzner, Israel (1963), *Market Theory and The Price System*, Princeton: Van Nostrand.
Menger, Carl (1892), 'On the Origin of Money', *Economic Journal*, June.
Mises, Ludwig von (1949), *Human Action*, New Haven: Yale University Press.
Mises, Ludwig von (1952), 'Profit and Loss', in *Planning for Freedom*, South Holland, IL: Libertarian Press.
Rothbard, Murray N. (1962), *Man. Economy, and State*, Princeton: Van Nostrand.
Stigler, George J. (1961), 'The Economics of Information', reprinted in *The Organization of Industry*, Homewood, IL: Richard D. Irwin, 1968.

23 Non-price rivalry

W. Duncan Reekie

Non-price competition includes rivalry between firms based upon advertising, product differentiation and product and process innovation. The neoclassical approach to the first two is epitomized by the Dorfman–Steiner theorem (1954) which applies the marginal equivalency principle in a normative fashion to describe the partial equilibrium conditions for a profit-maximizing firm. (Specifically, the single product firm should equate each of price elasticity, the marginal sales effect of advertising and the product of quality elasticity times mark up over average cost.) This equilibrium approach, however, is unsuited to innovation (whether product or process) as indeed it is to changes in consumer preferences (which themselves could be brought about by advertising). Taste and technology changes are then presumed to be exogenous to the system and are 'explained' respectively as shifts in either consumer preference maps or production functions. These changes then result in consequential new equilibria. Neither of the concepts of equilibrium or exogeneity, however, are particularly helpful in understanding such an important and obtrusive part of the market process as non-price rivalry.

Although less obviously so, Austrian economics, like the neoclassical mainstream, is also somewhat deficient in its approach to non-price rivalry. The common reason is that in both schools of thought price is centre stage. Advertising, product differentiation and innovation are secondary considerations. However, in the Austrian approach, what is stressed is *price differences* arising from ever-changing subjective variations in value, while in the neoclassical approach what matters is *price homogeneity* in equilibrium. Consequently, Austrianism can handle non-price rivalry rather more readily. Non-price rivalry, a dynamic activity, can be incorporated into an understanding of the market process in a way it cannot be in static neoclassical theory.

In the standard neoclassical approach price is a given in a situation of equilibrium and perfect knowledge. Transactors can make once-and-for-all exchanges at ruling prices. Or, if the knowledge assumption is relaxed, then, in the presence of imperfect information about the optimal equilibrium, time and effort and other costs can be incurred by transactors to find out the terms on which goods are available on the market. After a point, search will be abandoned in favour of purchase because the marginal costs of search themselves are about to exceed the marginal benefits of further search. Advertising (for example) can then be embodied in the system as a cost incurred to provide information to decision makers who simply include it as a search cost preceding an achieved framework of equilibrium. This type of knowledge acquisition via search implies that the advertiser already knows what the recipient of the advertising message does not know. Advertising which is not informative (that is, which is persuasive) is then an 'imperfection', as is product differentiation. To neoclassicists, these aspects of non-price rivalry are simply characteristics of imperfectly, as opposed to perfectly, competitive equilibrium.

More discrete aspects of non-price rivalry such as product or process innovation (or technological changes) are handled exogenously as explaining why new and different equilibria are appropriate. That is, innovation changes – exogenously – the indifference curves of the consumer and production isoquants of the producer so that new and different equilibrium points with new and different equimarginal rates of substitution can hold. Austrianism does not view such an equilibrium as the norm. Rather, it sees non-price differentials nudging the system towards (a never attained but) higher equilibrium as entrepreneurs seek to profit from exploitation of price differentials and non-equivalent marginal rates of substitution.

These alternative starting-points can result in two sharply differing interpretations of the reasons for and functions of non-price rivalry. Neoclassicists tend to view non-price rivalry as a *substitute* for price competition, while Austrians view it rather as a *necessary complement*. Much discussion in modern industrial organization theory of non-price rivalry views various aspects of it as necessary strategic managerial devices. These devices may be selected by firms to avoid upsetting fragile oligopolistic equilibria based on price alone. Alternatively, many of the non-price rivalry activities are perceived as pre-emptive barriers discouraging the appearance of new competitors by raising the cost of new market entry. A third view is that in regulated industries, where prices are legally held above the equilibrium level which would otherwise hold, non-price rivalry will be engaged in to a significant extent as a surrogate for lower prices. Each of these explanations is to a greater or lesser degree linked to a concept of equilibrium and each also implies that non-price rivalry offers protection in some sense to profit margins of price over cost which would not exist absent the non-price rivalry.

To Austrians, however, competition is a discovery process, not an equilibrium. Profits are the rewards to alertness to the discovery of opportunities where consumer wants remain unsatisfied, where marginal rates of substitution are not equal, or would not be equal even if all trade opportunities were viable. As Menger ([1871], 1976, p. 242) put it: 'Commodities that are little known ([or] "articles that have not yet been introduced") have very small clienteles, simply because they are not known. Producers are therefore accustomed to make their commodities "known" often at great economic sacrifice, in order to increase the number of persons to whom they are saleable. This accounts for the economic importance of ... advertisements ... etc.' Israel Kirzner (1974) expanded on this explanation of advertising as a means of inducing in consumers entrepreneurial alertness to purchase opportunities using the example of cars and gasoline. Advertising not only informs potential traders that an exchange may be viable; it alerts them to its existence. 'Supposing,' argued Kirzner, 'I set up a gas station ... I have a pump carefully hidden behind the bushes, and cars that come down the road can buy gas if they know I'm here. I don't put out a sign. Well, gas without information is like a car without gas.' Even with a sign, cars may speed down the road but fail to see it. 'People are looking for that information. It's my task as an entrepreneur not only to have gas available but to have it in a form which is known to consumers. It is my task to supply gas-which-is-known-about, not to provide gas *and* information'. The way to perform that entrepreneurial task is to have highly overt advertising, preferably with the price visible, and even more preferably with a price lower than that of nearby known-about gas stations.

It is this indivisibility of the tangible product from the information about it, and in turn from the overt transmission mechanism (for example, noise, color, form, words and so on) of that information which makes Austrians reject the charge that advertising is 'wasteful'. Neoclassicists do not accept this indivisibility of production costs on the one hand and selling costs on the other. Advertising (and other forms of product differentiation), they claim, is typically supplied at zero price. Yet, they argue, it has a positive social cost. In consequence more advertising will be demanded (and so supplied) than if it were provided at a positive price. This raises the problem that some people may buy a product and receive the benefits of advertising whether they want them or not, while others receive the benefits of the advertising without incurring the burden of paying; that is, they do not buy the product. The result, in terms of a social demand curve for advertising, is 'waste'.

Austrians deny that explicit demand and supply analysis can be used in this way. Quite apart from the conceptual problem of aggregating individual demands to obtain a social demand for advertising, it is fallacious to accept the notion that a derived demand can be extracted from the demand for the final product in the way that the demand for flour is determined by the demand for cakes. A 'product-which-is-known-about' is not the same as a 'product plus information'.

If derived demand analysis is inappropriate for advertising, then equally the notion that 'waste' due to the quantity demanded having a marginal value below that of its marginal social cost is not apposite. Rather, advertising (and other forms of product differentiation) must simply be seen as a necessary cost. Furthermore, the wealthier society is the greater is the range of potential choices facing consumers and hence more and more provocative advertising messages must be imparted to them to alert them to that breadth and depth of choice. Advertising is an unavoidable cost of generating consumer alertness. As Kirzner put it, it may be 'something that we'd much rather do without if we could; but we can't'. To engage in a trading opportunity, to move towards a situation of more equal marginal rates of substitution, requires that the opportunities be in a form which cannot be missed. That is the role of advertising. As the opportunities grow the advertising becomes more shrill.

This might imply that advertising is a selling expense. Austrians, however, do not distinguish between selling and production costs. Neoclassicists often argue that a rise in the latter increases supply, while an increase in the former raises demand. Mises (1966, p. 322) emphasizes that all costs of production (including non-price rivalry costs) are 'expended with the intention of increasing demand'. A manufacturer who differentiates his product by using a higher quality and more costly raw material aims at increasing demand just as much as if he makes the product's appearance or packaging more attractive or spends more on advertisements.

Non-price rivalry is thus an essential endogenous element in the competitive process. It alerts buyers and sellers to profitable trading opportunities so that price differentials can be reduced and the system can move towards equilibrium. Non-price rivalry also includes the (neoclassically exogenous) process of innovation, which Schumpeter (1939) defined to include not only the introduction of new products and techniques but also the opening up of new markets and supply sources, the improvement of management techniques and new distribution methods. The person responsible for doing these 'different things' is the entrepreneur or innovator. To Schumpeter, the entrepreneur is a factor input and like other factor inputs must be rewarded. His payment is entrepreneurial profit (Schumpeter, 1948, p. 83): 'the premium put upon a successful innovation in a capitalist society ... will vanish in the subsequent process of competition and adaptation'. This interpretation of innovation as non-price rivalry highlights apparent (but not real) differences between Schumpeterian and Misesian/Kirznerian entrepreneurs in the Austrian approach. The latter, like the former, acts for anticipated gain. But the latter is *any* human actor motivated by gain and alerted to the opportunity. The entrepreneurial spotting of the opportunity has to be done by both producer and consumer (and possibly a middleman). It is possible that each incurred similar entrepreneurial effort and reaped similar rewards, but it is more probable that one of the three assumed the greatest part (but never the whole) of the entrepreneurial role. Thus the decision to engage in advertising and product differentiation implies that the producer carries out the bulk of the entrepreneurial role. But that is simply making it possible for the consumer more readily to spot and be alert to his trading opportunities. It does not remove from him the total responsibility to spot potentially gainful opportunities to engage in trade. No one can be wholly passive, no one can take totally predictable actions, no one can opt out of the Misesian/Kirznerian responsibility to be an entrepreneur, except in equilibrium.

Both the Schumpeterian innovator and the Misesian/Kirznerian entrepreneur act for gain. The apparent difference is that the former moves the economy *away* from one equilibrium towards another higher one, while the Misesian/Kirznerian entrepreneur helps move the economy *towards* an equilibrium, but this equilibrium is itself an ever-changing and unattainable objective. The Misesian/Kirznerian entrepreneur notes, ex ante, that the indifference curves of consumers are different tomorrow from what they are today. He notes, ex ante, that the production isoquants of producers are not the same tomorrow as they are today. If he is correct in the trades he attempts to initiate by engaging in or prompting non-price rivalry, he makes profits and, if not, losses. As the market process unfolds his ignorance and uncertainty are reduced and equilibrium is progressively approached as he adjusts his bids and/or offers including any non-price activities.

The use of neoclassical language to explicate how the Kirznerian/Misesian entrepreneur moves traders to equilibrium and an equimarginal situation has tended to exclude innovation and Schumpeterian entrepreneurship from both Austrianism and neoclassicism until the last decade or so. Innovation is exogenous. Kirzner's (1982, p. 154) work, however, has reconciled the two. The fact that equilibrium was unattainable has always been central to Austrians but while it was presumed to be 'ever-receding' this phrase was as meaningful in terms of innovation as the word 'exogenous' was to non-Austrians. Innovation, as a form of non-price rivalry, is now fully embodied in the Austrian mainstream. Other aspects of non-price rivalry relate to single-period entrepreneurship (that is, alertness to present facts, requiring future actions to bring about mutually beneficial future trades). Innovation, however, requires multi-period alertness. As Kirzner put it (1982, pp. 154–5):

> the entrepreneur may, by his creative actions ... *construct* the future as *he* wishes it to be ... [instead of simply being alert to currently overlooked facts] ... alertness must include ... the perception of the way in which creative and imaginative action may vitally shape the kind of transactions that will be entered into in [the future] ... One must now possess ... vision, boldness, determination and creativity ... rather than ... merely [being the first to see] that which stared one in the face.

However, the essential entrepreneurial function remains the same in this multi-period case as in the single-period case: it is directed at coordinating transactions in different parts of the market. The incentive (of profit) is also the same. Thus, to Austrians, non-price rivalry is a device which facilitates the workings of the market process. It matches (or tends to match) willing buyers with willing sellers. In all its facets it is endogenous, not exogenous. It is above all, in a dynamic world with ever-expanding tastes, technologies and choices, an essential complement to price rivalry, not an inefficient or 'wasteful' alternative.

See also:
Chapter 24: The economics of information; Chapter 25: Prices and knowledge; Chapter 14: Competition

Bibliography
Dorfman, R. and P. Steiner (1954), 'Optimal Advertising and Optimal Quality', *American Economic Review*.
Kirzner, I.M. (1974), 'Advertising', *The Freeman*, September.
Kirzner, I.M. (1982), 'Uncertainty, Discovery and Human Action', in I. Kirzner (ed.), *Method, Process and Austrian Economics*, Lexington: D.C. Heath.
Menger, C. [1871] (1976) *Principles of Economics*, New York: New York University Press.
Mises, L. (1966) *Human Action*, Chicago: Henry Regnery.
Schumpeter, J. (1939), *Business Cycles*, London: Harrap.
Schumpeter, J. (1948), *Capitalism, Socialism and Democracy*, London: Harrap.

24 The economics of information

P.D.F. Strydom

The economics of information developed rapidly from the early 1960s following two pioneering publications by Stigler (1961) and Machlup (1962). The first was based on an application of conventional utility maximization analysis combined with search theory. The second was primarily concerned with the so-called 'knowledge industries', with the dissemination of knowledge as the focal point of interest. The general equilibrium framework underlying the first approach created important logical problems and Austrian economics set off on a different route where the dissemination of knowledge featured prominently (Hayek, 1945), but the exposition was supported by a dynamic framework with uncertainty where market participants faced an unknowable future (Shackle, 1958). Moreover, this exposition was based on a particular view of markets as a process (Kirzner, 1973) where individuals added value to the information in terms of a subjectivist approach (Lachmann, 1986).

Information and equilibrium economics

The general equilibrium models fall into two categories. One deals with event uncertainty (Hirshleifer and Riley, 1979) or the exogenous data of the economic system where individuals overcome uncertainty through information-generating activities. The other is more closely associated with Stigler's analysis where disequilibrium emerges because of market uncertainty and where search theory plays an important part (Rothschild, 1973), while uncertainty about the exogenous features of the economic system is assumed away. The analysis focused heavily, but not exclusively, on prices as the main element of market information. In this exposition market participants are supposed to adopt a decision rule such as a fixed sample size or a sequential procedure whereby they engage in price search activity. The literature finally opted in favor of a sequential search procedure to ensure optimal outcomes. This reasoning clearly demonstrates the intellectual framework of the equilibrium approach, namely its bias in favor of equilibrating processes, in the sense that the pursuit of information through search or the dissemination of information through any process is regarded as a disequilibrium-correcting activity (Hirshleifer and Riley, 1979). Fundamentally, these models of economic behavior were characterized by the overriding feature of equilibrating forces which overruled disequilibrating processes. Disequilibrium analyses were nevertheless suggested by several authors, in the sense that the searching procedure did not generate sufficient information to attain market equilibrium (Rothschild, 1973), but the deterministic nature of these models disqualifies them as meaningful instruments in explaining human behavior.

Equilibrium economics has particular methodological features which are not very helpful in understanding the economics of information. These features are evident in terms of the static nature of the analysis which means that time is effectively eliminated. In equilibrium economics the future and the present collapse into a single dimension of logical time where what is happening now will also happen in the future. The exposition is characterized by instantaneous adjustments because market participants have the correct information about equilibrium prices and quantities which is supplied without cost. The analysis is concerned with a world with no uncertainty, which means that speculative gains and losses which characterize the real world are absent. Equilibrium economics has nothing to say about non-equilibrium situations, since no trading is allowed at non-equilibrium prices. Within this static intellectual framework, where uncertainty is absent, information dissemination through the market process or Machlupian 'knowledge industries' has no meaning. We can address the problem of information economics meaningfully if we discard the intellectual framework of equilibrium economics. Information only has meaning in a world of uncertainty.

Information and knowledge
Linguistically, knowledge refers to the sum of what is known, while information is associated with items of knowledge. Machlup (1962) drew attention to the *act* of informing and the *state* of knowing. We could, therefore, follow Lachmann (1986) and distinguish between the stock of knowledge and the flow of information. In a changing world, the flow of information is not only important in the sense that one may alter one's plans according to the latest information, but one should constantly assess one's stock of knowledge for revision.

Information and markets
The application of the static market concept of equilibrium economics to the problems of information economics has met with criticism, as indicated by Rothschild (1973). Moreover, this exposition usually defended markets within a paradigm of efficiency with particular optimum conditions which could not be satisfied in the real world and therefore neoclassical economics elaborated on the possibility of market failure. The markets of equilibrium economics could be considered as mental systems associated with human behavior in an imperfect world as if they were dealing with a perfectly working system. Information cannot play a meaningful role in this paradigm.

Austrian economics introduced a dynamic market framework in terms of market processes (Kirzner, 1973) where private plans are important while market pressures and market spillovers (Lachmann, 1986) generate dynamic adjustments in an uncertain world with a time dimension (Torr, 1988). Within this dynamic framework markets are social institutions which disseminate information (Strydom, 1990). In the efficiency framework of equilibrium economics, markets are restricted to performing an allocative role, but, in the dynamic exposition where uncertainty prevails, markets disseminate information. Individual plans which Lachmann (1986) defined as a web of thought which accompanies and guides observable action, feature prominently in the exposition. A plan may be put into practice or it may be modified because of new information and in other instances the information may change to such a degree that a particular plan may be abandoned. This series of changes in individual plans generated by the flow of market information was identified as the market process by Kirzner (1973) and Lachmann (1986) extended this dynamic analysis by elaborating on the different types of processes.

The subjectivist approach
The concept of change and the formulation of a dynamic process with a time dimension which dispenses with the static framework of equilibrium economics signals the importance of the subjectivist approach, since these dynamic processes in time are uniquely related to the actions of human beings. Analysing these actions introduces the subjectivist approach (Kirzner, 1960), the essence of which is that human beings apply their reason to prevailing and known circumstances to perceive a preferred state of affairs, and in doing so they become active within a time dimension, going from the present to the future; that is, they have private plans to attain the preferred state of affairs. The present is analysed and understood in terms of our stock of knowledge which is updated and altered by the flow of new information and, following the process of updating, the individuals change their plans. The perceived preferred state of affairs introduces the importance of the future. The future cannot be analysed systematically in terms of our present stock of knowledge, but expectations play an important part in generating a dynamic framework comprising the future and the past. Expectations about the future can be derived by applying our imagination (Shackle, 1958) to conceive certain states of affairs which are different from the past. The subjectivist view of expectations is important because it introduces a dynamic relation between the past and the future.

By applying our imagination to the future we are able to plan, and the divergence of human plans is the basis for dynamics. By applying one's imagination the human mind conceives a future state of affairs which is preferred to that of the present and this new state is achieved by means of a systematic plan, setting out a programme of action to attain the goal. We are not merely concerned with the individual plans in isolation because actions taken by others have an important bearing on the plans of market participants. The plans of a particular person will partly depend on his actions and partly on his expectations regarding the likely actions of other market participants. Information is of crucial importance because changing circumstances are identified through information. As soon as new information becomes available expectations regarding the future change and new plans are drawn up to guide the actions of market participants. In such a dynamic framework it becomes important to be informed, that is to know the latest information. One could ensure a competitive advantage by becoming informed ahead of others and working according to a new revised plan of action.

The individual plans which guide the actions of a particular person are based on private information, which brings us to another dimension of the subjectivist approach in the economics of information. The significance of private information has been recognized explicitly by Lachmann (1986) in the sense that individuals interpret the information. Interpretation is a function of the human mind and it is always private and subjective. Machlupian 'knowledge industries' are active in the distribution and transmission of information and this flow of knowledge is interpreted by individuals; they change their plans in terms of their latest assessment and expectation of the future and their actions which follow become part and parcel of market processes through which information is disseminated within markets and through spillover effects from one market to the other. The interpretation of information is a focal point of the analysis in the economics of information.

We have already emphasized the importance of the divergence in human plans as a basis for dynamic analysis. This is a different approach from that of rational expectations, where expectations are introduced within a static framework according to which utility and profit-maximizing economic agents employ all useful available information as envisaged by the relevant economic theory. This is in sharp contrast with the analysis in information economics where diverging human plans are possible because of different interpretations of the information and/or diverging expectations. As demonstrated by Torr (1988), the rational expectations approach does not acknowledge diverging expectations, which means that uncertainty and speculative market behavior are excluded from the analysis; therefore, the exposition falls back on the same mental processes of static analysis, as opposed to the dynamic processes envisaged by the economics of information.

See also:
Chapter 25: Prices and knowledge; Chapter 17: Risk and uncertainty

Bibliography

Hayek, F.A. (1945), 'The use of knowledge in society', *American Economic Review*, **35**, 519–30.

Hirshleifer, J. and J.G. Riley (1979), 'The analytics of uncertainty and information : an expository survey', *Journal of Economic Literature*, **17**, 1375–1421.

Kirzner, I.M. (1960), *The Economic Point of View : An Essay in the History of Economic Thought*, Princeton: Van Nostrand.

Kirzner, I.M. (1973), *Competition and Entrepreneurship*, Chicago: University of Chicago Press.

Lachmann, L.M. (1986), *The Market as an Economic Process*, Oxford: Basil Blackwell.

Machlup, F. (1962), *Production and Distribution of Knowledge in the United States*, Princeton: Princeton University Press.

Rothschild, M. (1973), 'Models of market organisation with imperfect information: a survey', *Journal of Political Economy*, **81**, 1283–1308.

Shackle, G.L.S. (1958), *Time in Economics*, Amsterdam: North-Holland.

Stigler, G.J. (1961), 'The economics of information', *Journal of Political Economy*, **69**, 213–25.

Strydom, P.D.F. (1990), 'Markets, information and liberty', *South African Journal of Economics*, **58**, 377–90.

Torr, C. (1988), *Equilibrium, Expectations and Information: A Study of General Theory and Modern Classical Economics*, Oxford: Basil Blackwell.

25 Prices and knowledge

Esteban F. Thomsen

Introduction: Hayek's argument

As part of the almost explosive growth of the economics of information, a theme that has gained wide acceptance in economics is that market prices, in reflecting relative scarcities reasonably faithfully, perform some type of informative function. F.A. Hayek (1945) was the first to present this argument explicitly. Until he wrote his classic 1945 article, 'The use of knowledge in society', economists explained prices almost exclusively as useful incentives for adjusting individual plans to scarcity. According to Hayek, however, market prices also perform an informational role. This point can be conveyed by describing his often cited tin example. Assuming that one source of supply has disappeared, the resulting rise in the price of tin leads its consumers to economize on it and other suppliers to increase their output. The price is not only an incentive for this economizing to occur: the adaptation happens also without most of the people who are carrying out the necessary adjustments 'knowing anything at all about the original cause of these changes' (Hayek, 1945, p. 86). The real function of prices, Hayek said, is to communicate information.

The informational role of prices has since been examined quite closely, particularly because of the development of the 'economics of information' in the 1960s, and of the resurgence of interest in modern Austrian economics in the 1970s. Market prices are now understood to perform, more or less effectively, at least three different informational roles (Thomsen, 1992):

1. prices as 'knowledge surrogates' may inform the actions of an individual (without informing *him*): this is essentially what Hayek was saying in 1945;
2. prices as 'signals' may be 'read' by individuals to infer some information or be used by them to transmit it; and, lastly,
3. price disparities may provide profit opportunities that spark the entrepreneurial discovery of new knowledge.

Prices: knowledge surrogates or signals?

Many authors have interpreted Hayek as saying that prices constitute 'sufficient statistics'. The argument, which appears in an early version in Koopmans (1957) and which nowadays is found even in economics textbooks, is that market prices are signals that convey all the information traders need to act in a Pareto optimal way. Nobody needs to know everything about the economy and 'the final competitive allocations are as if an invisible hand with all the economy's information allocated resources' (Grossman, 1981, p. 555). This is a caricature of Hayek's point: he was only saying that prices *reduce* the amount of detail that an individual needs to know to adjust his behavior efficiently. Furthermore, he did not have in mind the achievement of Pareto optimality. This part of his argument may have been misunderstood because, although he was not centering his analysis on equilibrium states, in 1945 he had not developed a process-oriented view of the market as fully as he, and younger Austrians, would later on. The market process theory of Austrian economics leads to a different notion of what 'efficiency' means.

The interpretation of Hayek's argument in terms of 'sufficient statistics' has been carefully, and critically, examined. One of the most detailed critical analyses is that of S.J. Grossman and J.E. Stiglitz, in several papers gathered in Grossman (1989). They try to show that Hayek's argument is not correct for situations with *costly* information, where it is most important, and that in the latter situations prices are 'informationally inefficient'. Their argument is that if, as they interpret Hayek to be saying, prices fully reflect all available information, no equilibrium exists when information is costly. If market prices reflect all the necessary information, there is no incentive for anyone to engage in the costly activity of acquiring it: each trader could do equally well by observing only the price, instead of buying the information. But then, paradoxically, prices will not reflect information because it is not rewarding for anybody to collect it.

On the other hand, Grossman and Stiglitz argue, the situation in which no one collects information is not an equilibrium either: in this case a given individual will find it profitable to gather costly information because, owing to the price-taking assumption of the perfectly competitive model, he believes his activity will not affect the equilibrium price. (This belief assures him that his information will not become freely available to other traders, allowing him an advantage.) However, as soon as many individuals start collecting information, the equilibrium price is affected and aggregates their information perfectly. This, again, provides an incentive for individuals to stop gathering costly information and to obtain it costlessly from the price. As a result, they argue, a breakdown of markets occurs when price systems reveal too much information.

The source of this paradox is a problem of externalities. As Grossman has pointed out, when prices are taken as *sources* of information they create an externality by which a given individual's information gets transmitted to all other traders. In the case of costly information, uninformed traders will free-ride on the information-gathering activity of informed traders. The latter, unable to reap the full rewards of their (costly) activity, will tend, as in standard externality analysis, to seek information in a non-optimal fashion.

The other possibility is that prices do not aggregate information perfectly (that is, they are 'noisy'). Then it is not possible for individuals to obtain all the necessary information from prices. In this case it may become worthwhile for traders to engage in costly information-gathering activities, and an equilibrium is possible. However, this means Hayek's argument, as generally interpreted, breaks down. When the price system is 'noisy', prices are not sufficient statistics. Hayek's argument that a higher price is sufficient to lead agents to react in an efficient way is apparently shown to be wrong. The answer to this criticism is not only that Hayek's argument was not referring to equilibrium states, but also that it is confusing different possible informational roles of prices, attributing them all to Hayek. Hayek was saying that agents, by economizing with respect to market prices, respond to events of which they are not – or, rather, need not be – aware. (An individual engaged in central planning, Hayek's argument went, would have to know about these events.) Although Grossman and Stiglitz seem to understand this, they analyse situations in which individuals infer information from market prices. In other words, individuals facing market prices do not act *as if* they knew the relevant information but, instead, they obtain information from prices. In Grossman and Stiglitz's models, the agents are assumed not to know what the value of the good is to them, so they need to obtain this information. In these particular models, they get the information from prices. A higher price of land, for example, could indicate to a potential buyer that other traders now expect higher future income flows from land, which could perhaps increase his interest in it.

Grossman and Stiglitz's work exemplifies one of the instances in which the agents' beliefs about the quality of what is being traded depend on its price (Stiglitz, 1987). Besides these cases, there is also the literature on rational expectations, which often assumes agents obtain information from observed prices to form their expectations of future occurrences. Most of this work, however, is concerned with an informational role of prices different from that emphasized by Hayek, whose main point, in fact, is that prices *make it unnecessary* that individuals become informed of large numbers of facts. Prices in Hayek's argument are more appropriately described as knowledge *surrogates*, while in the approach exemplified by Grossman and Stiglitz they are sources for the inference of knowledge. Kreps (1988, p. 115) seems to be making this distinction when he refers to a 'classic (Walrasian) notion of "information communication" by prices, that should be distinguished from the information communication function of prices in a rational expectations equilibrium. The information Hayek finds reflected in equilibrium prices refers only to relative scarcities. The information disseminated in Grossman and Stiglitz's framework is about some quality of the traded good.

Whatever the case may be, a large body of literature, both in microeconomics and in macroeconomics, relies on the notion of inferring knowledge from prices, frequently – and mistakenly – citing Hayek's 1945 article as its origin. There is no need to deny the possible existence of this informational role of prices: individuals in a Hayekian world could attempt to infer information from prices if it were profitable for them to do so. Nevertheless, it is a different informational function. And, insofar as it is with the inference kind of activity that Hayek's critics are dealing, their analysis is largely irrelevant to his argument.

The Austrian view of prices
Grossman and Stiglitz's argument is that prices cannot be perfect transmitters of information if they are to provide a reward for the activity of obtaining information. On the other hand, modern Austrians, when viewing markets in disequilibrium terms, agree that prices cannot be taken 'literally', as price takers are supposed to take them, because out of equilibrium they provide wrong information about relative scarcities. For Grossman and Stiglitz this means that prices are informationally inefficient. Austrians, on the other hand, argue that disequilibrium prices perform a more important informational role (and that, insofar as they do so effectively, they may also serve as reasonable knowledge surrogates).

For Austrians, real markets are not states of perfect knowledge, or even of 'individually optimal' ignorance, as the 'economics of information' would have it. Markets are full of yet undiscovered, but profitable, 'facts'. The ignorance of economic agents leads to disequilibrium prices. By definition, disequilibrium prices provide pecuniary profit opportunities. These opportunities attract the attention of alert entrepreneurs, stimulating them to discover the previously unthought of alternatives. Strictly speaking, from this perspective it is *profits*, rather than prices directly, that perform an informational role.

Prices translate the situations of ignorance in the market into profit opportunities and thus provide the incentive for their elimination. Agents are always in an unending process of discovery. The claim is not that price-taking agents, by deciding on the basis of known prices, act as if they know more than they actually do, but rather that profits lead them to find out about better available courses of action. As Kirzner (1984, p. 205) puts it, 'the social function served by market prices is captured far more significantly by the concept of discovery, than by that of communication'. This role of prices may not seem original: economic theory has usually interpreted profits as incentives for action in a market economy. But, with their perception of the knowledge problem, market-process economists make a distinction between two types of incentives (Kirzner, 1985, pp. 34–6, 94–8; Lavoie, 1985, pp. 143–4).

1. Incentives, in the standard sense, are rewards that encourage the agents' adoption of certain courses of action already perceived and known by them. Profits, from such a point of view, make it worthwhile for the agent to engage in these actions. These actions, however, were known to him before, but were not worth the costs involved without the reward.
2. Incentives, in the sense emphasized by market-process economists, are rewards that encourage the discovery of opportunities that have until now been perceived by no one at all. Without this type of incentive, the problem would not be 'that people will be insufficiently motivated to do the right things but, more fundamentally, that they will not know what the right things to do are, even if they passionately wanted to do them' (Lavoie, 1985, p. 21).

The discovery role of prices has received little attention from economists because of the concentration of their analysis on equilibrium states. There is no room for such an informational role in a framework that confines itself to the analysis of equilibrium. The 'real' (as opposed to optimal) ignorance that is dissipated through (successful) entrepreneurial discovery cannot exist in equilibrium – equilibrium excludes it by definition. However, this informational role is crucial because the extent to which prices may reflect information, both as surrogates and as signals, will be a result of the rival bids and offers of entrepreneurs stimulated by disequilibrium profit opportunities.

See also:
Chapter 24: The economics of information; Chapter 22: The Austrian theory of price; Chapter 20: Supply and demand; Chapter 4: Market process

Bibliography

Grossman, S.J. (1981), 'An introduction to the theory of rational expectations under asymmetric information', *Review of Economic Studies*, **48**, October, 541–59.

Grossman, S.J. (1989), *The Informational Role of Prices*, Cambridge, Mass.: MIT Press.

Hayek, F.A. (1945), 'The use of knowledge in society', *American Economic Review*, **34**, September, 519–30; reprinted in F.A. Hayek, *Individualism and Economic Order*, London: Routledge & Kegan Paul, 1976.

Kirzner, I.M. (1984), 'Prices, the communication of knowledge, and the discovery process', in K.R. Leube and A.H. Zlabinger (eds), *The Political Economy of Freedom, Essays in Honor of F.A. Hayek*, Munich: Philosophia Verlag.

Kirzner, I.M. (1985), *Discovery and the Capitalist Process*, Chicago: University of Chicago Press.

Koopmans, T.C. (1957), *Three Essays on the State of Economic Science*, New York: McGraw-Hill Book Co.

Kreps, D.M. (1988), 'In Honor of Sandy Grossman, Winner of the John Bates Clark Medal', *Journal of Economic Perspectives*, **2**, spring, 111–35.

Lavoie, D. (1985), *Rivalry and Central Planning: The Socialist Calculation Debate Reconsidered*, Cambridge: Cambridge University Press.
Stiglitz, J.E. (1987), 'The causes and consequences of the dependence of quality on price', *Journal of Economic Literature*, **25**, March, 1–48.
Thomsen, E.F. (1992), *Prices and Knowledge. A Market-process Perspective*, London: Routledge.

26 The boundaries of the firm

Richard Langlois

Why are there organizations called firms? And what determines the allocation of productive activities among various organizational and contractual alternatives like firms and 'markets'? These are not questions that have seized the center of attention among writers in the Austrian tradition. They are, however, questions that are beginning to attract – and to yield to – insights and approaches one could characterize as fundamentally Austrian. Among these insights are the importance of economic process and the tacit and decentralized character of economic knowledge.

Knight and Coase

Questions of the boundaries of the firm – as we will call this bundle of issues – have only recently returned to a place of any significance among neoclassical economists, who in the 1930s largely abandoned the vision of Alfred Marshall, Allyn Young and others in pursuit of a formalistic 'production function' approach to the firm. It is not perhaps surprising, therefore, that writers in the Austrian tradition (who are far less numerous) have also been slow in allotting significant effort to this area. On the other hand, part of the explanation for the lack of interest in these questions among Austrians may have to do with a traditional focus on entrepreneurship at the level of the individual economic agent. For questions of pure economic theory, issues of organization are immaterial details that speak only to the form rather than to the nature of the entrepreneurial role.

A concentration on the abstract category of the entrepreneur did not, however, prevent Frank Knight (1921) from formulating an explanation for the existence of the firm. This explanation is more often misunderstood than not; but, properly cast, Knight's theory of the boundaries of the firm anticipates some of the idea detailed below (Langlois and Cosgel, 1993). In effect, Knight argued that, because of the pervasiveness of radical uncertainty, much of economic action must rely on human judgement. Judgement is an economic function that cannot be hired through contract and thus entails some measure of effective control over and ownership of productive assets. The result of a continuing need for the exercise of judgement is a form of economic cooperation in which some incomes are determined through contract and others as residual claims of ownership – that is, a firm.

Knight's views in this matter, as in others, might easily be classed as 'Austrian'. But Knight's theory of the firm has had an effect on Austrian writers only slightly greater than that on writers in the mainstream. The far more influential source of present-day ideas on the boundaries of the firm is Ronald Coase's 'The Nature of the Firm' (1937). Coase begins with an observation that is something of a central theme in Austrian writing: the price system is an institution that provides rather marvelous information and coordination functions. In view of these remarkable qualities, Coase wonders, why do we observe some transactions to be removed from the price system and carried out within the business firm? The answer is that there must be a cost to using the price system. Since a cost is a forgone benefit, this implies that there is a benefit to using an institution alternative to – or, at any rate, additional to – the price system at its most abstract. Wherein lie the benefits of such institutions? Although the case cannot be made here, it is arguable that Coase saw the benefits in terms of improved coordination and flexibility in the face of changing circumstances.

Transaction cost economics
The Coase-inspired literature that has blossomed since the 1970s casts these benefits in a rather different light, however. Rather than seeing the firm as a coordinating institution, theorists have focused on the role of the firm in solving various kinds of incentive problems. The modern transaction cost theory of the firm, as this literature is called, feeds from two different but related streams: one is the moral hazard or measurement cost approach; the other is the asset specificity approach. In the first case, the abstract institution of the market generates transaction costs in situations in which the incentives of the cooperating parties diverge and monitoring is costly. In the second case, the market can lead to transaction costs when, in the presence of highly specific assets, one of the parties might threaten the other with non-cooperation in order to extract a larger share of the quasi-rents of cooperation. In both cases, common ownership of the cooperating assets – that is to say, a firm – may avoid these transaction costs.

In his original formulation, Coase conceived of the dichotomy between firm and market in simple terms. A transaction uses the price system if the cooperating capital is separately owned and the intermediate product or service exchanged in an arms' length arrangement. A transaction is carried out within a firm when the relevant cooperating capital is commonly owned and the operative contract is a more open-ended employment contract. However, it is clear that the categories are more complicated. On the one hand, separate capital owners might cooperate using an open-ended or 'relational' contract; on the other hand, transactions within the domain of commonly owned capital – as between the divisions of a large firm – might be carried out using prices and simple arms'-length contracts. Those who look only at the contractual aspects are thus led to a kind of agnosticism about the very definition of the firm, a position we might call the nexus of contracts view. Looking at ownership gives a clearer, and to the present author more appealing, definition of the firm, one arguably more consistent with Knight's conception. (For a discussion, see Langlois, 1992b; Langlois and Cosgel, 1993.)

This neoclassical theory has vastly enriched our understanding of the nature of and rationale for extra-market organization. As in many other areas of theory, however, the neoclassical approach has its limits. In particular, the transaction cost literature shows its neoclassical legacy in posing the problem of the firm in terms of a maximization problem perceived *ex visu* of a point in time. In present-day transaction cost economics, one explains particular business institutions we observe in the world as having arisen to minimize the sum of production costs and transaction costs. Those costs are normally understood implicitly to have arisen from the environment in existence at the moment under analysis. Seldom does the theory give thought to the possibility that organizational forms may be influenced as much by environments that exist only as future possibilities, imagined or feared. Neither does it pay much attention to the possibility that organizational forms observable today may owe their shape importantly to a legacy of past environments (Langlois, 1984).

Moreover, although these theories often pay due homage to the concept of bounded rationality, they do not in fact see coordination in a world of limited knowledge as a fundamental problem. To put it another way, they see the firm as solving various kinds of incentive problems, never as solving a coordination problem.

The capabilities view

There is, however, a developing theory of business institutions that does take seriously these Austrian concerns about process and limited knowledge. In the work of Edith Penrose and G.B. Richardson, and more recently of Nelson and Winter and David Teece, one gets a picture of the firm as possessing certain 'capabilities'. (For a fuller discussion, see Langlois, 1992b.) Unlike neoclassical theory, this approach does not take production in the economy to be a purely technical question, a matter of combining given inputs according to known blueprints. Instead, it sees economic activity as requiring skills and organization. Neither of these is in any sense 'given'. Economic actors must struggle with the limitations to human knowledge and what those actors do know is mostly know-how, the inarticulate form of knowledge Michael Polanyi described as 'tacit'. As a result, capabilities – individual and organizational skills – develop in idiosyncratic and historically dependent ways. And competition is the learning process through which capabilities are created in the economy.

This is a way of looking at a firm that should appeal to writers in the Austrian tradition. To see firms as possessing limited and distinctive capabilities accords well with Hayek's (1945) insights about the decentralized nature of knowledge. Indeed, it is a vision of the evolution of the firm that also accords well with Hayek's writings on cultural evolution. The machines and personnel of a firm follow, invent, learn and imitate routines that persist over time. As in Hayek's theory of culture, the routines are often tacit and skill-like, followed unconsciously because they produced success in the past. And it is these routines upon which the mechanism of selection operates.

As in the case of rules in cultural institutions, the rules in an organization serve a coordinating function. This may at first seem at odds with the thesis of Hayek (1945). Is not the point of decentralized knowledge and the coordinating virtues of the price system that such a system is superior to central planning, especially in situations of economic change? There is no contradiction. First of all, the capabilities view suggests that the internal workings of the firm are far less in the nature of conscious planning than popular accounts would have it. Moreover, Hayek's argument is about the ability of the price system to coordinate multifarious plans. It is not an argument that the price system must always be a superior way to coordinate specific plans at what we may think of as a 'lower' or more concrete level of the hierarchy. In arguing for the coordinating benefits of the price system, Hayek (1945, p. 523) pointed out that 'economic problems arise always and only in consequence of change'. And, indeed, the respective merits of firm and market as institutions of coordination appear most clearly when we consider economic change and the response to it.

Towards a dynamic theory of organizational boundaries
Just as firms possess capabilities, so also can we think of markets as possessing capabilities, in the sense that one can choose to produce a good or service using one's internal capabilities or one can use the capabilities of others by acquiring the good or service on the market. When will internal organization prove superior to market procurement in a world of economic change? The answer depends (a) on the existing level of capabilities in the market and (b) on the nature of the economic change involved.

Situations in which existing market capabilities are limited, or in which those capabilities are ill-adapted to an innovation, would tend to favor internal organization, *ceteris paribus*. This effect would be more significant in the case of a systemic innovation, that is, an innovation that involves coordinating change in many different routines simultaneously. Consider the case of the American car industry (Langlois and Robertson, 1989). In the early days of that industry, car makers were all assemblers; that is, they contracted for almost all the parts that went into the cars, reserving only the assembly stage for themselves. They could do this because the American economy – and the Detroit region in particular – possessed a high level of general-purpose machining and metal-working capabilities available in the market. However, the innovation of the moving assembly line at Ford rendered these capabilities obsolete, in that Ford could mass-produce parts much less expensively than it could buy them on the market. Because Ford could not quickly and cheaply convey to suppliers the (partly tacit) nature of the innovation – which was in any case a slowly unfolding process – it was forced to integrate vertically into parts manufacture. It is in this sense, then, that an organization can be a coordinating institution: it can sometimes avoid the coordinating costs of informing, negotiating with and persuading potential contracting parties who may not share one's faith in the proposed innovation or even, in a fundamental sense, one's view of the world (Silver, 1984; Langlois, 1988). This suggests the importance of a neglected set of 'transaction' costs (or, more properly, governance costs) in explaining the firm: the costs of changing one's capabilities or, to put it another way, the costs of not having the capabilities you need when you need them (Langlois, 1992b). Such coordination costs are related to uncertainty and, in fact, arguably to the kind of radical uncertainty one often reads about in the Austrian literature (Langlois, 1984).

Economic change may also favor the market over internal organization. This might be the case when the existing level of capabilities is high in the market relative to those within the organization proposing to innovate. The market will also gain advantages when the innovation involved is largely autonomous; that is, when the innovation does not require change in many different routines. Consider the example of the IBM personal computer (Langlois, 1992a). In entering the PC market in the early 1980s, IBM understood both that the market possessed a high level of capabilities and that IBM's own capabilities were severely lacking. This latter was the case partly because the company had focused on larger computers and did not possess all the capabilities necessary for producing smaller machines. But it was also and more importantly because the company's hierarchical structure, internal sourcing procedures and elaborate system of controls made it too inflexible to respond well to a rapidly changing market. As a result, IBM chose in effect to disintegrate vertically into the production of PCs. The company 'spun off' a small group of executives and engineers, exempted them from IBM internal sourcing and other procedures, and treated them as, in effect, a venture-capital investment. The original IBM PC was in fact almost completely assembled from parts available in the market, very few of which were produced in IBM plants. IBM's motives for *disintegration* were in this regard strikingly similar to Henry Ford's motives for *integration*: the need to gain rapid access to capabilities that would not otherwise have been available in time. The coordinating virtues of the market here are very much those Hayek praised.

See also:
Chapter 55: Industrial organization and the Austrian school; Chapter 27: The Coase Theorem; Chapter 24: The economics of information

Bibliography
Coase, Ronald H. (1937), 'The Nature of the Firm', *Economica* (NS), **4**, 386–405.
Hayek, F.A. (1945), 'The Use of Knowledge in Society', *American Economic Review*, **35**, (4), 519–30.
Knight, Frank H. (1921), *Risk, Uncertainty, and Profit*, Boston: Houghton Mifflin.
Langlois, Richard N. (1984), 'Internal Organization in a Dynamic Context: Some Theoretical Considerations', in M. Jussawalla and H. Ebenfield, (eds), *Communication and Information Economics: New Perspectives*, Amsterdam: North-Holland, pp. 23–49.
Langlois, Richard N. (1988), 'Economic Change and the Boundaries of the Firm', *Journal of Institutional and Theoretical Economics*, **144**, (4), 635–57.
Langlois, Richard N. (1992a), 'External Economics and Economic Progress: The Case of the Microcomputer Industry', *Business History Review*, **66**, (1), spring, 1–50.
Langlois, Richard N. (1992b), 'Transaction-Cost Economics in Real Time', *Industrial and Corporate Change*, **1**, (1), 99–127.
Langlois, Richard N. and Metin M. Cosgel (1993), 'Frank Knight on Risk, Uncertainty, and the Firm: A New Interpretation', *Economic Inquiry*, **31**, July, 456–65.
Langlois, Richard N. and Paul L. Robertson (1989), 'Explaining Vertical Integration: Lessons from the American Automobile Industry', *Journal of Economic History*, **49**, (2), 361–75.
Silver, Morris (1984), *Enterprise and the Scope of the Firm*, London: Martin Robertson.

27 The Coase Theorem

Donald J. Boudreaux

Named after Ronald H. Coase, winner of the 1991 Nobel Prize in Economic Science, the Coase Theorem initiated a fundamental overhaul of the economic theory of regulation. Prior to Coase's analysis, the typical neoclassical economist saw negative externalities as a problem to be solved by government regulation or taxation. Regulators would determine the socially optimal amount of externality reduction and require those parties whose activities generate negative externalities to achieve this specified reduction. Alternatively, taxation could achieve the same result by forcing private costs into line with social costs. The factory spewing soot on neighboring houses would take the cost of this soot damage into account if the factory were taxed by an amount equal to the marginal cost of this soot damage at each level of factory output. Regulation or taxation was believed to be necessary to entice the factory to produce the socially optimal amount of output and pollution. Coase demonstrated that this view of externalities – associated most closely with British economist A.C. Pigou – overlooks the ability of people acting within their private spheres to seek out and exploit all available gains from trade.

Coase first published his Theorem in a 1959 article about the United States' Federal Communications Commission, but developed it more fully one year later (Coase 1959, 1960). Put in its most succinct form, the Coase Theorem states that the particular assignment of legal liabilities has no effect on economic outcomes *if and to the extent that* people can bargain amongst themselves for the exchange of these liabilities. That is, when transaction costs are not so high as to stifle bargaining, the ability of persons ('victims') harmed by the activities of others ('injurers') to pay injurers to reduce or stop their harmful ways necessarily induces injurers to internalize the costs that their activities impose on victims. Whenever bargaining is possible, no government intervention beyond the specification and enforcement of property rights is required to achieve the socially optimal level of economic activities (see also, for example, Buchanan, 1984; Polinsky, 1989). But this fact was not always recognized.

Pre-Coasean analysis of externalities
Consider the following example. A manufacturer earns a net profit of $1000 per month. However, this manufacturer's production process generates soot

179

that falls on a nearby home, resulting in monthly damages to the home owner of $700. To be rid of the pollution, the home owner sues the manufacturer, seeking an injunction forcing the factory to stop polluting. The court must decide whether to grant the injunction or not. Stated differently, the court must decide if the home owner has the right to be free from pollution from the factory, or if the factory has the right to pollute. If the court dismisses the case, in effect awarding the right to pollute to the factory, then the factory continues to produce and to pollute as before.

However, if the court instead grants the home owner an injunction to stop the factory from polluting, pre-Coasean analysis says that the factory will stop producing (assuming that the only way to reduce the pollution is for the manufacturer to shut down). Under these assumptions, the outcome differs according to which party receives the property right from the court. If the manufacturer wins in court, it keeps producing; if the home owner wins, the manufacturer ceases operations. Both output and pollution are greater if the manufacturer wins the legal battle than if the home owner wins.

Coasean analysis of externalities
The pre-Coasean analysis is wrong. Real-world outcomes will not always vary with different winners in court. In this example, the factory will produce the same quantity of output and pollution if it loses as it would if it wins. The manufacturer will pay the home owner for the right to pollute because the value to the manufacturer of continued production exceeds the cost to the home owner of putting up with the soot. Thus, if the household can enjoin the manufacturer from polluting, the manufacturer will offer the home owner some amount between $700 and $1000 per month for the right to pollute. Clearly, the home owner will find any such offer to be advantageous. A mutually beneficial trading possibility exists which will not remain unexploited.

A few variations on this example are useful. Suppose now that the dollar amount of the monthly soot damage to the household is $1200 rather than $700. With the manufacturer's monthly net profits still at $1000, the efficient solution is to close the factory. The Coase Theorem shows that this solution will occur regardless of the court's decision. In this scenario, if the court awards an injunction to the home owner, the manufacturer will not pay the home owner for the right to continue producing. The producer shuts down. And the same result occurs if the court dismisses the home owner's complaint. When the manufacturer owns the right to pollute, the home owner will offer the manufacturer a monthly sum between $1000 and $1200 to entice the manufacturer to stop polluting. The manufacturer will accept the home owner's offer; it ceases producing and polluting.

Let us abandon the assumption that the only way pollution damage can be mitigated is for the manufacturer to shut down. Suppose now that the manufacturer can purchase a scrubber for its smokestack that will completely eliminate soot discharge. Operation of this scrubber costs a total of $400 per month. With the manufacturer's monthly profits (without the scrubber) at $1000, and the home owner's monthly damage at $700, the efficient solution is for the manufacturer to install the scrubber. Shutting the factory down costs $1000, continuing to pollute costs $700, while eliminating pollution with the scrubber costs $400. Again, this efficient solution will be employed regardless of the court's decision. If the court awards an injunction to the home owner, the manufacturer will install the scrubber, continue producing but not polluting, and be left with monthly net profits of $600. If, instead, the court dismisses the home owner's suit, the home owner will offer to purchase the $400/month scrubber for the manufacturer – an offer the manufacturer has no incentive to reject. In this case, the manufacturer's monthly net profits are $1000 and the soot emissions are eradicated. The home owner spends $400 per month to avoid a loss of $700 per month.

Many more variations on this example are possible, but there is no need to pursue them here. The general lesson is that it is a fallacy to believe that the party with the legal right to 'cause' harm to another party does not internalize the cost his damage imposes on the other party. The home owner can offer the manufacturer an amount of money up to the value of the damages caused by the soot in exchange for the manufacturer's promise not to pollute. The manufacturer who continues to pollute must forgo the amount the home owner would pay him to stop polluting. Analogously, if the court awards the home owner the right to enjoin the factory from polluting, the factory can offer the home owner an amount of money up to the value of its net profits in exchange for the home owner's agreement to allow the factory to continue producing. The home owner who insists on enforcing the injunction against the manufacturer forgoes the amount the manufacturer would pay to him for his agreement not to enforce the injunction.

Regardless of the court's ruling, if the home owner's damages are less than the manufacturer's profits, production continues. If the home owner's damages exceed the manufacturer's profits, the manufacturer shuts down. *The possibility of voluntary exchange between injurer and victim is sufficient to internalize all externalities*. Thus, so long as affected parties can bargain with each other, the efficient allocation of resources will emerge. Stated differently, the Coase Theorem says 'that the legal right to take an action does not necessarily translate into an economic motivation to take that action. Legally recognized and enforced rights are distinct from economically rational exercises of these rights. If the owner of a right is free to sell it, whoever values the right most highly will buy it' (Boudreaux and Ellig, 1992, pp. 578–9).

The effect of excessive bargaining costs

What happens when bargaining costs are so high as to block the exchange of a legal right from the party who values it less to the party who values it more? In this situation, the particular assignment of rights chosen by the court *does* potentially affect economic outcomes. Suppose that 1000 home owners, rather than a single home owner, collectively incur damages of $1200 per month from the factory's soot emissions. Monthly damages are $1.20 per household. The manufacturer's monthly profits are $1000. Assuming that pollution damage can be reduced only by shutting the factory down, the efficient solution is for the factory to cease operations. Closing the factory causes the manufacturer to lose $1000 per month while increasing the aggregate welfare of the home owners by $1200 per month, thereby improving social welfare by $200.

If the manufacturer has the right to pollute, and if the home owners as a group bargain with the manufacturer, they would offer to pay the manufacturer some monthly sum between $1000 and $1200 in return for the manufacturer's agreement to stop producing. However, familiar collective action problems created by such a large number of home owners make this bargain unlikely. Thus the manufacturer does not internalize the costs that its soot emissions impose on neighboring home owners. The manufacturer continues to produce and pollute, even though this is not the efficient outcome. For the efficient outcome to occur, the court must enjoin the manufacturer from polluting. No production and no pollution: this is the outcome that would have occurred, even if the court refused to enjoin the manufacturer, if the home owners could effectively bargain with the manufacturer.

Note that the situation is similar if the aggregate monthly cost to home owners of the pollution is less than the manufacturer's monthly profits of $1000. If the homeowners' aggregate monthly cost from pollution is $700, the efficient outcome is for the factory to continue production. But if the court awards the home owners the right to enjoin the factory from polluting, the large number of home owners with which the manufacturer must bargain in order to purchase the right to produce and pollute stands in the way of this efficient outcome. The manufacturer is forced to shut down despite the fact that, if bargaining costs were not inordinately high, home owners would all agree to sell to the manufacturer the right to pollute.

The lesson to be learned from these high bargaining costs examples is that, when bargaining costs are prohibitive, efficient outcomes are possible only if the court awards the property right to that party, or to those parties, that value the right most highly. This means that, in the face of excessive bargaining costs, the party with the highest cost of coping with the externality should be awarded the property right. This lesson is not a corollary of the Coase Theorem; rather, this lesson is a normative – although immensely valuable –

prescription about appropriate legal remedies for situations to which the Coase Theorem does not apply (see, for example, Coase, 1988, p. 15). To repeat: the Coase Theorem is the explicit recognition that ability to bargain induces people who exercise their property rights to internalize the costs of these exercises – that is, that an owner of a right includes non-owners' assessments about a particular exercise of that right as part of his own assessment. The Coase Theorem puts analysts, courts and policy makers on notice that observed instances of one party's actions causing detrimental effects to another party's person or property are not necessarily instances of market failure.

Of course, recognizing and dealing with the myriad situations in which bargaining costs are excessive is important. The courts cannot escape this task. However, it is also a task that the law cannot be expected to perform flawlessly: maximum efficiency, after all, requires the courts to guess correctly what the outcomes of voluntary exchange would have been in the absence of excessive transaction costs. Coasean analysis highlights the role of bargaining in reducing dramatically the burden faced by the courts. When bargaining costs are not prohibitive, courts need only define the scope of the property right and make clear who owns it and how that ownership is protected. With this done, voluntary exchange ensures that only, and all, mutually beneficial uses of resources will occur. The resulting exchange process respects subjective preferences and utilizes individual and local knowledge. The law does not have to allocate initial holdings correctly. Thus law makers are not called upon to perform a task that requires virtual omniscience. As Coase says, 'in the absence of transaction costs, it does not matter what the law is, since people can always negotiate without costs to acquire, subdivide, and combine rights whenever this would increase the value of production' (Coase, 1988, p. 14). Only when bargaining is impossible does the law's particular allocation of property rights matter for the economy (as opposed to the individual).

Obviously, individual parties *do* care whether they win or lose a case in court. The winner is wealthier and the loser is poorer than each would have been if the court had rendered the opposite decision. But assuming that the change in wealth prompted by a court decision has only slight effects on the supply and demand conditions in the market, the economic outcome – what is produced, in what quantities and sold at what prices – will essentially be unaffected by the court's ruling if bargaining is possible (see Demsetz, 1988, pp. 12–27).

When are bargaining costs excessive?
Traditionally, and as discussed above, only large numbers of affected parties were thought to create excessive bargaining costs. Recently, however, schol-

ars have argued that bargaining involving *small* numbers may yield excessive bargaining costs because one or both parties may maneuver strategically to extract as much of the available surplus as possible from the other party. Hence such situations are not accurately described by the Coase Theorem. For example, William Landes and Richard Posner claim that bilateral monopoly is 'an important source of transaction costs' and, as a consequence, 'the Coase theorem's assumption of zero (or negligible) transaction costs may not be fulfilled even in the apparently simple two-party ... case' (Landes and Posner, 1987, p. 34; see also Cooter and Ulen, 1988, pp. 99–108). This line of reasoning leads to the conclusion that bargaining costs are excessive whenever the parties to a potential bargain do not face perfectly competitive conditions for the sale and purchase of the legal right in question. It is not so much the numbers that bargainers face, but the options that each bargainer has, that determine if mutually beneficial exchanges will occur. If any potential seller or buyer of a legal right has any market power, that party can suppress his willingness to sell or to buy solely in order to out-duel the other party. Each party rejects offers by the other, not because each would not benefit from the offer, but because each seeks to extract greater gains from the other. Without the discipline of a competitive market in these legal rights, strategizing dominates trading. Applicability of the Coase Theorem is severely attenuated.

This small-numbers argument is based on a misunderstanding of Coase's essential insight. The fact that a bargain does not take place does not mean that conditions required for applicability of the Coase Theorem are not present. It is the *ability* to strike a bargain that internalizes the costs of property use on the owner of that right. If a potential party to an exchange is observed to hold out strategically for a larger share of the gains from trade, all we – as consistent subjectivists – can conclude is that the value to this party of exchanging on the terms most recently offered by his bargaining partner is lower than the value of not exchanging at this time. Without knowing the subjective preferences of a party, we cannot legitimately conclude that an inefficient refusal to trade is taking place. A party who refuses an offer solely to extract a greater proportion of the gains from trade nevertheless faces an offer to exchange, and such an offer forces this strategically behaving party to internalize the costs his activities impose on the other party.

Consider again the two-party example of the single home owner and the polluting factory. Assume that the factory earns monthly net profits of $1000 and that the monthly damages to the home owner from the factory's soot emissions are $1200. Also assume that the court awards to the manufacturer the right to continue dumping this quantity of soot on the home owner. Standard Coasean analysis says that the home owner will purchase from the manufacturer the right to be free of soot damage for some price between

$1000 and $1200 per month. However, introducing strategic behavior into the analysis casts doubt on this outcome: the manufacturer will strategically refuse to stop polluting for any price much less than $1200 (say, 1199) per month, while the home owner will strategically refuse to offer much more than $1000 per month (say, $1001) in exchange for the manufacturer's agreement not to emit soot. Holding out by both of these 'bilateral monopolists' stops mutually beneficial trading. The inefficient solution results: the factory continues producing and polluting.

Examining this situation more closely, however, we see that the offer by the homeowner of $1001 to the manufacturer internalizes on the manufacturer the cost felt *at this time* by the home owner. By not accepting this offer, the manufacturer forgoes $1001. This sum is the current subjective monthly cost to the home owner of the factory's pollution, and it is fully internalized by the manufacturer. The fact that the homeowner is willing to sweeten its offer to the manufacturer at some future point only means that the subjective cost of the pollution to the home owner *within the existing institutional and legal framework* changes over time. The home owner incurs soot damage today as part of the price he pays today for higher chances of securing a lower price for its purchase tomorrow of the manufacturer's right to pollute. Consistent application of subjectivist principles demands that the analyst not regard the monthly cost of current soot damage to the home owner as being more than $1001.

Likewise, the manufacturer's strategic refusal of any offer less than $1199 per month for its agreement to stop polluting represents the manufacturer's currently felt cost of selling its right to pollute. The manufacturer obviously believes that holding out now for a higher price potentially increases the value of its right to some figure close to the maximum amount the home owner is willing to pay to be free of soot damage. Thus the current monthly cost to the manufacturer of selling its right to pollute is no less than $1199. No inefficiency can be inferred by outside observers given the *ability* of these two parties voluntarily to bargain and exchange (see also Buchanan, 1986).

Those skeptical of this analysis should consider the following situation. Suppose a friend owns the world's only remaining bottle of 1961 Château Latour; and to make this situation a true bilateral monopoly, also assume (contrary to fact!) that you and your friend are the only two people in the world who have any taste at all for this particular vintage. You make an offer to your friend of $2000 to purchase this bottle. This offer immediately internalizes on your friend a cost of at least $2000 of keeping, or himself consuming, this bottle of wine. If he refuses your offer, he forgoes $2000. You may be willing to offer up to $3000 for this bottle, but not now. The reason you hold your offer to $2000 is because the value to you now of offering more than $2000 and thereby gaining a higher chance of immediate acceptance by your friend is lower than the value of offering only $2000 and thereby 'purchasing' an increased chance of eventually getting the bottle at a price close to $2000. The point is that the current cost to you of your friend's keeping or consuming the wine is no higher than the price you offer your friend for the wine. And this cost is internalized on your friend by your offer.

Unquestionably, alternative assignments of liabilities (or of rights, depending on how you look it) often result in different demand and cost conditions faced by individual economic actors. And different conditions result in different patterns of efficient resource allocation (Demsetz, 1988, p. 16). Rather than focus on what James Buchanan (1986, p. 95) calls the 'invariance version' of the Coase Theorem – according to which alternate assignments of liability generate the very same physical allocation of resources – it is truer to Coase's essential message to focus on the fact that ability to bargain freely is practically necessary, and almost always sufficient, to internalize the full subjective costs of resource use upon owners of property rights.

Ability of property rights owners to bargain voluntarily with each other internalizes on property rights owners the costs that their exercises of these rights impose on all potential parties to the bargain. This is Coase's message.

See also:
Chapter 26: The boundaries of the firm; Chapter 38: Law and economics

Bibliography
Boudreaux, Donald J. and Jerome Ellig (1992), 'Beneficent Bias: The Case Against Regulating Airline Computer Reservation Systems', *Journal of Air Law & Commerce*, **57**, spring, pp. 567–97.
Buchanan, James M. (1984), 'The Coase Theorem and the Theory of the State', in J.M. Buchanan and R.D. Tollison, *Public Choice II*, Ann Arbor: University of Michigan Press, pp. 159–73.
Buchanan, James M. (1986), 'Rights, Efficiency, and Exchange: The Irrelevance of Transactions Cost', in J.M. Buchanan, *Liberty, Market, and State*, New York: New York University Press, pp. 92–107.
Coase, Ronald H. (1959), 'The Federal Communication Commission', *Journal of Law & Economics*, **2**, October, 1–40.
Coase, Ronald H. (1960), 'The Problem of Social Cost', *Journal of Law & Economics*, **3**, October, 1–44.
Coase, Ronald H. (1988), *The Firm, the Market, and the Law*, Chicago: University of Chicago Press.
Cooter, Robert and Thomas Ulen (1988), *Law and Economics*, Glenview, IL: Scott, Foresman.
Demsetz, Harold (1988), *Ownership, Control, and the Firm*, Oxford: Basil Blackwell.
Landes, William M. and Richard A. Posner (1987), *The Economic Structure of Tort Law*, Cambridge, Mass.: Harvard University Press.
Polinsky, A. Mitchell (1989), *An Introduction to Law and Economics*, 2nd edn, Boston: Little, Brown.

28 Self-organizing systems

Friedrich Hinterberger

In the works of Friedrich Hayek we find on several occasions a plea for using a 'theory of complex phenomena' when describing economic processes (see, for example, Hayek, 1967, pp. 22–42). An important feature of social and economic order is that law, language, markets and so on are the 'results of human action but not of human design'. Hayek places the development of the economic order between (a) natural and (b) artificial phenomena. He relates it back to Adam Smith who used the famous metaphor of an 'invisible hand', which drives society to an end which was no part of the individual's intention. Although the process is based on 'nothing but the private intentions, beliefs, goals, and actions of the participating individuals, in a specified set of circumstances' (Ullmann-Margalit, 1978, p. 273), the outcome 'is shown to be the product neither of centralized decisions nor of explicit agreements to bring it about; rather, it is presented as the end result of a certain process that aggregates the separate and "innocent" actions of numerous and dispersed individuals into an overall pattern which is the very phenomenon we set out to account for' (ibid. p. 265). Such a process is often said to take place in an equilibrating economic system, working infinitely fast. Other methods explicitly miss the point by postulating, for example, an exogenous auctioneer. Hayek's main point is that neither individual participants in the market process nor an observing scientist can have the knowledge necessary to be able to predict the outcome of uncoordinated individual behavior.

As a scientific method for describing such a process Hayek repeatedly refers to biological theories of complex phenomena (see, for example, Hayek, 1967, p. 26). In terms of contemporary science we may talk about 'self-organizing systems' to be examined by so-called 'self-organization theories'. One of the most important – though not unanimously accepted – approaches is that of Ilya Prigogine (see Prigogine and Stengers, 1984). From thermodynamics we know that in an isolated system entropy rises until it reaches a maximum in the thermodynamic equilibrium; this implies that order is permanently diminishing. (Note that the thermodynamic concept of equilibrium is quite different from the usual economic one.) Apart from artificially designed test conditions the only really isolated system seems to be the universe as a whole. Every other system is either open (exchanging energy and matter with the environment) or closed (exchanging only energy). In such systems complexity can be increased through a self-organizing process by exporting entropy out of the system. This takes place, according to Prigogine, within so-called 'dissipative' structures, which are far from a thermodynamic equilibrium. Biological evolution on earth is possible because of the system's opportunity to use external energy (provided by the sun). Advancements in non-linear mathematics make it possible to describe the behavior of complex structures the parts of which are interrelated by positive and negative feedbacks (self-reinforcing processes); these structures are able to form cohesive 'wholes' – without external, deliberate steering.

Many physical and chemical processes are successfully described that way. Certain applications to biological and social processes are convincing, though still under debate. Markets provide the fundamental structures of an 'economy as an evolving complex system', as suggested by the title of a book that has already become a standard reference in this field (see Andersen, Arrow and Pines, 1988). Concepts like communication and information gain a specific importance in self-organizing systems, where macro processes are not fully understandable by examining the (mechanistic) behavior of the particular units.

Some of the theoretical aspects of complex systems make it reasonable that they be considered in an economic context too. Because of their complexity, non-linear, complex mathematical systems cannot be solved analytically, so that numerical computer simulation plays an important role in helping us to understand their behavior. Radzicki (1990) presents a system dynamics computer simulation model, in which individual preferences can be revised according to the way an agent perceives the reactions of the environment to his or her actions. It is an inductive method where human behavior is not deducted from general principles. The subjective wants and perceptions directly create and change the socioeconomic results. Such an approach provides an opportunity to combine the institutionalist research program of describing how institutions influence individual behavior and the Austrian point of view that institutions are nothing other than the outcome of individual human action and thought but not necessarily of human design. The individual is allowed to re-evaluate step by step his or her own behavior and thus learns by means of a trial and error procedure. If the computer simulation leads to results which are isomorphic to the respective empirical data from real-world economic processes, we find it plausible to argue that the structure of the models exhibits important features of the real processes. What has been successfully used for global models of environmental socioeconomics within the 'limits to growth' studies can be further developed to support a dynamic micro foundation of socioeconomic processes. Instead of equilibria such models use the concept of attractors, which are defined as temporal situations of steady state; this can be related to the Marshallian concept of partial equilibria.

Dopfer (1991) points out that non-linear equations can be used to describe the emergence and change of institutional patterns in a complex evolving world. In a special case, the mathematical description of such processes leads into what has become known as 'chaos' (see Briggs and Peat, 1989, for an excellent presentation in a popular scientific way). A simple example is frequently used to show the general problem:

$$x_{t+1} = a \cdot x_t \cdot (1 - x_t). \tag{1}$$

Here the development of x shows qualitatively different paths for different specifications of the parameter a. Small numerical changes in the parameter a (especially within the range between 3 and 4) can lead to a qualitative change of the system: in some cases the system is 'ordered' (regular, repeated), but in a famous special case it becomes 'chaotic' (irregular, non-repeating; see Dopfer, 1991, pp. 47–8). From this it follows that similar causes do not in every case lead to similar results. Non-linear mathematics exhibits features which correspond to features of 'reality' that can hardly be described by the tools of standard linear economics: path-dependency, non-ergodicity, lock-ins, inflexibilities, multiple equilibria, strange attractors and, in certain cases, inefficiencies. The problem disappears when we use linear equations, but non-linearity provides a better description of many real-world problems. In the case of 'chaotic' behavior, we are confronted with non-predictability which restricts the possibilities of economic forecasting as well as of economic policy. But the methodology can also be used for describing how individuals behave when they associate.

Dopfer (1991, pp. 67–9) also shows that there is a way out of the problems created by the probability of chaos. Non-linear dynamics is said to have the properties of quasi-determinacy and historical accidentality. This is due to the fact that non-linear models form new structures that Prigogine and Stengers (1984) describe as 'order out of chaos'. It is compatible with observations in economic history that at certain points after relatively stable developments the institutional or technological framework changes fundamentally, with severe implications for economic outcomes. Chaos theory describes such situations as bifurcations.

Processes like these, which lead to association and cooperation between individuals, are also described by so-called 'synergetics' (see Haken, 1977). Here individual behavior depends on the behavior of the other individuals (not of a metaphysical 'whole'). This can be formulated mathematically with the master equation approach in order to describe the interdependency of changes in individual behavior in algebraic and numerical models. We are now able to differentiate situations in which individuals act relatively independently of each other while under certain circumstances they happen to associate so that their behavior seems to be guided by a pattern imposed by an invisible hand – especially if scarcity exists. In the case of street congestion, for example, cars form a cohesive pattern compared to a road with enough space to allow every driver to choose his or her speed (see Briggs and Peat, 1989). Still they are not really guided by an exogenous rule – they only behave 'as if'. (Analogous phenomena can be shown in turbulent fluids and many other examples; see Prigogine/Stengers, 1984). In this sense self-organization theory provides a middle course between radical individualism and 'wholism'. Individuals associate to form cohesive wholes, which are to be explained by examining individual behavior *and* the boundary conditions (the congestion, for example). But everything is still based on individual behavior.

Another approach to systems theory is much less accepted by the scientific community: Humberto Maturana's and Francisco Varela's works about biological systems and their concept of autopoiesia (see Maturana and Varela, 1980). The basic units of that approach are relations between certain items and not these items themselves, so that we may term the approach as non-individualistic. Distinguishing between 'the economy' on the one hand and 'society' on the other has important implications for the question whether a self-organizing economy can be externally influenced by means of state activity (which will be discussed below). Only if the economy is seen as a system isolated from policy can we truly speak of 'impairments' in the economy – otherwise it is an interaction within the socioeconomic system itself. Although using a systems-theoretical argumentation, Luhmann (1989) delimits the economy from society in total analogy to traditional economic approaches. Conceptually he leans very heavily on the autopoiesian concept. The economy is defined as the system whose final elements are payments that have been produced and reproduced by the economic system, while the elements of the political system are collective decisions; in Luhmann's eyes the difference between the economy and policy is proved by everyday experiences and by international trade (see Luhmann, 1989, pp. 17, 52–9). A connection to the evolutionary economics paradigm becomes evident. The economic environment of one individual agent consists of nothing else than the interacting totality of all other agents. Seen from a systems-theoretical point of view, the relations between the economy and state activity are characterized by differences based on their functions and by parallel construction, especially with regard to the instabilities in both systems (see ibid., p. 26).

The transfer of the systems-theoretical approaches to economics has not yet reached a point where an application to important problems of real-world economic phenomena and economic policy can be put in very concrete terms. All the methods and theories discussed above have recently been applied to biological problems and are now entering the social sciences. However, the scope of such applications is still under debate. The literature mentioned in this contribution should give an overview of the range of applications that are worth consideration if a world in which social institutions are 'the results of human action but not of human design' (Hayek, 1967, pp. 96–105) is to be described.

See also:

Chapter 78: Evolutionary economics; Chapter 29: 'Invisible hand' explanations; Chapter 30: Spontaneous order; Chapter 43: Resource economics

Bibliography

Andersen, Ph.W., K.J. Arrow and D. Pines (1988), *The Economy as an Evolving Complex System*, Redwood: Addison-Wesley.

Briggs, J. and F.D. Peat (1989), *Turbulent Mirror. An Illustrated Guide to Chaos Theory and The Science of Wholeness*, New York: Harper Row.

Dopfer, K. (1991), 'The Complexity of Economic Phenomena: Reply to Tinbergen and Beyond', *Journal of Economic Issues*, **25**, 39–76.

Haken, H. (1977), *Synergetics*, Berlin: Springer.

Hayek, F.A. (1967), *Studies in Philosophy, Politics and Economics*, London: Routledge & Kegan Paul.

Luhmann, N. (1989), *Die Wirtschaft der Gesellschaft*, Frankfurt am Main: Suhrkamp.

Maturana, H. and F. Varela (1980), *Autopoiesis and Cognition: The Realization of the Living*, Dordrecht, Holland: D. Reidel Publishing Co.

Prigogine, I. and I. Stengers (1984), *Order out of Chaos*, New York: Bantam Books.

Radzicki, M.J. (1990), 'Institutional Dynamics, Deterministic Chaos, and Self-Organizing Systems', *Journal of Economic Issues*, **24**, pp. 57–102.

Ullmann-Margalit, E. (1978), 'Invisible Hand Explanations', *Synthese*, **39**, 263–91.

29 'Invisible hand' explanations

Roger G. Koppl

The metaphor of the 'invisible hand' seems to have first been used by Adam Smith (Vaughn, 1987). Today, the term 'invisible hand explanation' identifies any argument that proposes to show how some regular social phenomenon emerged or could have emerged 'spontaneously' or 'unintendedly' from the actions of many persons. A social structure emerges 'spontaneously' or 'unintendedly' when the actions that bring it about were not fully coordinated in advance and the ends of those actions did not include the realization of that structure. 'Invisible hand' explanations describe the unintended consequences of individual action.

The unintended consequences of individual action may be beneficial or harmful. Austrian economists generally argue that a liberal social order, an 'open society', tends to produce beneficial unintended consequences, whereas central planning and interventionism are more likely to generate harmful unintended consequences. Austrians also tend to view the traditions that gave rise to the open societies of the Western world as being, themselves, unintended consequences of individual action. Among Austrian economists, the standard example of an 'invisible hand' explanation is Carl Menger's explanation of the origin of money.

Some 'invisible hand' explanations describe the operation of existing social and economic institutions. Others describe the emergence or evolution of social and economic institutions. An account of the operation of a system of fractional reserve banking is an example of the first type of 'invisible hand' explanation. A theory of the evolution of fractional reserve banking is an example of the second type. In a standard article on the subject, Ullmann-Margalit (1978) describes several features of ('aggregate mold') invisible hand explanations (pp. 277–8). (Ullmann-Margalit uses the term 'invisible hand explanation' to describe models in which the function of an institution is a part of the explanation for its existence and in which no clear link is established between the 'invisible hand' explanandum and individual actions undertaken without regard to its existence. In keeping with the methodological individualism and methodological subjectivism of the Austrian school, the term will not be used for such 'structural–functionalist' arguments.) The features are the following:

1. The domain of explanation: 'invisible hand' explanations seek to explain social phenomena rather than natural phenomena (Ullmann-Margalit, 1978, p. 265).
2. The explained phenomena: the social phenomena to be explained appear to be designed but are not. They are 'the results of human action but not of human design' (Hayek, 1967, pp. 96–105).
3. The nature of the explanation: an 'invisible hand' explanation is a 'genetic' explanation: it describes a process unfolding in time that is supposed to account for the origin of the explained phenomenon.
4. The mode of explanation: the explanation displaces an argument that attributes the phenomenon to design with the process story mentioned under (3) above. This process story shows how dispersed actions of individuals, seeking various particular ends and not any overall social result, may nevertheless result in the emergence and replication of the phenomenon being explained.
5. Idiosyncrasies of the explanation: the explanation does, indeed, explain the phenomenon. The explanation is plausible in the sense that each stage of the process story depicts an 'ordinary and normal course of events'. 'It cannot hinge on the extraordinary and the freaky, or on strokes of luck or genius' (Ullmann-Margalit, 1978, p. 271). Moreover, the explanation must contain an element of 'surprise' (ibid., pp. 271–2).

To construct an 'invisible hand' explanation, an analyst must do three things. First, he must provide a description or representation of the 'invisible hand' phenomenon to be explained. Second, he must provide a description or representation of the actions that (unintendedly) brought about the phenomenon, together with an account of the causal linkages amongst those actions. Finally, the analyst must provide an explanation of those actions showing how they could have occurred in spite of the actors' supposed disregard for the 'invisible hand' results of their activities.

Because 'invisible hand' phenomena are unintended, they can have no meaning. They may have considerable significance for human action in the sense that their existence influences the course of human events and the life chances of individuals, but they cannot be interpreted in quite the way we interpret a written text or an individual action. In this sense they are 'mechanistic'. Because of this mechanistic character of such phenomena it is often useful and appropriate to represent them with graphs and algebraic equations. The models of 'neoclassical' economics, general equilibrium theory included, may often be used for this purpose.

Just as the unintended consequences of individual action are 'mechanistic', the causal linkages between individual action and these unintended consequences, being themselves equally unintended, are meaningless and may also be described as 'mechanistic'. Thus, when constructing an 'invisible hand explanation', it may be useful to represent individual actions and interactions with 'mechanistic' models such as the rational optimizing agent. However 'mechanistic' the analyst's representation of individual action may be, he will need to establish the causal linkages among actions. This will generally entail the use of 'adjustment models', as described by Machlup:

1. *Initial position.*   The analyst first specifies the set of interrelated variables of interest to him and identifies a constellation of values for those variables that is self-consistent and thus embodies no 'inherent tendency to change'. This situation is the 'initial equilibrium'.
2. *Disturbing change.*   The analyst introduces a change in one of the 'exogenous' variables specified in step 1. It is this cause whose effect(s) the model is intended to isolate.
3. *Adjusting changes.*   The analyst now specifies the process whereby the 'endogenous' variables specified in step 1 'adjust', that is, the process by which those variables change in value in reaction to the change introduced in step 2.
4. *Final position.*   This is the 'final equilibrium', a position in which the values of the variables are once again mutually consistent. It is 'a situation in which, barring another disturbance from the outside, everything could go on as it is. In other words, we must proceed until we reach a "new equilibrium", a position regarded as final because no further changes appear to be required under the circumstances' (Machlup, 1963, p. 48).

When constructing an 'invisible hand' explanation, the analyst may wish to use several concatenated adjustment models to explain the sequence of causal linkages to which he attributes the 'invisible hand' phenomenon.

While the 'invisible hand' consequences of individual action are without meaning by virtue of their unintended character, the actions themselves are meaningful. We may hope to understand them in something like the way we understand the Book of Job, a letter from home or the instructions on a tube of toothpaste. An analyst cannot claim to have 'explained' an 'invisible hand' phenomenon if he cannot provide us with such an understanding of the actions that generated the phenomenon.

The actions chronicled in an 'invisible hand' explanation may be considered 'explained' if the analyst has made them '"understandable" ... in the sense that we could conceive of sensible men acting (sometimes at least) in the way postulated' (Machlup, 1955, p. 17). To this end, it is sufficient that these actions appear in an 'understandable' adjustment model. For an adjustment model to be 'understandable', it must satisfy the following conditions, discussed in Koppl (1992) and in Langlois and Koppl (1991):

1. *Methodological individualism.* The sequence of adjusting changes must at the same time be a sequence of individual actions. For instance, the change in price level brought about by an increase in quantity of money must be accounted for in terms of the buying and selling decisions of individuals.
2. *Subjective interpretation.* The individual (re)actions that bring about the changes chronicled in the model must themselves be explained or accounted for in terms of the knowledge, preferences and expectations of the individuals doing the acting.
3. *Subjective plausibility.* The actions and reactions involved must seem reasonable and understandable in commonsense terms to both the actors themselves and their fellow men. (This is similar to Ullmann-Margalit's requirement that the 'invisible hand' story depict an 'ordinary and normal course of events'.)
4. *Anonymity.* The richness and specificity with which the knowledge, preferences and expectations of the actors are characterized must be neither greater nor less than required in order to ensure that the actions take place and are plausible in the sense explained earlier. (For a discussion of anonymity, see the entry on 'Ideal Type Methodology' in this volume.)
5. *Causal adequacy.* The requirement of causal adequacy is a double requirement. On the one hand, it requires that the knowledge, preferences, propensities, purposes and expectations attributed to the actors provide sufficient cause for their actions. On the other hand, these actions must in turn provide sufficient cause for the specified effects. (In both cases the analysis presupposes an invariant institutional regime within which these causes operate.)
6. *Complete determinateness of the result.* If the condition of causal adequacy is satisfied, both the individual actions and the overall effects specified in the model will be the only ones possible.

Explanations of the origins or evolution of institutions, too, should be understandable adjustment models. They should be 'understandable' in the sense indicated above to ensure that the actions creating the institution may be considered to be explained. They should be adjustment models to ensure that the proposed causes of the institution are sufficient and that, in consequence, the institution may be said to be 'explained'. Understandable adjustment models explaining the origins of social and economic institutions will generally fit the following scheme, described in Koppl (1992):

1. *Initial institutional regime.* The analysis begins with a description of an initial constellation of action patterns or institutions.

2. *Identification of unexploited profit opportunities.*   The analyst then identifies profit opportunities available to at least some of the individuals in the model. The profit opportunity is exploited by acting on a new ends/means framework, by innovating.
3. *Innovation.*   The analyst then supposes some of the actors to recognize the opportunity before them and to act on it.
4. *Reaction and imitation.* The analyst then identifies the sequence of adjustments, reactions and imitations that follow from the innovative action(s) identified in step 3.
5. *New institutional regime.*   The sequence of actions detailed in step 4 is pursued until no further acts of imitation or adjustment are called for.

The use of understandable adjustment models to explain the unintended consequences of individual action allows Austrian economists to combine radical subjectivism with causal accounts of the origin and operation of many orderly social phenomena. The dispersed actions of many individuals, each animated by the spontaneous activity of an independent human mind, may produce orderly and, often, beneficial overall results even though there is no overarching design intended to realize such results.

See also:
Chapter 14: Competition; Chapter 21: Profit and loss; Chapter 28: Self-organizing systems; Chapter 30: Spontaneous order

Bibliography
Hayek, F.A. (1967), *Studies in Philosophy, Politics, and Economics*, Chicago: University of Chicago Press.
Koppl, Roger G. (1992), 'Invisible-Hand Explanations and Neoclassical Economics: Toward a Post Marginalist Economics', *Journal of Institutional and Theoretical Economics*, **148**, (2), 292–313.
Langlois, Richard N. and Roger Koppl (1991), 'Machlup and Methodology: A Reevaluation', *Methodus*, **3**, (2), 86–102.
Machlup, Fritz (1955), 'The Problem of Verification in Economics', *Southern Economic Journal*, **22**, (1), 1–21.
Machlup, Fritz (1963), *Essays on Economic Semantics*, Englewood Cliffs: Prentice-Hall.
Ullmann-Margalit, E. (1978), 'Invisible-Hand Explanations', *Synthese*, **39**, (2), 263–91.
Vaughn, Karen I. (1987), 'Invisible Hand', in John Eatwell, Murray Milgate and Peter Newman (eds), *The New Palgrave: A Dictionary of Economics*, London: Macmillan, pp. 997–8.

30 Spontaneous order

Ulrich Fehl

Modern economies are characterized by a high degree of division of labor and, correspondingly, of knowledge. The division of labor, of course, only makes sense if the activities of the involved subjects are – at least to some degree – integrated; in other words, if they are in a sense 'coordinated'. To understand the complex phenomena the division of labor entails, one is bound to form an idea as to what is meant by 'integration', or by 'coordination'. If economists say that the activities of the subjects concerned are integrated or coordinated they mean that these activities form a kind of 'order'.

Spontaneous order as an unintended outcome
In principle, 'order' can be interpreted as the intended outcome of planned activities or as the consequence of a process of self-structuring generated, but not intended, by the activities of the human beings involved. It is this latter case we circumscribe as a 'spontaneous order'. Its counterpart is the order created by 'organization' or – if the procedure is applied to the whole economy – by 'central planning'. Although organizations are important elements of modern economies, it is not implied that there will not emerge a spontaneous order, provided that the economy as a whole is not itself treated as an organization. Hayek's verdict of 'constructivism' refers to this form of central planning, but it is, of course, not confined to it. The notion of a planned or designed order should not be obscured by the fact that the goal of such an attempt in most cases will not be achieved: Austrian economists in particular have always stressed the importance of the unintended consequences of planned activities leading to outcomes that were not anticipated by the planning human beings. Thus the 'order' created by organization as a rule exhibits elements of spontaneity. Nevertheless, we cannot identify the resulting structure as a 'spontaneous order', because, as will be shown in the following, some formal prerequisites of such an order are lacking. Therefore our analysis primarily refers to the spontaneous order generated by market processes.

Spontaneous order and equilibrium
The distinction between an order created by the single mind of an individual (or by an organization) and an order emerging from the interaction process of

many individuals (and/or organizations) relates to the way the 'order' is generated, but tells us nothing about the attributes of a state we qualify as 'order'. Consequently, we have to add a concept telling us something about the properties that constitute 'order'. The concept traditionally used by economists to identify 'order' is the idea of equilibrium. An equilibrium is a state of affairs where agents have adapted the 'variables' they control in an optimal manner to some 'data'. The concept of equilibrium can be applied at different levels of analysis: thus we may ask which conditions must hold for a household or a firm to be in equilibrium, or we may investigate what is meant by the state of equilibrium of a single product market; finally, we may refer to the economy as a whole and ask which conditions constitute a state in which all agents have adjusted to each other in an optimal manner; in other words, there is a general equilibrium.

Equilibrium theory has a long tradition in economics. When, in this tradition, economists investigated whether the autonomous actions of individuals lead to an order or not, they actually meant a partial or general equilibrium, generated by the price system. Thus classical and neoclassical economic theory developed around the concept of 'equilibrium', in order to get a deeper insight into the working of the 'invisible hand', which was Adam Smith's metaphor to circumscribe the process of bringing about 'order' by virtue of the price system. Basing the 'spontaneous order' on an equilibrium concept does not by any means require the economy to be permanently in equilibrium. Actually, it would suffice for there to be at least a strong tendency towards equilibrium; or, in other words, the economy should be kept 'near' equilibrium. Otherwise it would not be very useful to identify 'order' with 'equilibrium'. The real issue, therefore, is whether the economy has to be assessed as 'near to' or 'far from' from equilibrium, in the sense of a perfect coordination.

Although the answer to this question cannot be given without a certain degree of discretion, there is something to be said in favor of the economy's being 'far from' equilibrium. Thus we have only to look at the modus operandi by which equilibrium analysis deals with its standard questions: does an equilibrium *exist*: that is, can the agents ensure perfect coordination on the basis of price informations alone, if the equilibrium price vector is 'given' (see Schmidtchen, 1990)? Is this equilibrium unequivocal or not? Is this equilibrium *stable*, in the sense that the economy will approach or return to the equilibrium state once disturbed?

In order to answer these questions, equilibrium analysis not only has, as has already been mentioned, strictly to distinguish 'data' from 'variables', but it also cannot allow for changes in the 'data', lest the argumentation should lose its stringency: by this procedure equilibrium theory is bound to eliminate central features of real life, at least as far as it is not in a position to give an adequate picture of what is going on in market processes. In other words, equilibrium theory excludes *real time* and *human creativity* from its investigation.

It is not difficult to see that *time* is excluded from the analysis when the existence problem is under discussion. But does not the investigation of the stability problem require us to consider 'time'? The answer must, of course, be 'yes'. If we scrutinize the way time is introduced into the analysis, however, we soon realize that only its 'Newtonian' aspects are accounted for or, what amounts to the same, time is conceived of only as a homogeneous, not as a heterogeneous matter (see O'Driscoll and Rizzo, 1985). This approach could be accepted, at least as an approximation, if the time elapsing between a change of a 'datum' and the attainment of the new equilibrium is very short. Then equilibrium will be reached more or less instantaneously, as may be the case when an individual reacts immediately to a changed 'datum' or when on certain product markets purchasers and sellers adjust very quickly to changed conditions. But equilibrium theory tells us little, and often even nothing, of the Newtonian time span needed for the economic system to arrive at a new equilibrium state. Equilibrium analysis and especially the implied Newtonian time concept seem to be inadequate, if the time needed to approach the new equilibrium after a change in the 'data' has taken place is substantial, as for instance in the case of the economy as a whole. Then one 'datum' or another will change and thus general equilibrium theory has to be assessed as a rather problematic approach.

Creativity of the human being is ignored by neoclassical general equilibrium economics as well. But individuals, households and firms do not just have preferences and use a given technology, they are inclined to change them autonomously in the very process of time. Thus what is classified as 'data' by general equilibrium theory actually is not constant over time. It is just this creative activity of human beings which leads to the conclusion that economic theory in principle must be conceived of as an *evolutionary process* in order to overcome the shortcomings of received neoclassical theorizing. Actually the creativity of man may be considered even more challenging for equilibrium theory than is the time problem, if time is restricted to its purely Newtonian aspects. The data variables concept seems to grow less adequate the more the data themselves change in the very process needed for the economy to arrive at a new equilibrium. If on the one hand change took place in the 'data' and the economic system was able to adapt to this change very quickly by approaching a new equilibrium state, and if on the other hand we could assume a change in the 'data' to be less probable the shorter the time span taken into consideration, then equilibrium would be a useful concept. It is by no means clear whether this assumption of equilibrium theory holds or not. In any case we have to keep in mind that outcomes of human *ingenuity* cannot be predicted and that *innovations* may occur even in states of equilibrium. But if 'data' and 'variables' change simultaneously, the difference between them becomes spurious. Thus, at least with respect to the economy as a whole, the equilibrium concept – with the implied great span of time required to restore equilibrium – should not be used to characterize 'order' of an economy understood as a continuing process.

Spontaneous order and the market process (selection order)

If, on the one hand, the spontaneous order of the market cannot be interpreted as the intended outcome of an organization and, on the other hand, it cannot be illustrated by the final state of a process, that is, an equilibrium state, it has to be brought into close connection with the ongoing market process itself; that is, we have to look for an order, *sui generis*, referring to the process as a process. As Austrian economists stress the importance of the market process – in contrast to the equilibrium view – such a concept of spontaneous order should be more adequate to their views.

To understand the kind of 'order' that is generated by the market process it is necessary to have a look at its driving forces. The driving forces of the market process are *innovation, arbitrage* and *production–accumulation*. Innovation and arbitrage refer directly to the entrepreneurial activities brought into focus by Schumpeter and von Mises or, respectively, to the consequences resulting from these activities. It should be noted that to combine the driving forces of the market process means nothing but to stress their simultaneity. Thus the world of the market process must necessarily be a world of disequilibrium and hence – according to the equilibrium concept – a world of 'disorder'. If we still want to maintain the notion of 'order' in the market process, where else should we look for it?

First it should be realized that the market process is embedded in a framework of *legal and moral institutions* which, at least in principle, do not change during the process. To this extent, then, the data variables approach can be used. But, as will be discussed below, even this 'constancy' does not hold in the strict sense: the insight that the legal and moral system is adapted by the activities of the actors in the very process of interaction reveals another trait of the spontaneous order. To identify the legal and moral framework as an important prerequisite of the spontaneous order is an essential point. As is well known, such 'rules' generate an order in themselves. They enable the individuals to make plans involving the interaction with other individuals, insofar as the execution of contracts can, in principle, be expected by the actors. Thus plans can be carried out, even if the goals of the participating individuals are conflicting (see Hayek, 1973, 1976, 1979). In any case, the 'order of exchange' by no means requires an equilibrium environment. On the contrary, while being 'executed' in a technical sense, some plans will not achieve the intended goals. As a consequence the revision of plans and the adaptation of activities will take place permanently.

Secondly, it can be shown that equilibrium theory overemphasizes the importance and the speed of *arbitrage* as a driving force of the market. To study it together with innovation as a simultaneous driving force must lead to a generalization of neoclassical argumentation. This, however, has far-reaching consequences. To state that the neoclassic, that is equilibrium-centered, theory overemphasizes arbitrage activity is only correct insofar as innovation as a driving force is ignored. That is to say, in a disequilibrium or market process context, arbitrage has to be attributed an even higher importance. In an ongoing market process with price setters the conduct of the participants cannot be modeled as a mere adaptation procedure – in the sense that the agents adapt to changing, but 'given' prices – rather, the individuals have to perceive better opportunities they can offer or use, respectively. Discovering better opportunities does not only refer to prices, but to other properties of the exchange process as well. Although all people are bound to react to the permanent process of reshuffling in the market in order to survive in this context, their ability to discover better opportunities will differ to a high degree. This factor is stressed by Kirzner's theory of the Misesian entrepreneur, whom he tends to interpret as an equilibrating force (Kirzner, 1973). This is an adequate explanation insofar as one is inclined to accept the equilibrium framework, but the entrepreneur as an arbitrageur in the sense of Kirzner can be interpreted in a market process-oriented or evolutionary context, too: it is the entrepreneur who perceives the better opportunities, and in doing so he will discover the kind of order implied in the market process, namely the *selection order*, which can then be used by other market participants as well. In other words, the spontaneous order generated and perpetuated in the market processes is nothing but a selection order or a collection of such selection orders.

To see what is meant by such a selection order, we have to take into full account *innovation* as a driving force. Innovation is understood here in a broad sense. Whereas arbitrage refers to something which already 'exists', by innovation something 'new' is introduced into the market process, be it a new resource, a new product, a new production process or a new form of organization. The term 'new' is applied to all grades of 'improvement'. They do not need to be revolutionary at all. It is clear that the market process would eventually come to an end if innovation came to a standstill. Finally, all differences between sellers would be eliminated by the working of arbitrage. To put it otherwise: while the ongoing market process is characterized by heterogeneity the emerging equilibrium resulting from the activity of arbitrage alone would be characterized by homogeneity (see Fehl, 1986). Thus the selection profile of market opportunities would have vanished. It is clearly to be seen that it is the permanent 'input' of innovations that prevents the selection profiles disappearing, whether these innovations be caused by the need to react in order to survive in the market or whether they be implemented spontaneously. It should be noted that innovation as a driving force of the market process cannot do this job alone, nor can arbitrage. The market process is in need of the bounding mechanism to create order in the dynamic sense used here: without arbitrage the price system would not reflect actual processes of valuation, and thus innovations could not be judged as 'good' or 'bad'. On the other hand, the arbitrage mechanism is useless without innovation processes creating variety. It should be noted that the ability to innovate differs greatly between human beings, as does the ability to arbitrage; for this reason Heuß, following Schumpeter, introduced a whole spectrum of entrepreneurs differing with regard to their faculty of innovating (Heuß, 1965).

To gain a full understanding of the selection profiles constituting themselves in the ongoing market process one has to keep in mind the third driving force, *production–accumulation*. Arbitrage in the sense of perceiving new opportunities would have no consequences at all if it was not followed by production and accumulation; innovations could not spread their effects without production and accumulation. In short the driving forces of the market processes depend on each other and it is their concerted action which produces the selection profiles of the markets, that is, the set of different opportunities in the product markets as well as in the economic system as a whole. These selection profiles will be present if, and only if, the market process is going on (see Fehl, 1986).

If it is accepted that selection profiles are continuously generated by the market process, how can we conceive of order being established by the very existence of such process-dependent profiles? We can qualify a system as 'ordered' if it delivers signals for the individuals to improve their situation, if it 'guides' the individuals' behavior. The spontaneous order of the market system – being understood as a system of ongoing processes – is constituted by two separate systems of guidance or, more precisely, by two systems of *orientation*. The first is the system of legal and moral rules already discussed above. The second is the system of selection profiles emerging in the market process. The selection profiles reflect the heterogeneity being built up as a consequence of 'advancing' and 'following' (challenge and response) in the market as a dynamic process. It is precisely heterogeneity being revealed by the activity of the entrepreneurs in the sense of von Mises which delivers *differentiated signals* to the participants of the market system.

Thus, on the one hand, purchasers as well as sellers are told where 'good' and where 'less good' opportunities can be realized; at the same time, the firms receive different information as to their relative positions. Some will receive the information that they can raise their prices, others that they will have to lower their prices or leave the market, or improve their performance, for instance by innovating. In this way the selection profiles make it possible for the market participants to be guided by differentiated messages. This does not only apply to the single product market, but to branches as well: thus different profit margins in different industries may guide investment decisions. In short, if in the ongoing market process, for one reason or another, the selection profiles vanished, then a vital 'instrument' of orientation would be missing.

The interpretation of the spontaneous order as an order furnishing a schedule of orientation, in the sense that the selection profiles exhibit differential signals to the market participants, is obviously related to the coordination problem. While the equilibrium concept of order focuses on the perfect (ultimate) state of coordination, the concept of selection order is concerned with the very process of coordination. The relevant question here is: what kind of procedure is furthering coordination in the dynamic or even evolutionary sense? Or what are the factors leading to such a self-structuring order which can serve as a guide for a more adequate adaptation of the individuals involved? Being understood as the consequence of the concerted action of innovation, arbitrage and production–accumulation, the spontaneous order can be viewed as the prerequisite and simultaneously as the result of a process of self-organization. Or to put it differently: in an evolutionary economy the relevant concept of spontaneous order must be a selection order. In sum, then, the order of the market as a medium for discovery procedures has to be oriented to the process of coordinating and not to the final state of a perfect coordination in the equilibrium sense.

It should not be overlooked, however, that the spontaneous order in the sense of a selection order does not represent a perfect order. The formation, the revelation and the interpretation of the emerging selection profiles rest on subjective interpretations, expectations and decisions. Austrian economists, though to a differing degree, have always stressed the importance of subjectivity in economic analysis, but where there is subjectivity in the sense described there is scope for error. It can be shown, however, that, at least in principle, subjectivity of expectations extends the realm of heterogeneity and thus reinforces the working of the selection order (see Fehl, 1986). On the other hand, the possibility that errors may occur makes it clear that the spontaneous order in the sense of the selection order is restricted in its performance to the working of a trial-and-error process. There are many reasons why errors may appear: the selection profile itself may be incomplete, it may be revealed imperfectly or even in a 'wrong' manner, and the differentiated messages may be interpreted in an inadequate way or may be answered by inadequate measures. As a consequence, a firm with a 'bad' performance could stay in the market, while a 'better' firm might be eliminated. In this respect the term 'selection order' should not be interpreted in a normative sense. On the whole, however, the selection or spontaneous order of the market should be 'workable'.

Spontaneous order and its evolution in the longer run
As a direct consequence of subjectivity and the possibility of errors, one should take into consideration that individuals, being confronted with the existence of a selection order reflecting the market system as being 'far from' equilibrium, have to face a high level of uncertainty, which they will tend to reduce. In such a situation the market participants will look for new institutions to reduce uncertainty. They will thereby improve the working of the spontaneous order (see Schmidtchen, 1990). This, of course, can be interpreted in itself as a spontaneous process. It has already been mentioned above that the creation of the legal and moral rules, as well as that of other institutions, is explained in this way by some Austrian economists. But this is a controversial point. Of course there are examples which clearly show that the institutional framework may change during the market processes, owing to the activities of the market participants, without the interference of some central authority. Thus legal and moral rules may change or come into existence along with other institutional innovations (see Kunz, 1985). Seen in this way we can speak of a spontaneously generated spontaneous order of the market.

But what about an institutional reform being executed by a central authority and by 'organisation'? Are we allowed to interpret this as a 'spontaneous' action and to classify the resulting order as a 'spontaneous order'? At first sight we are inclined to answer this question in the negative. If we have a closer look at the problem, we may, however, come to the conclusion that the emerging order as a whole may be rather a 'spontaneous' as opposed to a 'constructivistic' order. If the institutional innovation aims at improving the working of the spontaneous order (Schmidtchen, 1990), the innovators have to clarify whether the new or the amended rule or institution fits in the received system of rules or institutions. If this implementation is 'reflected' the new rule or institution is 'intended' but its working cannot be understood without recourse to the received system of the other rules or institutions. In this view the result of the innovation is not a constructivist order, but a spontaneous one. The crucial point is that the emerging order of the rules and institutions as a whole is not instantaneously 'constructed', but is based on the experience of the past. In this sense the institutional framework as a whole is not 'made'. Rather, we may interpret the received system of rules as a vehicle transferring experience from the past to the future, experience we cannot 'understand' or 'reconstruct' in its entirety. This is Hayek's thesis of the 'spontaneous' generation of spontaneous order, which is often misunderstood. A crucial point which should be acknowledged is that the intention must be to improve the system of rules in existence, but not to create a system as a whole. It should be realized, too, that the intention of improving the existing system of rules and institutions may be misguided. Error cannot be excluded at this level of argumentation either. We have to take comfort from the notion that the ensemble of rules and other institutions as a system in action is permanently testing whether the latter fit together or not; or, more precisely, the permanent test will reveal whether some improvements have to be made. It is, so to speak, a 'total analysis' at work.

See also:

Chapter 4: Market process; Chapter 15: Entrepreneurship; Chapter 29: 'Invisible hand' explanations; Chapter 28: Self-organizing systems

Bibliography

Fehl, U. (1986), 'Spontaneous Order and the Subjectivity of Expectations: A Contribution to the Lachmann–O'Driscoll Problem', in J.M. Kirzner (ed.), *Subjectivism, Intelligibility and Economic Understanding*, New York: New York University Press.

Hayek, F.A. (1973), *Law, Legislation and Liberty, vol. 1: Rules and Order*, London/Henley; Routledge & Kegan Paul.

Hayek, F.A. (1976), *Law, Legislation and Liberty, vol. 2: The Mirage of Social Justice*, London/Henley: Routledge & Kegan Paul.

Hayek, F.A. (1979), *Law, Legislation and Liberty, vol. 3: The Political Order of a Free People*, London/Henley: Routledge & Kegan Paul.

Heuß, E. (1965), *Allgemeine Markttheorie*, Tübingen-Zürich: J.C.B. Mohr (Paul Siebeck) – Polygraphischer Verlag AG.

Kirzner, I.M. (1973), *Competition and Entrepreneurship*, Chicago: University of Chicago Press.

Kunz, H. (1985), *Marktsystem und Information*, Tübingen: J.C.B. Mohr (Paul Siebeck).

O'Driscoll, G.P. Jr. and M.J. Rizzo (1985), *The Economics of Time and Ignorance*, Oxford: Basil Blackwell.

Schmidtchen, D. (1990), 'Neoclassical and Austrian Theory of Economic Policy: Differences in Constitutional Policies', in A. Bosch, P. Koslowski and R. Veit (eds), *General Equilibrium or Market Process*, Tübingen: J.C.B. Mohr (Paul Siebeck).

PART II

FIELDS OF RESEARCH

31 Capital Theory

Peter Lewin

Carl Menger the discoverer of subjective value

In the economic mainstream the Austrian school is most often associated with the Austrian theory of capital, especially with the work of Böhm-Bawerk (1884, 1889). It is to the earlier work of Carl Menger (1871), however, that we must look for the beginnings of this theory. It was Menger's remarkable vision that provided the inspiration for the development of a comprehensive view of the economic system as a process driven by the subjective preferences of consumers. He showed that it is the value that consumers put on products that determines the value of the inputs that are used to produce those products and not the other way round, as had so often been thought. Value is a *forward-looking* rather than a *backward-looking* concept. A unit of capital equipment is valued because its owner can look forward to its producing a valued (by prospective consumers) output, rather than because it used scarce resources in its own production. The value of the inputs is derived from the value of the outputs. Many important insights follow from this simple, yet subtle contention.

Menger characterizes production as a sequential process in which *goods of higher order* (capital goods) become transformed into *goods of lower order* (consumption goods). Capital goods are varied in nature but can be classified by where they fit, along a time continuum, into the production process. The lowest, or first, order goods are consumption goods. The lowest order capital goods are second order. The next highest are third order, and so on. With this model he makes clear that the element of time is inseparable from the concept of capital. Rewards to saving result only if more time-consuming methods of production are adopted (Menger, 1871, p. 153). The higher order goods that men come to own must allow for greater production if there is to be progress. That is, they must (in combination with other goods) be able to produce a greater volume of consumption goods in the future or, in other words, they must be able to extend consumption further into the future. Menger envisaged the time-consuming creation of specific capital goods (however accomplished) to be a necessary condition for achieving economic progress. Böhm-Bawerk's later discussion of the greater productivity of more 'roundabout' methods of production (those production techniques 'embodying more time' being more productive) is clearly drawn from Menger, although there are important differences in perspective (and in methods of analysis) between the two.

Menger first introduces these ideas in connection with processes in nature. Men find the fruits of nature valuable, but at an early stage in the development of civilization they learn that they can do more than simply wait for nature's yield. They can intervene in natural processes and affect the quantity and quality of the subsequent yield. The earlier a producer intervenes, the greater are the opportunities to tailor the production process to suit his own purposes: 'This provides an intuitive basis for the notion that the more "roundabout processes" tend to have a greater yield in value terms' (Garrison, 1985b, p. 165).

At any point in time there is a capital structure characterized by capital goods of various orders: 'The value of goods of higher order is always and without exception determined by the prospective value of the goods of lower order in whose production they serve' (Menger, 1871, p. 150). These values manifest themselves in the market as prices. As long as these prices remain (and are expected to remain) constant and as long as there are no technical changes in methods of production, the capital structure will remain constant. But if there should be a permanent change in the price of even one consumption good, this would almost always imply the need to change the capital structure in some way (Menger, 1871, pp. 65–6; Skousen, 1990, p. 19). The level and pattern of the employment of resources (including labor) is thus determined and depends on *the strong link between the structure of consumption and the structure of production.* Changes in the demand for one (or some) consumption good (*relative to others*) cause changes in the evaluation and use of *particular* capital goods and in employment. The implication in Menger is that the market can accomplish this smoothly. The economic consequences of human error are implicit in Menger's view of capital but (unlike Keynes) he does not see them as destabilizing. Menger was aware of the possibility of error and of the importance of expectations. He says, 'The prospective value of goods of lower order is often – and this must be carefully observed – very different from the value that similar goods have in the present' (1871, p. 152). It is thus possible to say (anticipating later Austrian developments), 'The "correctness" of the valuations of higher order goods depends completely on entrepreneurial abilities' (Garrison, 1981, p. 21).

Böhm-Bawerk

From the above discussion it is evident that Menger laid the groundwork for a comprehensive theory of capital. It is to his most famous disciple, Eugen von Böhm-Bawerk, however, that most economists look when thinking about capital. Böhm-Bawerk was primarily interested in the relationship between capital and interest and, indeed, in the very existence of interest as a phenomenon. He advanced three independent reasons for the existence of a positive interest rate, the third of which was the higher productivity of 'roundabout' methods of production. Our focus here will be on his theory of capital.

Böhm-Bawerk's characterization of a capital-using economy is, in many ways, very similar to Menger's. (We rely heavily here on Garrison, 1981, pp. 23–9). He adds a geometric device to Menger's reasoning. The production process is viewed as a series of concentric circles, with time progressing outward from the center. The outermost ring represents the value attained by consumption goods, while the center represents the origin of the production process. The respective rings, starting at the outside and progressing toward the center, thus correspond to Menger's first, second and higher order goods. In a world without change, a stationary state, the rings have two interpretations: '(1) The area of the rings can represent the amount of the different kinds (maturity classes) of capital that exist at a given point of time, or (2) the initial inputs of the production process can be seen as radiating outward through the several maturity classes until they finally emerge at the outermost ring as consumer's goods' (Garrison, 1981, p. 24). Though this is the view that was to surface later in the famous debate with John Bates Clark, the stationary state was not central to Böhm-Bawerk's view. He was concerned with the question of how an increase in capital occurs and what that meant for economic events (1884, p. 109). His recurring theme is 'that real saving is achieved at the expense of the lower maturity classes (the outer rings) and that the saving makes possible the expansion of the higher maturity classes (the padding of the inner rings) and the creation of higher maturity classes than had previously existed' (Garrison, 1981, p. 24). Garrison points out that this hints at the presence of the entrepreneur 'who brings such structural changes about and ... [who] is guided by changes in relative prices of capital in the various maturity classes' (ibid., p. 25). The point to be stressed is that, for Böhm-Bawerk, as for Menger, an increase in capital, a condition we normally associate with the progress of a capital-using economy, involves a change in the *time structure of production* in some way. It is not simply an augmenting of each type of capital good at each level of maturity.

Böhm-Bawerk tried to capture the relationship between the various maturity levels with a single number, 'the average period of production'. This concept was designed to measure the amount of time on average that it took to produce the product or, alternatively, the amount of time on average that the inputs in the production process spend in production before emerging as outputs. In this way he hoped to have found the elusive element that would cement the heterogeneous elements of the capital *structure* into a single measurable *stock*. The element of measurement was time – 'embodied time'. This involved a radical departure from Menger's forward-looking vision and was later criticized by the Austrians for that reason.

In order to calculate the average period of production, one is required not only to identify definite starting and ending points for each production process, one is also required to formulate each production process in terms of physically defined inputs, physically defined outputs and the elapse of calendar time between them. This is only possible in a world where unexpected change is absent, where all production techniques are known. This implies that all production plans are consistent with one another – where plans are inconsistent some must fail and this implies the occurrence of unexpected events. In such a situation, it is impossible to derive unambiguously an average period of production for all production processes and, therefore, for the economy as a whole. So, in this respect, though not in his essential vision of capital, Böhm-Bawerk departed from Menger and the Austrians who came after him. But it was this specific aspect of Böhm-Bawerk's work that Clark attacked from an entirely different point of view.

Clark attacked Böhm-Bawerk's emphasis on the importance of time for understanding capital by concentrating on his 'average period of production'. The essence of his criticism can be understood as follows. We have seen that the average period of production can only be calculated when the production process is describable in a very particular way. A favorite example in the literature is the case of wood production from a forest in which a fixed number of young trees is planted while the same number of trees is cut down each period. It should be clear that it is possible to say that, since production and consumption go on steadily each period, they are in effect simultaneous. Production and consumption are synchronized and occur together all the time (Clark, 1893, p. 313). In this example of the woodlot, it *is* possible to calculate the period of production. It is the time that it takes, on average, for a tree to grow from a seedling into a mature tree ready to be cut. If we assume that this time is the same for each tree, we have an even clearer measure. Clark's criticism can be understood to say that this time period is irrelevant since the forest is, after all, a permanent source of wood. Since production and consumption are in effect simultaneous, the relevant period of production is zero. This is the kind of vision one is offering in suggesting that capital should be thought of as a 'permanent' fund yielding a flow of income. A 'capitalist' economy is then one in which capital plays this role.

This view is valid only for an economy that has reached a state of stationary equilibrium – a situation in which the capital stock has been built up, is suitably maintained and yields a continuous income (net of maintenance cost). In terms of the forest example, the forest is already grown and yielding a steady output when our analysis begins. It tells us nothing about the decisions to grow the forest in the first place, when questions relating to the 'period of production' must have been important. Consequently, it can tell us nothing about the effect of changes to the structure of production and the decisions that motivate them, or, indeed, what types of (consumption and production) decisions are necessary to expand or contract the production flow. In a fundamental sense, production and consumption only appear to be simultaneous to the observer who does not care about the production plans which gave rise to the production process in the first place. One plants seedlings today not in order to cut trees today but in order to cut trees some years from now. One cuts trees today only because one planted seedlings some years ago. One cannot ignore the time element. Unless we are able to relate the production process to these production decisions, we will not be able to understand changes in that process. Furthermore, in the real world, where the capital structure and the array of consumption goods is continually changing, production and consumption frequently do not even appear to be simultaneous. If we are to understand the meaning and effects of changes in economic policy, such as changes in tax rates, public expenditures and so on that affect the pattern of production, we cannot remove the time element from view.

Modern developments: Hayek, Kirzner and Lachmann

Later developments in Austrian capital theory occurred in two distinct and separate areas: Austrian business cycle theory and Austrian market process theory. F.A. Hayek (building on earlier work of Mises) attempted to construct an Austrian theory of the business cycle. He included an account of the way the capital structure was altered by ill-conceived monetary policies and thus affected employment. In his early work on this subject, Hayek introduced his famous triangles (1931) but later struggled, over a protracted period (during which he produced many works), to find a more appropriate characterization of the capital structure. This culminated in his intricate and difficult work, *The Pure Theory of Capital* (1941). This period was also one of intense debate between Hayek and Frank Knight. In many ways, this echoed the earlier Clark–Böhm-Bawerk debate. In essential respects, Hayek failed to go much beyond Böhm-Bawerk's time structure conception and remained wedded to aspects of a 'period of production' approach.

The essentials and limitations of this 'period of production' approach were incisively surveyed in Israel Kirzner's work (1966). Kirzner showed clearly how a commitment to subjective value notions precludes a meaningful aggregate measure of the capital stock and points the way to a vision of the capital structure as the result of a dynamic, entrepreneurially driven market process. Ludwig Lachmann's contribution to capital theory (1978), indeed, proceeded from a conviction that it was necessary to break completely from Böhm-Bawerk's conception. Lachmann provided an account of the nature of the capital structure in a dynamic economy and discarded any attempt to measure the capital stock. Nevertheless, he felt it was possible to preserve the essence of Böhm-Bawerk's valid insights and to reinterpret Böhm-Bawerk's thesis about the higher productivity of 'roundabout production' (p. 73).

The capital structure can only be understood in terms of the individual plans from which it derives. A production plan involves the combining of individual capital goods and labor resources in order to produce particular outputs. These capital goods stand in a *complementary* relationship to one another within the plan. As individual bits of machinery, raw materials, buildings and so on, they make little sense, but when seen as part of an overall plan, they assume immediate significance. Understanding capital in terms of plans provides two important benefits. First, the plans provide reference points for interpreting any given capital structure. We understand and relate to capital goods in terms of the plans that they help to fulfil. And as long as plans are successful the structure will be maintained. But, second, and perhaps more important, when plans fail, completely or in part, or succeed beyond the planner's expectations, they will be revised and the capital structure will be changed. And it is in understanding this change that we must refer back to individual production plans.

Whatever its motivating cause, a plan revision entails the *substitution* of some resources for others. (Though capital goods are specialized – more suited to the production of some things rather than others – this is a matter of degree. Capital goods in general can be characterized as having *multiple specificity*, that is, a limited range of competing uses.) Substitutability is a phenomenon of change. It is part of the process of capital regrouping that follows upon the revision of disappointed (or surprised) expectations. Thus, while complementarity is an aspect of any given plan, one type of capital good combining with others to help fulfil a specific production plan, substitutability is an aspect of contemplated *changes* in plans. Together these two concepts characterize different aspects of the capital structure, namely, its coherence and its adaptability.

In the economy as a whole many firms will be acting in the manner described, planning and replanning their production activities. Out of the interaction between them will emerge a flow of goods and services. The logic of these interacting plans provides the (unperceived) logic of the capital structure. At the firm level the entrepreneur–manager establishes the plan structure. At the market economy level, the market process establishes the capital structure. Whereas Böhm-Bawerk characterizes economic development in terms of an increasing 'average period of production', Lachmann characterizes economic development in terms of the increasing *complexity* of the capital structure as evidenced by the increasing number of production stages. Adam Smith identified the 'division of labor' as the key to economic progress. In modern capitalistic production a 'division of capital' may indeed be more important (Lachmann, 1978, pp. 78–85).

While these modern developments provide a coherent, suggestive picture of capital and its nature, the full integration of capital into monetary theory and macro policy still remains to be done.

See also:
Chapter 32: Austrian business cycle theory; Chapter 67: The debate between Böhm-Bawerk and Hilferding; Chapter 18: Marginal productivity; Chapter 43: Resource economics

Bibliography
Böhm-Bawerk, E. (1884), *Capital and Interest*, translated by George D. Huncke and Hans Senholz, Spring Mills: Libertarian Press, 1959.
Böhm-Bawerk, E. (1889), *The Positive Theory of Capital*, translated by George D. Huncke and Hans Senholz, Spring Mills: Libertarian Press, 1959.
Clark, J.B. (1893), 'The Genesis of Capital', *Yale Review*, November, 302–15.
Garrison, R.B. (1981), *The Austrian–Neoclassical Relation: A Study in Monetary Dynamics'*, PhD dissertation, University of Virginia.
Garrison, R.B. (1985a), 'Intertemporal Coordination and the Invisible Hand: An Austrian Perspective on the Keynesian Vision', *History of Political Economy*, summer, 309–21; reprinted in R.M. Ebeling, *Austrian Economics: A Reader*, Hillsdale: Hillsdale College Press, 1991, pp. 531–52.
Garrison, R.B. (1985b), 'A Subjective Theory of a Capital Using Economy', in G.P. O'Driscoll Jr. and M.J. Rizzo, *The Economics of Time and Ignorance*, Oxford: Basil Blackwell.
Hayek, F.A. (1931), *Prices and Production*, London: Routledge.
Hayek, F.A. (1933), *Monetary Theory and the Trade Cycle*, translated by N. Kaldor and H.M. Croome, London: Jonathan Cape.
Hayek, F.A. (1941), *The Pure Theory of Capital*, Chicago: University of Chicago Press.
Kirzner, I.M. (1966), *An Essay on Capital*, New York: Augustus M. Kelly.
Lachmann, L.M. [1956] (1978), *Capital and Its Structure*, Menlo Park: Institute of Humane Studies.
Menger, C. (1871), *Principles of Economics*, translated by James Dingwall and Bert Hoselitz, New York: New York University Press.
Skousen, M. (1990), *The Structure of Production*, New York: New York University Press.

32 Austrian business cycle theory

Robert J. Batemarco

Whereas theories of the business cycle currently in vogue are mathematical models of economic aggregates which, in the tradition of positive economics, seek merely to predict quantitatively (that is, mimic) cyclical phenomena (Lucas, 1981, p. 219), Austrian business cycle theory (hereafter referred to as ABCT) is an altogether different kind of theory. Derived using the method Ludwig von Mises dubbed praxeology, it is the logical consequence of the axiom of human action in conjunction with its corollaries of time preference, interest, the vertical structure of production and capital complementarity, and the nature of the institution of central banking. Praxeology dispenses with mathematical tools, restricts aggregation to within individual stages of production and refrains from proffering predictions of either timing or magnitude. Austrians perceive economic theory as a means of understanding (*verstehen*) rather than as a tool for prediction.

This method breaks every taboo of the regnant positivist orthodoxy. The most salient implication of the theory itself, that business cycles do not arise from mere policy error, but rather from the very institution of fractional reserve central banking, attacks one of the central icons of the mixed economy policy-making establishment. Unsurprisingly, mainstream economists and policy makers have viewed ABCT with scorn when they have not simply ignored it. Nevertheless, the perceived shortcomings of mainstream economics during the last two decades have led increasing numbers of economists to reconsider the praxeological approach and its offshoot, ABCT.

Developed by Ludwig von Mises (1912, pp. 396–404) and refined by F.A. Hayek (1928, 1931, 1939), ABCT is unique in including real capital goods among its elements in a manner which does not assume away their essential heterogeneity. Austrian treatment of capital goods owes much to Böhm-Bawerk's structure of production analysis and the notion of capital complementarity (Lachmann, 1956, pp. 3, 117–18). The theory demonstrates the connection between this structure of capital and monetary policy by way of Wicksell's natural rate of interest theory and Mises's integration of money into general economic theory.

Outline of the theory
Under modern central banking with fractional reserves, new money is created when the central bank makes loans. Sometimes these are made directly to

banks, although usually they are not. In any event, those loan proceeds come to be deposited in the banking system and, because those proceeds are liabilities of the central bank, they constitute bank reserves. As reserves, they can be loaned out by the banks. To induce borrowers to seek these new funds, banks will reduce interest rates from what their levels would have been in the absence of this credit expansion (the natural rate of interest). Because lower interest rates will increase the present discounted value the most for those investment projects the benefits of which will be realized in the most remote future (in Austrian terminology, they raise the relative prices of higher order goods to those of lower order goods and reduce the profit margins between the stages of production), they encourage resources to be reallocated so as to make greater provision for a more distant future and less for the more proximate future.

Money creation can never be neutral because some people must receive the new money before others. Those who receive the new money first have resources redistributed to them at the expense of those who receive that money last (after it has been used to bid prices up). In the case under discussion, those who receive the new money first are those who want to invest in capital goods which will not yield consumer goods until the most distant future. Thus the structure of capital will diverge from what it would have been in the absence of the credit expansion. As Austrians would put it, the structure of production has been lengthened.

Higher order capital goods industries will experience a boom as a result. At the same time, the resources which are supporting this boom are being drawn away from the consumer goods industries. Thus consumers will have to curtail satisfaction of their immediate needs (although, in a growing economy, this curtailment would be relative rather than absolute) in a phenomenon known as forced saving (Hayek, 1939, pp. 183–95). Only a continued expansion of credit to firms investing in higher order goods can sustain this boom.

Typically, however, the credit expansion will have to be slowed down, if not halted completely, because it will generate substantial price inflation. Not long after the credit creation ceases, so will the boom. As the new money spent on the higher order capital goods gets paid to productive factors as incomes and spent on consumer goods, forced saving will come to an end. It will become clear that the consumers wanted to provide for a less distant future than entrepreneurs did. Reflecting those desires, interest rates will rise. This will restore profitability to consumer goods industries and, thus, increase the opportunity costs of investing in higher order goods. This enables producers of consumption goods as well as the lower order capital goods to bid labor, raw materials and non-specific capital goods away from the higher order capital goods industries. Investments which appeared profitable in an easy money, low interest rate environment are now revealed to be malinvestments, as the complementary capital goods necessary for their successful completion are no longer available. These malinvestments must now be completed at a lower than expected profit (or even a loss), liquidated, or in the most extreme case abandoned. Available capital must be redeployed to satisfy more proximate needs.

In a world of perfectly homogeneous capital goods, this adjustment might occur without a hitch. However, we do not live in such a world and our understanding of business cycles will not be furthered by assuming such a world. On the contrary, capital goods are heterogeneous, of various degrees of specificity, and must often be used in certain well-defined configurations. As a result, the adjustment process needed to restore the capital structure to a state of compatibility with consumers' desires will inevitably entail temporary reductions of output (that is, a recession or depression, depending on its severity and duration). Immobility of labor and wages which are slow to adjust will bring about unemployment in this situation as well.

To elaborate, many of the capital goods whose production was financed by credit creation in the boom are highly specialized. They are all but useless in any function except that for which they were originally intended. Other capital goods are not so specialized. They can be shifted at fairly low cost to other uses and, once credit expansion abates, they will be transferred to the lower stages of production. This process will take time. During this time, production in the higher stages is severely curtailed because of the unavailability of those complementary capital goods which have been diverted to the lower stages of production. While there is some increase in output at the lower stages of production, it is unlikely to make up for the decline of the higher stages because such a large portion of the capital goods originally devoted to those higher stages is specific and can neither be used in those higher stages nor redeployed at the lower stages. This is the paradoxical situation of which Hayek speaks, in which the shortage of capital makes capital unsaleable (1931, p. 94). It results in a shortage of capital looking very much like a surplus of capital (Buchanan and Wagner, 1977, p. 68).

I emphasize capital complementarity as a distinctive feature of ABCT because it has been practically ignored by other theories of business cycles. Modern economists treat capital as an amorphous putty which will always be as productive as was expected (through the assumption of a fixed capital–output ratio) when the investment in it was made. This, in turn, is based on the older tradition of J.B. Clark and Frank Knight, which saw capital as a permanent fund of wealth which synchronizes production and consumption (Skousen, 1990, pp. 28–33, 68–70). In these models, capital cannot be wasted. As a result, their proponents find capital of no relevance to business cycles.

In a nutshell, ABCT sees the creation of credit under a fractional reserve system misleading entrepreneurs into using capital wastefully, generating a boom. The cessation of the credit creation reveals the extent of the waste and initiates a process of correcting the errors committed in the boom. This process constitutes the recession. ABCT, then, explains the generation of the boom and the inevitability of the turning-point.

Empirical applications

The method of praxeology does not find empirical data appropriate to prove or disprove the theories derived from it. As praxeological theories are nothing more than the logical implications deduced from the human action axiom, supporting axioms and institutional data, proof (or disproof) can only be obtained from the truth (or untruth) of the axioms and the correctness (or error) in the deductive reasoning used (Mises, 1962, p. 71).

Economic theory is intended to permit us to interpret the facts of history. Examinations of the historical record can be used to determine the range of applicability of praxeological theories in doing so. Even a cursory reading of that history shows the applicability of ABCT to be wide. ABCT provides a cogent explanation of certain characteristics of business cycles which are regularly observed. It explains why recessions invariably follow deceleration of money supply growth, why higher order good industries experience larger fluctuations in their prices and output both in the boom and in the recession, and why predictions that we are in a new era in which the business cycle has been vanquished will be wrong as long as our banking institutions remain as they are.

Particular cyclical episodes which have been interpreted in the light of this theory include the USA in the 1850s (Batemarco, 1983, pp. 68–120), Germany in the 1920s (Bresciani-Turroni, 1937; Batemarco, 1983, pp. 121–72), the Great Depression (Rothbard, 1963; Robbins, 1934; Phillips, McManus and Nelson, 1937) and the USA in the 1960s and 1970s (Wainhouse, 1984; Batemarco, 1983, pp. 173–229). A detailed account of the behavior of relative prices in the first four decades of the twentieth century in the USA which ABCT explains was provided by Mills (1946).

Critiques and rebuttals

The objections most commonly raised by mainstream economists against Austrian business cycle theory regard issues of existence, initial conditions, proportionality, inevitability, learning, policy and universality. In this section, each set of objections will be described, along with some Austrian rebuttals.

Existence

The cycles to which ABCT pertains consist of booms and recessions which are caused by a single set of factors. Recent statistical tests have been interpreted to deny the very existence of cycles of this type, and to claim instead that business fluctuations are merely a random walk (Tullock, 1988, p. 74). New Classical theories of the cycle (that is, equilibrium business cycle theory and real business cycle theory) also attribute business fluctuations to a series of random shocks (monetary–fiscal shocks for equilibrium cycle theory (Lucas, 1975, p. 1114) and 'shocks to preferences, technologies/opportunities, or resources and endowments' for real cycle theory (Plosser, 1989, p. 57)).

Austrians reject the empirical objection because they deem the type of tests used incapable of saying anything about causality. Statistical tests are irrelevant, as only theory can enable us to recognize cycles (Salerno, 1989, p. 142). Austrians also find New Classical theories irrelevant because those theories do not seek to derive implications of known facts, but rather strive to create 'a fully articulated artificial economy which behaves through time so as to imitate closely the time series behavior of actual economies' (Lucas, 1981, p. 219). Their type of theory assumes cycles of the Austrian type do not exist.

Initial conditions
It has often been alleged that ABCT cannot explain unemployment because it starts by assuming full employment. Actually, the opposite would be closer to the truth, since any unemployment already assumed in deriving ABCT could not be explained by it. In any event, Hayek showed that, even from a state of less than full employment, credit creation would still generate a boom–bust cycle (1931, pp. 96–9; 1939, pp. 3–70).

It should be noted here that it is not full employment per se which is necessary, but merely scarcity (Lachmann, 1956, p. 113). The failure of some critics to recognize this primordial fact led them to criticize the theory's contention that there was a necessary trade-off between higher order and lower order goods (Evans, 1969, p. 333; Hansen, 1951, p. 387). Some of this confusion was due to a failure to see that increases in production of both higher and lower order goods over time was not inconsistent with a trade-off at a single point in time.

Proportionality
Some authors were skeptical that the levels of forced saving and interest rate movements normally observed over the course of typical cycles were sufficiently high to generate the fluctuations in output and employment of the magnitudes usually found during actual business cycles (Haberler, 1937, p. 56; Kaldor, 1942, pp. 153, 175; Lucas, 1981). This was true particularly of the Great Depression. Three points can be made regarding this. In the first place, it is possible that our measures of interest rate changes, for example, are too low. The correct comparison is not between interest rates at the beginning of the credit expansion and interest rates at the end of the credit

expansion (which is readily available), but between interest rates at the end of the credit expansion and what interest rates *would have been* in the absence of that credit expansion (a counterfactual which is unavailable). Secondly, an event of relatively small magnitude can lead to consequences of much larger import (for example, the shooting of the Archduke Franz Ferdinand and the First World War). Finally, ABCT only explains why there will be an upper turning-point. The severity of the subsequent recession will depend on many factors other than the severity of the boom.

Inevitability

It is a commonplace of modern economics of almost all varieties that skilful policy making can permit an economy to enjoy an inflationary boom yet escape the bust which Austrians regard as inevitable (Tullock, 1989, p. 149). This would seem an easy proposition to prove, since a single example would suffice. The evidence of an inflationary boom not followed by a recession has yet to be presented, however.

Indeed, while the recession can be postponed for a while by accelerating the pace of credit expansion, it cannot be held off forever. In the post-First World War German hyperinflation, for instance, unemployment started to increase in the summer of 1923, while the rate of money creation continued to accelerate through November of that year (Batemarco, 1983, pp. 130, 137).

Learning

The rational expectations school has argued that entrepreneurs should never be fooled more than once into mistaking falling interest rates due to credit creation for falling rates due to more voluntary saving. Thus they could not generate cycles in the manner described by ABCT more than once. Austrians find this argument wanting, on at least three grounds. In the first place, entrepreneurs do not possess rational expectations in the sense of 'perfect familiarity with economic theory and a careful scrutiny of current monetary and credit phenomena [which alone] could save a man from being deceived and lured into malinvestments' (Mises, 1943, p. 252). In the second place, the distortions caused by credit expansion would create temporary profit opportunities to which entrepreneurs would respond as suggested by ABCT. The more astute of those entrepreneurs, however, would be able to unload their investments on the less astute shortly before they were exposed as malinvestments (O'Driscoll, 1977, pp. 166–8). Furthermore, malinvestment implies plans which are inconsistent on an economy-wide basis. This is possible even if there are no inconsistencies within individual firms (Garrison, 1989, p. 9).

Policy
A prime implication of ABCT is that inflationary credit expansion causes the cycle. It has been argued that, while this may be correct, the emphasis of the boom's inflationary origins would lead to counterproductive policies in the slump, where the immediate problem was deflation (Robbins, 1971, p. 154). While not urging deliberate deflation, Austrians point out that new credit creation intended to halt a recession is what would be counterproductive. ABCT stands alone in noting that the recession, however painful, is actually the recovery phase of the cycle, in which entrepreneurial errors are exposed and corrected (Rothbard, 1963, pp. 20–21). Attempts to prevent it from running its course simply create new malinvestments and sow the seeds of another cycle.

Universality
The claim of ABCT to be the only valid explanation of cycles has been criticized even by authors who do consider it a valid explanation of some cycles (Schumpeter, 1939, pp. 296, 303; Lachmann, 1956, p. 113). The claim is based largely on a narrow definition of a cycle. By defining slumps not caused by the same factors which caused the preceding booms as fluctuations rather than part of the cycle, Austrians are able to maintain this claim (Rothbard, 1963, pp. 12–14, 28). This contention might be more convincing if its proponents pointed out historical examples of fluctuations which were not cycles.

See also:
Chapter 31: Capital theory; Chapter 68: The Hayek–Keynes macro debate; Chapter 62: Political business cycles; Chapter 63: The Great Depression

Bibliography
Batemarco, R. (1983), 'Studies in the Austrian Theory of the Cycle', PhD dissertation, Georgetown University.
Bresciani-Turroni, C. (1937), *The Economics of Inflation*, translated by M.E. Sayers, London: George Allen & Unwin.
Buchanan, J.M. and R.E. Wagner (1977), *Democracy in Deficit: The Political Legacy of Lord Keynes*, New York/San Francisco/London: Academic Press.
Evans, M.K. (1969), *Macroeconomic Activity*, New York/Evanston/London: Harper & Row.
Garrison, R.W. (1989), 'The Austrian Theory of the Business Cycle in the Light of Modern Macroeconomics', *The Review of Austrian Economics*, **3**, 3–29.
Haberler, G. (1937), *Prosperity and Depression*, new revised and enlarged edition, Cambridge, Mass.: Harvard University Press, 1958.
Hansen, A. (1951), *Business Cycles and National Income*; expanded edition, New York: W.W. Norton, 1964.
Hayek, F.A. (1928), *Geldtheorie und Konjunkturtheorie*, Vienna/Leipzig; translated by N. Kaldor and H.M. Croome as *Monetary Theory and the Trade Cycle*, New York: Harcourt, Brace & Co, 1933; reprinted New York: Augustus M. Kelley, 1966.
Hayek, F.A. (1931), *Prices and Production*; 2nd edn, revised and enlarged, London: G. Routledge & Sons, 1935; New York: Augustus M. Kelley, 1967.

Hayek, F.A. (1939), *Profits, Interest and Investment and Other Essays on the Theory of Industrial Fluctuations*, reprinted New York: Augustus M. Kelley, 1969.

Kaldor, N. (1942), 'Professor Hayek and the Concertina Effect', *Economica*, NS, 9; reprinted in *Essays on Economic Stability and Growth*, Glencoe, IL: Free Press, 1960.

Lachmann, L.M. (1956), *Capital and Its Structure*, London: G. Bell; reprinted Kansas City: Sheed Andrews & McMeel, 1977.

Lucas, R. (1975), 'An Equilibrium Model of the Business Cycle', *Journal of Political Economy*, **83**, June, 1113–44.

Lucas, R. (1981), 'Understanding Business Cycles', in *Studies in Business Cycle Theory*, Cambridge, Mass.: MIT Press.

Mills, F.C. (1946), *Price–Quantity Interactions in Business Cycles*, New York: National Bureau of Economic Research.

Mises, L. von (1912), *Theorie des Geldes und der Umlaufsmittel*, Munich/Leipzig: Duncker & Humbolt; translated by H.E. Batson as *The Theory of Money and Credit*, London: Jonathan Cape, 1934; reprinted Indianapolis: Liberty Classics, 1981.

Mises, L. von (1943), '"Elastic Expectations" and the Austrian Theory of the Trade Cycle', *Economica*, NS, 10, August, 251–2.

Mises, L. von (1962), *The Ultimate Foundations of Economic Science*, Princeton: Van Nostrand; reprinted Kansas City: Sheed Andrews & McMeel, 1976.

O'Driscoll, G. (1977), *Economics as a Coordination Problem: the Contributions of Friedrich A. Hayek*, Kansas City: Sheed Andrews & McMeel.

Phillips, C.A., T.F. McManus and R.W. Nelson (1937), *Banking and the Business Cycle*, New York: Macmillan.

Plosser, C.I. (1989), 'Understanding Real Business Cycles', *The Journal of Economic Perspectives*, **3**, summer, 51–77.

Robbins, L. (1934), *The Great Depression*, London: Macmillan.

Robbins, L. (1971), *Autobiography of an Economist*, London: Macmillan.

Rothbard, M.N. (1963), *America's Great Depression*, Princeton: Van Nostrand; 3rd edn, Kansas City: Sheed & Ward, 1975.

Salerno, J.T. (1989), 'Comment on Tullock's "Why Austrians Are Wrong About Depressions"' *The Review of Austrian Economics*, **3**, 141–5.

Schumpeter, J.A. (1939), *Business Cycles*, New York: McGraw-Hill.

Skousen, M. (1990), *The Structure of Production*, New York/London: New York University Press.

Tullock, G. (1988), 'Why the Austrians Are Wrong About Depressions', *The Review of Austrian Economics*, **2**, 73–8.

Tullock, G. (1989), 'Reply to Comment by Joseph T. Salerno', *The Review of Austrian Economics*, **3**, 147–9.

Wainhouse, C.E. (1984), 'Empirical Evidence for Hayek's Theory of Economic Fluctuations', in B.N. Siegel (ed.), *Money in Crisis*, San Francisco: Pacific Institute for Public Policy Research.

33 Comparative economic systems
David L. Prychitko

Austrian economists are rather well known for their defense of capitalism and criticism of planning and intervention. Comparative economic systems – the comparative analysis of a society's fundamental organizational principles – has emerged as a popular, and powerful, field of study within contemporary Austrian economics. Here, many of the Austrian school's key theoretical concepts regarding prices and knowledge, profit and loss accounting, and rivalrous competition have been rigorously applied to examine the nature and logic of capitalism, socialism and interventionism. While the Austrians have developed a theory of comparative economic systems over the past several decades, only recently, since the collapse of 'really existing socialism' in the former Soviet Union and Eastern Europe, has their analysis – particularly of the problems of rational planning under socialism – become accepted by mainstream economists.

Roots of comparative systems analysis
The field of comparative economic systems is neither an Austrian invention, nor unique to the school. Economists of all stripes have studied the theory and practice of capitalist and socialist systems. Its roots travel back to the nineteenth century. If, as contemporary economists commonly believe, Adam Smith's *An Inquiry into the Nature and Causes of the Wealth of Nations* offers the first attempt to study the economics of free market capitalism (which Smith dubbed the 'system of natural liberty'), then Karl Marx arguably provides the first major 'comparative' analysis: most notably, Marx's *Das Kapital* established both a critical (if not hostile and damning) analysis of capitalism and also an implicit, general vision of socialist economic organization.

Marx's inquiry suggests that society may be founded upon three systemically distinct organizational principles: tradition, market or plan. These categorical distinctions have, with some important exceptions to be discussed later, been generally accepted by contemporary comparative systems economists from both the neoclassical school (Grossman, 1963, for example) and the Austrian school (Lavoie, 1985, for example). A tradition-based society, such as primitive communal groups or hunter–gatherer tribes, tends to be organized along the following institutions: common ownership of (very simple) means of production; production for direct use; barter; little, if any, division of labor (at best, along gender lines without regard to rationality or efficiency); a consistent aversion to risk-taking behavior. Alternatively, a market-based society (capitalism) affords a very different organizational logic. (According to Marx, in fact, the market is the antithesis of traditional society.) De facto private ownership of (technologically advanced) means of production replaces common ownership; commodity production and exchange wipes out production for direct use and face-to-face bartering; both a highly technical and a hierarchical division of labor is created in the workplace, and a spontaneous, undesigned social division of labor emerges with the development of labor markets and specialized industrial production. The market system requires a panoply of entrepreneurial risk taking, in the form of discovering new avenues of investment, alertness to economic error, and technological and organizational innovation. Money – a universal medium of exchange – provides the basis for appraising the relative scarcities of consumer goods and the means of production (capital) in the form of competitive prices and profit–loss accounting.

For Marx, the market system is ultimately 'anarchic', based upon an 'anarchy of production', in both a descriptive and pejorative sense. Marx argued that the market system is an undesigned, uncontrollable series of commodity exchanges for the sake of personal gain and profit (here essentially agreeing with Smith's descriptive 'invisible hand' phrase). Consequently, for Marx, the market would be plagued with ever-increasing bouts of recessions and depression, economic chaos and, ultimately, utter collapse (a pejorative sense of 'anarchy of production' which has no counterpart in Smith's 'invisible hand'). Hence Marx predicted that, just as sure as market has abolished tradition in the battle over organizational principles, so too, would the plan extinguish the market and usher in a final type of economic system: socialism. (Employing the dialectic, Marx tried to demonstrate that socialism represented the inevitable synthesis between primitive communal society – tradition – and industrial capitalism – market.)

Socialism is a system based upon de facto public or social ownership of the means of production, the abolition of a hierarchical division of labor in the enterprise and a consciously organized social division of labor. Under socialism, money, competitive pricing and profit–loss accounting would be destroyed. The 'anarchy of production' would be replaced outright with a scientifically settled, comprehensive economic plan. Tradition, market and plan thus emerge, with Marx, as three conceptual systems with unique organizational logics. This is not to say that people within a market-based system, for example, fail to be influenced by certain customs and traditions, or fail to create and pursue plans. Rather (and this is the point of capitalizing each system), the *underlying economic principle* upon which the plans and purposes of people are coordinated within the market – a competitive and spontaneous profit–loss system – is conceptually distinct from a society organized by a scientific, comprehensive plan or by a pre-modern, cooperative pattern of face-to-face bartering, essential to a tradition system.

Austrian contributions to comparative systems analysis
Tradition-based economies have been interpreted by most economists, including Austrians, as having only historical–anthropological relevance (for understanding the emergence of civilization, for example), while offering little or nothing to the grand debate over economic organization under modernity. The traditional economy, in other words, has generally been relegated to a conceptual organizational scheme with little contemporary empirical relevance. Economists who have worked within the field of comparative systems have, for the most part, directed their attention to the question of whether a plan-based system (which we shall subsequently refer to as socialism) can achieve the same, if not a higher, level of economic rationality or efficiency as a market-based system (which shall now be referred to as simply capitalism).

On this question, the conclusions drawn by Austrian economists have been notoriously consistent. Shortly following Eugen Böhm-Bawerk's (1896) relentless critique of the Marxian labor theory of value, the chief Austrian insight in comparative systems theory – that socialism will fail to calculate rationally the relative scarcities of goods and resources, and must therefore fail in practice – first surfaced in Friedrich von Wieser's *Theorie der gesellschaftlichen Wirtschaft* (1914). Wieser had claimed that plans in a capitalist system can be coordinated

> far more effectively by thousands and millions of eyes, exerting as many wills; they will be balanced, one against the other, far more accurately than if all these actions, like some complex mechanism, had to be guided and directed by some superior control. A central prompter of this sort could never be informed of countless possibilities, to be met with in every case, as regards the utmost utility to be derived from given circumstances, or the best steps to be taken for future advancement and progress. (pp. 396–7)

But the *locus classicus* of the Austrian criticism of socialism appears in Mises's 1920 essay, 'Die Wirtschaftsrechnung im sozialistischen Gemeinwesen' (translated as 'Economic Calculation in the Socialist Commonwealth').

The core of Mises's argument can be stated concisely: (1) socialism aspires to replace private ownership of the means of production with social ownership, and seeks to destroy spontaneous (anarchic) market exchange in favor of central economic planning; (2) therefore, the means of production (that is, higher order capital goods) will not be produced for, and exchanged within, a competitive market process; (3) without this market process, competitively established prices – those that normally allow individuals to appraise the relative scarcities of the means of production – will be erased; (4) therefore the primary economic goal of a socialist system – rational economic planning – will be impossible. The knowledge required for successful economic planning is dispersed among individuals within society, and cannot be effectively collected and used without competitive market pricing. As Hayek would later emphasize (1945), the relevant information is contextual, particular to time and place. More recently, younger Austrians (especially Lavoie, 1986) have argued that the type of knowledge supplied by rivalrous market pricing and profit loss accounting is predominantly 'tacit' or inarticulate, and have thereby developed a phenomenological–hermeneutical analysis to defend their claim that this knowledge cannot be collected by even the most advanced computer systems.

Mises maintained that, at best, socialism 'is only conceptually possible' (1920, p. 109; also see Mises, 1927, pp. 70–75). Rational economic calculation may not pose a problem in the pure theory of a static socialist society (or in any theory that depends upon such extreme assumptions as, for instance, the end of scarcity, or full and complete information). Nevertheless, Austrian economists maintain that calculation is an eminently practical problem, one which must lead to the downfall of real-world socialist planning. (The Austrians were not, of course, free from criticism or misunderstanding. Soon Oskar Lange would attempt to answer Mises's claim by erecting a neoclassical model of 'market socialism' (Lange, 1936). Joseph Schumpeter, who should have been more aware of the intricacies of the Austrian position, would later follow Lange's lead (Schumpeter, 1942). The confused socialist calculation debate had resulted.)

The collapse of the Soviet Union and the Eastern Bloc after 1989 seems to suggest that there is empirical power to the Austrian analysis, and has already rekindled some outside interest in the school's approach to comparative systems analysis (see Kornai, 1990, for example). But this collapse may also, perhaps ironically, suggest that the Austrian analysis will need to be clarified and critically re-evaluated as we move into the next century. Why is this so? The Austrians have claimed that socialism, as a plan-based system, is only a conceptual possibility, void of empirical viability. Hence, although they have accepted the original Marxian systems schema of tradition–market–plan, they have demonstrated that, for all practical purposes, the empirical status of a plan-based system falls far short of that found even among traditional systems. After all, traditional economies *have* existed at one time or another, while a successfully functioning socialist system is, according to Austrian theory, a real-world impossibility. Here, the Austrian contribution to the comparative systems literature is nothing short of radical, and arguably represents a tremendous intellectual feat, one which distinguishes Austrian economists from Marxists and neoclassical comparative systems economists.

Moreover, the Austrians have consistently criticized the notion of a potential 'Third Way' – as proposed by models of market socialism, indicative planning, redistributive welfare states, corporatism and the like. The Austrians have remained firm that market and plan are conceptually distinct economic systems, undergirded by different organizational logics. A notion of a 'third' system (barring tradition), which purports to 'combine' market and plan, is grounded on a logical confusion, and either collapses into a system of central economic planning (as argued in Hayek, 1944, and Prychitko, 1991) or remains a market-based system with mere state intervention (Mises, 1929: Littlechild, 1979; Lavoie, 1985).

Yet, if their analysis is correct, Austrians must ask themselves exactly what *did* collapse in the late 1980s and early 1990s. To be consistent, Austrian economists cannot claim *socialism* finally collapsed, otherwise they face the embarrassing task of explaining how socialism – an economic system which they purport to be empirically impossible – lasted several decades, or indeed, how it lasted at all. Here lay a potential weakness of applied Austrian systems theory, for Austrian economists, unfortunately, are traditionally prone to commit this intellectual mistake. Michael Polanyi's (1957, p. 36) criticism of Mises and Hayek is the most glaring:

> Of all the intellectual triumphs of the Communist regime – and they are vast – it seems to me the greatest is to have made these eminent and influential writers [Mises and Hayek] so completely lose their heads. Could anything please that regime better than to hear itself proclaimed by its leading opponents as an omnipotent, omniscient, omnipresent socialist planner? That is precisely the picture of itself which the regime was so desperately struggling to keep up. Such accusations supply the Soviet government with an incontestable 'testimony' of having achieved the impossible aspirations of socialism, when in fact it has simply set up a system of state capitalism – a goal which leaves the regime next door to where it started.

To claim today that the collapse of the Soviet economy represents a collapse of socialism (and a final vindication of the Austrian position) may simply prolong the above misunderstanding.

Fortunately, some younger Austrians (such as Boettke, 1990, 1993 and Lavoie, 1986–7) and others sympathetic to the Austrian position (Roberts, 1971, for example) have interpreted so-called socialist economies as market systems with a tremendous degree of state intervention. In this manner, so-called socialist economies differ *in kind* from a comprehensively planned system because they crucially depend upon world market prices and a stupendous underground economy for scarce resources – which engenders de facto private property relations in spite of a de jure socialist constitutional framework.

But Austrians might now harbor a greater tendency to undermine the strength of their own analysis by interpreting the latest events in Eastern Europe as 'proof' of socialism's failure. Perhaps as the excitement over these economic reforms begins to wane, and new problems emerge, Austrian economists will be better prepared to interpret more carefully the history of interventionism in the twentieth century, while avoiding unnecessary scholarly confusion.

See also:
Chapter 69: The socialist calculation debate; Chapter 77: The 'new' institutional economics'; Chapter 64: The collapse of communism and post-communist reform; Chapter 74: Marxisms and market processes

Bibliography
Boettke, Peter J. (1990), *The Political Economy of Soviet Socialism: The Formative Years, 1918–1928*, Boston: Kluwer Academic.
Boettke, Peter J. (1993), *Why Perestroika Failed*, New York: Routledge.
Böhm-Bawerk, Eugen (1896), *Zum Abschluss des Marxschen Systems*, translated as *Karl Marx and the Close of His System* (1898); New York: Augustus Kelley, 1949.
Grossman, Gregory (1963), 'Notes for a Theory of the Command Economy', *Soviet Studies*, **15**, (2), October.
Hayek, F.A. (1944), *The Road to Serfdom*, Chicago: University of Chicago Press.
Hayek, F.A. (1945), 'The Use of Knowledge in Society', *American Economic Review*, **XXXV**, (4), September.
Kornai, Janos (1990), *The Road to a Free Economy*, New York: W.W. Norton.
Lange, Oskar (1936), 'On the Economic Theory of Socialism', reprinted in Benjamin E. Lippincott (ed.), *On the Economic Theory of Socialism*, New York: McGraw-Hill, 1964.
Lavoie, Don (1985), *National Economic Planning: What is Left?*, Cambridge, Mass.: Ballinger Publishing Co.
Lavoie, Don (1986), 'The Market as a Procedure for Discovery and Conveyance of Inarticulate Knowledge', *Comparative Economic Studies*, **28**, (1), spring.
Lavoie, Don (1986–7), 'Political and Economic Illusions of Socialism', *Critical Review*, **1**, (1), winter.
Littlechild, Stephen C. (1979), *The Fallacy of the Mixed Economy*, San Francisco: Cato Institute.
Mises, Ludwig von (1920), 'Die Wirtschaftsrechnung im sozialistischen Gemeinwesen', *Archiv für sozialwissenschaften*, **47**, translated as 'Economic Calculation in the Socialist Commonwealth', in F.A. Hayek (ed.), *Collectivist Economic Planning: Critical Studies on the Possibilities of Socialism*, (1935); Clifton, NJ: Augustus M. Kelley, 1975.
Mises, Ludwig von (1927), *Liberalismus*, translated as *Liberalism: A Socio-Economic Exposition*, Kansas City: Sheed Andrews & McMeel, 1962.
Mises, Ludwig von (1929), *Kritik des Interventionismus*, translated as *A Critique of Interventionism*, New York: Arlington House, 1977.
Polanyi, Michael (1957), 'The Foolishness of History', *Encounter*, **9**, (5), November.
Prychitko, David L. (1991), *Marxism and Workers' Self-Management: The Essential Tension*, Westport, Conn.: Greenwood Press.
Roberts, Paul Craig (1971), *Alienation and the Soviet Economy*, Albuquerque: University of New Mexico Press.

Schumpeter, Joseph A. (1942), *Capitalism, Socialism, and Democracy*, New York: Harper & Row, 1976.
Wieser, Friedrich von (1914), *Theorie der gesellschaftlichen Wirtschaft*, translated as *Social Economics* (1927); New York: Augustus Kelley, 1967.

34 Financial economics

Mark Skousen

The Austrian school of economics has only recently begun to publish articles and books about the raging debates in finance theory. Are stock prices predictable? Can investors beat the market? Is it possible for an investor to minimize risk and maximize return on his investment portfolio? What is the role of government in the securities industry? Let us consider how Austrian economic theory can provide insights into these issues.

Are stock prices predictable?

There is no consensus today on the question of whether economic or financial events are forecastable. Many Wall Street practitioners, technical analysts and financial gurus are convinced that they can predict the future prices of stocks and other financial assets. They rely on a variety of tools, including economic theories, econometric models, company fundamentals, technical chart patterns and complicated mathematical systems, to determine the direction of markets. Many technical chartists see each financial market as some kind of a living organism, destined like lemmings to repeat the same instinctive behavior over and over again. Other analysts, steeped in engineering, mathematics, computer science or the natural sciences, see the market in an entirely mechanistic way, like the movement of the stars and planets. To them the stock market is just a complicated numbers-crunching puzzle.

At the other end of the spectrum are the academic 'random walkers' who deny that anyone on Wall Street has a crystal ball. These theoreticians of finance, including Harry Markowitz, Fischer Black, Merton Miller, William Sharpe and Paul Samuelson, assert that prices of financial assets are completely unpredictable, at least in the short term. Their saint is Louis Bachelier, a nineteenth-century French mathematician, who stated, 'The mathematical expectation of the speculator is zero.' In other words, at any given instant, the probabilities are 50 per cent that stock prices will rise and 50 per cent that they will fall. Bachelier also claimed that stock prices vary according to the square root of time, which bears a remarkable resemblance to molecules randomly colliding in space. This phenomenon, known as Brownian motion, came to be called 'random walk' in the literature of finance (Bernstein, 1992). The random walk theory asserts that stock prices are essentially random, that 'short-term' changes in stock prices cannot be predicted. Investment advisory services, earnings predictions, and complicated chart patterns are useless' (Malkiel, 1990, p. 24).

Market analysis and human action

Austrian economic theory can shed light on this never-ending debate between these two polar positions. The world of finance often appears as a sophisticated game of numbers and chart patterns, but Austrians stress that behind the mathematics and geometry are thousands of buy-and-sell transactions between individuals. In short, the financial markets represent human action.

According to Austrians, human action is fundamentally distinct from nature. Unlike animals, plants and inorganic matter, human beings possess free will and free choice. People adopt values and employ means to achieve specific ends to improve their condition. They are always evaluating their situation, changing their mind, acquiring new skills, learning from their mistakes, and sometimes overreacting. In short, human beings are neither machines nor lemmings. As such, unlike the events in nature, human action is not completely predictable. Economics, the science of human action, is inherently subjective. It is qualitative, not quantitative (Mises, 1966).

In applying this dualistic epistemology, Austrians refer to any misapplication of the physical sciences to economics and finance as 'scientism' (Hayek, 1942). A natural scientist can predict with considerable precision the outcome of a chemical or physical experiment. But an economist will not be able to make a similar prediction about the prices and output of next year's wheat harvest. He may be able to say with some authority that prices will fall if the expected harvest is double the previous year's output, assuming other factors remain unchanged. But he may have considerable difficulty in accurately forecasting *how much and when* the price of wheat will fall. Predicting the direction of interest rates is an even more arduous task. An increase in the supply of money may not necessarily result in a reduction in interest rates. Rates may actually rise and bond prices fall if inflationary expectations are strong enough. The outcome is uncertain because an increase in the money supply does not simply shift the supply curve for loanable funds, but may shift the demand curve as well. In any case, it is extremely difficult to forecast the direction of interest rates, let alone the magnitude of change.

Events and price action in the economy and the financial markets are based on the actions and emotions of people, not things, and therefore cannot be precisely measured. Sir Isaac Newton summed it up best when he said, 'I can calculate the motions of heavenly bodies, but not the madness of people.' Investors should be wary of any financial adviser or economist who predicts exact dates, sets precise price targets, or attempts seriously to answer the question, 'What will the Dow Jones Industrial Average be on 31 December?' All such efforts are guesswork. The future of human activity is always uncertain to some extent: 'There are no constant numerical relations in human action, and therefore there are no coefficients that can be included in this law that are not simply arbitrary and erroneous' (Rothbard, 1980, p. x).

Austrian economists are also suspicious of technical trading systems that rely on cycles, trends or other mechanical devices linked to historical data. They take the warning, 'past performance is no guarantee of future performance', very seriously. Unreliable financial theories include the Kondratieff cycle theory, the Elliott wave theory, the Dow theory, and the gold–silver ratio. These forecasting systems depend on an objective standard which is inconsistent with subjective expectations (Browne, 1987).

Austrians in the middle
Austrian theory does not suggest, however, that market action is completely unpredictable. If a choice is made (Figure 1) between one extreme, those who say the market is totally predictable, and the other extreme, those who say that the market is totally unpredictable, the Austrians fall somewhere in between (Garrison, 1984).

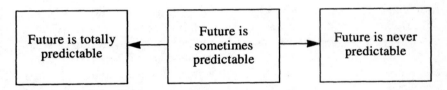

Figure 1

Prices of stocks and other financial assets can be predicted with some degree of accuracy because the actions of the market are always non-random. All financial events and prices are linked to human decision making. There is always a cause-and-effect relationship in the financial market-place. By properly understanding and assessing the policies of a nation and the behavior of the market players, an analyst can get a sense of where the market is headed. This is where the role of the economist *qua* entrepreneur comes into play. However, because of the complex set of variables that operate in the market-place, it is impossible to be precise about the future of market behavior. There is *always* uncertainty.

How important is the stock market?
Austrians reject the view held by many mainstream economists that the stock market has little or nothing to do with the economy and that economists can safely ignore the machinations of Wall Street. It is unfortunate that neoclassical economics has become 'the economics of capitalism without capitalists,

capital assets and financial markets' (Minsky, 1986, p. 120). The stock market cannot be divorced from the industrial system; while it occasionally becomes overvalued or undervalued, it 'tends to reflect the "real" developments in the business world' (Rothbard, 1983, p. 75). Nor is Wall Street a gigantic casino, as Keynes alleged. A share or stock is not a lottery ticket; it is partial ownership in a company (Skousen, 1992b). The stock market is a major source of capital in a nation, a concept easily forgotten in a world of day trading, telephone switching, butterfly spreads and the OEX.

In the long run, the performance of the stock market is determined by the profitability of individual companies and, in a profound way, reflects the robustness of a nation's economy. A nation's economic and political policies have tremendous influence on the direction of the markets. Stock prices will tend to perform best in countries that provide a stable legal system, enforce property rights, impose low taxes on investment assets, minimize commercial regulations and provide the broadest degree of freedom in the production, distribution and consumption of goods and services. Wise investors will find the best investment opportunities in the most stable and free economies, where stock exchanges are well developed, and will avoid investing in countries with a high degree of socialism and government intervention.

In addition, investors can gain or lose as a result of changes in tax rates, money supply, regulations and other forms of government policy. Such shifts in economic policy can dramatically affect the value of stocks, bonds, real estate and other financial assets. The investor who better understands the significance of these changes will profit the most. For example, in the late 1960s, it became apparent to a few astute investors that Western governments could not maintain their policies of fixed exchange rates and an official gold price of $35 an ounce. Investors who recognized early the effects of inflation on the financial markets profited handsomely (Skousen, 1988).

Short-term forecasting
But what about the movement in stock prices from day to day or week to week? While the short-term behavior of prices is much more difficult to predict, there are guidelines to watch for. In studying financial history, investment analysts may recognize patterns of market psychology. For example, at the bottom of a long bear market, the public frequently appears pessimistic. Contrarians and value-seeking investors look for these 'sold-out' conditions to buy. At the top, the public is frequently overly enthusiastic, and intelligent speculators look for opportunities to sell. Speculators and analysts often rely on price patterns, volume figures and other technical data to assess the psychological attitudes of the general public to determine tops and bottoms of markets. Thus some forms of technical analysis may be valuable to the market forecaster as long they reflect 'human nature' and the psychology of investors.

In addition, financial forecasters can profit immensely if most other analysts and investors misread or misunderstand the fundamental inner workings of the economy, the markets and the effects of government policy, or use an inappropriate trading system. Naive and misguided investors can create a lot of 'noise' in the market-place, giving wise investors an opportunity to get in early before the public realizes it has misread the situation. As the old Wall Street adage says, 'In the land of the blind, the one-eyed man is king.' For example, in the 1980s, Europe established an exchange rate mechanism (ERM) between major currencies. After a decade, it became apparent to many currency traders and international bankers that the ERM, like all forms of price controls, could not last, despite the efforts of central banks. Strong currencies such as the German mark were undervalued and weak currencies such as the British pound were overvalued. Speculators who took advantage of the situation profited handsomely when ERM collapsed in September 1992. The public, who had little understanding of the economics underlying the ERM, lost out.

Another example: in the early 1970s most investors continued to hold bonds in the face of an easy money policy. Meanwhile, shrewd bondholders sold their position in anticipation of rising price inflation and an eventual fall in bond prices. The general public, not recognizing how the inflation transmission mechanism worked, lost out when price inflation surfaced and bond prices fell. Thus the market rewards those investors who understand sound economics and punishes those who do not. However, forecasters must not assume that market psychology always remains the same. In a very real sense, each financial event is unique. The stock market action of 1987–90 was not a repeat of 1929–33. Both began with a crash, but performed quite differently afterwards. There are always new factors involved in each financial event, many of which are difficult to anticipate.

Moreover, as rational expectations theory notes, the public can learn from its mistakes and become more knowledgeable about the economy and the markets. The next time the government adopts an easy money policy, the public, remembering the past, may react right away and sell bonds, reducing the profit opportunities for nimble speculators. Finally, because the factors affecting the market vary over time, it is difficult to predict when the trend will change. For instance, after a long bear market, an investor may not know whether a price rise is the beginning of a bull market or just a bear market rally. Such entrepreneurial decision making is more of an art than a science.

Modern portfolio theory

Modern portfolio theory (MPT) is an academic approach developed by professors of finance to assist individuals and institutions in measuring risk and in selecting a portfolio that maximizes their return, given the level of risk they wish to take. Three financial economists – Harry Markowitz, Merton

Miller and William Sharpe – received the Nobel Prize in economics in 1990 for their efforts to quantify risk in stock and portfolio selection. These finance professors have reached three main conclusions: (1) rates of return are related directly to investment risk; (2) investors should not try to beat the market; and (3) investors should diversify their portfolios as much as possible. What can Austrian economics say about these assertions?

First, MPT states that, to induce an investor to bear more risk, the expected return must be higher. Return is related to risk. Wildcatters will not drill for oil if all they can hope for is a return equal to a bank savings account. Investors will not buy growth stocks if the expected return is no greater than blue chip stocks that pay high dividends. Clearly this assertion is based on common sense. However, mainstream methods of measuring risk and uncertainty in the market are often suspect. *Beta* is considered the most useful gauge to measure risk against expected return. Beta is a statistic created to estimate a stock's volatility beyond the general ups and downs of the whole market. By measuring a stock's volatility relative to the entire market, Beta is intended to estimate systematic risk relative to general market cycles.

The capital asset pricing model (CAPM) is a technique designed to help investors select securities with expected rates of return that match the risk investors wish to take. In order to achieve higher rates of return, CAPM calls for investors to select a broad portfolio of high-Beta stocks. Initial studies showed that over the long run the rate of return is higher for investments with high-Beta coefficients. However, recent studies have raised serious doubts about CAPM and the usefulness of Beta coefficients in estimating risks. Some studies indicate that the low-Beta stocks have at times outperformed high-Beta stocks. (Malkiel, 1990, pp. 238–63).

Austrian economic theory raises doubts about the CAPM as a reliable model for stock selection. There is no guarantee that companies whose stocks have been traditionally volatile will offer a higher rate of return in the next bull market, or that low Beta stocks will underperform the market. The underlying assumption behind CAPM is that Beta coefficients are relatively constant throughout market cycles, a violation of the principle that history never quite repeats itself. There is no reason why a stock's Beta cannot change radically over time, as the result of modifications in company management, the product line or customer demand.

Risk and the structure of production: an Austrian contribution
Finance professors dissatisfied with Beta and the CAPM have searched for alternative theories. The Arbitrage Price Theory (APT), developed by Stephen A. Ross, is a popular alternative method of measuring systematic risk in various sectors of the securities market according to changes in inflation, the yield curve and the business cycle. Austrian economics suggests that further

advances could be made along the lines of what might be called an 'intertemporal pricing model' (IPM). IPM disaggregates stocks into sectors according to their place along the intertemporal transformation process. The model predicts that stock prices will tend to be more volatile in industries located in the earlier stages of processing and less volatile in industries located in the final stages of consumption.

According to IPM, the time structure of production and consumption pervades the entire economy and the financial markets. The Austrian theory of the business cycle asserts that changes in the money supply, interest rates and government policy affect the structure of the economy and the financial markets systematically (Rothbard, 1983). When the government artificially lowers interest rates and expands the money supply, it creates an artificial boom in the capital goods industries and in capital assets. Industries engaged in the early stages of production tend to expand more rapidly than industries engaged in the later stages of production. Unfinished higher order goods have a longer period of production, are more capital-intensive and are more interest rate-sensitive than most lower order consumer goods. Equally, when real interest rates rise and the economy contracts, the capital goods industries tend to shrink more rapidly than the consumer goods industries. We can see this phenomenon using the Aggregate Production Structure (APS) of an economy, shown in Figure 2 below. APS measures the annual gross output of all stages of production, from natural resources to final consumer goods. The vertical axis measures the time it takes for goods and services to be produced, from the earliest raw commodity stage to the final consumer stage, while the horizontal axis measures the gross output or revenue of each stage of production.

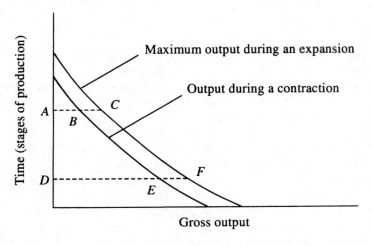

Figure 2

The APS illustrated in Figure 2 demonstrates what happens to the economy during the business cycle. Throughout the cycle, the early stages (capital goods industries) tend to expand and contract on a magnitude much greater than that experienced by the later stages (consumer goods industries). Note that *BC/AC* is substantially smaller than *EF/DF*. Historical studies confirm that output, prices, employment and inventories in capital goods industries tend to be more volatile than those in consumer goods industries (Skousen, 1990).

This Austrian insight can be applied to the securities market. The IPM explains why the stock prices of mining, manufacturing and other early-stage companies tend to be more volatile than those of retail and other consumer-oriented firms. Prices of mining stocks usually fluctuate more than those of utilities or grocery store companies. Even within industries, the stage of processing to which a publicly traded company belongs matters a great deal. Prices of junior oil stocks, which engage in early-stage exploration and development, tend to fluctuate more than those of major oil companies that sell fuel at the pump.

The IPM can also explain apparent exceptions to this phenomenon. For example, car and residential housing stocks are considered retail stocks, yet they are cyclical in nature. This is because cars and housing are durable goods that take years to be used up. Therefore car and housing stocks are just as sensitive to changes in interest rates as are mining and natural resource stocks. According to IPM, stock volatility is a function of the total period of production *and* consumption (Skousen, 1990).

Can investors beat the market?

The second principal debate in finance is whether individuals are smart enough to outperform the stock market averages consistently. Proponents of the efficient market theory (EMT) assert that it is next to impossible to beat the market over the long term. According to the strong version of EMT, the stock market is so efficient that all new information is quickly discounted in the financial markets: no one can outperform the market except by occasional luck. Proponents point to numerous studies indicating that most professional money managers, stockbrokers and investment advisers are unable to beat the averages or to perform better than a randomly selected portfolio of stocks. Nor can security analysts accurately predict earnings by major corporations over a one-year or five-year period (Malkiel, 1990). Since bull and bear markets are unforecastable, the EMT proponents recommend buying a large portfolio of stocks (or a stock index fund) and holding for the long term. Trading is considered counterproductive, not only because of transaction costs and taxes, but because it cannot improve upon the averages.

Proponents of EMT raise serious doubts about the possibility of either a 'high return/low risk' or a 'low return/high risk' investment. Figure 3 demonstrates the possibilities.

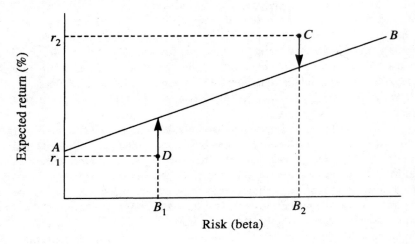

Figure 3

Line *AB* represents the average risk–reward ratio of various investments. As return increases, so does the risk. Point *C* represents an undervalued situation; that is, a higher return compared to other investments with similar risk (high return/low risk). According to the EMT, this condition cannot last because investors will recognize the advantage of this investment and rush out to buy it, thus driving up the price. The risk stays the same, but the higher price reduces the return for new buyers, thus bringing the risk–reward ratio into line with other investments. The same principle applies to point *D*, an overvalued investment (low return/high risk). Investors, recognizing the situation, will sell the investment. The risk remains the same, but the lower price makes the asset more appealing, and the return higher, thus bringing the risk–reward ratio into line with other investments.

Once again, the Austrians take a middle ground between those who say that the market is always and everywhere efficient, and those who say that the market is always in a state of irrational disequilibrium. The market is neither perfect nor broken. The truth lies somewhere in between (Garrison, 1984). While containing much truth, the EMT does not tell the whole story. In some ways, the strong version of EMT is the perfect competition model of the financial markets (Skousen, 1991). The primary objection to EMT is that it assumes that the entrepreneur *qua* arbitrager always moves the markets rapidly and immediately towards equilibrium. It denies that the entrepreneur can create new disequilibrium conditions, or that disequilibrium conditions last long enough for investors to make consistent above-average returns. According to Austrians, the entrepreneur is the central figure in the economic system. The investor *qua* entrepreneur has the uncanny ability to see things that other analysts do not see, to find temporarily undervalued stocks and to get out of overvalued investments. The fact that many money managers have been able to outwit other market participants for decades (Arnold Bernhard and his Value Line Investment Survey, John Templeton and his Templeton Funds, Peter Lynch and his Magellen Fund, Warren Buffett and his Berkshire Hathaway Partnership, as well as many commodity traders) is proof that superior speculators do exist.

In the above illustration, Austrians would ask: *Who* are the first investors to discover point *C* (undervalued) and buy, and point *D* (overvalued) and sell? These alert entrepreneurs are able to profit by acting before everyone else. MPT fails to explain how undervalued (high return/low risk) and overvalued (low return/high risk) situations arise in the first place. Clearly a more complete theory of finance must explain how above-average profitable opportunities arise and not simply how they disappear.

Austrian economics may offer a more dynamic theory of investment markets. Schumpeter emphasizes how entrepreneurs upset the supply or demand factors and create an above-average investment opportunity as the market shifts *away* from equilibrium conditions (Schumpeter, 1950). Kirzner suggests that alert entrepreneurs discover an above-average investment and, through competitive bidding, move *towards* equilibrium conditions (Kirzner, 1973). Oskar Morgenstern, an Austrian economist who later worked closely with John von Neumann and Clive Granger on the theory of games and finance, concludes that entrepreneurs are so successful in moving prices rapidly towards equilibrium that markets can be regarded as highly efficient. In fact, Morgenstern was a firm believer in the EMT and the random movement of stock prices (Granger and Morgenstern, 1970). While Morgenstern considered himself a follower of Menger and Böhm-Bawerk, his spectral analysis of stock prices clearly falls outside the Austrian middle ground.

EMT is of course not without merit. Clearly, everyone cannot beat the market because everyone *is* the market. For the same reason, it is impossible for everyone to get out at the top or get in at the bottom. Accurate forecasting by the vast majority of businessmen and investors is a priori self-contradictory. Suppose, for example, that everyone expects a crash. The result will be a crash *before* the time everyone expects it: 'The very fact that people are putting faith in the forecast of a crash results in the annulment of the prediction: it instantly produces the crash' (Mises, 1956). What is left out of the EMT equation is the role of a few investors who have the unique capacity to act in a way opposite to the rest of the public. While it is impossible for the vast majority of investors to outperform the market, to get out at the top, or get in at the bottom, a small minority of speculators can consistently outperform everyone else. These superior forecasters have a better understanding of market psychology and the way the economy really works, and therefore are able to stay ahead of all the others. But they tend to be loners (Neill, 1980). Of course, there are no guarantees that a top-performing money manager or adviser will stay ahead of the pack. Human nature is such that it is easy to fall from the top. Many shrewd money managers have discovered undervalued gems in one year, only to be disappointed in the next.

Is there an ideal investment portfolio?
MPT supporters maintain that broad diversification reduces risk and increases the overall return in an investment portfolio. The more diversified the portfolio, the less volatile the return will be and the better the chance of profiting from unexpected market advances. According to their research, it is better to buy stocks across several industries, not just within an industry; better to buy a stock index fund rather than a dozen stocks; better to buy a broad mix of stocks, bonds and money market funds than just stocks; and, finally, better to buy stock, bonds, real estate, gold and other liquid investments both here and abroad. According to MPT, an internationally diversified mixed asset portfolio is the ideal low-risk portfolio.

Once again, however, the MPT process of selecting an ideal portfolio relies on past performance rather than sound economic analysis to make its case. For instance, in the early 1980s, many professors of finance recommended that institutions add real estate to their portfolios because it had a long record of rising prices and showed very little volatility. As a result, institutions invested billions of dollars in commercial and residential property, only to see real estate prices fall sharply in value as the economy and government policies shifted in the 1980s.

The role of government
Does government have a legitimate role in protecting investors against bad investment decisions and potential fraud? What should the role of government be in regulating the securities industry? Federal and state securities regulations began in earnest in the 1930s and 1940s, following the 1929 stock market crash. Supporters of regulation alleged that securities fraud and manipulations by syndicates and pools were widespread during the 'roaring twenties'. A series of laws were passed by Congress requiring the registration of publicly traded companies, the licensing of brokers and investment advisers, the imposition of criminal and civil penalties on a variety of 'fraudulent' securities activities and the establishment of the Securities and Exchange Commission (SEC). States also passed 'blue sky' laws requiring similar

measures at a state level. Later the Commodities Futures Trading Commission (CFTC) was created to regulate futures markets.

However, it is important to point out that the New York Stock Exchange and major brokerage houses had already begun to take measures prior to the Security Act of 1933 to eliminate fraud and stock manipulation. Milton Friedman and other free-market advocates have long emphasized the importance of private industry in providing methods of monitoring and controlling ethical standards in industry and commerce (Friedman, 1962). There is no reason why stringent ethical standards cannot be established by stock exchanges, brokerage houses, the National Association of Securities Dealers and publicly traded corporations. Furthermore, the financial media play an important role in educating the investment public and exposing fraud, abuse, insider trading and other inappropriate activities.

Even when government rules and regulations are deemed necessary in the financial industry, the high costs of regulation, both apparent and hidden, should be considered. For example, federal and state registration expenses are so high that many small growth companies find it prohibitive to take their companies public in the USA. State regulators impose burdensome regulations and sometimes limit the types of investments available to individual investors. The existence of the SEC and state regulatory agencies also creates a false sense of security, giving the impression that brokers, investment advisers and mutual funds are less likely to defraud investors or lead them astray (Skousen, 1992a).

Summary
According to the Austrian school, the financial markets reflect the actions and emotions of individual investors and institutional managers. As such, the stock market represents their assessment of the future. Austrians believe that the securities markets will perform best when enlightened individuals are given the freedom to make their own investment decisions. Bureaucratic restrictions, burdensome regulations and high tax rates will tend to stifle the financial markets.

Stock prices, like all prices in the market economy, are determined by human decision making, and are therefore never random. Austrians rely primarily on fundamental analysis, including political and economic factors, to determine future prices of investments, and use technical analysis only to the extent that it represents the psychology of investors. However, because investors can change their mind and are constantly acquiring new information, it is difficult to predict the future of stock prices. Austrians emphasize the unique ability of the entrepreneur in forecasting and profiting in the competitive market-place and are critical of academic theories that ignore the role of risk-taking entrepreneurs in the investment markets and their ability to predict the future and earn above-average returns.

See also:
Chapter 61: Financial regulation; Chapter 25: Prices and knowledge

Bibliography
Bernstein, Peter L. (1992), *Capital Ideas: The Improbable Origins of Modern Wall Street*, New York: Free Press.
Browne, Harry (1987), *Why the Best-Laid Investment Plans Usually Go Wrong*, New York: William Morrow.
Friedman, Milton (1962), *Capitalism and Freedom*, Chicago: University of Chicago Press.
Garrison, Roger W. (1984), 'Time and Money: The Universals of Macroeconomic Thinking', *Journal of Macroeconomics*, spring.
Granger, Clive W.J. and Oskar Morgenstern (1970), *Predictability of Stock Market Prices*, Lexington, Mass.: Heath Lexington.
Hayek, Friedrich A. (1942), 'Scientism and the study of society', *Economica*, **IX**, 35, August.
Kirzner, Israel M. (1973), *Competition and Entrepreneurship*, Chicago: University of Chicago Press.
Malkiel, Burton G. [1973] (1990), *A Random Walk Down Wall Street*, 5th edn, New York: W.W. Norton.
Minsky, Hyman P. (1986), *Stabilizing an Unstable Economy*, New Haven: Yale University Press.
Mises, Ludwig von (1956), 'The Plight of Business Forecasting', *National Review*, 4 April.
Mises, Ludwig von [1949] (1966), *Human Action*, 3rd edn, Chicago: Regnery.
Neill, Humphrey B. [1954] (1980), *The Art of Contrary Thinking*, 4th edn, Caldwell, Idaho: Caxton Printers.
Rothbard, Murray N. (1980), 'Foreword', in James B. Ramsey, *Economic Forecasting – Models or Markets?*, San Francisco: Cato Institute.
Rothbard, Murray N. [1963] (1983), *America's Great Depression*, 4th edn, New York: Richardson and Snyder.
Schumpeter, Joseph A. [1942] (1950), *Capitalism, Socialism and Democracy*, 3rd edn, New York: Harper & Row.
Skousen, Mark (1988), 'Murray Rothbard as Investment Advisor', in Walter Block and Llewellyn H. Rockwell, Jr. (eds), *Man, Economy, and Liberty: Essays in Honor of Murray N. Rothbard*, Auburn, Ala.: The Ludwig von Mises Institute, pp. 151–74.
Skousen, Mark (1990), *The Structure of Production*, New York: New York University Press.
Skousen, Mark (1991), 'The Economist as Investment Advisor', *Economics on Trial*, Homewood, IL: Business One Irwin, pp. 255–73.
Skousen, Mark (1992a), *The Investor's Bible: Mark Skousen's Principles of Investment*, Potomac, Maryland: Phillips Publishing.
Skousen, Mark (1992b), 'Keynes as a Speculator: A Critique of Keynesian Investment Theory', in Mark Skousen (ed.), *Dissent on Keynes*, New York: Praeger, pp. 161–9.
Skousen, Mark (1993), 'Who Predicted the 1929 Crash?', in Jeffrey M. Herbener (ed.), *The Meaning of Ludwig von Mises*, Auburn, Ala.: The Ludwig von Mises Institute, pp. 247–83.

35 Industrial organization

Jerome Ellig

Industrial organization sports a curious mélange of theory and empirical work, and the Austrian contribution to the field is no exception. Discussing the Austrian contribution is made more difficult by the fact that prominent scholars not normally identified with the Austrian school have developed and applied important Austrian insights. Relevant authors include a number of familiar figures, such as Dominick Armentano, Friedrich Hayek, Israel Kirzner, Ludwig von Mises, Murray Rothbard and Joseph Schumpeter, but a list of contributors to 'Austrian' industrial organization would be seriously incomplete without a second group of names, many of which are associated with the Chicago school. They include, among others, Robert Bork, Harold Demsetz and Frank Knight.

As in many other fields, the Austrian perspective on industrial organization hinges on the concept of uncertainty. Uncertainty, in this context, is 'Knightian' uncertainty: a situation in which not all possible future states of the world can be identified, and not all can be assigned probabilities (Knight, 1971). Uncertainty makes a perfectly competitive equilibrium unattainable, because a fundamental assumption of general competitive analysis is that traders possess all the relevant information they need about opportunities, constraints, technologies and so on. The basic question for industrial organization is thus why various business institutions arise in response to uncertainty.

In addition, most Austrians would endorse the stronger statement that uncertainty makes the perfectly competitive model irrelevant as a welfare ideal. The genuine economic challenge, in this view, is not the optimal allocation of known means to achieve given ends, but the discovery and commercialization of new technologies and products (Hayek, 1978). In terminology popularized by Bork (1978), Austrian industrial organization emphasizes productive efficiency, almost to the exclusion of allocative efficiency (High, 1984–5).

Competition and entrepreneurship

Because products, technologies, equilibrium prices and other data are not given and known, real-world markets can best be characterized as a rough-and-tumble competition to find all of these things out. Prices convey a great deal of information, but because observed prices are not general equilibrium prices, other forms of communication and organization are also necessary to promote efficiency. Thus, for Austrians, 'the market' does not mean the perfectly competitive model composed of atomistic, arms'-length exchanges. Instead, it comprises a complex web of interactions that includes relationships ranging from spot market transactions to integrated firms. The market includes both competition and cooperation; hence the firm is part of the market, not an 'island of planning in a sea of markets' (compare Cheung, 1983).

Like economic theorists before the 1920s, Austrians view competition as a rivalrous process in which entrepreneurs strive to outperform each other (DiLorenzo and High, 1988). It is essentially a race with many finish lines. The really crucial form of competition is not the addition of another producer offering the same product to drive price closer to marginal cost, but rather the producer who enters the market with an entirely lower set of cost curves, or a brand new demand curve. In short, the Austrian view of competition bears a close resemblance to the innovative competition in the evolutionary models of Nelson and Winter (1982). Schumpeter (1942, p. 84) stated the distinction most eloquently:

> In capitalist reality as distinguished from the textbook picture, it is not that kind of competition which counts [competition producing known products within known constraints] but the competition from the new commodity, the new technology, the new source of supply, the new type of organization ... competition which commands a decisive cost or quality advantage and which strikes not at the margins of the profits and the outputs of existing firms but at their foundations and their very lives.

Within this swirl of creative destruction, the entrepreneurs who most effectively exercise the qualities of alertness and judgment reap profits. Kirzner (1973, 1985) argues that pure entrepreneurship is costless, but the prospect of profit nevertheless 'switches on' entrepreneurial alertness. (The carrying out of entrepreneurial plans, of course, involves resource costs.) In his view, therefore, entrepreneurial profit is truly a residual. However, it is not merely the amount of profit that motivates entrepreneurs, but also the 'open-endedness' of the situation, the prospect of inestimable profit opportunities. As a result, it is impossible to ascertain the amount of return that is adequate to elicit a given level of entrepreneurial activity. Therefore not even persistently high profits can be taken as a sign of monopoly.

Barriers to entry
The above proposition holds even in the presence of barriers to entry. Neoclassical economics defines barriers to entry as sunk costs – investments that cannot be recovered if the firm leaves the industry. But if heterogeneity and continuous improvement are the hallmarks of competition, then truly effec-

tive competition actually creates barriers to entry (see Demsetz, 1982; High and Gable, 1992). An entrepreneur who tries a new path, introduces a new technology or offers a new product shoulders substantial sunk costs: if the entrepreneur's judgement proves wrong and he must abandon his project, he incurs a capital loss. The more difficult to imitate is the innovation, the less elastic is the entrepreneur's demand curve; hence, entrepreneurial competition conveys monopoly power, in the traditional neoclassical sense of ability to influence price. Nevertheless, the resulting 'monopoly profits' are not a sign of inefficiency, but a prize that induced the innovation in the first place.

In their informal stories of competition, economics textbooks generally recognize a role for short-run entrepreneurial profits. In similar fashion, Austrian authors frequently speak as if entrepreneurial profits are always short-lived. However, nothing in the logic of the Austrian approach precludes long-lived entrepreneurial profits, depending on the nature of the specific entrepreneurial activity. For example, consider the case in which a profitable natural monopoly arises on the free market, perhaps as the result of very large economies of scale combined with sunk costs. A consistent Austrian account would have to recognize the monopoly's profits as entrepreneurial profits. In the case of a natural monopoly, these profits may be large and quite long-lasting. They provide a significant incentive for entrepreneurs to discover low-cost technologies, implement them quickly and invent new technologies to circumvent the old natural monopolies.

This process of entry barrier creation may appear to jeopardize economic efficiency and, in fact, dynamic competition may often sacrifice short-run allocative efficiency. However, in the Austrian view, competition does not create its principal benefits by beating prices down to marginal costs. Rather, competition for profits forces down costs, and prices eventually follow. Competition for profits also generates value for consumers by spurring entrepreneurs to create new products and services.

Firm conduct
This realization helps explain the Austrian tolerance for a wide variety of seemingly monopolistic practices. Austrians would essentially endorse the Chicago school analysis of vertical business relationships; vertical restraints and vertical integration both serve as powerful tools to promote productive efficiency. Likewise, Austrians would draw similar conclusions in their analysis of market concentration; for Austrians, as for Chicago economists, large market shares and high concentration are the endogenous results of efficiency-enhancing entrepreneurship, not exogenous conditions that signify inefficiency. (Compare Bork, 1978; Armentano, 1982.)

What is monopoly?
When it comes to identifying monopoly, two distinct Austrian approaches are apparent. In general, Austrians look for monopoly wherever there are barriers to exercising entrepreneurship. Government restrictions on entry, and on market activity generally, certainly qualify under this definition. Whether a firm can gain monopoly purely through private market activity is a matter of some debate.

Kirzner (1973) and Mises (1966, pp. 357–79) argue that monopolies may occasionally arise in the free market if someone owns the entire supply of a resource essential for producing a product. A person who owned all of the orange trees (and orange seeds!) in the world would thus be a monopolist, because he controls an essential resource for making orange juice. This person is in a position to block other entrepreneurs who may have better technologies for producing or marketing orange juice, because there exists only one source of oranges.

Others, such as Armentano (1982), O'Driscoll and Rizzo (1985), Rothbard (1977) and High (1985), would question whether even this rare example really constitutes a monopoly. In their view, an economically meaningful concept of monopoly cannot be defined without reference to legal and ethical principles. As a result, O'Driscoll and Rizzo propose that the term 'monopoly' be restricted to situations in which a producer has a government-enforced property right to a market or market share. For this group of scholars, the general implication should be clear: only government can be the source of monopoly power.

Whither efficiency?
It would be a mistake to regard this attitude towards antitrust and regulatory policy as ideology overtaking analysis. Rather, the policy differences between Austrians and other economists reflect fundamentally different beliefs about the nature and importance of the two different types of economic efficiency. Austrian economists often subscribe to the empirical generalization that the most significant increases in human welfare occur because of productive efficiency: the introduction of new products and techniques. The 'structure–conduct–performance' school of industrial organization tends to emphasize the importance of allocative efficiency, which is derived from the perfectly competitive norm and requires that prices equal marginal costs. In this schema, the Chicago school occupies a middle ground, for Chicago scholars sometimes stress allocative efficiency, sometimes productive efficiency. As a result, Austrians find much to agree with in the Chicago school, but also much to criticize.

See also:
Chapter 26: The boundaries of the firm; Chapter 55: Industrial organization and the Austrian school; Chapter 57: Mergers and the market for corporate control

Bibliography
Armentano, Dominick (1982), *Antitrust and Monopoly: Anatomy of a Policy Failure*, New York: John Wiley.
Bork, Robert H. (1978), *The Antitrust Paradox*, New York: Basic Books.
Cheung, Steven N.S. (1983), 'The Contractual Nature of the Firm', *Journal of Law and Economics*, **26**, (1), April, 1–21.
Demsetz, Harold (1982), 'Barriers to Entry', *American Economic Review*, **72**, (1), March, 47–57.
DiLorenzo, Thomas and Jack High (1988), 'Antitrust and Competition, Historically Considered', *Economic Inquiry*, **26**, July, 423–35.
Hayek, Friedrich A. (1948), 'The Meaning of Competition', reprinted in *Individualism and Economic Order*, Chicago: University of Chicago Press, pp. 33–56.
Hayek, Friedrich A. (1978), 'Competition as a Discovery Procedure', in *new Studies in Philosophy, Politics, Economics, and the History of Ideas*, Chicago: University of Chicago Press.
High, Jack (1984–5), 'Bork's Paradox: Static vs. Dynamic Efficiency in Antitrust Analysis', *Contemporary Policy Issues*, **3**, 21–34.
High, Jack and Wayne Gable (eds) (1992), *100 Years of the Sherman Act: A Century of American Economic Opinion*, Fairfax, VA: George Mason University Press.
Kirzner, Israel (1973), *Competition and Entrepreneurship*, Chicago: University of Chicago Press.
Kirzner, Israel (1985), *Discovery and the Capitalist Process*, Chicago: University of Chicago Press.
Knight, Frank (1971), *Risk, Uncertainty, and Profit*, Chicago: University of Chicago Press.
Mises, Ludwig von (1966), *Human Action*, 3rd revised edn, Chicago: Contemporary Books.
Nelson, Richard and Sidney Winter (1982), *An Evolutionary Theory of Economic Change*, Cambridge, Mass.: Harvard University Press.
O'Driscoll, Gerald P. Jr. and Mario Rizzo (1985), *The Economics of Time and Ignorance*, Oxford: Basil Blackwell.
Rothbard, Murray (1977), *Power and Market*, Mission, Kansas: Sheed Andrews & McMeel.
Schumpeter, Joseph (1942), *Capitalism, Socialism, and Democracy*, New York: Harper.

36 International monetary theory

Joseph T. Salerno

Austrian analysis of the balance of payments and the exchange rate originated in Ludwig von Mises's *Theory of Money and Credit*, first published in German in 1912 (Mises, 1981, pp. 195–213). In formulating his theories, Mises built on the analysis of the monetary adjustment process under a specie standard pioneered by eighteenth-century writers, most notably David Hume and Richard Cantillon, and on the extensions of their analysis to the case of an inconvertible paper money undertaken by the British bullionists of the early nineteenth century, especially David Ricardo. Important elaborations and applications of Mises's theoretical framework were subsequently undertaken by Mises (1978, pp. 1–55) himself, writing during the German hyperinflation, and, later, by his student F.A. Hayek (1971) and other economists associated with the London School of Economics during the 1930s, notably Lionel Robbins (1937, 1971) and Frank Paish (1950, 1966).

Among Continental economists, the Polish-born Michael A. Heilperin, Mises's colleague at the Geneva Institute of International Studies in the 1930s, is especially noteworthy for following a basically Austrian approach in his writings on a broad range of international monetary issues (Salerno, 1992; Heilperin, 1968; Heilperin, 1978). In German-language publications of the 1920s and 1930s later translated into English, Misesian monetary theorists such as the early Fritz Machlup (1964a, 1964b), the early Gottfried Haberler (1985) and Wilhelm Röpke (1969) developed the implications of the Austrian approach for the solution of the so-called 'transfer problem' of unilateral payments and capital movements. More recently, Murray N. Rothbard (1975, 1990, 1994) has criticized the case for fluctuating exchange rates and analysed twentieth-century international monetary experience, particularly the workings of the gold exchange standard, from an Austrian perspective; and Joseph T. Salerno (1982, 1984) has restated the Austrian analysis in the light of the modern monetary approach and applied it to re-evaluating the performance of the classical gold standard.

Austrian analysis of the balance of payments begins with the insight that disequilibria in payments balances between exchanging parties can never arise in a system of barter and therefore that money in its role as the general medium of exchange is the active element determining the balance of payments and not merely an item moving to and fro in passive response to discrepancies that arise in the trade of commodities, services and assets

(Mises, 1981, p. 208; Salerno, 1982, p. 248). Balance of payments phenomena are thus treated, as they were by Cantillon, Hume and the bullionists, as an integral part of the market process by which the purchasing power of money and its distribution among regions and nations sharing a common currency are adjusted to variations in the relationship between the demand for and supply of money. For example, under an international gold standard, an increase in the supply of money in a gold-mining nation that disrupts a pre-existing monetary equilibrium by furnishing some residents with excess cash balances leads to excess demands in goods and asset markets, and this results – sooner or later, depending on the concrete data of the case – in a net outflow of money through the nation's current and capital accounts and, hence, a deficit in its 'money account' or overall balance of payments. When residents have succeeded in ridding themselves of their excess cash, equilibrium is restored in the domestic 'money market' and subsequently in the balance of payments as the net outflow of money ceases.

In thus analysing the balance of payments as a phase in the monetary adjustment process, the Austrian theory focuses closely on the actions of individual money holders linked to one another in a sequence of monetary exchanges. The steps in this sequential adjustment process are then accounted for by examining the causes and effects of the decisions to equilibrate their cash balance positions undertaken by individuals who occupy different links in the microeconomic income and spending chains that reach back to the originating cause of the monetary disequilibrium. As Hayek (1971, pp. 19–24) and Salerno (1982, pp. 490–91) in particular have shown, it is therefore the interrelated variations in the complex of individual cash balances, incomes and prices – and not brute up-and-down movements in national money supplies, nominal GDPs and price levels – that drive this equilibrating process.

One of the more significant implications of this analysis is that balance of payments adjustment under a common international money such as gold does not require or promote monetary inflation and deflation, as is commonly asserted in the textbook characterization of the 'price-specie-flow mechanism' (Robbins, 1937, pp. 280–90; Salerno, 1982, pp. 491–2). Under the international gold standard, the transfer of money from one nation to the rest of the world as a result of, say, a decline in world demand for the former's exports, will be quickly reversed, unless, as is likely to happen, it is accompanied by a relative decrease in the demand for cash balances on the part of workers and entrepreneurs experiencing falling real incomes in the contracting export industry. In the latter case, the reduction in the nation's money supply does not represent a 'deflation', properly defined as a reduction in the money supply of a closed system or 'currency area', but merely the same type of redistribution of cash balances between individuals, industries and regions that regularly occurs when demand shifts from the product of one domestic industry to that of another within, for example, the present-day US fiat dollar area.

According to Austrian theory, the monetary and balance of payments equilibrium that the market is continually driving towards can be described as one in which the purchasing power of money (the 'PPM' for short) is everywhere absolutely equal. Interspatial equalization of the PPM is not taken to mean, however, that national price indexes ever tend towards equality. Indeed, Austrians deliberately eschew the use of such statistical constructs when theorizing about changes in the PPM, restricting their use only to obtaining rough historical estimates of PPM variations (Mises, 1971, pp. 187–94; Heilperin, 1978, pp. 259–69). For Austrian theorists geographical equalization of the value of money refers to an equilibration of the unaveraged and heterogeneous array of alternative quantities of goods which are exchangeable for a unit of money.

Thus conceived, equilibration of money's purchasing power array cannot be expected to yield equality between the prices of physically identical goods available in different locations, let alone between the arbitrarily selected and weighted price indexes of different nations or regions. The reason is to be found in Mises's subjectivist insight that the situation of a good in space may affect its perceived usefulness and thus its subjective value in satisfying human wants (Mises, 1981, pp. 195–203). A good available at its place of production, for example, coffee in Brazil, is evaluated by coffee drinkers in New York City as a capital good which must be combined with additional labor and complementary capital goods, that is, the means of transportation, before it can attain the (higher) subjective value of the consumption good, coffee in New York. Indeed, an important respect in which the money commodity differs from non-monetary commodities is that, in the case of the former, the routine acceptance of items which substitute for it in exchange ('money substitutes') and which are virtually costless to transfer physically, such as checkable deposits and bank notes, in conjunction with the existence of clearing systems, renders money's position in space a matter of indifference to economic agents. Thus stocks of money, wherever they may be situated within the unitary market area, for all practical purposes, constitute parts of a supply of a perfectly fungible commodity, subject to the operation of the Jevonian Law of Indifference, also known as the Law of One Price.

But the Austrian insight regarding the influence of the spatial element on the quality of (non-monetary) goods does not merely embrace the pure distance between the location of the consumer and the location of the good, but also the consumer's positive or negative psychic response to the very site of purchase or consumption. For example, even in equilibrium, the same brand of men's shirt may simultaneously sell for different prices at a mall boutique and at a downtown clothing store, because, at the margin, consumers are prepared to offer a higher price for the shirt purchasable at the mall location, which is perceived to be more easily accessible and more pleasant. Or consider that a glass of beer consumed in a restaurant situated on top of a skyscraper in New York City, which offers a breathtaking view of Manhattan and its environs, commands a much higher price than a glass of the same beer imbibed in a street-level pub located a few blocks away. Surely, we do not expect would-be bar patrons at the former establishment to react to knowledge of such a price discrepancy by a mad scramble to the elevators, precisely because such a discrepancy does not represent a genuine interlocal disequilibrium in the PPM. Taking into account their spatial quality components, the two glasses of beer represent different goods. This is not to deny, of course, that, whenever consumers are neutral with respect to alternative locations of stocks of a technologically identical good ready for consumption or purchase, the spatial equilibration of the PPM implies the complete eradication of interlocal price differences.

Thus, from the Austrian point of view, the equilibration of the PPM is accomplished as part of the same microeconomic process that gives rise to the structure of relative prices. As Phillip H. Wicksteed (1967, vol. 1, pp. 140–45) has shown us, this process culminates in a state in which, barring further change in the data, mutual gains from further exchange between any two market participants are impossible, because the ordinal value rankings of equal-sized units of each of the various goods and of money are identical for all those possessing them. This state also reflects the *absolute* equalization of the objective exchange value of money between any two locations, because it implies that interlocal differences between prices of physically homogeneous goods exactly equal their costs of transportation (abstracting from time in transit) between their consumption and production centers and, more generally, that no individual can achieve a more desirable outcome, that is, an increase in total utility, from the exchange process by diminishing his expenditures on consumer goods available at one location and substituting expenditures on goods, whether physically homogeneous or not, offered at alternative locations.

The reference to Wicksteed suggests why Austrian balance of payments theorists, like their bullionist forerunners, consider monetary equilibrium to be relatively rapidly established. Wicksteed (1967, vol. 1, pp. 219–28) begins his analysis by assuming that consumer value scales and the stocks of all goods (including money) remain constant over the course of a logically stipulated 'market day' that dawns in disequilibrium and terminates in a pure exchange equilibrium. This procedure permits him to analyse the short-run arbitrage and speculative processes that lead to the equilibrium structure of relative prices (the inverse of the equilibrium PPM array) in isolation from the complex phenomena of entrepreneurship and production. It also serves to emphasize the point that the geographical equalization of the PPM is a pure exchange phenomenon which is constantly being approximated by real-world market processes and does not await the time-consuming adjustment of the production structure that characterizes the long-run equilibration of the overall economy. Austrians are thus inclined to speak of 'the' purchasing power of money with only slightly less confidence than they and other economists refer to 'the' market prices of oil, steel, wheat and other broadly traded commodities.

Austrian analysis of the determination of the exchange rate between two independent moneys is based on the purchasing power parity (PPP) theory as it was first formulated by Mises in 1912 (Mises, 1981, pp. 205–13; Wu, 1939, pp. 115–16, 233–5), four years before Gustav Cassel published the first of his many statements of it. In Mises's version of the theory – which, unlike Cassel's later version, is 'absolute' and exclusively monetary – the long-run equilibrium or 'final' exchange rate between two currencies is always exactly equal to the inverse of the ratio between the purchasing powers of the two currencies. This implies that a given depreciation of the overall purchasing power of currency A relative to that of currency B brings about an increase of the final price of B in terms of A in precisely the same proportion, regardless of the inevitable changes in relative prices that are produced by the non-neutral depreciation process.

The marked differences between the Misesian and Casselian versions of the PPP theory can be traced back to Mises's analytical coup in perceiving the artificiality of the distinction long maintained in classical monetary theory between the case of a parallel standard, that is, two different moneys circulating side by side in domestic use, and the case in which there is only one kind of money employed in domestic transactions while another kind is in use abroad (Mises, 1981, pp. 206–7; Robbins, 1971, pp. 22). According to Mises, as long as exchange relations exist between two different currency areas, economically, the money of one area necessarily functions as the money of the other area, since both moneys must be utilized in effecting an exchange between the two areas.

Most importantly, in the Misesian version, the exchange rate between two different national currencies is no longer determined, as it was for Cassel, by the 'quotient between the general levels of prices in the two countries'. National price indexes, which generally include purely domestic goods, for example the 'houses and haircuts' of textbook fame, whose spatial quality components render their prices interlocally and, a fortiori, internationally incommensurable, are wholly irrelevant to the issue, because there is no longer a reason to distinguish between internationally 'tradeable' goods and domestically produced and consumed 'non-tradeable' goods. As in the case of domestically coexisting parallel currencies, all goods entering into the exchange nexus, including each and every spatially differentiated good, find expression in the purchasing power array of each of the two national currencies, because all goods are potential objects of international trade, even though many may be 'immovable' or 'non-transportable'. Certainly, one of the lessons learned from the exchange rate gyrations of the 1980s was that American real estate and consumer services, when rendered sufficiently cheap by a depreciated dollar, are purchasable by foreign speculators and tourists.

The apparent problem presented to the PPP theory by the existence of goods whose position in space is fixed is thus easily soluble when the spatial dimension of quality is taken into account. For example, if the final or PPP exchange rate between the US dollar and the British pound is two to one, then the pound price of a house located in London must be exactly one-half the dollar price of this same house. Of course, owing to consumer perceptions of the difference in quality between the two cities as residential locations, the final price in dollars (pounds) of an identically constructed house situated in Manhattan may be triple that of the London house also expressed in dollars (pounds). To maintain purchasing power parity, therefore, it is not necessary that technologically identical but immovable goods available in *different* locations maintain equal prices in the same currency, but only that the ratio of the prices in two different currencies of an immovable good in the *same* location equals the inverse of the exchange rate between these two currencies. If the ratio of currency prices for any given commodity diverges from the prevailing exchange rate, equilibrium has not yet been attained and profit opportunities will exist for selling the good for the relatively overvalued currency, employing the sale receipts to purchase the undervalued currency, and then using the latter to repurchase the original good. These arbitrage operations will drive the exchange rate and the ratio of currency purchasing powers towards a mutual and final adjustment (Rothbard, 1990, p. 42).

For the Austrian, then, the problems arising from 'fixed' or 'pegged' exchange rates between national fiat currencies are the same as the problems confronting a domestic bimetallic standard. Gresham's Law, which, as Mises (1981, pp. 90–93, 282–6) first recognized, is merely the application of the general theory of price controls to the monetary sphere, operates to cause a chronic shortage on foreign exchange markets or disappearance from domestic monetary circulation of the artificially undervalued national currency or metal.

Another feature which significantly distinguishes Mises's formulation of the PPP theory from Cassel's involves the question of whether the exchange rate is exclusively a monetary phenomenon or whether changes in the real data via movements in relative prices are capable of bringing about a permanent departure of the equilibrium exchange rate from the rate which maintains strict PPP between the two currencies. Like Cassel, especially in his later writings, most modern writers pursue what might be termed an 'inclusive' approach to exchange rate determination, that is, one which includes references to non-monetary factors as codeterminants of the exchange rate. They therefore reject the absolute version of the PPP theory, because it is incapable of accounting for the influence on the equilibrium exchange rate of variations in the nation's 'real terms of trade', that is the relative price between its imports and exports, or in the internal relative price between its exports and non-tradeable goods.

Whatever the validity of this criticism against the PPP theory expressed in terms of relative national price levels, it has no bearing whatever on a theory referring to the relative purchasing powers of parallel currencies coexisting in a unitary market area. The Misesian version of the PPP theory remains intact in its absolute and exclusively monetary formulation. To illustrate, let us consider the case of a monopolistically induced increase in the price of oil, the US import, relative to the US export, wheat. While the terms of trade turn against the USA, *ceteris paribus*, that is, in the (unlikely) absence of any induced changes in the monetary data, there will be no long-run depreciation of the US dollar against the Saudi riyal, because both currencies experience an equal reduction of their purchasing powers in terms of oil and, assuming the demand for oil is inelastic along the relevant segment of the global demand curve, equal increases of their purchasing powers in terms of wheat. Of course, this is not to deny that short-run and self-reversing fluctuations in the exchange rate may accompany the market's adjustment to the alteration in relative prices. Thus US consumers may initially respond to the increased price of oil with increased expenditures on oil without a corresponding reduction in their spending on wheat, allowing their cash balances to run down temporarily. This response implies a planned 'overabsorption' of output relative to their shrunken real income by US residents, creating an excess demand for riyals in the foreign exchange market and necessitating a temporary rise in the exchange rate and a depreciation of the dollar. The movement in the exchange rate will thus assist in clearing excess demands in output markets and adjusting the terms of trade to prevent overabsorption and preserve balance of payments equilibrium, but only until US residents' expenditures adjust, cash balances are re-established at their former equilibrium levels, and the exchange rate floats back down to its unchanged PPP level.

Moreover, other things are not likely to remain equal; in particular, we can expect a change in the relative demands for the two currencies which results from the redistribution of income and wealth from US entrepreneurs and laborers to their Saudi counterparts and leads to a long-run depreciation of the dollar. But it is the relative decline in the cash balance demand for the dollar and therefore in its purchasing power *vis-à-vis* the riyal, and not the deterioration of the US terms of trade, which is the direct cause of the change in the *final* exchange rate.

The foregoing analysis, of course, implies that Austrians conceive purchasing power parity between currencies as a condition which fully holds only in equilibrium and that real factors do play a role, albeit subordinate and transient, in the determination of the spot exchange rate that is actually realized at each moment on the foreign exchange markets. With regard to the spot exchange rate, Austrians, taking their cue from Mises (1981, pp. 243–6; 1978, pp. 27–8, 51), also emphasize its responsiveness to expectations of future variations in currency purchasing powers and in national money supplies. In recognizing that movements of the exchange rate generally anticipate adjustments forthcoming on the domestic money market, however, the Austrian approach must be distinguished from the rational expectations approach. While adherents of both approaches view the foreign exchange market as an asset market characterized by instantaneous market clearing and the participants' orientation to new information, Austrian theorists reject the 'efficient market hypothesis' as a realistic description of the operation of this market. Rather, they explain the behavior of the exchange rate as governed by the conflicting forecasts of ever-shifting aggregations of bears and bulls, who are differentiated from one another and from non-participants in this market by their varying individual experiences and market situations in conjunction with their innate and widely varying entrepreneurial abilities to interpret their experiences and informational discoveries in developing an understanding of future market conditions.

See also:
Chapter 81: Monetarism; Chapter 86: The new monetary economics; Chapter 75: Pre-Keynes macroeconomics; Chapter 59: Free banking

Bibliography

Haberler, Gottfried (1985), 'Transfer and Price Movements', in *Selected Essays of Gottfried Haberler*, ed. Anthony Y.C. Woo, Cambridge, Mass.: MIT Press, pp. 133–42.
Hayek, F.A. [1937] (1971), *Monetary Nationalism and International Stability*, New York: Augustus M. Kelley
Heilperin, Michael A. (1968), *Aspects of the Pathology of Money: Monetary Essays from Four Decades*, London: Michael Joseph.
Heilperin, Michael A. [1939] (1978), *International Monetary Economics*, Philadelphia: Porcupine Press.
Machlup, Fritz (1964a), 'Foreign Debts, Reparations, and the Transfer Problem', in *International Payments, Debts, and Gold: Collected Essays by Fritz Machlup*, New York: Charles Scribner's Sons, pp. 396–416.
Machlup, Fritz (1964b), 'Transfer and Price Effects', in *International Payments, Debts, and Gold: Collected Essays by Fritz Machlup*, New York: Charles Scribner's Sons, pp. 417–24.
Mises, Ludwig von (1978), *On the Manipulation of Money and Credit*, ed. Percy L. Greaves, Jr., translated by Bettina Bien Greaves, Dobbs Ferry, NY: Free Market Books.

Mises, Ludwig von [1953] (1981), *The Theory of Money and Credit*, 2nd edn, Indianapolis: Liberty Classics.

Paish, F.W. (1950), 'Causes of Changes in Gold Supply', in *The Post-War Financial Problem and Other Essays*, London: Macmillan, pp. 149–86.

Paish, F.W. [1936] (1966), 'Banking Policy and the Balance of International Payments', in Howard S. Ellis and Lloyd A. Metzler (eds), *Readings in the Theory of International Trade*, Homewood, IL: Richard D. Irwin, pp. 35–55.

Robbins, Lionel Charles (1937), *Economic Planning and International Order*, London: Macmillan.

Robbins, Lord (1971), *Money, Trade and International Relations*, London: Macmillan.

Röpke, Wilhelm [1930] (1969), 'On the Transfer Problem in International Capital Movements', in *Against the Tide*, translated by Elizabeth Henderson, Chicago: Henry Regnery, pp. 1–23.

Rothbard, Murray N. (1975), 'Gold Vs. Fluctuating Fiat Exchange Rates', in Hans F. Sennholz (ed.), *Gold Is Money*, Westport, Conn.: Greenwood Press, pp. 24–40.

Rothbard, Murray N. (1990), *What Has Government Done to Our Money?*, 4th edn, Auburn, Ala.: Praxeology Press.

Rothbard, Murray N. (1994), 'The Gold Exchange Standard in the Interwar Years', in Kevin Dowd and Richard Timberlake (eds), *Money and the Nation States*, Oakland, CA: Independent Institute.

Salerno, Joseph T. (1982), 'Ludwig von Mises and the Monetary Approach to the Balance of Payments: Comment on Yeager', in Israel M. Kirzner (ed.), *Method, Process, and Austrian Economics: Essays in Honor of Ludwig von Mises*, Lexington, Mass.: D.C. Heath, pp. 247–56.

Salerno, Joseph T. (1984), 'The International Gold Standard: A New Perspective', *Eastern Economic Journal*, **10**, October/December, 488–98.

Salerno, Joseph T. (1992), 'Gold and the International Monetary System: The Contribution of Michael A. Heilperin', in Llewellyn H. Rockwell, Jr. (ed.), *The Gold Standard: Perspectives in the Austrian School*, Auburn, Ala.: The Ludwig von Mises Institute, pp. 81–111.

Wicksteed, Phillip H. [1932] (1967), *The Common Sense of Political Economy and Selected papers and reviews on Economic Theory*, 2 vols, ed. Lionel Robbins, New York: Augustus M. Kelley.

Wu, Chi-Yuen (1939), *An Outline of International Price Theories*, London: George Routledge & Sons.

37 Labor economics
Don Bellante

Historical development

The Austrian tradition in labor economics dates back to the very origins of the Austrian school itself. While this tradition begins with Menger (1871), the full development of a theory of factor prices whose values are imputed from utility in consumption is traced to Friedrich von Wieser (1889). Conventional wisdom places the marginalism of Menger on an equal footing with that of Jevons and Walras. However, the Austrian recognition of the marginal utility of consumption as determining not only output prices but also factor prices distinguishes this approach from the non-Austrian developments of marginalism. This distinction is important, as this uniquely Austrian application of subjective value theory to factor markets has had a profound impact on modern labor economics. Profound as this influence may be, its historical lineage in the Austrian school is not often appreciated. Consequently, J.B. Clark's (1899) development of marginal productivity theory, with its more objectivist framework, is more often given credit for the provision of the foundations of modern labor economics. Clark's exposition, however, simply took the supply of labor as a given, thereby removing from consideration all subjective considerations from the supply of labor. Nonetheless, mainstream labor economics today contains significant elements of subjectivism in the analysis of labor supply. These elements include the very basic notion of labor supply as a consequence of a labor–leisure trade-off, and the more complex notion of subjective worker preferences in the determination of equalizing pay differences.

Despite the greater congeniality towards subjectivism in labor economics than in other branches of the neoclassical mainstream, Austrian economists have not in recent years contributed significantly to the enormous and highly specialized literature in labor economics. Several reasons can be speculatively offered. First, Austrian economics comes closer than the mainstream to being a unified social science seeking to explain human action on the basis of a small number of axioms. This axiomatic approach does not lend itself to fragmentation into specialized areas of inquiry – Austrian economists have not focused on narrow areas of specialization such as urban economics, public finance and so on. Working in the Misesian tradition, Austrian economists have focused their efforts on applications of methodological individualism that span particular markets and deal more with the interrelatedness of markets. By analogy, their analysis is focused more on the forest and less on the trees.

Second, and related to the first point, the Austrian tradition increasingly over time has developed a focus on the problem of market coordination, particularly intertemporal coordination. To the extent that there is specialization at all, it is in those areas where the causes and most severe consequences of intertemporal coordination failures are evident; these are in the areas of monetary economics, and capital and interest theory. The focus of the Austrian research program is more often on market processes than on the details of equilibrium states in particular markets – for example, the emphasis on entrepreneurship and the discovery process that characterizes the work of Israel Kirzner (1985). Despite these observations, one can find numerous analytical treatments of the workings of the labor market throughout the writings of twentieth-century contributors to the Austrian school. Analysis of the workings of the labor market figures most prominently in Austrian theory of the trade cycle, as in Hayek's *Prices and Production* (1935). In these earlier analyses, disruptions in the labor market are the residual consequences of the complementarity of labor and capital, and derive from the consequences of monetarily induced distortions in the structure of capital. Unemployment, for example, results from the necessity of restoring an appropriate capital structure following a period of malinvestment. But the problem of readjustment in labor markets is seen as less severe than in capital markets because capital, once in place, is far more specific and thus less adaptable to use in other production processes. It has been argued more recently (Bellante, 1983) that specialization and the division of labor have increasingly over time rendered labor skills nearly as specific as physical capital. Given the putty–clay nature of human capital, malinvestment is as possible in human resources as in physical capital. Thus the process of adjustment of the structure of production to a period of malinvestment involves a realignment of both the physical and human capital dimensions of that structure. Analytically, structural unemployment cannot be separated from cyclical unemployment, as it is in the usual neoclassical treatment.

Theoretical core
The core methodological elements of the Austrian approach are methodological individualism, subjective value theory and a focus on market processes. The application of Austrian method yields insights into the functioning of labor markets and an evaluative framework for public policy that go beyond the contributions of the neoclassical mainstream. The demand side of the labor market is derived from the demand for the outputs of the production process, which in turn is derived from the marginal utility of that output. This aspect of marginalist analysis has been well accepted and incorporated into

the standard neoclassical model of the labor market. The subjectivism of the Austrian school is particularly insightful in examining the more complex phenomena of the supply side of the labor market. The fact that value is subjectively determined is arguably of greater consequence in labor markets than in commodity markets, largely because workers cannot be separated from the work effort that they provide. Thus all aspects of the work environment in which labor is employed have an effect on the price of labor. A worker exchanges his labor for a wage rate, but perhaps also for a set of non-wage benefits, some of which are easily converted to a monetary equivalent (such as defined contributions to a pension plan) and some of which are not (such as a seniority system). There are a variety of other utility-affecting attributes that attach to the job as well. These include degree of injury risk, relative uncertainty of employment and earnings stability, and opportunities for training and promotion. The wage rate, fringe benefit and other attributes combine in an employment 'bundle' of characteristics that are not separable in any one job. Nonetheless, each of these characteristics in a genuine sense has an implicit market. Thus, within what is thought of as the supply side of the labor market, there is both a demand and a supply side for job characteristics. Employers choose the quantities of each characteristic to 'supply' in combination with the wage rate, subject to any relevant legal constraints. Presumably, these characteristics are subject to diminishing returns: desirable characteristics (such as paid sick leave) can be marginally increased, or undesirable characteristics (such as probabilities of physical injury) can be incrementally removed, but at an increasing marginal cost. These costs will likely vary substantially across industries, occupations and firms. An employer will be willing to incur the costs of expanding along any of these margins to the extent that their provision enables more than equivalent savings elsewhere, such as in the basic wage rate.

The demand for these job characteristics is derived from the subjective (and marginally diminishing) values placed upon them by individual workers. In a world of perfect information, perfect divisibility, zero transactions cost, static preferences and continuous general equilibrium, workers would face a market price for each characteristic and would simply choose the utility-maximizing combination of wage and job characteristics. These equilibrium prices would reflect the rates at which the utility of consumers would trade against the utility of workers on the margin at which all gains from trade have been exploited.

In the real world none of these conditions exists, and an entrepreneurial pursuit of pure profit is necessary in order to move the relevant markets in the direction of perfect coordination. The employer as entrepreneur coordinates the subjective and thereby heterogeneous values of workers with his own necessity of securing labor services. The return to successful efforts at discovering the relevant trade-offs is the savings in the costs of labor that can be realized. The entrepreneur's success in this process depends on (a) his ability to perceive and act upon the disequilibrium that exists both within and across the 'markets' for job characteristics that make up the labor market and that exists between the labor market and output markets, and (b) his ability to perceive, and perhaps even create, changes in underlying tastes and technologies. The disequilibria referred to across the markets for job characteristics consists of the discrepancies that exist between (a) the effects on the firm's non-wage production costs arising from a marginal change in any job characteristic, and (b) the effects of that marginal change on the wage costs that must be paid by the firm in order to obtain the desired mix of workers. Since workers are heterogeneous in preferences and circumstances, the package of pay and characteristics that each firm offers will tend to attract those workers for whom the package is most attractive. In this manner a sorting and matching process takes place between workers and firms, and this process is subject to continual change and readjustment. In the real world, incremental maximization of utility by workers is never literally possible, but the extent to which it can be approached depends on the degree of variability that exists in the combinations of job characteristics associated with the range of jobs available to the worker.

Policy applications
The Austrian's thoroughly subjectivist perspective on the labor market leads to a specific framework for the analysis of public policy. The Austrian perspective suggests that institutions, including governmental and legal institutions, should be evaluated in terms of whether the particular institution advances or retards the dual processes of economic coordination and discovery. Against this criterion, Bellante and Porter (1990) have examined a number of state interventions in US labor markets. These include: minimum wage legislation, unemployment insurance, workers' compensation, regulation of occupational safety, pension regulation and mandatory health insurance. In the case of occupational safety, for example, the best that can be accomplished, under ideal conditions, is the freezing into law of the best standard of safety technology that exists at the time of codification, assuming the impossible – that the centralized authority possesses the relevant information. But the incentive for entrepreneurial alertness to, and discovery and implementation of, new safety possibilities is greatly diminished, if not eliminated. Thus the provision of detailed codification of safety rules would be dynamically inefficient, even if they could be statically efficient. Whether any type of regulation of private labor markets can ever even be statically efficient (in terms of coordination) is seen as questionable, however, if it reduces the variety of job packages available to actors in the labor market.

Another example of the subjectivist critique is its application to comparable worth issue by Deborah Walker (1984). Proponents of comparable worth tend to argue that pay determination should be based on 'job analysis'. This method, while theoretically rationalized on the contention that job characteristics have intrinsic (objective) values, in practice substitutes what must be the at least partly subjective values of the job analyst for the subjective values that determine behavior in the actual labor market.

The Austrian perspective on collective bargaining is not easily generalized. Austrian economists, unlike the neoclassical mainstream, do not see monopoly as necessarily inefficient so long as the monopoly position is not established and maintained through governmental or other coercive power. In principle, Austrian economists would find freely established collective bargaining no more objectionable than product monopolies in a free market (Bellante, 1990). Throughout the industrialized world, however, trade unions have succeeded in obtaining legislation that lends to them in varying measures the ability to impose collective bargaining. Some Austrian economists, however, view a closed shop arrangement, even if it results from a non-coerced agreement between a firm and union, as a coercive imposition on individual employees (Shand, 1984).

This discussion has touched upon some of the insights that subjectivist method brings to the analysis of the processes at work in labor markets. Aside from simple product demand theory, there is probably no area of mainstream economics where subjective value theory has made greater inroads than in labor economics. Nonetheless, the area remains relatively unexploited by self-identified Austrian economists.

See also:
Chapter 52: Economics of gender and race; Chapter 53: The Phillips curve; Chapter 31: Capital theory; Chapter 18: Marginal productivity

Bibliography
Bellante, D. (1983), 'A Subjectivist Essay on Modern Labor Economics', *Managerial and Decision Economics*, **4**, (4), 234–43.
Bellante, D. (1990), 'Labor Markets and the Welfare State', in K. Groenveld, J.A.H. Maks and J. Muysken (eds), *Economic Policy and the Market Process: Austrian and Mainstream Economics*, Amsterdam: North-Holland.
Bellante, D. and P. Porter (1990), 'A Subjectivist Economic Analysis of Government-Mandated Employee Benefits', *Harvard Journal of Law and Public Policy*, **13**, (2), 657–87.
Clark, J.B. (1899), *The Distribution of Wealth*, New York: Macmillan.
Hayek, F.A. (1935), *Prices and Production*, 2nd edn; reprinted New York: Augustus M. Kelley, 1967.
Kirzner, I. (1985), *Discovery and the Capitalist Process*, Chicago: University of Chicago Press.
Menger, C. (1871), *Grundsätze der Volkswirtschaftslehre*, translated as *Principles of Economics*, ed. by J. Dingwall and B. F. Hoselitz, Glencoe, IL: Free Press, 1950.
Shand, A.H. (1984), *The Capitalist Alternative: An Introduction to Neo-Austrian Economics*, New York: New York University Press.

Walker, D. (1984), *Value and Opportunity: Comparable Pay for Comparable Worth*, Washington, DC: Cato Institute.

Weiser, F. von (1889), *Der Natürliche Werth*, translated as *Natural Value*, ed. by W. Smart, London: Macmillan, (1893).

38 Law and economics

Donald J. Boudreaux

During the past three decades economics has been applied with increasing vigor to areas once believed to be impervious to the 'rational' mode of analysis characteristic of economic reasoning. Activities and institutions as diverse and as far removed from the domain of profit-seeking business as politics (Buchanan and Tullock, 1962), the family (Becker, 1981) and sports (Goff and Tollison, 1990), among others, have been successfully investigated with economic tools. In this same spirit, law and economics connotes the use of economics to analyse common-law doctrines and, to a somewhat lesser extent, statutory and administrative law. (Use of economics to investigate the origin and operation of statutory and administrative law is unambiguously part of the law and economics movement; however, this part of the movement overlaps almost completely with the work of public choice scholars. The focus in this essay is on the unique and core enterprise of law and economics, namely, the use of economics to explain common – that is, judge-made – law.)

The uniqueness of law and economics lies in the explicit use of economic analysis to understand and explain the emergence of legal doctrines in areas of law that do not seem, on the surface, to be susceptible to economic reasoning. It is one thing to use economics to analyse antitrust and common-carrier laws; these areas of law are readily identified as dealing with commercial matters. But it is quite another thing – a more creative and ambitious endeavour – to use economics to explain the full body of common-law doctrines, most of which touch only sporadically, or not at all, upon commercial relationships.

Why does anglo-american contract law generally allow a promisor to breach and pay money damages rather than perform? Why does the law disallow breach in certain instances? Why does property law sometimes allow squatters to acquire full legal title to real property that they use? These and many other questions have traditionally been answered by lawyers using terms such as 'equity', 'fairness', 'justice' and 'precedent'. In contrast, economists, and economics-minded legal scholars, answer these questions by examining the plausible efficiency properties of these rules and their alternatives. A surprisingly large number of traditional common-law doctrines are sensibly understood as efficient solutions to interpersonal conflicts over scarce resources. Here we examine just two examples.

Application of economics to law: efficient breach

Suppose Goodyear agreed on 1 July to ship 100 000 standard 15" automobile tires to General Motors on 1 December, at a price of $30 per tire. On 15 November, Goodyear informs GM that it cannot perform. The law will not require Goodyear to perform, but it will require Goodyear to pay money damages to GM in an amount sufficient to make GM indifferent to Goodyear's performance and Goodyear's breach. Is it efficient – indeed, is it fair or just – that the law allows Goodyear to break its promise to GM as long as it is willing to pay money to do so? The answer is yes.

Assuming the courts assess money damages correctly, GM truly does not care whether Goodyear performs or breaches. (If GM does care, then the courts either under- or overestimate the monetary value of the breach.) GM is indifferent to breach. And Goodyear obviously finds it less costly to breach and pay money damages than to perform – else it would perform. Thus, whenever courts can accurately assess money damages caused by a breach, it makes little sense to compel specific performance. Allowing promisors to buy their way out of performing by paying money damages allows contracting parties to avoid unexpected and unnecessarily costly obligations without disappointing expectations held by other parties to the contract.

It is thus efficient for the law generally to allow breach-with-damages. This policy reduces the cost to all contracting parties of entering into contracts and, hence, increases the use of contracts as a method of reallocating resources. The reason is that each party knows that chances are greater than zero that some unexpected event can occur between the time of the contract's signing and its performance date that makes performance significantly more costly than anticipated at the time the contract is entered into (for example, one of Goodyear's factories might burn down). Awareness of the option of breaching and paying monetary damages gives both parties to the contract assurance that (1) each will receive full satisfaction from the other party, and (2) each will not be compelled to undertake inefficiently expensive steps to uphold his end of the bargain.

The few occasions on which the law disallows breach – that is, requires specific performance – involve unique goods. For example, if I agree to sell to you my house at 201 Boggs Street in Clemson, South Carolina, the law will not allow me to breach. The reason is that the existence of unique goods makes it sufficiently unlikely that the law will be able to determine the amount of money damages that makes the non-breaching party indifferent between performance and breach. And the law regards each piece of real property as being unique. Because the law is generally quite sensitive to protecting people's subjective expectations about their contracts, the law refuses to allow breach in situations in which it is too difficult for courts adequately to assess money damages.

Application of economics to law: adverse possession

If you own a piece of land you have the right to use that land as you wish as long as you do not violate rights held by others. Typically included in your ownership right is your legal ability to exclude other people from using your land. But suppose someone enters your land uninvited, and that person builds a house on your land and openly occupies that house and your land continually over the course of many years without your ever objecting in any way. According to the legal doctrine of adverse possession, after a certain number of years (often seven) the squatter becomes full and legal owner of the land. You lose any and all legal interests you had in this land. Is this efficient?

Economic analysis shows that the doctrine of adverse possession promotes efficiency. Note all the requirements for the squatter to become fee-simple owner of the land: he must not be invited (thus he is not a tenant of yours); he must occupy the land openly and continually for the full period required for adverse possession to become effective (thus his occupation is no secret to you or to anyone else); and you must not have objected (thus you as owner have evidenced no interest in the land during the adverse-possession period). Experience shows that a few owners of real estate will be neglectful both in using their properties *and* in ensuring that no one else uses their properties. Given that land is a scarce resource, the doctrine of adverse possession discourages owners from being neglectful. For those parcels of land owned by the chronically neglectful, this doctrine helps ensure that neglected land is brought back to productive use. (Note that the doctrine of adverse possession does not penalize an owner who wishes to leave his land to lie fallow or unspoiled. All the owner must do to maintain ownership rights is to protest within a reasonable time if some other party squats on his land. Erecting and maintaining fences and 'No Trespassing' signs are some of the ways available for owners to give notice to squatters and to other members of the community that the owner is not neglecting his land and does not approve of squatters.)

Are terms such as 'justice' and 'morality' synonyms for 'efficiency'?

Many additional examples from other areas of law can be offered to show that common-law rules typically serve the goal of efficiency despite being couched in language such as 'fairness', 'justice', 'morality' and 'reasonableness'. This fact suggests that these terms are often reserved by the law to describe actions and outcomes that are efficient. Thus application of economic tools to the study of law has not shown that the law pursues efficiency *at the expense* of 'fairness' or 'justice' or 'morality', or that the law *should* pursue efficiency at the expense of these high principles. Rather, law and economics demonstrates that terms with moral connotations such as 'fairness' and 'justice' are applied with surprising consistency in the law as labels for efficient behavior and outcomes. (For one of innumerable examples, see the case of *Eastern S.S. Lines, Inc.* v. *United States* (125 Ct. Cl. 422, 1953) in which the court allowed the promisor to breach efficiently by paying money damages. The court argued that this solution solved the dispute between the parties 'with perfect fairness' – although the court's reasoning shows clearly that this solution was viewed by the court as 'fair' because it was efficient.) (See, more generally, Posner, 1992, pp. 261–4.)

Of course, such bold claims about efficiency and about the power and stretch of economic reasoning elicit objections from those who see moral principles as something apart from the maximization of wealth or utility. The literature on law and economics has consequently been full of interesting debates, at various philosophical levels, about the applicability of economic reasoning to law. Yet another source of interesting debate is the attempt by legal scholars to protect their intellectual turf from trespass by economists. Trespass by one discipline into the domain of another naturally prompts practitioners of the trespassed discipline to regard the trespassers as invaders, and to find fault with the invaders and their weapons. In the case of trespass by economics into law, legal scholars have advanced several objections to the economic analysis of law. Only two of these objections are considered here.

Two frequent objections to law and economics
Objection 1: law and economics scholars derive their conclusions about the efficiency of common law from excessively flexible assumptions regarding preferences, production functions and consequences of legal rules. These assumptions are constructed after the fact to guarantee that each common-law rule analysed can be shown to serve efficiency ends (Malloy, 1990, pp. 60–66).

Of course, as with all uses of economics, those who apply economics to the study of law can never prove beyond dispute the validity of the stories they tell to argue that this legal doctrine or that common-law precedent promotes efficiency. An intellectual antagonist can always assert that people's preferences, producers' production functions and the full consequences of a particular legal doctrine differ substantially from the preferences, production functions and consequences explicitly or implicitly assumed by the law and economics analyst. But when plausibility – rather than certainty – is the standard used to judge hypotheses, law and economics fares quite well in making common-law doctrines understandable.

Is it not plausible that two parties to a potential contract both prefer, ex ante, that the law allows one or both of the parties to breach and pay damages? Is it not plausible that society is well served by the rule of adverse possession? Plausible, yes; certain, certainly not. But plausible explanations of legal rules are the most that can be asked for. At the same time, however, they are also the minimum that should be accepted. Often, of course, a legal rule will have two or more plausible explanations. In choosing among such competing explanations, it makes sense to choose the one yielded by the analytical engine boasting the most success at generating plausible explanations of other areas of the law. Although many scholars find approaches to law other than law and economics that better fit this criterion, law and economics can legitimately claim to provide sensible and consistent explanations of nearly all areas of law. (See, for example, Posner, 1992; Cooter and Ulen, 1988; Goetz, 1984.)

Objection 2: efficiency itself is either a meaningless or a corrupt concept because all discussions of efficiency take property distributions as given. Change the distribution of property and you change the set of efficient outcomes. Therefore proponents of the efficiency criterion necessarily endorse the current distribution of wealth – which itself is not explained on efficiency grounds (see, for example, Coleman, 1988). Judges should thus address distributional concerns rather than narrow efficiency considerations (see, for example, Kennedy, 1976).

There are several weaknesses in this objection, not all of which can be examined here. First, it confuses positive explanation with normative justification. Using economics and its concept of efficiency to explain legal rules is not to endorse such rules or the wealth distribution that gives rise to these rules. Second, it is wrong to suggest that even a radical redistribution of wealth would alter the content of efficient rules. The legal rule generally allowing breach of contract will not become inefficient if the identities of the haves and have-nots in society change, or if wealth or income is radically equalized across all members of society. The efficiency property of this rule, like that of many other common-law rules, is quite independent of distributional concerns. Third, this complaint misconstrues the task judges face. Judge Richard Posner (1992, p. 255) – the most diligent and consistent proponent of the use of economics to analyse law – notes that

> efficiency is highly controversial when viewed as the only value a society's public institutions should pursue, but much less controversial when viewed as just one value. And effective redistributive policies require taxing and spending powers that judges lack. As they cannot do much as common law judges to alter the slices of the pie that the various groups in society receive, they might as well concentrate on increasing its size.

Moreover, those who argue that judges should radically restructure society forget that courts sit to adjudicate disputes only between identifiable parties; courts are not legislatures. More importantly, proponents of radical redistribution of property overlook the incurable fallibility of all humans, whether they be judges, legislators, bureaucrats or taxi drivers. It is easy to say that property should be redistributed; it is substantially more difficult to determine what the best pattern of distribution is and how best to accomplish this distribution. Surely, enormous danger accompanies attempts by individual judges to achieve massive restructurings of society (Heyne, 1988).

Conclusion

Absent their ability to re-engineer society every time they hear a case, judges are generally left with little incentive to do other than what is best for the parties standing before them. And 'doing best' is surprisingly consonant with making efficient decisions. Perhaps the greatest single achievement to date of law and economics is the demonstration that anglo-american common law evolved over the years to arrive at rules that, with a few exceptions, are plausibly efficient. What is not yet so clear is *why* the common law evolved this way. Some attempts have been made to explain why the common law is efficient (for example, Rubin, 1977), but more work needs to be done in this regard. Economists trained in the Austrian tradition – with their appreciation of evolutionary processes, spontaneous order and methodological individualism – should be especially well equipped to contribute to this research.

See also:
Chapter 77: The 'new' institutional economics; Chapter 39: Legal philosophy; Chapter 42: The economic theory of regulation; Chapter 41: Public choice economics

Bibliography
Becker, Gary S. (1981), *A Treatise on the Family*, Cambridge, Mass.: Harvard University Press.
Buchanan, James M. and Gordon Tullock (1962), *The Calculus of Consent*, Ann Arbor: University of Michigan Press.
Coleman, Jules L. (1988), *Markets, Morals and the Law*, New York: Cambridge University Press.
Cooter, Robert and Thomas Ulen (1988), *Law and Economics*, Glenview, IL: Scott, Foresman.
Goetz, Charles (1984), *Law and Economics*, St Paul: West Publishing Co.
Goff, Brian L. and Robert D. Tollison (eds) (1990), *Sportometrics*, College Station, TX: Texas A&M University Press.
Heyne, Paul (1988), 'The Foundations of Law and Economics: Can the Blind Lead the Blind?' *Research in Law and Economics*, **11**, 53–71.
Kennedy, Duncan (1976), 'Form and Substance in Private Law Litigation', *Harvard Law Review*, **89**, June, 1685–1778.
Malloy, Robin Paul (1990), *Law and Economics: A Comparative Approach to Theory and Practice*, St Paul: West Publishing Co.
Posner, Richard A. (1992), *Economic Analysis of Law*, 4th edn, Boston: Little, Brown and Co.
Rubin, Paul H. (1977), 'Why Is the Common Law Efficient?', *Journal of Legal Studies*, **6**, January, 51–63.

39 Legal philosophy

Bruce L. Benson

Carl Menger (1963) proposed that the origin, formation and ultimate process of all social institutions, including law, is essentially the same as the spontaneous order Adam Smith described for markets. Indeed, 'customary law' develops from the bottom up through the voluntary actions of self-interested individuals, and the resulting legal system will support private property, induce fulfilment of obligations and recognize freedom of contract (Benson, 1990). Markets coordinate interactions and so does customary law. They both develop the way they do because the actions they are intended to coordinate are performed more effectively under one system or process than under another. More effective institutional arrangements replace less effective arrangements. As long as the resulting rules and institutions are allowed to evolve without coercive imposition of a different system (for example, through military invasion, or a concentration of force by some inside group) then the basic legal framework necessary for a free market economy will arise spontaneously as the market system evolves (Benson, 1989).

Reciprocity, reputation effects and law
If all interactions between individuals involve discrete, simultaneous once-and-for-all contacts, then mutually beneficial interaction, including cooperation in the form of collective recognition and compliance with a set of behavioral rules, is unlikely. An individual, person A, that bears costs from adopting some type of self-constraining conduct (for example, respecting someone's possession of property as a right) will get nothing in return if the other individual, B, does not adopt similar behavior (for example, if B does not recognize A's property rights). Uncertainty about the behavior of B in the resulting prisoners' dilemma type situation induces non-cooperative behavior. This does not characterize many kinds of interactions, however. Individuals' choices regarding interaction with others are frequently part of a continuous process, with each decision representing one link in a long time-chain of relationships. For example, most businessmen expect to be involved in repeated transactions with other businessmen. The same is true of members of families, primitive kinship groups, stable neighborhoods, religious organizations and many groups who contract for joint production.

In a repeated interaction setting with a finite uncertain horizon, cooperation becomes possible (Axelrod, 1984). Specifically, repeated interaction facilitates recognition of common standards of behavior as each individual recognizes that the long-term benefits of remaining on good terms with another party by behaving as expected are likely to be greater than the immediate benefits of not cooperating (that is, taking another person's property or committing fraud). As Hayek (1973, pp. 96–7) explained, many issues of law are not

> whether the parties have abused anybody's will, but whether their actions have conformed to expectations which other parties had reasonably formed because they corresponded to the practices on which the everyday conduct of the members of the group was based. The significance of customs here is that they give rise to expectations that guide people's actions, and what will be regarded as binding will therefore be those practices that everybody counts on being observed and which thereby condition the success of most activities.

Even a repeated game situation involves weaker incentives to recognize a common set of rules (customs, practices) than the incentives which often exist. In particular, each individual enters into several different relationships with different players. Thus refusal to recognize widely held rules within one relationship can affect the person's reputation and limit entry into other relationships to the extent that reputation travels from one relationship to another. Under these circumstances, the potential for cooperation in the form of recognition of commonly recognized behavioral rules is even greater than in simple repeated games (Schmidtz, 1991, p. 102). In order to maintain a reputation for fair dealings or 'high moral standards', each individual's dominant strategy is to behave as expected throughout each interaction.

The evolution of legal institutions
Law is not simply a system of rules. Fuller (1964, p. 30) contended that 'law' involves 'the enterprise of subjecting human conduct to the governance of rules'. Thus law consists of both rules of conduct and the mechanisms or process for applying and expanding upon those rules. When a situation arises in which the implications of existing rules are unclear, for example, a dispute becomes likely, so dispute resolution institutions are required. Individuals may also require additional incentives to accept the adjudicated rulings beyond those arising from reciprocity and reputation effects, so institutions for applying sanctions may be part of the enterprise of law. Furthermore, conditions change, so mechanisms for legal evolution must exist.

The self-interest impetus for institution formation can arise when individuals want to interact with others, but because of uncertainty about someone's reputation (that is, some relatively new entrant into the community) they may be reluctant to initiate their first interaction without some sort of assurance that the person shares the same set of behavioral rules. Each party's commitment to adopt commonly expected behavior must be credible. One way to help ensure a credible commitment by another party is to maintain a position of personal strength, of course, in order to threaten violent retaliation if the other party does not behave as expected. However, this can be quite costly. Thus individuals with mutual interests in long-term interaction (as with kinship ties or business dealings) have strong incentives to form 'contractual' groups or associations for mutual support. This reduces the probability that an individual will have to defend his property and reduces the likelihood that violence will have to be employed to resolve a dispute following some form of interaction. Mutual support groups are, therefore, particularly attractive if group members are obliged to act as or provide access to third parties to arbitrate or mediate disputes, assess judgements to make sure that they are just and consistent with the group's customs and practices and, if necessary, help enforce the adjudicated rulings (Benson, 1990).

A customary legal system is based on individual self-interest but it is ultimately achieved through collective action, because each member of a mutual support group finds it beneficial to agree in advance to obey commonly recognized evolving rules (even though each probably recognizes that these rules may occasionally work to his disadvantage) and to contribute to the costs of enforcement, in anticipation that the long-term benefits will exceed the costs. As a result, total resources devoted to the production of the defense of property should fall relative to what individuals acting on their own would have to invest, and the property itself will become more valuable as the potential for interaction expands.

If a dispute between group members arises, a mutually acceptable arbitrator or mediator might be chosen from a group's membership or from an approved pool of specialists. Since the arbitrator/mediator must be acceptable to both parties in the dispute, 'fairness' becomes embodied in the adjudication process. As Buchanan emphasized (1975, p. 68), 'Players would not consciously accept the appointment of a referee who was known to be unfair in his enforcement of the rules of the game or at least they would not agree to the same referee in such cases. "Fairness" or "justice" may emerge, therefore, in a limited sense from the self-interest of persons who enter into an enforcement contract.'

The arbitrator or mediator need have no vested authority to impose a solution on disputants, however. Under such circumstances, the ruling must be acceptable to the group to which both parties in the dispute belong. An arbitrator or mediator's only real power in such a system is that of persuasion. Given that the adjudicator has convinced the individuals in the affected group that a judgement should be accepted, his ruling can then be backed by a threat of ostracism by the members of the entire community. That is, refusal to cooperate (for example, to behave according to the accepted rules of conduct, including acceptance of fair judgements) can then be 'punished' by boycott (exclusion from some or all future interaction with other members of the group). Similarly, individuals in the group will lose support if they do not agree to arbitration when a dispute arises and yield to a judgement that is acceptable to the other individuals in the group. Fear of this boycott sanction reinforces the self-interest motives associated with maintenance of reputation and reciprocal arrangements. After all, each individual has made an invest-ment in establishing himself as part of the community (for example, estab-lishing a reputation), but the value of that investment is specific to that community, so the boycott threat helps ensure that the commitment to coop-erate is credible. Thus arbitration decisions under customary law can be enforced without the backing of the coercive apparatus typically associated with a nation-state.

The formation of 'localized' mutual support groups can take on even more functions (note that the basis for these groups can be geographic proximity, but it need not be; other possibilities include kinship proximity, religious proximity or functional proximity, as in a commercial group). For example, some member of one group may wish to interact with some member of another group in a cooperative fashion (for example, trade), but the two individuals may not expect to interact frequently, so the dominant strategy is one of non-cooperation. After all, reputation affects are localized within the group, and there is no potential for a boycott sanction to be applied against someone who is not in the group. However, it may be that there is consider-able potential for mutually advantageous interaction between the two groups as a whole even though each individual within each group may not anticipate frequent interactions with members of the other group. That is, the groups may be in a repeated game situation with one another, with fairly large potential benefits from cooperation that can be internalized, even though this is not necessarily true of any of the specific individuals in the two groups (at least initially, before inter-group relationships are established). If members of each group recognize the potential benefits from inter-group interaction, then an inter-group acceptance of a common law becomes possible and inter-group legal cooperation may evolve.

Inter-group cooperation is hindered by a significant assurance problem, however. Each individual must feel confident that someone from the other group will not be able to take advantage of him and then escape to the protection of that other group. Thus some sort of inter-group insurance ar-rangement becomes desirable, as well as establishment of an apparatus for inter-group dispute resolution. For instance, each group might bond its mem-bers in the sense that they will guarantee payment if a member is judged by a mutually acceptable arbitrator to be in the wrong in a dispute with someone from the other group: the mutual support group becomes a surety group as well (Rothbard, 1973). A judgement involving an inter-group dispute will have to be considered to be a fair one by members of both groups, of course. If it is, then a member for whom a surety group has to pay will owe that group's membership rather than someone from a separate group. In this way the boycott threat comes into play once again. Membership in a group then serves as a signal of reputable behavior to members of another group, and lack of membership serves as a signal that an individual may not be reputable.

The evolution of customary behavioral rules

Recognition of private property rights is likely to constitute the most important rules in a legal system built on reciprocity and reputation (Benson, 1990). After all, individuals must expect to gain as much or more than the costs they bear from voluntarily constraining their behavior. Recognition by others of a person's private property is a very attractive benefit. This gives individuals incentives to enter into cooperative arrangements in order to reduce their individual costs of defending property for which they have possession claims, and to enhance that property's value by increasing the potential for interaction, including exchange.

Demsetz (1967) explained that property rights will be defined when the benefits of doing so cover the costs of defining and enforcing such rights. Such benefits may become evident because a dispute arises, for example, perhaps implying that existing rules do not adequately cover some new situation. The parties involved must expect the benefits from resolving the dispute and clarifying a rule to outweigh the cost of resolving the dispute and enforcing the resulting judgement, or they will not take it to the adjudication system. The adjudicator will often have to make more precise those rules about which differences of opinion exist, and at times even extend existing rules, in effect supplying new rules because no generally recognized rule exists to cover a new situation (Hayek, 1973, p. 99). An adjudicated decision becomes part of customary law only if it is seen as a desirable rule by all affected parties, however. Good rules which facilitate interaction tend to be adopted over time, while decisions that do not turn out to establish useful rules do not influence future behavior (Benson, 1990). For new rules to be accepted by the members of an affected group, they generally must be consistent with individuals' expectations; that is, they must build upon or extend existing rules. Thus fundamental rules of private property are simply extended to cover new situations.

Dispute resolution is not the only source of evolving rules. Individuals may simply observe that others are behaving in a particular way in the light of a new situation and adopt similar behavior themselves, recognizing the benefit of avoiding a confrontation by trying to establish a different type of behavior. As a consequence of adopting such behavior, the individuals create an obligation to one another to continue the behavioral pattern.

As rules and their accompanying institutions evolve and are improved upon, they tend to become more formal and, therefore, explicitly contractual. In addition, as inter-group interaction develops and expands wherein the trust relationships that characterize intra-group interaction do not apply, conflicts are avoided by explicitly stating the rules as they affect the terms of the interaction a priori; that is, by contracting. A carefully constructed and enforceable contract can substitute for kinship or some other localized source of trust. Thus freedom of contract naturally evolves in customary law as well. Indeed, contracts become another source of legal change, as individuals explicitly agree to behave in a certain way and, if that contractual arrangement proves to be beneficial and widely applicable, it spreads through the affected group or groups.

There are many examples of societies whose values and legal systems have evolved over fairly long periods of time from incentives such as those outlined above (Benson, 1990; Rothbard, 1973). The international merchant community of medieval Western Europe is one such example (Benson, 1989, 1990) and it was from the resulting system of customary law that modern international commercial law, the backbone of free trade, emerged. Other societies also started down this road, only to have these evolutionary processes interrupted and perhaps even stopped by coercive forces before a full-blown free market order was able to emerge.

See also:
Chapter 48: Social contract theory; Chapter 80: Social institutions and game theory; Chapter 77: The 'new' institutional economics

Bibliography
Axelrod, Robert (1984), *The Evolution of Cooperation*, New York: Basic Books.
Benson, Bruce L. (1989), 'The Spontaneous Evolution of Commercial Law', *Southern Economic Journal*, **55**, January, 644–61.
Benson, Bruce L. (1990), *The Enterprise of Law: Justice Without the State*, San Francisco: Pacific Research Institute.
Buchanan, James M. (1975), *The Limits of Liberty*, Chicago: University of Chicago Press.
Demsetz, Harold (1967), 'Toward a Theory of Property Rights', *American Economic Review*, **57**, May, 347–59.
Fuller, Lon (1964), *The Morality of Law*, New Haven: Yale University Press.
Hayek, F.A. (1973), *Law, Legislation, and Liberty*, vol. 1, Chicago: University of Chicago Press.
Menger, Carl (1963), *Problems of Economics and Sociology*, translated by Francis J. Nook, ed. Louis Schneider, Urbana: University of Illinois Press.
Rothbard, Murray (1973), *For a New Liberty*, New York: Macmillan.
Schmidtz, David (1991), *The Limits of Government: An Essay on the Public Goods Argument*, Boulder, Colo.: Westview Press.

40 Public goods theory
Anthony de Jasay

The notion of public good presupposes a relevant 'public', a set of persons similarly placed in some respect, such as location, language, legal status, interest or need, who all have free access to the good by the sole virtue of being members of the set. Publicness implies that, though some or all members of the public may contribute to the cost of the good, for example by paying tax, their access to it is not 'bought' by their contribution. (Public goods differ from 'club goods' in that access to the latter is open to contributors only, for example, to those who pay membership fees. However, the member may make greater use of the club good without paying more fees. Thus, while it is private intramarginally, the 'club good' is a public good at the margin in that consumption of an additional unit is virtually costless to the consumer, any increase in total cost being borne by the membership as a whole.)

The dissociation of contribution from benefit is the determining attribute of publicness. It is common to both the traditional theory of public goods and its emerging generalized version. In contrast to the traditional theory in which voluntary contribution to the cost of a public good by non-altruists is irrational, the contemporary approach treats the expected value of an individual's benefit from a public good as being probabilistically contingent on his own contribution and either smaller or larger than the contribution. By relaxing the traditional presupposition, the more general theory implies that, if the public good is valuable enough, it is potentially rational for non-altruists to contribute to it; that is, that private provision is consistent with free access.

The traditional theory
It may be held on some agreed ground (interpersonal welfare judgement, Pareto optimality or cost–benefit judgement) that producing a certain good is better than letting the necessary resources be used to some other purpose. If, however, the good cannot be provided for one member of the public without being provided for all others, the latter receive it as an externality. The contribution of anyone to the cost would benefit mainly the others, and the incremental benefit to the contributor would be small, typically imperceptible, and in any event smaller than the contribution. The problem is so defined as to make this the case. Hence everyone is better off if the good is provided,

but for each it is better not to contribute; public provision requires compulsory contribution.

The goods in question have come to be defined by two properties, 'non-rivalry' or 'jointness' (greater use of the good by one user does not reduce the benefits available to the others) and non-excludability (a member of the public cannot be denied access to the good). Goods having both properties are 'pure' public goods. Traditional theory recognized that there are few or no produced goods that are 'purely' public. However, it sufficed that access to the good was not or could not be made contingent upon a contribution to its cost for a problem of public finance and public welfare to arise, for, left to the interplay of free choices, the good would either not be provided at all, or only in 'suboptimal' quantities. The fulfilment of widely accepted optimum conditions would therefore require mutual coercion (Baumol, 1952). (Note that the prediction that the good will be 'underprovided' by the market, rather than not provided at all, is open to the objection that, if it is irrational to contribute to its cost, it is no less irrational to contribute a little rather than a lot.)

Normative consequences

If a good is in fact in non-rivalrous joint supply, it is suboptimal to exclude anyone from access to it, since an additional beneficiary can be admitted to access without any increase in cost. Conversely, if a good is non-excludable, it must be provided in joint, non-rivalrous supply to permit non-discriminatory access to all members of the public.

How much of which public goods should be provided from resources made available under fiscal coercion? A necessary condition of optimal resource allocation is that, for every member of the public, the marginal 'utility' he derives from the public good should be the same as the marginal 'utility' yielded by every private good he consumes, and that no resources are left unused. This, in turn, implies that the marginal rates of transformation and of substitution between any two goods are equal to each other and to their relative prices. However, an individual cannot normally effect substitutions between the resources he devotes to private and to public goods. His marginal rates of substitution are neither adjusted in nor revealed by market transactions. Nor do public goods have prices. A suggested solution to this conundrum was to aggregate all individual marginal rates of substitution for a public good (relative to a *numéraire* private good) as it were, 'vertically', and to consider the sum of all individuals' taxes devoted to the public good as its price (Samuelson, 1954).

This, however, merely yields a formal statement of the optimum in terms of unknowns which may or may not be capable of closer identification. Some may be defined by the preferences of a given individual, but the latter will have no opportunity to act upon them, and therefore cannot reveal them in the course of his ordinary market transactions. Various non-market mechanisms have been suggested for inducing people to reveal their preferences for public goods, notably by ranking alternative tax-cum-public good proposals. The basic idea is that the optimal proposal will be the one that is unanimously or near-unanimously chosen (Wicksell, 1896). Taxation as voluntary exchange between the users and the provider of public goods is a common feature of these non-market mechanisms (Musgrave, 1939, 1959; Buchanan, 1968). They have a close affinity to contractarian political theory and to its manner of deriving the legitimacy of the state (Buchanan 1965, 1975).

However, intrinsic obstacles to such solutions subsist. If it is really the case that an individual's benefit from a public good is not contingent on his contribution to it, it is always best for him not to contribute, and not to honor any undertaking he may have given to the contrary. If revealing his preference for the good imposes on him a binding obligation to contribute to it accordingly, it is best for him to conceal (understate) his preference. In agreements requiring (quasi-) unanimity, his incentive to sell his veto right dearly would give rise to bargaining problems that may be intractable, or find resolution in redistributive bribes that cast doubt upon the putative merits of voluntary exchanges of the Wicksell–Lindahl type. Beyond these objections, the very meaning of Pareto comparisons between coerced and non-coerced levels of public goods provision is open to serious doubt.

Escape routes
Among suggested escape routes from the apparent dilemma, two have aroused wide interest. One is based on the game-theoretical finding that, when a prisoners' dilemma situation is indefinitely repeated, it is pay-off maximizing for each player to contribute as long as the others do (Axelrod, 1984) and this may make non-coerced provision of public goods consistent with self-interest (Taylor, 1976, 1987). This argument has considerable force in contexts where the members of a non-excluded public have good visibility of each other's conduct and must count on interacting with one another in similar situations in the future. Accordingly, close-knit communities of various kinds would have good chances of providing public goods for themselves without recourse to coercion. Cases of successful voluntary cooperation and self-restraint in the use of common pool resources (whose incentive structure resembles that of public goods) bear this out (Ostrom, 1990). Large, anonymous and amorphous groups with poor mutual visibility, however, would according to this argument presumably not resolve public goods problems, however recurrent.

The other suggested escape route is the coupling of the non-excludable public good with an excludable private good, with the latter serving as bait, as a 'selective incentive' (Olson, 1965). For the sake of getting the private good, a self-interested person may be induced to contribute both to it and to the public good. One contribution, that is, the price charged for the private good, must cover the cost of both goods for this solution to work. However, this is only possible if supplying the private good yields a supernormal profit, which can be devoted to subsidizing the public good. Competitors would then seek to supply the private good or its close substitutes at a lower price. A strong monopoly would be needed to defeat such attempts. How the monopoly permitting the supernormal profit could arise and persist is not clear, and the supposed role of 'selective incentives' correspondingly ill-defined.

'Government failure'

Taking it for granted that voluntary provision of public goods must be aborted by 'market failure' due to non-excludability, traditional theory considers provision by the government, financed by taxes, as patently superior to the purported alternative of no public goods, lawlessness and a 'nasty, brutish and short life'. It seems to go without saying that, since only the government can, it ought to supply public goods: 'the only question which arises is whether the benefits are worth the costs' (Hayek, 1960, p. 222). If this is the only question (and in a trivial sense there is indeed no other), it is a large one. There is no agreed way of answering it. How much of which goods are to be provided are matters decided in complex political processes. For well-known reasons explored in social choice theory, it is highly problematical to take the outcomes of these processes as the 'true', credible, reliable expressions of 'society's preferences'. Yet, if available social choice mechanisms are not to be trusted, what other indications should one follow? On what grounds can one affirm that the benefit of a public good is not worth its cost?

Any political process offers opportunities for a winning coalition to distribute the benefits and costs of public goods asymmetrically, skewing the 'product mix' to favor its own interests and tastes, and making the costs fall more heavily on the losing coalition. 'The benefits are worth the cost' to the winners, but perhaps not to the losers. Some or all of this redistributive effect is concealed from view, and some of it may be unintentional. Neither feature should commend it.

Secondly, there is a presumption that the political process is systematically biased to overprovide the good relative to some putative Pareto optimum. The bias may arise from 'fiscal illusion' – people vote for incremental expenditure without perceiving a connection between it and their own incremental taxes – from asymmetry between those who vote for public goods and those who are made to pay for them, and from the ability of single-issue groups to press for and obtain expenditure on some special public good, of interest to the single-issue 'public', by strategic voting or 'log-rolling'. As Hayek put it, a public good must satisfy 'collective wants of the community as a whole and not merely ... of particular groups' (Hayek, 1978, p. 111), but this merely begs the question of how we tell what 'the community as a whole' wants, and how we make the political process deliver it (rather than some dubious aggregation of several particular wants).

Thirdly, there is a tendency to systematic overprovision of public goods as long as their production responds to their use, consumption, or to 'need'. The marginal cost to the user is imperceptible, hence he has no inducement to use the good economically; a bias towards wasteful use is probably inevitable and is confirmed by experience, notably in publicly financed health care and education. On these and similar grounds, the provision of public goods by compulsory contributions is surrounded by 'government failure' that takes the place of 'market failure'. However, the balance of the argument might still lean in favour of compulsory provision of at least some goods if voluntary provision were, as the traditional view used to hold, clearly infeasible.

Generalizing the theory
The received view of public goods is a special theory in that it rests on three particular and demanding assumptions: (a) the goods in question are non-excludable; (b) they are in joint supply; and (c) an individual's contribution to the cost of providing the good increases his benefit from it by less than his cost. Each assumption can be usefully relaxed, rendering the theory capable of explaining a wider range of phenomena.

Excludability is not a binary, yes-or-no relation, but a matter of degree, best seen as a continuous function of the cost of excluding access to the good. This exclusion cost is, in fact, the cost of protecting (enforcing) full property rights in the good (Demsetz, 1964). Part of the enforcement may itself be supplied as a public good (through the maintenance of law and order), while some of it is normally assumed by the holder of the right, the owner. By incurring the cost, the owner (typically the original producer or the reseller) ensures that access to the good is contingent on his consent, which he sells at a price. The exclusion cost can vary from the very low (such as measures to prevent shoplifting) to the prohibitively high. Some exclusion costs are 'objective', a matter of technology and logistics; others may be subjective (for example, the pity, shame and social odium involved in refusing medical treatment to the indigent, or in excluding poor children from school, instead of treating such categories of people as a non-excluded public). A political decision to provide a good publicly may be due to its high 'objective' exclusion cost which would prevent profitable production for sale, or to a high imputed, 'subjective' cost, such as social disapproval, unrest or the risk of electoral defeat.

In principle, it seems possible to provide all goods freely to a defined community, subject to a budget constraint. This is actually the case in many families where minor children get 'all they want within reason', and it was meant to be the case for entire societies or the whole world under full communism. These considerations help us to see all goods as public, with private goods as a special case, or vice versa. A good is treated as a special case according to its exclusion cost. The differential advantage of providing a good publicly can be taken as the saving of this cost. This is trivially true if exclusion cost is defined all-inclusively. In a non-trivial sense, there is a balance of advantages and disadvantages. Among the latter is the encouragement of wasteful use.

There is some evidence that exclusion cost is sometimes ill-judged and overestimated, deterring otherwise feasible private provision and militating for publicness. The for-profit provision of intellectual property, broadcasting, adjudication, contract compliance and public safety are among suspect areas where exclusion costs may be lower than generally thought. In these and perhaps other areas, publicness may not be indispensable and for-profit production may be feasible. A notorious case is the lighthouse; it has long been cited as a paradigmatical non-excludable good, yet it turns out that English for-profit lighthouse operators, from the seventeenth century to their nationalisation, were perfectly able to collect lighthouse dues from shipping. In fact, shipowners petitioned for operators to be granted the right to erect lighthouses and collect dues (Coase, 1974).

Non-rivalry or jointness is a special case where the supply of a good is abundant enough relative to its 'relevant public' for every member to consume it, or otherwise benefit from it, at least up to some culturally conditioned standard which may, but need not, imply satiety, and where adding one more member to the public does not make the good less abundant. In the general case, supply may fall short of this level or exceed it, moving from inadequate to redundant. However, except for rare instances mainly confined to non-produced goods (such as daylight or language) as supply is decreased or as the public is increased, the benefit to the representative member of the public sooner or later declines perceptibly. Access to the good becomes 'crowded' and sets off some process of non-price allocation. The latter may be wholly informal (the cheekiest consumer with the sharpest elbow gets the greatest benefit and the shy one gets none) or formalized, as in queues, lotteries, rationing and so on. Arguably, there will be some threshold degree of crowdedness, hence a threshold quantity of the good, past which the benefit yielded by the good is so impaired that it no longer satisfies the criteria, notably free access to some standard of benefit, that qualify it as a public good.

If this is the case, the good is discrete, 'lumpy', indivisible up to the threshold. Some goods are, of course, 'lumpy' intrinsically, regardless of the size of the public they are destined to serve: a road bridge has a minimum length set by the breadth of the river and a minimum width set by a single carriageway. But even technically divisible, continuous goods may take on a discrete, 'lumpy' character when provided publicly, because they must be tailored to a given public with given customs, standards and expectations. Unlike the case of private goods, the supply of public goods and the size of their public are not reconciled by prices. That public goods have an inherent scale aspect determined by the scale of their public has an important consequence for the thesis, crucial for the traditional theory, that an individual's benefit is not (or virtually not) contingent on his contribution (see below).

An individual's contribution to the total cost of providing a public good may, but by no means must, increase his expected benefit from it by less than his cost. It is perfectly possible that it will increase it by more. The question cannot be prejudged. The contrary supposition in traditional theory is rooted in the idea that the effect of a marginal contribution to total cost is a marginal increase in total benefit; this is heavily diluted among all members of the public, most of it accruing as an externality to its other members, the part accruing to the individual contributor being (except in freak cases) imperceptibly small. However, for this to be the case, the total benefit from the good must be a continuous function of the total cost devoted to it, each small increment of the latter producing a small increment in the former. If, on the contrary, the good is discrete, 'lumpy', the benefit from it will vary discontinuously at some threshold or thresholds. (Actual supply may be inadequate or redundant relative to the threshold size that corresponds to the relevant public). Marginal benefit may be nil (if the good is redundant) or equal to the total benefit (if without the marginal contribution the critical threshold supply would not be forthcoming). There may indeed be several critical levels corresponding to successive 'lumps' of the good, or the good may be 'lumpy' up to some level and continuous beyond it (Hampton, 1987).

In general, therefore, the individual's valuation of the (uncertain) benefit he thinks he would get from contributing some sum of money or effort to the cost of a public good depends, in addition to the advantage of the public good over private ones, on his subjective estimate of the probability that the total benefit (or a 'lump' of it) is contingent on his own contribution. The traditional theory can be viewed as a special case of this general theory, namely the case where for all (or virtually all) members of the public this probability is small enough. But there is no a priori reason why this case should predominate. If not less than k members of an N-member public must make some predetermined contribution in order to secure some threshold supply of the public good, it may be reasonable for each member to assume that the probability of his contribution being required is k/N – though of course he may have particular grounds for forming a higher or lower probability estimate. This quotient, combined with the advantage of having a good provided publicly rather than devoting the resources in question to private substitutes, determines whether the expected value of the benefit from one's own contribution is greater or less than its cost.

Spontaneous cooperation to produce public goods

The provision of public goods cannot properly be analysed without some use of game-theoretical tools, for an individual's best course of action depends on what others choose to do, and in the absence of coercion or self-enforcing mutual promises (either of which would remove the kernel of the public goods problem) the actions of others can at best be anticipated, surmised or inferred from what may seem best for them to do. The special assumptions of the traditional theory give rise to a game of prisoners' dilemma. It is best for each not to contribute, regardless of what the others may choose to do. In a more general theory, there may be no such clear and simple imperative. If the differential advantage of having some public good is sufficient, the expected (probability-weighted) value of the benefit derived from one's own contribution may exceed its cost. The relevant 'game', then, is no longer a prisoners' dilemma, for out of four possible stylized outcomes, non-contribution will then produce either the best or the worst (instead of the third-best), while contribution will produce either the second-best or the third-best (instead of the worst).

In the face of this pay-off structure, a rational non-altruist has no dominant strategy. Contribution involves paying for oneself and for the free-riders who choose not to pay and get the good all the same; the unfairness of playing 'sucker' and missing out on the chance of a free ride argues against it. Non-contribution may yield a free ride, but it involves the risk of forgoing the benefit of the public good (or of a 'lump' of it) if too many others also choose to bet on the uncertain chance of a free ride, and contributions fall short of the threshold level. Each individual's subjectively best strategy depends in some manner on the probability he attaches to others taking or not taking this risk. In fact, the choice of strategy is the choice between two risks: the risk of finding oneself in the role of 'sucker', and the risk of losing all or a large lump of the benefit of the public good for lack of contributions.

Taking either risk to avoid the other is perfectly rational, and one is not a priori 'more rational' than the other. The relevant subjective probability judgements and public goods preferences may vary widely from one person to another. Expectations of each other's behavior therefore need not be mutually consistent; it would indeed be surprising if they were. Logically there is, then, room for schemes of voluntary cooperation for the provision of a public good, with or without 'political entrepreneurs' organizing them. In such schemes, 'sucker' and 'free-rider' roles would be adopted spontaneously according to risk choices, instead of being allotted by the government, that is, imposed by a politically stronger coalition on the weaker one.

See also:
Chapter 41: Public choice economics; Chapter 44: Austrian welfare economics; Chapter 15: Entrepreneurship; Chapter 65: Privatization

Bibliography

Axelrod, Robert (1984), *The Evolution of Cooperation*, New York: Basic Books.
Baumol, W.J. (1952), *Welfare Economics and the Theory of the State*, Cambridge, Mass.: Harvard University Press.
Buchanan, J.M. (1965), 'An Economic Theory of Clubs', *Economica*, **32**.
Buchanan, J.M. (1968), *The Demand and Supply of Public Goods*, Chicago: Rand McNally.
Buchanan, J.M. (1975), *The Limits of Liberty*, Chicago/London: University of Chicago Press.
Coase, R.H. (1974), 'The Lighthouse in Economics', *Journal of Law and Economics*, **17**, reprinted in Tyler Cowen (ed.), *The Theory of Market Failure*, Fairfax, VA: George Mason University Press, 1988.
Demsetz, Harold (1964), 'The Exchange and Enforcement of Property Rights', *Journal of Law and Economics*, 7, reprinted in Tyler Cowen (ed.), *The Theory of Market Failure*, Fairfax, VA: George Mason University Press, 1988.
Hampton, Jean S. (1987), 'Free-Rider Problems in the Production of Collective Goods', *Economics and Philosophy*, **3**.
Hayek, F.A. (1960), *The Constitution of Liberty*, Chicago: University of Chicago Press.
Hayek, F.A. (1978), *New Studies in Philosophy, Politics, Economics and the History of Ideas*, London: Routledge & Kegan Paul.
Musgrave, R.A. (1939), 'The Voluntary Exchange Theory of Public Economy', *Quarterly Journal of Economics*, **53**.
Musgrave, R.A. (1959), *The Theory of Public Finance*, New York: McGraw-Hill.
Olson, Mancur Jr. (1965), *The Logic of Collective Action*, Cambridge, Mass.: Harvard University Press.
Ostrom, Elinor (1990), *Governing the Commons*, Cambridge/New York: Cambridge University Press.
Samuelson, Paul A. (1954), 'The Pure Theory of Public Expenditure', *Review of Economics and Statistics*, **36**.
Taylor, Michael (1976), *Anarchy and Cooperation*, London/New York: John Wiley.
Taylor, Michael (1987), *The Possibility of Cooperation*, Cambridge: Cambridge University Press.
Wicksell, Knut (1896), *Finanztheoretische Untersuchungen*, Jena: Gustav Fischer.

41 Public choice economics

*Charles K. Rowley**

Positive public choice – or the economics of politics – is a relatively new field of scientific endeavor, located at the interface between economics and politics. It was founded in 1948 by Duncan Black, whose paper on the rationale of group decision making (Black, 1948) showed that, at most, only one motion, before a committee or an electorate, can secure a simple majority over every other motion. Specifically, if voter preferences are single-peaked over policy issue space, a unique equilibrium exists in the motion most preferred by the median voter.

In 1957, Anthony Downs moved positive public choice from its initial preoccupation with committee voting and direct elections to its subsequent concern with democracy and representative government. In a far-reaching contribution (Downs, 1957), he skilfully moved the median voter theorem from the realm of committees to the more complex environment of representative government. In so doing, he laid the foundations for a major research program that applies rational choice theory to every aspect of the political market-place. Public choice, thus defined, is a positive science concerned with what is or what conditionally might be. Its practitioners seek to understand and to predict the behavior of political markets by utilizing the analytical techniques of economics, most notably the rational choice postulate, in modelling non-market decision-making behavior (Rowley, 1993a).

Normative public choice – or social choice – is concerned with the appropriate relationships between individuals and society, the extent to which individuals' preferences can and should be aggregated into some overall notion of social welfare, social judgement or social choice. This research program examines relationships between ethics, economics and the state, combining moral philosophy, economics and political science to explore the rationale and implications of a range of alternative and sometimes conflicting social goals.

Because of the pre-eminence of Virginia political economy in normative public choice, the dominant ethics are widely seen to be conservative (Buchanan and Tullock) or classical liberal (Rowley and Wagner). However, the socialist ethic is well represented (Arrow and Rawls), as is the social

* I am indebted to The Lynde and Harry Bradley Foundation for continuing financial support for my research activities.

democrat ethic (Mueller and Olson). Normative public choice provides a much larger ethical tent than many of its practitioners and many of its critics are willing to concede (Rowley, 1993b). As public choice extends its influence beyond the North American sub-continent, ethical diversity, predictably, will increase even as scientific knowledge begins to converge.

Rational choice

The most distinctive single characteristic of positive public choice is its reliance on the rational choice model of neoclassical economics in modeling the behavior of all participants in political markets. Indeed, it is unlikely that public choice as it is now would survive the jettisoning of this principle as the protected core of its research program. Yet the resolute application of this principle has provoked strong scholarly criticism, not least from within the Austrian school (Rothbard, 1989). Rothbard's specific criticism of rational choice is his belief that public choicers carry economic determinism to the extreme of denying any motivation in human history except monetary gain. As he sees it, the only argument in the utility functions of those individuals who are modeled in public choice is expected wealth: 'Accumulate, accumulate: that is Moses and the prophets.' In this respect, Rothbard is misinformed. Public choicers, with but few exceptions, view individual utilities as multidimensional, albeit with expected wealth playing an important role. There is a considerable literature, for example, exploring the role of altruism and ideology in political market behavior (Rowley, 1993a).

What does appear to be incontrovertible is the remarkable empirical power of the expected wealth variable in models purporting to explain and to predict the demand and supply of public policies. Rothbard may wish that this were not so, may choose to stand in front of water that flows downhill and command it to reverse its flow, but he is about as likely as was Canute to be successful in a similar endeavour. Much of public choice analysis is directed at the margins and not the totality of individual behavior. If the expected cost of a course of behavior increases, the evidence indicates that supply, almost without exception, falls; if the expected return increases, the evidence indicates that supply, almost without exception, rises. Once the *ceteris paribus* conditions are acknowledged, Rothbard's criticism is seen to be misplaced.

An important presumption of the Austrian research program is the unknowability of the future and the problem of disseminating information, yet Rothbard (1989) is particularly shocked by one of the truly important paradoxes of public choice, namely the concept of the rationally ignorant voter. One of the earliest discoveries of positive public choice (Downs, 1957) was an explanation as to why many rational potential voters are ill-informed about political matters. Given the extremely low probability that an individual's vote will be decisive in an election (one in one million in a typical presidential election in the USA), the expected benefit of well-informed voting is small to the point of invisibility and much less than the cost of search.

Since the cost of voting is relatively high, abstention is the rational policy for the investment-oriented potential voter. Those who vote for consumption reasons are rationally ignorant of the competing candidates' policy positions and may indeed pull the election levers randomly or on the basis of valence considerations. Such behavior in no sense implies a judgement that individual voters are unconcerned about acquiring knowledge as a basis for human betterment. It implies that knowledge will move, readily acquired, in areas over which individuals have some influence, to the neglect of areas which are largely beyond an individual's control. Such a notion is entirely consistent with Hayek's writings on the use of knowledge (Hayek, 1945).

Equilibrium
A great deal of positive public choice scholarship applies the equilibrium analysis of neoclassical economics to political markets, indeed is viewed by many political scientists as straightforward imperialism on the part of neoclassical economists. To the extent that this approach is influential, it runs counter to the broad thrust of Austrian economics which analyses markets as disequilibrium processes, which views individuals as subjective decision makers in environments characterized by radical uncertainty and which emphasizes alertness to as yet unperceived opportunities as the principal criterion of entrepreneurial success (Kirzner, 1987).

Without doubt, the most committed applications of neoclassical economics to public choice stem from the Chicago political economy program (CPE) which was launched in 1971 by George Stigler's article on economic regulation. The leading practitioners of CPE are Becker, Peltzman, Landes and Posner. CPE views government primarily as a mechanism exploited by rational, self-seeking individuals to redistribute wealth within a society. *Homo economicus* is modeled almost exclusively as a wealth maximizer. The thrust of the theory is towards instantaneous and durable equilibrium, with political markets clearing continuously. Politicians broker political markets without invading them as principals. They are driven by constraints and not by preferences. Their own ideologies are tightly suppressed (Rowley, 1993a).

The auxiliary hypotheses of CPE ensure that political market equilibrium is both tight and instantaneous. All individuals are assumed to be price takers, transacting at market-clearing prices consistent with optimizing behavior. All individuals are assumed to engage in optimal search and prices thus reflect all economically relevant information. All constraints on economic behavior are viewed as technically efficient, the outcome of wealth-maximizing behavior on the part of those who create or modify them. The equilibria predicted by

CPE are not based on perfect foresight and uncertainty conditions individuals' behavior in political markets. However, individuals respond to uncertainty stochastically as expected utility maximizers, and not as entrepreneurs groping towards profit opportunities in an environment characterized by Knightian uncertainty. For the most part, CPE views political markets as technically efficient, parlaying the preferences of the decisive actors into well tailored public policies.

CPE is a body of literature that analyses political markets from the perspective of price theory and positive economics. Its models are precisely formulated in the language of mathematics. The predictions of its models are rigorously evaluated through state-of-the-art statistical techniques. In all these respects, it is sharply at odds with the methods of Austrian economics, which to a significant extent eschews as inappropriate modern mathematical and econometric techniques (Kirzner, 1987). It is noteworthy that two scientific programs that are so mutually incompatible are advanced by scholars who share much the same anti-government ideology.

The scientific approach of the Virginia political economy program (VPE), though still emphasizing equilibrium analysis, is distinctly closer to that of Austrian economics. Government is analysed from the perspective of price theory as a vehicle exploited by rational, self-seeking individuals to redistribute wealth. In this respect, the protected core of the VPE research program closely resembles that of Chicago. Yet its central hypotheses – suggestive of universal government failure – could not be more different. In explaining such a divergence in predictions, important differences in the auxiliary statements of the two programs must be identified. Virginia, unlike Chicago, does not assume that individuals are always price takers in political markets. Significant discretionary power is anticipated. Virginia does not assume as generally as Chicago that political markets clear instantaneously and continuously. It does not as frequently assume that the future should be analysed in terms of risk rather than Knightian uncertainty. It does not generally perceive political equilibria to be durable, nor does it as easily excise human error from its theories of political markets. In general, its approach is that of diffuse rather than tight prior equilibrium. However, it does not regularly analyse political markets from the perspective of disequilibrium, nor does it regularly employ the radical subjectivism of the Austrian school in its analysis of public choice.

Although Virginian theories are formulated generally at a lower level of mathematical sophistication than those of Chicago and with more concern about institutional details, the methods of hypothesis testing are much the same. Once again, Virginian and Austrian scholars, who have much in common in the field of ideology, and whose understanding of political market failure is much closer than is the case with CPE, derive their results through radically different scientific methods.

Catallactics

The term 'catallactics' meaning the 'science of exchanges', was first proposed as a replacement for the term 'political economy' by the Reverend Richard Whately in his 1831 Drummond Lectures delivered at Oxford University. Whately denounced Adam Smith's definition of the scope of political economy as the science of wealth (Rothbard, 1987), instead defining man as 'an animal that makes exchanges'. This shift of emphasis led Whately in the direction of a subjective theory of value and to the judgement that differences in subjective value are the foundation of all exchanges. Catallactics made heavy weather in the powerful currents of neoclassical economics and all but died out after 1905 following the death of Arthur Latham Perry, the foremost proponent of the approach in the USA. It was resurrected as a central pillar of Austrian economics by Ludwig von Mises in his major treatise on economics (Mises, 1949). Mises embedded catallactics in the wider discipline of 'praxeology', the science of human action, thus setting out the core of the modern Austrian economics research program.

Only in the Virginian political economy program does catallactics play a significant role in public choice analysis, and then almost exclusively at the constitutional level. Under the intellectual leadership of James M. Buchanan and Gordon Tullock, catallactics has been renamed as the contractarian approach (Buchanan, 1987) and has drawn its intellectual inspiration more from the writings of Knut Wicksell than from Ludwig von Mises. It made its initial dramatic entry in 1962, arguably in the most important single contribution to public choice, *The Calculus of Consent* (Buchanan and Tullock, 1962). Remarkably enough, this text has become a focal point of hostile attack by one of Ludwig von Mises's most devoted pupils, Murray Rothbard, precisely because of its reliance upon the catallactic method (Rothbard, 1989). In *The Calculus of Consent*, Buchanan and Tullock attempted to delineate the logical foundations for constitutional democracy vested in universal consent, rather than in conflict, conquest and subjugation of some individuals by others. By assuming that individuals make constitutional decisions under conditions of generalized uncertainty, they claimed to derive, on the basis of strict methodological individualism, universal consent for constitutional rules designed to minimize the joint cost of external effects and of collective decision making. Simultaneously, such universal consent was seen as defining the range and extent of collective action, and as delineating the constitutional constraints within which the ordinary processes of politics must take place.

Rothbard's attack on this model claims that it is predicated on a fatally flawed attitude towards government, in that it fails to grasp the crucial distinction between a voluntary exchange, where both parties gain, and a coerced exchange, where one party gains at the expense of the other. Instead of regarding the state as the organization of the political means – as the systematization of theft and coercion on a grand scale – the Virginian public choicers are viewed by Rothbard as regarding the state much more benignly, as merely one large firm, albeit a particularly inefficient firm. Rothbard is categorically incorrect in this reading of *The Calculus of Consent.* For Buchanan and Tullock, the state is the product of universal consent, offering gains from trade to those who otherwise must exist in the Hobbesian state of nature, suffering the privations brought on by the war of each against all. Its existence, as referee, as provider of public goods and as rectifier of market failure, is based entirely on rules that are endorsed universally in the constitutional settlement. There can be no coercion within this concept of government, as long as the parchment of the constitution is systematically upheld. Evidently, Rothbard confuses the logic of constitutional democracy with the malignancy that is *realpolitik.*

The relevant criticisms of Buchanan and Tullock's catallaxy of politics lie elsewhere. First, they require all individuals residing within prespecified geographical limits to participate in the constitutional settlement. No one is free to remain in the state of nature. In this sense, the constitutional settlement is a political and not a private act, in contravention to the Lockian tradition. Second, there is no right of secession in the contractarian constitution, no prospect for disaffected citizens either to return to the state of nature or to Balkanize into independent nation-states. Third, there is no recognition that real-world parchments are of a very different texture from that of any calculus of consent, the derivative at best of a transient supermajority, ultimately dependent for its survival upon the competing guns of often minority interests. All of these issues have been reviewed in detail by Virginian scholars (Rowley and Wagner, 1990; Rowley, 1993c; Wagner, 1993) from a perspective not too distant from Rothbard's own libertarian thrust. From such perspectives, real political markets behave in a manner much closer to Rothbard's Satan than to any calculus of consent, largely by dishonoring the constitutional calculus.

Political markets
In the public choice approach, politicians are modeled as providing a brokerage function in the political market for wealth transfers. Individual voters and special interest groups capable of effective political organization 'demand' such transfers evidencing willingness to pay in some combination of votes and campaign contributions. Other voters and interest groups, less capable of effective organization, 'supply' such transfers, albeit at some price in terms of displaced votes and campaign contributions. Politicians effect market equilibrium, balancing benefits against costs at the margin, in order to maximize their own utility functions, weighted variously in terms of expected wealth, expected votes and ideology.

The concepts of 'demand' and 'supply', in this stylized model, require a somewhat special interpretation. Demand is forthcoming only when the wealth transfers that are sought are perceived to carry a positive net present value to those concerned. Such positive returns represent rent, and not profit, insofar as overall wealth is not enhanced by political transfers. The existence of rent induces rent-seeking behavior which dissipates wealth by diverting scarce resources to non-productive ends (Tullock, 1967). The rent seekers who predictably represent demand are not limited to the ultimate beneficiaries of wealth transfers. Typically, they are joined by those departments of government and those government-dependent private contractors whose budgets and/or profits can be augmented by engaging in the political transfer program.

Supply consists of the unwillingness or inability of those from whom wealth transfers are sought, at the margin, to protect themselves with countervailing offers of money transfers or votes to the politicians who broker policies. The existence of supply is fully consistent with the existence of inframarginal rent protection outlays, since political market equilibrium is not necessarily equivalent to political market domination. It also has connotations of coercion that are absent in private markets, hence Rothbard's vigorous defense of anarchy.

When Duncan Black discovered the median voter theorem, he truly believed that he had identified a unique connection between the voting process and the actual outcomes of committees and direct elections. Unfortunately, this initial confidence was misplaced, as Black's subsequent work, consolidated by Kenneth Arrow, quickly established. Separately, they identified a set of mathematical problems sufficiently difficult to suggest that democracy is either an illusion or a fraud (Tullock, 1987), most notably because of the prevalence of vote cycles and the consequential path dependence of the vote mechanism. If cycles exist, in essence there are two possibilities when we observe such voting bodies as The House of Representatives in the USA or The House of Commons in the UK and review the outcome. The first is that the outcome is random and due to chance, since the order of the agenda dictates the outcome and no one realizes this within the chamber. The alternative is that the outcome is manipulated by some evil agenda setter who understands the situation and uses it to dictate solutions. Among public choice scholars, Gordon Tullock (1987) is almost a lone voice playing down the significance of this problem. No doubt Murray Rothbard would be sympathetic to the views of Arrow on this matter and would deploy the cycling problem as further evidence of the evils of democracy.

Even should single-peakedness conditions hold, the uniqueness of the median voter theorem is suspect once the ideal conditions posited by Anthony Downs (1957) are relaxed. If elections comprise three or more competing parties, or if abstentions due to alienation are possible, or if policy issue space is multidimensional, or if political parties are immobile across policy issue space, or if voters are rationally ignorant, the median solution is much less dominant, even if an equilibrium should exist. Furthermore, there is no guarantee that a government elected on a median voter platform will honor its political pledges. As the 1992 Clinton presidential victory demonstrates, elected officials may cynically jettison *all* their electoral pledges immediately following an election and rely upon voters' failing memories to carry them forward to subsequent electoral success. As long as they recognize the logic of collective action (Olson, 1965) and concentrate political benefits on well organized special interest groups while dispersing the political costs across the electorate at large, such deviant politicians stand every chance of continuing success in the rent-seeking environment of democratic politics.

Conclusions

For Rowley and Wagner (1990) a knowledge of public choice, drawn largely although not exclusively from neoclassical economic analysis, confirms a dislike of big government that is shared, perhaps for different reasons, by most scholars of the Austrian school. For us, the principle of liberty, linked to the lessons of public choice, leads not to the parchment of even some widely endorsed *limited* transfer state, but rather to the classical liberal doctrine of the *minimal* state, in which government is small, heavily constrained and acts only as nightwatchman for an otherwise unconstrained market economy. Such a solution would not be enough for Murray Rothbard; but it is a long way further in his direction even than the position of contractarian public choicers like Buchanan and Tullock, who are not known for their love of non-market decision making.

See also:

Chapter 49: Interventionism; Chapter 42: The economic theory of regulation; Chapter 62: Political business cycles

Bibliography

Arrow, K.J. (1951), *Social Choice and Individual Values*, New York: John Wiley.
Black, D. (1948), 'On the rationale of group decision-making', *Journal of Political Economy*, 56, 23–34.
Buchanan, J.M. (1987), 'The Constitution of Economic Policy', *American Economic Review*, 77, (3), 243–50.
Buchanan, J.M. and G. Tullock (1962), *The Calculus of Consent*, Ann Arbor: University of Michigan Press.
Downs, A. (1957), *An Economic Theory of Democracy*, New York: Harper & Row.
Hayek, F.A. (1945), 'The Use of Knowledge in Society', *American Economic Review*, 35, (4), 519–30.
Kirzner, I. (1987), 'Austrian School of Economics', in John Eatwell, Murray Milgate and Peter Newman (eds), *The New Palgrave A Dictionary of Economics*, New York: The Stockton Press, vol. 1, pp. 145–50.

Mises, L. von (1949), *Human Action: A Treatise on Economics*, New Haven: Yale University Press.

Olson, M. (1965), 'The Logic of Collective Action', Cambridge, Mass.: Harvard University Press.

Rothbard, M.N. (1987), 'Catallactics', in John Eatwell, Murray Milgate and Peter Newman (eds), *The New Palgrave: A Dictionary of Economics*, New York: The Stockton Press, vol. 1, pp. 377–8.

Rothbard, M.N. (1989), 'Public Choice: A Misshapen Tool', *Liberty*, 3, (1), 20–21.

Rowley, C.K. (ed.), (1993a), *Public Choice Theory*, vols 1–3, Aldershot: Edward Elgar.

Rowley, C.K. (ed.), (1993b), *Social Choice Theory*, Vols 1–3, Aldershot: Edward Elgar.

Rowley, C.K. (ed.), (1993c), 'Liberty and the State', *Shaftesbury Papers*, No. 4, Aldershot: Edward Elgar.

Rowley, C.K. and R.E. Wagner (1990), 'Choosing Freedom: Public Choice and the Libertarian Idea', *Liberty*, 3, (3), 43–5.

Tullock, G. (1967), 'The Welfare costs of tariffs, monopolies and theft', *Western Economic Journal*, 5, 224–32.

Tullock, G. (1987), 'Public Choice', in John Eatwell, Murray Milgate and Peter Newman (eds), *The New Palgrave: A Dictionary of Economics*, New York: The Stockton Press, vol. 3, pp. 1040–44.

Wagner, R.E. (1993), 'Parchment, Guns and Constitutional Order', *Shaftesbury Papers*, No. 3, Aldershot: Edward Elgar.

42 The economic theory of regulation

Gary M. Anderson

Economists have long devoted considerable time and attention to the economics of regulation, particularly antitrust regulation. Meanwhile, prior to the 1970s, the problem of why government regulation occurs – that is, the economics of the regulatory process per se – received relatively little attention. This neglect began to end in 1971, with the publication of Stigler's seminal article.

Previous to Stigler's contribution, the economics profession mostly held that government regulation was instituted primarily to protect and benefit the general public, and represented a social response to various kinds of 'market failure'. From this perspective, regulations represented government efforts to improve social welfare, even though in some cases the true effectiveness of regulation in achieving this goal was questionable. Therefore any costs imposed by regulation on the economy were really costs associated with achieving some social goal. In this view, government regulators were implicitly assumed not to be self-interested actors responding to economic incentives, but public interested maximizers of the social welfare.

Stigler offered a true economic theory of the regulatory process which, despite the title of his article, is readily extendable to all forms of government regulation, and is not restricted to regulation traditionally described as 'economic' (for example, antitrust regulation) as opposed to 'social' regulation (such as environmental laws). He models regulation as a profit-seeking enterprise in which self-interested groups and individuals attempt to gain via the use of government coercion. Regulation, in this view, is not some idealized attempt to maximize a social welfare function but rather the seeking of competitive advantages through the intervention of government.

Stigler concentrates his analysis on the use of government regulations by industries to provide cartel status and enforcement for themselves. Private cartel arrangements, where a group of firms cooperate to raise prices and restrict quantities in pursuit of monopoly profits for themselves, are unreliable and unstable. Individual member firms know that they can make themselves even better off by secretly undercutting the cartel, and therefore 'cheating' by cartel members usually causes disintegration from within. Also outsiders who see the cartel earning monopoly profit have an incentive to enter that market and undercut the cartel price to consumers. The problem a cartel faces, then, is how to prevent competition from breaking out and rendering the cartel ineffective.

Government regulation can be an effective device for achieving this end. By legally limiting entry into the industry by new competitors, and imposing mandatory price and output restrictions, government can provide the necessary 'services' required to make a cartel both effective and stable. Stigler argues that many real-world regulations represent attempts by cartel-seeking industry groups to obtain cartel rents through the mechanism of government. Thus the Stigler model of government regulation emphasizes the role of groups of producers seeking rents by using government to reduce the competition they face.

The political process imposes a variety of costs on the cartelizing industry, which take the form of limitations on government regulation-assisted cartel profit maximization. The distribution of control of the industry among firms changes; small firms tend to have relatively greater political influence than their market share would suggest. Reviews, oversight and bureaucratic hurdles of various sorts significantly increase the transactions costs associated with change in response to new conditions. Finally, the political process by its very nature introduces political players, outsiders, into industry decision making, often with uncertain and unpredictable results. These various factors constrain the pursuit of cartel rents by producer groups via the mechanism of regulation.

Regulation has two important economic consequences: it reallocates wealth and it imposes deadweight costs on the economy. As Stigler notes, 'When an industry receives a grant of power from the state, the benefit to the industry will fall short of the damage to the rest of the community' (1971, p. 217). While regulation may represent a rational strategy on the part of an industry group seeking cartel profits, the associated deadweight costs reduce the welfare of society from what it might have been in the absence of regulation, other things held equal. According to Stigler's model of regulation, then, the competition by economic interest groups to secure benefits from the governmental process is a kind of market-place, albeit one with important differences from the free market. Stigler emphasizes that, unlike the free market, the pursuit of regulatory rents represents competition for coercive transfers of wealth. Further, in a democracy, the familiar public choice problems associated with majority rule tend to produce regulatory outcomes which are inefficient and wasteful.

Another critical building-block in the development of the economic theory of regulation was contributed by Peltzman (1976). This article formalized Stigler's basic model but, more importantly, filled in major gaps in the latter's reasoning. One obvious difficulty with Stigler's theory is that it fails to explain the origin of some forms of government regulation which appear to transfer resources from producer groups to (some) consumer groups, or else share benefits between producers and consumers. Peltzman argues that no single economic interest is likely to 'capture' a regulatory body. Both producer and consumer groups can organize and compete for influence over regulatory bodies. He derives an equilibrium in which the political decision maker allocates benefits across groups in a manner designed to maximize that politician's utility. At the risk of oversimplifying, Peltzman suggests that politicians 'sell' regulation to the highest 'bidder', in a market where 'bids' take the form of money bribes, votes and other resources valuable to political decision makers.

Thus Peltzman's model accepts the possibility that government regulation need not be solely driven by producer interests. Consumers may be able to offer some votes or money to regulators for a small departure from the cartel equilibrium. In such an event, pure producer protection will not, in general, be the dominant political strategy. Peltzman's model predicts that government regulation will commonly be designed to appeal to both organized producer interests and organized consumer interests at the same time. Regulations will tend not to benefit all producers or all consumers, but rather subgroups which can organize with the appropriate characteristics for effectively obtaining a regulatory benefit. Regulators will allocate benefits across organized consumer and producer groups so that the regulators' total utility is maximized. All politically effective groups will share in the rents at the regulators' disposal.

In his 1983 article, Gary Becker extends the economic theory of regulation still further and develops a model of the effect of interest group competition on the economic efficiency of government regulation. In Peltzman's (1976) model, the economic inefficiency of regulation is implicitly constrained by the need for political suppliers of regulatory rents to satisfy both producer and consumer interest groups; this process presumably limits the tendency of government to enact regulations that waste resources while redistributing wealth. Becker adds a significant constraint on the inefficiency of the regulatory process. According to him, groups organize to exert pressure on the political process to grant them benefits or exempt them from paying benefits to others. The actual regulatory regime at any given time represents an equilibrium in the competition between these opposing forces. Becker's key argument is that under these conditions deadweight losses are a constraint on inefficient regulatory policies. Deadweight loss is the winner's gain from the regulation minus the loser's loss. These gains and losses are what motivate the competing pressures on the political process. Therefore rising marginal deadweight costs reduce the incentive to pursue more regulation and power the incentive to oppose it as well, from the perspective of the respective interest groups. In other words, regulatory outcomes which reduce deadweight cost (economic waste) tend to dominate because reducing deadweight cost makes the size of the 'pie', for distribution between competing pressure groups, bigger. Rational self-interest on the part of the competing pressure groups tends to force more efficient outcomes.

Becker argues that the political process will be drawn to efficient modes of redistribution in general and to efficiency-enhancing regulation in particular. The reason is that neither winners nor losers would rationally oppose changes that eliminated some deadweight loss. This model does not, however, imply that the process of competition between opposing pressure groups produces an economically ideal outcome, only that existing regulation reveals where marginal benefit equals marginal cost. Social welfare would almost certainly be higher if all pursuit of rents from government regulation could somehow be assumed away. In particular, democratic governments are not very efficient markets for transacting about coercive transfers, for familiar public choice reasons. Competition between pressure groups contributes to the survival of public policies that raise output, in the long run. Regulation still generates allocative inefficiency in the form of deadweight cost; competition merely serves to minimize this loss. Both Peltzman and Becker recognize the continuing nature of regulatory competition by pressure groups. The continuation of a given regulatory regime requires a continuing investment of resources by its beneficiaries as they lobby to fight off actual and potential attempts on the part of anti-regulatory interests to reduce the regulatory burden.

In an important 1987 paper, McChesney helps explain some apparent anomalies in the market for regulation. Some important government regulations are difficult to explain simply as expressions of interest group competition between groups of potential winners and losers in the private sector. For example, in a 1985 paper, Stigler himself finds no coherent empirical explanation for the passage of the Sherman Act, the first US antitrust law. McChesney points out that the economic theory of regulation has tended to neglect one vital participant in the market for regulation – the government itself. Government officials and politicians may stand to gain rents from the act of providing regulation to industries seeking cartel enforcement services, and/or from the act of threatening interest groups with onerous regulation if they fail to 'bribe' government to stop. In effect, McChesney points out that government itself represents a large and well-organized interest group in the market for regulation, with its own economically motivated agenda. The legislature will sometimes pass a vaguely defined statute to be enforced in an unpredictable manner, in order to identify and pressure interest groups to make payment, and to increase the demand from those groups for relief from cost-increasing government regulation. McChesney refers to this process as 'rent extraction'. Tollison (1991) notes that it is analogous to fishing: 'the government is simply trolling for business'.

The economic theory of regulation has spawned a rich empirical literature. These studies range widely and include applications of the model to the following problems: the role of heterogeneous costs within an industry in determining support for industry regulation in the case of pollution regulation (Maloney and McCormick, 1982); the determinants of farmer opposition to futures markets (Pashigian, 1988); the influence of interest groups in affecting the rise and decline of nations (Olson, 1982); the role of competition among pressure groups in explaining the rise of free enterprise in seventeenth-century England (Ekelund and Tollison, 1981); as well as a wealth of other diverse applications. This large and growing series of applications attests to the explanatory power of the economic theory of regulation (see Tollison, 1991, for a thorough survey of this literature).

One marked advantage Peltzman and Becker have over Stigler's original approach concerns deregulation. Stigler's basic model fails to explain occasional regulatory relaxation or deregulation. But, with their broader emphasis on the competition between pro- and anti-regulation pressure groups in the market for government transfers, both Peltzman and Becker lay the foundation for an extension of the economic theory of regulation to the problem of deregulation as well. Government regulation of particular industries tends to relax in cases where marginal benefits, marginal costs or both shift in relation to relevant interest groups on either side of the policy.

In a 1989 article, Peltzman examines the major examples of federal deregulation in the late 1970s and 1980s. He reviews the cases of the most economically significant examples of federal government deregulation in the period – railroads, airlines, stock brokerage, bank deposit interest rates, oil price controls – and argues that in each case a decline in the marginal benefits from regulation received by producer interests combined with an increase in marginal costs borne by consumers to cause a shift in the political equilibrium, resulting in a change in regulatory regime. This implies that, at least in most important cases, careful examination of the basic facts suggests that the recent experience of deregulation can be adequately explained within the framework of the economic theory of regulation.

Peltzman admits that the economic theory of regulation, at least in its present form, does not seem to provide a convincing explanation for some other recent deregulation (such as on trucking or long-distance telecommunications). However, these loose ends may in fact really be consistent with the economic theory of regulation, correctly interpreted. This is an important problem for future research.

The economic theory of regulation has helped to inspire related developments in the literature, such as the interest group theory of government (see Tollison, 1988, for a review) and the theory of rent seeking (see Rowley, Tollison and Tullock, 1988 for a review). These two literatures extend the basic insights at the heart of the economic theory of regulation to all coercive wealth transfers, regardless of their ostensible purpose.

The economic theory of regulation has been a product of the Chicago school. However, it has developed in a manner generally consistent with Austrian economic theory. Unlike the mainstream 'public interest' alternative, the economic theory of regulation is based on methodological individualism and extends market reasoning to the problem of explaining the behavior of government actors as rational, self-interested agents. Consequently, the literature devoted to the theory and its applications deserves serious consideration from Austrian economists.

See also:
Chapter 41: Public choice economics; Chapter 50: The political economy of price controls; Chapter 61: Financial regulation; Chapter 51: The economics of prohibition

Bibliography
Becker, G.S. (1983), 'A Theory of Competition Among Pressure Groups for Political Influence', *Quarterly Journal of Economics*, **98**, August, 371–400.

Ekelund, R.E. and R.D. Tollison (1981), *Mercantilism as a Rent-Seeking Society*, College Station: Texas A&M Press.

Maloney, M.T. and R.E. McCormick (1982), 'A Positive Theory of Environmental Quality Regulation', *Journal of Law and Economics*, **25**, April, 99–124.

McChesney, F.S. (1987), 'Rent Extraction and Rent Creation in the Economic Theory of Regulation', *Journal of Legal Studies*, **16**, January, 101–18.

Olson, M. (1982), *The Rise and Decline of Nations*, New Haven: Yale University Press.

Pashigian, P. (1988), 'Why Have Some Farmers Opposed Futures Markets?', *Journal of Political Economy*, **96**, April, 371–82.

Peltzman, S. (1976), 'Toward A More General Theory of Regulation', *Journal of Law and Economics*, **19**, August, 211–40.

Peltzman, S. (1989), 'The Economic Theory of Regulation After a Decade of Deregulation', in Martin Neal Baily and Clifford Winston (eds), *The Brookings Papers on Economic Activity*, Washington: Brookings Institution, pp. 1–41.

Rowley, C.K., R.D. Tollison and G. Tullock (eds) (1988), *The Political Economy of Rent Seeking*, Boston: Kluwer.

Stigler, G.J. (1971), 'The Theory of Economic Regulation', *Bell Journal of Economics and Management Science*, **2**, spring, 3–21.

Stigler, G.J. (1985), 'The Origin of the Sherman Act', *Journal of Legal Studies*, **14**, 1–12.

Tollison, R.D. (1988), 'Public Choice and Legislation', *Virginia Law Review*, **74**, March, 339–71.

Tollison, R.D. (1991), 'Regulation and Interest Groups', in Jack High (ed.), *Regulation: Economic Theory and History*, Ann Arbor: University of Michigan Press, pp. 59–76.

43 Resource economics

Charles N. Steele

Resource economics is concerned with issues in the utilization, conservation and allocation of natural resources, both renewable and non-renewable. The field dates back at least to Hotelling's 1931 study of resource extraction and has followed the development of mainstream neoclassical economics, in that it consists primarily of equilibrium models of decision, either under conditions of uncertainty, or with stochastic variables of commonly known distribution. The main Austrian contribution to resource economics has come through replacing these strong assumptions concerning information, and the notions of equilibrium and optimality which arise from them, with a more adequate treatment of knowledge and learning. In order to analyse the Austrian contribution, it is necessary to make a brief excursion into standard resource economics.[1]

The first 'fundamental theorem' of resource economics holds that the owner of a resource stock sees it as a capital asset, and can capitalize future values. Thus he will either earn the normal rate of return on it, or will dispose of it (Clark, 1990, p. 4). The second 'fundamental theorem' maintains that with an open access resource (one in which rights to use are common and no exclusion is possible) resource exploitation will rise to a level where revenue flow exactly equals opportunity cost, as it is not possible for users to capitalize future values and conserve the resource (ibid., pp. 6–7). This 'commons problem' can be seen as a form of externality, and has led resource economics into a heavy concern with 'market failure' type problems and regulatory solutions. Utilizing equilibrium models, a common tendency in this approach is to calculate an optimal allocation of resources and then use this to prescribe a particular regulatory policy or management decision.

The Austrian contribution to resource issues has come primarily through the new resource economics (NRE) paradigm.[2] NRE augments traditional resource economics by introducing ideas from property rights economics, public choice and Austrian economics.[3] The main contribution of property rights economics to the NRE is a more thorough analysis of the various possible structures of property rights and in turn of what potential costs and benefits decision makers face and what margins they operate on. Public choice turns the focus to the incentives facing government officials and issues of government failure. More to the point of this essay, Austrian economics provides a theory of the role of information and how it is generated and utilized both within a market process and under a governmental command system.

The NRE explicitly utilizes Austrian entrepreneurial theory to account for the movement of the economic system towards coordination and equilibrium.[4] The price system offers a method of calculating relative values of resources in various uses. By observing price signals, and discovering and pursuing profit opportunities, entrepreneurial action moves resources to more highly valued uses. Under a market system, the diffused knowledge of individuals is thus spontaneously assembled and used to coordinate economic activities. Austrian entrepreneurial theory thus makes at least three points which are important for resource economics. First, it provides a theory of equilibration. Rather than simply assuming equilibrium, entrepreneurial theory provides a causal 'mechanism', a process rooted in individual action, to account for systematic adjustment of economic activity. This theory, augmented by relevant specifications of the structure of property rights, gives a more fruitful explanation of economic processes than does the simple assertion of equilibrium.

Second, Austrian theory consistently recognizes that much of the most basic economic information is of a subjective nature. In particular, costs are always opportunity costs, and necessarily are the subjective estimates of individuals of the relative worth of opportunities which will never be realized. Further, Austrian entrepreneurial theory includes a theory of ignorance and learning. Even in a world of costless information, it is necessary that information be discovered or learned (Kirzner, 1973, p. 229). These points call into question the concept of an optimal allocation of resources. If economic data are subjective, dispersed and sometimes ignored or unknown, then it is impossible to calculate an optimal state, even if one might be able to characterize what such a state would be like in principle. In particular, the optimal states suggested by equilibrium models appear to be artifacts of the strong informational assumptions.

Third, the above two points together raise doubts about the abilities of government regulators wisely to manage the use of resources. Even if regulators' incentives are such that they seek to optimize some measure of social welfare, their abilities to do so are limited, particularly in the case of state-owned resources and common resources for which markets are poorly developed or absent. With information subjective and dispersed, even the best intentioned regulator, induced by appropriate constitutional constraints to pursue naught but the public weal, faces serious information problems when he tries to improve on market outcomes. Thus the Austrian critique of government resource management complements, and is also more fundamental than, the public choice analysis of government incentives.

Several studies working within the NRE paradigm have extended the application of Austrian theory to resource economics, most notably by applying the Austrian 'socialist calculation' argument to resource issues.[5] Centrally planned economic systems can be seen as the limiting case of regulatory control of resources, and it is here that informational problems for government officials are most severe and entrepreneurial discovery most constrained. Socialist calculation arguments have proved particularly useful in explaining persistent resource waste and environmental crises in communist states such as China and the now defunct USSR.

Another contribution of Austrian thought to resource economics, one quite unrelated to the NRE paradigm, is the use of neo-Austrian capital theory in evolutionary models.[6] In this approach a version of Austrian capital theory emphasizing time and time irreversibility as well as entrepreneurial innovation or discovery is incorporated into a mathematical model economy and environment. These models take explicit account of the evolutionary and irreversible nature of economic and biological/environmental processes, and are used in simulations of an economy and environment moving through time. This form of modeling also relaxes the extreme information assumptions of standard neoclassical models and allows for the emergence of novelty, or entirely unforeseen possibilities.

Notes
1. The following discussion is largely from Clark, 1990. See also Johansson, 1987, for a mainstream treatment of environmental aspects of resource issues.
2. See Anderson (1982) for a thorough discussion of NRE. The present account relies heavily on this article. Anderson and Leal (1991) employ the NRE paradigm in a popular treatment of environmental problems and solutions.
3. Of these three sets of ideas, Austrian economics has arguably had the least impact, likely owing to the reliance of the property rights approach on equilibrium assumptions. For a seminal contribution in the non-Austrian vein, see Cheung (1970).
4. See Kirzner (1973) for the definitive presentation of the theory of entrepreneurship.
5. See Smith (1982) and Steele (1992).
6. See Faber and Proops (1991) for a full presentation of this form of model and the theory behind it.

See also:
Chapter 77: The 'new' institutional economics; Chapter 78: Evolutionary economics; Chapter 15: Entrepreneurship; Chapter 42: The economic theory of regulation

Bibliography
Anderson, Terry L. (1982), 'The New Resource Economics: Old Ideas and New Applications', *American Journal of Agricultural Economics*, December, 928–34.
Anderson, Terry L. and Donald R. Leal (1991), *Free Market Environmentalism*, San Francisco: Pacific Research Institute for Public Policy.
Cheung, Steven N.S. (1970), 'The Structure of a Contract and the Theory of a Non-Exclusive Resource', *Journal of Law and Economics*, **13**, 49–70.
Clark, Colin W. (1990), *Mathematical Bioeconomics: The Optimal Management of Renewable Resources*, 2nd edn, New York: John Wiley.
Faber, Malte and John L.R. Proops (1991), *Evolution, Time Production, and the Environment*, Berlin/New York: Springer-Verlag.

Hotelling, H. (1931), 'The Economics of Exhaustible Resources', *Journal of Political Economy*, **39**, 137–75.

Johansson, Per-Olov (1987), *The Economic Theory and Measurement of Environmental Benefits*, Cambridge/New York: Cambridge University Press.

Kirzner, Israel M. (1973), *Competition and Entrepreneurship*, Chicago: University of Chicago Press.

Smith, Robert J. (1982), 'Privatizing the Environment', *Policy Review*, spring, 11–50.

Steele, Charles N. (1992), 'Environmental Consequences of Central Planning', working paper, Political Economy Research Center, Bozeman.

44 Austrian welfare economics
Tyler Cowen

Welfare economics, the normative side of economic science, encompasses the criteria for analyzing economic policies and how to evaluate trade-offs using these criteria. In neoclassical economics, welfare economics is based on the theory of Paretian optimality and the practical application of cost–benefit analysis. Welfare economics has received only sporadic attention from those economists usually classified as Austrian. In some cases, the Austrians argue explicitly that welfare economics is an empty box. Nonetheless, several attempts have been made to develop an Austrian approach to welfare economics. The Austrian views that have been developed are based, in varying degrees, upon the underlying principles of subjectivism, methodological individualism and the view of the market as a dynamic process.

Wertfreiheit
Many Austrian economists stress the theme of *Wertfreiheit*, or value-freedom. Economics is seen as a science that contributes to our understanding of market phenomena, but which does not evaluate policies as good or bad. Policy evaluation requires the explicit introduction of ethics. The doctrine of *Wertfreiheit* was emphasized by Max Weber and has been defended subsequently by Kirzner (1976) and Rothbard (1977), among others. *Wertfreiheit* does not necessarily eliminate the practice of welfare economics, but it does change the scientific status of the propositions of welfare economics. Welfare economics cannot yield substantive conclusions about policy without relying upon ethical judgements.

Paretian welfare economics comes to terms with *Wertfreiheit* by accepting certain underlying ethical assumptions (for example, taking the initial distribution of wealth as given, assuming that informed trade makes people better off, and so on). Upon auxiliary ethical assumptions, Paretians use economic logic to analyse the efficiency and ethical trade-offs involved in policy choices. The Austrian economists have generally taken a different approach. Whereas (some) neoclassical economists agree upon the ethical presuppositions behind Paretianism and debate the logic of the trade-offs that follow, the Austrian economists have focused upon the fundamental issues involving the relationship between ethics and economics. The Austrian literature emphasizes the underlying ethical presuppositions behind other kinds of welfare economics, whether economics is (should be?) a value-free science and the normative implications of the subjectivity of costs. By considering fundamental issues, the Austrians have anticipated the recent post-Paretian revolution in welfare economics (Amartya Sen, the new cardinalism, and so on; see Cowen, 1987, for a survey). The Austrians, however, have not dealt explicitly with most of the specific issues debated in the post-Paretian literature. Following the earlier arguments of Robbins (1932), most Austrians have dismissed approaches that postulate cardinal, interpersonally comparable utilities.[1]

Although most Austrians accept the doctrine of *Wertfreiheit*, there is not complete agreement on this issue. High (1985) argues that the very definitions of property rights and market exchange involve reference to ethical concepts. Without an underlying moral theory, for instance, we cannot distinguish between voluntary and involuntary transactions. Even the concepts used in so-called 'positive' economics involve implicit reference to ethical criteria. High believes that economic science cannot and should not be value-free.

Criticisms of Paretianism and cost–benefit analysis
The Austrian literature has been nearly unanimous in rejecting welfare economics as practiced by most neoclassical economists. Austrians do not generally dispute the Paretian principle of exhausting the gains from trade; however, Austrians have criticized Paretian theory for its framework of given means and ends. Paretian theory treats welfare as a problem of what Kirzner (1973) calls 'Robbinsian maximizing'. In contrast, the Austrians stress innovation and the discovery of previously unknown possibilities, rather than mathematical optimization techniques.

Cost–benefit analysis has also been the subject of much Austrian criticism. By its very nature, cost–benefit analysis must sum up dollar magnitudes and aggregate across different individuals. Numerous Austrians have argued that this procedure violates methodological individualism and assumes that the relevant costs are objectively measurable (see Vaughn, 1980; Thirlby, 1981; Formaini, 1990). The Austrian emphasis upon the subjectivity and incommensurability of costs implies that aggregative judgements about welfare cannot be made scientifically.

Many Austrian essays on welfare economics emphasize the value-laden nature of efficiency or public policy judgements. One of the best known essays in this vein is that of Rizzo (1980), who focuses upon the concept of efficiency used in the modern law and economics movement. Rather than sneak in ethical judgements under the guise of an efficiency concept, Rizzo would prefer policy evaluation to take place in explicitly ethical terms. In an earlier essay, Yeager (1978) examines and rejects some of the implicit ethical assumptions behind Paretian welfare economics.

Extant Austrian approaches to welfare

Rothbard (1977) argues that welfare economics should be based upon the concept of 'demonstrated preference'. Observed market choices are the only source of data for personal well-being. If a person is observed as preferring *A* to *B*, we can say that the person's choice of *A* over *B* improves his welfare. Furthermore, we cannot make inferences about a person's preferences concerning *A* and *B* under any other circumstances.[2]

Presumably, the claim that we should prefer to further a person's welfare involves an ethical value judgement. Nonetheless, Rothbard argues for a one-to-one identification between observed market choices and personal welfare. This identification is possible within the realm of positive economics alone. Note that, under Rothbard's theory, assertions of market failure due to public goods and externalities problems are not well-defined. Unless we observe persons preferring a public good, we cannot say it is valued. If markets fail to produce a dam, for instance, we can only conclude that market participants did not want to have the dam produced. But here, Rothbard's approach appears to offer a tautologous definition of welfare and beg the question about how well markets solve coordination problems.

A less extreme position on welfare economics has been taken by Kirzner (1979) who, unlike Rothbard, allows for the possibility of market failure. One instance of market failure arises when entrepreneurs fail to notice available profit opportunities. Kirzner, however, also places very strong restrictions upon the economist's ability to make positive claims about welfare by adhering to a strict form of methodological individualism. Definite statements about changes in welfare can be made only under those criteria that also satisfy the standard of Paretian optimality; some individuals must benefit and no individuals can be made worse off.

Another approach to Austrian welfare economics, suggested by the work of Hayek, is to evaluate economic systems with respect to an external standard or set of standards involving discovery, innovation, coordination, complexity and so on. The economic system that does a better job in furthering coordination, for instance, is preferable. Nelson and Winter (1982) and O'Driscoll and Rizzo (1985) present more detailed treatments of this approach, which is only implicit in Hayek.[3]

Cowen (1991) analyses the logic of using non-Paretian standards for evaluating economic systems. On the positive side, non-Paretian standards such as discovery and innovation add a dynamic element to welfare economics lacking in the Paretian literature. But they also involve serious conceptual problems. The choice of standard appears to rely upon some other underlying theory of economic welfare. We might choose the standard of innovation, for instance, but it is easy to imagine economic systems that produce too much innovation at the expense of other values.[4] More generally, for any standard we might choose we must face the possibility of evaluating trade-offs between this standard and other values. Evaluating the relevant trade-offs without invoking some version of Paretianism, or some other theory of welfare, is difficult. But if non-Paretian standards are parasitic upon other theories of economic welfare, such standards are not fundamentally distinct approaches to welfare economics.

In sum, Austrian welfare economics is an area in disarray. Extant Austrian approaches share certain common dissatisfactions with Paretian welfare economics, but there has been no agreement upon an operational or even coherent alternative. Austrian approaches will likely remain defined by their skepticism towards neoclassical practices, rather than the construction of an alternative set of methods for the normative economist. Whether this is a strength or weakness of current Austrian approaches probably depends upon one's own views concerning the relationship between ethics and economics.

Notes

1. Shearmur (1990), however, defends a modified form of cardinalism and argues that the early Austrians, such as Menger, were more sympathetic to a cardinal notion of well-being.
2. Rothbard's notion of demonstrated preference differs from Samuelson's revealed preference theory in several respects; see Rothbard (1956). Perhaps most importantly, Rothbard's theory does not assume that preference orderings remain constant.
3. The choice of standard might be an ethical judgement; alternatively, the choice of standard might be considered descriptive. The decision to adhere to this standard for policy choices would then be the relevant ethical decision.
4. Massive subsidies to research and development might create this result, for instance.

See also:

Chapter 15: Entrepreneurship; Chapter 45: Value-freedom; Chapter 47: Utilitarianism; Chapter 19: Efficiency

Bibliography

Cowen, Tyler (1987), 'Recent developments in Social Choice Theory', *Market Process*, **5**, (1), spring, 4–8, 25.
Cowen, Tyler (1991), 'What a Non-Paretian Welfare Economics Would Have to Look Like', in Don Lavoie (ed.), *Economics and Hermeneutics*, London: Routledge.
Formaini, Robert (1990), *The Myth of Scientific Public Policy*, New Brunswick, NJ: Transaction Books.
High, Jack (1985), 'Is Economics Independent of Ethics?', *Reason Papers*, **10**, spring, 3–16.
Kirzner, Israel M. (1973), *Competition and Entrepreneurship*, Chicago: University of Chicago Press.
Kirzner, Israel M. (1976), 'Philosophical and Ethical Implications of Austrian Economics', in Edwin G. Dolan (ed.), *The Foundations of Modern Austrian Economics*, Kansas City: Sheed and Ward.
Kirzner, Israel M. (1979), 'Perception, Opportunity and Profit: Studies in the *Theory of Entrepreneurship*', Chicago: University of Chicago Press.
Nelson, Richard R. and Sidney G. Winter (1982), *An Economic Theory of Evolutionary Change*, Cambridge, Mass.: Belknap Press.

O'Driscoll, Gerald P. and Mario J. Rizzo (1985), *The Economics of Time and Ignorance*, Oxford: Basil Blackwell.

Rizzo, Mario J. (1980), 'The Mirage of Efficiency', *Hofstra Law Review*, **8**, (3), spring, 641–58.

Robbins, Lionel (1932), *Essay on the Nature and Significance of Economic Science*, London: Macmillan.

Rothbard, Murray N. [1956] (1977), *Toward a Reconstruction of Utility and Welfare Economics*, New York: Center for Libertarian Studies.

Shearmur, Jeremy (1990), 'From Hayek to Menger: Biology, Subjectivism and Welfare', in Bruce Caldwell (ed.), *Carl Menger and His Legacy in Economics*, Durham: Duke University Press.

Thirlby, G.F. (1981), *L.S.E. Essays on Cost*, New York: New York University Press.

Vaughn, Karen I. (1980), 'Does it Matter that Costs are Subjective?', *Southern Economic Journal*, **46**, January, 702–15.

Yeager, Leland B. (1978), 'Pareto Optimality in Policy Espousal', *Journal of Libertarian Studies*, **2**, (3), fall, 199–216.

PART III

APPLIED ECONOMICS
AND PUBLIC POLICY

A   Political philosophy

45 Value-freedom

Israel M. Kirzner

The doctrine of *Wertfreiheit* (of which the term 'value-freedom' is the literal translation) prescribes for the social scientist a methodological stance aimed at carefully separating and insulating scientific work from the personal ('unscientific') preferences of the researcher. (A standard work on the meaning and history of the doctrine is Hutchison, 1964.) The doctrine rests on several premises, each of which has been subjected to debate. First, the doctrine affirms a sharp qualitative distinction between scientific statements presenting empirical or theoretical assertions, on the one hand, and 'unscientific' expressions of personal preference, on the other. The latter, 'judgements of value', are in fact in *Wertfreiheit* discussions often held to be inherently incapable of being established on objective, scientific grounds that might convince an impartial observer insisting on proof. Second, the doctrine of *Wertfreiheit* assumes the possibility of in fact being able to engage in scientific work in a manner ensuring that personal value judgements are in no way expressed in the substantive content of the science. It *is* possible, that is, to enunciate scientific propositions the validity of which can be equally apparent to detached scientific observers holding opposing judgements of value. Third, the *Wertfreiheit* doctrine maintains that, both in order to maintain the integrity of the scientific enterprise and in order to ensure widespread confidence in the validity of the conclusions reached by scientists, it is necessary to insist on *Wertfreiheit*, and to ensure that the public be convinced that science is not simply an elaborate facade expressing the personal interests and preferences of scientists. *Wertfreiheit* is a tenet to be adhered to, in other words, not only in order to guard the integrity of science, but also in order to ensure that its integrity be recognized and appreciated.

The doctrine has had, of course, particular reference to economics, where the pronouncements of economists have often (justifiably) been dismissed as simply expressing the political or ideological positions of the economists or of those whom the economists are supporting. *Wertfreiheit* has often been urged as the only way to correct this unfortunate situation. In particular, Austrian economists have traditionally been outspoken on the need for *Wertfreiheit* in economics. Despite certain murmurings of apparent dissent on this matter within the ranks of contemporary Austrian economists, as we shall see, *Wertfreiheit* is still stoutly upheld as an ideal within the mainstream of contemporary Austrian economics (for examples, see Rizzo, 1992; White, 1992).

In what follows we shall (1) draw brief attention to well-known major pronouncements by important figures in the Austrian tradition which have argued for *Wertfreiheit* in economics; (2) refer briefly to some recent statements on the part of some Austrian economists which appear, at first glance, to challenge some of the assumptions upon which the *Wertfreiheit* doctrine must rest; and (3) explore the thesis that, for economists steeped in the Austrian tradition in economics, the doctrine is likely to seem especially plausible and, indeed, well-nigh essential to the methodological underpinnings of that tradition.

Value-freedom in the Austrian tradition
The Austrian tradition was, of course, born into a struggle with the German historical school of economics. The outstanding figures in that school tended to fuse their economics with their personal ethical views on social justice and morality, sometimes addressing their lecture classes almost as if they were political rallies. It was against this style of economics that Max Weber was, at the start of the present century, to rebel vigorously in his call for an austere *Wertfreiheit* in scientific economic research and discussion. It is no surprise, therefore, to discover that the first statement on the *Wertfreiheit* issue made within the Austrian tradition was indeed directed – years before Max Weber – against the German historical school. In his 1883 *Untersuchungen* (in which he threw down the methodological gauntlet in his criticisms of the historical method), Carl Menger wrote an appendix in which he briefly but emphatically criticized the tendency of the German economists to confuse ethical positions with the conclusions of economics.

The next prominent statement arising out of the Austrian tradition that should be cited is that of Robbins. Lionel Robbins wrote his classic *An Essay on the Nature and Significance of Economic Science* under strong Austrian influence (see, for example, Robbins, 1935, pp. xv–xvi). It can be persuasively argued that it is due to Robbins that the early Austrian commitment to *Wertfreiheit* came to be routinely accepted within mainstream neoclassical post-Second World War economics. An important element in Robbins's position in his *Essay* was his enthusiastic adoption of Max Weber's position on *Wertfreiheit*: 'Economics is neutral as between ends. Economics cannot pronounce on the validity of ultimate judgments of value ... Between the generalizations of positive and normative studies there is a logical gulf fixed which no ingenuity can disguise and no juxtaposition in space or time bridge over ... [Economic Science] is fundamentally distinct from Ethics' (ibid., pp. 147–52). What is distinctive in Robbins's statement of the *Wertfreiheit* doctrine is the fact that the doctrine emerges organically from Robbins's conception of the very nature of economic science (we shall take up this feature of his work in a later section of this essay). Robbins's 'positivism' was sharply attacked by his critics, who denounced his refusal to accord the name 'science' to normative disciplines, but Robbins stood his ground in the second edition of his book, emphasizing his continued acceptance of Max Weber's position (ibid., pp. xif).

Since Robbins, the most emphatic voice within Austrian economics on the issue of *Wertfreiheit* has certainly been that of Ludwig von Mises. It seems fair to say that it is due to Mises's insistence on this matter that Austrian economics is today widely recognized as endorsing the Weberian doctrine. The theme seems to have been foremost in Mises's mind over the last several decades of his scientific career. In 1933, Mises dwelt at length on the obligation of the economic scientist to maintain objectivity and neutrality in regard to judgements of value: 'What is impermissible ... is the obliteration of the boundary between scientific explanation and political value judgement' (Mises, 1933, p. 37). Mises had no doubt that this boundary can be clearly drawn: 'The objectivity of bacteriology ... is not in the least vitiated by the fact that the researchers in this field regard their task as a struggle against the viruses responsible for conditions harmful to the human organism' (p. 36). In his 1949 magnum opus, *Human Action*, Mises again carefully addressed this issue, concluding that economics 'is perfectly neutral with regards to all judgments of value, as it refers always to means and never to the choice of ultimate ends'. The fact that this discussion comes in the very last chapter of the book is surely significant. It serves to highlight Mises's concluding sentence in the book, in which he calmly declares that disregard of the warnings of the neutral science of economics must 'stamp out society and the human race' (Mises, 1949, p. 881). Mises returned to the *Wertfreiheit* theme in one of his last books, *Theory and History* (1957). Here the discussion does not conclude the book, but is in fact the substance of the first chapter and generally pervades the whole of Part One of the book. It serves as a prelude to a trenchant dismissal of Marxist (and other) charges that the teachings of economics are the product of bias.

Of course the *Wertfreiheit* doctrine is not peculiar to the Austrian tradition. In a comprehensive critique of the doctrine, Subroto Roy links the doctrine to Hume's insistence upon a categorical distinction between 'ought' statements and 'is' statements (with the concomitant denial of the possibility of deducing the former from the latter). Roy cites close to 20 of the most renowned figures in nineteenth and twentieth-century economics as having subscribed to some form of this doctrine (Roy, 1989, p. 17 and p. 194, note 1). Yet, despite the apparent near-universal acceptance of the doctrine among both mainstream and Austrian economists, a case does appear to be able to be made that Austrian economics tends to support the *Wertfreiheit* doctrine in a peculiarly characteristic way. We shall take up this argument in a later section of this essay. Here we pause to take brief note of certain intimations of apparent dissent concerning the *Wertfreiheit* doctrine, which might at first suggest a possible incompleteness in the unanimity of contemporary support for the doctrine.

Dissent within the Austrian camp?

Although several statements by Austrian economists during recent decades seem to point in a direction opposite to that taken by the proponents of *Wertfreiheit*, careful examination of them reveals that the disagreements involved (with the traditional Austrian position on the matter) are relatively minor. In several papers, Murray Rothbard has challenged, not so much the *Wertfreiheit* doctrine itself, as the claim that economic policy pronouncements can be made without violating the doctrine. Whereas Mises and other Austrians have appealed to *Wertfreiheit* as the basis for the possibility of economic policy pronouncements being made independently of any ethical presuppositions, Rothbard flatly denies any such possibility. While Misesian 'economic theory is extremely useful in providing data and knowledge for framing economic policy, it cannot be sufficient by itself ... to advocate any public policy whatsoever' (Rothbard, 1976, p. 109). Economic policy, Rothbard argues, necessarily involves some ethical foundation. Although this conclusion of Rothbard's *appears* diametrically opposed to Mises's claims that the objectivity of value-free economic science ensures the unbiased character of implied policy pronouncements, one may question the extent of the substantive disagreement between Mises and Rothbard. Rothbard, too, insists that sciences, including economics, are in themselves value-free; he merely claims that policy prescriptions by economists cannot fail to transcend such value-freedom. Although there is room for differences in nuance between the Misesian and Rothbardian approaches to economic policy advice, it seems that they share a basic commitment to the Weberian ideals.

Jack High (1985) sharply criticizes the thesis that economics is 'independent of ethics'. High argues that in fact the very definitions of basic entities crucial to economic inquiry must necessarily implicitly rely upon ethical norms for their very meaning. We cannot sensibly distinguish between market and government without resort to ethical standards (needed in order to assign meaning to the concepts of 'voluntary', 'coercive' and 'ownership'). It might seem, on a first reading, that High is attacking that separation between economics and ethics which served Menger and Weber as the foundation of the *Wertfreiheit* doctrine. Indeed, High cites critically those very observations of Menger on the subject which we saw earlier to be the foundation of *Wertfreiheit* in the Austrian tradition. Yet it becomes clear, upon further study, that High does *not* wish to challenge the doctrine itself. In fact he concludes his paper by assuring the reader that his central thesis leaves 'the much-cherished "value-freedom" of economic science' untouched. In other words, what High has argued is not at all that economic science is committed to a *particular* set of values, but that *some* set of values must be supplied before the propositions of economic science can be applied to concrete situations. For example, High writes, we can characterize the market economy as 'acquisition and use of resources that respect natural rights' without endorsing the ethical correctness of natural rights. So that High accepts, after all, the central foundation of the *Wertfreiheit* doctrine, that any ethical content implied in substantive economic propositions *can* be disentangled and separated from the non-ethical components in such propositions.

It is true that Rothbard's (and perhaps High's) position expresses disagreement with the thesis (central to at least many statements of the *Wertfreiheit* doctrine) which declares the correctness of value-judgements to be incapable of scientific demonstration. (In this they are concurring with a number of recent philosophical contributions.) But their position is nonetheless entirely consistent with traditional Austrian emphasis on the desirability of pursuing economic analysis in a way which protects it from dependency upon any particular ethical norms whatsoever. We conclude, therefore, that, while the degree of enthusiastic support for the centrality of the *Wertfreiheit* doctrine may vary among at least some Austrian economists, it yet remains valid to assert that acceptance of the doctrine remains characteristic of the Austrian tradition. Let us further explore this connection.

Wertfreiheit and the Austrian approach

Although, as noted, the *Wertfreiheit* doctrine has been accorded general acceptance by many schools of modern economic thought, it may be argued that its affinity to Austrian economics is an especially natural and organic one. It may be argued, that is, that the very way in which Austrian economics has conceived of its subject-matter entails a methodological stance which can hardly fail to be highly sympathetic to the *Wertfreiheit* doctrine.

No doubt the initial thrust of the Austrian tradition, its affirmation of the independence of theory from historical context, helped crystallize the ideas which were to mature into the *Wertfreiheit* doctrine. To declare the validity of propositions showing chains of causation which apply across widely differing institutional and historical backgrounds must certainly help promote understanding of the objectivity of such causation chains and their independence of the analyst's ethical evaluation of any of the specific situations in which they may manifest themselves. But Austrian economics, of course, was not the only school of modern economics to reject the position of the German historical school.

More to the point, perhaps, has been the Austrian focus on *individual choice* as the analytical unit in economics. The implications for *wertfreiheit* are perhaps most clearly seen in Robbins. Because economics is the logic of choice, the working out of the systematic consequences of the circumstance that man's actions are dictated by the configuration of his scarce *given* means and multiple, ranked, *given* ends, it follows that the propositions of economics depend not one whit on the ethics underlying the choice of ends or the morality of the distributive system responsible for the given means. For Robbins, writing under Austrian influence, the independence of economic science from ethics was explicitly seen as flowing out of his definition of the science. To be sure, Robbins's ideas on economics as the logic of choice have become the foundation for mainstream (non-Austrian) treatments of microeconomics, yet we should not lose sight of the characteristically Austrian influences which appear to have helped shaped Robbins's *Wertfreiheit* commitment.

Mises's own commitment to *Wertfreiheit* appears to have emerged in a manner parallel to (although not quite identical with) that which we have seen in Robbins. As is well known, Mises saw economics as praxeology, the pure science of human action. Because Mises saw praxeology as consisting of propositions developed a priori from economic reasoning, and applying in the real world wherever the relevant circumstances pertain, it followed that the positive truths of economics will manifest themselves whether we like them or not, whether we approve of the ethics of any particular set of circumstances (in which these truths manifest themselves) or not. Through appropriate demonstration, it is then possible to hope, these truths can appear as reasonable and persuasive to open-minded students of economics, regardless of any ethical prejudgements which they may hold.

The notion of human action, central to the very idea of Misesian praxeology, appeared to have confirmed, for Mises, the underpinnings of the *Wertfreiheit* doctrine: 'The significance of value judgments consists precisely in the fact they are the springs of human action. Guided by his valuations, man is intent upon substituting conditions that please him better for conditions which he deems less satisfactory. He employs means in order to attain ends sought' (Mises, 1957, p. 20). Mises sees this as the basis for asserting a sharp distinction between ultimate judgements of value and the propositions of economics: 'As soon as we start to refute by arguments an ultimate judgment of value, we look upon it as a means to attain definite ends. But then we merely shift the discussion to another plane. We no longer view the principle concerned as an ultimate value but as a means to attain an ultimate value' (Mises, 1957, pp. 22–3).

It seems to follow that Mises's commitment to the doctrine of *Wertfreiheit* does not depend on the assertion that the correctness of value judgements can never be demonstrated or disproved by scientific methods. His commitment to the doctrine rests merely on the contention that, in the context of any economic problem, the correctness of the relevant judgements of value is not itself the issue. In this respect Mises and Robbins appear to concur in every significant respect.

Austrian economics has often been understood to support the free market political program. What we have seen is that, despite the fact that many Austrian economists (Mises in particular!) were indeed emphatic in their belief that economic science lends support to proponents of the free enterprise system, they have consistently maintained that the theoretical basis of such support is by itself politically neutral. Precisely because the support by economists for free market institutional arrangements has often been sharply attacked as the product of bias, Austrian economists have felt it necessary to emphasize the need for their science to be absolutely untainted by such bias. They have, we have seen, found the basis for such a possible 'purity', unstained by judgements of value, in the most fundamental of their conceptions of what makes a science of economics possible. It is because of their conviction of the soundness of this possibility, and their lively awareness of the need to escape unfair charges of pro-market bias, that Austrians have again and again felt impelled to uphold the doctrine of value-freedom.

See also:
Chapter 5: Aristotelianism, apriorism, essentialism; Chapter 2: Methodological individualism; Chapter 3: Subjectivism

Bibliography
High, J. (1985), 'Is Economics Independent of Ethics?', *Reason Papers*, No. 10, spring.
Hutchison, T.W. (1964), *'Positive' Economics and Policy Objectives*, Cambridge, Mass.: Harvard University Press.
Mises, L. von (1933), *Grundprobleme der Nationalökonomie*, translated as *Epistemological Problems of Economics*, Princeton, NJ: Van Nostrand, 1960.
Mises, L. von (1949), *Human Action*, New Haven: Yale University Press.
Mises, L. von. (1957), *Theory and History*, New Haven: Yale University Press.
Rizzo, M.J. (1992), 'Afterword: Austrian Economics for the Twenty-First Century', in Bruce J. Caldwell and Stephen Böhm (eds), *Austrian Economics: Tensions and New Directions*, Boston: Kluwer Academic.
Robbins, L. (1935), *An Essay on the Nature and Significance of Economic Science*, 2nd edn, London: Macmillan.
Rothbard, M.N. (1976), 'Praxeology, Value Judgments, and Public Policy', in E. Dolan (ed.), *The Foundations of Modern Austrian Economics*, Kansas City: Sheed and Ward.
Roy, S. (1989), *Philosophy of Economics*, London/New York: Routledge.
White, L.M. (1992), 'Afterword: Appraising Austrian Economics – Contentions and Misdirections', in Bruce J. Caldwell and Stephen Böhm (eds), *Austrian Economics: Tensions and New Directions*, Boston: Kluwer Academic.

46 Classical liberalism and the Austrian school
Ralph Raico

The theoretical basis of classical liberalism, of what we shall refer to here simply as *liberalism*, is the conception of civil society as by and large self-regulating when its members are free to act within the very wide bounds of their individual rights. Among these, the right to private property, including freedom of contract and the free disposition of one's own labor, enjoys a high priority. Historically, liberalism has displayed a hostility to state action, which it aims to reduce to a minimum.

From its beginnings, Austrian economics was associated with liberalism, an association that has become more intimate over time. Austrian economists have always been at pains to affirm the *Wertfreiheit* (value-freedom) of their theory and thus its conformity to Weberian strictures on the character of scientific theories. Its neutrality as regards values and, hence, ideologies, may be granted in the formal sense that no Austrian doctrines yield liberal claims without the interposition of particular value judgements. Nonetheless, the manifold connections between liberalism and Austrian economics have been recognized by adherents and opponents alike. These links exist on the levels of methodology, economic theory (to the degree that this can be separated from Austrian methodology) and the historical development of the school.

Methodology
Methodological individualism has been a keystone of Austrian economics since the publication of the first Austrian work, Menger's *Principles*, in 1871. This approach implies the elimination of holistic systems that treat entities like race, nation or class as irreducible primaries (major grounds for opposition to Austrianism from both right and left). Thus, while it is certainly possible for non-liberals to advocate methodological individualism, the procedure has the effect of precluding some important ideologies incompatible with liberalism, such as classical Marxism and varieties of racism and hypernationalism. To this extent, then, it is not simply *methodological* individualism.

Political factors have played a role in the debate over Austrian methodology from the start. It was on the basis of Menger's method that Gustav Schmoller, leader of the German historical school, accused him of adhering to *Manchestertum* (laissez-faire) in his review of Menger's *Investigations* (1883). Many decades later, F.A. Hayek, in a sense, concurred with Schmoller.

The central idea of his most extensive work on methodology, *The Counter-Revolution of Science* (1952), is precisely the historical and theoretical connections between 'scientism', which represents the denial of methodological individualism, and the growth of socialism.

Marxist writers have criticized Austrian methodology for allegedly stunting the understanding of social reality by concentrating on the psychology of isolated, atomistic individuals, and thus diverting attention from the crucial questions of *political economy* that had been the focus of classical economics (including Marxism). The abstracting approach of Austrianism, however, pertains – necessarily – to its *theory*. Most Austrians, it is true, have neglected to *apply* their theory to elucidate concrete, 'real-life' history, but that this omission is not intrinsic to their economic approach is shown by the work of Murray N. Rothbard, a strict methodological individualist, who has undertaken the analysis of highly important questions of political economy on an Austrian foundation.

An allied feature of Austrian methodology is its *subjectivism*. Austrian economics begins with and places in the forefront the action of the individual human being. As Ludwig Lachmann put it: 'The significance of the Austrian school in the history of ideas perhaps finds its most pregnant expression in the statement that here man *as an actor* stands at the center of economic events.' In contrast to the neoclassical school, Austrian subjectivism highlights the perpetually active role of all participants in market processes, stressing the alertness, inquisitiveness and resourceful creativity of individuals. This is especially the case in respect to entrepreneurs and the entrepreneurial function, yet even consumers are viewed, not as fixed loci of consumption functions, but as sources of incessant change.

In this whole area there are strong congruities with central elements of classical liberalism. Austrian subjectivism finds analogues in essential liberal modalities, such as individuality, individual creativity, and differences and inequalities among individuals. These all have implications for both social theory and political policy. In combating authoritarian ideologies, liberals historically focused on the individual human being as the fountainhead of creativity and social progress. From this they derived the chief and most general liberal demand, the need to concede as wide a latitude as possible to individual freedom of choice and action.

On the level of economic policy, Austrianism's individualist and subjectivist methodology tends to produce skepticism in regard to the macroeconomic models of mainstream economics, with their assumption that various global magnitudes act upon one another – a precondition of much state interference in the economy. Austrian subjectivism generates a similar skepticism towards conventional welfare economics, which serves to justify statist welfare measures by attempting, as Israel Kirzner has written, 'to aggregate, in some sense, the tastes, the purposes, or the satisfaction of individuals into an entity that it is the ideal of economic policy to maximize' (Kirzner, 1976, pp. 84–5).

Individuality bears an intimate, perhaps even logical, connection to diversity, and Austrianism, in contrast to neoclassical economics, accentuates the role of diversity in economic life. To the degree that weight is given to individual differences and diversity, a statist approach to policy becomes more problematical. Thus, it seems clear that distinctive Austrian emphases – on the role of the individual's alertness to opportunities in his specific setting, on the market as a process of discovery, on the heterogeneity of the factors of production, and so on – are so many points telling against the possibility of either socialist planning or efficient state intervention in the economy. That individuality implies inequality is affirmed by both Austrian economics and liberal social philosophy. As against the neoclassical school, the Austrian approach, as Lachmann pointed out, views men as *highly unequal*, with different needs and abilities that decisively affect market transactions. Here again the methodological underscoring of human inequality has an affinity with the liberal principle of inequality of wealth and income. Ludwig von Mises, who believed in the innate physiological and intellectual inequality of human beings, stated outright: 'The inequality of incomes and wealth is an inherent feature of the market economy. Its elimination would entirely destroy the market economy' (1949, p. 836).

Finally, in the area of methodology, a rather odd claim of both T.W. Hutchison and Milton Friedman may be mentioned. These authors have asserted that the strictly a priori approach of Mises and his followers (praxeology) is *incompatible* with the values and spirit of liberalism. Neither Hutchison nor Friedman, however, has provided a sufficiently coherent argument to warrant, or even allow for, serious rebuttal.

Economic theory
There is a sense in which any analytical economics can be said to be relatively favorable towards the market. But Austrian economics has been so often and so closely tied to liberalism that it is plausible to seek a connection in its distinctive economic principles. The sustained attack on the possibility of rational economic planning under socialism that was led by Mises and Hayek has doubtless played a major role in associating the school with liberal doctrine. To the extent that Austrian principles rebut the possibility of viable socialism, they obviously lend support to the liberal case.

A widely explored Austrian concept employed in the anti-socialist attack particularly by Hayek – that of prices as surrogate information – militates against interventionism as well. Interventionist measures, as Erich Streissler points out, eliminate 'the mechanism of the creation and dissemination of information about economically relevant circumstances, i.e., market pricing', thus impeding economic efficiency (Streissler, 1988, p. 195). In addition, the Austrian analysis of the market as a process precludes certain interventionist or socialist moves, for example, viewing the total of incomes of individuals and firms within a national jurisdiction as a kind of 'national cake' to be divided up at will. The concept of the market as process also serves to validate the social inequalities and hierarchical structures inherent in capitalism. As Mises wrote:

> The selective process of the market is actuated by the composite effort of all members of the market economy ... The resultant of these endeavors is not only the price structure but no less the social structure, the assignment of definite tasks to the various individuals. The market makes people rich or poor, determines who shall run the big plants and who shall scrub the floors, fixes how many people shall work in the copper mines and how many in the symphony orchestras. None of these decisions is made once and for all; they are revocable every day. (1949, p. 308)

But probably the most convincing grounds for linking Austrian economics and the free market have to do with the general conception of economic life propounded by the Austrians, beginning with Menger.

Israel Kirzner has offered an explanation of why, despite the differing policy views of its founders (see below), Austrianism was immediately perceived as *the* economics of the free market. It was because their works

> expressed an understanding of markets which, *taken by itself*, strongly suggested a more radical appreciation for free markets than the early Austrians themselves displayed. It is this latter circumstance, we surmise, which explains how, when later Austrians arrived at even more consistently laissez-faire positions, they were seen by historians of thought as somehow simply pursuing an Austrian tradition that can be traced back to its founders. (Kirzner, 1990, p. 93)

Kirzner appropriately refers to the novelty in Menger's 'overall vision of the economy'. It was seen as

> a system driven entirely and independently by the choices and valuations of consumers – with these valuations transmitted 'upwards' through the system to 'goods of higher order', determining how these scarce higher-order goods are allocated among industries and how they are valued and remunerated as part of a single consumer-driven process. (ibid., p. 99)

In contrast to the classical economists, who saw the capitalist system as producing the greatest possible amount of material goods, Menger's view was that it was 'a pattern of *economic governance exercised by consumer preferences*'. (Later, W.H. Hutt coined the term 'consumer sovereignty' for this.) Kirzner observes that 'it was this thoroughly Mengerian insight which nourished Mises's lifelong polemic against socialist and interventionist mis-understandings of the market economy' (ibid., p. 100). And, it may be added, it was this insight that terrified the Marxists.

Another major Austrian concern has also forged a close connection with liberalism. Since liberalism is based on the recognition of the self-regulating capacities of civil society (that is, the social order minus the state), any social theory that centers on those capacities may be expected to furnish support for the liberal position. From a very early point, Austrianism was noted for its emphasis on 'spontaneous order' in society. In his *Investigations*, Menger raised the question, 'How can it be that institutions which serve the common welfare and are extremely significant for its development come into being without a common will directed toward establishing them?' He pointed out that 'Law, language, the state, money, markets, all these social structures are to no small extent the unintended result of social development.' Menger went on to provide a brilliant and famous explanation, based on methodological individualism, of the origin of money (Menger, 1985, pp. 139–59).

Hayek, in particular, continued this Mengerian quest, declaring, 'The point … which was long not fully understood until at last Carl Menger explained it clearly, was that the problem of the origin or formation and that of the manner of functioning of social institutions was essentially the same' (Hayek, 1967, p. 101). Still, it is not entirely clear to what degree the Menger–Hayek view of the spontaneous origin of institutions is serviceable to liberalism. As Menger stated:

> But never, and this is the essential point in the matter under review, may science dispense with testing for their suitability those institutions which have come about 'organically'. It must, when careful investigation so requires, change and better them according to the measure of scientific insight and practical experience at hand. No era may renounce this 'calling'. (Menger, 1985, p. 234)

Thus, a certain – undefined, but presumably substantial – area would seem to exist for 'social engineering'.

Historical development of the school

Historically, the emergence of Austrian economics, and of neoclassicism in general, appeared to many to signal both the rescue of market-oriented economic theory from the impasse to which Ricardian and Millian economics had led, and the decisive refutation of Marxism. Outraged socialist critics, aware of the danger, pilloried marginalism as a rationalization for the capitalist system. Karl Kautsky, the Pope of German Marxism before the First World War, took note of the Austrian challenge and declared: 'Böhm-Bawerk's and Marx's theories of value are mutually exclusive. … That means, therefore: either–or.' Nikolai Bukharin, who attended Böhm-Bawerk's lectures, devoted a major work to refuting Austrianism as 'the economic theory of the rentier class'. From the other side, Frank A. Fetter, after describing the battle between the subjective-value theory and Marxism, exulted in 1923 that 'it would be difficult to find in the whole history of economic thought a more complete victory of one idea over another'.

Although the generally liberal direction of Austrian theory was widely agreed upon from an early point, less agreement has obtained respecting the extent of commitment to laissez-faire of the founders of the school. While Friedrich von Wieser was fairly obviously a statist, the precise positions of Eugen von Böhm-Bawerk and, above all, Carl Menger, have been a matter of dispute. Until recently, it was generally held, on the basis of a few published articles, that Menger was a 'social', rather than a classical, liberal. Erich Streissler has maintained, however, that the recently discovered notebooks of Menger's pupil, the Crown Prince Rudolf, show the tutor 'to have been a classical liberal of the purest water with a much smaller agenda for the state than even Adam Smith' (Streissler, 1990, p. 110). It appears, however, that Streissler exaggerates the value of these notebooks and that Bruce J. Caldwell is probably correct in stating: 'One suspects that the final chapter on Menger's policy views remains to be written' (Caldwell, 1990, p. 7).

Another historian of Austrianism, Emil Kauder, maintained that the founders of the school, including Böhm-Bawerk, displayed an 'uneasy swinging back and forth between freedom and authority in their economic policy', the result of contradictory forces working on their thought. On the one hand, according to Kauder, they were influenced by the Austrian tradition of state paternalism. On the other, they were 'social ontologists', holding that 'a general plan of reality exists. All social phenomena are conceived in relation to this master plan. ... The ontological structure does not only indicate what is, but also what ought to be.' Kauder takes as an example Böhm-Bawerk's *Positive Theory of Capital*, which demonstrates 'the natural order under the laissez-faire mechanism. In "beautiful harmony" the economic fabric is fitted together by marginal utility, discount theory of interest, and roundabout production, if the long run price (Dauerpreis) of free competition is reached' (Kauder, 1957). This 'social ontology' – exemplified in other landmark Austrian works, above all Mises's *Human Action* – is deeply congruent with the liberal vision.

Especially beginning with Mises and Hayek, the links of Austrian economics to liberalism are strong and pervasive. Mises and Hayek were themselves probably the two most eminent liberal thinkers of the twentieth century. In the minds of many scholars as well as of much of the informed public, the association of Austrianism with liberalism was greatly enhanced by the famous debate over the possibility of rational economic calculation under socialism. Mises himself effectively inaugurated the debate in the early 1920s, in articles and in his *Socialism*, and he and his disciple Hayek were the acknowledged leaders of the anti-socialist camp through the 1930s and 1940s. In the same period and later, each in his own way elaborated and restated the social philosophy of liberalism for the age. Hayek in particular also devoted himself to studies in the intellectual history of liberalism, expounding in his article, 'Individualism: True and False', a version of that history tending to buttress his own rather 'Whiggish' slant.

Even leaving aside the differing focuses and temperamental undertones of the two great thinkers, there is a clear distinction in the degree of liberalism they evidenced. This may be symbolized by the fact that Hayek always avoided using the term 'laissez-faire' to describe his view, quite unlike Mises, who gloried in it. Mises, perhaps influenced here by Böhm-Bawerk's dismal experience in government, virtually never had a good word to say for politicians, while Hayek was always more open to the useful possibilities of state action. Hayek had been a student of Wieser's, originally attracted to him, as he stated, by Wieser's 'mild Fabian Socialism'. Throughout his career, Hayek displayed a penchant for *Sozialpolitik* and distanced himself from the authentic liberal position by declaring, in 1960, for instance, that 'though a few theorists have demanded that the activities of government should be limited to the maintenance of law and order, such a stand cannot be justified by the principle of liberty'. The state, Hayek insisted, is not solely 'a coercive apparatus', but also 'a service agency' (1960, pp. 257–8). Mises, on the contrary, viewed the state in the classical manner, as merely 'the social apparatus of compulsion and coercion', and stressed the possibilities of meeting charitable and other 'social' needs through the resources of civil society.

Contemporary Austrian economists, following in Mises's footsteps, have by and large adopted a radical form of liberalism. At least one of them, Murray N. Rothbard, has gone even further in his anti-statism. It is to a large degree due to Rothbard's work that Austrianism is often associated with a defense of the free market and private property to the point of the very abolition of the state and thus the total triumph of civil society. Rothbard has also extended his analysis to international affairs, a highly significant dimension of liberal theory mostly ignored by earlier Austrians.

See also:
Chapter 13: Cost; Chapter 29: 'Invisible hand' explanations; Chapter 12: Marginal utility

Bibliography
Caldwell, Bruce J. (ed.) (1990), *Carl Menger and His Legacy in Economics*, annual supplement to vol. 22, *History of Political Economy*, Durham, NC: Duke University Press.
Dolan, Edward G. (ed.) (1976), *The Foundations of Modern Austrian Economics*, Kansas City: Sheed and Ward.
Hayek, F.A. (1948), *Individualism and Economic Order*, Chicago: University of Chicago Press.

Hayek, F.A. (1955), *The Counter-Revolution of Science*, Glencoe, IL.: Free Press.
Hayek, F.A. (1960), *The Constitution of Liberty*, Chicago: University of Chicago Press.
Hayek, F.A. (1967), *Studies in Philosophy, Politics, and Economics*, Chicago: University of Chicago Press.
Hayek, F.A. (1992), *The Fortunes of Liberalism. Essays on Austrian Economics and the Ideal of Freedom*, in *The Collected Works of F.A. Hayek*, Vol. IV, ed. Peter G. Klein, Chicago: University of Chicago Press.
Kauder, Emil (1957), 'Intellectual and Political Roots of the Older Austrian School', *Zeitschrift für Nationalökonomie*, **17**, (4), December, 411–25.
Kirzner, Israel M. (1976), 'Philosophical and Ethical Implications of Austrian Economics', in Dolan (1976).
Kirzner, Israel M. (1990), 'Menger, Classical Liberalism, and the Austrian School of Economics', in Caldwell (1990).
Menger, Carl [1883] (1985), *Investigations into the Method of the Social Sciences with Special Reference to Economics*, ed. Louis Schneider, translated by Francis J. Nock, New York: New York University Press.
Mises, Ludwig von (1949), *Human Action: A Treatise on Economics*, New Haven: Yale University Press.
Mises, Ludwig von (1969), *The Historical Setting of the Austrian School of Economics*, New Rochelle, NY: Arlington House.
Mises, Ludwig von [1927] (1985), *Liberalism in the Classical Tradition*, translated by Ralph Raico, Irvington, NY/San Francisco: Foundation for Economic Education/Cobden Press.
Raico, Ralph (1992), 'Prolegomena to a History of Liberalism', *Journal des Économistes et des Études Humaines*, **3**, (2/3), 259–72.
Rothbard, Murray N. (1970), *Power and Market, Government and the Economy*, Menlo Park, CA.: Institute for Humane Studies.
Rothbard, Murray N. (1973), *For a New Liberty*, New York: Macmillan.
Rothbard, Murray N. (1988), *Ludwig von Mises: Scholar, Creator, Hero*, n.p.: Ludwig von Mises Institute.
Streissler, Erich (1987), *Wie Liberal Waren die Begründer der Österreichischen Schule der Nationalökonomie?*, Vienna: Carl Menger Institute.
Streissler, Erich (1988), 'The Intellectual and Political Impact of the Austrian School of Economics', *History of European Ideas*, **9**, (2), 191–204.
Streissler, Erich (1990), 'Carl Menger on Economic Policy: The Lectures to Crown Prince Rudolf', in Caldwell (1990).

47 Utilitarianism
Leland B. Yeager

Moral philosophy tries to identify the grounds for appraising behavior, character traits, institutions and public policies as good or bad, right or wrong. Utilitarianism is one particular orientation. One or another version seems to be the house brand of ethics accepted, at least tacitly, by most economists who concern themselves with normative questions.

Throughout his writings, Ludwig von Mises forthrightly called himself a utilitarian. Although ordinarily shunning that label, F. A. Hayek is also a utilitarian (or so I have argued, 1984). In an excellent but inadequately appreciated book, Henry Hazlitt (1964) elaborates on the utilitarian doctrines of Mises and Hayek and of David Hume, who inspired both. However, some contemporary Austrian economists, mentioned later, repudiate utilitarianism in favor of a natural-rights approach to ethics and political philosophy.

An extreme *act* version of utilitarianism calls on each person to act on each individual occasion in whatever way he calculates will contribute most to total pleasure or happiness, aggregated over all persons and perhaps even over all sentient beings and over all time. Scarcely anyone clearly asserts so unappealing a version nowadays (though it is sometimes attributed to the nineteenth-century Benthamites and though Edgeworth, 1881, might also count as a near example). Act-utilitarianism serves as a hypothetical benchmark for illuminating more plausible versions by contrast – and also as an easy target for superficial critics.

A rules or indirect utilitarianism, espoused by several twentieth-century philosophers and sometimes attributed to John Stuart Mill (1863; see Gray, 1983), rejects trying to determine the best course of action afresh from case to individual case. Instead, people should ordinarily heed established rules. It is the rules that are to be counted good or bad, right or wrong, according as they tend to support or to undermine social cooperation. The same criterion applies in appraising attitudes and character traits, institutional arrangements, and laws and public policies. Social cooperation is the complex of activities, supported by appropriate institutions, rules and attitudes, that accomplish or promote specialization and exchange and other mutually beneficial interactions among individuals as they strive to make good lives for themselves in their own diverse ways.

Ludwig von Mises and Henry Hazlitt, in particular, have stressed this criterion. As Mises says, preserving 'the peaceful course of social cooperation ... is in the interest of everyone' (1927, p. 165). Further,

> Morality consists in the regard for the necessary requirements of social existence that must be demanded of each individual member of society. ... For the life of the individual in society is possible only by virtue of social cooperation.... In requiring of the individual ... that he should forgo an action that, while advantageous to him, would be detrimental to social life, society does not demand that he sacrifice himself to the interests of others. For the sacrifice that it imposes is only a provisional one: the renunciation of an immediate and relatively minor advantage in exchange for a much greater ultimate benefit. The continued existence of society as the association of persons working in cooperation and sharing a common way of life is in the interest of every individual (ibid., pp. 33–4; compare pp. 155ff, as well as other writings of Mises quoted and paraphrased in Yeager, 1992).

Neither the concept nor the term 'social cooperation' originated with Mises and Hazlitt. Herbert Spencer repeatedly used it in his *Principles of Ethics*; and the concept itself, though not the term, goes at least as far back as Thomas Hobbes, who emphasized the importance of peace and security to human prosperity and indeed to survival (1651, notably chapter 13). David Hume made much of social cooperation, although without using the term, and linked justice with promoting or subverting it. He observed that

> the circumstance of utility, in all subjects, is a source of praise and approbation: That it is constantly appealed to in all moral decisions concerning the merit and demerit of actions: That it is the sole source of that high regard paid to justice, fidelity, honour, allegiance, and chastity: That it is inseparable from all the other social virtues, humanity, generosity, charity, affability, lenity, mercy, and moderation: And, in a word, that it is a foundation of the chief part of morals, which has a reference to mankind and our fellow-creatures. ... everything which promotes the interest of society must communicate pleasure, and what is pernicious give uneasiness. ... whatever conduct promotes the good of the community is loved, praised, and esteemed by the community, on account of that utility and interest, of which every one partakes. (Hume, 1777, pp. 66, 67, 79)

(Hume obviously does not give the word 'utility' the technical meaning it has in modern microeconomics. For him it clearly means usefulness – usefulness for social cooperation and so for promoting human well-being.)

The following passage from Hume (1777, pp. 148–9) is widely quoted:

> Public utility requires that property should be regulated by general inflexible rules; and though such rules are adopted as best serve the same end of public utility, it is impossible for them to prevent all particular hardships, or make beneficial consequences result from every individual case. It is sufficient, if the

whole plan or scheme be necessary to the support of civil society, and if the balance of good, in the main, do thereby preponderate much above that of evil.

Social cooperation is not itself the *ultimate* criterion of good and bad, right and wrong. The ultimate utilitarian criterion is hard to specify precisely, but any plausible attempt uses words alluding to the happiness or satisfaction or fulfilment of individuals. Precision is unnecessary; for social cooperation, although not the ultimate end, is the indispensable means to what human beings find good for themselves individually and jointly. It serves as a surrogate criterion: institutions, rules, laws, actions and attitudes are deemed good or bad, right or wrong, according as they maintain or subvert it. These considerations recommend truth telling, promise keeping and respect for property rights and other human rights; they condemn opposite behaviors and character traits.

As already implied, utilitarian ethics has two components: consequentialism and a criterion. The first demands attention to the *consequences* of adopting or rejecting various behaviors, notions of rights and duties, and so forth. The ultimate criterion of appraisal rests on a fundamental value judgement favoring happiness (in some suitably stretched sense of the word) and deploring misery. A relatively specific value judgement is one for which reasons can be given. Someone who judges Jones a scoundrel could probably explain why; likewise, he could probably explain that he admires honesty and deplores deceit because of their effects on social cooperation and so on prospects for human happiness. A *fundamental* value judgement, by contrast, is one that cannot be argued for (for argument involves appealing to other, more nearly fundamental, judgements). Someone pressed to explain why he favors happiness and deplores misery probably could give no reasons. His recourse to fact and logic has come to its end; he has no more to say to someone who does not share his fundamental intuition. While utilitarianism thus does appeal to an irresolvable kernel of intuition, it does not appeal to intuitions *prematurely* and *promiscuously*. (Such an appeal to numerous specific intuitions, as the philosopher R.M. Hare properly insists, is the opposite of disciplined argument. Or, as Mises said, the tenets of intuitionist ethics 'are irreconcilable with scientific method' and 'have been deprived of their very foundations' (1922, p. 360).

Like almost any other ethical doctrine, utilitarianism has a third characteristic – often called generalizability, universalizability or impartiality. Its precepts are *not* chosen to favor specific individuals and groups and to put special burdens on others. As Ludwig von Mises says about classical liberalism – for which he offers a utilitarian grounding – it demands the preservation of society and opposes special favors for particular groups (1927, especially pp. 175–9). He writes:

Liberalism has always had in view the good of the whole, not that of any special group. It was this that the English utilitarians meant to express – although, it is true, not very aptly – in their famous formula, 'the greatest happiness of the greatest number'. Historically, liberalism was the first political movement that aimed at promoting the welfare of all, not that of special groups. (ibid., p. 7)

Some philosophers argue that ethical precepts are universalizable *by definition*, by the very meaning of ethics; but one may argue at least as well that this impartiality follows from utilitarian considerations. An ethical code arbitrarily rigged to favor some specific persons and victimize others would not be defensible by reasoned argument, could not command general adherence, and so would not be workable and could not promote the general welfare. It is reasonable to expect impartiality of an ethical code but *not* to expect it of persons in their own decisions. No code could be workable if it demanded routine self-sacrifice – if it required each person to subordinate his closest concerns to some sort of aggregate social utility, if it required each person to be impartial between the interests and projects of himself and his family, friends, associates and fellow-countrymen and the interests and projects of everyone else. Only a straw-man version of utilitarianism expects that. Such an expectation would waste information and undercut incentives, would not and could not be faithfully heeded, would arouse feelings of resentment or guilt or both, and so would be subversive of a good society. Self-interest within the restraints of ethics, zeal in pursuing one's own projects, loyalty to family and friends, and an honorable patriotism are themselves ingredients of a good society and necessary to human happiness. Ethical precepts recognizing the value of special interests and ties can be impartial in the sense under discussion. What *would* violate impartiality or universalizability in this sense would be rules entitling some specific persons to show special concern for themselves and their friends while denying this entitlement to others.

To promote the common good, meaning the interests that individuals share in common, an ethical code must be *workable*, which presupposes that the individual find it in his own interest, by and large, to abide by it. As John Rawls said (1971, section 29), a workable social system must be able to stand the 'strains of commitment'. Abiding by the usual precepts of morality is indeed likely to serve self-interest, as many philosophers and economists have explained (including, in our century, Moritz Schlick 1930; Mortimer Adler, 1970; Henry Hazlitt, 1964; Robert Frank, 1988). A disposition to behave otherwise – opportunistically, exploitatively, out of narrow and short-run self-interest – is likely to harm even the individual himself. Being in a position to reap the gains from trade and other forms of cooperation with other persons presupposes coming across to others as a cooperator rather than defector or exploiter. The best way to do so is actually to *be* a cooperator, and to have the corresponding emotions. Because one's emotions provide a short-run pay-off to behavior that might otherwise pay off only probabilistically in the long run, emotions help overcome the human tendency to underrate one's long-run interest relative to short-run interest (see Frank, 1988, in particular).

Cooperativeness includes an aversion to unfairness and even a disposition to take revenge in extreme cases. These attitudes and their supporting emotions (possessed, incidentally, by the hypothetical impartial benevolent spectator in the doctrines of David Hume and Adam Smith) tend to serve both the private interests of individuals and also their shared interest in a good society. As the columnist Stewart Alsop once wrote, 'the man who makes a justified fuss does a public service'. A disposition to exhibit honesty, cooperativeness, fairness, and even justified indignation tends, but merely *tends*, and *in the long run*, to serve an individual's own interest. Many people have flourished through dishonesty, theft, or 'going along to get along'; and many have ruined or lost their lives through honesty and decency. Nothing guarantees that morality will pay off. We have to go by the probabilities, which do recommend morality. What an individual recognizes as in his own interest largely depends, furthermore, on his upbringing and social environment. The characters of a society and of its individual members interact.

Contrasting ethical doctrines further illuminate what utilitarianism means. Can the will of God, somehow ascertained, provide a distinct basis for ethics? Can the supreme criterion be not the well-being of people in general but the flourishing of the few noblest and most creative specimens of the human race (a view sometimes attributed to Nietzsche, rightly or wrongly, as by Rawls, 1971, pp. 25, 325)? Can knowledge or beauty form the supreme criterion, quite apart from what they might contribute to human happiness?

Some suggest *duty* as the foundational concept of ethics – absolute duty to be known and performed quite apart from any thought of consequences. But what counts as duty, and why? Identifying duties by the consequences of performing and neglecting them takes us back to utilitarianism. Immanuel Kant and his ethics of duty incurred sharp criticism from Mises: 'His desperate attempt to uproot Eudaemonism has failed. In ethics, Bentham, Mill, and Feuerbach triumph over Kant. The social philosophy of his contemporaries, Ferguson and Adam Smith, left him untouched. Economics remained foreign to him. All his perception of social problems suffers from these deficiencies' (1922, p. 388).

Some philosophers and economists (for example, Rothbard, 1982) trumpet an alternative to utilitarianism focusing on natural (or human, or individual) rights. They appeal to widespread intuitions that rights are great and noble things. But can we conceive of rights as objective if intangible entities that exist prior to other ethical concepts and prior to considerations of human aspirations and social structure? Rights are important, but assertions of them cannot serve as the foundation or centerpiece of morality because they themselves are propositions or implications of morality: rights presuppose morality. They may be sensibly understood as ethical precepts of a particularly binding character – precepts about how people should treat one another. They are identified by considering facts of the very kinds that support a utilitarian ethics, facts concerning what sorts of interpersonal relations are necessary for human flourishing and happiness. Human beings have rights because of the sorts of creatures they are. It would make nonsense to attribute rights to life, liberty, property and the pursuit of happiness to social insects, say, whose entire lives are biologically programmed in detail. In short, rights are ethical precepts but no alternative to a utilitarian *grounding*.

Another supposed alternative to utilitarianism, at least in the realm of political philosophy and public policy, is the contractarianism espoused by some philosophers (including Jan Narveson and David Gauthier) and by James Buchanan and other economists of the public choice school. Economist contractarians allude to contract and consent, to unanimous consent of some 'conceptual' rather than literal sort, and to consent on some sort of constitutional level as distinguished from legislative and administrative levels. A test of institutions and policies is whether everybody *could* agree to them or *would* agree to them under idealized conditions. Anyway, ones that people would *not* agree to are ruled out. A contractarian feels entitled to recommend a policy only tentatively, only as a hypothesis that it is in accord with a unanimously made contract, or that it conceptually commands agreement, or that it could command agreement after sufficiently enlightening public discussion. But how does the contractarian judge whether some policy could or could not command agreement? Must he not consider its consequences, as for social cooperation and thereby for happiness? It seems operationally empty to try to distinguish between propounding hypotheses about what policies could ideally command agreement and recommending policies because they are expected to enhance social cooperation and so serve human happiness. Contractarianism appears to be utilitarianism disguised by particular bits of rhetoric.

Contractarianism does have this merit: its emphasis on agreement, even if only 'conceptual' agreement, highlights the individuality and diversity of the persons whose welfare forms the ultimate criterion. The contractarian knows the dangers of supposedly pursuing some aggregate utility, the utility of some entity transcending mere individual human beings. He knows that the happiness of individuals is the only kind attainable. But critics of utilitarianism have no monopoly on recognizing facts like these.

Utilitarianism routinely gets a bad press nowadays. Jan Narveson (1988) and Loren Lomasky (1987) make sweeping criticisms, characteristically without naming the writers to whom they supposedly apply. Utilitarianism, Narveson suggests, calls on each person to work towards maximizing the aggregate of cardinally measurable and interpersonally comparable utilities, remaining impartial between his own and other persons' aspirations (1988, pp. 150–53 especially). The doctrine allegedly invokes 'equality of the value to *anyone* of a unit of *anyone*'s utility" (p. 92). 'For a utilitarian,' says Lomasky, 'persons turn out to be convenient loci at which and through which value can be realized. Because rightness of action is entirely a function of utility production, it is necessarily utility that counts primarily, persons only derivatively' (1987, p. 54). Since each person is merely a soldier in a common cause, nothing is 'suspect about sacrificing one of the troops for another just as long as more impersonal value is thereby attained' (ibid. p. 53). 'Because utilitarian morality takes all value to be impersonal, utilitarianism makes no room for individualism. It values humanity but not individuals' (ibid., pp. 196–7).

Yet critics of this stripe have no monopoly on recognizing facts of reality that any even halfway perceptive utilitarian also recognizes. These include the distinctiveness of individuals and their understandable partiality to their own interests and projects and those of their relatives and friends. Trying to cultivate an unnatural impartiality would itself be subversive of human happiness. The happiness of individuals is the only kind available; there is no distinct kind pertaining to some sort of social aggregate instead.

Utilitarianism, some critics say (for example, Kerner, 1990, chapter 7), entails or requires dishonesty and self-deception. The committed utilitarian is willing to override moral rules for the sake of utility, yet he recognizes that firmly believing in and heeding them does serve social utility. Therefore he tries to conceal their merely utilitarian basis from ordinary people. If I know you are a utilitarian and you know that I know, and so forth, then 'my relying on your word will become unintelligible. For then I know that you know that I know that you will always let utility override honesty' (Kerner, 1990, p. 64).

Such critics do not understand how seriously utilitarians can take moral rules (a seriousness that R.M. Hare explains well in several books). One does not weaken the authority of rules by openly recognizing their valid or best available grounding (instead of deceiving oneself and others about their grounding). If a critic finds the utilitarian grounding of moral rules shaky, what better one can he offer? That some other grounding might compel firmer allegiance to the rules – if it were valid – does not make a rival grounding valid. Besides exposing the critics' misconceptions, an adherent of the utilitarianism that takes a well-functioning society as its near-ultimate and 'happiness' as its ultimate criterion can throw down a challenge to the critics. What better foundation can they offer for appraisals of good and bad, right and wrong?

Utilitarianism emphasizing social cooperation is the strand of moral philosophy most closely overlapping social science. Economics and ethics join in helping to explain how people can get along with one another to their mutual benefit, even without any central planning of their interactions. Economics deals with coordination and cooperation through markets, ethics through the mostly voluntary observance of mostly imprecise and tacitly articulated restraints on how people may treat one another. The satisfactory operation of markets even presupposes ethical standards. Ideally, though ideals can be infringed, law and public policy help reinforce ethical standards. Governments are instituted, as the Declaration of Independence says, to secure (protect) rights that people already possess and that do not originate with any lawgiver.

Recognizing utilitarian ethics as a branch of social science points the way towards resolving several dangling issues. If satisfying the preferences and desires that people have (or think they have) may be distinguished from promoting their actual happiness or flourishing, which one is the ultimate utilitarian criterion? In assessing the desirability of states of affairs, what weight should one give to the interpersonal distribution of utilities (that is, the degree of equality or inequality) and what weight to the general level of utilities – assuming that these concepts are meaningful? The ethicist as social scientist would investigate the operational meanings of this or that version of the ultimate criterion and of this or that distributional principle. What would implementing the criterion or the principle mean in practice? What institutions would be necessary? To what kind of society would these practices and institutions lead? Social scientists can push their factual and logical analysis further and further, narrowing any appeal to sheer intuition and flowery rhetoric. Utilitarianism has a close affinity with the comparative-institutions approach to understand the good society.

See also:
Chapter 5: Aristotelianism, apriorism, essentialism; Chapter 44: Austrian welfare economics; Chapter 11: Praxeology; Chapter 3: Subjectivism

Bibliography

Adler, Mortimer J. (1970), *The Time of Our Lives*, New York: Holt, Rinehart & Winston.
Edgeworth, Francis Y. (1881), *Mathematical Psychics*, London: Kegan Paul; photoreprint, New York: Kelley, 1961.
Frank, Robert H. (1988), *Passions within Reason*, New York: W.W. Norton.
Gray, John (1983), *Mill on Liberty: A Defence*, London/Boston: Routledge & Kegan Paul.
Hazlitt, Henry (1964), *The Foundations of Morality*, Princeton: Van Nostrand.
Hobbes, Thomas (1651), *Leviathan*, London: J.M. Dent, Everyman Library, 1943.
Hume, David (1777), *An Enquiry Concerning the Principles of Morals*, reprinted Chicago: Open Court, 1930.
Kerner, George C. (1990), *Three Philosophical Moralists*, Oxford: Clarendon Press.

Lomasky, Loren E. (1987), *Persons, Rights, and the Moral Community*, New York: Oxford University Press.

Mill, John Stuart (1863), *Utilitarianism*, various editions.

Mises, Ludwig von (1922), *Socialism: An Economic and Sociological Analysis*, translated from the 1932 edition by J. Kahane; reprinted with a Foreword by F.A. Hayek, Indianapolis: Liberty Classics, 1981.

Mises, Ludwig von (1927), *Liberalism in the Classical Tradition*, translated by Ralph Raico, 3rd edn, Irvington-on-Hudson: Foundation for Economic Education/San Francisco: Cobden Press, 1985.

Mises, Ludwig von (1949), *Human Action*, New Haven: Yale University Press.

Mises, Ludwig von (1957), *Theory and History*, New Haven: Yale University Press.

Narveson, Jan (1988), *The Libertarian Idea*, Philadelphia: Temple University Press.

Rawls, John (1971), *A Theory of Justice*, Cambridge, Mass.: Belknap Press of Harvard University Press.

Rothbard, Murray (1982), *The Ethics of Liberty*, Atlantic Highlands, NJ: Humanities Press.

Schlick, Moritz (1930), *Problems of Ethics*, translated by David Rynin, 1939; reprinted New York: Dover, 1961.

Yeager, Leland B. (1984), 'Utility, Rights, and Contract: Some Reflections on Hayek's Work', in Kurt R. Leube and Albert H. Zlabinger (eds), *The Political Economy of Freedom: Essays in Honor of F.A. Hayek*, Munich/Vienna: Philosophia Verlag.

Yeager, Leland B. (1992), 'Mises and His Critics on Ethics, Rights, and Law', in Jeffrey Herbener (ed.), *The Meaning of Ludwig von Mises*, Boston: Kluwer Academic.

48 Social contract theory

Viktor Vanberg

The principal claim of social contract theory is that political authority derives its legitimacy from the consent of the governed. The interpretation of political organization in such terms had, in one version or another, long been an element in Western political thought, yet it was primarily in the seventeenth century, in the wake of the Reformation, that it developed into a systematic and coherent philosophical argument, paradigmatically stated in Johannes Althusius's *Politica methodice digesta* (1603), and brought to prominence, most significantly, in Thomas Hobbes's *Leviathan* (1651) and John Locke's *Two Treatises of Government* (1690). As it rose to a dominant mode of thought, social contract theory drew increasing criticism, one of the most well known and most effective examples of which is David Hume's essay, 'On the Original Contract', (1748). When Jean-Jacques Rousseau published his *Contrat Social* (1762), it had already passed its zenith, and it has been said that, by the nineteenth century, 'the age of Social Contract theory was virtually at an end' (Levin, 1973, p. 262).

The argument that the age of social contract had come to an end is actually not entirely correct. It would be more accurate to say that what had come to an end was its prominent role in academic philosophical discourse, not, however, its role in practical political discourse. In its Rousseauian version, social contract theory became part of the intellectual underpinnings of the French Revolution. In its Lockean version, it was of major intellectual influence in the founding of the United States of America, as reflected in many of its documents (Gough, 1957, pp. 229ff), most prominently in the Declaration of Independence with its affirmative avowal that governments derive 'their just powers from the consent of the governed'. In fact, it can be said, more generally, that the social contract view of political legitimacy has become *the* implicit commonsense philosophy of modern liberal democracies.

Though already pronounced dead, social contract theory as a philosophical doctrine has recently been proved to be no less robust than its commonsense counterpart. There has been a remarkable modern revival of social contract theory, primarily associated with the name of John Rawls, whose *Theory of Justice* (1971) seems, indeed, at present to dominate the field of political philosophy (Lessnoff, 1986, p. 97). Another principal contribution to the modern revival of contractarianism is James M. Buchanan's *constitutional political economy*, as developed, in particular, in *The Calculus of Consent*

(1962, co-authored with Gordon Tullock) and in *The Limits of Liberty* (1975). Along with Rawls and Buchanan, Robert Nozick with his *Anarchy, State, and Utopia* (1974) has been classified as one of 'The New Contractarians' (Gordon, 1976), a classification that, as will be argued below, may need to be qualified.

Though one may justly speak, as I have done above, of a 'principal claim of social contract theory', it needs to be added that the theory has been given, through its history, differing interpretations and that it has been employed to support such divergent constitutional constructs as Hobbes's absolutism, Locke's concept of a limited government under the law, Rousseau's unconstrained rule of the 'general will', and Rawls's moderate welfare state. The various, more or less distinct versions of the theory can be usefully classified into three categories, according to the ways in which they specify the notions of *contract* and *consent*, namely either as a contract that *has (originally) been* agreed upon, as a contract that *could (hypothetically) be* agreed upon, or as a contract that continuously *is (tacitly or implicitly)* agreed upon (Ballestrem, 1983).

As the interpretations of the social contract notion have differed, so have their criticisms. The notion of a historical, original contract has been the easiest, but also least interesting target of criticism. Obvious objections, articulated by Hume and others, have been that hardly any political regime can truly claim such historical origins and, even if it could, this fact would hardly be of moral relevance for those who currently live under the regime, many generations removed from the original contract. If a regime's *current* legitimacy is at issue, the criterion applied should relate to the regime's current properties and, in this regard, the concepts of a hypothetical or implicit contract are clearly more relevant than that of an original contract. The main objection against the notion of a hypothetical contract, that is, the idea that a criterion for legitimacy may be found in what *could* have been agreed upon, has been that one can conjecture many things that persons *could* agree upon under hypothetical conditions and that, therefore, this notion is much too unconstrained to offer a workable criterion. Though such criticism seems to raise a serious challenge to the criterion of hypothetical agreement, it nevertheless is the case that the concept of implicit agreement remains the only serious candidate for an informative and operational social contract theory.

When implicit agreement is suggested as a criterion for the legitimacy of a political regime, it is supposed that such behavioral choices as maintaining residence within the territorial domain of a state and not voicing opposition can be viewed as indicators of tacit consent to the existing regime. According to widely held opinion, this version of the social contract idea has also fallen victim to Hume's biting criticism in 'On the Original Contract', where Hume uses the example of a man who, while he was totally drunk, had been brought on a ship and, waking up, found himself on board in the middle of the ocean. The point of Hume's story is, of course, to suggest that it would be clearly unreasonable to take the fact that the man does not jump off the ship, and does not rebel against the captain, as an indicator of his implicit agreement to the regime he finds himself in. And Hume wants his reader to conclude that the whole concept of implicit agreement rests on equally shaky grounds because of the high costs typically associated with the choice to emigrate. Yet, what Hume, and those who have taken his argument as the last word in these matters, may not have sufficiently appreciated is the fact that political regimes can vary considerably in terms of barriers to emigration and costs of voicing opposition, and that, therefore, regimes can be meaningfully compared as to the degree to which available evidence can be considered indicative of genuine tacit consent (Vanberg, 1993, chapter 12). Even though emigration tends always to be a costly act, the history of the communist empire has provided ample proof of how significant an attribute of political regimes the right to emigrate is.

The fact that the social contract idea has been given different interpretations, and has been employed in support of different constitutional regimes, does not mean that these interpretations and advocated regimes are all equally consistent with the essential thrust and inherent logic of a contractarian approach. There is a set of ideas that appear to form the essential core of a coherent contractarian paradigm, in the light of which the different versions of the social contract notion can be critically examined as to their plausibility and coherence. Most fundamentally, social contract theory embodies the idea that voluntary consent, as opposed to coercion and oppression, is the constituting principle of a good polity, the appropriate standard for judging the legitimacy of political institutions. It embodies an 'ascending thesis' of government (Levin, 1973, p. 254), that is the assumption that political authority is delegated upwards, from the ruled to the rulers, as opposed to a 'descending thesis' of government that derives political authority from other sources. In more modern terminology, it views the relation between rulers and ruled as an *agent–principal* relationship. Governments are considered to hold authority only in trust for their citizens, the ultimate principals or sovereigns, in whose interest such authority is supposed to be exercised.

As was clearly noted in Althusius's early statement of the social contract idea, a principal–agent relationship is only meaningful if the agent is constrained by rules that secure responsiveness to the principal's interests. For Althusius, in order to qualify as legitimate, political authority has to be based on consent and to be constrained by constitutional rules, a view that may well be argued to provide a more adequate elaboration of social contract theory than, for instance, Hobbes's absolutism or the model of a constitutionally unconstrained direct democracy that Rousseau suggested. Althusius clearly recognized the crucial distinction between the *constitutional* and the *sub-constitutional* level of choice, a distinction that, as Buchanan suggests, was 'one of the essential logical purposes or aims of the contractarian approach' (Buchanan and Tullock, 1962, p. 311). Recognition of this distinction is a prerequisite for an adequate answer to the question of legitimacy in government: the proximate answer is that political authority is legitimate if it has been acquired and is exercised in accordance with the constitutional rules of the polity. The more fundamental answer is that the constitutional framework itself is legitimate to the extent that it can reasonably be assumed to be based on continuing consent of the members of the polity, where what 'can be reasonably assumed' would have to be argued along the lines suggested in the above comments on the notion of implicit consent. Awareness of the distinction between the constitutional and the sub-constitutional is a prerequisite for an understanding of the fact that people may voluntarily – and rationally – choose, at a constitutional level, to submit jointly to rules that constrain their sub-constitutional choices. And it is the understanding of the nature of such joint commitment that allows one to reconcile 'the apparently conflicting claims of liberty and law' (Gough, 1957, p. 254), a reconciliation that, as Gough (ibid.) asserts, has been the 'ultimate raison d'être for the contract theory, all through its history'.

There is a further sense in which Althusius can be said to have proposed a more coherent version of social contract theory than most of its other advocates. While the contractarian tradition, in general, confined its attention largely to that particular social entity, the state, it was Althusius who systematically turned the social contract idea into a general theory of human associations, a theory that is meant to apply to all kinds of collective arrangements, private and public, from families and economic organizations to local communities and nation states (Gough, 1957, p. 75; Lessnoff, 1986, p. 36). He used, in effect, the concept of a social contract in an analytical or structural sense, suggesting that the contractual relations that underlie the various kinds of human associations or organizations have certain characteristics in common. It is in such a generalized, analytical sense that the concept of a social contract appears to be of particular interest for modern social theory.

In its generalized, analytical use the concept of a social contract is meant not only to emphasize that all human associations can be understood in terms of *contractual* relations. The attribute 'social' is supposed to indicate that these are contractual relations of a particular kind. To be sure, *all* contracts involve two or more persons and they are all 'social' in this sense; if the 'social' in 'social contract' were to imply no more than that, it would be redundant. It is meaningful only if it is intended to distinguish the contracts that underlie organized human associations from other kinds of contractual relations. The relevant distinction here is between what one may juxtapose as *exchange contracts* on the one side, and *constitutional contracts* on the other, two types of contracts that are concerned with two characteristically different kinds of social arrangements, with discrete transactions on the one side and continuing relations on the other. Exchange contracts are concerned with the kinds of problems that can arise in exchange transactions, in particular in cases of non-simultaneity where one party performs first, while the other party promises to do its part at some point in the future. By contrast, constitutional contracts are not about particular transactions and acts of promising. They are concerned with the rules that constitute an organized collective enterprise, they define the terms of participation in a continuing joint endeavor (Vanberg, 1994, chapter 8). Exchange contracts can be said to be about acts of promising, constitutional contracts about joint commitments, mutuality of constraints. Social contract theory is clearly about constitutional contracts and it is misconceived if interpreted in categories of exchange contracts. Indeed, one may suspect that some of the confusion around the social contract issue has been caused by the failure clearly to distinguish between obligations arising from acts of promising and obligations arising from 'mutuality of restrictions' (Lessnoff, 1986, pp. 120f).

If social contract theory is understood, in the sense suggested above, as a theory of constitutional contract, it is somewhat misleading, as indicated earlier, to include Nozick (1974) among the 'new contractarians'. To be sure, Nozick seeks to understand the emergence of a minimal state as a process of voluntary contracting and he shares, in this regard, a common perspective with Rawls and Buchanan. Yet his account critically differs from theirs insofar as he does not invoke a social or constitutional contract at all, but describes the contractual process as if it were exclusively about exchange contracts. In other words, he implicitly identifies voluntary contracting with exchange contracts and fails to see the distinctive *constitutional* nature of the contracts that underlie an organization like the state. Nozick's blindness to the role of social or constitutional contracts is reminiscent of a broader issue, concerning the relationship between a classical liberal and a social contract perspective. According to a not uncommon presumption, articulated by F.A. Hayek and others, classical liberalism and social contract tradition are somehow incompatible (Vanberg, 1994, chapter 12) and, indeed, authors such as, in particular, Rousseau have interpreted the social contract idea in ways that are clearly in conflict with a classical liberal framework. Yet, while the problems with such interpretations certainly need to be recognized, this should not distract attention from the fundamental affinity between the contractarian emphasis on *voluntary consensus* and the concept of voluntary market exchange that has been central to the classical liberal tradition.

Social contract theory and classical liberalism can be said to share two fundamental principles, *individualism* and *voluntarism*; both take the individual participants as the starting-point for their understanding of social structures, and both view voluntary contract as the core principle of social cooperation. What is different is their respective focus in applying these principles: classical liberalism concentrates on voluntary exchange in markets, social contract theory concentrates on voluntariness in constitutional choice. Viewed in this way, the two perspectives cannot only be said to be compatible; the social contract paradigm, as exemplified by J.M. Buchanan's contractarian constitutionalism, can be argued to provide a natural complement to classical liberalism, a complement that may be labeled *contractarian liberalism* (Vanberg, 1994, chapter 13).

See also:
Chapter 44: Austrian welfare economics; Chapter 39: Legal philosophy; Chapter 80: Social institutions and game theory

Bibliography
Ballestrem, K. (1983), 'Vertragstheoretische Ansätze in der Politischen Philosophie', *Zeitschrift für Politik*, **30**, (NF), 1–17.
Buchanan, J.M. (1975), *The Limits of Liberty – Between Anarchy and Leviathan*, Chicago: University of Chicago Press.
Buchanan, J.M. and Tullock, G. (1962), *The Calculus of Consent – Logical Foundations of Constitutional Democracy*, Ann Arbor: University of Michigan Press.
Gordon, S. (1976), 'The New Contractarians', *Journal of Political Economy*, **84**, 573–90.
Gough, J.W. (1957), *The Social Contract – A Critical Study of its Development*, Oxford: Clarendon Press.
Lessnoff, M. (1986), *Social Contract*, Atlantic Highlands, NJ: Humanities Press.
Levin, M. (1973), 'Social Contract', *Dictionary of the History of Ideas*, New York: Charles Scribner's Sons, vol. IV, pp. 251–63.
Nozick, R. (1974), *Anarchy, State, and Utopia*, New York: Basic Books.
Rawls, J. (1971), *A Theory of Justice*, Cambridge, Mass.: Belknap Press of Harvard University Press.
Vanberg, V. (1994), *Rules and Choice in Economics*, London: Routledge.

B   Public policy economics

49 Interventionism

Sanford Ikeda

'Interventionism' is the doctrine or system based on the principle of the limited use of government's discretionary powers (intervention) to address problems identified with the private ownership of the means of production and the unregulated market process. An 'intervention', according to Ludwig von Mises (1966, pp. 718–19)

> is a decree, issued directly or indirectly, by the authority in charge of society's administrative apparatus of coercion and compulsion which forces the entrepreneurs and capitalists to employ some of their factors of production in a way different from what they would have resorted to if they were only obeying the dictates of the market.

Interventionism begets the so-called 'mixed economy' or what Mises has termed the 'hampered market order'.

Because interventionism assigns to government discretionary powers to intercede in the market process, it is distinct from a system in which the state operates only to protect the integrity of the private property, market order (laissez-faire capitalism). However, because it does set some limits on the use of these discretionary powers, interventionism is also distinct from complete state ownership of the means of production and central planning (pure socialism).

To its supporters, interventionism stands for an alternative economic system that lies between the extremes of laissez-faire capitalism and pure socialism – an ideal blend of both systems that manages to avoid the worst aspects of each. They contend that laissez-faire capitalism, or 'the free market', performs certain desirable tasks ineffectively or produces certain undesirable outcomes. Yet, because they find aspects of pure socialism equally unattractive, and the failures of capitalism sufficiently small in number and scope, they advocate the judicious use of limited intervention to preserve capitalism's best features, such as the effective adjustment in the use of resources to changing economic conditions, while achieving the best features of socialism, such as social justice and equity. However, three presumptions underlie the concept of interventionism: (1) that interventionism is a logically consistent and intellectually defensible alternative economic system: (2) that the state is able to identify 'capitalist failures', determine the relative importance of these failures, and construct a coherent program of limited intervention that will, from the point of view of its sponsors, achieve an outcome more desirable than the problems that it was intended to solve; and (3) that the state is free from the influence of redistributive coalitions and the self-interested behavior of its own agents.

An exhaustive Austrian critique would scrutinize every facet of interventionism, including the soundness of the arguments leveled against laissez-faire capitalism and the reality of the benefits of socialism. Since other essays included in this volume address these issues, however, the next section will confine itself to the Austrian response to the above three presumptions.

The Austrian critique of interventionism: Mises's contribution

An important role of standard economic analysis has always been to trace the effects of particular public policies on private market decisions and to point out their often obscure and unexpected repercussions. The unique Austrian contribution to the analysis of the mixed economy, and that of Ludwig von Mises in particular, is a general critique of the doctrine of interventionism itself, centered on an examination of the dynamics of an interventionist economy. The following passage conveys the nature of Mises's (1977, 37–8) critique: 'The middle system of property that is hampered, guided, and regulated by government is in itself contradictory and illogical. Any attempt to introduce it in earnest must lead to a crisis from which either socialism or capitalism alone can emerge'. Thus Mises criticized interventionism for its logical inconsistency (the first presumption) and the undesirability of its effects (the latter part of the second presumption). Mises argued that interventionism, unlike either socialism or capitalism, is untenable as a doctrine and inherently unstable as a system because it is at odds with fundamental economic forces. Profit-seeking actors in both the market and political processes tend to respond to particular interventions in ways that frustrate or circumvent these interventions and that the authorities, for whatever reason, fail to anticipate. Because of these responses, there is a tendency for interventionism to 'bring about a state of affairs, which – from the viewpoint of its advocates themselves – is much more undesirable than the previous state they were intended to alter' (Mises, 1977). The accumulated problems of piecemeal intervention must inevitably lead policy makers to choose between more coherent, thoroughgoing government planning (socialism) or minimal interference with the market process (capitalism). In this sense interventionism as a system is 'self-defeating'. (The next section outlines the process by which this occurs.)

Mises was well aware that the influence of distributive coalitions and narrowly self-interested public agents could pervert the political process (the third presumption). One of the strengths of Mises's contribution, however, is that it manages to explain how the interventionist state tends to expand in the direction of complete central planning even when government officials are well intentioned, act only as public servants and do not deliberately aim for central planning. Nevertheless, most Austrians today share a sense of intellectual kinship with the public choice approach to political economy, which applies a form of praxeological reasoning to political processes and institutions. To Austrians, one of public choice's most important contributions to the overall critique of interventionism is its penetrating analysis of the pernicious effects of narrowly self-interested behavior in the political process, the waste associated with the use of coercion and compulsion to redistribute wealth, and the forces that influence the size of government. Although the method most of its practitioners use at present is equilibrium-oriented, Austrians can appreciate public choice's fundamental insight that purposeful behavior in the context of the political process can produce unintended consequences for the system as a whole.

While Mises's critique represents the logical starting-point for a more general theory of interventionism, it leaves open a number of questions, only some of which have been addressed. First, Mises himself conceived of interventionism in terms of state activity beyond the minimum necessary to promote social cooperation and coordination of the market process. That is, coercion and compulsion in the pursuit of the (minimal) state's proper functions is for Mises not interventionism, yet he overlooked the question of whether problems similar to those that plague intervention beyond the minimal state might also confront the minimal state itself. Thus Mises took it for granted that the minimal state is, in some sense, both stable and optimal. This is, however, open to question.

Second, in his earlier studies (1977, p. 19), Mises excluded partial socialization and nationalization from his concept of interventionism, a position that his later writings have apparently left unchanged (Lavoie, 1982, p. 175). This exclusion is consistent with a view of intervention as a means of industrial regulation, which is distinct from outright ownership of a private business or industry. The state does not 'intervene' with respect to property it owns when it determines the use of that property. However, this means Mises's categories of alternative economic systems are non-exhaustive, since a system in which the state has nationalized less than total domestic production capacity would be, in his framework, neither interventionism nor socialism, and certainly not capitalism. (See Lavoie, 1982, for elaboration on and a critique of this aspect of Mises's argument as well as of Rothbard's categorization, presented next.)

Murray N. Rothbard (1977), using the Misesian analysis as his starting-point, has offered a more complete categorization, which classifies partial socialization or nationalization as a variety of interventionism. He divides interventionist policies into the following three categories:

Autistic intervention: interference into private, non-exchange activities. These include, for example, invasions of private matters such as private religious practices, personal expression, travel and choice of lifestyle.

Binary intervention: forced exchange between an individual and the state; for example, taxation, compulsory consumption of publicly provided goods and the nationalization of industries.

Triangular intervention: forced exchange between individuals. Examples include price control, fiscal and monetary policy, trade and contract restrictions, and environmental, safety, health and civil rights regulations.

Finally, a theory of interventionism should explain why authorities acting in the public interest would continue to embrace interventionism in the face of mounting problems emanating from that policy. The 'self-defeating' nature of interventionism leads one to wonder why such an inherently unstable system is evidently so widespread and tenacious. Mises emphasized the importance of ideology – a statist or anti-capitalist mentality – that induces authorities to opt for more intervention at critical decision points, but he did not directly confront the issue at the very heart of his critique: why the interventionist state consistently fails to foresee the negative side-effects of its decisions. Mises did not explicitly examine the nature of the knowledge constraints that prevent authorities in mixed economies from realizing the existence of problems and correctly identifying their source (the first part of the second presumption) before it is too late. It is possible, however, to use Mises's own insights into the nature of socialist calculation, as extended by Hayek and Lavoie, to fill in this gap in the theory of interventionism. Indeed, while not explicit in his critique, Mises may have simply taken for granted something like the 'knowledge problem' (see below) in exposing the unstable and the self-defeating nature of interventionism. The next section shows how integrating insights from the knowledge problem into Mises' critique of interventionism will also illuminate the dynamics of the resulting process and indicate the direction that a more general theory of interventionism might take.

The interventionist process
Implicit in Mises's critique is the Austrian perspective that further inquiry into the operation of non-equilibrium processes will contribute more to our understanding of real phenomena than continued efforts to characterize equilibrium end states. In the present case, a policy implementing the doctrine of interventionism sets into motion a series of effects that create outcomes which even those who initially favored the policy deem undesirable. Unexpected, intervention-created profit opportunities and eager, opportunity-seeking actors combine to produce these outcomes. The typical response of state authorities is to further expand the scope of state activity, although this is by

no means inevitable since, however unlikely, it is possible for them to reduce state activity at these critical points. Thus one can view interventionism as a non-equilibrium dynamic process, in which the decisions of partially ignorant actors provide the internal dynamic that drives the mixed economy.

One example which could serve as a paradigm for this approach is the Mises–Hayek theory of the business cycle. In this theory, the state authorizes a monopolistic central bank to expand credit in order to stimulate short-term economic activity. The resulting impact on relative intertemporal prices induces producers to increase the future supply of goods relative to future demand. Credit expansion continues so long as the state is unaware that this intertemporal reallocation of resources generates shortages in the present and surpluses in the future. Monetary authorities realize the extent of the coordination problems only when a financial crisis threatens, at which time they have an opportunity to reverse the easy-money policy. However, the unemployment and dislocation that would attend such a readjustment may reinforce political and ideological pressure to continue the credit expansion. With its better, though less than complete, knowledge the state at this critical point must decide whether to continue an expansionary policy that will produce a crisis of even greater though unknown proportions in the indefinite future, or take steps now to reverse the policy and weather the more immediate repercussions. What the policy makers decide depends on their awareness of the nature and scope of the crisis, the perceived costs of continuing or discontinuing their policy and their willingness to abandon the interventionist ideology.

In the analysis of interventionism as a process, lack of complete knowledge, or the existence of at least partial *genuine* ignorance (in contrast to *rational* ignorance owing to high information costs) plays an indispensable role in creating the conditions that produce interventionism's unexpected side-effects. In particular, knowledge relevant to the state's decisions is dispersed among anonymous individuals in both the private and public sectors of the economy – this is the 'knowledge problem', which Austrians have underscored in discussions relating to economic calculation under socialism. In the previous example, in order to offset the negative effects of credit expansion, the monetary authorities would need to know, among other things, not only the path the new credit would take as it trickled through the economy, but also how the private sector *as well as* all branches of the government would respond to countervailing interventions. They would need to know such things as how antitrust enforcers and non-subsidized areas of the economy would respond to public spending that might be aimed at specific industries to augment the supply of consumer goods underproduced owing to prior credit expansion.

The presence of the knowledge problem means not only that the promoters of intervention will be unable to foresee all of the negative repercussions of their policies before embarking upon them, but that a great deal of time may pass before they become aware of these repercussions. In the meantime, the economy could have moved quite far along the path towards collectivism, supported by statist ideological tendencies. One implication of the Misesian analysis is that the inevitable economic crisis that follows the build-up of undiscovered (by authorities) past errors and discoordination creates conditions for a possible radical policy shift back towards laissez-faire capitalism. That is, the emergence of the crisis could reveal its fundamental source to authorities, making plain the radical choice they face: reject interventionism and release markets from control, or 'organize' and 'rationalize' piecemeal interventions by embracing more thoroughgoing collectivist economic planning.

Thus, although Mises did not frame his critique of interventionism explicitly in terms of the informational constraints imposed on the interventionist state, aspects of the 'knowledge problem' originally introduced in the debate over the possibility of economic calculation under complete socialism are applicable to, and indeed indispensable for, a more detailed understanding of more limited forms of state intervention.

Suggestions for further research
A great deal of work remains to be done in this largely undeveloped area of Austrian economics. There are at least two aspects of a research program in the theory of interventionism. The first concerns the 'micro' implications of the theory for particular industries. More specifically, the theory suggests that regulation unintentionally breeds further regulation, until it creates an environment in which deregulatory reform might or might not take place. An analysis of the history of regulation in some industries, airlines for example, can serve to illustrate how a crisis resulting from gradually increasing regulation over time leads relatively suddenly to dramatic deregulatory reforms. In addition, with appropriate adjustments, Mises's critique could provide a framework for analysing the links among social policies pertaining to civil rights, the environment and health and safety issues.

A second area for research concerns the relations among certain 'macro' variables. The theory of interventionism suggests, for example, that the rate of growth in regulation should be inversely related to the rate of productivity growth and the rate of private wealth accumulation. While disaggregation is perhaps more consistent with traditional Austrian fastidiousness, regularities in the overall pattern would be of some interest (although finding and measuring the appropriate empirical values would be problematic). Historical and international comparisons of policy decisions at critical points – for example, the USA in 1929, Weimar Germany in 1932 and Eastern Europe in the late

1980s – could also serve to illustrate the consequences of interventionist processes.

See also:
Chapter 22: The Austrian theory of price; Chapter 57: Mergers and the market for corporate control; Chapter 50: The political economy of price controls; Chapter 51: The economics of prohibition

Bibliography
Kirzner, Israel M. (ed.), (1982), *Method, Process, and Austrian Economics*, Lexington, Mass.: Lexington Books.
Lavoie, Don (1982), 'The Development of the Misesian Theory of Interventionism', in I.M. Kirzner (ed.), *Method, Process and Austrian Economics*, Lexington, Mass.: Lexington Books.
Lavoie, Don (1985), *Rivalry and Central Planning: The Socialist Calculation Debate Reconsidered*, Cambridge: Cambridge University Press.
Mises, Ludwig von [1949] (1966), *Human Action: A Treatise on Economics*, 3rd edn, Chicago: Henry Regnery.
Mises, Ludwig von [1929] (1977), *A Critique of Interventionism: Inquiries into Economic Policy and the Economic Ideology of the Present*, translated by Hans F. Sennholz, New Rochelle, NY: Arlington House.
Rothbard, Murray N. (1977), *Power & Market: Government & the Economy*, Kansas City: Sheed Andrews & McMeel.

50 The political economy of price controls
E.C. Pasour

Prices perform a key role in the discovery, coordination and transmission of information to market participants (Hayek, 1948). Despite the importance of price signals in the production and consumption of goods and services, there is a long history of government-mandated price controls (Mises, 1966, chapter 30). Depending upon which groups the political authority wishes to favor, governments sometimes resort to minimum prices, as in the case of farm price supports. In other cases, price ceilings such as rent controls are instituted. The widespread involvement of government in raising and lowering prices suggests two key questions. First, what are the different types of price controls? Second, what are their economic effects?

Price controls: types and implementation problems
Mises (1977, p. 142) describes two types of price controls – 'sanctioning controls' and 'genuine controls'. A sanctioning price control is defined as one in which government attempts to set price at the level that would prevail in a competitive or unhampered market. For example, it is sometimes argued that government can and should reduce uncertainty on the part of market participants in agricultural and other highly competitive markets by setting price at the competitive level, thereby reducing market instability. Similarly, leading economic theorists have argued that government should institute marginal cost pricing in the case of public utilities and other monopolies, thereby forcing sellers to charge competitive prices instead of higher monopoly prices (Coase, 1988).

A genuine control, in contrast to a sanctioning control, is considered to be one in which government deliberately sets the price above or below the level that would prevail in an unhampered market (Mises, 1977, p. 144). Examples include price ceilings and price floors in the form of agricultural price supports, price controls for food, rent controls, minimum wages, and so on. As shown below, however, this seemingly plausible distinction between sanctioning and genuine controls is more apparent than real. Moreover, any government program that attempts to set price deliberately, whatever the purpose, faces formidable information and incentive problems.

Information problems are endemic in price controls because of the separation of power and knowledge. In the case of a price control to raise or lower price deliberately, the authority having the power to act in the political process does not have and cannot obtain the information to determine what the price of a good or service *should* be. The idea of a 'just' price, aside from the price determined through the competitive market process, has no economic content (Mises, 1966, pp. 727–8). No price of wheat, however high, appears unjust to the farmer. No price of bread, however low, appears unjust to the consumer. A price support, if effective, benefits producers at the expense of consumers. A price ceiling tends to have just the opposite effect – at least in the short run.

In so-called welfare economics, attempts have been made to justify government intervention, which benefits some people at the expense of others. However, as F.A. Hayek (1979) emphasizes, attempts to measure the relative utilities or satisfactions of different people lack a scientific foundation. Therefore there is no legitimate way to compare the benefit afforded to one group of people with the harm endured by a different group of people, and the idea of basing prices 'on such fantasies is clearly an absurdity' (Hayek, 1979, p. 202).

The information problem confronting government officials who attempt to use sanctioning controls to simulate the competitive market is scarcely less formidable. Consider, for example, the authority who attempts to set a price support for corn at the equilibrium price level. If the price support at planting time were set at the market-clearing level at harvest, uncertainty confronting market participants could be reduced without creating a surplus or shortage (Pasour, 1990, chapter 8). To simulate the performance of the market, however, it is necessary to know in advance what the discovery process of the market will reveal only with the passage of time (Kirzner, 1985, p. 131). Moreover, the market price varies from place to place and changes frequently in response to constantly changing economic conditions throughout the world. Thus the knowledge necessary to determine now the market-clearing price that will prevail in a future time period clearly is impossible. Consequently, there is little likelihood that government officials can increase market stability by using such sanctioning price controls.

Marginal cost pricing, as in public utility regulation, is no less problematic (Coase, 1988). Information problems pose an insurmountable obstacle to the implementation of the marginal cost pricing rule because the opportunity cost and expected revenue data that influence entrepreneurial decisions are subjective (Mises, 1966; Buchanan, 1969). A governmental injunction to set price equal to marginal cost is an empty one because the most profitable response to anticipated market conditions depends upon the decision maker's unique knowledge and attitude towards risk and uncertainty. Consequently, there is no reason to expect the regulatory authority and the firm decision maker to assess future market conditions in the same way, or to reach the same conclusion concerning price and output implied by the pricing rule.

Furthermore, even if the government authority were omniscient, it would face a formidable *incentive problem*. There is a separation of power and responsibility on the part of decision makers in the political process because those having the power to act do not bear the consequences of the decisions they make – at least not to the same extent as decision makers in a private property system. Entrepreneurial decisions are guided by perceptions of profit opportunities, and those firms that best anticipate market conditions are most likely to survive. In contrast, there is no comparable 'bottom line' or reliable indicator of success in the case of governmental agencies (Mises, 1966). Moreover, it is highly unlikely that government regulators will assess information about demand and supply conditions as accurately as market participants who have their own money at risk.

Implementation problems are endemic in government price controls, whatever the type. Moreover, in practice there is no clear distinction between a price control whose aim is to simulate the competitive market and one designed to raise or lower price from the competitive level. In a world where future economic conditions are shrouded in uncertainty, subjectivity is unavoidable either in estimating what the unhampered market price will be at a future point in time or in determining how high price *should* be when price ceilings or floors are legally mandated. Furthermore, as shown below, legislated price controls hamper operation of the market process, reduce the output of goods and services, and provide no long-run benefit to those the controls presumably are designed to assist.

Economic effects of price controls

The seen as well as the unseen is important in government price controls (Bastiat, 1968). The direct effect of rent controls, for example, is easily seen – an effective price ceiling lowers the nominal rental price below the market-clearing level. The resulting economic shortage is also quite predictable when the money price is legally prevented from rising to the market-clearing level in rationing a scarce good or service to competing demanders. When market price is not permitted to ration goods and services, some other method must be used. Indeed, an economic shortage typically can be identified by the presence of non-monetary costs in the acquisition of goods and services, most notably waiting time in queue rationing (Heyne, 1991, chapter 4).

The indirect effects of price controls are no less important but much less obvious. First, any price control impedes the operation of the entrepreneurial market process. Market prices provide correct signals to market participants only when prices are free to respond to changing economic conditions. A price control distorts both the information communicated by the price to consumers about product availability and that communicated to producers about consumer choices. For example, a government policy that forces price below the competitive level can be viewed as a type of legal censorship that prevents consumers from transmitting accurate information to producers. In the case of rent control, consumers place a higher value on housing than that conveyed by the price ceiling to present and prospective providers of rental property. Consequently, the lower price reduces the construction and availability of rental housing, thereby exacerbating the shortage caused by the price control.

In the near term, owners of rental property adjust to the government-mandated price ceiling both by converting rental property to alternative uses and by reducing costs, including a reduction in maintenance of properties they continue to rent. In the longer term, lower rents reduce the quantity of rental housing. Thus the perverse effects of rent controls increase with the passage of time.

There is a strong tendency in a competitive market system for investments of similar risk to have similar expected returns. This result has profound implications both for the short- and long-term effects of price controls in a world of specialized resources. A legislated increase in the price of wheat, for example, will not increase the long-run profitability of wheat production in a market economy. That is, regardless of how high the price of wheat is set, competitive market forces will bring about increases in prices of land and other resources used in the production of wheat so that the expected rate of return from producing wheat will be no higher than that from competing investments of comparable risk.

Moreover, an agricultural price support mainly benefits owners of land and other specialized farm resources at the time the price control is instituted; any gains to resource owners from a government-mandated price floor are 'once and for all'. Farmers who begin to produce wheat after a price floor is instituted and resource prices increase do not gain from it because higher costs of production offset the benefits of the higher product price. In short, a price floor raises product price, thereby inducing overproduction and harming consumers and taxpayers as long as it remains in effect, and it yields only transitional benefits to owners of specialized capital assets.

Second, the economic effects of price ceilings are quite different, depending upon the length of adjustment period. When rent controls are instituted, for example, current renters benefit at the expense of owners of either rental houses or property potentially developable for use as rental housing. The effect of a rent ceiling hinges both on the expected life of the rent controls and on how much the rental price is reduced below the free market level. And the wealth effects on owners of affected property, as in the case of price floors, tend to be 'once and for all'. Market values of rental real estate are quickly reduced in response to the lower expected income from rental properties over time. And on the supply side of the market, it is the owners of affected property at the time the price ceiling is instituted who bear the largest cost. After a rent control is instituted, costs must be lowered sufficiently for the expected rate of return in the rental housing industry to be comparable to that from other investment alternatives. The fact that owners or developers of rental property expect to achieve competitive rates of return under rent controls does not mean, of course, that the price ceiling has no harmful effects. As shown above, an effective rent control brings about adjustments that adversely affect the availability of rental housing in both the near and long term.

Third, price controls spawn further government intervention. For example, rent controls reduce the availability of rental housing. Then government programs are instituted to subsidize both the construction of housing and housing itself for low-income consumers.

Finally, price controls and the programs instituted in response to the problems created by them are an important source of support to the politicians and political bureaucracy in a democratic society. Legislators having a rural constituency, for example, use agricultural price supports to maintain political support. Urban legislators use rent controls, rent subsidies, subsidized credit for construction of low-income housing and similar programs in the same way. Moreover, price controls of all types are an important source of financial support to the political bureaucracy, including economists employed by universities and the state, which administers and evaluates them.

What is the explanation in a democratic system for the existence of price ceilings and floors that benefit the few at the expense of the many? Those benefiting generally have much more at stake on an individual basis than those who bear the cost. Despite their small numbers, these factions are able to influence the political process to their advantage through lobbying, campaign contributions and so on.

Conclusions and implications
The competitive market process is important, both in the communication of existing knowledge and as a discovery process, in generating awareness of previously unperceived opportunities (Hayek, 1948, 1978). Thus a price ceiling not only creates an economic shortage, it also hampers innovation. The artificially low price reduces output under known production conditions; it also makes the discovery of new production opportunities less likely (Kirzner, 1985). A price floor, in contrast, creates an economic surplus that is exacerbated with the passage of time by the discovery and use of substitute products.

All governments, including democratic ones, frequently intervene in the pricing of goods and services to serve the interests of the few, including the regulators, at the expense of the many. Moreover, price controls create artificial shortages and surpluses, regardless of the type of political and economic system. Although the harmful effects of price controls are exacerbated by perverse incentives that are endemic in the political decision-making process, price controls would generate economic confusion and reduce economic productivity even if the regulators were completely dedicated to the public weal. In short, price controls hamper and stifle the information and incentives conveyed through market price signals, whatever the type of political and economic system.

See also:
Chapter 49: Interventionism; Chapter 25: Prices and knowledge; Chapter 20: Supply and demand

Bibliography
Bastiat, F. (1968), *Selected Essays on Political Economy*, translated by S. Cain and edited by G.B. de Huszar, Irvington-on-Hudson, NY: The Foundation for Economic Education.
Buchanan, J.M. (1969), *Cost and Choice: An Inquiry in Economic Theory*, Chicago: Markham.
Coase, R.H. (1988), *The Firm, The Market, and the Law*, Chicago: University of Chicago Press.
Hayek, F.A. (1948), *Individualism and Economic Order*, Chicago: University of Chicago Press.
Hayek, F.A. (1978), 'Competition as a Discovery Procedure', in *New Studies in Philosophy, Politics, Economics and the History of Ideas*, Chicago: University of Chicago Press.
Hayek, F.A. (1979), *Law, Legislation and Liberty*, vol. 3, *The Political Order of a Free People*, Chicago: University of Chicago Press.
Heyne, P. (1991), *The Economic Way of Thinking*, 6th edn, New York: Macmillan.
Kirzner, I.M. (1985), *Discovery and the Capitalist Process*, Chicago: University of Chicago Press.
Mises, L. von (1966), *Human Action: A Treatise on Economics*, 3rd edn, Chicago: Henry Regnery.
Mises, L. von [1929] (1977), *A Critique of Interventionism: Inquiries into Economic Policy and the Economic Ideology of the Present*, trans. by Hans F. Sennholz, New Rochelle, NY: Arlington House.
Pasour, E.C., Jr. (1990), *Agriculture and the State: Market Processes and Bureaucracy*, New York: Holmes and Meier.

51 The economics of prohibition

Mark Thornton

Prohibition is an extreme form of government intervention that outlaws a good, harming both producers and consumers. Inevitably, illegal production and consumption occur in response to the prohibition. The public policy of prohibition should be sharply distinguished from the voluntary and mutually beneficial membership conditions and rules of behavior established by organizations such as civic and social groups, firms, neighborhood associations and religions.

Prohibition is an important component of statecraft for conservative, socialist and theocratic rulers. Used under the guise of pursuing the public interest, prohibition is a powerful tool for the repression of minorities and social change. However, when viewed from a long historical perspective, prohibitionism has diminished in scope as the economy develops and as prohibitions are repealed in favor of more stable policies, such as regulation. Noteworthy among modern prohibitions are the national alcohol and narcotics prohibitions established in the USA during the Progressive Era. Preceded by numerous local restrictions and state prohibitions, national prohibition against the production, distribution and sale of alcohol (1920–33) was enacted by the Eighteenth Amendment to the Constitution of the USA and was enforced by the Volstead Act. The National prohibition of narcotics developed from the Harrison Narcotics Act of 1914. This legislation was also preceded by numerous state prohibitions on opium, cocaine and other narcotics, but, unlike alcohol prohibition, narcotic prohibition survived and developed into an international prohibition, with legal consumption strictly limited and highly controlled.

Prohibition is of special methodological interest because of its link with the development of mathematical (neoclassical) modeling and the decline of subjective utility theory in economics. Irving Fisher was an ardent prohibitionist who wrote three books in support of the Eighteenth Amendment and one on the dangers of alcohol. However, the foundation of his analysis of prohibition and his primary contribution to the development of neoclassical economics occurred in his doctoral thesis, where Fisher (1892) attempted to translate the theory of value and prices into the language of physics and mathematics (that is, utility = energy). Despite crucial shortcomings, Fisher's efforts were praised by Francis Ysidro Edgeworth and Vilfredo Pareto for his distinction between utility of 'that which cannot be useful [read: alcohol], and that which is really useful'. Paul Samuelson (1950, p. 254) labeled Fisher's dissertation the 'best of all' in economics. Despite its scientific trappings and fundamental flaws, Fisher's distinction provides a guide to the perennial failure of prohibitions if his distinction is understood as utility 'as it really is, and that which the prohibitionists would like it to be'.

Prohibition, from the public interest perspective, is seen as a cure for markets where addiction, consumer ignorance, lack of will or exploitation by the entrepreneur is said to be present. By restricting access to a certain good, it is argued, prohibition can improve public health and hygiene. It can reduce crime, corruption and the disintegration of the family. It can improve education and increase participation in the democratic process. Whatever the specific benefits offered, the basic justification of prohibition is that politicians and bureaucrats know more about an individual's utility than the individual does.

The economic justification for prohibiting a good is that its consumption impairs decision-making ability, reduces productivity, increases absenteeism and causes negative externalities. There is no theoretical or empirical justification for these claims. It is often argued, for example, that products such as alcoholic beverages burden the taxpayer because their consumption increases the demand for public health and welfare programs. This increased burden, however, is the result of programs that do not discourage irresponsible behavior or encourage responsible behavior, not the nature of the goods themselves. History indicates that prohibitions do not reduce the tax burden, they increase it.

The important economic results of prohibition can be usefully derived and organized by applying Kirzner's (1978) discussion of regulation. The first result is that support for prohibition represents a failure to understand how a free market promotes the discovery of solutions to the problems prohibitionists wish to solve. Some prohibitionists fail to perceive the market's problem-solving capacity and therefore promote prohibition and government intervention as the only solution. Others view the market as an instantaneous problem-solving mechanism, rather than a process whereby scarce resources are allocated to solve problems efficiently. If the market's capabilities are overestimated, all existing problems become evidence of market failure and the need for government intervention. Kirzner refers to this as the *undiscovered discovery process* because prohibition is seen as the result of a failure to fully understand the capability of the market and the scarcity of resources. It should also be recognized that special interest groups play an important role in initiating prohibitions.

Prohibition replaces the market process with a bureaucratic process. Bureaucracy is institutionally incapable of duplicating or 'simulating' the evaluation, allocation and creation of the market's discovery process. The well-

recognized efficiency and incentive problems of bureaucracy are only deriva-
tives of the insurmountable information and calculation problems described
by Ludwig von Mises. As a result, even intelligent and public-spirited bureaucrats are incapable of duplicating or improving on the solutions of the
market process. Prohibition is an *unsimulated discovery process.*

Unfortunately, in the case of prohibition, the bureaucratic process cannot
even augment the market's discovery process because it completely suppresses it. Prohibition represents a completely *stifled discovery process* that
suppresses new techniques, information, safety features, product characteristics, forms of business organization and institutions that would both improve
consumer satisfaction and make the call for prohibition unnecessary. This
cost of prohibition increases over time as more discoveries are forgone. The
most noteworthy results of prohibition are the 'unintended consequences'.
Prohibition creates the *wholly superfluous discovery process* of the illegal or
underground economy (black market). Among the outcomes of this alternative discovery process are more dangerous products and organizational techniques that would not survive in the free market. These results are antithetical
to both the free market process and the public interest rationale for prohibition.

In the case of narcotic drugs and alcohol, prohibition encourages suppliers
to increase potency, decrease quality and ignore product safety in the pursuit
orprofits. Under prohibition, suppliers enforce contracts and sales territories
with violence and resort to organizational forms such as street gangs and
crime syndicates. Crime rates increase because prohibition destroys legal
income opportunities. Addicted criminals commit crimes to pay higher prices
for drugs, police are diverted from property crime to prohibition enforcement, and the police and politicians are corrupted by suppliers.

Profit opportunities in the black market make effective prohibition impossible. To the extent that it succeeds in reducing consumption, prohibition
exacerbates the underlying social problems it was intended to solve. Most
importantly, by resorting to prohibition, government has opened the ultimate
Pandora's box of dictating what the consumer can and cannot choose. If
government continues to 'improve' on consumer decisions in this manner,
more jobs will be destroyed in the economy, more individuals will turn to a
life of crime and people will lose respect for law and order. The attempt to
bolster the social order through prohibition will, at the limit, lead to its
disintegration.

See also:
Chapter 50: The political economy of price controls; Chapter 49: Interventionism; Chapter 42:
The economic theory of regulation

Bibliography

Buchanan, James (1986), 'Politics and Meddlesome Preferences', in Robert Tollison (ed.), *Smoking and Society: Towards a More Balanced Assessment*, Lexington, Mass.: Lexington Books, pp. 335–42.

Fisher, Irving (1892), *Mathematical Investigations in the Theory of Value and Prices*, reprinted New Haven: Yale University Press, 1926.

Kirzner, Israel M. (1978), 'The Perils of Regulation: A Market Process Approach', reprinted in *Discovery and the Capitalist Process*, University of Chicago Press, 1985.

Mises, Ludwig von (1944), *Bureaucracy*, reprinted New Rochelle, NY: Arlington House, 1969.

Samuelson, Paul (1950), 'On the Problem of Integrability in Utility Theory', *Economica*, **17**, November.

Thornton, Mark (1991), *The Economics of Prohibition*, Salt Lake City, UT: University of Utah Press.

Warburton, Clark (1932), *The Economic Results of Prohibition*, New York: Columbia University Press.

52 Economics of gender and race

Deborah Walker

Since the passing of Title VII of the Civil Rights Act of 1964, the public policy arena has witnessed one proposal after another, all designed to promote equality of opportunity and to remedy both historical and current injustices in hiring practices. The Civil Rights Act itself forbids employers from hiring on the basis of race or sex. The policy agenda since 1964 includes legislation that would force many employers to offer family leave benefits, require many employers to change pay scales for entire occupations within firms, require or induce employers to hire a given number of women and minorities, and much more.

Economists can contribute a great deal to this public policy debate, which has centered around perceived social injustices and not around basic economic and legal principles such as private property rights, freedom of contract, and supply and demand. When the analyses of all types of affirmative action legislation lends itself to sound economic reasoning, its surface attractiveness is quickly lost. Basically, economists who find fault in legislation such as Title VII of the Civil Rights Act of 1964, the 1991 Civil Rights Act, mandatory employment benefits and pay equity reforms do so on the grounds that the costs of the legislation will outweigh its benefits. Furthermore, the legislation will not accomplish what it intends to accomplish, there will be unintended and undesirable consequences, and the legislation will undermine freedom of contract and the rule of law, both prerequisites for an efficient market economy. It is also argued that the market is actually superior, in many cases, at dealing with the problems that this legislation is designed to correct. In other words, a free market-place is not the problem, but is, at least in part, the answer to the problem.

Discrimination allegedly manifests itself in such ways as segregated labor markets, pay gaps and 'glass ceilings'. But statistics cannot tell us the whole picture, and in fact are very misleading. If certain markets are segmented by sex, for example, is discrimination a major, or even minor, reason behind that segmentation? Or are people in those markets making choices themselves which simply lead to some occupations being predominantly female and others being predominantly male? It is these kinds of questions that are most often overlooked by those who jump to the conclusion that discrimination is the cause of every 'undesirable' statistical finding in labor markets.

The problem to be addressed, then, cannot be found in statistics. This is true even with the presence of discrimination, which is certainly still alive and well, because the fact is we cannot know what the statistics should or should not be. The number of blacks who will choose a particular occupation is unknown to us before their choices are made. As economist Thomas Sowell points out, there is no reason to believe that in a population composed of 50 per cent blacks all occupations would also be composed of 50 per cent blacks in the absence of discrimination (Sowell, 1981). Generally, we cannot say that labor market discrimination is the problem. This is because there is a large amount of discrimination that takes place which is undesirable neither from an economic standpoint nor from an ethical standpoint. Instead, equality of opportunity is the general focus of the discussion and the problem is discovering the best means of attaining it. However, there are several interpretations of equality of opportunity. One needs to be clear as to which interpretation or definition is being used.

Equality of opportunity can mean that everyone should be able to offer their services for a given job. This means that if I, as an adult, want to apply for a job, there are no legal restrictions keeping me from making an offer and there are no legal restrictions on the content of the offer, or on the acceptances of the offer (apart from force and fraud) (see Epstein, 1992). This would be the interpretation of classical liberals and the interpretation that is used in this essay. Or equality of opportunity can mean that employers have an obligation to consider everyone who makes an offer. Furthermore, certain characteristics of persons (such as sex, race or age) making the offers generally cannot be used as criteria for choosing whether or not to accept the offers. This is the interpretation which led to the passage of Title VII of the Civil Rights Act.

A reliance on free markets, devoid of legal restrictions, underlies the first interpretation or definition of equality of opportunity. However, if this is the case, we are then faced with two questions. First, does a reliance on, or endorsement of, free markets mean that one must assume there is no labor market discrimination and/or that it is not a social problem? If not, then how will the freedom of contract/market alternative address this, or will it actually do so? And second, does this also mean that one must be happy with the status quo? Is cultural change desirable and, if it is, can free markets bring about desirable change, at least to some degree? And if so, why and how are free markets superior to other means for cultural change, especially, for example, legislative means? This second question will be addressed later. First, let us address the question of discrimination as studied by market economists.

Let us begin by stating that there is discrimination in the market and in some circumstances it is a social problem. On the other hand, in many cases discrimination is quite rational and, from a market perspective, should be allowed to persist. We first consider arguments regarding how discrimination is decreased (but not erased) by market forces; then why some discrimination in markets is rational and/or actually desirable; and lastly, why government anti-discrimination policies have not only failed but have actually worsened economic and social problems in general.

Do markets decrease discrimination?

Discrimination on the basis of race or sex can, in many cases, be costly. Consider the case where the discrimination is racism or sexism in its purest form. That is, as Thomas Sowell explains, 'where people are treated differently because of group membership as such'. If a firm decides that it will only hire men, for example, the firm must spend more time searching for qualified applicants who also must be men. This added search effort can be very costly, especially if there are very few qualified people in the relevant labor market. If this is the case, the discriminating firm can even face additional costs. In order to attract the few qualified men to that firm, it must pay them relatively higher wages. If other firms are not discriminating on the basis of sex, their labor pools are larger and they may not have to offer such high wages in order to attract qualified workers to their firms. The discriminating employer faces higher costs, then, in two ways, through longer and more extensive searches, the costs of which also include lost productivity, and through effectively decreasing the available (acceptable) labor supply, driving up wage rates (Sowell, 1981; Williams, 1982).

Given, then, that firms only survive in markets if they make monetary profits, discriminating firms with higher costs will be at a competitive disadvantage and will have to either stop the discriminating behavior in order to remain competitive or lose profitability and perhaps even close their doors. In this way, competition in markets can, at times, decrease pure discrimination. The less competitive a market is, the more likely a discriminating employer will be able to bear the costs of discriminating. In industries, for example, where there are legal restrictions to entry, discrimination is more likely to persist.

In some cases, however, it is third parties, not employers themselves that discriminate. For example, customers or existing employees can insist that certain 'kinds' of potential employees be eliminated from consideration. If this is the case, it can actually be economically desirable to continue the discrimination. The motives behind the discrimination can be purely innocent: for example, a woman may prefer a female physician or a man may prefer to have his hair cut by another man. When discrimination is third party discrimination the market can still, at times, play a role in diminishing it. In the case of customer discrimination, for example, if the customers do not have direct contact with all employees, they will not be able to push their preferences onto the entire firm (or production process) without undergoing a considerable amount of costs. In the case of employees preferring to work with 'likes', for example, a firm can sometimes segment internally, such that its hiring practices in general are not discriminatory.

We turn now to the case where employers might discriminate on the basis of group characteristics. Whether these characteristics are real or falsely perceived is important. For example, an employer may perceive *all* blacks to be less productive than other races in general. Therefore, the employer will refuse to hire blacks. Insofar as the employer's perception regarding blacks is false, other employers can take advantage of this false perception and hire productive blacks, while the discriminating employer must again search for productive workers that are not black. Again, the discriminating employers will face higher search costs and will be forced through competition to re-evaluate their perceptions regarding all blacks.

An employer may also refuse to hire a member of a group, not because all members of the group are perceived to be unproductive, for whatever reason, but because the average member of the group is perceived to be less productive than the average member of other groups. In that case, if the perception is correct, those members of the group who fall in the upper range of the scale (that is, are more productive than the average member) are punished simply for being a member of a particular group. Here again, if the perception regarding the group average is incorrect, competitive forces will tend to punish discriminating employers. On the other hand, if the perception is correct, then employers might continue to discriminate because the high costs of screening individual employees in order to discover if they fall in the upper range of the distribution outweigh the estimated benefits of doing so.

But on the other hand, most employers would rather be able to screen individual employees and hire the most productive workers of any group. In essence, then, employers face a knowledge problem regarding which employees to hire. They must trade off the costs of screening individual employees against the costs of missing out on hiring very productive workers. This is why firms, indeed market forces, have produced different ways by which they can screen employees at lower costs. These include employment agencies, interviews, references, different types of employment tests, such as aptitude or skill level tests, as well as brand names in educational and vocational institutions. All of these devices decrease screening costs for employers and thereby increase the likelihood that potential employees will be hired on the basis of their individual attributes rather than on the basis of their group membership. Anything which increases the flow of information regarding individual employees will lead to a decrease in employer discrimination based on group membership. Insofar as the flow of information is interrupted, employers' screening costs remain high and they resort to hiring on the basis of statistical averages. Legislation that prohibits the use of employment tests, for example on the basis that the tests are biased against particular groups in society, will actually decrease the likelihood that individual members of these groups can set themselves apart from the group and be hired on individual merit considerations (Epstein, 1992).

This knowledge problem that employers sometimes face can also be a source of opportunity for employers who are also members of the groups who are being discriminated against. As a member of the group, a person will have more knowledge about the true characteristics of individual members and will therefore be at an information advantage over other employers. This can then translate into a cost advantage. This can explain why many ethnic groups, for example, hire from within; they are able to hire the 'cream of the crop' because other employers are not bidding for these workers' services. Again, over time, as this information about individual employees becomes more prevalent, discrimination decreases (Sowell, 1981, Williams, 1982).

Lastly, another very important source of information for employers who are willing to hire from any group of employees, as long as they can in some ways ascertain information regarding their individual merit prior to employment, is the employment contract itself. This can be especially important for women, who may all be seen as less productive than men because of the biological ability to give birth. Through individual contract terms a woman can assure an employer that she will not leave the job within a specific period of time, will not ask for an extended leave if she does choose to have a child, and so on. In other words, she can legally promise the employer that she will take full responsibility for her personal choices and will not expect the employer's costs to increase because of those choices. In this way, women who have chosen to make their market career their top priority can signal that fact to employers and be judged on their individual merits. The freedom to make creative, individualized employment contracts can be a very important source of information to employers and thereby decrease discrimination (Walker, 1988).

When is discrimination in markets necessary?
Although the above arguments demonstrate how competitive markets can decrease discrimination, in many cases discrimination persists. There are several reasons for this. First, markets are not static and the information contained within them is very dispersed and is constantly changing (Mises, 1949). Therefore, as much as employers may attempt to hire the most productive employees, the inability to ascertain information on individual applicants may lead them to continue using statistical averages.

Furthermore, also because markets are dynamic and information is never perfect, markets are never in a perfectly competitive scenario whereby all monetary profits are maximized. In fact, it is impossible for a firm to know if profits are maximized or not. Therefore what employers actually do is make enough monetary profits to satisfy the owners of the firm to the extent that they will not move the firm's resources elsewhere. It may be the case, therefore, that some employers are able to trade off monetary profit for personal satisfaction. In other words, because markets are not perfect, some discrimination may persist because employers would rather discriminate than earn more money. This behavior is amplified when there are legal barriers to entry which decrease the ability of non-discriminating employers to compete with existing discriminating employers. For example, when governments grant monopoly privileges to firms, costs become less important, making discrimination more likely. Many economists, such as Thomas Sowell (1981) and Walter Williams (1982) have frequently noted how discrimination against blacks has been much more prominent in public, not private, institutions.

Furthermore, legal barriers to entry can also decrease or diminish the ability of an entire group to enter an occupation. The most blatant examples of this were laws in the USA which specifically stated that women were not allowed to work in bars or mines, or many other places of employment. But much less blatant are barriers such as state licensing requirements which, because of the specific nature of the required qualifications, prohibit most, if not all, members of particular groups from entering the occupations. Economist Walter Williams, for example, explains how occupational licensing requirements in fields such as cosmetology, plumbing and electrical work have effectively reduced the number of blacks in those occupations by setting standards that most blacks cannot meet (Williams, 1982). Along these same lines are government policies such as minimum wage laws and prevailing wage laws (such as those stated in the Davis–Bacon Act for example). Not allowing employers to hire workers at wages they are willing and able to pay to unskilled labor means that many unskilled workers simply will not be hired. This can translate into fewer racial minority workers and fewer female workers being employed simply because these groups have a relatively larger proportion of unskilled workers.

Notice should be taken that, when wages are free to vary as the market sees fit, discriminatory practices are broken down. If an employer is faced with hiring a highly skilled male employee or a less skilled female employee (and in some cases the difference in skill level or productivity is only perceived, not real) an employer can be induced to hire the less skilled woman if the difference in the wage rates between the two workers justifies the difference in productivity. Two important points must follow. First, if the perception regarding the skill or productivity level is correct, then hiring the less skilled worker enables the worker to gain valuable experience and skills, increasing the worker's market value and wage rate over time. Second, if the perception of the productivity is incorrect, hiring a woman over an equally productive male at a relatively lower wage rate allows the woman to obtain the job and prove her productivity, thereby also allowing her to increase her wage over time – sometimes almost immediately upon the discovery that the employer's perception was incorrect.

We now return to the case where it is existing employees who have preferences for working with people who are similar to themselves. The employer may find it profitable to go along with these preferences simply because it will decrease governing costs within the firm. When employees are very diverse, the costs of reaching a consensus regarding rules within the firm can be very high. On the other hand, when the employees are very similar, they are more likely to agree easily and efficiently to rules (both formal and informal) that govern the work environment. A good example here is smokers preferring to work with smokers because the cost of negotiating with non-smokers can be very high. Women may prefer to work with other women in some cases because they may be more sympathetic to short-term periods of absence due to child care responsibilities and are therefore more likely to cover for their fellow female employees. A firm must therefore weigh these governing costs against the potential benefits of having a more diverse workforce. For example, if a firm's customers are primarily black, the firm will want to hire black employees who will have special knowledge regarding not only how to market the products, but also how the products should be designed. A good example of this is cosmetics companies who make cosmetics specifically designed for women of color. In this case, not hiring black women could be very costly for the firm. Again, however, a firm's options can also include segmenting within the firm itself, thereby taking advantage of diversity but keeping governing costs to a minimum (Epstein, 1992).

In order to minimize conflict, groups will sometimes have a tendency to self-select. When this process of self-selection is left alone, worker satisfaction will increase and, as Richard Epstein argues (1992), income of all workers may also increase. This is because, if racists and chauvinists tend to group together in particular firms, then the rest of the workforce will not have to deal with them; therefore, although the number of opportunities may go down for any given woman or minority, the quality of the opportunities left will go up.

The failure of legislative change
Thus far it has been argued that free markets and freedom of contract go a long way towards decreasing labor market discrimination. Furthermore, much of the discrimination that does remain in markets is desirable both from the employer's point of view and from that of minorities and women. We must now address the question as to whether legislative means for desirable cul-

tural change are superior to free markets. We begin by focusing on the unintended consequences of the legislation that has already taken place and ask whether the goal of equality of opportunity is being met through this means.

Insofar as Title VII has forced employers to hire workers on the bases of race or sex instead of on the basis of productivity (although the Act was allegedly designed to do just the opposite) economic efficiency has decreased. Now one may say that this is a justified cost. However, let us see how this consequence has actually hurt the very people Title VII was designed to help. If firms are less efficient, they have fewer resources to put back into the firm and less growth takes place, meaning fewer jobs are created. Fewer jobs mean fewer opportunities for everyone looking for work, including minorities and women (Bellante, 1989; Frankel Paul, 1989; Sowell, 1981; Walker, 1984, 1988; Williams, 1982).

Employers may hire minorities and/or women out of the fear of a Title VII lawsuit. If so, they may also fear a lawsuit if they fire a minority or a woman. In an attempt to avoid having to do this, employers will hire the 'cream of the crop' from both the minority hiring pool and the female pool. In general, these individuals would have been able to find employment in the absence of anti-discrimination laws. It is the minorities and women who are not part of the 'cream of the crop' that these laws are designed to help, yet employers will not even give these people a chance, not because of discrimination per se, but because they do not want to have to fire them (on productivity grounds) and face a lawsuit under Title VII.

Furthermore, there are numerous psychological costs to affirmative action legislation. First, many qualified individuals feel it is not fair that they are not given opportunities because they are not a minority or a woman and, instead of blaming the laws, turn their anger towards the minorities and women. This only tends to increase race and sex discrimination, not decrease it. Employers, too, may feel a sense of unfairness because they are forced to hire people they otherwise would not choose to hire and may turn their anger towards minorities and women. Second, again, in order to avoid lawsuits, employers may hire women and minorities who are not actually qualified for the jobs. Then, when the employees fail, it only tends to confirm stereotypes that women and minorities are unproductive in general. This also serves to decrease the self-esteem of these workers. Also, when women and minorities do achieve excellence through their own hard work, they often do not receive the recognition they deserve because it is assumed that it was the legislation, and not hard work, that allowed them to make achievements (McElroy, 1992). Finally, affirmative action legislation sends the message to people that they do not have to achieve advancement on their own, that government will open opportunities for them, thereby decreasing their incentives to better themselves through education and training or by decreasing their incentives to create their own opportunities through entrepreneurship.

These unintended, and undesirable, consequences of anti-discrimination laws have come about because of the attempt to legislate cultural change in a very complex market economy (Hayek, 1973). The cultural climate that evolves from the interaction of many diverse individuals cannot be planned or engineered without these kinds of unintended consequences taking place. Can, however, a market system effectively deal with undesirable discrimination and produce the cultural changes that many would like to see take place? When one considers the arguments already given for the way markets have a tendency to decrease discrimination, thereby inducing discriminating employers to change their behavior, not through legislation, but through their own choices, the answer is a probable yes. The advances that both minorities and women have made in labor markets have not come about because of legislation, but instead because of market forces themselves. Cultural change through markets is slow, most assuredly, but it is cultural change from within the system itself, coming about through voluntary changes on the part of individuals acting within the market system. The only other alternative is to have changes imposed by outside legislation, which forces people to act in ways they otherwise would not choose to act. This breeds the unintended consequences that have been discussed, which have actually moved us in the opposite direction to that intended by the legislation. Free markets and freedom of contract have produced positive changes for women and minorities without the unintended negative consequences that legislative means have brought us. Markets can and do bring cultural change, but only as long as the actual actors within the market-place desire it, not because a few politicians or interest groups desire it.

See also:
Chapter 37: Labour economics; Chapter 49: Interventionism; Chapter 42: The economic theory of regulation

Bibliography
Bellante, D. (1989), 'Subjective Value Theory and Government Intervention in the Labor Market', *Austrian Economics Newsletter*, spring/summer.
Epstein, R. (1992), *Forbidden Grounds: The Case Against Employment Discrimination Laws*, Cambridge, Mass.: Harvard University Press.
Frankel, Paul E. (1989), *Equity and Gender: The Comparable Worth Debate*, New Brunswick, NJ: Transaction Publishers.
Hayek, F.A. (1973), *Law, Legislation and Liberty: Volume I, Rules and Order*, Chicago: University of Chicago Press.
McElroy, W. (1992), 'Preferential Treatment of Women in Employment', in Caroline Quest (ed.), *Equal Opportunities: A Feminist Fallacy*, London: IEA Health and Welfare Unit.
Mises, L. von (1949), *Human Action*, New Haven: Yale University Press.
Sowell, T. (1981), *Markets and Minorities*, New York: Basic Books.

Walker, D. (1984), 'Value and Opportunity: The Issue of Comparable Pay for Comparable Worth', *CATO Institute Policy Analysis*, no. 38, 31 May.
Walker, D. (1988), 'Mandatory Family-Leave Legislation: The Hidden Costs', *CATO Institute Policy Analysis*, no. 108, 8 June.
Williams, W. (1982), *The State Against Blacks*, New York: McGraw-Hill.

53 The Phillips curve

Don Bellante

Conceptual development

The Phillips curve is named after the British economist A.W. Phillips (1958), who in a pathbreaking article investigated the statistical relationship in the UK between the annual rate of change of money wages and the annual rate of unemployment. Later versions of the Phillips curve examined the relationship between unemployment or the rate of growth of output and, alternatively, the rate of change of product prices, and the deviation between actual and 'expected' inflation.

Inasmuch as the Phillips curve is an important component of mainstream economics, its development remains a curious paradox. Logical positivism is the conventional methodology of the neoclassical mainstream and this methodological doctrine has been severely criticized by economists working within the Austrian methodological perspective. Logical positivism involves the construction of theory that is tested by empirical evidence. The resulting empirical evidence may lead to modification of the theory and further testing, but the initial theory construction always precedes empirical testing. The Phillips curve developed purely as an empirical relationship with only ad hoc theoretical rationalizations provided. Only later were attempts made to develop a theory that would 'explain' the statistical relationship. This method is more akin to that of the German historical school, of which criticism by the Austrian school has been much more severe. The series of currently recognized policy errors that followed from attempts to exploit the Phillips curve serves as an excellent but unfortunate example of the problems associated with 'letting the facts speak for themselves'.

In the first phase of the development of the concept, the Phillips curve was commonly viewed as providing a missing link to the Keynesian perspective on inflation, which had been previously seen as incompatible with any level of unemployment greater than 'full' employment. While this first phase involved merely the observation of a negative inflation–unemployment relationship, the second phase involved the development of the aforementioned policy prescription. Samuelson and Solow (1960), for example, presented the presumably stable negative relationship between inflation and unemployment as a menu of choice facing national governments. Through the 1960s, as policies were pursued in the USA that appeared to accept more inflation in exchange for a lower unemployment rate, the apparent negative relationship appeared to move in a north-east direction: any rate of unemployment seemed to be associated with sequentially higher rates of inflation. This apparent shift of the curve led to a third phase involving attempts to explain the shift on the basis of exogenous, microeconomic changes, such as increases in the degree of union power or industry concentration. A fourth and more consequential phase followed from the recognition that the apparent north-eastern shifts of the curve were the result of attempts to exploit the curve and were thus endogenous. This recognition is associated with the development of the collateral concepts of adaptive expectations and the natural rate of unemployment. The development of these concepts is associated with monetarism, and its earliest exposition is in Friedman (1968). In this line of reasoning, the ability of a government to achieve lower unemployment through inflation is seen as a strictly short-run phenomenon: once a higher rate of inflation comes to be expected, unemployment returns to its natural level; hence, the long-run Phillips curve is vertical. A fifth phase involved introduction of the concept of rational expectations. In this view, any monetary policy involving a feedback rule would eventually be learned by market participants; once the rule was learned, even a short run trade-off between inflation and unemployment could not successfully be exploited. While mainstream economists continue to debate the existence of a short-run trade-off, and whether that trade-off leaves a role for stabilization policy, a consensus has developed which accepts the position that no permanent trade-off is possible.

Austrian criticism
Despite the fact that the Phillips curve concept has been criticized by modern Austrian economists to varying degrees in each of its five phases, there is generally a recognition among Austrian economists that there is a considerable element of truth in the developments of the fourth and fifth phases. Most particularly, the central contemporary policy conclusion – that any success in lowering unemployment through stimulative monetary policy is at best transitory – is well accepted by Austrian economists. Indeed, this essential insight into the transitory nature of the alleged trade-off was part of Austrian monetary analysis long before the incorporation of adaptive and then rational expectations into treatment of the Phillips curve. In fact, such recognition predates even the original treatment of A.W. Phillips. Ludwig von Mises (1953) briefly described the process by which inflation could create a boom provided that the effects of money growth affected product prices before fully affecting money wages. But the increase in employment would last only for as long as the actual money wage remained below the money wage that would provide an equilibrium real wage, given the levels of product prices. Though not fully developed, the essence of the Misesian insight is that the deviation of the real wage from its equilibrium value is the causal factor that

produces the movement in employment. Following the implication of Mises, Gallaway and Vedder (1987) have attempted to measure such deviation and find that it does a good job of explaining movements in employment through a number of episodes, including the great depression. The discussion of a temporary inflation–unemployment trade-off is notable not only because it predates by five years the initial treatment of Phillips, which treatment failed to recognize both the transitory nature of the trade-off and the role that monetary expansion plays in inducing a self-reversing change in unemployment. Mises's discussion is more notable because it precedes by 15 years the publication of Friedman's treatment (which incorporated the two insights that Phillips failed to recognize).

Despite this apparent congeniality between Friedman's and Mises's perspectives, both the primitive (intertemporally stable relationship) version and the now prevalent long-run vertical Phillips curve versions have been seen as at odds with actual experience and with the Austrian view of cyclical activity. Jeffrey Herbener (1992), for example, has criticized Phillips's original article for its lack of a market process foundation. Herbener has also argued that only by the use of very questionable econometric technique applied to unnecessarily aggregated data was Phillips able to derive an apparent negative relationship. Moreover, for Phillips's subperiod of best fit, 1861–1913, elimination of only the three years of highest wage inflation removes any suggestion of a negative relation. With no data points eliminated, a scatter diagram of the annual observations contained in the Samuelson–Solow analysis of the USA reveals no apparent relation. Herbener's analysis suggests that attempts to determine why the primitive version later collapsed are pointless if the 'apparent' earlier statistical regularity was in fact non-existent.

Austrian cycle theory and the Phillips curve

Whether there existed an apparently intertemporally stable Phillips curve prior to 1960 is perhaps moot in the light of the broad current consensus across schools of thought that the unemployment–inflation trade-off is transitory and self-reversing. This consensus is subject only to the qualification of the rational expectations school to the effect that the inflation must be the result of a change in the monetary regime for the trade-off to materialize. However, the Austrian explanation of the market process by which the trade-off unfolds and dissipates is different and in important respects at odds with the neoclassical description. Whereas the neoclassical explanation is based on erroneous perceptions within the labor market, the Austrian explanation focuses on intertemporal discoordination, particularly in the market for capital goods. The first effort to reformulate the Phillips curve explanation in terms of Austrian monetary and capital theory was provided by Gerald O'Driscoll (1977, pp. 115–18). An extensive comparison of Friedman's (monetarist) and Hayek's (Austrian) explanations of the processes that transmit a monetary injection into a self-reversing decrease in unemployment is provided in Bellante and Garrison (1988).

A simplified version of the Hayekian description begins with an injection of newly created money by the central bank into the market for loanable funds. This injection lowers the market rate of interest below the Wicksellian 'natural' rate of interest – the rate consistent with time preferences and which, unlike the market rate, is sustainable in the long run. In the language of Böhm-Bawerk, the structure of production is made more 'roundabout', meaning that capital is redirected towards stages of production that are more remote from final output, and away from less remote stages. The relative prices of capital goods more remote from final output are also bid upwards in this process. As what might be called 'goods in process' move towards later stages of production, the problem of intertemporal discoordination emerges: the requisite resources to complement the earlier stages of production are not available, as they would have been if the initiating fall in the interest rate had reflected a genuine and sustained increase in the willingness to save. In response to these shortages, the relative prices of capital goods shift in the reverse direction – towards the capital goods needed in the later stages of production. If all capital goods were virtually homogeneous and could easily be employed in any stage of the production process, production could be profitably completed, but, despite the fiction of perfectly homogeneous capital that characterizes the neoclassical model, capital goods once put in place are highly specific and most are not readily substitutable across stages of production. Hence the contractionary stage of the cycle inevitably sets in. In time, the structure of production is reformulated along lines consistent with the natural rate of interest; but given the specificity of capital, this is likely to be a drawn-out process. The length of time required for recovery depends on, among other things, the extent to which the capital structure was initially distorted.

Since the typical telling of the Austrian interpretation of the cycle focuses on the capital structure, modern adaptations have had to deal with the reactions in the labor market in order to translate the scenario into one that traces out a pattern of movements of unemployment that would fit a modern Phillips curve scenario. Certainly, if labor were perfectly homogeneous, perfectly and costlessly mobile, and continuously substitutable for capital in production processes, then a complete Austrian cycle could unfold without affecting the unemployment rate. Recognizing that labor is none of these, and that in fact many types of labor are highly complementary to specific forms of capital, is all that is necessary in order to draw out the implications for the labor market: there is a net increase in the demand for labor during the early phase of the cyclical process, as the newly created credit is used not only to draw some workers away from later stages, but also to attract new workers. This effect corresponds to the reduction in the rate of unemployment below its natural rate. In the later phase of the cycle, owing to labor–capital complementarity, there will be decreases in the demand for labor in the earlier stages of production. The increases in the demand for labor in the later stages of production cannot completely offset this decrease, primarily because of the shortage of complementary capital, but also because of the lack of perfect substitutability of labor across stages of production and other frictions in the labor market. These frictions will account for substantial and persistent rises of the unemployment rate above its natural rate. The return to the natural rate cannot be completed until the appropriate capital structure is restored.

The disruptions to the labor market are, however, secondary to and a by-product of the distortions that occur in the capital market. Even so, it can be argued that the Austrian perspective on the Phillips curve yields more significant insights into the actual responses of the labor market to money-induced cycles than does the neoclassical alternative. For example, Richard Wagner (1979) has argued that the Austrian approach sheds light on the social cost associated with the 'waste' that results from the necessity of using some of the labor resource to restore the appropriate capital structure, a waste that is ignored if the unemployment rate is used as the indicator of the social cost of a money-induced recession. Moreover, since the neoclassical explanation of the Phillips phenomena depends primarily on informational disequilibria, the 'persistence' of cycles is a puzzle to be explained. Considerable efforts have been put forth to rationalize this persistence problem, including incorporation of 'time-to-build' considerations into the model. In the Austrian explanation, with its emphasis on capital market distortions, and what might be called 'time-to-correct', no such puzzle exists.

See also:
Chapter 32: Austrian business cycle theory; Chapter 31: Capital theory; Chapter 58: Inflation; Chapter 81: Monetarism

Bibliography
Bellante, D. and R.W. Garrison (1988), 'Phillips Curves and Hayekian Triangles: Two Perspectives on Monetary Dynamics', *History of Political Economy*, **20**, (2), summer, 207–34.
Friedman, M. (1968), 'The Role of Monetary Policy', *American Economic Review*, **58**, (1), March, 1–17.
Gallaway, L. and R.K. Vedder (1987), 'Wages, Prices, and Employment: Von Mises and the Progressives', *Review of Austrian Economics*, **1**, 33–80.
Herbener, J.M. (1992), 'The Fallacy of the Phillips Curve', in M. Skousen (ed.), *Dissent on Keynes: A Critical Appraisal of Keynesian Economics*, New York: Praeger.
Mises, L. von (1953), *The Theory of Money and Credit*, New Haven: Yale University Press.
O'Driscoll, G.P. Jr. (1977), *Economics as a Coordination Process: The Contribution of Friedrich A. Hayek*, Kansas City: Sheed Andrews & McMeel.

Phillips, A.W. (1958), 'The Relation Between Unemployment and the Rate of Change of Money Wage Rates in the United Kingdom, 1867–1957', *Economica*, **25**, (4), November, 283–99.

Samuelson, P.A. and R. Solow (1960), 'Analytical Aspects of Anti-Inflation Policy', *American Economic Review*, **50**, (2), May, 177–94.

Wagner, R.E. (1979), 'Comment: Politics, Monetary Control, and Economic Performance', in M.J. Rizzo (ed.), *Time, Uncertainty, and Disequilibrium*, Lexington, Mass.: DC Heath.

54 Taxation

Roy E. Cordato

Unlike most other schools of economic thought, Austrian economics provides no efficiency justification for taxation. The primary rationale for taxation found in more orthodox economic literature, derived from Pigouvian welfare economics, is inconsistent with Austrian methodology and has been criticized extensively by Austrian writers.

The basic issue is the same as that raised by Mises and Hayek in regard to rational economic calculation under socialism. The standard rationale for taxation requires what Hayek (1978) called a 'pretence of knowledge' on the part of the economist or policy maker. The information that would be necessary to first construct the tax and then implement it is impossible even to comprehend let alone gather and utilize. Therefore no allegedly efficiency-enhancing tax can be invoked in a way that is consistent with the economic theory that gives rise to its advocacy.

To illustrate this point, imagine a simple Pigouvian excise tax meant to correct for problems brought about by a negative externality. In the presence of such externalities, markets are said to fail, in that prices are lower and outputs are greater than they would be in a perfectly competitive general equilibrium (PCGE). This situation is said to provide a justification for an excise tax placed on the generator of the externality equal to the marginal social costs of the external effect. Such a tax, if implemented in a way that is consistent with the underlying economic theory, would correct for the market failure by forcing the price–output combination to conform to the PCGE result. In this way, such an excise tax would enhance economic efficiency. As one staunch advocate of such taxes has argued: 'The primary function of such taxes is to make the economy function more efficiently. Through their use we have the opportunity to employ the tax system, not only to raise revenues but also to enhance the operations of the economy' (Oates, 1988, p. 254).

The Austrian critique is fundamental. Information problems ultimately render the PCGE standard of economic welfare both non-operational and conceptually vacuous. Therefore any efficiency properties that the tax might have within the theoretical framework of general equilibrium analysis will necessarily disappear when an attempt is made to put it into practice. The tax only enhances efficiency or social welfare when it is implemented as part of an overall PCGE. The problem is twofold. For any moment in time the PCGE solution for a given real-world situation is impossible to identify.[1] Information about costs and benefits is inherently subjective and therefore unmeasurable. Furthermore, the necessary technical knowledge is ungatherable because it is highly diffused throughout the population and because it is often in the form of 'tacit' knowledge, that is, it cannot be made explicit by those who hold it.

To further complicate what, even in a static sense, is an impossible problem to solve, all relevant information is in a constant state of flux. Therefore the necessarily hypothetical PCGE pattern of outcomes changes from moment to moment. Even if the efficient tax could be identified for a point in time it would be out of date before it was implemented. O'Driscoll and Rizzo have pointed out that these are precisely the problems facing the socialist planner:

> In the Mises–Hayek analysis, socialism is intervention carried out systematically in all markets. It substitutes ... non-market allocations for ... market institutions. Particularistic intervention at the micro-level is socialism writ small ... If a tax rate is to be optimal, policy makers must know the optimal level of the taxed activity ... The information requirements for [optimal taxation] are simply those for non-price resource allocation. There can be no theory of optimal ... taxing behavior until there is a theory of non-price resource allocation that actually addresses the original Mises–Hayek argument. (1985, p. 141)

Similar arguments, based on knowledge problem considerations, can be made with regard to the theory of neutral taxation.[2] It is typically argued that a tax will not hinder economic efficiency so long as its relative price effects are neutral. Neutrality, though, typically means neutral with respect to relative prices as they would arise in a PCGE without taxation. Once this is made explicit, all of the knowledge problems that are faced in trying to construct the efficient externalities tax also apply to the construction of a neutral income tax. To construct and implement such a tax the analyst must 'pretend' that he is able to identify the 'efficient' array of prices and outputs both before and after the tax.[3]

Unfortunately, most analysis of taxation by Austrian economists has remained at the level of criticizing the more traditional theoretical justifications for taxation. Very little effort has been made to analyse the effects of different kinds of taxation on economic behavior.[4] In this regard Austrians have an opportunity to build on important insights of some supply-side economists, who, like Austrians, reject aggregative macroeconomic analysis of taxation as a meaningful starting-point. Furthermore, they make the praxeologically sound point that, while people ostensibly pay taxes, from the perspective of economic analysis, it is particular activities that those people are pursuing that the tax penalizes. The task of positive tax analysis is to identify the penalized activities and to draw out the consequences, both intended and unintended, of the tax policy.

The unique Austrian contribution would come in linking the tax analysis to Austrian time preference and capital theory. Like Austrian business cycle theory and the more general analysis of the non-neutral effects of money supply changes on economic activities, Austrian tax analysis could offer insights that, because of their insufficient capital theory, more orthodox schools tend to miss. As a brief example, consider the effects of a broad-based income tax on saving. Supply-side economists argue, correctly, that such a tax penalizes saving relative to consumption (see Turé, 1983). Without reviewing the analysis, a broad-based income tax that includes returns to savings, that is interest, dividends, capital gains and so on, in the tax base has the effect of reducing the returns to consumption once, while reducing the returns to saving at least twice, that is, saving is 'double taxed'. As a consequence, arguing in a traditional neoclassical (or more strictly speaking, Knightian) vein, it is concluded that broad-based income taxes cause the capital stock to be smaller and therefore interest rates and the cost of capital to be higher.

Austrian capital theory would allow a much richer analysis to be pursued, with additional insights being brought to light. From an Austrian perspective the adverse effect on saving of such a tax would have consequences for the entire 'time structure of production'. When saving is penalized, the time horizon of market participants is shortened. Therefore, in addition to reducing capital accumulation in general, such taxes would affect the composition of investment such that relatively shorter-term investments, investments that take a shorter period of time to be completed, would be encouraged relative to longer-term investments. This is due to the fact that the reduced supply of loanable funds causes interest rates to be higher, reducing the profitability of longer-term investments relative to shorter-term investments.

An Austrian insight that tends to be missed in the more standard supply-side analysis is that the time structure of production is truncated as a result of the tax.[5] A research program of tax analysis from an Austrian perspective would likely result in similarly unique insights with respect to the effects of other forms of taxation such as value added taxes and other broad-based consumption taxes, in addition to the economic effects of different kinds of rate structures. This is an almost completely untouched field of analysis from an Austrian perspective.

Conclusion
In recognizing that there is truly no efficiency justification for taxation, Austrians have shied away from trying to evaluate normatively the relative inefficiencies of different kinds of taxation. In other words, there has been no attempt by Austrians to take the presence of taxation as a given, and to consider what kinds of taxation will do the least amount of damage to the

economic pursuits of market participants. Tax policy debates are continuous and, as was demonstrated by Keynesians in the 1960s and supply-side economists in the late 1970s and early 1980s, economic analysis, for better or worse, can have an impact on the direction of these debates. Austrian tax analysis could have an influence, but it first needs to be more thoroughly developed and then applied on a case-by-case basis.

Notes

1. It should be pointed out that to assume actual market prices are general equilibrium prices, as is often done, involves a logical contradiction. If an externality problem exists, then, by definition, the world is deviating from the conditions of general equilibrium. On the other hand, as is suggested by the theory of second best, partial equilibrium analysis is not a way to eliminate this problem. From the perspective of welfare economics and therefore tax analysis, there is only general equilibrium analysis and disequilibrium analysis. Any partial equilibrium analysis ultimately must collapse into general equilibrium.
2. For a discussion that argues convincingly that no tax can ever be 'neutral' see Rothbard (1981). Rothbard's approach is not from the perspective of tax analysis per se but argues from the more general perspective that no government activity, by its very nature, can be neutral.
3. It should be pointed out that this does not prevent the tax analyst from analysing, without the pretense of trying to construct *the* neutral tax, the way in which different kinds of taxes can penalize some activities relative to others. Standard supply-side analysis of the way in which the income tax penalizes work relative to leisure or saving relative to consumption is a good example of this kind of 'incentive effects' analysis.
4. As in many other areas related to political economy, Rothbard has done the most work in analysing different kinds of taxation. But even here, the emphasis has been on the political and ethical ramifications of taxation and not the particular economic effects of taxation. See Rothbard (1970).
5. For a lengthier discussion of this, see Cordato (1992b).

See also:

Chapter 44: Austrian welfare economics; Chapter 19: Efficiency; Chapter 15: Entrepreneurship; Chapter 4: Market process; Chapter 25: Prices and knowledge; Chapter 82: Supply-side economics

Bibliography

Cordato, Roy E. (1992a), *Welfare Economics and Externalities in an Open Ended Universe: A Modern Austrian Perspective*, Boston/London: Kluwer Academic.

Cordato, Roy E. (1992b), 'Taxation and Market Economies: Some Guiding Principles for Eastern Europe', in Robert McGee (ed.), *The Market Solution to Economic Development in Eastern Europe*, New York: Edwin Mellen.

Hayek, F.A. (1978), 'The Pretence of Knowledge', in *New Studies*, Chicago: University of Chicago Press.

Oates, Wallace E. (1988), 'A Pollution Tax Makes Sense', in Herbert Stein (ed.), *Tax Policy in the Twenty-First Century*, New York: John Wiley.

O'Driscoll, Gerald P., Jr. and Mario J. Rizzo (1985), *The Economics of Time and Ignorance*, Oxford: Basil Blackwell.

Rothbard, Murray (1970), *Power and Market*, Kansas City: Sheed Andrews & McMeel.

Rothbard, Murray (1981), 'The Myth of Neutral Taxation', *Cato Journal*, fall.

Turé, Norman B. (1983), 'The Accelerated Cost Recovery System: An Evaluation of the 1981 and 1982 Cost-Recovery Provisions', in Charles E. Walker and Mark A. Bloomfield (eds), *New Directions in Federal Tax Policies for the 1980s*, Cambridge, Mass.: Ballinger.

55 Industrial organization and the Austrian school

Thomas J. DiLorenzo

From the 1930s to the early 1970s, industrial organization (and antitrust policy) was dominated by the structure–conduct–performance (SCP) paradigm, which holds that

> *performance* in particular industries or markets is said to depend upon the *conduct* of sellers and buyers in such matters as pricing policies and practices, overt and tacit interfirm cooperation, product line and advertising strategies, research and development commitments, investment in production facilities, legal tactics ... and so on. Conduct in turn depends upon the *structure* of the relevant market, characterized by the number and size distribution of sellers and buyers, the degree of physical or subjective differentiation distinguishing competing sellers' products, the presence or absence of barriers to the entry of new firms, the shapes of cost curves, the degree to which firms are vertically integrated from raw material production to retail distribution, and the extent of firms' product line diversification. (Scherer and Ross, 1990)

Thus the SCP paradigm, which is still very popular, holds that market structure determines industrial conduct, which in turn determines performance in terms of efficiency and equity. It is a derivative of the perfect competition model, which contends that one of the assumptions of a competitive market is that there are 'many' firms. Having fewer firms leads to oligopoly or monopoly. Market structure, according to this paradigm, is the main determinant of competition.

Primarily because of Chicago school scholars, there has been a virtual revolution in industrial organization (and in antitrust policy) since the early 1970s. The SCP paradigm has been turned on its head: the 'new learning' in industrial organization now holds that market structure is determined by conduct and performance, not the other way around (McGee, 1971; Goldschmid, Mann and Weston, 1974; Bork, 1978; Armentano, 1982; Brozen, 1982). More often than not, according to this research, a concentrated industry got that way because of the superior efficiency of one or a few firms, not because of collusion or monopolistic mergers. From a policy perspective, the implication is that forced deconcentration can be harmful to efficiency (and ultimately to consumers).

The new learning also looks more favorably upon an array of business practices – from advertising and product differentiation to R&D spending, interfirm cooperation and price cutting – than the SCP paradigm does. Although it is not widely recognized, this so-called 'new learning' has its roots in Austrian economics, particularly the notion of competition as a dynamic, rivalrous process.

The meaning of competition

According to the perfect competition model and the derivative SCP paradigm (hereafter called the PC/SCP model), an ideal or perfectly competitive industry presupposes homogeneous commodities supplied by a 'large' number of sellers, none of which can unilaterally affect price. There is free entry into the market, resources can move freely and there is complete knowledge of the relevant factors on the part of all participants in the market. But to the Austrian economists, 'competition is by its nature a dynamic process whose essential characteristics are assumed away by the assumptions underlying static analysis', that is, the PC/SCP model (Hayek, 1972). The essence of the Austrian theory of competition is its emphasis on the continuing process of rivalry, as opposed to the static equilibrium conditions of the PC/SCP model.

The Austrian theory also provides a prominent role for entrepreneurship, which is all but ignored by the SCP paradigm. The Austrian theory of entrepreneurship as developed by Mises (1949) and Kirzner (1973) emphasizes how human action in the competitive market-place directs (and redirects) the flow of resources to best satisfy human wants. The Kirznerian entrepreneur sees profit opportunities that others have ignored and takes advantage of them by satisfying consumers better than others have.

Because it virtually ignores the *process* of competition and the role of entrepreneurship, the PC/SCP model simply assumes away many of the most significant aspects of competition as viewed by the Austrians. Business firms do not raise or lower prices, differentiate their products, advertise or do any of the things that businesses do in a dynamic, competitive environment.

Advertising

Consider the case of advertising. The PC/SCP model has long held that advertising expenditures can constitute a barrier to entry. Firms making heavy use of advertising allegedly impose prohibitive entry costs on some potential rivals. This perspective, however, ignores or de-emphasizes the informational role of advertising and the function of entrepreneurship as described by Kirzner (1973):

> As part of his *entrepreneurial* role, it is the function of the producer to go beyond the mere fabrication and delivery of a commodity to be available for the con-

sumer. He must also *alert* the consumer to the availability of the product, and sometimes he must even alert the consumer to the *desirability* of an already known product ... this latter role cannot be understood merely as that of 'producing knowledge' for the consumer concerning prospective or existing opportunities. Rather, it consists in *relieving the consumer of the necessity to be his own entrepreneur.* In order for him to perform this role, 'costs of production' must be higher than they would otherwise be. (Emphasis in original)

Application of the PC/SCP model has also led some economists to label some advertising as 'wasteful' or as 'unnecessary duplication'. But 'in calling such duplication wasteful one is presumably passing judgement from the perspective of assumed omniscience. In the absence of such omniscience, to criticize competitive duplication as wasteful is to criticize the very process through which the market assembles the entrepreneurial knowledge required to perceive the occurrence of waste' (Kirzner, 1973). In short, by comparing the real-world competitive process to a yardstick of perfect knowledge, one quite naturally concludes that such expenditures are wasteful. But what appears from the viewpoint of omniscience to be waste is precisely the instrument employed by the competitive process to eliminate imperfections in knowledge, imperfections that hinder market exchange.

Empirical research by economists who do not necessarily consider themselves to be Austrians has supported the Austrian view of the role of advertising. Studies have shown that government-imposed advertising *restrictions* on items ranging from eyeglasses to attorneys' and physicians' services have resulted in less competition and higher prices to consumers. Other research has shown that advertising intensity does not lead to more stable profit levels, contrary to the 'barriers to entry' theory of advertising. This new view of advertising is compatible with, if not inspired by, the Austrian tradition.

Product differentiation

The PC/SCP model has also led to the idea that product differentiation can be a monopolizing device by creating 'spatial monopolies', as discussed in the monopolistic competition literature. From a market process or Austrian perspective, product differentiation is best construed as part of the normal competitive process. From this perspective an 'efficient' organization of industry is one that maximizes the net gains from trade to buyers, sellers and entrepreneurs. It is likely to be reflected by a unique matching of a multitude of consumer wants with producer outputs. There will be many unique exchanges involving many differentiated products within any one 'industry' because of the enormous variation in consumer preferences and production possibilities over time.

The market process view of product differentiation suggests that it is *legal barriers* to product differentiation that may constitute a restraint of trade.

One example of this phenomenon is a 1980 antitrust case where the US Federal Trade Commission prosecuted Kellogs, General Foods and General Mills for allegedly 'sharing' a monopoly in the ready-to-eat cereal industry. The firms were accused of improperly increasing sales by offering consumers a wider range of choice (product differentiation). So-called 'brand prolifera- tion' did cause a divergence from the perfectly competitive ideal, but the three cereal companies could not have increased their market share if con- sumers were not satisfied by the wider range of choice (which their competi- tors were slow to develop). From a market process perspective, it is a mark of competition for firms continually to experiment with new brands to *discover* what will best satisfy consumers – precisely the kind of knowledge that the PC/SCP model unrealistically assumes already exists in a competitive indus- try. The case was decided in favor of the cereal companies (and of consum- ers).

Market concentration

Perhaps the most important element of the PC/SCP paradigm is the market- concentration doctrine, which holds that a concentrated industry is more likely to be monopolistic than a less concentrated one. The presumed link between market concentration (measured by concentration ratios) and profit- ability is the likelihood of collusion. It is assumed that collusion is more likely to take place when there are relatively few 'dominant' firms in an industry. The standard approach of adherents to the market concentration doctrine has been to take a snapshot look at an industry at a point in time and, if the industry happened to have a high concentration ratio, to categorize the industry as oligopolistic or monopolistic. What constitutes a 'high' concen- tration ratio has always been purely arbitrary.

Dozens of empirical studies have refuted the market concentration doc- trine by showing that there is not always a positive correlation between concentration and profitability (Brozen, 1982) and, when there is, the correla- tion is often caused by the superior efficiency of one or a few firms, not by a monopolistic conspiracy. This entire body of research is an illustration of the Austrian theory of competition as a process, although it is not always ac- knowledged as such. For example, this research has recognized that indus- tries tend to *become* concentrated – at least for a short period of time – precisely because of competitive rivalry. Market concentration can increase as smaller firms become larger as the result of increased efficiency and economies of scale, as innovation of new products or production processes increases the market share of the innovating firms, as mergers result in economies of scale in production, distribution, R&D, capital financing and other areas, and as corporate takeovers discipline inefficient managers and provide economical alternatives to bankruptcy.

Of course, mergers and takeovers do not always work out; many acquired firms are spun off after several years. Consequently, some adherents of the PC/SCP model have criticized such 'unsuccessful' takeovers as 'wasteful' and have advocated government regulation ostensibly to permit only 'good' takeovers. But mergers or takeovers that do not directly enhance efficiency are only 'wasteful' if one compares real-world markets with the perfectly competitive ideal whereby information is costless. Trial and error in the market-place is the only way to learn which type of corporate structure is most efficient. Therein lies the social value of 'unsuccessful' takeovers. Such information cannot simply be assumed to exist in the minds of economists or federal regulators.

The 'new learning' turns the market concentration doctrine on its head by demonstrating that the process of competition can cause markets to become concentrated because of the continuing quest by competitors to satisfy consumers better than their rivals. The market concentration doctrine virtually ignores this entire process and focuses instead on the simple statistics of concentration ratios. These ratios may reveal how concentrated an industry is at a point in time, but they say nothing about the process by which it became that way.

A fatal blow to the market concentration doctrine was delivered by a line of empirical inquiry initiated by Yale Brozen (1982) which tracked the profitability of industries with varying degrees of concentration over time. Brozen studied a number of industries where other researchers had found a simple correlation between concentration and profitability (and had simply *assumed* the profitability to be caused by monopoly power) and examined the question of the persistence over time of the correlation. He found that the correlations degenerated within a few short years, and high and low profit rates tended to converge towards a common level. The high profit rates of the concentrated industries tended to collapse and, along with them, the market concentration doctrine. Like other Chicago school economists, Brozen may not consider himself an Austrian, but his research program is inspired – implicitly or explicitly – by the Austrian tradition.

Historical perspectives

The Austrian tradition and the 'new learning' in industrial organization are both compatible with the way in which Adam Smith and the classical economists viewed competition as rivalry. Until about the 1920s the Smithian/Austrian view of markets dominated the thinking of American economists. With very few exceptions, turn-of-the century economists saw the trust movement and corporate mergers as desirable aspects of the competitive process (DiLorenzo and High, 1988). Richard T. Ely, co-founder of the American Economic Association, wrote in 1900 that 'large scale production is a thing which by no means necessarily signifies monopolized production' (DiLorenzo and High, 1988). His colleague and AEA co-founder, John Bates Clark, wrote in 1888 that mergers will undoubtedly 'play an increasingly important part in economic affairs', but 'that competition is to be to a corresponding extent destroyed ... should not be too hastily accepted'. Other prominent economists of that period, such as Herbert Davenport, Irving Fisher, Edwin R.A. Seligman, Henry Seager and Arthur Hadley, echoed these views.

The economics profession was virtually unanimously opposed to the idea of antitrust regulation on the grounds that it was inherently incompatible with competitive rivalry (DiLorenzo and High, 1988). These opinions were a direct consequence of the essentially Austrian (or Smithian) view of competition as a dynamic, rivalrous process that dominated economic thinking in the USA until about the 1920s. Once the PC/SCP model became widely accepted in the post-Depression era, however, the economics profession became more supportive of antitrust regulation. The 'new' skepticism over antitrust that has developed in recent years is essentially a rediscovery of the old economic truths about competition that were held by Adam Smith and the classical economists. The 'new learning' is not so new after all.

The problem of monopoly
Once one views competition as a dynamic, rivalrous process and acknowledges the importance of entrepreneurship, many of the business activities that the PC/SCP model views suspiciously as monopolistic are interpreted as essential parts of the competitive process. This is not to suggest that monopoly is not a problem, but that its origins are not likely to be the free market. There have long been 'two systems of belief' about monopoly, as Harold Demsetz has written (Goldschmid, Mann and Weston, 1974). One system of belief, the PC/SCP model, sees monopoly as primarily the result of the divergence of real-world markets from the perfectly competitive ideal. The alternative system – often associated with the Austrian school – sees government as the source of monopoly through protectionism, monopoly franchises, occupational licensure, government enterprises and myriad other mercantilistic laws and regulations.

To Austrian economists, the search for so-called 'free-market monopoly' is a misallocation of intellectual resources. It is socially wasteful for an economist to spend his career seeking to uncover the extent to which price diverges from marginal cost at a point in time or spinning endless oligopoly tales. Cloistered in his windowless office, he ignores the fact that he is paying a monopolistic price for his cable TV, is forced to cater only to the US Postal Service's monopoly in first-class mail, he must send his children to a monopolistic public school system, have his garbage collected by a government monopoly, pay gas, electric and water bills to other government-sponsored monopolies, pay supracompetitive prices for the services of taxi drivers, physicians, attorneys, hairdressers, undertakers and myriad other service providers because of supply-reducing occupational licensing laws, he is victimized by misguided antitrust regulation which encourages inefficient businesses to sue their more efficient rivals for *cutting* their prices or expanding their product lines, and he pays higher food prices caused by acreage allotments and other forms of farm protectionism.

These are just a few examples of government-sponsored monopolies that have been largely ignored by most industrial organization economists because of the PC/SCP model's preoccupation with market structure as the benchmark of competition.

See also:
Chapter 26: The boundaries of the firm; Chapter 14: Competition; Chapter 24: The economics of information; Chapter 15: Entrepreneurship; Chapter 4: Market process; Chapter 57: Mergers and the market for corporate control; Chapter 23: Non-price rivalry

Bibliography
Armentano, Dominick (1982), *Antitrust and Monopoly: Anatomy of a Policy Failure*, New York: John Wiley.
Bork, Robert (1978), *The Antitrust Paradox*, New York: Basic Books.
Brozen, Yale (1982), *Concentration, Mergers and Public Policy*, New York: Macmillan.
DiLorenzo, Thomas J. and Jack C. High (1988), 'Antitrust and Competition, Historically Considered', *Economic Inquiry*, **26**, July, 423–35.
Goldschmid, Harvey J., H. Michael Mann and J. Fred Weston (eds) (1974), *Industrial Concentration: The New Learning*, Boston: Little, Brown.
Hayek, Friedrich (1972), 'The Meaning of Competition', in *Individualism and Economic Order*, Chicago: University of Chicago Press.
Kirzner, Israel (1973), *Competition and Entrepreneurship*, Chicago: University of Chicago Press.
McGee, John (1971), *In Defense of Industrial Concentration*, New York: Praeger.
Mises, Ludwig von (1949), *Human Action*, New Haven: Yale University Press.
Scherer, F.M. and David Ross (1990), *Industrial Market Structure and Economic Performance*, Boston: Houghton Mifflin.

56 Advertising

Robert Hébert

Advertising is the provision of information about various aspects of commodities, services, events or human activities. As such, it is widely engaged in by virtually every segment of society. Advertising therefore has social and economic connotations. From the more narrow economic standpoint, advertising is a commercial activity associated with the sale of goods and services in organized economic markets. This more narrow definition constitutes the point of focus here. Few topics offer a better mirror of the differences between mainstream neoclassical economics and Austrian economics than advertising. These differences, as well as practically all others between the two schools, can be traced to deep divisions in *gestalt* and in method.

Is competition therapeutic or prophylactic?

How one views advertising is largely a function of how one views competition. Consider two broad visions of competition. A *prophylactic* notion of competition prevents the intrusion of ignorance and error into the decision nexuses of production and consumption, thus 'solving' the most difficult problems by simply assuming them away. The prophylactic view of competition (adopted, in the main, by mainstream neoclassical economics), regards advertising as incompatible with the notion of perfect competition, a 'frictionless' model that assumes the existence of perfect information and simultaneous adjustments by all economic actors. Advertising, in this view, is both an irritant and a waste. By contrast, a *therapeutic* notion of competition (embraced by Austrian economics) recognizes error and ignorance as part of the human condition, and searches for palliatives. Advertising, in this view, is, in fact, one of the palliatives. It is a means at the disposal of the entrepreneur to make consumers aware of consumption opportunities and to stimulate the production of those things that increase consumers' utility.

Since E.H. Chamberlin's (1933) early attempt to treat advertising formally in economics, the concept and practice has attracted increasing attention from economists. Most of the early literature on the subject was critical, finding advertising both unnecessary and wasteful. Following Kaldor (1950), most early neoclassical economists stressed advertising's persuasive character and argued that advertising establishes entry barriers, encourages concentration, misallocates resources and reduces price elasticities of demand within markets. Lacking from this early literature was the awareness that judgements about waste can only be made unambiguously if one assumes that all decision makers are omniscient: once one leaves the rarefied atmosphere of perfect competition, the assumption cannot be sustained. As Rothschild (1954, p. 307) acknowledged almost four decades ago, 'even in its most ideal practical form [competition] is therapeutic, not prophylactic'.

Beginning with Telser (1964), certain economists have defended advertising by stressing its informational nature, arguing that it *increases* elasticities and *lowers* barriers to entry. This new departure is based on the assumption of imperfect information. Superficially, this new, neoclassical theory appears to meld with the Austrian approach; and in fact, the two approaches share some of the conclusions about advertising. Yet a fundamental difference remains: the new, neoclassical theory does not go so far as to accept the notion of competition as therapeutic. It is scientifically more conservative in its analysis of human decision making. It circumscribes the decision-making process in such a way as to exclude the existence of surprises (not merely the unknown but the unknowable).

Open-ended v. closed-ended decisions

Mainstream neoclassical economics concentrates on market decisions made under certain assumptions about the nature, form and extent of information possessed by decision makers. In its early development, neoclassical theory assumed that an individual decision maker, say a consumer, always knows the full range of choices available at any particular moment, as well as the cost of each choice, and the full extent of his/her demand. Under such assumptions, advertising (as part of a discovery process) is unnecessary and, presumably, wasteful. Kirzner (1988, p. xiv) has categorized the kind of world in which such decision processes rule as a 'closed universe'. In a closed universe, the decision maker is confronted by a finite number of clearly perceived alternatives, each leading to a certain outcome. There is no room for, nor any conceptual admission of, any *surprises* in such a model. Nor is there any scope for the decision maker to exercise creative imagination. Decisions are made mechanically by rational calculation, and all decisions produce actions that rapidly converge to equilibrium.

Contemporary neoclassical economics has progressed one stage beyond this early formulation by recognizing the existence of imperfect or incomplete information. Stigler (1961) and others have enriched mainstream neoclassical economics by pioneering 'the economics of information', 'search theory' and 'transactions-cost theory', all integuments of the admission of imperfect information in economic markets. Austrians, however, claim that these developments are insufficient because mainstream neoclassical economics retains the assumption that all decision alternatives are known beforehand. The new developments modify (and enrich) the concept of the 'closed-ended universe', but they do not go so far as to embrace what Kirzner calls 'the open-ended universe'. The open-ended universe insists that decision makers not only do not know the full range of choices available to them at any particular moment, they also do not know the extent of their ignorance! In other words, the open-ended universe assumes more than merely imperfect information, it assumes that surprise (that is, discovery) is genuinely possible. It is in such a world as this that advertising finds its most powerful role and function.

The Austrian perspective

Since Menger, competition has been viewed in the Austrian tradition as a discovery process. Hayek (1948) refined this view by defining markets as mechanisms that generate and mobilize dispersed information. Thus contemporary Austrian economics treats advertising as merely one particular dimension of competitive activity, albeit an important one. In the Austrian tradition, competition, entrepreneurship and advertising are intricately interwoven concepts. The most forceful modern proponent of this view is Israel Kirzner (1973), who argues that advertising is an integral and inescapable aspect of the market economy.

Kirzner has simultaneously welcomed contemporary neoclassical embellishments (for example, the economics of information, search and transaction costs) and complained that these advances do not go far enough. The economics of information, as pioneered by contemporary neoclassical theorists, treats information as something apart from the particular commodity or service demanded. This separation of information *about* a product or service from the product or service itself allows information to be analysed by standard demand and supply concepts (see, for example, Stigler, 1961; Telser, 1966). Kirzner finds fault with this approach, on the following grounds. To treat all informational aspects of advertising exclusively as providing a separate, distinct service is to overlook completely the important role of the entrepreneur as one who presents to consumers available purchasing opportunities. Kirzner maintains that there are informational aspects of advertising beyond those that attach themselves to known products. There are, for example, opportunities and products about which consumers know little or nothing. Entrepreneurs seek to bring these opportunities to the attention of consumers in a process called 'demand discovery'. The point of demand discovery is that, not only do consumers not know everything about existing consumption possibilities, they do not know all of the consumption possibilities themselves.

To illustrate Kirzner's point, consider the following comparison. Suppose a homeowner knows that he wants to purchase a dehumidifier to make the living space in his basement more comfortable, but he does not know which brand of dehumidifier provides the highest quality or the best price. Advertising aimed at disclosing (even amidst some puffery) information about different brands, and/or a list of stores at which each brand may be purchased, clearly provides utility to the homeowner/consumer by reducing his/her search and transaction costs. In this case, the information may be treated analytically as something apart from, albeit complementary to, the product in question. But suppose we turn back the clock to the time when dehumidifiers entered the market as new products. The same homeowner with a dank basement may not even know that such a product as a dehumidifier exists, or that the product is capable of making life more comfortable. It makes no sense to speak of a demand for something not known to exist. In this case, advertising provides utility in the form of a new opportunity, one that was previously unknown. In other words, advertising is an integral aspect of 'demand discovery'. An Austrian perspective requires that the second aspect of information be recognized, even though it does not lend itself to economic analysis in the same manner as the first.

In a more general sense, the Austrian view forces a reconsideration of standard neoclassical demand theory. This theory treats the demand curve – the driving force behind production decisions (thus the basis for consumer sovereignty) – as given and known *apart* from the production decisions that occur. By contrast, the Austrian view holds that demand curves are entrepreneurial guesses as to what consumers want, and that actual, or ex post, demand cannot be manifested until *after* production has taken place. Unlike mainstream neoclassical analysis, the Austrian notion of competition accommodates error as well as ignorance, aspects denied by the situational notion of perfect competition.

Agenda for future research

Overall, advertising does not emerge from the empirical (neoclassical) literature as an important determinant of consumer behavior. Empirical research in this area is, however, beset by a number of serious problems. Distinctions between informative and persuasive advertising have little meaning empirically, because it is practically impossible to separate the two. Few if any advertisements present facts in a way that does not attempt to persuade, however subtly. Even advertisements without any apparent factual content demonstrate the fact that the seller has invested resources in grabbing consumers' attention. Indeed, we often observe very intensive advertising in markets where consumers are generally familiar with the product, as in beer and soft drinks. Finally, because advertising is endogenous it makes econometric analysis of the effects of advertising on consumer spending patterns extremely difficult. Advertising reflects sellers' decisions and therefore gives rise to simultaneity problems in econometric analysis.

Attempts to measure the welfare effects of advertising have been inconclusive. Some have argued that advertising fosters the long-term growth of materialism, but no one has offered anything like a rigorous test of this proposition. The evidence on market concentration and scale economies is mixed (Schmalensee, 1972). On the one hand, reduction in the number of sellers is expected to reduce advertising, whereas, on the other hand, increased market concentration may be expected to allow sellers to raise price considerably above marginal costs, thereby providing increased incentives to advertise. As to whether or not there are scale economies in advertising, despite observed variable intensities of effort, no one has presented conclusive evidence that a doubling of advertising expenditures will more than double demand. In general, the neoclassical literature can support neither the proposition that market-determined levels of advertising are socially optimal, nor its opposite proposition that they are suboptimal.

The Austrian paradigm, in contrast to the orthodox neoclassical approach, demands research that explores the therapeutic nature of competition, the dynamics of disequilibrium states, the centrality of entrepreneurial activity, the essences of creativity and imagination, and the elements of surprise. Pursuit of this agenda undoubtedly will take us into the more esoteric aspects of human behavior. Nevertheless, these are the areas that contain the challenges of future research into the economics of advertising.

See also:
Chapter 14: Competition; Chapter 24: The economics of information; Chapter 15: Entrepreneurship; Chapter 4: Market process; Chapter 23: Non-price rivalry

Bibliography
Chamberlin, E.H. (1933), *The Theory of Monopolistic Competition*, Cambridge, Mass.: Harvard University Press.
Hayek, F.A. (1948), *Individualism and Economic Order*, Chicago: University of Chicago Press.
Kaldor, N. (1950), 'The economic aspects of advertising', *Review of Economic Studies*, **18**, (1), 1–27.
Kirzner, I.M. (1973), *Competition and Entrepreneurship*, Chicago: University of Chicago Press.
Kirzner, I.M. (1988), 'Foreword: advertising in an open-ended universe', in R.B. Ekelund, Jr. and D.S. Saurman (eds), *Advertising and the Market Process*, San Francisco: Pacific Research Institute.
Rothschild, K.W. (1954), 'The wastes of competition', in E.H. Chamberlin (ed.), *Monopoly and Competition and Their Regulation*, London: Macmillan.
Schmalensee, R. (1972), *The Economics of Advertising*, Amsterdam: North-Holland.
Stigler, G.J. (1961), 'The economics of information', *Journal of Political Economy*, **69**, June, 213–25.
Telser, L.G. (1964), 'Advertising and competition', *Journal of Political Economy*, **72**, December, 537–62.
Telser, L.G. (1966), 'Supply and demand for advertising messages', *American Economic Review*, **56**, (2), 457–66.

57 Mergers and the market for corporate control
Peter G. Klein

The theory of merger is a subset of the theory of the optimal size and shape of the firm, a relatively undeveloped area in the Austrian literature. A firm seeking to expand its activities, whether into new product lines or within existing ones, can do so either via internal growth or by acquiring another firm. Acquisition will be preferred if the firm believes it can buy and redeploy the assets of an existing firm more cheaply than it can purchase new capital equipment and increase its current operations. In this sense, we can think of merger or takeover as a *response to a valuation discrepancy*: acquisition occurs when the value of an existing firm's assets is greater to an outside party than to its current owners. Put differently, merger can be a response to economies of scope, in that the value of the merging firms' assets combined exceeds their joint values separately. As with any exchange, the transaction is (ex ante) advantageous to both parties and should thus be welfare-enhancing. Such a valuation discrepancy typically exists because the buying firm believes that its management – or a new management team it installs – can operate the target firm more effectively than the target firm's incumbent management. Hence we can also think of mergers as a *form of monitoring institution*: takeover, or the threat thereof, is a disciplinary device that constrains the managers of a firm. If managers fail to maintain the market value of the firm, new owners will quickly arrive and replace them.

Mergers and acquisitions may take a variety of forms. An acquiring firm can try to reach a merger agreement directly with the management and board of directors of a target firm, paying with cash or its own stock, and then submitting the agreement to shareholders for ratification. Or it may appeal directly to the target firm's shareholders, asking them to 'tender' their shares at a stated price. (If the incumbent management resists the tender offer, this is called a 'hostile takeover'.) In either case a new, larger entity will be formed, combining the two initial firms under a single ownership. Corporations can be restructured in other ways as well: under a leveraged buy-out or other 'going private' transaction, a group of investors, often including incumbent management, buys out the firm's equity and replaces it with debt, usually in the form of high-yield ('junk') bonds. This class of transactions, like proxy contests and share repurchases, establishes a new ownership arrangement without necessarily affecting the physical assets of the firm. Additionally, spin-offs and divestitures can be used to break large firms into smaller pieces.

Following convention, we typically refer to all these reorganizations as *mergers and acquisitions* (M & A). The reason for M & A activity is straightforward: as economic theory tells us, in a market economy resources tend to move towards their highest valued uses. Mergers and acquisitions, as changes in the ownership pattern of assets, are simply part of the market process of adjusting the structure of production to meet consumer wants. Resources are shifted, from owners whose stewardship is poor, to those the market believes can do a better job.

While a certain amount of corporate restructuring is expected at all times, aggregate merger activity has tended to be concentrated in particular periods, commonly known as merger waves. (See Shugart and Tollison, 1984, however, for an argument that the timing of merger activity is equally well characterized as a random walk with drift.) The first significant merger movement in the USA occurred from about 1895 to 1904, with a series of horizontal mergers establishing the great trusts, particularly in railroads, coal and heavy manufacturing (Lamoreaux, 1985). The end to this movement is linked with a 1904 Supreme Court case, *U.S.* v. *Northern Securities*, which established that mergers could be successfully challenged under Section One of the Sherman Act. The 1920s brought a wave of vertical merger activity, primarily in public utilities, banking, food processing, chemicals and mining, as large industrial concerns in these areas integrated backwards into materials and equipment and forwards into marketing and distribution.

Perhaps the most significant, and least well-understood, merger movement in American history is the conglomerate merger boom of the 1960s. The great conglomerates of the period, like ITT, Gulf & Western and Litton Industries, were formed by deliberate strategies of aggressive acquisition into unrelated product lines. ITT, for example, branched out from its original base in telephone switching equipment to buy such companies as Aetna, Avis Rent-a-Car and Sheraton Hotels. As many of the large conglomerates turned out to be unsuccessful, the takeover and buy-out movement of the 1980s is sometimes viewed as an attempt to break such firms up into smaller, more manageable parts (Shleifer and Vishny, 1991). Indeed, product diversification in general has become a much-studied phenomenon in the field of business strategy, though the timing of the conglomerate movement in particular may be explained by non-economic factors, such as aggressive antitrust restrictions on horizontal expansion and the prosperity of the aerospace and defense-related industries associated with the Vietnam era military build-up. Many of the model 1960s conglomerates diversified from their initial areas of specialization precisely to get into more lucrative defense-related work.

The nature of the firm

Why, in general, do firms expand and diversify? And why do they sometimes retreat and 'refocus'? In the perfectly competitive model, firms as such do not exist at all; the 'firm' is a production function, its efficient output range and mix given by economies of scale and scope. Outside the textbook model, however, economies of scale and scope cannot explain the size and shape of the firm as *ownership structure*. Economies of scale, for example, imply that certain quantities of output can be produced more efficiently when produced together. But this does not explain why the joint production must take place in a single firm. Absent transactional difficulties, two independent firms could simply contract to share the same plant or facility and jointly produce the efficient level of output.

Ronald Coase, in his celebrated 1937 paper on 'The Nature of the Firm' was the first to explain that the size of the firm depends not only on productive technology, but also on the costs of transacting business. In the Coasian framework, as developed and expanded by Williamson (1975, 1985) and others, the decision to organize transactions within the firm as opposed to on the open market – the 'make or buy decision' – depends on the relative costs of internal versus external exchange. Use of the market mechanism entails certain costs: discovering the relevant prices, negotiating and enforcing contracts, and so on. Within the firm, the entrepreneur may be able to reduce such costs by coordinating these activities himself (though internal procurement will face its own information and incentive problems as well). In short, the boundary of the firm depends on organizational, as well as technological, considerations. These can in turn be broken down into a series of operational factors: the presence of transaction-specific assets, uncertainty and employee opportunism, and the like. Recently, this transaction cost theory of the firm has been challenged and extended by the concept of economic 'capabilities', an explanation for the scope of the firm based on complementarities in knowledge and organizational routine (Nelson and Winter, 1982; Langlois, 1992).

Unfortunately, the growing literature on the theory of the firm has yet to produce a fully satisfactory explanation of the limits to firm size (Williamson, 1985, chapter 6). In Coase's words, 'Why does the entrepreneur not organize one less transaction or one more?' Or, more generally, 'Why is not all production carried on in one big firm?' (Coase, 1937, pp. 42–3). Theorists have offered various span-of-control arguments to account for the limits to internal coordination, but none of these has been completely adequate. Here Austrian theory has an obvious contribution to make, by the application of Mises's theorem on the impossibility of economic calculation under socialism. Rothbard (1962, pp. 545–8) has shown how the need for monetary calculation in terms of market prices not only explains the failures of central planning under socialism, but also places an upper bound on the size of the firm.

The large, integrated firm is typically organized as groups of semi-autonomous business units or 'profit centers', with each unit or division specializing in a particular final or intermediate product. The central management of the firm uses statements of divisional profit and loss to allocate physical and financial capital across the divisions: more profitable divisions are rewarded and expanded, while those showing lower profits are scaled back. The role of economic calculation can be illustrated as follows. Consider a decentralized, vertically integrated firm with an upstream division selling an intermediate component to a downstream division. To compute the divisional profits and losses, the firm needs an economically meaningful 'transfer price' for the component. If there is a market for the component *external to the firm*, then the firm can use that market price as a benchmark for its own internal calculations. Without a market price, however, a transfer price must be estimated in some way – usually on a cost-plus basis, or as negotiated between the divisions – but these substitute transfer prices will necessarily contain less information than true market prices; firms relying on them will suffer. The firm is thus constrained by the need for external markets for all internally traded goods. In other words, no firm can become so large that it is both the unique producer and user of an intermediate product; then no market-based transfer prices will be available and the firm will be unable to calculate divisional profit and loss and therefore be unable to allocate resources correctly between divisions. Like the centrally planned economy, the firm needs market signals to guide its actions; without them the firm cannot survive. The mainstream literature on the firm has yet to incorporate this Austrian insight, though recognition that the socialist calculation debate covers the main issues of organization theory is beginning to appear (Williamson, 1991).

Managerial discretion and the financial markets
As mentioned above, a vital function of mergers and corporate restructuring is to limit managerial discretion. Critics of the corporation, at least since Berle and Means (1932), have argued that the modern firm is run, not by its owners, the shareholders, but by salaried managers, whose interests are different from those of shareholders and include executive perks, prestige and similar rewards. If the corporation is diffusely held, no individual shareholder has sufficient motivation to engage in (costly) monitoring of managerial decisions and hence discretion will flourish at the expense of the market value of the firm (what we would now call a principal–agent problem). Henry Manne's seminal paper, 'Mergers and the Market for Corporate Control' (1965), responded that managerial discretion will be limited as long as there exists an active market for control of corporations. When managers engage in

discretionary behavior, the share price of the firm falls, inviting takeover and subsequent replacement of incumbent management. (Other mechanisms to limit managerial discretion are also present, including the market for managers itself; see Fama, 1980.)

Interestingly, the central insight of Manne's paper is also found in Mises's *Human Action* (1949), in the passage distinguishing what Mises calls 'profit management' from 'bureaucratic management' (pp. 302–4). It is true, Mises argues, that the salaried managers of a corporation indeed hold considerable autonomy over the day-to-day operations of the firm. Nonetheless, the shareholders make the ultimate decisions about allocating resources to the firm, in their decisions to buy and sell stock:

> [The Berle–Means] doctrine disregards entirely the role that the capital and money market, the stock and bond exchange, which a pertinent idiom simply calls the 'market', plays in the direction of corporate business .... The changes in the prices of common and preferred stock and of corporate bonds are the means applied by the capitalists for the supreme control of the flow of capital. The price structure as determined by the speculations on the capital and money markets and on the big commodity exchanges not only decides how much capital is available for the conduct of each corporation's business; it creates a state of affairs to which the managers must adjust their operations in detail. (p. 303)

Mises does not identify the takeover mechanism per se as a means for capitalists to exercise control – takeovers were much less popular before the late 1950s, when the tender offer began to replace the proxy contest as the acquisition method of choice – but the main point is clear: the true basis of the market system is not the product market, the labor market or the managerial market, but the capital market, where entrepreneurial judgements are exercised and decisions carried out.

Mises's treatment of the importance of financial markets is also the key to his final rebuttal in *Human Action* to Lange, Lerner and the other market socialist critics of his calculation argument (pp. 694–711). The market socialists had claimed that a central planner could solve the calculation problem by ordering managers of industrial enterprises to fix prices at some level (say, price equal to marginal cost) and then make adjustments up or down according to conditions in the consumer goods market. Mises replied that the market socialists misconceive the nature of the 'economic problem': the main task performed by a market system is not the pricing of consumer goods, but the allocation of capital among the various branches of industry. By focusing on production and pricing decisions within a *given* structure of capital, the socialists ignore the vital role of capital markets. The financial sector, in which decisions are made about what resources will be available to each branch of production, is the true hallmark of a capitalist economy.

Are mergers efficient?

Mergers and acquisitions, like other business practices that do not conform to textbook models of competition, have long been viewed with suspicion by economists and regulatory authorities. While some critics are hostile to vertical and conglomerate expansion, most discussions of antitrust law and public policy towards mergers focus on horizontal expansion and the accompanying rise in 'market power'. There the debate centers on the presumed trade-off between 'productive' and 'allocative' efficiency. Productive efficiency refers to innovations in technology and process that reduce cost. Allocative efficiency describes the condition that price equals marginal cost. To promote innovation, it is argued, some deviation from the perfectly competitive ideal must be allowed, since monopoly profits are needed to finance research and development. Antitrust law, then, must balance the loss of consumer surplus associated with monopoly power against the gains from technological progress (Williamson, 1968; Bork, 1978).

Austrian economists have long argued that the perfectly competitive model is a hugely inappropriate guide to public policy; estimation of price–cost margins, far from being a useful tool for locating market failure and justifying government intervention, is irrelevant to the real problems of economic organization. In the actual world of uncertainty, error and constant change, allocative efficiency means nothing other than directing resources towards higher valued uses, which can only be measured by the successes and failures of firms as determined by the market. What is good for the firm, then, is good for the consumer. There are also obvious potential benefits from horizontal expansion and even cartel agreements: reduction of uncertainty about rivals' actions, pooling of promotion and distribution costs, establishment of standards, and so on (High, 1984–5). In short, absent legal restrictions on market structure, 'dynamic theory presumes efficiency' (p. 31). Any merger that is not known to be a response to legal restrictions or incentives must be assumed to create value.

The paradox of contemporary merger analysis is the recognition that there seems to be a sharp divergence between market participants' pre-merger expectations about the post-merger performance of merging firms and the firms' actual performance rates. Ravenscraft and Scherer's (1987) large-scale study of manufacturing firms, for example, found that, while the share prices of merging firms did on average rise with the announcement of the proposed restructuring, post-merger profit rates were unimpressive. Indeed, nearly one-third of all acquisitions during the 1960s and 1970s were eventually divested. Ravenscraft and Scherer conclude that mergers typically promote managerial 'empire building' rather than efficiency, and they support increased restrictions on horizontal expansion. Other observers suggest changes in the tax code to favor dividends and share repurchases over direct reinvestment, thus limiting managers' ability to channel 'free cash flow' into unproductive acquisitions (Jensen, 1986).

But the fact that some mergers – indeed, many mergers, takeovers and reorganizations – turn out to be unprofitable does not imply 'market failure' or prescribe any policy response. In a world of uncertainty, errors will always be made. Even the financial markets, which aggregate the collective wisdom of the entrepreneurs, capitalists and speculators who are the very basis of a market economy, will sometimes make the wrong judgement on a particular business transaction. Sometimes the market will reward, ex ante, a proposed restructuring that has no efficiency rationale. But this is due, not to capital market failure, but to imperfect knowledge. Final judgements about success and failure can be made only ex post, as the market process plays itself out. Throughout this process information is revealed over time, as market forces work to weed out the relatively inefficient organizational forms. Certainly, there is no reason to believe that courts or regulatory authorities can make better judgements than the financial markets. The decisions of courts and government agencies will in fact tend to be far worse: unlike market participants, judges and bureaucrats pursue a variety of private agendas, unrelated to economic efficiency. Furthermore, the market is quick to penalize error as it is discovered: no hearings, committees, or fact-finding commissions are required. In short, that business often fails is surprising only to those committed to static equilibrium models in which failure is defined away. Such models are surely no guide to public policy.

Finally, it is difficult to justify recent proposals to penalize 'insider trading' and reform securities law to discourage takeovers in favor of internal investment. All market participants act on the basis of private information. Their actions benefit third parties as well: where insider trading is allowed, stock prices more accurately represent the true prospects of the firm. In addition, disclosure rules that protect incumbent management naturally weaken the disciplinary role of takeovers, and not surprisingly are favored by established corporations and brokerage houses. But proponents of such restrictions on the market for corporate control have yet to provide a convincing economic rationale for their existence.

See also:
Chapter 14: Competition; Chapter 15: Entrepreneurship; Chapter 55: Industrial organization and the Austrian school; Chapter 4: Market process; Chapter 21: Profit and loss

Bibliography
Berle, Adolph A. and Gardiner C. Means (1932), *The Modern Corporation and Private Property*, New York: Macmillan.
Bork, Robert H. (1978), *The Antitrust Paradox*, New York: Basic Books.

Coase, Ronald H. (1937), 'The Nature of the Firm', reprinted in Coase, *The Firm, The Market and the Law*, Chicago: University of Chicago Press, 1988, pp. 33–55.

Fama, Eugene F. (1980), 'Agency Problems and the Theory of the Firm', *Journal of Political Economy*, **88**, April, 288–307.

High, Jack (1984–5), 'Bork's Paradox: Static vs. Dynamic Efficiency in Antitrust Analysis', *Contemporary Policy Issues*, **3**, 21–34.

Jensen, Michael C. (1986), 'Agency Costs of Free Cash Flow, Corporate Finance, and Takeovers', *American Economic Review*, **76**, May, 323–9.

Lamoreaux, Naomi R. (1985), *The Great Merger Movement in American Business, 1895–1904*, Cambridge: Cambridge University Press.

Langlois, Richard N. (1992), 'Transaction Cost Economics in Real Time', *Industrial and Corporate Change*, **1**, 99–127.

Manne, Henry G. (1965), 'Mergers and the Market for Corporate Control', *Journal of Political Economy*, **73**, April, 110–20.

Mises, Ludwig von (1949), *Human Action: A Treatise on Economics*, New Haven: Yale University Press.

Nelson, Richard R. and Sidney G. Winter (1982), *An Evolutionary Theory of Economic Change*, Cambridge, Mass.: Harvard University Press.

Ravenscraft, David and F.M. Scherer (1987), *Mergers, Sell-Offs, and Economic Efficiency*, Washington, DC: Brookings Institution.

Rothbard, Murray N. (1962), *Man, Economy, and State: A Treatise on Economic Principles*, 2 vols, reprinted Los Angeles: Nash Publishing, 1970.

Shleifer, Andrei and Robert W. Vishny (1991), 'Takeovers in the '60s and '80s: Evidence and Implications', *Strategic Management Journal*, **12**, 51–9.

Shugart, William F. and Robert D. Tollison (1984), 'The Random Character of Merger Activity', *Rand Journal of Economics*, **15**, 500–509.

Williamson, Oliver E. (1968), 'Economies as an Antitrust Defense: The Welfare Tradeoffs', *American Economic Review*, **58**, March, 18–35.

Williamson, Oliver E. (1975), *Markets and Hierarchies: Analysis and Antitrust Implications*, New York: Free Press.

Williamson, Oliver E. (1985), *The Economic Institutions of Capitalism*, New York: Free Press.

Williamson, Oliver E. (1991), 'Economic Institutions: Spontaneous and Intentional Governance', *Journal of Law, Economics and Organization*, **7**, 159–87.

58 Inflation

Steven Horwitz

The Austrian analysis of inflation uses a number of the school's most fundamental theoretical insights, including its capital theory, its monetary theory
and its explanation of the relationship between prices and knowledge. In
examining this analysis, we can distinguish four issues: definitions, causes,
effects and policy responses.

There is not one sole Austrian definition of inflation. Austrians offer two
similar, though potentially contradictory, definitions. On one side is the notion of inflation as any increase in the money supply not connected with an
increase in the monetary commodity (for example, gold under a gold-driven
system), which is preferred by Rothbard (1962). More recently, a number of
younger Austrians have preferred to see inflation as simply 'an excess supply
of money', as in Selgin (1988). The latter definition allows for increases in
the money supply unmatched by increases in some monetary commodity as
long as the money supply increases maintain monetary equilibrium; that is,
they keep the money supply equal to the demand for money without an
intervening change in the price level. Although these two definitions are at
odds with each other, their differences are less important for Austrian analyses of the causes and effects of inflation, while being more important for the
various policy proposals to eliminate inflation. For the purpose of clarity, we
will adopt the second definition in the discussion below.

It is also important to note that both definitions differ from more neoclassical ones. A standard textbook definition of inflation is usually something like
'a rise in the general level of prices'. For Austrians, like monetarists, inflation
is always a monetary phenomenon, and both Austrian definitions express that
belief. A further reason for rejecting the neoclassical definition is that non-
monetary phenomena can cause a rise in the general price level (as with a fall
in the supply of oil). However, this price rise is not inflationary because the
higher prices are simply accurately reflecting the increased relative scarcity
of a factor of production. Making such knowledge available through price
changes is precisely what markets are supposed to do according to Austrians,
and these price changes should not be thought of as inflationary any more
than an efficiency-generated decline in prices should be seen as a problematic deflationary trend.

Austrians see two causes of inflation. The first is self-interest on the part of
political actors. In a world of government-run or overseen central banks,

inflation is profitable for political actors. By creating excess supplies of money, political actors can transfer resources (seignorage) from the money-using public to the central bank and the government. Such funds can be used to pay for various vote-getting projects and inflation is thus an attractive way for incumbent politicians to please their constituents. Austrians generally accept the broad notion of a political business cycle and have offered more detailed analyses of the benefits inflation can provide political actors (Wagner, 1980; Horwitz, 1991).

The second cause of inflation is simply mistaken bank policy. A central bank faces the same sort of knowledge problem that haunts more comprehensive central economic planning. The knowledge required to accurately track the demand for money is voluminous and, more importantly, inarticulate, making it impossible to marshal and analyse in one central location. As a result, even public-spirited central bankers stumble around in the dark in their attempts to maintain monetary equilibrium. Even if one ignores the political incentives that favor inflation, mistaken policy by unavoidably ignorant central bankers, or entrepreneurial errors by non-governmental banks, can be causes of unwarranted increases in the money supply.

The main effect of inflation is the way in which it alters the structure of relative prices. Unlike the neutrality arguments of the Quantity Theory, where changes in the money supply equiproportionally scale up the array of prices, Austrians emphasize that inflation affects prices differentially. This insight is normally credited to Richard Cantillon, and the changes in relative prices are referred to as 'Cantillon effects'. Because excess supplies of money enter the economy at specific times and places (normally as the result of central bank open market operations), those who receive the money first disproportionally affect the prices of the goods they purchase. The sellers of those goods can, to a slightly lesser degree, affect the prices of the goods they buy, and so on. The pattern of relative price changes will depend on both the location of the injection of the excess supply of money and the preferences of the recipients. There is no reason to expect that the outcome of this process would leave the array of relative prices unchanged.

The importance of these relative price changes is that they undermine the process by which prices facilitate the social use of knowledge. Entrepreneurs rely on prices as signals about the preferences and behavior of other market actors. During inflation, this communication process becomes more difficult because entrepreneurs need to disentangle the underlying economic preferences from the temporary noise coming from the spenders of the excess supply of money. Prices become less reliable as knowledge surrogates and the entire coordination process of the market suffers and resources are less efficiently allocated.

Moreover, these changes in relative prices will spill over into the capital structure via derived demand. As the prices of particular goods rise from inflation, resources will flow into the production of these goods, and the inputs necessary for such production will be more highly valued. This forces entrepreneurs to decide whether to invest in more capital, or train more labor, to meet the increased demand for their output. If they believe the increased demand to be genuine and long-term, they may well do so. If the demand is interpreted to be inflation-generated, and therefore temporary, major changes in production are likely to be unprofitable. The problem is that entrepreneurs have no way of knowing the cause of the increased demand. Price increases do not come stamped with 'inflationary' or 'non-inflationary'. Knowledge of the central bank's intentions is of no help because it tells the entrepreneur nothing about the *specific* path the inflation is taking and whether that path includes the entrepreneur's firm. To the extent that entrepreneurs guess wrong, resources are wasted as purchasing capital and labor involves both transaction costs and the irretrievable costs of adapting machinery and training labor. For Austrians, inflation is a major drag on economic growth because it unnecessarily complicates the entrepreneur's job and leads to error and wasted resources.

In general, Austrians agree with many of the points raised by Leijonhufvud (1981) concerning the inadequacy of neoclassical accounts of inflation. Whereas neutrality approaches see only the costs of maintaining higher nominal money balances and remarking prices, Austrians see the more fundamental chaos engendered by the disruption of the price system's ability to aid in the process of resource allocation. Austrian analyses of inflation also point to what might be called the 'coping costs' of inflation. Inflation forces actors to spend time and resources on coping with the effects of inflation: for example, negotiating a cost of living adjustment, or hiring a financial expert to track central bank policy, involve expenditures of resources that would not occur in a zero inflation regime. It is also of note that, even when such coping strategies are *successful*, they still involve wasted resources in comparison to zero inflation.

It can also be argued that aggregate measures of economic growth underestimate the costs of inflation (or overestimate the health of inflationary economies) because GDP figures do not distinguish between exchanges that are genuinely productive and those that arise in response to the problems caused by inflation. The payment to a financial expert who devises a strategy to outguess the central bank adds to GDP, even though the resources involved would be used directly for want satisfaction in a zero inflation economy. Breaking a window will raise GDP by the cost of fixing it, but this is not what Austrians would call economic growth, as window breaking forces the owner to replace what he already had, rather than add to society's total product. To the extent that inflation disrupts price and wage coordination and reduces economic growth, it would appear to contradict the traditional Phillips curve picture of an inflation and unemployment trade-off. The Austrian analysis suggests that inflation of any notable duration will *cause* unemployment and lower economic growth. This parallels the suggestion made by Friedman (1977) that the Phillips curve may be positively sloped, given enough sustained inflation.

A further possible effect of inflation is the beginning of the business cycle. Excess supplies of money leave banks with additional reserves, enabling them to lower their market rates of interest and attract new borrowers. As the Austrian theory of the business cycles argues, these lower market rates will be below the prevailing natural rate of interest (that is, the rate that equates ex ante savings and investment) and will lead entrepreneurs to invest in longer-term projects, thus setting off the cycle (see Rothbard, 1983). Whether or not a significant cycle occurs will depend upon the length and severity of the inflation and whether or how the excess supplies of money make their way into the hands of producers.

Finally, inflation leads to growth in the political sector's influence over the economy. As market coordination becomes more problematic because of price distortions, individuals are more likely, on the margin, to turn to the political process in order to acquire wealth or attempt to redress the undesirable consequences of an inflation-ridden market. Self-interested political actors will take advantage of this situation to promise wealth and programs in exchange for votes. Once these inflation-induced programs come into existence, they become very hard to eliminate, even if the inflation that necessitated them should end. Creating government programs means creating beneficiaries who will not easily give up their benefits. Even a moderate spell of moderate inflation can lead to this political feedback, which will have long-term effects on the economy. To the extent that Austrians tend to see politics as an inefficient allocator of resources, such structural shifts away from markets towards politics as the preferred resource allocation process will be seen as undesirable consequences of inflation and likely causes of diminished economic growth.

Austrian economists have also been concerned with the kinds of policies or institutions that will best reduce or eliminate inflation. Though Austrians differ on their preferred solution, they do agree that the source of the problem is with the institution of government central banking (see the essays in Siegel, 1984; Rockwell, 1985). The neoclassical choice between rules and discretion is viewed as a false dichotomy applicable only if one takes central banking as given. Even with central banking, neither policy regime can effectively prevent inflation (Horwitz, 1992). Discretionary regimes are plagued by the aforementioned knowledge problem. Although discretionary policy makers might try to track the demand for money, they cannot obtain the knowledge needed to do so. A regime of rules, on the other hand, suffers from insufficient flexibility. What growth rate should one pick and what ensures that the demand for money will stay sufficiently stable to match that growth rate? Rules have the advantage of avoiding significant political ma- nipulation, but they are not significantly less likely than discretion to gener- ate unintended inflation.

To move beyond the policy paradoxes posed by central banks, earlier Austrians adopted various versions of the gold standard. The desire for some sort of non-political 'automatic' monetary policy pointed Austrians in the direction of the classical gold standard (as in the work of Mises and the younger Hayek) or a 100 per cent gold reserve banking system (see Murray Rothbard's essay in Rockwell, 1985). The advantage of gold standard sys- tems was that the high cost of increasing the supply of base money would, according to their supporters, put a limit on increases in the total money supply. More recently, younger Austrians have shown an interest in the notion of free banking (Selgin, 1988). In a free banking system, banks would competitively produce currency which would be redeemable in some outside money, perhaps gold, but not necessarily. Banks' interest in maximizing profits would lead them to produce neither more nor less money than the public wished to hold. Banks that underproduced money would bear the opportunity cost of forgone interest on the loans that would put such money into circulation, while overproducing money would lead to a drain of bank reserves, creating a possible liquidity crisis. Jointly minimizing these interest and liquidity costs would lead to an optimal holding of reserves and, thus, a supply of money equal to the public's demand to hold. With the appropriate structure of property rights, the self-interest of bankers would unintentionally lead to monetary equilibrium and the virtual elimination of inflation.

As with many other parts of Austrian economics, the analysis of inflation draws on uniquely Austrian insights and suggests that neoclassical approaches fall short because they fail to take seriously the institutional context in which economic action occurs. Inflation is first and foremost a monetary phenom- enon, but monetary phenomena do not exist in isolation from the rest of economic activity, or from the political process. Understanding both the economic effects of inflation, and how these effects interact with the institu- tions and incentives of the political process, defines the Austrian approach to inflation.

See also:
Chapter 32: Austrian business cycle theory; Chapter 59: Free banking; Chapter 68: The Hayek–Keynes macro debate; Chapter 60: The history of free banking; Chapter 62: Political business cycles

Bibliography

Friedman, Milton (1977), 'Nobel Lecture: Inflation and Unemployment', *Journal of Political Economy*, **87**, (3), June.

Horwitz, Steven (1991), 'The Political Economy of Inflation: Public and Private Choices', *Durell Journal of Money and Banking*, **3**, (4), November.

Horwitz, Steven (1992), *Monetary Evolution, Free Banking, and Economic Order*, Boulder, Colo.: Westview Press.

Leijonhufvud, Axel (1981), 'Costs and Consequences of Inflation', in *Information and Coordination*, Oxford: Oxford University Press.

Rockwell, Lew (ed.) (1985), *The Gold Standard: An Austrian Perspective*, Lexington, Mass.: D.C. Heath.

Rothbard, Murray N. (1962), *Man, Economy and State: A Treatise on Economic Principles*, 2 vols, Los Angeles: Nash Publishing, 1970.

Rothbard, Murray N. (1983), *America's Great Depression*, 4th edn, New York: Richardson and Snyder.

Selgin, George A. (1988), *The Theory of Free Banking: Money Supply Under Competitive Note Issue*, Totowa, NJ: Rowman and Littlefield.

Siegel, Barry N. (ed.) (1984), *Money in Crisis: The Federal Reserve, the Economy, and Monetary Reform*, Cambridge, Mass.: Ballinger.

Wagner, Richard (1980), 'Boom and Bust: The Political Economy of Economic Disorder', *Journal of Libertarian Studies*, **4**, (1), winter.

59 Free banking

Kevin Dowd

A banking system is free when it is unregulated. A free banking system has no central bank or other monetary authority such as a government deposit insurance agency, it has no legislated currency monopoly, and banks are free to do as they wish subject only to the normal laws of contract. There are consequently no reserve or capital adequacy requirements, no interest rate ceilings and no restrictions on the types of loan that banks can make. Advocates of free banking claim that it would provide a safer and sounder banking system than central banking systems have provided, and the free banking school was prominent in controversies over banking reform in a number of countries in the early to mid-nineteenth century (see Smith, 1936; White, 1984). Sooner or later, however, decisions were made to opt for central banking instead, and the free banking issue slipped into oblivion. Free banking was almost largely forgotten by the beginning of the twentieth century and, to the extent that they gave it any thought at all, twentieth-century economists were usually quick to dismiss the idea as a patently unsound one that would lead to a monetary explosion and hyperinflation if it were ever implemented. The idea of free banking was then rehabilitated in the 1970s when Friedrich Hayek recommended the privatization of money as the only solution to the monetary instability created by central banks and their political masters (Hayek, 1978). The idea attracted a lot of attention, and a large literature on the subject soon developed (for example, White, 1984; Selgin, 1988; Dowd, 1989; Glasner, 1989).

Theoretical issues
The basic argument for free banking is very simple. If markets are generally better at allocating resources than governments and their officials, then what is 'different' about 'money' and the industry that provides it, the banking industry, that should lead one to believe that money and banking are an exception to that general rule? Each product and each industry is different from others, of course, but no serious economist would argue that the difference between clothes and shoes requires us to examine the clothing industry in a fundamentally different way from the footwear industry. The differences that exist are not relevant for policy purposes. But if we treat these two industries in much the same way, free bankers argue that there is a presumption that we should treat the banking industry in the same way as well. This

line of reasoning suggests that there should be a presumption in favor of free banking, and the onus of proof is on its critics to demonstrate that that presumption is wrong.

An attempt to do so is Goodhart (1988). He argues that banking is 'different', for three separate reasons. The first and most important, he suggests, arises because information is scarce and imperfect. While imperfect information is not unique to banking, he argues that imperfect information in banking implies that asset values may be difficult to assess. As a result, it is much easier to transfer bank liabilities from one institution to another than it is to transfer assets, and this imbalance leaves banks vulnerable to runs. There is also a danger that runs might be 'contagious' – that currency holders might run on a bank simply because they see others running on other banks – and therefore pose a threat to the banking system as a whole. According to Goodhart, these factors create a need for a lender of last resort to protect the banking system by standing ready to provide banks with emergency loans should they need them. Free bankers would accept that banks are typically subject to *potential* runs, but they would dispute the claims that runs would be contagious or that banks need the protection of a central bank. A depositor or note-holder will only run if he has reason to do so, and the normal reason to run is to avoid the losses he might expect if he believed that the bank was weak (that is, had a low or negative net worth) and he would suffer losses if he kept his funds in the bank and the bank subsequently proved to be unable to honor its debts. However, in that case a fractional reserve bank faced with the possibility of a run would try to reassure its customers that it was in a sound financial position. It would therefore avoid excessive lending risks and maintain a strong capital position that would reassure its customers that it could honor its debts even if it suffered unexpected losses on its loans. It would also maintain sufficient liquidity (and lines of back-up credit, if necessary) for it to be able to meet demands for redemption from the public without defaulting on its redemption obligations. A bank that pursued such policies would give its customers no reason to doubt its soundness and, given its liquidity, no reason to run on it. It follows that runs are a realistic possibility only for weak banks that do not command public confidence, but there is a strong argument such banks should be eliminated anyway, and a bank run provides the means to do so. In short, the threat of a run is what encourages the 'good' banks to maintain their financial strength, and the occurrence of occasional runs is what eliminates weak and badly managed banks that ought not to be in business anyway. It follows as a corollary that there is little reason to expect runs to be contagious. Customers will only run on banks if they have good reason to doubt their soundness, and the observation that a weak bank is in difficulties gives the customers of a 'good' bank no reason to run themselves. We would not expect to observe bank run contagion under laissez-faire.

Goodhart also suggested that banking was 'different' for a second reason. Free bankers had made much of the argument that the clearing-house disciplines banks that overissue by returning excess issues promptly for redemption. Goodhart argued, however, that this discipline was inadequate because it only applied to individual banks, and the clearing-house does nothing to discipline banks if the banking system as a whole overexpands its issues in concert. He also argued that even individual banks could overexpand if they made their issues more attractive to hold (for example, 1988, p. 30). For both these reasons he argued that free banking provided only a weak discipline against overissue and would be subject to recurrent financial crises as a result (for example, 1988, pp. 30–31). One reply to this argument is that the clearing-house discipline is not meant to discipline overissues by the system as a whole, but only overissues by individual banks, and what disciplines the system as a whole is the commitment to redeem liabilities when required to do so. If the system as a whole overexpands and issues more bank money than the public wish to hold, then the public will simply return the excess issues to the issuing banks and the latter will be forced to redeem them. The fact that a typical bank involved would have a zero clearing balance is irrelevant. Then there is the argument that a bank might be able to expand its issues and make them more attractive to hold at the same time. Making its liabilities more attractive might not always be easy – how would a bank encourage people to hold more non-interest-bearing notes? – but even if one grants that it can be done, the critical issue is not whether it *could* do so, but whether it *would*. If a bank is initially maximizing its profits – and if it is not, it ought to be – then the marginal benefit from further issues is roughly equal to the marginal cost. We would normally expect the former to be falling with further issues and the latter to be rising. A bank that increased its issues by making them more attractive would therefore decrease its profits. The fact that it could expand in this way makes no difference because a profit-maximizing bank would not want to do so anyway.

Finally, Goodhart argued that competition on the lending side would lead banks to engage in damaging cycles of excessive bank expansion followed by financial crisis and subsequent contraction, and he drew the conclusion that a central bank was needed to rein the banks in and dampen these cycles down (for example, 1988, pp. 47–9). This argument, however, is open to similar objections as the previous argument that banks would overexpand on the liability side. Individual banks have an incentive to expand their lending up to a certain point only, and to expand beyond that is to make excessively risky loans and possibly endanger the bank. Nor is there any reason to believe that competition somehow forces banks to engage in excessive lending that they would otherwise have avoided. It is not in a bank's interest to engage in excessive lending regardless of whether its rivals are engaging in such lending or not. Indeed, far from competition encouraging excessive lending, there is good reason to believe that it does just the opposite. If a bank sees its rivals recklessly expanding their lending, it has every incentive to distance itself from them and cultivate a reputation for soundness that will stand it in good stead when the other banks start to take losses and lose public confidence. The 'bad' banks will then experience runs and the 'good' banks will be in a position to win over their market share by encouraging the customers of 'bad' banks to switch their accounts over to them. 'Good' banks may have to bide their time, but they will win out in the long run as banks that engage in excessive risk taking eventually lose their market share.

Empirical evidence

Recent research has uncovered a large number of historical experiences that can be regarded as approximations to free banking (see, for example, Schuler, 1992, and the various other readings in Dowd, 1992). Most existed in the nineteenth century and virtually all were successful – some spectacularly so. These experiences included some that lasted the best part of a century or even longer (for example in Australia, Canada and Scotland) and some that operated apparently successfully despite very turbulent political conditions (for example in Colombia and Revolutionary France). Free banking ended, not because it had 'failed' economically, but because it was suppressed for essentially political reasons, the usual reason being that it was an obstacle to the government's desire to extract seignorage revenues from the banking system (for example, Dowd, 1989; Glasner, 1989; Selgin, 1988). A number of specific points also stand out. The first is that historical free banking was *not* prone to inflation. In apparently every case, historical free banking systems issued convertible currencies whose real values were determined by the monetary standard – usually the gold standard – on which the banks operated. The monetary standard imposed a discipline against the overissue of currency, and such inflations and deflations as occurred were due to changes such as gold discoveries that affected all banking systems on that standard regardless of whether they were free banking systems or not. No free banking system ever abandoned convertibility and there is no evidence that competition in banking leads to a monetary explosion and rapid inflation.

Another point that stands out is the high degree of stability of free banking systems. Overissues of currency were corrected rapidly by the banks' clearing system operating on the basis of the commodity standard (for example, White, 1984; Selgin, 1988). There is evidence that interest rates were more stable under free banking, and the less regulated banking systems of Scotland and Canada were apparently better able to weather shocks than their more regulated counterparts in England and the USA. There is also evidence that shocks tended to originate in the more regulated systems and spread to the less regulated ones, rather than the other way round. Banks typically observed high capital ratios by modern standards and, in the absence of 'official' regulation, bank management was monitored by the market. The evidence seems to confirm that banks that were not considered sufficiently sound would lose their market share, and competition for market share would force banks to maintain the margins of safety and soundness that their customers desired (see, for example, Kaufman, 1988). But perhaps the most striking evidence is that, in the absence of any 'official' lender of last resort or deposit insurance, banks only rarely faced runs, and the runs that did occur were typically confined to small numbers of banks, and often only a single bank, which had suffered some shock (such as the revelation of loan losses) which led their customers to doubt their soundness. When more than one bank was involved in a run, there was usually an identifiable cause (for example, they all suffered region- or industry-specific losses). Bank runs appear to have been 'rational' affairs triggered off by reasonable doubts about the soundness of particular banks, and there is very little evidence of bank run 'contagion' in which customers ran on their own banks simply because they saw people running against theirs. The typical scenario was one where one or more weak banks received bad news that triggered off a run against them – and more often than not put them out of business – but the funds withdrawn would then be redeposited with sounder banks. There would thus be a 'flight to quality' and little or no withdrawal of funds from the banking system as a whole.

The historical experience also flatly contradicts the idea that banking is in any reasonable sense a natural monopoly. Historical free banking systems show evidence of scale economies – branch banking would replace unit banking, for example – and a small number of large nationwide branch banks would typically develop. Each of these banks would engage in all the usual banking activities, including the issue of notes, but the economies of scale were never sufficiently pronounced for one bank to be able to eliminate the others or acquire any position of supremacy over them. Besides the 'big' banks, there would also be a large number of other institutions that might specialize in some way or other. They might take deposits, but not issue notes, or they might specialize on a regional or industrial basis. The evidence also indicates that free banking systems were highly competitive and efficient. Even where the number of banks was small, as in early eighteenth-century Scotland, competition was fierce and the fight for market share developed bankers' entrepreneurial skills and produced a number of innovations in banking. Amongst these were the payment of interest on deposits; the option clause, which allowed banks temporarily to defer redemption demands provided they subsequently paid compensation; the cash credit account, an early form of overdraft; and the development of branch banking. The spreads between borrowing and lending rates appear to have been relatively small, and the fact that the banks appear to have been earning normal profits most of the time suggests that the economic surplus was competed away to their customers.

See also:
Chapter 61: Financial regulation; Chapter 60: The history of free banking; Chapter 58: Inflation; Chapter 62: Political business cycles

Bibliography
Dowd, K. (1989), *The State and the Monetary System*, Hemel Hempstead: Phillip Allan, and New York: St. Martin's Press.
Dowd, K. (ed.) (1992), *The Experience of Free Banking*, London: Routledge.
Glasner, D. (1989), *Free Banking and Monetary Reform*, Cambridge/New York: Cambridge University Press.
Goodhart, C. (1988), *The Evolution of Central Banks*, Cambridge, Mass.: MIT Press.
Hayek, F.A. (1978), 2nd edn, *Denationalisation of Money*, London: Institute of Economic Affairs.
Kaufman, G.G. (1988), 'The Truth about Bank Runs', *Cato Journal*, 7, 559–87.
Schuler, K. (1992), 'The World History of Free Banking: An Overview', chapter 2 in K. Dowd (ed.), *The Experience of Free Banking*, London: Routledge, pp. 7–47.
Selgin, G.A. (1988), *The Theory of Free Banking: Money Supply Under Competitive Note Issue*, Totowa, NJ: Rowman and Littlefield.
Smith, V.C. (1936), *The Rationale of Central Banking*, London: P.S. King.
White, L.H. (1984), *Free Banking in Britain: Theory, Experience, and Debate, 1800–1845*, Cambridge/New York: Cambridge University Press.

60 The history of free banking

Kurt Schuler

Free banking is a system of competitive issue of bank-notes and deposits, with low legal barriers to entry by competitors and no central control of reserves. In most free banking systems, governments have monopolized coinage and established the monetary standard (usually gold or silver) by law, but a completely laissez-faire approach would allow coinage and the choice of standard to be determined through competition, as they have been in some cases.

The first Austrian economist to investigate the history of free banking was Vera C. Smith (1990), in a dissertation written under F.A. Hayek. Keynesian influence largely submerged interest in free banking until Hayek's (1978) *Denationalisation of Money*. Hayek envisioned a system of competing fiat currencies and made no appeal to historical cases of free banking. Austrian economists soon began to find such cases, however; the work of Roland Vaubel (1978) is noteworthy here.

A breakthrough came with Lawrence H. White's (1984) *Free Banking in Britain*. White showed that the Scottish free banking system had operated for over a century (1716–1845) in a stable, efficient and competitive manner. White's book complemented the work of non-Austrian economists who had found that American 'free banking' was more stable than previously believed. (These and other articles on free banking are collected in White, 1993.) American 'free banking' is more accurately termed 'bond-deposit banking', for it required banks to buy certain approved bonds as a condition for issuing notes. Real free banking without bond deposit requirements existed in some American states (such as Virginia and Louisiana) alongside bond-deposit 'free banking' in other states from 1837 to 1863. In 1863 the Union government adopted a nationwide bond-deposit system as a means of financing its Civil War spending.

The work of White and of writers on bond-deposit banking unsettled received opinions that had prevailed since the mid-1800s among monetary theorists, and sparked further historical research. To date almost 60 countries have been found to have had free banking (Schuler, 1992; some of these cases are discussed in Dowd, 1992). Much work remains to be done, but the general features of historical experience with free banking are clear: free banking was for the most part stable; it was no more subject than central banking of the time to bank runs or financial panics; it showed no inherent tendency towards monopoly in note issue or concentration of reserves. Central banking was not a natural evolutionary step, as some writers have claimed (Goodhart, 1988), but a development forced on banking systems by governments, often to promote favored political interests.

Free banking originated in China about 1004, when the first private competitive bank-notes were issued. Competitive deposit banking was millennia older than that. China had several periods of free banking, interrupted by monopoly government note issue that was usually inflationary. The last period of Chinese free banking lasted from 1644 to 1928. An unusual feature of Chinese free banking was that copper and silver coexisted for centuries as monetary standards. Different forms of bank organization competed with each other, including Western banks established in port cities, beginning in the 1840s (Shiu, 1990). Chinese free banking had little explicit regulation, although the government or local warlords often extracted forced loans from banks.

Free banking developed in Japan by the late 1600s, when bills of exchange circulated like bank-notes; at about the same time, free banking began in Europe in the British Isles. It spread so far that, by the 1800s and early 1900s, most economically advanced nations had free banking, for periods of a few years to more than a century. Free banking was prevalent in Western Europe, the Americas, the Orient and the British Empire. For example, all nations in the Americas that became independent before 1900 had free banking. On the other hand, free banking never reached Eastern Europe and most colonies of nations other than Britain, which generally established monopoly banks of note issue. Most of Africa and the Middle East never had free banking either, because they had no note-issuing banks at all when free banking was widespread elsewhere.

In some cases, especially in the Americas, free banking came after experience with inflationary note issues by government. In the USA, colonial governments and the revolutionary Continental Congress had issued forced legal tender notes that depreciated against gold and silver. France had a similar experience with the *assignats* issued by its revolutionary government. After governments retired from the scene, free banks sprang up to issue notes convertible at fixed rates into gold or silver. In these and other cases, notes and deposits of free banks were not fiat currencies, as Hayek envisioned, except where governments allowed or forced banks to nullify convertibility contracts with customers.

Free banking systems typically had large numbers of banks in their early years. Competition and the advantages of economies of scale typically reduced the number of banks in mature systems to two to twenty, all with extensive nationwide branch networks. Economies of scale, however, were never so extensive that they resulted in a monopoly of note issue. Despite rivalry for customers, free banks cooperated in ways that advanced their common interests. They established clearing arrangements, which reduced the need for reserves all around. Often they institutionalized clearing with clearing-houses, which then became focal points for other forms of cooperation, such as rescue operations to save banks that were fundamentally solid but temporarily short of reserves. Attempts to use clearing-houses to establish cartels failed and there seems to be no record of any lastingly successful effort by free banks to collude in fixing interest rates.

What little evidence exists concerning rates of economic growth under free banking is favorable to free banking. Far more evidence exists concerning stability of exchange rates and prices. Free banking systems had better records at maintaining convertibility into gold or silver, and hence in maintaining long-run stability of prices, than the central banking systems that succeeded them. This suggests that free banking was an important, neglected factor in making the classical (pre-1914) gold standard truly 'automatic' and smoothly operating. Peacetime financial panics and bank runs were also rare in the least regulated free banking systems. Wartime panics were no more common than in central banking systems. The cause of many wartime panics was not fear that banks themselves were insolvent, but fear that governments would suspend the gold or silver standard. Scottish banks devised a voluntary contractual arrangement to permit them to suspend convertibility, the option clause. In return for the right to suspend convertibility for up to six months, Scottish banks promised to pay a higher than normal rate of interest to note-holders and depositors. The option clause was outlawed in Scotland in 1765 for political reasons, and even when legal was not widely imitated outside Scotland. The option clause would have been a good alternative to forced suspension of convertibility.

If free banking was so successful, why did it disappear? The causes were a combination of economic theory, experience with bank failures in heavily regulated free banking systems and the desire of many governments to use the monetary system as a means of taxation. The most important battle between central banking and free banking occurred in Britain. The English banking system was heavily regulated: before 1826, only the Bank of England could have more than six stockholders, and after 1826 it had a monopoly of note issue in the London region. Because Scotland had a legal system independent of England, the Scottish banking system was little regulated and the Bank of England had no part in it. Writers of the British currency school appealed to English experience with bank failures and financial panics to show that competitive issue of notes was inherently unstable. The currency school wished to monopolize note issue with the Bank of England and subject the note issue (though not deposits) to strict reserve requirements. The rival free banking school pointed to Scottish experience of stable banking to show that competitive issue of notes was stable if unregulated. The free banking school advocated abolishing the privileges of the Bank of England. Policy makers, who were mainly English, were convinced by the currency school, and made its program law with Peel's Bank Charter Acts of 1844 and 1845. The Bank of England thus became a central bank because of the one-to-one convertibility of other banks' deposits into Bank of England notes.

England was the most economically advanced nation of the time, and its example had a powerful effect. The German central bank (established 1875) was one of many modeled upon the Bank of England. Many British colonies replaced free banks with currency boards. Currency boards were not central banks, because they did not accept deposits and had no discretion in monetary policy, but most were monopoly issuers of notes and coins.

Like England, the USA had a heavily regulated free banking system. Restrictions on branch banking and note issue made American banks small and unstable, causing waves of bank failures during periodic panics from 1819 to 1907. The Canadian banking system, which permitted nationwide branching and more liberal note issue, was immune from panics except in 1837. Rather than adopt the Canadian model, which was feared by rural banks without branches, the USA retained restrictions on branching and solved problems of note shortage after a fashion by establishing the Federal Reserve System, which opened in 1914.

As in England and the USA, several other nations experienced financial panics under free banking, and adopted central banking as a way to try to prevent them. Most of these free banking systems were heavily regulated. The greater stability of free banking systems that were less regulated suggests that the problem in nations that experienced panics was too much regulation rather than too little. The less regulated free banking systems had no apparent need of a lender of last resort, nor, contrary to the claims of some writers (Goodhart, 1988), did they rely on central banking systems with which they had close links to provide them with a lender of last resort.

During the First World War, most countries suspended the gold or silver standard and used their banking systems as means of inflationary finance. Having experienced the possibilities of government control of the money supply, they were reluctant subsequently to return to free banking. Furthermore, the intellectual fashion for central banking made free banking appear unscientific and out of date. Free banking diminished during the 1920s; it became nearly extinct with the Great Depression, when Canada, New Zealand and most other nations that still had free banking replaced it with central banking. The last free banking system was that of South-West Africa (Namibia), which ended in 1962.

Central banks have not accomplished the goals hoped for them. Even the best performers, such as the Federal Reserve and the Bank of Japan, have worse records of fighting inflation than the free banking systems they succeeded. Nor have central banks vanquished the business cycle. Bank runs have been largely eliminated by nationalizing bank risk, but in the USA that has been enormously costly. Despite the poor performance of central banking, free banking appears politically impossible at the moment. It may yet return by two paths, however. Recent political upheavals in Eastern Europe have broken old coalitions of interests and it is conceivable that one or more countries will allow competitive issue of notes and abolish reserve requirements, which are a tax on banks. In the West, recent developments in communications and financial markets may eventually eliminate the need for bank-notes and make other means of central bank control easy to evade (Burstein, 1991), allowing free banking to return through the back door. Whether free banking comes through the back door or the front door, historical experience suggests that there is nothing to be feared from denationalizing money, provided that bank risk is also denationalized.

See also:
Chapter 61: Financial regulation; Chapter 59: Free banking; Chapter 58: Inflation; Chapter 62: Political business cycles

Bibliography

Burstein, M.L. (1991), *The New Art of Central Banking*, New York: New York University Press.
Dowd, K. (ed.) (1992), *The Experience of Free Banking*, London: Routledge.
Goodhart, C. (1988), *The Evolution of Central Banking*, Cambridge, Mass.: MIT Press.
Hayek, F.A. (1978), *Denationalisation of Money*, 2nd edn, London: Institute of Economic Affairs.
Schuler, K. (1992), 'The World History of Free Banking: An Overview', in K. Dowd (ed.), *The Experience of Free Banking*, London: Routledge.
Shiu, M.C. (1990), 'Free banking in China: A preliminary study', unpublished MS, George Mason University.
Smith, V. [1936] (1990), *The Rationale of Central Banking and the Free Banking Alternative*, Indianapolis: Liberty Classics.
Vaubel, R. (1978), *Strategies for Currency Unification: The Economics of Currency Competition and the Case for a European Parallel Currency*, Tübingen: J.C.B. Mohr (Paul Siebeck).
White, L. (1984), *Free Banking in Britain: Theory, Experience, and Debate 1800–1845*, Cambridge/New York: Cambridge University Press.
White, L. (ed.) (1993), *Free Banking*, Aldershot: Edward Elgar.

61 Financial regulation

*Randall S. Kroszner**

The financial system is one of the most heavily regulated sectors in modern capitalist economies. While regulations vary widely across nations and over time (see Kindleberger, 1984), this entry will focus primarily on the types of regulations found in the USA. First, we examine the origins of financial regulation relating to the demands of government finance. Second, we turn to the problems caused by the socialization of risks through government guarantees of deposits. Third, the essay considers the broader implications of financial regulation for the organization and monitoring of firms and entrepreneurs.

Public finance motives for early banking regulation
Most banking and financial regulation originates in the demands of government finance. The oldest surviving central bank, the Bank of England, was founded in 1694 to facilitate war finance. Although government finance is not the only force shaping the financial regulation, it is certainly an important and long-standing one.

After the US Constitution prevented the states from issuing fiat money, they turned to bank regulation, taxation and ownership as a source of revenue (Sylla, Legler and Wallis, 1987). Bank-related share of total state revenues exceeded 10 per cent in a dozen states in the first half of the nineteenth century; in states such as Massachusetts and Delaware, a majority of total state revenue was bank-related. States received fees for granting bank charters, taxed bank capital and purchased shares in banks. To enhance the value of bank charters that the states were 'selling', the state legislatures devised ways to restrict competition. First, they prohibited banks incorporated in other states from operating in their territory. Second, most states adopted restrictions upon branching in order to provide a series of local monopolies within the state. Some states went so far as to adopt 'unit banking', in which a bank could have no branches.

These geographical and branching restrictions were not relaxed during the so-called US free banking era, from about 1838 until the Civil War. During this time, many states were experiencing a change in their financial requirements as they undertook increasingly large capital expenditures on, for exam-

* Thanks to Peter Boettke, Tyler Cowen and Daniel Klein for helpful comments.

ple, infrastructure projects. The chartering fees and share dividends were no longer sufficient to satisfy the growing demands for funds. States thus needed to borrow and wished to ensure a ready market for their debt. They did so by making bank charters much more freely available and requiring that banks hold state bonds in their portfolio (see Rockoff, 1972). When faced with the sharp increase in borrowing necessary to finance the Civil War, the Union followed the states' practice and created a new class of financial institutions to absorb the supply of Union bonds. With the National Currency Act of 1863 and National Banking Act of 1864, the federal government began to compete with the states by issuing national bank charters (see White, 1983). National banks were obliged to use federal government bonds as backing for their note issues. To encourage more state banks to switch their charters, the federal government in 1865 effectively outlawed state bank-note issuance by levying a 10 per cent tax on state bank-notes. Thus the origin of the 'dual banking' system in the USA, with the banks being able to choose to be supervised by either the state or the federal government, is war financing.

National banks were restricted to dealing in government and, to some extent, private, debt instruments. There was, however, much competition from state-chartered banks and trusts, which had no such activity restrictions. To avoid these regulations, many banks began to set up securities affiliates after the First World War in order to engage in investment banking. The financial system thus appeared to be evolving towards universal banking. The Glass–Steagall Act in 1933 thwarted this movement and has become one of the most debated – that is, lobbied over – pieces of US financial regulation (Kroszner and Rajan, 1994). This separation is at the heart of the differences between, for example, the US and German financial systems and has important consequences for firm governance in the USA. Powerful vested interests have emerged to maintain the separation of commercial and investment banking.

The market for financial regulation, like all regulation, involves competition among special interest groups. There is a strong tendency for regulatory bodies, in part or in whole, to be 'captured' by the industry which is to be regulated (Stigler, 1971; Peltzman, 1976). How could we then experience some forms of deregulation in the early 1980s? Technology changed the value of geographic restrictions to the banks: (1) transport improvements eroded locational monopoly rents; and (2) the advent of the automatic teller machine, which was deemed by the courts not a bank 'branch', allowed banks to provide depositor services across state lines. Since the value of the geographical restrictions was declining for the incumbent banks, the balance tipped in favor of a new coalition of consumer groups and expansion-minded banks.

The recent round of international regulatory 'harmonization' again returns to the government finance theme. Under the auspices of the Bank for International Settlements in Basle, the major economic powers adopted uniform 'risk-adjusted' capital requirements (sometimes called the Basle accords) for banks operating in their territories. The risk adjustment classifies government securities as riskless, and financial institutions need hold no capital against these assets; in contrast, the institutions must hold capital against all corporate obligations in their portfolios. Since the risk associated with some of the OECD government debt may be roughly on par with (and in some cases greater than) that for top quality private firms, the capital standards reduce the cost of holding government debt relative to holding private instruments. Commercial banks now have a special incentive to purchase government rather than private debt. Thus concerns about the safety of the banking system and the costs of government deposit 'insurance' to the taxpayer are not the only forces shaping these capital regulations.

Deposit insurance and the crisis in the savings and loan industry
The Misesian notion of the 'interventionist dynamic' can be applied fruitfully to explain the regulation of financial services: an initial government regulation, which is supposed to redress a 'failure' of the private markets, causes unintended problems which may call forth further interventions, in a continuing cycle. Nationalization may be the logical conclusion of this process, which the development of the crisis in the US savings and loan (S & L) industry well illustrates. The modern regulatory structure of the S & L industry was created during the early years of the New Deal in its ill-fated attempts to revive the economy. To stimulate the housing and construction sector, the Federal Home Loan Bank Board was set up to oversee and encourage savings and loan institutions, whose primary activity was making long-term, fixed-rate mortgage loans. The Federal Savings and Loan Insurance Corporation (FSLIC) provided government insurance for the depositors in the member thrifts, in parallel to the role of the Federal Deposit Insurance Corporation for commercial banks. Government insurance, it was believed, would provide stability to the banking system by preventing 'panic' runs and, thereby, help to reduce the costs of financial intermediation. The assessments charged by the FSLIC were based on simply the size of deposits, regardless of the riskiness of the portfolio of the thrift.

This structure was a recipe for disaster – a 'time bomb' in the words of George Benston. Federal deposit guarantees short-circuited the market discipline that the depositors would have exercised. Depositors no longer had to be compensated for the risk of failure of the thrift since the government insured their deposits. Since the insurance scheme reduced the cost of taking risks, the thrifts were naturally willing to take on more risk in striving for a higher return than they otherwise would have. The portfolio choices exposed them to enormous losses if interest rates were to rise. The thrifts' primary assets were long-term, fixed-rate mortgages, so they bore all of the risk of an increase in interest rates over the life of the mortgage. They financed the 20 to 30-year loans through shorter-term deposits – savings deposits and certificates of deposit with maturities of no longer than a few years. In addition, they typically failed to diversify, for they held primarily one type of asset – real estate loans in the local community.

The quadrupling of interest rates to 20 per cent in the late 1970s and early 1980s triggered the bomb (see White, 1991). The value of the thrifts' portfolios dropped so much that the net worth (difference between assets and liabilities) became negative. Without government guarantees, depositors would have withdrawn their funds from the insolvent institutions, causing bankruptcy. Instead, we had forbearance – the blind hope of the regulators that things would get better. On the contrary, things became worse – 'zombie' thrifts with negative net worth, which normally would have been forced out of business, were able to survive. These institutions were willing to 'bet the bank' to gamble for resurrection from insolvency. The large risks translated into losses which bankrupted the FSLIC and have led to a taxpayer-financed bail-out of the industry which entails the government seizure of insolvent thrifts. The perverse incentives of deposit insurance have thus led to the largest nationalization in US history. Estimates of the total cost to the taxpayer range between a quarter and a half trillion dollars.

Consequences of financial regulation for firm governance
Regulation of financial intermediaries has important consequences not only for taxpayers and, of course, the intermediaries themselves, but also for the governance and efficiency of firms (see Roe, 1990). As an enterprise grows, an entrepreneur–owner–manager looks to outside sources of capital to finance expansion. The sole proprietorship organization of production then typically gives way to the public corporation, in which numerous, dispersed equity owners hire managers who specialize in the control and operation of the firm. To deal with the so-called Berle and Means (1932) problem of the separation of ownership and control, firm owners develop a complex web of contracts to align the incentives of the managers with the desires of the owners. In addition to such 'internal' governance devices as proxy voting rules and compensation based upon firm performance, there is the 'external' governance by the capital market through takeovers and purchases of large blocks of (voting) shares.

Restrictions on ownership by large institutional investors and financial institutions reduce the discipline exercised by the 'external' governance mechanism in the market for corporate control. The Glass–Steagall Act of 1933 prevents commercial banks from taking direct equity stakes in firms and from being involved in underwriting or dealing in equity issues. The regulations governing insurers, open-ended mutual funds and pension funds effectively prohibit them from purchasing controlling stakes in corporations or actively engaging in the market for corporate control (see Roe, 1990). These restrictions hinder these important pools of financial expertise and funds from contributing to the operation of the capital market as a monitor of corporate performance. With this source of external monitoring reduced, managers enjoy greater scope to act in their self-interest rather than in the owners' interest. In consequence, the corporate efficiency could suffer throughout the economy as managers pursue perks rather than profits.

Conclusion

The demands of government finance have had a major impact on the financial regulations lawmakers adopt. Vested interests emerge to support the prevailing regulations and capture the regulatory bodies, at what may be high costs to the users of financial services and taxpayers. Financial regulations also affect the efficiency of capital markets and corporate management. Laissez-faire for the financial system obviously would have very different consequences, but the evolution of an unregulated financial system continues to be much debated (contrast Selgin and White, 1987; Cowen and Kroszner, 1994).

See also:

Chapter 34: Financial economics; Chapter 86: The new monetary economics; Chapter 59: Free banking

Bibliography

Berle, Adolf and Gardiner Means (1932), *The Modern Corporation and Private Property*, New York: Commerce Clearing House.
Cowen, Tyler and Randall Kroszner (1994), *Explorations in the New Monetary Economics*, Oxford: Basil Blackwell.
Kindleberger, Charles (1984), *A Financial History of Western Europe*, London: George Allen & Unwin.
Kroszner, Randall and Raghuram Rajan (1992), 'Is the Glass–Steagall Act Justified? A Study of the U.S. Experience with Universal Banking before 1933', *American Economic Review*, **84**, September.
Peltzman, Sam (1976), 'Toward a More General Theory of Regulation', *Journal of Law and Economics*, **19**, August.
Rockoff, Hugh (1972), 'The Free Banking Era: A Re-Examination', PhD thesis, University of Chicago, Department of Economics.
Roe, Mark (1990), 'Political and Legal Restraints on Ownership and Control of Public Corporations', *Journal of Financial Economics*, **27**, September, 7–42.
Selgin, George and Lawrence H. White (1987), 'The Evolution of a Free Banking System', *Economic Inquiry*, **25**, July, 439–58.
Stigler, George (1971), 'The Theory of Economic Regulation', *Bell Journal of Economics and Management Science*, **2**, spring.
Sylla, Richard, John Legler and John Wallis (1987), 'Banks and State Public Finance in the New Republic: The United States, 1790–1860', *Journal of Economic History*, **47**, June, 391–403.

White, Eugene (1983), *The Regulation and Reform of the American Banking System, 1900–1929*, Princeton: Princeton University Press.
White, Lawrence J. (1991), *The S & L Debacle*, New York: Oxford University Press.

62 Political business cycles

Richard E. Wagner

Business cycles have motivated a large body of economic scholarship of all varieties, including Austrian. Much of this scholarship has been driven by a prescriptive concern with avoiding, or at least mitigating, business cycles. Where some scholars call for an activist government that offsets private sources of instability, others call for a passive, or even rule-bound government, generally under a belief that activism is at least as likely to confound as to support the corrective forces of the market. These controversies mostly involve cognitive disputes about the nature of the economic process and whether a government could know enough to promote economic stability.

The literature on political business cycles starts by asking whether a government would truly want to promote economic stability, even if it knew how. In democracies, incumbent governments periodically must face re-election; if electoral survival is of paramount interest, whether economic stability or instability will be promoted depends upon which better enhances electoral prospects. Government is not some unified being with a selfless dedication to economic stability, but a collection of individual politicians who will need periodically to win an election and will seek to craft policies that they think will enhance their electoral prospects.

Vote motives and electoral cycles

With few exceptions, the literature on political business cycles has been developed within the highly aggregative confines of macroeconomic theory, with the variables of analytical interest being the rates of inflation, unemployment and growth in GNP. Models of political business cycles typically involve two primary elements. One is a representation of the way voter evaluations of incumbent politicians and, hence, electoral outcomes, will depend upon macroeconomic performance. The other is a characterization of the way in which politicians can use policy measures to influence macroeconomic performance and, thereby, electoral prospects.

Over the past 20 years, quite a large empirical literature has emerged on the relationship between election outcomes and macroeconomic variables (see, for instance, Tufte, 1978; Hibbs, 1987; Willett, 1988). The general tenor of this literature is that the share of votes going to the incumbent party varies inversely with the rates of inflation and unemployment, and directly with the rate of growth in GNP. If such relationships are assumed to be stable, an incumbent party could acquire useful information about its prospective electoral fortunes by consulting the state of those macroeconomic variables prior to a forthcoming election. If those variables, thought to hold clues to electoral fortunes, can themselves be influenced through policy measures under the control of the incumbent party, it would seem only natural to expect that party to try to influence those variables, at least so long as it did not feel confident about re-election. Models of electoral cycles seek to describe how what might otherwise be a stable economy can be subjected to electoral shocks that can create business cycles. (It is, of course, not necessary to assume that the economy would otherwise be stable, but this is done simply as a modeling strategy to focus on the impact of periodic elections on business cycles.)

To be sure, how an incumbent party might pursue an electoral cycle depends on some important institutional details, details that are often glossed over in the modeling exercises. Electoral cycles are typically modeled as a game between an incumbent political party and voters. This setting perhaps fits closest a parliamentary system of government that also has the central bank as a component of the treasury. In this case it would seem plausible to speak of an incumbent party choosing an expansionary program prior to an election. But a central bank with some degree of independence restricts the options open to the incumbent party because the party cannot control the extent to which government debt is monetized. A presidential system of government with a bicameral legislature further restricts the incumbent party's options, particularly if party discipline is weak, for then it might be ambiguous even to refer to an incumbent party. Rather there would be many incumbent politicians, from different parties, all of whom are seeking to promote their electoral prospects.

The idea of a political business cycle can be illustrated in simple fashion by assuming a parliamentary system where the central bank is part of the treasury (Nordhaus, 1975, initiated the contemporary literature). Suppose the economy is characterized by some Phillips curve trade-off between inflation and unemployment in the short run. Further suppose that, with an election approaching, prevailing economic conditions, represented by the rates of inflation and unemployment, face the incumbent party with 52:48 odds of success. If a properly timed expansionary policy is then pursued and the short-run Phillips trade-off exploited, the odds of success for the incumbent party might rise to, say, 56:44. The expansionary policy is able, in this framework, to enhance electoral prospects temporarily. But if there is no long-run Phillips trade-off, the expansionary program will have weakened the future electoral prospects of the incumbent party, for, after the expansion, the rate of inflation is permanently higher, but the rate of unemployment is no lower. Under these circumstances, the incumbent party will face lower odds of success at the next election, say, 48:52.

At this point there are two paths the story can take. One has the incumbent party doing the same thing as before, only with less prospect of success: rather than starting from a 52 per cent chance of success, the incumbent party starts from a 48 per cent chance. A new expansionary program might raise those odds to, say, 50:50. This path reveals a story of ever-increasing inflation inspired by the search for electoral support, yet ending eventually in the defeat of the incumbent party. The other path has the incumbent party following a deflationary policy after the election, which initially sends its popularity with voters plummeting. Subsequently, however, the economy is restored to its original state, where the incumbent party again faces 52:48 odds of success. The incumbent party is thus poised to initiate another cycle before the next election. This path reveals a story of pre-election expansions followed by post-election contractions.

Simplicity, complexity and macro modeling

Most of the literature on political business cycles has been formulated within a standard macroeconomic framework, where the phenomena under examination are simple and not complex (Hayek, 1967). The entire economic process can be apprehended in terms of two or three variables. One good is produced – 'output' –which can be measured in real terms (growth in GNP), in nominal terms (inflation) and with respect to the number of people engaged in producing it (unemployment). Everyone is identical or rendered effectively so through a focus on averages as being analytically determinative, which effectively creates a one-person world. The world of macroeconomic modeling, within which the literature on political business cycles has largely developed, clearly violates the elemental propositions about the impossibility of collectivist planning.

Indeed, the political business cycle is a model of collectivist planning. In this case it is the incumbent party that plans the pattern of economic activity so as to enhance its electoral prospects, through the generation of an electoral cycle involving a recurring pattern of pre-election feasts followed by post-election famines. For incumbents to be able successfully to practice such economic manipulation, it would be necessary to presume either that voters are ignorant of the pro-cyclical policies being pursued or that they are highly myopic. For such reasons as these, political business cycle models went into eclipse for a while, during the ascendancy of rational expectations modeling (see, for instance, McCallum, 1978). For within the standard macro presumption that economic phenomena are inherently simple, political business cycles would seem to violate some reasonable requirements of rationality.

No doubt this is so, but there are some severe problems with the entire enterprise of seeking to explain economic events and processes through standard macro formulations. To model electoral processes as driven by macro magnitudes is surely incoherent, regardless of whatever statistical fits might be achieved. What is a macro policy, as distinct from what might be called a micro policy? The only reasonable answer must be that it is one for which people care only about its magnitude and not about its distribution – whether over space, among people or along any other dimension. If government spending was to be increased by $100 billion, it would be irrelevant how that money was spent. Political support would be garnered by the mere fact of the expenditure. Distributional issues would be irrelevant. To illustrate the point, suppose an incumbent party secures a $100 billion increase in government spending, in a polity that contains ten electoral districts. Two of those districts are absolutely safe for the incumbent party, three are absolutely safe for the opposition, and five are tightly contested. The standard macro story would say that success for the incumbent party resides in getting the $100 billion spent, and with the party being indifferent as to how or where that money is spent. Such a story teller would surely fail as a politician, for a successful party would concentrate the money in the five contested districts – for money spent in the other five districts will have no influence over the election's outcome.

Empirically, according to the standard Phillips curve stories, the increased spending would reduce unemployment and increase support for the incumbent party in those five districts. Such an outcome is fully consistent with a regression equation estimated for national magnitudes, which shows that the incumbent party's vote share varies inversely with the unemployment rate. But such consistency is an incidental by-product of aggregation. Those macro aggregates themselves do not generate any understanding of economic and political processes. The very idea of macroeconomic policy is surely chimerical. Macroeconomic measures are simply aggregations over individual variables. There is no such thing as a policy measure that sets some aggregate level of unemployment, some average rate of change in prices, or some rate of increase in GNP. Rather, there are thousands of measures enacted each year, each of which is supported by subsets of the population, subsets that, when joined together, may constitute a winning coalition.

Traditional Austrian cycle theory emphasized how money-financed credit expansion generated unsustainable adjustments in the structure of prices. A reasonable approach to political business cycles would have a similar emphasis on the way electoral politics generate unsustainable shifts in the pattern of economic activity (O'Driscoll, 1979; Wagner, 1980). One of the central features of public choice scholarship is that any program of wealth redistribution that secures majority approval can be defeated through majority vote by an indefinite number of other programs. Such voting cycles are commonly presented as a feature of the logic of majority rule, but when viewed historically they suggest that political programs enacted this year will to varying degrees be subject to reversal in subsequent years as new coalitions replace old ones.

Political competition generates a churning of policy measures that continually inject shocks into the economic process (De Jasay, 1985). Perhaps the year prior to an election would see more such shocks, though this is not clear. Politicians no doubt seek to use policy measures to influence their odds of future success, and when faced with the proximity of an election it would be understandable if they became a bit more frantic in looking for another margin of support here or there. Booms and busts there can be, and the political search for gain, by injecting shocks into the economic process, can be a source of economic discoordination. But there would seem to be little point in looking for regular cyclical patterns. A cycle as a recurring pattern seems to be more a product of ease in modeling than a feature of history, as Lachmann (1986, pp. 30–31) notes.

The centrally valid principle behind the literature on political business cycles is that politicians who are nervous about their electoral prospects will seek policy measures that will improve those prospects. There is no reason to presume that this will lead to the neat, rhythmic patterns that can be squeezed out of certain macro modeling. The macro focus on regular, recurring cycles guided by elections must give way to a focus on the development of policy measures to secure the support of *particular* groups of voters. Both the macro focus and the presumption that economic processes are inherently simple and, hence, easily controllable must give way to a recognition of the inherent complexity of economic processes and the adoption of a micro-oriented perspective towards political and economic processes. A focus on cycles per se will be replaced by a recognition that the pursuit of electoral gain induces a flow of legislation that changes the relative profitability of different activities, though with that profitability being subject to subsequent reversal as political exigencies change.

See also:
Chapter 59: Free banking; Chapter 41: Public choice economics

Bibliography
De Jasay, A. (1985), *The State*, Oxford: Basil Blackwell.
Hayek, F.A. (1967), 'The Theory of Complex Phenomena', in *Essays in Economics, Politics, and Philosophy*, Chicago: University of Chicago Press.
Hibbs, D.A., Jr. (1987), *The American Political Economy: Macroeconomics and Electoral Politics*, Cambridge, Mass.: Harvard University Press.
Lachmann, L.M. (1986), *The Market as an Economic Process*, Oxford: Basil Blackwell.
McCallum, B.T. (1978), 'The Political Business Cycle: An Empirical Test', *Southern Economic Journal*, **44**, 504–15.
Nordhaus, W.D. (1975), 'The Political Business Cycle', *Review of Economic Studies*, **42**, 169–90.
O'Driscoll, G.P., Jr. (1979), 'Rational Expectations, Politics, and Stagflation', in M.J. Rizzo (ed.), *Time, Uncertainty, and Disequilibrium*, Lexington, Mass.: D.C. Heath.
Tufte, E. (1978), *Political Control of the Economy*, Princeton: Princeton University Press.

Wagner, R.E. (1980), 'Boom and Bust: The Political Economy of Economic Disorder', *Journal of Libertarian Studies*, **4**, 1–37; reprinted in James M. Buchanan and Robert D. Tollison (eds), *The Theory of Public Choice – II*, Ann Arbor: University of Michigan Press, 1984.
Willett, T.D. (ed.) (1988), *Political Business Cycles*, Durham, NC: Duke University Press.

63 The Great Depression

Mark Skousen

The Great Depression of the 1930s was the most traumatic economic event of the twentieth century. It was especially shocking when one considers the great advances that had been achieved in Western living standards since the turn of the century. The economic abyss represented a watershed in economic history and theory; its effects on attitudes and policies still linger at this dawn of a new century.

The brunt of the depression was felt in 1929–33. In the USA, industrial output fell by over 30 per cent. Nearly half the commercial banks failed. The unemployment rate soared to 25 per cent. Stock prices lost 88 per cent of their value. Europe and the rest of the world experienced similar turmoil. In addition, the recovery in the 1930s was slow and uneven; unemployment remained high (above 15 per cent) until the armament race heated up in the early 1940s. The prolonged depression created an environment critical of laissez-faire policies and favorable towards ubiquitous state interventionism throughout the Western world. It led to the Welfare State and boundless faith in Big Government. It caused most of the Anglo-American economics profession to question classical free-market economics and to search for radical anti-capitalist alternatives, eventually converting to the 'new economics' of Keynesianism and 'demand-side' economics. Prior to the Great Depression, most Western economists accepted the classical virtues of thrift, limited government, balanced budgets, the gold standard and Say's Law. While most economists continued to defend free enterprise and free trade on a microeconomic scale, they rejected traditional views on a macroeconomic level in the postwar period, advocating consumption over saving, fiat money over the gold standard, deficit spending over a balanced budget and active state interventionism over limited government. They bought the Keynesian argument that a free market was inherently unstable and could result in high levels of unemployed labor and resources for indefinite periods. They blamed the Great Depression on laissez-faire capitalism and contended that only massive government spending during the Second World War saved the capitalist system from defeat. In short, the depression opened the door to widespread collectivism in the USA and around the world.

Unfortunately, the causes of and cures for the Great Depression have been gravely misconceived by most economists and historians. The truth is that the free market performs well and provides an efficient use of labor and resources *if undisturbed by government interference*. The market economy is

431

not inherently unstable. The economic catastrophe of the 1930s cannot be blamed on laissez-faire capitalism, but rather on misguided government policies. Only recently have economists recognized the depth and extent of government mismanagement of the economy during this key period in world history. What was the real cause of the 1929–32 depression? Actually, there were several causes, all involving various forms of government intervention. Let us examine each one.

Cause 1: easy credit in the 1920s

In order to explain the cause and cure of the Great Depression, we must look at the economic events that led up to the stock market crash. Only the Austrian school maintains that the world's monetary system was defective in the 1920s and brought about the stock market crash of 1929 and economic crisis of the early 1930s. The monetarists and the Keynesians, both then and now, maintain a different view. They claim that there were few signs of an inflationary boom, excessive monetary growth, credit crunch, defective banking system or any other factor during the 1920s that might have precipitated an economic crash (Friedman and Schwartz, 1963). Some mainstream economists even argue that there was no speculative bubble on Wall Street in the late 1920s (Schwartz, 1987). It is not surprising, therefore, that neither the monetarists nor Keynesians of the day were able to forecast the stock market crash or depression (Skousen, 1992). Even today's academic descendants, using sophisticated time-series models, have concluded that the depression was 'unforecastable' (Dominguez *et al.*, 1988). The Austrians demur, suggesting that today's econometric forecasters are simply using the wrong model.

The Austrian theory of the business cycle

A correct model of the Great Depression should begin with the Austrian theory of the business cycle, as developed by Ludwig von Mises and Friedrich A. Hayek. The Mises–Hayek model offers a plausible cause for the initial downturn in 1929 and the crisis that followed. Mises and Hayek maintain that, as long as market interest rates reflect the natural rate of time preference of consumers, there can be no systematic business cycle. But if the government deliberately lowers interest rates below the natural rate of time preference, resources will be misallocated, changing the level and pattern of investment. An artificial boom begins in the higher-order capital goods industries (mining, manufacturing, construction and so on), but this boom is unsustainable. The imbalance between capital investment and consumption cannot last. Once expanded production is paid out in the form of wages, rents and profits, individuals will eventually spend their new money according to the *old* consumption/saving patterns. That is, individuals will increase consumption at the expense of investment. Consumer prices will start rising relative to producer prices. Inevitably interest rates will begin rising, cutting off the investment boom: the boom turns into a bust, or a depression. In fact, an inflationary boom requires a bust, a cleansing of malinvestments. The depression ends when the consumption/saving pattern returns to its equilibrium state, and market interest rates again reflect the natural rate of time preference. In short, the inflationary process – defined as a deliberate government policy of expanding the money supply and pushing interest rates below their natural rate – is self-reversing (Mises, 1953; Hayek, 1935; Rothbard, 1982).

1924–9: easy credit and the inflationary boom

The economic events of the 1920s closely followed the Austrian model. The expansionary phase of the business cycle, encouraged by an easy credit policy, began in earnest in the early 1920s and lasted until 1929. There has been a dispute among economists about the degree of monetary inflation in the 1920s. Milton Friedman and Anna Schwartz argue that there was no significant monetary inflation during the 1920s, but Murray N. Rothbard, using a much broader definition of money that included cash value in life insurance policies, demonstrates that a serious expansionism occurred in 1924–8 (Friedman and Schwartz, 1963; Rothbard, 1982). But the debate between the Austrians and the monetarists goes beyond the degree of monetary inflation in the 1920s. Both schools agree that the Fed pushed interest rates down in the mid-1920s. The real question is: did the Federal Reserve's easy credit policies distort the structure of the economy and create an unsustainable boom? The monetarists deny it; the Austrians affirm it.

J.M. Keynes, Irving Fisher and other leading contemporary economists, caught up in the 'New Era' optimism of the Roaring Twenties, remained unconcerned about the potential ill-effects of such an easy credit policy because consumer prices were relatively stable throughout the 1920s. And as long as prices were stable, they argued, there was no reason for concern. Thus the major schools of economics failed completely to foresee the coming economic storm. The economists in Vienna were not misled, however. They foresaw the structural imbalance created by the Federal Reserve's cheap money policy. The government's program may not have caused commodity or consumer prices to rise, but it did lead to an inordinate and unsustainable rise in manufacturing output, stock values and real estate prices. Easy money and low interest rates did not affect the economy and the capital structure uniformly. In the 1920s, the new money went into the investment markets and the manufacturing sectors. The stock market trebled in value from 1924 to 1929.

Once the central banks embarked on an inflationary course, it was only a matter of time until interest rates rose and cut short the economic expansion.

Although Mises and Hayek did not attempt to predict the exact date or the magnitude of the depression, they felt it had to occur rather quickly because of the international gold standard: relying on the Hume–Ricardo specie flow mechanism, Mises and Hayek predicted that the gold standard would force the Fed to reverse its course and restrict credit in short order. By 1927, gold started flowing out of the USA and, in late 1928, the Federal Reserve reversed its course. The money supply stopped growing and the central bank raised interest rates in early 1929 to stem speculation on Wall Street and to reduce potential gold outflows. By September 1929, the stock market had stopped climbing and on 24 October 1929, Black Thursday, Wall Street crashed.

Cause 2: Federal Reserve's deflationary policies
The recession following the 1929 crash need not have turned into a major depression. If government policy had remained neutral and allowed wages and prices to adjust freely, the economy could have recovered fairly quickly, just as it did in 1920–21. Unfortunately, Washington was not so benign.

The stock market collapse represented the first signs of a liquidity squeeze that accelerated in 1930. Economic activity declined rapidly and unemployment rose sharply, owing in part to Hoover's determination to keep wages high (see cause 6). In late 1930, a banking panic spread through the southeastern states and then, in December 1930, the Bank of the United States failed. Initially, the Federal Reserve responded to the banking crisis by reinflating, but the effect was countered when banks built up reserves and the public converted demand deposits into cash. Moreover, when Great Britain abandoned the gold standard in September 1931, the Federal Reserve, fearing a run on its gold reserves, sharply raised the discount rate. The gold drain was checked but the domestic effects were traumatic, resulting in massive bank failures and a rapid decline in the money supply up to March of 1933. Most Austrians would join the monetarists in concluding that the Federal Reserve made matters worse by raising interest rates, allowing banks to fail on a wholesale basis and causing the money supply to plunge (Friedman and Schwartz, 1963).

Cause 3: flawed banking system
While this monetary ineptness may have been the principal cause of the depression, the length and depth of the contraction were exacerbated by many other errors committed by government. One major factor was a flawed banking system based on the practice of centralized fractional reserve banking, which imposed uniform reserve requirements on commercial banks. Centralized fractional reserve banking often meant that withdrawals from one bank led to withdrawals from other banks, creating a 'domino effect'.

(According to free banking advocates, withdrawals from a weak bank would have been deposited in a strong bank under a decentralized competitive banking system.) Another major factor was the lack of nationwide banking in the USA. If commercial banks in the USA had been able to engage in inter-state branching, the contraction would have been limited. In Canada, where nationwide banking existed, the depression was less severe and there was no banking crisis (Selgin, 1988).

In addition, there were several political events in 1932–3 that worsened the banking crisis, including the publication of the names of banks that borrowed from the Reconstruction Finance Corporation, and the rumor that newly elected President Franklin D. Roosevelt would devalue the dollar. Both actions caused further runs on the banks and increased depositors' demands for gold, culminating in Roosevelt's declaration of a national emergency in March 1933 (Smiley, 1991).

Cause 4: Smoot–Hawley tariff

One of the most devastating measures passed by Congress (with President Herbert Hoover's support) was the Smoot–Hawley tariff in 1930. Smoot–Hawley imposed some of the highest tariffs ever on agricultural and manu-factured goods, thus compounding economic difficulties. The act raised the average tariff on imports to the USA from 19.8 per cent to 36.4 per cent. Many other countries responded in kind. The result was a sharp reduction in foreign trade, which in turn reduced economic growth and employment op-portunities.

Cause 5: tax increases

In 1932, facing a \$2 billion deficit, Congress (again with the approval of President Hoover) pushed through an extremely large peacetime tax increase. Personal income taxes were raised drastically, personal exemptions were sharply reduced and surtaxes on the wealthy were increased from a maxi-mum of 25 per cent to 63 per cent. The corporate income tax was raised from 12 per cent to nearly 14 per cent. The estate tax was doubled, and the gift tax was restored. Sales and excise taxes were imposed. A 2 per cent federal tax was placed on bank checks, which encouraged the shift from deposits to currency. Congress also sharply increased postal rates. Yet, despite the drastic increase in tax rates, revenues for 1932 declined (Rothbard, 1982).

Cause 6: government jawboning and wage controls

One of the fundamental reasons for the rapid rise in unemployment during the 1930s was the Hoover administration's efforts to maintain wage rates. In early 1930, Hoover invited major industrial leaders, including Henry Ford, Alfred P. Sloan and Pierre du Pont, to the White House and convinced them to maintain a high wage policy. With prices declining, that meant sharply higher *real* wages and, consequently, high and persistent levels of unemployment. By the end of the year, industrial leaders recognized the futility of their efforts and started cutting wages. Still, labor unions strongly resisted the wage cuts (Rothbard, 1982; Smiley, 1991).

Why did the depression last so long?

The Great Depression officially bottomed out in the second quarter of 1933, but the recovery was cut short. Unemployed resources and workers remained pervasive throughout the mid-1930s, and another deep contraction followed in 1938. As a result of the seemingly never-ending stagnation, most economists gave up free market solutions, including the Austrian model, and converted to Keynesian economics.

Why did it take so long for the economy to return to normality? Alvin Hansen and the Keynesians blamed hoarding, excess bank reserves, Washington's unwillingness to run a 'full employment' budget deficit, and 'secular stagnation' of the entrepreneurial spirit. Monetarists blamed an excessively tight money policy by the Fed. Certainly, a stable monetary policy would have been helpful, but many actions by Congress also inhibited a full recovery. Foremost was the National Industrial Recovery Act, one of the cornerstones of FDR's New Deal enacted in 1933. The National Recovery Administration (NRA) attempted to create government-sponsored cartels, shorten the work week, raise wage rates and prices, and force businesses to recognize labor unions and engage in collective bargaining. By reducing competition, production and investment, the NRA stopped the emerging recovery. Fortunately, the NRA was ruled unconstitutional in 1935, and industrial production increased until 1937.

The 1937–8 contraction was again caused by government's changing course. Keynesians point to a 'full employment' surplus in the federal budget, but more important was the Federal Reserve's doubling of bank reserve requirements. In addition, Congress passed pro-labor legislation (such as the National Labor Relations Act and the Wagner Act), giving labor unions excessive power. As a result, wage rates rose in early 1937, unmatched by increases in labor productivity. Increased unemployment was the result (Smiley, 1987, 1991).

What is the cure for depression?

What should the government do to get a country out of a depression? Judging from the causes of the depression listed above, the answer is clear. Government should establish a stable monetary and banking system, reduce taxes on individuals and businesses, remove regulatory barriers to business and international trade, avoid wage–price controls, stop fostering monopolistic practices that discourage flexible prices and wages, privatize and denationalize government programs, cut wasteful government spending, and encourage saving and investment (Robbins, 1934). In short, instead of engaging in an active interventionist role, government should get out of the way, and provide a steady, passive environment that allows productive citizens to do what is best for themselves, their families, their companies and their workers.

The depression and the Second World War

What about the Keynesian solution of deficit spending? Keynesians point to the Second World War as proof of the efficacy of a liberal fiscal policy as a cure for a depression. The Federal deficit rose from $6 billion in 1940 to $89 billion in 1944. At the same time, industrial production almost doubled, incomes rose and unemployment virtually disappeared. Yet Keynesians cannot use the 1940s as absolute proof of fiscal policy's potency. The monetarists are quick to demonstrate that monetary policy also changed dramatically during the 1940s. The money supply rose at an annual rate of 20 per cent during 1940–44. Furthermore, the war years saw an unprecedented rise in individual and business savings, which provided billions of dollars to finance the industrial war machine at extremely low interest rates (Skousen, 1988).

Then there is the question of how real the recovery was during the war, considering that most of the increased government spending, private savings and new money went into the production of war goods, and that the US armed forces drafted more than the 10 million unemployed in the USA. National income statistics for the war years are highly suspect, especially with regard to military expenditures. War output was significantly overpriced by the US Commerce Department. Meanwhile, other price indices consistently underestimated inflation. Price controls severely restricted the quantity and quality of consumer goods during the war. In fact, real per capita consumption reached a peak in 1941, declined, and then, though recovering, still did not reach the 1941 level until 1946. In conclusion, real prosperity arrived in 1946, after the war was over (Higgs, 1992).

Undoubtedly the liberal monetary and fiscal policies of the government during wartime created the *illusion* of prosperity, but neither reinflation nor deficit financing can provide a return to genuine, permanent prosperity. Reinflating only serves to boost the economy temporarily. It still creates distortions in the level and structure of investment that require a recessionary adjustment. The proper solution is to abolish the Federal Reserve and to establish a sound-money system. Austrians favor either a return to a classic gold standard or a free banking system. Critics argue that a return to gold is bound to be deflationary, as was the case with Great Britain in the 1920s. But that is not necessarily the case. The dollar and other major currencies can simply be revalued at a higher exchange rate with gold according to the amount of metal each country holds. Once a pure 100 per cent gold standard is established, the money supply is not likely to decline, nor is it likely to rise too fast (Skousen, 1991).

High deficit spending, the Keynesian prescription, also distorts the structure of the economy. New government spending must be financed by (1) new taxes, (2) borrowing, or (3) printing new money. New taxes transfer wealth from the productive private sector to the unproductive public sector. Treasury borrowing tends to raise interest rates and crowd out private investment. Monetizing the debt through new money creation tends to distort the capital structure, creating a boom–bust cycle. If government uses the new funds to compete with private business, the net benefit may be nullified (Egger, 1992).

A depression is usually characterized by a far greater collapse in the capital goods industries (mining, manufacturing, construction and so on) than the later stage industries (wholesale and retail markets). Unemployment is higher, inventories are larger and business losses are greater in the early stages of production (Skousen, 1990). Directing deficit spending primarily towards consumption can therefore exacerbate the depression by starving the higher-order investment sector even further. If new funds are spent directly on public infrastructure, they may revive the early stages of production, but only if the new projects do not crowd out private business. Capital-intensive businesses may reduce their own plans in favor of government programs. If the state creates projects that private enterprise does not choose to do (makework projects, pyramid building, war production), the general welfare of the country is reduced.

Can it happen again?
Is another Great Depression possible? Mainstream economists, from Milton Friedman to Paul Samuelson, contend that we are 'depression-proof'. They say that, if another depression threatens, big government will know what to do. Nevertheless, while the USA and other industrial nations may be depression-resilient, they are not depression-proof. As long as the world's central banks engage in volatile and unpredictable inflationary policies, the possibility of financial chaos and a subsequent economic cataclysm should not be discounted. In sum, the most recent economic crisis – whatever that may entail – will not be the last.

The impotence of the economics establishment in forecasting the last Great Depression is not a comforting feeling. If today's most sophisticated econometric models cannot predict the last Great Depression, how will they predict the next?

See also:
Chapter 32: Austrian business cycle theory; Chapter 31: Capital theory; Chapter 59: Free banking

Bibliography
Dominguez, Kathryn M., Ray C. Fair and Matthew D. Shapiro (1988), 'Forecasting the Depression: Harvard Versus Yale', *American Economic Review*, **78**, (4), September, 595–612.

Egger, John B. (1992), 'Fiscal Stimulus: An Unwise Policy for Recovery', in Mark Skousen (ed.), *Dissent on Keynes*, New York: Praeger.

Friedman, Milton and Anna J. Schwartz (1963), *A Monetary History of the United States, 1867–1960*, Princeton: Princeton University Press.

Hayek, Friedrich A. [1931] (1935), *Prices and Production*, 2nd edn, London: George Routledge.

Higgs, Robert (1992), 'Wartime Prosperity? A Reassessment of the U.S. Economy in the 1940s', *Journal of Economic History*, **52**, (1), March, 41–60.

Mises, Ludwig von [1912] (1953), *The Theory of Money and Credit*, 2nd ed., London: Jonathan Cape.

Robbins, Lionel (1934), *The Great Depression*, London: Macmillan.

Rothbard, Murray N. [1963] (1982), *America's Great Depression*, 4th edn, New York: Richardson & Snyder.

Schwartz, Anna J. (1987), 'Understanding 1929–1933', *Money in Historical Perspective*, Chicago: University of Chicago Press, pp. 110–51.

Selgin, George A. (1988), *The Theory of Free Banking: Money Supply Under Competitive Note Issue*, Totowa, NJ: Rowman and Littlefield.

Skousen, Mark (1988), 'Saving the Depression: A New Look at World War II', *Review of Austrian Economics*, **2**, 211–26.

Skousen, Mark (1989), 'Why the U.S. Economy is Not Depression-Proof', *Review of Austrian Economics*, **3**, 75–94.

Skousen, Mark (1990), *The Structure of Production*, New York: New York University Press.

Skousen, Mark (1991), 'Depression Economics', *Economics on Trial*, Homewood, IL: Business One Irwin, pp. 102–18.

Skousen, Mark (1992), 'Who Predicted the 1929 Crash?', *The Meaning of Ludwig von Mises*, Auburn: The Ludwig von Mises Institute.

Smiley, Gene (1987), 'Some Austrian Perspectives on Keynesian Fiscal Policy and the Recovery of the Thirties', *Review of Austrian Economics*, **1**, 146–79.

Smiley, Gene (1991), 'Can Keynesianism Explain the 1930s? Reply to Cowen', *Critical Review*, **5**, (1), winter, 81–114.

64 The collapse of communism and post-communist reform

James A. Dorn

The events of 1989 and 1990, which led to the collapse of communism and the rise of market liberalism in Eastern and Central Europe and the Soviet Union, brought the Marxist–Leninist vision of a socialist utopia to an abrupt end. In 1917, Russia began its socialist experiment with the hope of creating a new society where individuals would be free from want and able to realize their full potential. Vladimir Lenin (1963, p. 418) proclaimed: 'We have a right to say, with the fullest confidence, that the exploitation of the capitalists will inevitably result in a gigantic development of the productive forces of human society.'

The socialist dream of freedom and prosperity failed to become reality because the Communist Party prevented the development of private property and a rule of law. Under communism, there was no wall between the state and the individual. All economic and social decisions became political decisions, and everyone became a ward of the state. The loss of individual responsibility under socialism created what St Petersburg mayor Anatoly Sobchak (1991, p. 199) called a 'parasitic mentality', which destroyed civil society and crippled economic life. Under socialism, the elite of the Communist Party, not the workers, became the new class. Power, not freedom, prevailed in the Union of Soviet Socialist Republics; and corruption, not justice, was the outcome. Thus, at the end of the socialist experiment, Boris Yeltsin could say: 'The experience of the past decades has taught us Communism has no human face. Freedom and Communism are incompatible' (Rosenthal, 1992, p. A18).

In 1985, Mikhail Gorbachev instituted his policy of *glasnost* to open the Soviet Union to the West and to allow greater personal and political freedom. What he failed to realise was that, once the gates of freedom were open, they could not be shut. The fall of the Berlin Wall in November 1989 and the collapse of the Soviet Communist Party in March 1990 were death blows to the old political regime. By the end of 1991 the Soviet Union had ceased to exist. The rapidity of the political revolution that rocked Eastern and Central Europe in 1989 and the Soviet Union in 1990–91 astonished the world, as country after country left communism and adopted democracy without major bloodshed. The political change paved the way for economic reform and the transition to a free market system.

The course of the transition process, however, will depend on how successful ex-communist countries (ECCs) are in instituting private property, liberalizing prices, opening trade and establishing sound currencies. More fundamentally, unless the ECCs are able to nourish an ethos of economic liberty, there is little prospect of depoliticizing economic life and creating a private free market. In this sense, the creation of a civil society, in which the rights of persons and property are protected by law, is a process that must evolve naturally as the barriers to market exchange are removed and people are free to choose.

The failed socialist experiment

After experiencing a lifetime of socialism, Soviet philosopher Alexander Tsypko (1991, p. 290) wrote: 'During 70 years of socialist experimentation in Russia, not one major problem that the country was facing in 1917 has been solved.' The reason for that failure is not hard to discern. As Ukrainian physicist Igor Yukhnovsky observed, 'When something is ruled from the center, the optimization of life is impossible' (Greenhouse, 1990, p. A10).

Individuals require freedom to respond to change, to grow and to learn. By denying individuals their natural rights of liberty and property, the Communist Party created an artificial society and blocked the natural evolution of a spontaneous market order. And by substituting distributive justice for a rule of law, socialism violated the rules of just conduct that are the basis of a free society and that drive the competitive market process (see Hayek, 1982). At base, communism collapsed in Russia and Eastern Europe because of what F.A. Hayek (1988) called the 'fatal conceit', namely, the idea that an enlightened individual or group can bring about an outcome that is superior to the unplanned spontaneous order of a private free market. The problem, of course, is that no one person or group of persons – no matter how intelligent – can possess the knowledge that is dispersed among millions of people (Hayek, 1945). When communism replaces the invisible hand of market competition with the visible hand of government planning, the automatic feedback mechanism inherent in a free market price system is eliminated. Political power, not economic foresight, then determines who succeeds and who fails. Under such a system, the worst rise to the top (Hayek, 1944, chapter 10).

Without a profit–loss test and without the threat of bankruptcy, socialist firms have little incentive to adapt to changes in wants, resources or technology. Errors tend to accumulate and plans are revised only at great cost. Indeed, the longer inefficient state enterprises are allowed to survive, the greater is the ultimate cost of adjusting to the realities of the market. It is ironic that, by disallowing individual failure, the socialist system of central planning set itself up for total failure. That failure was predicted early on by the Austrian school of economics. Ludwig von Mises (1920, 1981) and F.A.

Hayek (1975) both recognized that rational economic calculation would be impossible without private property, and that the loss of property would mean the loss of freedom.

In sum, socialism failed because its institutions failed. The lack of private property and freedom of contract prevented the emergence of a spontaneous market order; and the lack of a rule of law and free expression prevented the emergence of a civil society. The socialization of risk, the absence of a price mechanism for rational economic calculation and the lack of any incentive for socialist enterprises to allocate resources to satisfy consumers' preferences combined to make central planning a poor alternative to the private free market. Although the Soviets and East Europeans sought in the 1960s and 1970s to reform the ossified system of central planning, their attempts at economic reform were limited by the absence of political reform. They tried to introduce markets and prices on a piecemeal basis, but none of the reforms abolished state property or introduced real competition. To have done so would have reduced the Communist Party's hold on economic life. Likewise, when Gorbachev introduced his policy of *perestroika* after 1985, he did not seek radical reform; he merely sought to create a hybrid of plan and market so that he and his Communist Party would retain a monopoly of power. That is why *perestroika* failed.

The very nature of socialism means that political reform must accompany economic reform. As Milovan Djilas remarked, 'You cannot change the form of property without changing the form of power.' Under communism, said Djilas, 'the economy is ruled and controlled by politics. You must change the political system first, because it is a tyrannical regime without respect for laws' (Hornik, 1990, p. 18).

The market–liberal revolution
Mikhail Gorbachev was, perhaps inadvertently, instrumental in launching the market–liberal revolution of 1989. He relaxed controls on freedom of expression and lifted the Iron Curtain that had prevented the Soviet people from seeing the vast gap between a planned and a free society. His promise to withdraw Soviet weapons from the countries of the Eastern bloc created the expectation that Moscow would not interfere with the liberalization movement that was taking shape in Poland and elsewhere. As a result, the liberalization process gained momentum.

In April 1989, Solidarity gained legal status; in September, East Germans were allowed to exit through Hungary to the West; in October, the Communist Party was abolished in Hungary; in November, the Berlin Wall was opened and Czechoslovakia ended the Communist Party's constitutional monopoly on power; in December, East Germany and Bulgaria also abolished the Party's privileged position, and Romania's provisional government was recognized by the USA and the Soviet Union. In 1990, further changes occurred: in January, Poland's Communist Party dissolved itself; in May, Poland held its first free elections since the Second World War; in October, East and West Germany were reunified; and in December, Lech Walesa was elected president of Poland.

The political upheavals in East and Central Europe reverberated back to the Soviet Union: in March 1990, the Congress of People's Deputies repealed the Communist Party's constitutional monopoly on power; in June 1991, Yeltsin was elected president of Russia by popular vote; in August, a failed coup d'état by hardliners solidified democratic forces behind Yeltsin; in December, the Commonwealth of Independent States was formed, Gorbachev resigned and the USSR was history. These dramatic political changes broke the grip of the Communist Party on economic life and provided a window of opportunity to make the transition from a planned economy to a free market.

Transition from plan to market

The collapse of communism and the failure of central planning created the opportunity for real reform. A free market system, however, requires privatization, price liberalization and a sound currency – all of which were lacking in Soviet-type economies. It would not be enough to tinker with the system of central planning; the entire system would have to be scrapped to revitalize economic and social life.

Private ownership is characterized by a bundle of rights: the exclusive right to use one's property, the right to sell and the right to partition property rights so that specialization in ownership or management is possible and risk can be diversified. When the rights associated with private ownership are protected by law, owners will bear responsibility for the uses of their property; they will capture the rewards from efficient use and incur the losses from inefficient use. The linkage between private property and individual responsibility is an important element of private ownership; it provides private owners with an incentive to search for new opportunities for mutually beneficial exchange. Private property, therefore, extends the range of market activity and is essential for a free market price system.

Private property rights will not be effective unless they are enforced. The newly emerging market economies in the East, therefore, must create a constitutional legal framework that safeguards the rights of property and creates a healthy environment in which the market can grow naturally without the threat of government intervention. But the law can only go so far; people themselves must develop a respect for private property, for the rights of others, for freedom of contract, for keeping promises, for honesty in business and for a rule of law. That psychological change requires abandoning socialism in spirit as well as in deed and recognizing that true justice is found in defending liberty, not in using the force of government to destroy property in the name of 'social justice'.

The Marxist–Leninist ideology imbued people with the notion that only government can create order and that market liberalism is a recipe for chaos. Experience has taught different lessons – that government failure is more prominent than so-called market failure and that, when individuals are free to choose within a private market setting, a natural spontaneous order will arise that is beyond the comprehension of any central planner. People in the East may not understand the logic of the price system, but they certainly understand the failure of central planning and the need for change. The question concerns not the direction change will take, but its magnitude and pace. Three reform strategies can be distinguished: the 'big bang' strategy, the Shatalin strategy and the market–socialist strategy. The first approach is characterized by radical and rapid reform, the second by comprehensive and evolutionary reform, and the third by piecemeal and gradual reform.

The idea behind the 'big bang' strategy is to make the transition to a market system in one fell swoop by privatizing, liberalizing and stabilizing the economy as rapidly as possible. Poland's reform strategy was of that sort. The Shatalin strategy, devised by Russian economist Stanislav Shatalin and his reform group, is to create an environment in which market institutions can evolve naturally. In his original 500-Day Program, Shatalin proposed that stabilization, privatization, price liberalization and other measures be *initiated* within 500 days, not that the transition to a market system be completed in that brief period of time. The idea was to get the reform train moving by enacting comprehensive reform measures and then let the market determine the pace of change (see Dorn, 1991, pp. 181–5). The task of reform, as viewed by the Shatalin working group, was that 'of taking everything possible from the state and giving it over to the people' (Shatalin *et al.*, 1990, p. i). The Marxist–Leninist vision was to be replaced by a market–liberal vision, and a primary principle of the 'new economic system' was to have been 'the maximum freedom for economic subjects' (ibid., part 1, p. 7). Gorbachev at first supported the Shatalin Program but later backed off under pressure from 'conservatives' who preferred a gradualist approach that might allow them to retain their power base.

The gradualist piecemeal strategy is to sequence the steps to a market economy and to negotiate with entrenched interests on the way to a market system. In contrast to the 'big bang' and Shatalin strategies, this approach places expediency before principle; and the result is apt to be a regulated market, not a private free market. Most ECCs have followed this route and, as a result, have ended up with market-socialism, not market-liberalism. An exception is the Czech Republic, where Vaclav Klaus has taken a principled stand in favor of market liberalism and has followed a Shatalin-like strategy.

Roadblocks to reform

If the ECCs are to create a free market order and not just another pseudo-market order, they will have to overcome four major barriers: (1) the rule of special interests, (2) the anti-capitalist mentality, (3) the credibility problem, and (4) the market–socialist syndrome.

In the absence of a rule of law, the rule of special interests is a powerful force in ECCs. The ruling elite under communism – managers of state-owned enterprises, directors of state and collective farms, top government bureaucrats and military commanders – continue to exercise considerable influence and have a strong incentive to protect their privileged positions. As a result, the effort to privatize state property in industry, trade and agriculture has been painfully slow.

If post-communist reform is to be successful in establishing a real market system, it will be necessary to embark on constitutional change and create a legal framework to insulate economic life from political life. Such a change, however, must be accompanied by an intellectual revolution that replaces the ingrained anti-capitalist mentality, which has been part of the culture of communism, with a market–liberal perspective. That perspective sparked the 1989 revolution, but the 'new thinking' needs to be cultivated and nourished if it is to survive. As one Russian liberal economist Larisa Piyasheva (1991, p. 294) noted, 'Unless we protect the fragile plant of liberal thinking now budding in our society, it will be very difficult to change things here.'

The leveling instinct is still very strong in ECCs and stands in the way of the competitive market process. Democracy, if unconstrained, could turn the former Soviet republics and other ECCs into giant welfare states. Thus, if a spontaneous market order is to emerge from the ashes of central planning, the parasitic mentality that Sobchak pointed to must be replaced by a widespread acceptance of the principles of market liberalism (as discussed in Hayek, 1967, chapter 11).

Another barrier to liberalization is the near-universal lack of confidence in government. The legacy of communism is mass distrust of government. To gain credibility, the ECCs must establish constitutional safeguards for private property and freedom of contract, create an independent judiciary, allow state enterprises to fail, stop printing money to finance government deficits, create a stable convertible currency and a competitive banking system, and institute a tax system that does not discourage free enterprise and foreign investment. Meaningful reform requires a credible, long-run commitment on the part of ECCs to limiting government and protecting individual rights. Once economic and personal liberties are secure, individuals will be free to choose and to plan for the future without fearing government intervention and policy reversals at every step of the way. Thus far the ECCs have failed to depoliticize economic life. In the former Soviet republics, for example, laws have been passed, but there is still no rule of law. No one knows what will happen next, or if the property that is being privatized today will be renationalized tomorrow. Such uncertainty is a major stumbling-block in making the transition to a free society and a private market system.

A final problem is that of leaving the market–socialist path and taking the road to a real market system. True markets are impossible without transferable private property rights. As long as the state controls property or regulates market prices, the information, incentive and allocative functions of the price system will fail to operate. The fatal conceit is to think that post-communist governments can plan the transition to a private free market. Rather, what they must do is to get out of the way and let voluntary exchange, under rules of just conduct, prevail to establish economic and social harmony.

The post-communist challenge
In his Nobel Memorial Lecture, Hayek (1989, p. 7) argued:

> If man is not to do more harm than good in his efforts to improve the social order, he will have to learn that in this, as in all other fields where essential complexity of an organized kind prevails, he cannot acquire the full knowledge which would make mastery of the events possible. He will therefore have to use what knowledge he can achieve, not to shape the results as the craftsman shapes his handiwork, but rather to cultivate a growth by providing the appropriate environment.

The post-communist challenge is to cultivate an ethos of economic liberty; to remove the remaining barriers to a market–liberal order; and to establish a new constitutional order based on individual, not state, sovereignty.

See also:
Chapter 74: Marxisms and market processes; Chapter 33: Comparative economic systems; Chapter 65: Privatization

Bibliography
Dorn, J.A. (1991), 'From Plan to Market: The Post-Soviet Challenge', *Cato Journal*, **11**, (2), fall, 175–93.
Greenhouse, S. (1990), 'To Ukrainians, Separation Follows Laws of Nature', *New York Times*, 28 December, A10.
Hayek, F.A. (1944), *The Road to Serfdom*, Chicago: University of Chicago Press.
Hayek, F.A. (1945), 'The Use of Knowledge in Society', *American Economic Review*, **35**, September, 519–30.
Hayek, F.A. (1967), 'The Principles of a Liberal Social Order', in F.A. Hayek (ed.), *Studies in Philosophy, Politics, and Economics*, Chicago: University of Chicago Press.
Hayek, F.A. (ed.) [1935] (1975), *Collectivist Economic Planning*, Clifton, NJ: Augustus M. Kelley.
Hayek, F.A. (1982), *Law, Legislation, and Liberty*, London: Routledge & Kegan Paul.
Hayek, F.A. (1988), *The Fatal Conceit: The Errors of Socialism*, vol. 1, *The Collected Works of F.A. Hayek*, ed. W.W. Bartley III, Chicago: University of Chicago Press.

Hayek, F.A. [1974] (1989), 'The Pretence of Knowledge', Nobel Memorial Lecture, 11 December; reprinted in *American Economic Review*, **79**, (6), December, 3–7.

Hornik, R. (1990), 'Why Perestroika Cannot Succeed', an interview with Milovan Djilas, *Time*, 19 February, 18, 27;

Lenin, V.I. [1917] (1963), *State and Revolution*, chapter 5, 'The Economic Base of the Withering Away of the State'; reprinted in J. Somerville and R. Santoni (eds), *Social and Political Philosophy*, Garden City, NJ: Anchor Books.

Mises, L. von (1920), 'Die Wirtschaftsrechnung im sozialistischen Gemeinwesen' ('Economic Calculation in the Socialist Commonwealth'), *Archiv für Sozialwissenschaft*, **47**, 86–121, reprinted in F.A. Hayek (ed.), *Collectivist Economic Planning*, Clifton NJ: Augustus M. Kelley, 1975, chapter 3.

Mises, L. von [1922] (1981), *Socialism: An Economic and Sociological Analysis*, Indianapolis, Ind.: Liberty Classics.

Piyasheva, L. (1991), 'Economic Reform: A Great Bubble or a Faint Chance to Survive?', *Cato Journal*, **11**, (2), fall, 293–8.

Rosenthal, A. (1992), 'Yeltsin Cheered at Capitol', *New York Times*, 18 June, A1, A18.

Shatalin, S. *et al.*, a working group formed by a joint decision of M.S. Gorbachev and B.N. Yeltsin (1990), *Transition to the Market*, Part 1: *The Concept and Program*; Part 2: *Draft of Legal Acts*, Moscow: Arkhangelskoe.

Sobchak, A. (1991), 'Transition to a Market Economy', *Cato Journal*, **11**, (2), fall, 195–205.

Tsypko, A. (1991), 'Revitalization of Socialism or Restoration of Capitalism?', *Cato Journal*, **11**, (2), fall, 285–92.

65 Privatization

Zenon Zygmont

Privatization is the transfer of the ownership of an asset or enterprise from the public to the private sector. The most frequently cited reasons for privatizing are anticipated improvements in enterprise performance because of increased efficiency and reduced state intervention. However, there are other important justifications for privatizing as well, such as reducing budget deficits, increasing share ownership among citizens and improving the provision of any remaining public sector goods and services.

It is generally accepted that state-owned enterprises (SOEs) are less efficient than their private sector counterparts. Absent ownership rights, a manager of a SOE does not have an incentive to consider the demands of consumers or the opportunity cost of scarce resources because neither profits nor losses can be internalized. State ownership also exacerbates the familiar principal–agent issue by making monitoring more difficult and less effective than in the private sector. In addition, a SOE is often a monopoly insulated from the discipline of competition. Because it is accompanied by profit seeking, competition and entrepreneurial discovery, privatization establishes an institutional setting in which economic efficiency is increased.

However, using efficiency to assess privatization can lead to ambiguities. Because efficiency suggests the Paretian criterion, comparative appraisals of privatization are shunted aside in favor of absolutist general equilibrium ones. For example, if a now privatized enterprise is believed to have market power, a narrow application of allocative efficiency may take precedence over a broader consideration of rivalrous competition. As a result, privatization is often accompanied by continued state intervention, particularly in the form of regulation and antitrust enforcement.

A second and related justification for privatization is to limit the state's participation in economic decision making. Well publicized attempts to 'turn back the tide of the state' were made by the Thatcher Government in Great Britain during the period 1979–90. The once-for-all sundering of state enterprise relationships was supposed to curtail the 'socialist ratchet' and reduce the number of margins on which the state could intervene. However, the British experience shows that, even with a reduced threat of nationalization, the remaining margins may be substantial. And evidence from Latin American privatizations illustrates that the benefits of privatization are often overwhelmed by discretionary state activities.

Two important prerequisites underlie privatization: the existence of an institutional infrastructure and credible state policies. In capitalist economies the transfer of property from the state to the private sector is facilitated by institutions such as banks, financial markets, commercial and legal codes, and accounting procedures. These institutions reduce the transactions costs of privatization, speed its implementation and help make it durable. State policies determine the responsibility of the state in carrying out privatization. Typically, the state is the initiator of privatization. It manages the transfer of a SOE to the private sector and retains responsibility for privatization. However, a state-managed approach to privatization assumes the state's policies will be credible and time-consistent. It also assumes the state is the recognized owner of the property and assets to begin with.

Privatization in the post-communist economies is qualitatively and quantitatively different from privatization in the capitalist economies. The institutional infrastructure is either non-existent or ossified, and the ability of the state to promote privatization, especially in an environment of emerging and unstable democracy, is uncertain. The task of privatization is extensive because thousands of large SOEs remain from the Soviet-type economy. These SOEs are autarkic, inefficient to the point of being characterized as 'negative value added', riddled by malinvestments and unresponsive to consumer demand. Geographic distortions compound these economic problems. In many locales citizens depend on a single factory for their livelihoods and view privatization as a threat. Notwithstanding the profound political and social problems and the enormity of the task, the need for privatization is clear. However, privatization experience from countries such as Great Britain makes for a mostly useless blueprint.

In response to the question, 'which strategies will be the most effective and rapid for the post-communist economies?', the three methods most often proposed are capital privatization, liquidation and mass privatization. Capital privatization converts a SOE to a joint stock corporation and distributes the equity to the private sector. Candidate firms – those evaluated by the state as the most viable in a competitive economy – undergo a period of restructuring to make them more commercially attractive to potential buyers. Following restructuring, equity shares are distributed, usually through direct sales, auctions or preferential allocations (for example, to managers and workers). The most commonly cited advantage of capital privatization is that it allows the scope and pace of privatization to be managed by the state, thus avoiding failures that might jeopardize the entire privatization program. It also raises revenue for the budget and ostensibly ensures the correct valuation of the SOE. There are disadvantages with capital privatization as well. Candidate SOEs must be privatized on a case-by-case basis. This limits the number of firms that can be privatized at one time and prolongs the period of privatization. Depending on the complexity of the transaction, this may be of several years' duration. For example, in Great Britain it took 11 years to privatize some 18 SOEs. Capital privatization is also relatively costly because it requires considerable assistance from business and legal consultancies. In addition, it is hindered by limited domestic investable funds, an often risk-averse citizenry and immature equity markets. Finally, during the period of restructuring, the state still retains ownership over the SOE and there is the potential for continued subsidization and similar 'soft budget constraint' problems.

Liquidation is defined by the distribution methods used. These include auctions, direct sales, management and employee buy-outs and leasing. The initiative to privatize usually originates with individuals in the SOE or with local and regional governments. The advantages of liquidation vary with the distribution method used. Management or employee buy-outs overcome political opposition to privatization especially if de facto (implicit) property rights are acknowledged. Auctions help reveal the subjective valuations (opportunity cost) of state assets and make distribution more transparent. Leasing helps surmount shortages of loanable funds and avoids permanent assignments of property that may be subject to competing claims. Liquidation has proved to be an especially useful and rapid method for privatizing retail establishments and small businesses. The disadvantages of liquidation include problems with applying it to larger SOEs and in designing the most transparent and competitive distribution methods possible. Liquidation is criticized because it appears the new owners (especially 'insiders') are acquiring collectively owned property at less than the true value. Because of the fear that many former members of the communist bureaucracy will be among the prime beneficiaries, liquidation is suspected of being merely another example of the discredited phenomenon of 'privatization by the bureaucracy' (Levitas and Strzalkowski, 1990).

Mass privatization is proposed as a way to promote rapid privatization while addressing concerns of fairness and justice. Under this method vouchers are distributed to citizens at no cost or at a nominal fee. The vouchers are used to bid for shares of the enterprises assigned to a pool of candidate SOEs. Bidding continues until the market clears. The vouchers are then converted into shares which can be traded in equity markets. The advantages of mass privatization include speed, the number of firms involved, widespread participation and fairness. Mass privatization also alleviates valuation problems and shortages of investable funds. The major disadvantage is its complexity. It requires a set of procedures that are understandable by all the participants. Because of these logistical problems, the use of financial intermediaries (like mutual funds) is proposed. Citizens would initially hold shares in the intermediaries and not in the enterprises. Early on, the intermediaries would relieve corporate control problems by serving as active investors. However, incentive-compatible contracts must be reached with the intermediaries to ensure their activities are congruent with the emergence of a market economy.

In the post-communist economies most of the authority and responsibility for privatization has been reserved by the state. It determines which privatization methods shall be used, approves the candidate SOEs and manages the privatization process through agencies such as the privatization ministry. The state-managed approach to privatization presumes that the state can collect the right information about SOEs, for example the relative valuation of the firm's assets. But as Frydman and Rapaczynski (1990, p. 13) note, privatization 'must place the burden of valuation on those parties which, like an ordinary investor in a market economy, will bear the consequences of their own decisions, since only the parties in this position can rely on their subjective estimates, without having to explain their reasons to ... anyone else'. Privatization in the post-communist economies is a process through which dispersed subjective knowledge about thousands of assets must be coordinated. As a result, planning and ex ante coordination by the state is likely to impede privatization just as it has impeded other market processes.

Underlying state-managed privatization is the idea of the state as a neutral agent or as a benevolent despot. If the right information can be acquired, the state can use it in a manner consistent with the objective. This presumption sidesteps the structure of political incentives. As both Mises (1983) and the public choice literature illustrate, the incentives of rational agents in political institutions lead to rent-seeking activities. Wealth transfers take precedence over wealth creation. Consequently, regardless of the intentions of the state's bureaucrats, any state-managed privatization program is constrained not only in an informational sense but also in an institutional sense and is therefore of limited effectiveness in promoting privatization.

Given the inherent weaknesses of state-managed privatization in post-communist economies, Austrian theory can contribute to privatization theory in at least four areas. First, private ownership of the means of production must continue to be supported on more than efficiency grounds alone. Efficiency, by itself, leaves a door open for continued intervention (which can impede privatization) and represents only a partial justification for private property being essential for economic progress. Second, the activities of the state must be defined in terms of abstract and general rules that promote privatization, not planning. This applies especially to enforcement of contracts, and to procedures though which privatization claims can be registered.

Third, Austrians should emphasize the need for experimental and evolutionary approaches to privatization rather than ex ante 'solutions' and constructivism. Privatization strategies that rely on design are not equivalent to those that rely on spontaneous order. All roads do not lead to Rome. It is ironic that, at the same time that the Austrian theory of socialism is being vindicated, a renaissance of economic intervention is appearing in the guise of economic transition policies (including privatization). Austrians must question whether privatization is establishing market outcomes or prolonging and strengthening state–enterprise relationships.

Fourth, Austrians should examine the conversion of de facto (implicit) property rights to de jure (explicit) rights. The idea that there are no property rights in the post-communist economies is fiction. To assume that some rights are poorly defined and fuzzy is very different from assuming that all rights reside with the central government. Under communism de facto property rights resulted in residual control rights exercised over property (the theoretical basis for this is provided by Polanyi, 1951, and Roberts's, 1971, work on economic organization). These control rights were held primarily by ministry bureaucrats and SOE managers. More recently, because of reforms, these rights have reverted more to workers, SOE managers and local governments (Schleifer and Vishny, 1992). State-managed privatization threatens to expropriate these rights; this 'disregards legal rights and ... does not aim at creating a revelation mechanism so that implicit rights could be taken into account' (Gligorov, 1992, p. 50). Not only does this create political problems, including the threats of renationalization and using privatization as a way to remedy past injustices, it ignores a foundation on which property rights can be developed.

Spontaneous privatization is one approach to privatization which might benefit from Austrian analysis. Spontaneous privatization occurs when an individual establishes control over a state asset with little or no government coordination. It encourages the discovery and revelation of the value of state assets by rational and self-interested agents who direct those assets to higher valued uses in response to anticipated profit opportunities. In general, spontaneous privatization looks similar to liquidation, only with fewer restrictions. There is already considerable evidence of spontaneous privatization, especially in the former Soviet Union. Even prior to the establishment of a formal privatization program, SOE managers are actively acquiring more control rights over assets and establishing different contractual forms over those assets (Johnson, 1991).

In order for spontaneous privatization to be understood it needs to be appraised on grounds other than efficiency. For example, spontaneous privatization is often equated with theft. While outright theft could be thought of as a type of spontaneous privatization, so too could liquidation, a legitimate method of distributing state assets. Like any market process, spontaneous privatization will operate most effectively within a framework of enforceable and general rules. Transparent procedures will allow the veil of illegality to be removed from spontaneous privatization and a system of dispute resolution to emerge. With the exception of conflict of interest clauses, there should be no prohibitions on participation by any members of society or foreigners. Conversely, the legal loopholes through which members of the former bureaucracy were able to accumulate property rights without diminishing their bundle of political entitlements must be closed. As Błaszczyk and Gruszecki (1991, p. 12) note, 'spontaneous privatization, unlike [privatization by the bureaucracy], does not entail any preferential treatment'. Undoubtedly, litigation will result from acts of spontaneous privatization; this is to be expected and should assist in the development of a body of property law.

Spontaneous privatization, by nature a rivalrous process, should be structured to encourage competition wherever possible. It should assist any individual SOE to initiate privatization but, absent its participation, spontaneous privatization should provide an entry mechanism for either domestic or foreign entities. Obviously, there is some trade-off between competition and recognition of de facto rights. Spontaneous privatization should help reconcile competing claims and implicit property rights within SOEs by providing a vehicle through which de jure rights can be formally established. In addition, spontaneous privatization may rapidly stimulate development of traditional roles of management, labor and ownership. In the post-communist economies this is an important sociological prerequisite for a market economy. The authority over spontaneous privatization can be devolved to local levels. The advantages of this decentralized distribution are that it allows political considerations to be incorporated (for example, it allows local authorities to decide how vigorously they want to pursue foreign buyers), it localizes responsibility and authority, and encourages experimentation. The objective of spontaneous privatization is to speed privatization and keep the state's discretion to a minimum.

See also:
Chapter 15: Entrepreneurship; Chapter 49: Interventionism; Chapter 39: Legal philosophy

Bibliography
Błaszczyk, Barbara and Tomasz Gruszecki (1991), *Privatization in Poland: Laws and Institutions, April 1990–January 1991*, Warsaw: The Stefan Batory Foundation.
Frydman, Roman and Andrzej Rapaczynski (1990), 'Markets and Institutions in Large Scale Privatizations', mimeo, New York University.
Gligorov, Vladimir (1992), 'Justice and Privatization', *Communist Economies and Economic Transformation*, **4**, (1), 45–58.
Johnson, Simon (1991), 'Spontaneous Privatization in the Soviet Union. How, Why and for Whom?', Working Paper 91, World Institute for Development Economics Research, Helsinki: United Nations University, September.
Hanke, Steve H. (1987), 'Privatization', in John Eatwell, Murray Milgate and Peter Newman (eds), *The New Palgrave: a Dictionary of Economics*, vol. 3, London: Macmillan, pp. 976–7.
Levitas, Anthony and Piotr Strzalkowski (1990), 'What Does "Uwłaszczenie Nomenklatury"

(Propertisation of the Nomenklatura) Really Mean?', *Communist Economies and Economic Transformation*, **2**, (3), 413–16.

Mises, Ludwig von (1983), *Bureaucracy*, Cedar Falls, Iowa: Center for Futures Education.

Polanyi, Michael (1951), *The Logic of Liberty*, Chicago: University of Chicago Press.

Roberts, Paul Craig (1971), *Alienation and the Soviet Economy*, Albuquerque: University of New Mexico.

Schleifer, Andrei and Robert W. Vishny (1992), 'Privatization in Russia: First Steps', Conference on Transition in Eastern Europe, February, National Bureau of Economic Research, Cambridge, Mass.

PART IV

HISTORY OF THOUGHT AND ALTERNATIVE SCHOOLS AND APPROACHES

A   Classic debates

66 The Methodenstreit

Samuel Bostaph

The conflict that is known to historians of economic thought as 'The Methodenstreit' was a debate concerning the methods and morphology of economics in which the primary participants were Carl Menger (1840–1921) and Gustav von Schmoller (1838–1917). It was inconclusive at the time and notable for the vitriolic nature of the language used by the contending parties. In addition, for the remainder of his life Menger was so preoccupied with the issues raised in the dispute, as well as with associated considerations, that he never completed the writing and publication of either a promised general economic treatise or one on economic method.

History of the debate

Menger began the debate with the publication of his *Untersuchungen ueber die Methode der Socialwissenschaften und der Politischen Oeconomie insbesondere* in 1883. This was 12 years after publishing his *Grundsaetze der Volkswirtschaftslehre* – the book that was to make his name and open a path to the prestigious economic theory chair at the University of Vienna. In the *Untersuchungen* Menger presented an argument against the concept of economics as an historically based discipline to be pursued solely by the application of an 'historical method' as, he contended, was the view among members of the German historical school. He also presented his own views on the nature, problems and limits of the discipline, as well as on the question of the methodology appropriate to both natural and social sciences and to each of the major divisions of political economy (theory, policy and finance).

It is not known exactly why Menger chose to attack the historical school, of which Schmoller was the leader and primary spokesman at the time. Menger's *Grundsaetze* had been dedicated to Wilhelm Roscher, the founder of the German school, and it had not been poorly or hostilely received by members of either the older or the younger generations of historicist scholars, although it certainly had not been hailed as the pathbreaking contribution to economic theory that it was. Whatever the reason for the subsequent several years of effort that Menger devoted to the *Untersuchungen*, the result was a broad-based attack on the historical method as well as on the historicists' basic conception of political economy as a discipline focused on the study of the economic development of national collectives.

Schmoller's reply to the attack took the form of a severe review in his *Jahrbuch* (1883), expressing strong opposition to key aspects of Menger's criticism of the historicists as well as to what he understood to be Menger's own position. Menger then responded in 1884 with a particularly insulting and cavalier treatment of Schmoller in *Die Irrthuemer des Historismus in der Deutschen Nationaloekonomie*. Schmoller made no rejoinder, instead returning *Die Irrthuemer* to Menger unreviewed. As the Austrian school formed around Menger, Wieser and Böhm-Bawerk in later years, there were sporadic outbreaks of conflict between representatives of the two schools. Thus, from an argument between Menger and Schmoller, the dispute escalated into a general opposition between the Austrian and historical schools, marked by periodic skirmishes.

The explanation of the root of this clash of scholars is by no means as simple a matter as it appears; nor did the conflict much involve personal or sociopolitical elements – although one of the results was that Schmoller's influence was rumored to have largely excluded adherents of the Austrian side of the argument from academic positions in Germany. Surprisingly, the Methodenstreit was not really even fundamentally a dispute over specific methods of economic research, but instead (Bostaph, 1976, 1978) was founded on their organizing and animating principles; that is, it stemmed from basic conflicts in the epistemological and metaphysical foundations of the complex of methods that constituted the respective methodologies of Menger and the historicists. The historical school was primarily informed by Humean nominalism, while Carl Menger is best understood in the context of nineteenth-century Aristotelian/neo-scholasticism. Unfortunately, neither Menger nor Schmoller recognized this and so never debated the most fundamental issues that separated them – their strongly differing theories of concepts, or universals, and of causality. Instead, they concentrated on the more superficial questions of the appropriate branches of economics, the goals, scope and phenomena addressed by each branch, how best to construct economic theory and to what degree the theory of economics provides an understanding of the economic activity from which it is somehow derived. On all these questions their respective answers stemmed from underlying and contrasting epistemological principles that inevitably produced contrasting methodologies. The Methodenstreit actually was the surface representation of the perennial and fundamental opposition between rival epistemological foundations of two basic methodological tendencies, the historical–empirical and the abstract–theoretical.

Historicist epistemology

Wilhelm Roscher (1817–94) was the founder and most important member of the Older Historical School, of which the other two most prominent members were Bruno Hildebrand (1812–78) and Karl Knies (1821–98). Gustav von Schmoller was the leader and primary spokesman for their successors, conventionally grouped under the label the Younger Historical School. There were a number of differences in major beliefs between the two generations; however, they were united in their primarily empiricist and holistic orientation. Both generations argued for the application of a descriptive 'historical method' to the data of history in order to derive economic laws; however, they differed concerning the scope or necessity of those laws.

Roscher argued that absolute laws of economic development could be found by intertemporal and interspatial comparisons between societies, social processes and social institutions. Such laws would be different in nature from the economic laws that would characterize a given 'stage' of a particular society. Such 'short-run' laws would describe the 'physiological' processes of specific economies and thus be relative in space and time, with no claim of universality. Hildebrand and Knies differed with Roscher concerning the 'absoluteness' of such laws of development, but they did not reject his empiricist and holistic method. This use of the same empirically descriptive approach to derive laws differing in their degree of necessity implied epistemological inconsistency – an inconsistency later eschewed by Schmoller, who denied entirely the possibility of any 'absoluteness' in the laws obtained through the descriptive historical method.

Roscher and the older historical school argued for the study of entire 'social organisms', while Schmoller turned to the study of social institutions and their interrelations, and of social processes within national economies. He argued for the observation, description, classification and formation of concepts of these institutions and of their relations as a necessary preparation for describing the 'general essence' of economic phenomena, or general theory. Schmoller's notion of causal relations, like his notion of concept formation, was also descriptivistic; it was directed to the discovery of 'short-run' empirically observed uniformities in the sequence of phenomena. The result would be economic 'laws' relative to, or contingent on, the context within which they were detected. The complex of concepts and laws resulting from the application of this historical method would be the sought-for economic theory – necessarily relative or contingent, as well as 'collectivistic' in nature. The notion of causality that best explains Schmoller's understanding of the epistemological nature of economic concepts, law and resulting theory is that of Humean nominalism. It was this philosophical position that supported his advocacy of an 'historical method' as the sole appropriate means of theory construction and guarantee of its relativity.

Carl Menger's epistemology

In his attack on the historical school, Carl Menger especially opposed the view that there was only one method by which to comprehend economic reality and to produce economic theory. He argued that economic history was only one branch of a discipline that also included economic theory and the practical sciences of economic policy and public finance, and that to claim that the same method was to be used in each was to claim an absurdity. Each subject area was to be pursued by the methods appropriate to research in the particular phenomena at issue and adequate to the goals sought. Menger was especially concerned with the historicists' claims for their method as a means of generating economic theory. By 'economic theory' Menger meant the explanation of the general nature and general connections of economic phenomena, as opposed to the description of the nature and connections of singular or collective individuals that he identified as properly being the subjects of economic history. He argued that economic theory could only be produced by one of two different methods, the 'exact' or the 'realistic–empirical'. Each produced theories that differed in the degree of 'strictness' or 'absoluteness' from the other.

Regularities in the coexistence and succession of phenomena discovered by observing the actual 'types' and 'typical relationships' of phenomena Menger termed 'realistic–empirical' theory, and these were subject to exceptions and to change with time. In a sense, this was the kind of theory that the historicists claimed to be able to discover, although they (and, especially, Schmoller) had a different (and to Menger, faulty) understanding of the way in which a 'type' or a 'typical relationship' was apprehended. On the other hand, regularities in the coexistence and succession of phenomena that were discovered by the 'exact' method admitted no exceptions because of the process of cognition involved in the method itself. Here, Menger presented his most abstract and arcane explanation and one still the subject of considerable differences in interpretation. The one found here is my own and results in the general attribution to Menger of an Aristotelian/neo-scholastic epistemology. It is generally agreed that Menger was strongly influenced by Aristotelianism of some sort; it is not agreed how this occurred or to what degree. Some varying views may be found in Smith (1986) and Caldwell (1990). Menger never specifically characterized his epistemology as Aristotelian and made no specific references to Aristotle's writings on either metaphysics or epistemology. Neither did he refer in his own publications to the epistemological writings of contemporary Aristotelian scholars or publish any purely epistemological books or papers.

Menger argued that regularities in the coexistence and succession of phenomena discovered by the 'exact' approach admitted no exceptions because of the process of cognition through which they were revealed. In order to derive 'exact' laws, it was first necessary to establish what were 'typical' phenomena. This was the identification of an essential *defining quality* or 'essence' (*das Wesen*) in individual phenomena *that made possible their recognition* as representatives of that type. In this solution of the problem of concepts, or universals, Menger said he sought the 'simplest' elements of everything real; and then, in the search for economic laws, he sought to isolate them and to use the 'simple elements' so obtained to deduce (1883, p. 61) 'how more complicated phenomena develop from the simplest, in part even unempirical elements of the real world'. Thus Menger sought not only the general knowledge exemplified in 'types', but also that exemplified in 'typical relationships'. He believed that those typical relationships, or general connections between economic phenomena, could be discovered in an 'exact' sense as 'exact' laws. An 'exact' or causal law was an absolute statement of necessity to which, Menger pointed out, exceptions were inconceivable because of the 'laws of thinking'.

An Aristotelian interpretation would be that Menger believed that entities in reality act according to their natures in 'typical' relationships. Thus a concept of an entity, if it embodies the essence of that entity as an instance of a type, will embody its nature. Reasoning which uses those conceptual 'simple elements' will be reasoning that proceeds according to their natures, and will construct (deduce) conceptual systems of causality corresponding to the causality of the real world. This is because the causal connection exists and is to be detected between determinate things in existence that have a determinate nature. To apprehend a causal relation is to apprehend this connection *by means of* the determinate things in the connection whose actions produce it, and which can only act or be acted upon in accordance with their natures. Thus conceptual or 'theoretical' causal laws are laws of the real – and, in Menger's words, they are 'absolute'.

It should not be difficult to understand the reaction of Schmoller to Menger's *Untersuchungen*, and to the deductive universalistic theory implied by Menger's 'exact' approach, given Schmoller's strong empiricistic orientation and fundamental rejection of any more abstraction from the whole empirical complexity of economic phenomena (as they occur in specific social contexts) than is pragmatically necessary. On the other hand, Menger refused to grant full theoretical status to any theory generated by an historical method because he held theories of concepts and causality that differed from those of the historical school. The essences of economic phenomena with which he was concerned were 'atomistic' general 'types' and their logically derivative 'typical' causal relationships; they were not the collectivistic individuals, and their contingent relations, of interest to the historicists. He had no use for a 'holistic' and contextual approach and refused to grant causal status to historicist empirical laws. Likewise, Menger's use of the 'simple element' of self-interest and his monocausal approach was unacceptably 'unrealistic' to Schmoller, who believed economic behavioral motives to be multitudinous, as were the causal influences in any empirical context.

See also:
Chapter 5: Aristotelianism, apriorism, essentialism; Chapter 2: Methodological individualism; Chapter 28: Self-organizing systems; Chapter 30: Spontaneous order

Bibliography
Bostaph, S. (1976), 'Epistemological Foundations of Methodological Conflict in Economics: The Case of the Nineteenth Century Methodenstreit', unpublished PhD dissertation, Southern Illinois University at Carbondale.

Bostaph, S. (1978), 'The methodological debate between Carl Menger and the German Historicists', *Atlantic Economic Journal*, 6, (3), September, 3–16.

Caldwell, B. (1990), *Carl Menger and His Legacy in Economics*, Durham, NC: Duke University Press.

Grassl, W. and B. Smith (1986), *Austrian Economics: Historical and Philosophical Background*, New York: New York University Press.

Menger, C. (1871), *Grundsaetze der Volkswirtschaftslehre*, translated (1950) as *Principles of Economics*, ed. J. Dingwall and B.F. Hoselitz; reprinted, New York: New York University Press, 1981.

Menger, C. (1883), *Untersuchungen ueber die Methode der Socialwissenschaften und der Politischen Oekonomie insbesondere*, translated (1963) as *Problems of Economics and Sociology*, ed. Louis Schneider; reprinted, New York: New York University Press, 1985.

Menger, C. (1884), *Die Irrthuemer des historismus in der Deutschen Nationaloekonomie*, Vienna: Alfred Hoelder.

Menger, C. (1889), 'Grundzuege einer klassifikation der wirtschaftswissenschaften', *Jahrbuecher fuer Nationaloekonomie und Statistik*, n.s., 19, 465–96, translated (1960), as 'Toward a systematic classification of the economic sciences', in *Essays in European Economic Thought*, ed. Louise Sommer, Princeton: Van Nostrand, pp. 1–38.

Schmoller, G. von (1883), 'Zur methodologie der Staats- und sozialwissenschaften', *Schmollers Jahrbuch fuer Gesetzgebung, Verwaltung und Volkswirtschaft*, 7, 975–94. This article was reprinted, with minor changes, as 'Die schriften von K. Menger und W. Dilthey zur methodologie der staats-und sozialwissenschaften', in G. von Schmoller, *Zur Litteraturgeschichte der Staats- und Sozialwissenschaften*, Leipzig: Duncker and Humblot, 1888; reprinted, Bibliography and Reference Series, No. 169, New York: Burt Franklyn, 1968.

Schmoller, G. von (1893), *Die Volkswirtschaft, die Volkswirtschaftslehre und ihre Methode*, reprinted, Frankfurt: Vittorio Klosterman, 1949.

Smith, Barry (1986), 'Austrian Economics and Austrian Philosophy', in W. Grassl and B. Smith (eds) (1986), pp. 1–36.

67 The debate between Böhm-Bawerk and Hilferding

Peter Rosner

The debate between Böhm-Bawerk and Hilferding concerned Karl Marx's theory of value and surplus value. Böhm-Bawerk was the plaintiff (1896), Rudolf Hilferding the defendant (1904). Although Böhm-Bawerk explicitly denied that a scientific refutation of Marx's theory of value and surplus-value is tantamount to a refutation of socialist ideas, this discussion had political overtones. An English translation of Böhm-Bawerk's essay appeared as early as 1898; Hilferding's reply was translated around 1919. They were made easily accessible, together with articles by Bortkiewicz on the transformation problem, by Sweezy in 1949.

Marx's economic theory was widely discussed in the 1880s and 1890s in Germany, Austria and Italy, particularly after Frederick Engels had published the second volume of *Das Kapital* in 1885. In his foreword, Engels already pointed to the problem that capital of equal size but unequal organic composition will earn different amounts of profit, if commodities are exchanged according to labor values. He promised that a solution to this problem would be provided in the third volume of *Das Kapital*, and asked all those who argued against the labor theory of value to compete with Marx by providing their own solution before the publication of the third volume. Articles and books dealing with the question whether the labor theory of value can be reconciled with the equilibrium condition in the capital market, namely that equal amounts of capital should earn equal profits, appeared in the years before the publication of the third volume in 1894 (see note 3 of Böhm-Bawerk, 1896). Immediately after the publication of the third volume, Marx's own solution was approvingly applauded by his adherents as final proof that his theory was a correct theory of the capitalist society, whereas his opponents considered the third volume as Marx's own rejection of his labor theory of value put forward in the first volume.

Most of the early articles on the value–price problem stuck closely to the concepts of Marx: that is, prices were argued to be solely determined by costs in the long run. The first important article on this problem which was firmly based on the then modern value theory was 'Zum Abschluß des Marxschen System' by Böhm-Bawerk, who had already discussed Marx's theory in his *Geschichte und Kritik der Kapitalzinstheorien* (1884) and in an article in

1890. A second, but less important, article on the third volume of *Das Kapital* from a modern perspective was published by Johann von Komorzynski (1896), like Böhm-Bawerk a pupil of Menger. Böhm-Bawerk put forward against Marx's theory of value and surplus value arguments which remained prominent in the discussions on Marx in the decades following. His central theme is the relationship between labor values (vol. I of *Das Kapital*) and prices (vol. III). He not only worked out that relative prices cannot be proportional to labor values – this was a fact which Marx had stated himself – but attacked all arguments of Marx that labor values are important for the determination of prices. He further wanted to elaborate where and why Marx, whom he considered to be an important thinker, went theoretically astray.

Hilferding's defense of Marx's theory moved the discussion of Marxian economics away from the problem of the determination of relative prices. His refutation of Böhm-Bawerk's critique served for decades, together with Nicolai Bukharin's *The Economic Theory of the Leisure Class* (1919) as the most important Marxist appraisal of the subjective value theory. His arguments remained topical for Marxists for decades. Böhm-Bawerk mentioned Hilferding's reply only in a footnote in the third edition of his *Geschichte und Kritik der Kapitalzinstheorien*, in which he stated that Hilferding had not made him alter his view.

Böhm-Bawerk's article (1896) begins with a short exposition of the theory of value and surplus value. He uses Marx's own words as far as possible and quotes *Das Kapital* extensively. According to this exposition the problems of relative prices and of the distributional shares are at the center of Marx's theory. In the second chapter, the theory of average profits and production prices as developed by Marx in the third volume is examined. It is shown that, in general, relative prices cannot be proportional to labor values and that there is in *Das Kapital* no theory to determine the profit rate. Marx's cost prices are therefore essentially the same as Adam Smith's natural prices. In the third chapter, Böhm-Bawerk evaluates the arguments in favor of the labor theory of value, which were put forward by Marx in spite of his knowledge that prices cannot be proportional to labor values. These arguments were: (1) aggregate values equal aggregate prices; (2) the law of values determines the movement of prices; (3) commodities were valued according to labor values in pre-capitalist market societies, when the immediate producers owned the means of production; and (4) aggregate surplus value equals aggregate profits. That Marx used these arguments is shown through quotations. Böhm-Bawerk then scrutinizes these four arguments in turn. First, since the problem of values is that of relative prices, the statement that aggregate values equal aggregate prices is meaningless, for it does not convey any information on relative prices. Marx's argument that on the average the price of a commodity equals its value is meaningless as well, as the average of deviations of prices from values taken over different kinds of goods is a pure arithmetical average without any economic content. Second, because the amount of labor necessary to produce a commodity is an important influence on its price, it does not follow that labor values determine values, as prices depend on the amount of capital necessary to produce a commodity as well. Third, in the case where the immediate producers own the means of production and there is no separation of classes, capital has to be rewarded too. This is due to the fact that, contrary to Marx's assertion, it does matter to the producers when the results of the combined effort of their labor and the means of production are rewarded. Furthermore, there is no proof that at any time commodities were valued according to labor values. Marx's argument that values are logically and historically prior to prices is on both accounts wrong. Finally, if values are proportional to the necessary amount of labor, the wage rate has no influence on values, as Marx emphasized again and again. However, it can be shown by simple arithmetic that a redistribution of income between workers and capitalists affects prices, as wage goods have to be valued by production prices. There is therefore no direct connection between aggregate prices, if one considers this aggregate to be identical with aggregate value, and the total surplus value. This aggregate therefore is different from total profits.

In the fourth chapter of his essay, Böhm-Bawerk evaluates the way Marx argues the labor theory of value in the first volume of *Das Kapital*: (1) he criticizes Marx for not trying to argue his case empirically or by referring to motives of human valuations as a basis for actions of exchange. To do so, it would have been necessary to inquire into the valuations of goods, something which Marx abhorred. However, besides excluding all goods which are not produced but nevertheless fetch positive prices, Marx relied on dialectical a priori reasoning which helped to exclude use values from any consideration of value. (2) The labor theory of value faces the problem that labor is not homogeneous. Marx argued that skilled labor is simple labor intensified. Böhm-Bawerk shows that this argument results in circular reasoning. The very standard by which skilled labor is to be reduced to embodied simple labor in the Marxian system was itself determined by exchange relations rather than determining them. In other words, Marx took as given what it was he set out to explain. (3) Marx's argument against taking demand and supply into consideration to the effect that, whenever demand equals supply, the two forces cancel each other out, is rejected by Böhm-Bawerk's pointing out the usefulness of equilibrium constructs in other sciences. In a fifth and final chapter, Werner Sombart's defence of Marx's theory, which appeared after the third volume had been published, is critically examined.

Hilferding conceded in his answer that Böhm-Bawerk's essay is the only one on Marx's theory, after the publication of the third volume, whose arguments are based on a coherent theory – the Austrian theory of value. But precisely because of this theoretical basis, Böhm-Bawerk is unable to grasp the essential points of Marx's analysis. His failure was not to consider the goods which are exchanged to be products of social labor, but to think of subjective valuations as being decisive for values. The individual is at the centre of Böhm-Bawerk's analysis, whereas for Marx the society as a whole, of which individuals are members, has to be looked at.

Because of this general point of reference for economic analysis, use values have no part to play. They only characterize an individual relationship between a commodity and an individual, and do not allow one to analyse the social relationships of human beings, which are twofold in modern societies. On the one hand, individuals exchange goods as products of their labor, because society is characterized by the division of labor and is bound together through exchange of commodities in markets. Individuals therefore approach each other as producers of commodities in markets. On the other hand, the society is a capitalist society, which means that commodities are not exchanged as products of independent individuals who meet in the market, but as products of capital employing workers by hiring labor power and therefore exploiting the workers. The labor theory of value was therefore never meant to be a theory of relative prices. Only the change in values over time can be argued for with the labor theory. Hilferding rejected Böhm-Bawerk's rebuttal that this is not a proper argument for the labor theory of value by pointing to the social character of all labor and of all change in labor productivity. The same argument is put forward against Böhm-Bawerk's critique of Marx's concept of simple labor intensified.

Böhm-Bawerk was right in pointing to the fact that relative prices could never be proportional to labor values since commodities were exchanged as products of capital, but this was no argument against Marx's theory, as he was well aware. Hilferding then goes on to argue against Böhm-Bawerk's four points. First, aggregate value is a meaningful concept as it is necessary to have such an aggregate to calculate the share of profits (and wages) – for Marxist political economy an important aspect. The Austrian theory of value could never provide such a calculation. Second, by claiming that a change in labor productivity changes values, Marx never meant to state that prices are proportional to labor values. Third, it is wrong to say that Marx assumed that workers who own the means of production do not have to value them. Böhm-Bawerk forgets the difference between capitalist and pre-capitalist market societies. In the latter, neither the differences in the organic composition of capital between different sectors of production nor the differences in the circulating time of capital were great and so they did not matter. It is therefore appropriate to assume that commodities were exchanged at prices which were not too different from labor values. Finally, it is true that the real wage affects relative prices – Hilferding himself constructs some examples of this fact – but this has nothing to do with values as the latter, according to Marx, must be independent of wages – the variable capital. Otherwise no law governing the shares of labor and capital can be calculated. One would be thrown back on Smith's theory of the natural price. But it was precisely the intention of Marx to overcome this defect of Smith's theory. The identification of aggregate surplus value with aggregate profits is the basis on which to calculate the income shares.

In the final part of his essay, Hilferding returns to basic differences between Marxist and subjective theory – which is labeled as being bourgeois. Whereas Marx and the Marxists consider society as a fundamental concept of economics, because all individuals and all human action can only be understood when seen as a part of society, the subjective theory of value can never understand the concept of society and consequently fails to understand that labor is the basic activity as nobody could survive without somebody working. The labor theory of value therefore does not rest on the subjective valuation of time spent working but serves as the basis for the materialistic approach to human society.

The beginning of the discussion between Marxist economists and the Austrian school also marked the end of that discussion. They spoke about completely different problems and this situation has remained until today. Böhm-Bawerk stressed the problem of relative prices and the importance of capital being scarce. This problem could not be handled without a theory of demand, which naturally was considered to be based on a theory of subjective valuations. This was anathema to Hilferding, as it has been to most Marxists since, as well as to some non-Marxist sympathizers of radical economics (for example, Robinson, 1950). According to them, to begin the analysis with independent individuals, as the Austrian school does, means the neglect of the social relations of these individuals and will therefore result in a static theory. Such a theory will not only give a false picture of the real world but serve a conservative cause as well, as it does not exhibit inner contradictions of the capitalist society and the tendencies which make a change of social relations necessary. Naturally, this point did not interest Böhm-Bawerk or any of his followers.

See also:
Chapter 31: Capital theory; Chapter 12: Marginal utility; Chapter 22: The Austrian theory of price; Chapter 18: Marginal productivity; Chapter 74: Marxisms and market processes

Bibliography
Böhm-Bawerk, Eugen von (1884), *Geschichte und Kritik der Kapitalzinstheorien*, Innsbruck.
Böhm-Bawerk, Eugen von (1896), 'Zum Abschluß des Marxschen Systems', in Otto von Boenigk (ed.), *Staatswissenschaftliche Arbeiten*, Festgabe für Karl Knies, Berlin.

Hilferding, Rudolf (1904), 'Böhm-Bawerks Marx-Kritik', in M. Adler and R. Hilferding (eds), *Marx-Studien*, vol. 1, Vienna.
Komorzynski, Johann von (1896), 'Der Dritte Band von Carl Marx' "Das Kapital"', *Zeitschrift für Volkswirtschaft, Sozialpolitik und Verwaltung*, 6.
Robinson, Joan (1950), 'Karl Marx and the Close of his System', *Economic Journal*, 60, 358–63.
Sweezy, Paul M. (ed.) (1949), *Karl Marx and the Close of his System By Eugen von Böhm-Bawerk's and Böhm-Bawerk's Criticisms of Marx By Rudolf Hilferding*, New York: Augustus M. Kelley Publishers.

68 The Hayek–Keynes macro debate

William N. Butos

The chronology

The Hayek–Keynes 'macroeconomic' debate was joined with Hayek's 'Reflections on the Pure Theory of Money of Mr. J.M. Keynes' in August of 1931. The review, a scathing attack on volume one of Keynes's *Treatise on Money*, was followed by Keynes's 'Reply' and Hayek's 'Rejoinder' in November of 1931, the second part of Hayek's 'Reflections' in February of 1932, and a series of letters from December to March.

The *Treatise*, published in December of 1930, preceded by just two months the sensation created by Hayek's University of London lectures, published the following September as *Prices and Production*. Though both dealt with issues central to business cycle theory and claimed to be building on Wicksellian foundations, they reached strikingly different conclusions. During the early 1930s economists felt obliged to decide which was right. It was by all accounts 'quite a drama' (Hicks, 1967, p. 203).

The context

Hayek and Keynes conducted their debate at a very abstract, technical level and directed it towards specialists in monetary theory. Keynes, whose earlier work in economics dealt mainly with international policy questions, intended the *Treatise* to be 'a definitive treatment of money which would confirm his stature as a serious academic scholar' (Dimand, 1988, p. 23). Hayek, the newly appointed Tooke professor at The London School of Economics, was eager to introduce to a British audience recent contributions by Swedish and Austrian economists in the theory of fluctuations. For Hayek this meant presenting the 'Wicksell–Mises' theory of the business cycle and the Austrian theory of capital.

The debate revealed deep and pervasive differences in the views of Hayek and Keynes concerning the operation of a market economy. They did not resolve these differences during their lives. Although some contemporary scholars propose a kind of synthesis of Hayek and Keynes on the grounds that they embraced 'subjectivism' and held similar theories of the cyclical downswing, Keynes (1973, p. 265) probably had it right when he remarked that between him and Hayek 'the abyss yawns'. The terrain of their debate was monetary theory, but its substance was the self-adjusting and coordinating properties of a market economy. On these foundational issues, they never agreed. For Hayek, his cycle theory analyses the inflationary consequences of the policies he accuses Keynes and his followers of advocating.

The debate over the *Treatise*

Keynes intended the *Treatise on Money* as a contribution to business cycle theory. He believed its theoretical core involved a 'novel means of approach' that would reveal the characteristics of a monetary system in disequilibrium and uncover the 'dynamical laws governing the passage of a monetary system from one position of equilibrium to another'. Regarding the book's policy significance, Keynes simply avers that properly understood it 'is of enormous practical importance to the well-being of the world' (1971, pp. xvii–xviii).

Keynes's 'novel approach' involved using the Wicksellian savings–investment framework to claim that aggregate income would rise or fall depending on whether savings were greater or less than investment. In the *Treatise*, Keynes defines the discrepancy between ex post savings and investment as unanticipated profits (Q), and it is these positive or negative 'windfalls' that drive the economy. If Q equals zero, entrepreneurs' expectations are satisfied and no changes in planned production for the next period are called for; the economy is in steady state equilibrium with stable prices and full employment. If savings exceed investment (and thus $Q < 0$), the *Treatise*'s model calls for a cumulative contraction to occur because income will not be sufficient to purchase aggregate output at prices which cover costs. The disequilibrium persists, along with increasing unemployment and falling prices and output, unless savings are reduced, investment is increased, or 'all production ceases' (1971, p. 160). Keynes omits the role of any self-correcting mechanisms endogenous to the system or, as in the case of real balance effects, dismisses them as unimportant.

In broad outline, the argument of the *Treatise* is not unlike that of *The General Theory* and the relation between the two is what Keynes (1936, p. vi) calls 'a natural evolution in a line of thought'. The insufficiency of aggregate demand (specifically investment) and the failure of intertemporal markets to coordinate plans effectively are prominent motifs in both works (see Garrison, 1985). While Keynes introduces in *The General Theory* the consumption function (and Kahn's multiplier) and his theory of involuntary unemployment, his treatment of expectations most sharply reflects the evolution of his thought. Expectations are not absent from the *Treatise*, but their importance is played down because their instability is confined to the very short run. In *The General Theory*, on the other hand, short-run expectations are stable but long-run expectations are not. Despite these differences, Keynes's essential message and vision is clear enough: a decentralized market system is subject to chronic instabilities and does not contain sufficiently robust self-corrective market mechanisms to overcome (or neutralize) these instabilities without third party intervention.

The debate centered on Hayek's claim that Keynes's *Treatise*, especially the core chapters contained in Books III and IV, failed to provide a coherent account of the relationship between savings, investment, output and money. Hayek held that Keynes failed to treat the central problems of monetary theory because, in his use of the Wicksellian savings–investment approach, he ignores its underlying capital-theoretic base. According to Hayek (1931– 2), Keynes failed to acquaint himself 'with the substance of [Böhm-Bawerk's] theory' (p. 280) – 'the most elaborate theory of capital we possess' (p. 279) – or to understand 'those fundamental theorems of "real" economics on which alone any monetary explanation can be successfully built' (p. 270). Hayek railed against Keynes's 'difficult, unsystematic, and obscure' exposition, in which 'the inconsistent use of terms produces a degree of obscurity which ... is almost unbelievable' (p. 271). It is little wonder that Hayek found it 'difficult to suppress some concern as regards the immediate effect which its publication ... may have on the development of monetary theory' (p. 271).

In Part I of the 'Reflections', Hayek's critique centers on the tools and constructs of Keynes's theory and in Part II on Keynes's explanation of the business cycle. Hayek persistently attacks Keynes's central theoretical points and conclusions, including, inter alia, the theory of investment ('the most obscure theme of the book'), the definition of saving, Keynes's 'fundamental equations' for the price levels of output and consumer goods, the theory of asset pricing and, of course, Keynes's account of the trade cycle.

Hayek argues that the *Treatise* was not only unfinished, as Keynes himself admits (1971, p. xviii), but that its theoretical superstructure was unrefined and idiosyncratic. Hayek claims, for example, that Keynes's treatment of aggregate profits as the mainspring of change is misleading. Keynes treats (total) profits as only a monetary phenomenon arising from changes in the direction of money flows and independent of underlying resource misallocation associated with 'relative demand for and supply of cost goods and their respective products' (Hayek, 1931–2, p. 273). Thus, according to Hayek, in treating the process of production as an 'integral whole', Keynes is perforce unable to analyse 'the possibility of fluctuation between ... stages' (p. 274). To illustrate that such refinements make a difference, Hayek provides an example where profits are zero in the aggregate but positive in the lower stages of production (that is, temporally closer to becoming available for consumption) and negative in the higher stages. This structural maladjustment will affect relative prices within the production structure, inducing effects that Keynes claims can only arise if (total) profits are not zero. The irony of Hayek's critique is that the macro-oriented Keynes employs a definition of profits that is suitable when applied to a single entrepreneur but inappropriate and misleading when applied to all entrepreneurs. That 'Mr. Keynes' aggregates conceal the most fundamental mechanisms of change' (p. 277) emerges as a persistent theme in Hayek's critique of the *Treatise*.

The concept fundamental to both Keynes's and Wicksell's analyses is the natural rate of interest, that is, the rate which equates saving and investment. For both Keynes and Wicksell, the significance of the natural rate resides in the consequences of a divergence between it and the market rate. Wicksell and most of his followers examine the inflation case of a positive deviation (lagging or lowered market rate); Keynes in the *Treatise* is primarily concerned with the deflation case of a negative deviation. Keynes's attempt to align his analysis with Wicksell's draws criticism from Hayek. First, Hayek contends that Keynes employs a peculiar conception of savings, implying that Keynes's equilibrium rate had to be different from Wicksell's. Keynes alters the 'ordinary' definition of savings – the excess of money income over consumption – to also include the shortfall of income accruing to entrepreneurs relative to their 'normal' income. In short, according to Keynes, if entrepreneurs sustained negative profits, they would reduce their consumption (increase their saving) by an equal amount. Since increased saving means reduced demand for consumption goods, 'the cruse becomes a Danaid jar which can never be filled up' since 'the effect of this reduced expenditure is to inflict on the producers of consumption goods a loss of an equal amount' (Keynes, 1971, p. 125).

Hayek rejects Keynes's 'Danaid jar' account as well as the obverse 'widow's cruse' example when profits are spent on consumption goods. For Hayek, an increase in savings would result in a build-up of consumer goods inventories that would serve to maintain consumption while more roundabout production processes are put on line. In contrast to Keynes, Hayek denies that an increase in saving constitutes a net decrease in demand and that investment will not rise to maintain equality with saving. Since Keynes assumes in the *Treatise* that investment decisions depend on anticipated profits and the interest (or bank) rate, an excess of saving or deficiency of investment would seem correctable by a reduction in the market rate of interest corresponding to the now lower natural rate as indicated by the increase in savings. Keynes, however, rules out this coordinating mechanism. He contends that savings are not channeled into investments (what he calls 'securities'); instead, owing to 'excess bearishness', they are hoarded (or, in his terminology, placed in 'bank deposits'), thus impeding the required fall in the market rate of interest (see Keynes, 1971, chapter 15 and pp. xxv–xxvii).

Hayek (1931–2) recognizes the theoretical significance of hoarding and the difficulty of finding a 'practical solution to these problems' (p. 34). He also notes that 'Mr. Keynes' elaboration of this contribution of Mr. Robertson is, in many respects, the most interesting part of his theoretical analysis' and that, in examining the 'relations between bank credit and the stock market', Keynes is 'breaking new ground' and 'has opened up new vistas' (pp. 34–5). Despite this, Hayek argues that Keynes's analysis is still 'not quite clear' and 'his solution of the problem not quite satisfactory' (p. 35) because he makes two questionable assumptions to support the proposition that the prices of securities are solely determined by hoarding. Keynes's first assumption (1971, pp. 224–5) is that the demand for securities is related to their current prices because a fall in their current prices strengthens the expectation of a future price rise. Hayek (1931–2) demurs, noting that 'any fall in the price of securities is just as likely to create a fear of a further fall as the expectation of a rise' (p. 37). Keynes's second assumption claims the banking system is able to determine the size of bank deposits (or the 'quantity of hoards'), a proposition, Hayek argues, requiring that deposits are unrelated to 'the terms on which the banking system is willing to lend' (p. 37). Thus, Hayek contends, Keynes's assumption makes the untenable claim that any 'excess deposits' created by the banking system will necessarily go into 'hoards' without affecting the market rate of interest.

Keynes's treatment carries the significant implication that 'bear speculators' will keep the interest rate above its equilibrium value, thereby depressing the value and volume of new investment. Thus the disequilibrium between the rate of savings and the rate of investment is caused by increased 'bearishness' and is unrelated to the standard Wicksellian assumption of changes in bank credit. Interestingly, in Keynes's 'Reply' to Hayek he insists there is 'no automatic mechanism in the economic system ... to keep the two rates equal' (1973, p. 251). Hayek (1931), however, responds specifically to this assertion by asking if it could 'be extended to the more general contention that there is no automatic mechanism in the economic system to adapt production to any other shift in demand' (p. 401).

In the *Treatise* and *The General Theory*, Keynes's explanation of the business cycle centers on investment instability. In the *Treatise*, the fear of falling prices instigates the disequilibrating role of 'bears'. This is present in *The General Theory* (see chapter 13), but the emphasis in 1936 is on 'the dark forces of time and ignorance which envelop our future' (p. 155) in the context of modern 'organized investment markets' (p. 150) that together cause 'animal spirits' to be vented in undesirable ways. Investment insufficiency and instability complicated by 'bears' keeping interest rates too high render the system susceptible to prolonged periods of 'stable equilibrium ... below full employment' (p. 30). The economy fails because it is unable to coordinate intertemporal plans effectively. While the specifics of Keynes's argument change from the *Treatise* to *The General Theory*, the essential claim in both is that intertemporal markets either do not exist or, if they do, generate perverse outcomes in the form of price deflation or aggregate output reduction.

Keynes largely ignores Hayek's critique that the *Treatise* neglects intertemporal market mechanisms. In his 'Reply' to Hayek's review, Keynes (1973) launches into a prolonged attack on *Prices and Production*, only to admit that capital theory 'would be highly relevant to my treatment of monetary matters' (pp. 252–3). Although he insists that 'there is no such theory at present', Keynes does 'substantially ... concede Dr Hayek's point' and that he will 'later on ... endeavor to make good this deficiency' (p. 253). Keynes, however, chose not to pursue seriously such questions; if anything, he drifted further away from such concerns, so that by 1936 the Wicksellian framework and its supporting capital theory are conspicuous by their absence.

The General Theory and after

Hayek did not specifically respond to *The General Theory*. This decision was based on his belief that *The General Theory* was just 'another tract for the times' whose popularity was sustained by 'momentary needs of policy' (Hayek, 1978, p. 284). But Hayek's withdrawal from the debate may also have been opportune: by the mid-1930s, Hayek's monetary theory and policy positions were losing much of their appeal with the continuing depression and the increasing clamor for more government economic activism. Even if it were true that Hayek had in the early 1930s 'largely demolished [Keynes's theoretical scheme' (ibid. pp. 283–4), it was evident that Keynes was winning decisively the policy battle. Hayek's isolation from an increasingly alien mainstream was surely a factor in persuading Hayek 'not to return to the attack' (ibid. p. 284).

The period following the publication of *The General Theory* and continuing through the postwar years was a time of great intellectual activity for Hayek. Three areas of inquiry – capital theory, 'the knowledge problem' and business cycles – may be briefly highlighted as areas of continuing interest for Hayek after 1936 that bear on questions germane to the debate with Keynes. Hayek, it will be recalled, claims that Keynes's theoretical framework in the *Treatise* is flawed because it lacks a coherent theory of capital. Hayek argues such a theory is essential to analyse the effects of monetary and real disturbances on output. During the 1930s, Hayek's debate with Frank Knight provided the opportunity to extend and refine the Böhm-Bawerkian theory of capital he first used in *Prices and Production*. The capstone of Hayek's efforts, and arguably the definitive treatment of Austrian capital theory, was published in 1941 as *The Pure Theory of Capital*. Regrettably, a planned second volume to extend the theory of capital into the monetary area was never written.

During the 1930s and 1940s, Hayek's papers on 'knowledge' argue that the price system, because it functions efficiently as an information network, enables intertemporal markets to coordinate effectively individuals' plans.

Despite the inevitability of our ignorance resulting from the decentralization of knowledge, the coordination of plans does not require complete knowledge; nor, in contrast to Keynes's view, does incomplete knowledge require markets driven by 'animal spirits'.

Hayek explicitly returns to business cycle theory in a 1939 essay, 'Profits, Interest and Investment'. The essay addresses the dynamic question of how 'cyclical fluctuations, once started, tend to be self-generating, so that the economy may never reach a position which could be described as equilibrium' (1939, p. 6). Hayek's model assumes, in contrast to *Prices and Production*, downwardly inflexible money wages, a fixed market of interest and an economy initially in recession. These new assumptions update his model without changing the theory. O'Driscoll (1977) notes that Hayek's later cycle work contributes significantly to the understanding of cyclical adjustment processes and the 'peculiarly discoordinating aspects of monetary disturbances' (p. 119).

See also:
Chapter 75: Pre-Keynes macroeconomics; Chapter 32: Austrian business cycle theory; Chapter 58: Inflation

Bibliography
Dimand, Robert W. (1988), *The Origins of the Keynesian Revolution*, Stanford: Stanford University Press.
Garrison, Roger W. (1985), 'Intertemporal Coordination and the Invisible Hand: An Austrian Perspective on the Keynesian Vision', *History of Political Economy*, **17**, (2), 309–21.
Hayek, F.A. (1931), 'A Rejoinder to Mr. Keynes', *Economica*, November, 398–403.
Hayek, F.A. (1931–2), 'Reflections on the Pure Theory of Money of Mr. J.M. Keynes', *Economica*, August and February, 270–95 and 22–44.
Hayek, F.A., (1939), *Profits, Interest and Investment*, Clifton, NJ: Augustus M. Kelley Publishers, 1975.
Hayek, F.A. (1978), *New Studies in Philosophy, Economics and the History of Ideas*, Chicago: University of Chicago Press.
Hicks, Sir John (1967), *Critical Essays in Monetary Theory*, Oxford: Clarendon Press.
Keynes, J.M. (1936), *The General Theory of Employment, Interest and Money*, New York: Harcourt Brace Jovanovich, 1964.
Keynes, J.M. (1971), *The Collected Writings of John Maynard Keynes*, Volume 6: *A Treatise on Money*, London: Macmillan.
Keynes, J.M. (1973), *The Collected Writings of John Maynard Keynes*, Volume 13: *The General Theory and After: Part I Preparation*, London: Macmillan.
O'Driscoll, Gerald P., Jr. (1977), *Economics as a Coordination Problem: The Contribution of Friedrich A. Hayek*, Kansas City: Sheed Andrews & McMeel.

69 The socialist calculation debate

Karen I. Vaughn

The socialist calculation debate is an episode in twentieth-century economic thought that has special significance for Austrian economics. On one side of the debate were economists either trained or influenced by the Austrian tradition of Menger, Wieser and Böhm-Bawerk who believed socialism and central planning could not improve upon the economic performance of a regime of private property and free markets. On the other side were professional neoclassical economists who were critical of market economics because of their perceived failures to achieve full employment, equitable income distributions and rational investment and who wished to find some method of central planning that would duplicate the potential efficiency of free markets without suffering their very real shortcomings.

The events of the debate are easily recounted (Vaughn, 1980). It began in 1920 when Ludwig von Mises wrote an article claiming that socialist central planning was inherently irrational and hence impossible to achieve. Mises was answered, directly and indirectly, by neoclassical economists such as H.D. Dickinson, Maurice Dobb, Abba Lerner and Oskar Lange who understood his reasoning but believed they could design a socialist economy that met Mises's objections and would actually improve upon the economic performance of market economies. Friedrich Hayek, Mises's younger colleague, entered the fray in the 1930s and wrote a series of profound critiques of socialism that were largely misunderstood by the opposition. By the mid-1940s, conventional opinion held that Mises had been wrong and socialism was in fact possible, and the Austrians lost the debate. That opinion was to hold for most of the next 40 years, until the disintegration of communism and the obvious economic failures of central planning required a re-evaluation of the Austrian arguments.

Despite the Austrian school's putative defeat, the debate was a watershed event in the development of Austrian economics. What began as a challenge to conventional views about the feasibility of central planning evolved into a debate not only about alternative political and economics institutions, but also about the status and usefulness of neoclassical economic theory itself. During the course of the more than 20 years during which the debate was carried on, Austrian economics underwent a transformation that eventually redefined what Austrian economics meant and what it had to contribute to economic science (Vaughn, 1990). Many of the issues first raised during this debate are unresolved in either the Austrian or the conventional neoclassical literature to this day.

Mises and the old Marxists

The set of writings that were to constitute the debate over economic calculation under socialism were generally responses to Mises's article, 'Economic calculation in the socialist commonwealth' (1920). This article was directed primarily at an audience of older Marxists who, despite their belief in the superiority of conscious control of economic life, were astonishingly unconcerned about the details of actually running a centrally planned economy (Lavoie, 1985, pp. 28ff). Many of them believed it was enough to eliminate private property and money in order to eliminate scarcity. What plans they did advocate for running a socialist society paid little attention to the accounting that would be necessary to make certain that income matched outgoings, let alone to efficient use of resources.

Mises, reiterating arguments made earlier by Wieser and Barone (Hayek, 1935, pp. 245ff) argued that the economic problem of managing scarcity was unavoidable in the real world and would be no less a problem for a socialist as for a capitalist economic order. In a capitalist regime, the way resources were managed was through private property and exchange in markets. The necessary accounting that makes certain that expenditures do not exceed income and that measures in some way the efficiency of resource use, he argued, were market prices. Prices are ratios of exchange values, and hence are necessary to allow people to weigh the relative values of alternatives and to make 'economic' decisions. Not only did Mises assert the importance of prices to making rational economics decisions, he also insisted that the only way in which meaningful prices could be established was in a regime of private property and free exchange. Central planners might try to decree prices for resource management but, unless these prices bore a close relationship to the way individuals value alternative goods, they would be meaningless. And the only way to ensure that prices bore the required relationship to individual judgements of value is to allow them to be established freely in markets. Socialist economy, therefore, was impossible.

Mises not only charged socialism with being unable to establish prices that actually measured relative resource scarcities, he also criticized the ability of central planning to produce the goods and services that needed to be priced. State-run firms, he argued, where managers were neither owners nor responsible to owners, would be riddled with inefficiencies. Without the incentives that flow from property ownership, managers would act irresponsibly with the resources under their direction, tending to take greater risks with the firm's resources than would private managers. There would be little direct accountability to consumers.

To modern ears, Mises's argument might seem incomplete, but it does not seem very radical. Certainly, the claim that prices are necessary for efficient economic choice is well established and that bureaucrats face different incentives from workers in the private sector is by now totally uncontroversial. What seemed intolerable to Mises's contemporaries, however, was his insistence that only free markets and private firms could establish economically meaningful prices and produce wealth efficiently. This was regarded as a gross overstatement of the advantages of the free market. Surely, given the economists' knowledge of mathematics and statistics, it would be possible for prices to be established in some other more 'equitable' way than through the rough and tumble of the market.

The socialist solution
While Mises's argument may not have convinced dyed-in-the-wool Marxists, he did present a challenge to conventional neoclassical economists who understood the necessity of prices for efficient resource allocation but who were also critical of the market failures associated with capitalism. They took it for granted that central planning was the way to correct those failures and concentrated their attention on trying to find ways to duplicate the efficiency of market pricing in socialist regimes.

Some of the proposals were reflections of the economics profession's newly developing romance with mathematics and statistics. Hence several economists (see in particular Dickinson, 1933) proposed variations on the theme of using extensive statistical sampling to estimate demand equations for all relevant goods and, together with estimated production functions, 'solving' for equilibrium prices. They were subject to swift and telling rebuttal by critics, the foremost being Friedrich Hayek. As a professor at the London School of Economics from 1932, Hayek was in the thick of the attempts by socialist economists to resolve the problem of planning. In his response to the proposals to set prices via central planning, Hayek raised issues that were to define the Austrian side of the socialist calculation debate.

Hayek basically had two kinds of arguments against the socialist proposals. The first had to do with the kind of knowledge socialist planners would be able to employ in their decision making and the second had to do with the incentives facing actors in socialist economic institutions. For example, contrary to the 'mathematical solution' to socialist planning, Hayek argued that, in an advanced economy, there are typically hundreds of thousands of products bought and sold every day. Even if it were possible to define all of the products to be priced, it would be a virtual impossibility either to gather enough relevant data to specify the demand and supply equations or to actually solve a system of hundreds of thousands of simultaneous equations (especially without the aid of computers, as was the case in 1930) (Hayek, 1935, pp. 209–13).

While Hayek had a number of other cogent criticisms the socialists took this one to heart immediately. As a consequence, one of their number, Oskar Lange, devised an ingenious system to generate economic prices in a centrally planned economy that did not require widespread statistical data gathering or the solving of numerous simultaneous equations but still yielded equilibrium prices that duplicated the success of the market while setting up an institutional structure that would also guarantee a fairer income distribution than capitalism was capable of achieving.

Lange's trial and error solution

Lange's solution (1939) to the problem of pricing in a centrally planned economy is worth examining for several reasons. First, for over 50 years it was regarded by professional economists as *the* answer to Mises and to the Austrian criticism of rational central planning. Second, it demonstrates in a clear-cut form the way economists understood both the workings of an actual economy and the relationship of economic theory to economic reality. The 'simultaneous equation' solution to pricing under socialism was an attempt to employ the mathematics of Walrasian general equilibrium theory. Lange also attempted to employ Walrasian theory, but from a different perspective. He argued that a socialist economy could be run in the following way. All consumer goods would be bought and sold in private markets, but 'the means of production' would be produced in state firms that would be under the direction of the central planning board (hereafter, CPB). The CPB would communicate a set of prices to the state firms and the firms would be instructed to minimize cost subject to those prices. The brilliance of Lange's plan was that it was irrelevant what the initial prices actually were since the firms would also be instructed to communicate to the CPB any surpluses or shortages of goods. From that information, the CPB, acting as Walras's auctioneer, would either raise or lower price accordingly. Hence, just as in real markets, prices would be the consequence of a 'tâtonnement' or trial and error process that would eventually settle into equilibrium. This obviated the need for detailed statistical knowledge of supply and demand and allowed the CPB to operate effectively on a minimum of information.

Hayek responded to this scheme by raising objections that were later to be recognized as being particularly Austrian insights into the nature of a market economy. He argued first that it would be virtually impossible for a CPB correctly to define all the products that are bought and sold even in capital goods markets. Lange was tacitly assuming all products were objectively definable and easily categorizable. Rather, Hayek argued, capital goods were heterogeneous in nature, often tailored to the individual user. In Lange's scheme, the CPB would set prices, not for real goods that people wish to buy and sell, but statistically tractable aggregates that suited no one in particular (Hayek, 1948, pp. 188–9, 193).

Hayek also argued that the products that people buy and sell are not solely objective entities. There is a large non-material component to goods, involving, for example, ease of availability, quality of service or reputation of supplier, that could not figure in government statistics. Even if goods could be correctly defined, however, Hayek believed that trial and error pricing was still doomed to failure because it could not respond as quickly or in the same way to changes in economic conditions as could individuals operating in decentralized markets. Lange's error was to presume that, once established, equilibrium prices would remain stable for long enough periods of time for CPB prices to be relevant to efficient decision making. At the time, Hayek argued that the socialists suffered from an excessive preoccupation with equilibrium states (1948, p. 188) to the exclusion of consideration of market processes. The implication was that equilibrium was a useful tool for organizing theories about the direction of change of market prices but that, in real life, prices were constantly undergoing a myriad of small adjustments made by actual buyers and sellers in response to changing conditions. Centrally directed trial and error pricing could not duplicate the efficiency of these small adjustments because they would be looking at statistics rather than actual conditions in markets.

This line of argument led Hayek to emphasize the importance of specialized, particularized knowledge for the efficient operation of market systems. The knowledge that is important in markets is not usually scientific, abstract knowledge such as is assumed, for example, in the theory of production functions, but detailed knowledge of 'time and place' that an actor may not even know he possesses until called upon to make a decision. Hayek was later to emphasize even more the role of tacit or inarticulate knowledge in markets, leading Austrians to adopt the 'knowledge problem' as a central concern of their research.

Like Mises before him, Hayek also objected to the cavalier way state firms were imagined to behave under socialism. Hayek also argued that the incentive structure facing state employees was relevant to their behavior and that they would be unlikely to behave in the same way as private workers (1948, pp. 198–9). Where Mises had argued that they would engage in more risky behavior since their own wealth was not at stake, Hayek presented a more convincing picture of state managers who would be loath to take any risk at all for fear that a negative result could not be justified after the fact. He reasoned that all production decisions were based on conjectures about future states of the world that could not be predicted with certainty. Even costs were not objective numbers but the subjectively estimated value of imagined forgone alternatives. Hence, where a manager's decision would be subject to review by a higher and more remote authority, that manager would try to make decisions that could easily be justified according to reportable criteria rather than the decision that seemed more profitable according to his own specialized or personal knowledge.

Despite Hayek's many telling criticisms of market socialism, by the middle of the 1940s the Austrians were considered by the economics profession to have lost the debate. The mainstream of the profession accepted the logical cogency of Lange's plan and regarded Hayek's criticisms as minor complications that in no way undercut the possibility of socialism. It was not until the 1990s, when the Soviet Union imploded, and when formerly communist countries all over the world were trying to reintroduce market economies as quickly as they could, that it was generally conceded that the Austrians had been correct after all in their assessment of the possibility of a centrally planned economy that could match the efficiency of capitalism.

While history may have presented a practical vindication of Mises and Hayek, on the theoretical level, aspects of the debate are still being waged. The heart of the Austrian critique (admittedly only fully articulated even by Austrians in the last decade) is that static equilibrium theory does not capture the important features of real market economies. Not only individual valuations are subjective in nature; so are expectations and the knowledge they hold about the real world. Indeed, Hayek's early conjectures about economics and knowledge have become a primary focus of the modern Austrian school. Similarly, the rejection of static equilibrium as a tool for designing an economic system has led to an investigation of the importance of real time to our understanding of economic theory. The early recognition of the incentives problem in socialist firms led Austrians to question the general relationship between institutions, rules structures and market activity. And finally, Hayek's frustrations during the calculation debate led him to reassert in more modern form the eighteenth-century discovery of markets as essentially unplanned and unplannable social orders, thereby providing Austrians with an articulation of their paradigm. How they will carry that research forward in the future is still to be seen.

See also:
Chapter 4: Market process; Chapter 25: Prices and knowledge; Chapter 14: Competition; Chapter 33: Comparative economic systems

Bibliography
Dickinson, H.D. (1933), 'Price Formation in a Socialist Community', *Economic Journal*, **43**, 237–50.
Hayek, Friedrich A. (1935), *Collectivist Economic Planning*, London: George Routledge & Sons.

Hayek, Friedrich A. (1948), *Individualism and Economic Order*, Chicago: University of Chicago Press.

Lange, Oskar (1939), 'On the Economic Theory of Socialism', in Oskar Lange and Fred M. Taylor (1938), *On the Economic Theory of Socialism*, ed. Benjamin E. Lippincott, New York: Augustus M. Kelley, 1970.

Lavoie, Don (1985), *Rivalry and Central Planning: the Socialist Calculation Debate Reconsidered*, Cambridge: Cambridge University Press.

Mises, Ludwig (1920), 'Economic calculation in the socialist commonwealth', republished in F.A. Hayek, *Collectivist Economic Planning*, London: George Routledge & Sons, 1935, pp. 87–130.

Vaughn, Karen I. (1980), 'Economic calculation under socialism: the Austrian contribution', *Economic Inquiry*, **18**, 535–54.

Vaughn, Karen I. (1990), 'The Mengerian roots of the Austrian revival', in Bruce Caldwell (ed.), *Carl Menger and His Legacy in Economics*, Durham, NC: Duke University Press, pp. 379–407.

B   Precursors and alternatives

70 The late scholastics

Alejandro A. Chafuen

Medieval scholasticism encompassed some seven centuries, from 800 AD to 1500 AD. The twelfth and thirteenth centuries constitute the most widely recognized period of scholastic contributions. The activity of the period from 1350 to 1500 AD is known as Late Scholasticism. In the field of economics the importance of scholastic thought did not wane until the late seventeenth century. The scholastic method examined opposing points of view to deduce an intelligent, scientific solution to relevant problems consistent with accepted authorities, known facts, human reason and Christian faith. Contributions of the late scholastics have been admired and recognized by Austrian school economists and their colleagues such as Murray N. Rothbard (1976), Joseph A. Schumpeter (1954), Raymond De Roover (1955) and Marjorie Grice-Hutchinson (1975).

It is widely believed that the economic contribution of the scholastic period rests principally with the Spanish scholastics, or the 'school of Salamanca'. It is, however, more accurate to describe the contributors as 'late scholastics', since some of the most important authors were not Spanish and many of them studied and taught at non-Hispanic universities. The Hispanic scholastics were deeply influenced by Aristotelic and Thomistic analysis. Key aspects of their theory of the value of economic goods can be attributed to a tradition of analysis which was initiated by St Augustine and continued by St Bernardino of Siena and St Antonino of Florence.

Thomas Aquinas (1226–74) was the foremost scholastic writer. His influence was so widespread that nearly all subsequent schoolmen studied, quoted and commented upon his remarks. The century following produced many scholastic authors whose works relate to economics. St Bernardino of Siena (1380–1444), St Antonino of Florence (1389–1459), Joannis Gerson (1362–1428), Conradus Summenhart (1465–1511) and Sylvestre de Priero (d. 1523) are those most frequently quoted by their successors. The writings of Cajetan (Cardinal Tomás de Vio, 1468–1534) represent the transition between these scholastics and their later Hispanic followers.

Francisco de Vitoria (c. 1480–1560) is often regarded as the founder of the Hispanic scholastics. He belonged to the Dominican order and studied and taught at the University of Paris where he helped edit one of the editions of Aquinas's *Summa Theologica* and the *Summa* of Saint Antonino of Florence. From 1522 to 1546 he taught at the University of Salamanca. Domingo de

Soto (1495–1560), also a Dominican, studied at Alcalá and under Vitoria in Paris. After his return to Spain, he taught at Alcalá and in 1532 was appointed professor of theology at Salamanca. His treatise *De Iustitia et Iure* went through no fewer than 27 editions in 50 years. Dominican Martín de Azpilcueta, 'Dr Navarrus' (1493–1586), regarded as one of the most eminent canon lawyers of his day, taught at Salamanca and Coimbra (Portugal). His *Manual de Confesores y Penitentes* (Azpilcueta, 1553) was one of the most widely used spiritual handbooks in the century, following its publication. Other important Dominican scholastics include Domingo de Bañez (1528–1604). Tomás de Mercado (c. 1500–1575), Francisco García and Pedro de Ledesma.

Franciscans Juan de Medina (1490–1546) and Henrique de Villalobos (d. 1637) employed scholastic sources and methods. Jesuit thinkers such as Luis de Molina (1535–1600), Juan de Mariana (1535–1624), Francisco Suarez (1548–1617), Juan de Salas (1553–1612), Leonardo Lessio (1554–1623), Juan de Lugo (1583–1660), Pedro de Oñate (1567–1646), Juan de Matienzo (1520–79) and Antonio de Escobar y Mendoza (1589–1669) made significant contributions.

Value and price
Nearly all the elements of modern value and price theory figure in the writings of the medieval schoolmen. For the scholastics, the price of goods depends on their ability to serve human utility and on the common estimation that market participants have regarding those goods. St Bernardino explained that water is usually cheap where it is abundant but, where it is extremely scarce, it could well be that water would be more highly valued than gold (Chafuen, 1986).

This utility is not something objective: as Molina said, 'it depends on the relative appreciation which each man has for the use of the good ... and on the fact that some men wanted to grant it value'. The just price was founded on those same principles. Using the price of pearls as an example, Molina argued that 'it is evident that the price that is just for them comes neither from the nature of these things nor their utility, but from the fact that the Japanese took a liking to them and esteemed them in that way' (Chafuen, 1986). The just price was based on common estimation even when it was the result of imprudent or foolish buyers.

For the schoolmen, value in exchange depends on value in use. Nonetheless, this value in use is not an objective quality. Since utility is more closely related to the mood and preference of the consumer (*complacibilitas* in the original Latin) than to the inherent capacity of the good to satisfy human wants (*virtuositas*), the scholastics found no objective way to establish the level of the just price. For this reason their theory of value must be understood as a subjective one. Sylvestre de Priero noted in his *Summa* that the estimation of a good reflects appreciation of it. If it is a productive good (*rei fructuosa*), he added, its price should depend on the revenue (*reditus*) it can produce (Chafuen, 1986). He thus advanced a consistent theory of value for the means of production.

Private property

The late scholastics repeated some of the arguments first presented by Aristotle and then further developed by Aquinas. Private property facilitates orderly production and division of labor, helps mitigate scarcity by encouraging a better use of the resources and promotes peace. According to Vitoria, if all goods are held collectively, 'evil men will take more and add less to the common barn'. Thieves and misers would achieve the highest positions in such society. Above all, the medieval schoolmen favored private ownership because it allows property to be used in a more ethical manner.

Trade

St Thomas Aquinas's justification of mercantile profits offered many examples of the benefits that commerce may bring to a society. He explicitly mentioned the usefulness of (a) the conservation and storing of goods, (b) the importation of useful goods that are necessary for the republic, and (c) the transportation of goods from places where they are abundant to places where they are scarce. Domingo de Soto defined trade contracts as obligations and acknowledged that both parties profit from the arrangements. The Jesuit Juan de Mariana carried this point further, suggesting that commerce favors the common good and that God gave man his nature of social dependency and his limited ability and capacity so that it would feel the need for commerce. This encourages man to live in society and to enjoy the benefits of social cooperation (division of labor): 'how much work and industry is involved in combing, spinning and weaving linen, wool, and silk ... The life of no single man is long enough to obtain all these things, however long he lives, unless the wonder and observation of many men, and collective experience, should come to the rescue' (Mariana, 1950).

One of the principal contributions of the late scholastics regarding commerce consists of the recognition of international free trade as subject to human laws, as Vitoria established in his *De Indis et de Iure Belli Relectiones* (Vitoria, 1964). Teófilo Urdanoz later stated 'that no one has realized, at least up to now, that Vitoria's vision of the right to free communication and unrestricted foreign relations represents an *explicit advance of the principles of economic neoliberalism and worldwide free market*' (Urdanoz, 1967). Eternal, natural and positive human law (*ius gentium*) favors international trade.

Public finance

The late scholastics' rejection of inflation as a method of overcoming financial difficulties paved the way for their balanced-budget proposals. They summoned authority to balance the budget by cutting spending, reducing subsidies and dismissing courtiers. They rejected financing budget deficits through public debt. In their experience, not only did excessive borrowing by the state fail to reduce the burden of excessive spending, it also jeopardized the future of the kingdom.

One of the schoolmen's primary concerns was the high level of taxation. To them, the purpose of taxation was to raise the necessary revenue for just government. They declared that taxes should be moderate and proportional, making no reference whatsoever to taxation as a tool for equalizing wealth. In his claim for moderate taxes, Navarrete realized that excessive taxation could reduce the king's income (as few will be able to pay such high rates): 'the origin of poverty is high taxes. In continual fear of tax collectors [the farmers] prefer to abandon their land, so they can avoid their vexations. As king Teodorico said, the only agreeable country is one where no man is afraid of tax collectors' (Chafuen, 1986). In the field of economic ethics, the late scholastics were careful to point out that certain tax laws could oblige legally but not morally.

Money

According to the late scholastics, the value of money should be determined in the same manner as the value of any other commodity. They saw utility and scarcity as the main factors influencing its value. Believing that the usefulness of money bore a close relationship to its quantity, the schoolmen noted that, when money undergoes continuous debasements, people try to reduce their real cash holdings. A reduction in the value of money will therefore cause a price increase of similar proportions. They also remarked that the value of money is greatest where it is most urgently needed for transactions (for example, at fairs).

The late scholastics in general, and Juan de Matienzo (1520–79) (Popescu, 1985) and Martín de Azpilcueta in particular (Grice-Hutchinson, 1975), have been credited as the first formulators of the quantity theory of money. Their contributions reached a peak with Juan de Mariana, author of one of the best monetary texts ever written; Mariana's *Tratado sobre la Moneda de Vellón* (Mariana, 1950), originally published in 1598, anticipated many of the anti-inflationary arguments of modern economists. In general, the late scholastics avowed that currency debasement caused a revolution in fortunes, undermined political stability and violated property rights. It also created confusion in commerce (internal and foreign), leading to stagnation and poverty. Currency debasement, at least for Mariana, represented an instrument of tyrannical plunder. This Jesuit also made an analogy between debasement and an excessive intake of alcoholic beverages, which in the short run might produce happiness but which, in the long run, generates calamitous effects. Mariana was referring to the short-term benefits that 'more money' might cause in commercial activity, and to the long-run damage caused by increased government spending.

Economic justice

A totally voluntary exchange would always be just (*volenti non fit injuria*) said Aristotle and so, later, the scholastics. It was implicit in the scholastic explanation that ignorance on the part of the buyer or seller could, in certain cases, render the transactions involuntary. Although the late scholastics tolerated the pursuit of profit due to better knowledge of the market, they morally condemned those who took advantage of an ignorant consumer. Lessio acutely reasoned that, if justice does not permit knowledgeable sellers to command the current price, 'buyers, following the same reasoning, should not be allowed to buy at the current price if they know that prices in the future will go up, and this is also false' (Chafuen, 1986).

The idea of discovery as a just basis for acquiring property was intrinsic to scholastic thought. The passage in the Gospels (Mattew 13:44–6) speaking about finding a treasure in another's property and then selling everything to buy that property and reap the profit, and of perceiving the special value of a unique pearl, were widely used by the late scholastics to prove that a 'finders keepers rule' can be consistent with a reign of justice. A major economic topic addressed by them in this context, apart from treasures, was the just property of underground discoveries, especially gold, and entrepreneurial trading opportunities. Pedro de Ledesma, following St Antonino's reasoning, remarked that those things that have never had an owner 'belong to the one who finds them, and the one who finds them does not commit theft by keeping them' (Chafuen, 1986). According to Ledesma, and most late scholastics, the finder has a natural right to appropriate such goods. Treasures, and other things that at one time had a proprietor, in certain circumstances may also belong to the one who found them. Chance, and luck, and not only industry and labor, gave in many cases a strong justification for acquiring ownership of found goods.

The schoolmen also had the wisdom to analyse wages, rents and profits in relation to contracts. They never regarded these topics as a matter of distributive justice. Rather the recommendations were consistent with their just price theory: the just wage, profit or rent should be determined or established by common estimation in the market.

Scholastic economics was not perfect and attracted its share of criticism. In 1955, for example, De Roover stated, 'the great weakness of scholastic economics was the usury doctrine'. The scholastics condemned charging interest for loans even when a lender freely agreed to the contract. Their thoughts on the higher value of money-in-hand in comparison with promissory notes, and other insights on the topic, made Schumpeter (1954) argue that the scholastics 'launched the theory of interest'.

See also:
Chapter 5: Aristotelianism, apriorism, essentialism; Chapter 22: The Austrian theory of price

Bibliography
Azpilcueta, M. (1553), *Manual de Confesores y Penitentes*, Coimbra
Chafuen, A.A. (1986), *Christians for Freedom: Late-Scholastic Economics*, San Francisco: Ignatius Press.
De Roover, R. (1955), 'Scholastic Economics: Survival and Lasting Influence from the Sixteenth Century to Adam Smith', *Quarterly Journal of Economics*, **69**, May, 161–90.
Grice-Hutchinson, M. (1975), *Early Economic Thought in Spain, 1177–1740*, London: George Allen & Unwin.
Mariana, J. de (1950), 'Del Rey y de la Institución Real, and Tratado sobre la Moneda de Vellón', in *Biblioteca de Autores Españoles*, Rivadeneyra, **31**, Madrid: Ediciones Atlas.
Popescu, O. (1985), Orígenes Hispanoamericanos de la teoría cuantitativa (Hispanic American Origins of the Quantity Theory), *Programa Bibleh-UCA-Conicet*, Buenos Aires, Serie Comentarios Criticos No. 2, ii., 60.
Rothbard, M.N. (1976), 'New Light on the Prehistory of the Austrian School', in E.G. Dolan (ed.), *The Foundation of Modern Austrian Economics*, Kansas City: Sheed & Ward.
Schumpeter, J.A. (1954), *History of Economic Analysis*, New York: Oxford University Press.
Urdanoz, Teófilo (1967), 'Síntesis teológico–jurídica de las Doctrinas de Vitoria', in Francisco de Vitoria, *Relectio de Indis o Libertad de los Indios, Corpus Hispanorum de Pace*, vol. V, critical edition by L. Perena and J.M. Perez Prendes, introductory studies by V. Beltrán de Heredia, R. Agostino Iannarone, T. Urdanoz and A. Truyol y L. Perena, Madrid: Consejo Superior de Investigaciones Científicas.
Vitoria, Francisco de (1964), *De Indis et de Iure Belli Relectiones*, ed. Ernest Nys, New York: Oceana.

71 German predecessors of the Austrian school

Erich W. Streissler

In the preface to his *Principles*, Carl Menger pointed out: 'It was a special pleasure to me that the field here treated, comprising the most general principles of our science, is in no small degree so truly the product of recent development in German political economy, and that the reform of the most important principles of our science here attempted is therefore built upon a foundation laid by previous work that was produced almost entirely by the industry of German scholars' (Menger, 1976, p. 49). This statement has to be taken seriously and is, in fact, true of the whole Austrian school at least up to about the beginning of the First World War. The close connection with German economics was forgotten (1) because of the dissociation of many of the later leaders of the Austrian school, both for political and for academic reasons, from German influence, and (2) because of the slightly earlier dissociation of a new tradition in German economics, the younger historical school, dominated by Schmoller and the universities under Prussian leadership during the Second German 'Reich', from the very fruitful older traditions of thought (from 1807 to around 1875) in the influential non-Prussian universities.

The Austrian school built upon the well-developed tradition of subjective value notions in a 'protoneoclassical tradition' of German economics (Streissler 1990a, 1990b). In particular, marginal productivity theory of factor valuation had been repeatedly formulated and was more or less accepted; and notions of diminishing marginal utility were frequently appealed to. Menger staged a 'reform' of this tradition insofar as he fully generalized and raised to the rank of paradigmatic and central ideas what had so far been matter-of-fact remarks and discussions in specialized treatises. In particular, the exact relationship of the supply (or cost) side to the demand side in price formation had remained unclear, so that Menger could truly remark that only he was 'placing all price phenomena (including interest, wages, ground rent, etc.) together under one unified point of view' (Menger, 1976, p. 49). The Austrian school continued the older German tradition insofar as it treated the same topics, which were not central to other branches of 'orthodox' economics: money, economic fluctuations ('crises'), entrepreneurship and the determination of profits. Only its theory of capital was exclusively Austrian. It differed most radically in its methodological precepts, though in the actual practice of scientific research and discussion the differences are not as noticeable. Each of these aspects will be addressed in turn below.

German 'protoneoclassical' subjectivism

The subjective value tradition in German economics during the first three-quarters of the nineteenth century did not come about through a revolutionary break with the past, but was rather due to its conservatism: the continental utility-oriented tradition, epitomized for example by Condillac, was continued and the cost-oriented value theory of the English classicists, of Ricardo and J.S. Mill, was rejected. In price theory German economics stuck to the pre-classical supply and demand framework of Sir James Steuart.

There were thus already (or still) basically subjectively oriented German economists in the early 1800s, for example, Storch and Fulda, but the outstanding pure subjectivist was Hufeland (1807), who first called 'goods, value, price, money and national wealth' the *'fundamental notions'* of economics and defined these concepts subjectively. (He was also the first to inquire into entrepreneurial remuneration.) For him things become goods because of human 'ideas of their value, of their suitability as means to an end that one wishes to reach', and not because labor has been used in procuring them.

The most important textbook written along subjective value lines was Hermann (1832). (In fact, Roscher, 1874, p. 1039, considered the young Menger as 'continuing in the road of Hermann'.) Hermann introduced the idea of 'free goods' to economics; he introduced the concept that costs are the 'objective' side to the determination of price while utility is the 'subjective' side and he presented a price theory in which 'the first and most important factor determining price is in all cases demand, the main roots of which are the value in use [utility] and the purchasers' ability to pay' (1832, p. 95). He defined wants as 'this sense of a deficiency with the endeavor to redress it' (Hermann, 1870, p. 5). He showed that prices will never be determined by supply conditions alone if the market supply curve is rising because of the differences in costs among suppliers; he suggests that costs themselves will eventually be changed if preferences change; and he uses opportunity cost concepts.

The most successful textbook around the middle of the century (with eight editions) was Rau (1826). Rau is more Marshallian than Mengerian. He is paradigmatic in treating all commodity and all factor prices symmetrically on the same demand and supply lines, the utility-determined demand price being the upper, the cost-determined supply price the lower limit to actual price. Entrepreneurial activity (a fourth factor of production!) and the reasons for its remuneration are treated extensively. The value 'which a commodity has for us' if we do not wish to exchange it is defined by 'the greatest sacrifice we are willing to make to obtain it' (1826, p. 110). 'Exchange is as a rule advantageous to both parties, as the two exchanged commodities are not valued equally highly by them' (Rau, 1855, p. 170), a purely subjective argument. Similarly, Rau derived something like an elasticity of demand along utility lines and drew a falling demand curve from his fourth edition (1841) onwards. Finally, Rau valued the social product in utility terms.

A strongly subjectivist treatment is given by Schäffle, Menger's immediate predecessor in Vienna: 'Value [is] a relationship between all goods in human consciousness ... [it is] predominantly of a *subjective* nature. It consists in a consciousness of purpose in matters economic ... All goods become comparable in terms of value ... Value [is] the significance of a good in the economic calculation of man. All economic calculation tries to determine the smallest sacrifice necessary to achieve full satisfaction' (Schäffle, 1867, pp. 51ff).

The most successful textbook writer of the second half of the nineteenth century, Roscher (1854, 26 editions) endorsed these subjective value notions and presented the labor theory of value not only as untenable, but as a 'national' English aberration, thereby implying a German patriotic duty to argue at least in part in subjective value terms.

Marginal utility and marginal productivity

Diminishing *marginal utility* was not new for Menger. In a passage which he calls 'often quoted', Hildebrand had stated (1848, p. 318): 'The more a quantity of a useful commodity is increased, the more the utility of each piece diminishes as long as the want has not changed.' Knies (1855) elaborated on this idea in a frequently cited article on the theory of value. Occasional remarks implying diminishing marginal utility abounded even earlier; and von Mangoldt (1863) presented a fully specified demand theory.

But the foremost achievement of German economics was the development of the *marginal productivity* theory of factor price remuneration. As early as 1826 Thünen gives numerous examples of optimal factor *use* up to the point where marginal product equals price – Rau, too (1826) presents a shorter, but also quantitative example to the same point – but only in 1850 does Thünen introduce the inverse, factor price determination by marginal productivity, and especially clearly for *capital*. By then the marginal productivity valuation at least of *labor* services was already well known. Hermann had pointed out (1832, p. 281): 'Only what the consumers give for the product constitutes the true remuneration of the service of the workers.' Schüz (1843, p. 286) had made this idea quite explicit and even used the term 'degree of [that is, marginal] productivity': 'In any business the wage is determined by the degree of productivity of labor and the remunerativeness of the occupation which is carried on with the cooperation of the labourer.' He suggests that this is only one instance of a general principle of all price determination. And Roscher (1864, p. 330) says: 'In each producing establishment the additional product which the worker who is last employed produces is regularly the maximum for the wages of workers of the same quality.' Thus marginal productivity theory could no longer be improved upon when Menger entered the stage, apart from the minor and already implicit point that marginal product had to be seen in utility terms.

Some of the Germans derived their marginal productivity analysis from Ricardo's theory of differential rent. Ricardo had suggested that invariable bundles (fixed as to their composition) of labor plus capital used on land received their marginal product. This idea was applied by German authors, for example, to a theory of the remuneration of machines of different quality (Hermann) and in particular to that of different kinds of labor, to the remuneration of human capital (Hufeland in 1807, that is before Ricardo). As many authors treated entrepreneurial effort as a kind of highly qualified labor, differential rent theory provided one explanation for entrepreneurial profit (von Mangoldt). Rent theory thus became a vehicle for rejecting over-aggregative concepts of factors and for suggesting that particular means of production had to be valued in terms of their usefulness.

Topics

Rau's formative textbook (1826) had treated not only *money*, but also banking and credit very extensively, in about one-sixth of the text. From then on these topics were considered to be of general importance, not only in textbooks (Roscher, 1854; Schäffle, 1867) but also in monographs, especially in the two volumes of Knies (1873, 1879), the teacher of Böhm-Bawerk and Wieser. It is thus no coincidence that Menger, Wieser, Mises, Schumpeter and Hayek became important monetary economists. In his brief treatment of *business cycles* ('crises') Rau (1826) had stressed their distributional consequences; but this topic became central only with Roscher, who devoted to it one of his early articles (1861), of monograph length and full of astounding insights. In his textbook summary of his arguments, Roscher explains business downswings by an asymmetry of expenditure functions in case of income redistribution, gainers being much slower in their increase than losers in their contraction of expenditure, and adds an *informational* argument: '...partly this is so already because the ones usually cannot judge their gains as well as the others their losses'. He also considers misjudgements about changes in the value of money as contributory factors (1864, pp. 446, 448). The monetary causes of business cycles, thus already important for Roscher, were further stressed by the two professors of German extraction in Vienna: Schäffle (1867, pp. 214 ff) saw informational problems and changes in interest rates as decisive, while von Stein (1858, pp. 225f) presented a full-fledged

'Austrian' theory of the cycle with expansions and contractions of *credit* causing waves of investment, an elaborate picture from which only the concomitant changes in the structure of capital were missing.

Lengthy discussions of the entrepreneurial role and of the causes of profit had been instigated by Rau (1826) and through him became a standard feature in the German literature. An extensive treatment can be found in Riedel (1839), who discusses innovation in a way which evidently strongly influenced Schumpeter. The insightful analysis of profits by von Mangoldt (1855) was, however, not appreciated by the Austrians.

Methodology

Hufeland (1807) had proclaimed a thoroughly subjectivist methodological position, including the treatment of institutions, after A. Smith, as unintended consequences of human action. In this he was followed by Hermann (1832), but partially also by Rau. In particular Rau (1826, p. 196) gives an explanation of money, very close to that of Menger, as an institution arising out of imperfectly understood social learning processes:

> The first introduction of a certain kind of money could have arisen neither as a consequence of the enforced command of a government nor of the explicit agreement among men, for it cannot be supposed that people had the concept of money and had known its advantages without having learned both from experience. One has therefore to assume that a commodity commonly thought desirable and in common demand was taken ever more frequently in exchange by those persons who did not themselves want to use it, and that in this way it acquired by degrees the nature of money, and at the same time step by step its concomitant utility was more and more clearly understood.

While German economics thus knew thoroughgoing positions of methodological individualism, many of the basic methodological tenets of the Austrians were more typical of a time 50 or even 100 years before they published (Silverman, 1990), so that Roscher (1886, p. 62) could criticize Menger as 'typical of the older[!] method, which abstracts from all reality and fails to recognize the organic whole of the economy and the life of a people'. The general German tendency was subjectivist, but it remained unclear whether the choices to be analysed were those of the average man or those of individuals in particular circumstances, whether subjective choices were not determined by an objectively knowable morality and as expressions of the general aims of human development, and whether they were not shaped by 'the organic whole of the economy and the life of a people'. Fundamentally at issue was the role of the state, in particular of the nation-state which, after 1871, the Germans had while the Austrians did not; or, as Roscher put it, the question was whether one did not have to recognize the importance of a 'public spirit' in decision making besides self-interest, while Menger insisted (1976, p. 260) that, for example, money came into being 'even without regard to the public interest'.

But up to around 1875 the statist positions of the Germans were subdued, Roscher's (1864, pp. 147ff) extensive treatment of the dangers of a socialist society for individual liberty ('a despotism to a degree that would hardly have yet existed in the world', p. 151) falling not at all short of the later strictures of Mises and Hayek. Thus the Austrians could find even their methodological positions prefigured in the wider German tradition. By around 1875 the general methodological tendency there was, however, one of 'anything goes'; in fact it was positively insisted that both empirical and theoretical methods were always to be used in every analysis. Thus the 'purism' of the Austrians, who insisted on whole-hearted subjectivism, methodological individualism and the pre-eminence of theoretical research, became divisive. Menger's deep epistemological arguments were not even understood by the Germans (Milford, 1990).

On the other hand, the Germans' extensive treatment of institutions and their development over time stimulated Austrian research as well. The German aversion to facile theoretical generalizing is one reason why the Austrians tended to shun aggregates and to see economic magnitudes as in many ways structured and diversified and to think of economic agents as typically differing as to their preferences or cost functions. Finally, Roscher's stand to the effect that perfect competition is at best a limiting case provided a framework for the Austrians for considering bargaining processes and for viewing the economy as in constant flux and certainly only rarely settled in the state of competitive equilibrium.

See also:
Chapter 12: Marginal utility; Chapter 3: Subjectivism; Chapter 66: The Methodenstreit

Bibliography
Hermann, Friedrich B.W. (1832), *Staatswirthschaftliche Untersuchungen*, Munich.
Hermann, Friedrich B.W. (1870), *Staatswirthschaftliche Untersuchungen*, 2d edn, Munich.
Hildebrand, Bruno (1848), *Die Nationalökonomie der Gegenwart und Zukunft*, Frankfurt am Main.
Hufeland, Gottlieb (1807), *Neue Grundlegung der Staatswirthschaftskunst durch Prüfung und Berichtigung ihrer Hauptbegriffe von Gut, Werth, Preis, Geld und Volksvermögen mit ununterbrochener Rücksicht auf die bisherigen Systeme*, Giessen and Wetzlar.
Knies, Karl (1855), 'Die nationalökonomische Lehre vom Werth', *Zeitschrift für die gesamte Staatswissenschaft*, **11**.
Knies, Karl (1873 and 1879), *Geld und Credit*, Vol. 1: *Das Geld*, Berlin; Vol.2: *Der Credit*, Berlin.
Mangoldt, H. von (1855), *Die Lehre vom Unternehmergewinn*, Leipzig.
Mangoldt, H. von (1863), *Grundriss der Volkswirthschaftslehre*, Stuttgart.
Menger, Carl [1871] (1976), *Grundsätze der Volkswirthschaftslehre*, Vienna, translated by J. Dingwall and B. Hoselitz as *Principles of Economics*, New York/London.

Milford, Karl (1990), 'Menger's methodology', in Bruce J. Caldwell (ed.), *Carl Menger and His Legacy in Economics*, Durham/London.

Rau, Karl H. (1826), *Grundsätze der Volkswirthschaftslehre*, Heidelberg.

Rau, Karl H. (1841), *Grundsätze der Volkswirthschaftslehre*, 4th edn, Heidelberg.

Rau, Karl H. (1855), *Grundsätze der Volkswirthschaftslehre*, 6th edn, Heidelberg.

Riedel, A.F. (1839), *Nationalöconomie oder Volkswirthschaft*, vol. 2, Berlin.

Roscher, Wilhelm [1849] (1861), 'Zur Lehre von den Absatzkrisen', in *Ansichten der Volkswirthschaft aus dem geschichtlichen Standpunkte*, section 6. Leipzig/Heidelberg.

Roscher, Wilhelm (1854), *Die Grundlagen der Nationalökonomie: Ein Hand- und Lesebuch für Geschäftsmänner und Studierende*, Stuttgart.

Roscher, Wilhelm (1864), *Grundlagen der Nationalökonomie*, 5th edn, Stuttgart.

Roscher, Wilhelm (1874), *Geschichte der National-Oekonomik in Deutschland*, Munich.

Roscher, Wilhelm (1886), *Grundlagen der Nationalökonomie*, 18th edn, Stuttgart.

Schäffle, Albert E.F. (1867), *Das gesellschaftliche System der menschlichen Wirthschaft*, Tübingen.

Schüz, Carl W. Ch. (1843), *Grundsätze der National-Oeconomie*, Tübingen.

Silverman, Paul (1990), 'The cameralistic roots of Menger's achievement', in Bruce J. Caldwell (ed.), *Carl Menger and His Legacy in Economics*, Durham, NC/London.

Stein, Lorenz von (1858), *Lehrbuch der Volkswirthschaft*, Vienna.

Streissler, Erich W. (1990a), 'Menger, Böhm-Bawerk, and Wieser: The Origins of the Austrian School', in Klaus Hennings and Warren J. Samuels (eds), *Neoclassical Economic Theory, 1870 to 1930*, Boston/Dordrecht/London.

Streissler, Erich W. (1990b), 'The influence of German economics on the work of Menger and Marshall', in Bruce J. Caldwell (ed.), *Carl Menger and His Legacy in Economics*, Durham, NC/London.

Thünen, Johann Heinrich von (1826), *Der isolirte Staat in Beziehung auf Landwirtschaft und Nationalökonomie*, Vol.1: *Untersuchungen über den Einfluss, den die Getreidepreise, der Reichtum des Bodens und die Abgaben auf den Ackerbau ausüben*, Hamburg.

Thünen, Johann Heinrich von (1850), *Der naturgemäße Arbeitslohn und dessen Verhältnis zum Zinsfuß und zur Landrente*, Part I, Rostock.

72 German market process theory

Wolfgang Kerber

In Germany since the Second World War, an original line of reasoning about competition and market processes has been developed. Based upon central ideas of Schumpeter and Hayek, competition has been interpreted as dynamic or, more exactly, evolutionary market processes. Central tenets of this approach are the importance of innovations and entrepreneurs, and the character of competition as a process. Simultaneously, these creative market processes have always been seen as the essential driving-force for economic development. This German approach, which has always regarded itself as critical of neoclassical economics, has many similarities to but also certain differences from Austrian market process theory. Since all these developments have been published and discussed only in German, they are practically unknown to English-speaking economists.

Beginning in the early 1950s, with the work of Helmut Arndt (1952), who viewed competition as a never-ending creative process consisting of the advancing pioneers, who take the lead by creating new products and new production techniques, and the following imitators, the notion of competition as a dynamic process has been developed and elaborated by a broad body of German economists (for example, Heuss, Hoppmann). The most influential source of this development was the second chapter of Schumpeter's *Theory of Economic Development* (1934) with his ideas of the entrepreneur, innovation and imitation, and endogenous change. But also the ideas of J.M. Clark (1961) with his notion of rivalrous competition consisting of initiatory actions and responses had an important impact. Since the 1960s the concept of a Schumpeterian 'dynamic competition' has been the dominant view in German competition theory. It also influenced German competition policy, which had been molded by the free market-oriented Freiburg School (ordoliberalism). In the 1970s and 1980s this concept was considerably broadened and developed further by the spreading and integrating of the Austrian ideas of Hayek and Kirzner, which has been due primarily to the work of Hoppmann. But also, independently of this development, German scholars elaborated further a theory of economic development, based upon an evolutionary concept of market processes (Röpke, Hesse), which increasingly tended to see itself as an alternative paradigm to neoclassical economics, and hence can be seen as one of the important streams within the new field of evolutionary economics.

It has always been an essential characteristic of German market process theory that competition was understood as producing economic and technical progress, which is the most important determinant of *economic development* and hence economic growth. Hence competition is seen less as driving down prices to the level of costs, as in traditional neoclassical price theory, than as creating new products, new production techniques and new forms of organization and so on. This idea that innovations and therefore new knowledge are being created and spread endogenously in the economic process has its roots in Schumpeterian thinking, but it was reinforced and – as regards the problem of knowledge – made much more explicit in Hayek's elaboration of the problem of knowledge and his concept of 'competition as a discovery procedure'. In particular, Jochen Röpke (1977) emphasized the importance of innovations for the survival and development of economic systems. According to this view the failure of the centrally planned economies is not so much a consequence of allocative inefficiencies but primarily follows from their inability to create and spread innovations in order to survive in an ever-changing world.

The concept of the *entrepreneur* has always been a central tenet in the German approach of dynamic competition and evolutionary market processes. It was Schumpeter's concept of the entrepreneur, who implemented innovations, and his analysis of the cognitive and motivational characteristics of the entrepreneur, which had a great impact. The concept of a creative entrepreneur was an essential part of Arndt's theory. Later on, Heuss contrasted the neoclassical *homo economicus*, who reacts like a robot, with the creative entrepreneur of Schumpeter, and he enriched the analysis by differentiating four types of entrepreneurs: the pioneer entrepreneur, the spontaneously imitating entrepreneur, entrepreneurs reacting under competitive pressure, and immobile agents, who are not able to adapt at all. From this point of view, Kirzner's introduction in the 1970s of the 'alert' entrepreneur, who discovers new opportunities, fitted in well. But whereas, on the one hand, Kirzner's view was rapidly accepted, many German market process theorists, on the other hand, emphasized more the creative aspect of the entrepreneur, sympathizing – with regard to this particular problem – more with Lachmann and Shackle than with Kirzner. In their striving to develop a more general approach to studying the evolutionary dynamics of the economy, Röpke and Hesse elaborated a model of the economic agent in which individual decision processes consisted of two phases: first, the creative constitution of the set of alternatives, which an agent perceives at a certain point of time (principle of cognitive creation) and, second, the subjectively rational choice from this set (principle of rationality). Hence the concept of economic agents in evolutionary market process theory includes both the notions of the creative entrepreneur (first phase) and the neoclassical *homo economicus* (second phase).

Returning to the earlier and more narrow concept of *dynamic competition*, competition has been seen since the early 1950s as a dynamic, rivalrous process, consisting of actions and reactions. The pioneer, improving his or her achievement (for example, through an innovation) or lowering the price, advances as compared with his competitors, and gains additional market shares and a market position, which would traditionally be interpreted as market power enabling him or her to reap supranormal profits. But these profits are necessary as an incentive for carrying out the competitive action. The decisive point for understanding the dynamic character of these competitive processes is that through this advance the competitors come under competitive pressure by losing market shares and/or suffering losses. This feedback mechanism forces them – under the threat of having to leave the market – to improve their own achievement and to catch up with or even outstrip the leading agents. They can thus imitate the advanced firm or innovate by themselves. Consequently, competitive processes can be interpreted as races for improving the opportunities for the agents of the other market side, in which a built-in motivator exists in the form of attributing profits and losses, depending on the relative position in this race.

Since nobody (including the entrepreneurs) can know, ex ante, which (new) products or services satisfy the consumer preferences best, the different products and services which the suppliers offer to the consumers can be interpreted as their hypotheses about the best way of satisfying the current wants of the consumers. By choosing from this set of different hypotheses the consumers exert the role of the referee in this contest and hence they decide which of these hypotheses are the best. Observing the relative success of the superior firms, the inferior competitors can take over their better knowledge. In that way, this rivalrous competitive process creates and spreads knowledge about the best way of satisfying the current preferences of consumers (*competition as a discovery procedure*). For German market process theorists it has always been a problem whether this dynamic character of the competitive process will be maintained, or slow down or even vanish. Hence they were interested in analysing the conditions for the *maintenance of these dynamic market processes*. In this respect, Clark had an important influence. He showed that certain market imperfections such as non-transparency, heterogeneity or a limited rapidity of reaction may foster instead of impede competition. This idea has been further elaborated by Heuss. In his theory of oligopoly, competitors learn about each other through experience. After a certain amount of time this may lead to the problem that competitors come to the conclusion that additional competitive actions will not be worthwhile, because they know that their competitors will follow them soon. Therefore they may refrain from making competitive advances. Heuss investigated which conditions foster or impede such behavior and therefore the slowing down or vanishing of the dynamics of competition.

Within German market process theory, Heuss (1965) also developed a *theory of market phases*. In this theory, markets – understood as whole industries such as the steel or the car industry – run through various phases. In the experimentation phase a new product has to be invented, and a suitable production technology found for it. If the new product happens to be successful, the expansion phase follows, in which the demand function is continuously moving to the right, and considerable improvements in product quality and massive cost reductions resulting from the accumulating experience from increased production, and hence large price reductions, are taking place. When this expansion of the demand, and the improvements and the cost and price reductions are slowing down, the market enters the maturity phase, to be followed by the stagnation phase, if there is no more growth. In these phases the market seems to approach the textbook notion of a market with given products and given cost and demand functions. If a new substitute product emerges (such as oil instead of coal), which leads to an expanding new market, the old market slips into the decline phase. The basic idea is that, in each of these market phases, typical situations with a typical pattern of data emerge, whose separate analysis allows for richer explanations of market processes. Since again and again new markets emerge and old markets wane, structural change with all of its adjustment problems is an inherent concomitant phenomenon of evolutionary market processes.

The concept of competition as a dynamic process consisting of perpetual advancing, catching up and outstripping among competitors has led to a *different view of market power*. In this notion the monopoly power of the advancing pioneer is a quite normal phenomenon in market processes and the resulting monopoly profits have to be seen as a legitimate reward and necessary incentive for the pioneers. Hence the observation that, at a certain point of time, a firm has a certain scope for determining prices does not imply that it is not being controlled by the competitive efforts of other firms. The crucial problem has rather been seen as whether other firms can catch up with the leading ones and thus nullify their market power. Consequently, German scholars tried to make the difficult differentiation between an unproblematic, temporary market power and a permanent one, which is protected from the competition of imitators and which may be a problem for competition policy. Actually, this is not far from the neoclassical notion, where market power is protected from being eroded by barriers to entry, but it is expressed in the richer and more descriptively accurate approach of market process theory.

In the USA the antitrust policy of the 1960s, which was dominated by the market power doctrine of the Harvard school and the structure–conduct–performance paradigm, has been successfully criticized by the Chicago school.

In Germany, this concept, which has primarily been upheld by Kantzenbach (and called *funktionsfähiger Wettbewerb*, 'workable competition'), was attacked by Hoppmann, who developed his own *concept of 'freedom to compete'*. On the one hand, Hoppmann rejected the notion of viewing competition as an instrument for pursuing economic goals. For Hoppmann, individual freedom is the ultimate value, and competition has to be seen as those market processes which emerge out of the freedom of the agents. From this notion, which comes close to the ordoliberal view of the Freiburg school, Hoppmann concluded that competition policy should protect individuals from restraints of their freedom to compete. Adhering to German market process theory, 'freedom to compete' means for him that the agents should be free to advance and pursue in the competitive process, and to choose among alternative buyers and sellers. But he also claimed that there is no incompatibility between individual freedom and the achievement of good economic results.

On the other hand, Hoppmann attacked the structure–conduct–performance paradigm, arguing that there is no clear causal relationship between market structure, market conduct and market performance. Consequently, he claimed that it is not possible to identify an 'optimal market structure' which could be pursued by competition policy. Hoppmann argued that individual market processes and their particular outcomes have to be viewed as unpredictable, and hence it is not possible to use market performance criteria in competition policy. For example, he vigorously criticized the attempts of the German Bundeskartellamt to enforce the control of abusive pricing by market-dominating firms, because it is impossible to determine the non-abusive 'competitive price'. To substantiate his argument, in the 1970s, he increasingly used Austrian reasoning, especially that of Kirzner and Hayek. Hoppmann described the market system as a coordination and evolution process (Hayek's 'spontaneous order'), but the central argument which he took over from Hayek was the knowledge problem, and the ensuing reproach of *'pretence of knowledge'* levelled at all those favoring regulation of or intervention in market processes. Also Hayek's insistence on the importance of general rules, which stabilize the expectations of the agents and, simultaneously, eliminate the discretionary power of government agencies had a great influence. Hence Austrian thinking, which fitted in well with earlier strands of evolutionary German market process reasoning, has had an important impact on the thinking about competition in Germany (for a short overview, see Herdzina, 1988).

From this tradition of German evolutionary market process theory, a broad strand of different lines of thought is being pursued by various groups of scholars. (For example, there are also close connections with institutional economics, especially on the emergence of institutions.) Here we consider a group which is much in the line of the whole tradition of German market process theory and which is particularly interested in an *evolutionary theory of economic development*. The basic idea of Röpke (1977) is that a system (such as a firm or a market system) can only survive in its environment if it constantly generates innovations. Since Röpke views the environment of the system as being perpetually changing and always more complex than the system itself, the survival of the system demands that it always have at its disposal a large variety of counteractions to parry the constantly emerging threats of a perennial and non-anticipatable changing environment. In being able to adapt successfully to these changes, the generation of innovations is the key strategy for a market system to survive in an ever-changing world. Since the testing of different ideas increases the chances of solving the emerging problems, a certain degree of heterogeneity among the agents is important, which has been especially emphasized by Heuss (1965) and Fehl (1986). Consequently, Röpke analyses the conditions for the emergence of innovations on three different levels: the psychic system (that is, the individual agent), the organizational system (the firm) and the market system. For that purpose, for example on the level of the psychic system, Röpke carries out thorough analyses of the ideas of Simon (bounded rationality), Shackle, Schumpeter, Knight (uncertainty) and the results of the behavioral sciences with regard to motivation and cognition. It is impossible to outline Röpke's argumentation here in more detail, but he elaborates various strategies by which firms try to avoid the necessity of innovating, and hence reduce the survivability of the whole market system. One possible means of achieving this is the utilization of the political system to protect their 'old' resource combinations from the devaluation caused through innovations by other entrepreneurs. Therefore Röpke emphasizes the importance of property rights, especially as regards innovations.

Another author in this group is Hesse, who is carrying out an extensive research project on long-term economic development. He especially wants to explain why industrialization first took place in north-western Europe and not in other parts of the world. In his evolutionary approach he proceeds from the basic idea that in all parts of the world human beings adapt innovatively to unalterable restrictions, leading them to different paths of development according to their particular problems, which – for example, for climatic reasons – are different in various parts of the world as, for example, between tropical and temperate regions. Thus one of his ideas is that in temperate regions farmers are not able to work during the whole year in agriculture, both inducing and enabling them in the idle winter season to develop innovatively capital equipment for speeding up agricultural work in the short summer period, whereas in other parts of the world with less seasonal change people can work in the fields all year. Hence the entailing different incentive structures result in the development of different kinds of human and real capital, and lead to a different path of economic development. But Hesse's whole approach consists of a bundle of interconnected theories, which cannot be even sketched here.

German market process theory has always been very critical of neoclassical equilibrium theory. American Austrians also reject the analysis of equilibrium states, but there has been a broad discussion, as to whether the activities of the entrepreneurs in the market processes are equilibrating and lead to greater coordination or not (for example, by Kirzner and Lachmann). Within German market process theory most scholars would sympathize more with the ideas of Lachmann, who contended that there exist both *equilibrating and disequilibrating tendencies* in market processes, reflecting the Schumpeterian tradition in German market process theory. In the 1950s, Arndt lucidly differentiated between 'adjustment competition', which leads to the clearing of markets, and 'development competition', meaning competition through innovations. Fehl (1986) elaborated the idea that in market processes there are both Schumpeterian entrepreneurs, who disequilibrate by carrying out non-anticipatable innovations, and entrepreneurs of the Mises–Kirzner type, representing the equilibrating forces (arbitrage). Both driving-forces are necessary for market processes and hence have to be seen as complementary. In Fehl's view, 'order' need not be identical to 'equilibrium', but the perennial stream of innovations created by Schumpeterian entrepreneurs, and the perpetual coordinating efforts of Kirznerian entrepreneurs, can lead to a new, different form of 'order' (order beyond equilibrium), which may be better able to cope with the challenges of the ever-changing world than a market system which is equilibrated in the traditional sense.

See also:
Chapter 14: Competition; Chapter 4: Market process; Chapter 15: Entrepreneurship

Bibliography
Arndt, Helmut (1952), *Schöpferischer Wettbewerb und klassenlose Gesellschaft*, Berlin: Duncker & Humblot.
Clark, John M. (1961), *Competition as a Dynamic Process*, Washington DC: Brookings Institution.
Fehl, Ulrich (1986), 'Spontaneous Order and the Subjectivity of Expectations: A Contribution to the Lachmann–O'Driscoll Problem', in Israel M. Kirzner (ed.), *Subjectivism, Intelligibility and the Economic Understanding: Essays in Honor of Ludwig M. Lachmann*, New York: New York University Press, pp. 72–86.
Hayek, Friedrich August von (1978), 'Competition as a Discovery Procedure', in *New Studies in Philosophy, Politics, Economics and the History of Ideas*, Chicago: University of Chicago Press, pp. 179–90.
Herdzina, Klaus (1988), *Möglichkeiten und Grenzen einer wirtschaftstheoretischen Fundierung der Wettbewerbspolitik*, Tübingen: J.C.B. Mohr (Paul Siebeck).
Hesse, Günter (1992), 'A New Theory of "Modern Economic Growth"', in Ulrich Witt (ed.), *Explaining Process and Change. Contributions to Evolutionary Economics*, Ann Arbor: Michigan Press, pp. 81–103.

Heuss, Ernst (1965), *Allgemeine Markttheorie*, Tübingen/Zürich: J.C.B. Mohr (Paul Siebeck) and Polygraphischer Verlag.
Hoppmann, Erich (1988), *Wirtschaftsordnung und Wettbewerb*, Baden-Baden: Nomos.
Röpke, Jochen (1977), *Die Strategie der Innovation*, Tübingen: J.C.B. Mohr (Paul Siebeck).
Schumpeter, Joseph A. (1934), *The Theory of Economic Development. An Inquiry into Profits, Capital, Credit, Interest, and the Business Cycle*, Cambridge, Mass.: Harvard University Press.

73 The Freiburg school of law and economics

M.E. Streit

The breakdown of socialist systems and the problems of their transformation into viable market economies and democratic regimes have further stimulated the revival of institutional analysis. Because it focused on the functional properties of the institutional framework of economic systems, the Freiburg school of law and economics belongs to those traditions in economic thinking which receive renewed attention when attempts are made to deal with the problems of transformation.

Founding members

The tradition is usually traced back to the economist among its founders, Walter Eucken (1891–1950). However, the real intellectual thrust developed as a result of the spontaneous cooperation of economists and jurists who happened to join the University of Freiburg in the 1930s. They discovered that they held similar methodological positions and chose research topics which were complementary. Furthermore, the choices were based on a pre-scientific interest which was rooted in a common value judgement in favor of liberty.

Eucken came to Freiburg in 1927, only two years after he had gained his first chair at the university of Tübingen. His early academic work was almost necessarily influenced by the historical school which dominated in Germany, but already his study of the German monetary problem (1923) had documented a change of course in the direction of theoretical analysis. To him, it was unacceptable that economists of the historical school had nothing to offer in terms of explanation and of policy advice in view of the German hyperinflation after the First World War. He continued his research in the field of monetary theory, frequently combining it with policy considerations. His theory of interest and capital (1934), which he based on Böhm-Bawerk and Wicksell, marked the end of a period of this kind of theoretical work. The introduction, in which Eucken posed the question, 'What does economic theory accomplish?', already sets the theme for his *Foundations of Economics* (first published in German in 1940) which focused on economic systems and became one of the building-blocks of the Freiburg approach.

In 1933, Hans Großmann-Doerth (1894–1944), a professor of civil and commercial law, left the University of Prague to join the Freiburg faculty. As early as the winter term of 1933/34 he initiated, together with Eucken, the joint seminar of jurists and economists which primarily dealt with problems of the economic order and its legal framework. Professors as well as students attended the seminar, and it became the organizational nucleus of the Freiburg school. In 1936 it was forced to close by political pressure, but this did not prevent its members from meeting privately, continuing their opposition to the Nazi regime and planning for the time after its fall together with other scholars from Freiburg and beyond.

The third key personality of the Freiburg school, Franz Böhm (1895–1977), joined the faculty after his time as a public prosecutor in Freiburg and as a civil servant at the cartel office of the Ministry of Economics in Berlin. Eucken and Großmann-Doerth were the appointed referees of his study (1933) which dealt with competition and monopolization and gained him access to a university career ('Habilitation'). Böhm stayed as assistant professor at Freiburg until 1936, when he moved to Jena. But instead of becoming a full professor, he was dismissed in 1939 because of his criticism of the regime's policy towards the Jewish citizens. After a second trial, he was reinstated as a public servant but was forbidden to teach. In 1945, he returned to Freiburg, became a full professor and served as vice-president of the University before he joined the University of Frankfurt in 1946. Thereafter he maintained close contacts with Freiburg and Eucken with whom he founded the journal ORDO which still serves today as a platform to present research related to problems of the economic order and its institutional framework.

Until Eucken's early death in 1950, the school attracted a number of bright scholars and established an intellectual network reaching well beyond Germany. Among those economists of the school who became internationally known, Friedrich A. Lutz, an assistant of Eucken, made contributions to the theory and policy of money, business cycles and exchange rates. Karl Friedrich Maier excelled in the field of balance of payments and monetary theory and gained original insights into the coordination of economic plans on a micro level. K. Paul Hensel established himself at the University of Marburg and initiated research on comparative economic systems, a tradition which is still alive today and has also been extended to the new institutional economics. Of those scholars who, like Eucken and Böhm, made important academic contributions to the formation of economic policy in post war Germany, Fritz W. Meyer and his scholar Hans Willgerodt should be mentioned. Willgerodt and Eucken's last assistant, Hans O. Lenel, are among the present editors of ORDO.

Among those economists abroad who held similar liberal convictions were Luigi Einaudi, Frank H. Knight, Ludwig von Mises, Lionel Robbins and Jacques Rueff. The school maintained scientific contacts with them, even during the politically difficult years. Of the German economists, who early on fled from the Third Reich, Wilhelm Röpke and Alexander Rüstow in particular were close friends of Eucken and Böhm. Most of the economists just mentioned welcomed the opportunity to strengthen their intellectual and personal ties to each other. They were given this opportunity when Friedrich A. Hayek (1899–1992) initiated the Mont Pèlerin Society in 1947 as a forum for the renaissance of classical liberalism under modern conditions. Hayek himself joined the faculty at Freiburg 12 years after Eucken's death, and he openly considered himself a successor of his late friend, despite the fact that he held different views on a number of important theoretical issues.

Methodological and historical background
The scientific approach and the central themes of the Freiburg school are to a considerable extent a creative response to methodological difficulties in economics and law as well as to the deplorable performance of economic policy during the inter-war period. Methodologically, the school formulated a new position concerning the relationship between history and theory. Economically and politically, the containment of power in order to secure a free society became its major focus.

Eucken (1940, p. 47) introduced the methodological problem by asking: 'Have economists succeeded, by a combination of history and theory, in understanding the economic process and its relationships in their entirety, thus overcoming what we are calling the Great Antinomy?' The German historical school had practically decided against theory by (1) postulating what is epistemologically impossible, namely first a perfect description of history and only thereafter a formulation of theory; (2) by subscribing to the diagnosis that, so far, economic theory had been useless in the formation of policy; and (3) that the solution of 'the social question' was of overriding importance, requiring state intervention and a reduction of competition as a major source of social problems. This kind of empiricism or even historicism was, to Eucken, as unacceptable as rationalistic theorizing in the sense of 'arbitrary model building'. He shared with Lord Robbins the view that, 'in the excitement of perfecting our instruments of analysis, we have tended to neglect a study of the framework which they assume' (cited in Eucken, 1948/ 65, p. 197).

Eucken's attempt to overcome this methodological dilemma involving Schmoller and Menger was strongly influenced by Edmund Husserl, Wilhelm Wundt and Max Weber. Husserl, with whom Eucken had close contact in Freiburg, had developed the principle of 'phenomenological reduction' which corresponded closely to what Eucken then described as 'isolating abstraction' (1940, p. 107) or as 'abstraction of significant salient features' (ibid., note 28, p. 332). Instead of 'generalizing abstraction' which seeks to identify what is common to many phenomena, Eucken was convinced that it should be possible to identify certain recurrent elementary forms in economic life.

Eucken's methodology induced him to start with the following question (1940, p. 80): 'If we were looking down on the world and its amazing swarm of human beings, on the variety of employments, the different patterns of related activities, and on the streams of goods, the first question we would ask is, "what is the order or system underlying all this?"' And then he asked his question relating to isolating abstraction (ibid., p. 81): 'Does one central authority direct everyday life, or do countless single individuals make their own decisions?' This led to his basic forms of an economic system: the centrally directed and the exchange economy. As to the latter, the important institutional issue to him was: 'If many individual economic units, though they make their plans independently, are dependent on and exchange with one another ... then the question arises as to the form of the system of exchange relationships. What are the rules of the game?'

Eucken's answer was Humean in the sense that he stressed private property, freedom of contract and liability as 'constitutive principles' of a 'competitive order' (for example, Eucken, 1952a). Of the additional principles, the one of 'open markets' reflects his insistence on competition as the element of control which prevents private property from leading to economic and social abuses. To him, 'the social question' was not, as the historical school believed, the result of excessive but rather of insufficient competition, reflecting the failure of the state to set and preserve the framework of a competitive order. The poor record of economic policy in terms of inflation and opportunistic, ephemeral interventionism with their eroding impact on the functioning of the market system led him to add to his constitutive principles those of 'monetary stability' and of 'steadiness of policy'. The diagnosis was shared by his co-founders, who provided complementary legal explanations for this failure. In his inaugural lecture, Großmann-Doerth (1933) drew attention to what he called 'self-created law of the business community' and to the fact that, for example, standardized conditions of sale were used to restrain competition and that the state tolerated the general private law's being bent into a law which served the vested interests of the business community. Böhm drew on his experience in the cartel office and on the jurisdictions whereby private attempts to close markets by forming cartels were considered legitimate applications of the freedom to contract, disregarding the corresponding reduction of the freedom to compete of third parties. Furthermore, 'adequate measures' for the implementation and enforcement of cartel policies, including boycotts and collective discrimination applied against outsiders, received support from the courts. The 1923 Cartel Regulation aimed to curb abuses, but it also meant that private closure of markets now received public support through regulation. Germany became known as the homeland of cartels.

As long as competition was not recognized as a constitutive element of the economic system which deserved protection and support by the law (as was the case in the USA following the Sherman Act), there was no jurisdictional possibility of reassessing the use of the freedom to contract and to trade. However, giving freedom to compete a legal status required not only thinking in terms of economic systems but also a value judgement, as well as the appreciation of the legal shapability of economic systems. This was an important insight which the jurists of the school shared with Eucken. But like Eucken in economics, they faced methodological problems in their own discipline. Basically they had to define their position somewhere between rationalistic approaches to the explanation of law, on the one hand, and positivism as well as historicism in the philosophy of law, on the other. Only by setting a basic value, freedom in a Kantian sense, did it become possible to avoid the fallacy of establishing norms by rational argument as well as to question law as it happens to develop in the course of legislation and history. With regard to the legal framework of the economy, the specific solution found by Böhm was the conception of the economic constitution. This reflects the recognition that the rules governing private autonomy in a market system and those securing the control of its use through competition have to be considered as complementary in view of the basic conflict between freedom and power. The structure of the economic constitution corresponds to the political constitution of a government under the law (*Rechtsstaat*): on the one hand, autonomy is granted to those who are entrusted to make laws and to govern, but since, on the other hand, autonomy tends to provide opportunities to exercise power, a sophisticated combination of checks and balances is required to prevent an arbitrary use of such power.

Characteristic features
Considering the economics of the Freiburg school, Hutchison (1979, p. 433) observed that it was much closer to classical political economy than mainstream Anglo-American economics. And in this sense Lord Robbins's (1952, p. 16) comparison of classical political economy with modern economic theorizing applies also to the Freiburg school: 'Their conception of the System of Economic Freedom was surely a conception of something more rough and ready, something much more dynamic and real than these exquisite laboratory models.' It reflected the pragmatic orientation of the school and its declared programmatic interest in economic policy motivated by traumatic experience with both interventionism and collectivism. This is well documented by the school's contributions to the economic and social programme for post war Germany which was the result of preparations begun in 1940. After the war, Eucken and Böhm served as advisers to the Western allies and then to Ludwig Erhard, the head of the economic administration office.

Thereafter, they joined the scientific council to the Federal Ministry of Economics. As a member of the Federal Parliament, Böhm was especially able to influence the development of the German antitrust legislation. In short, the formative period of the postwar economic order of Germany bears the mark of the Freiburg school.

Of the analytical achievements which belong to the scientific profile of the School, at least five should be mentioned. (1) The well-founded, institutionally based criticism of collectivist economic planning. It was formulated at a time when this form of economic system was still considered theoretically feasible within the standards of welfare economics. (2) The demonstration that institutions are important to the functioning of a market system. This represented a decisive deviation from conventional economics at that time. Given the programmatic approach, it was a well-founded 'setting of rules' and not an analysis of the 'choice among rules', in the sense of modern constitutional economics. (3) The recognition of what can be called the 'ethics of rules'. Given their pre-scientific interest but also the methodological position of the jurists of the school, they had fewer problems in accepting and elaborating the normativity of institutions than modern approaches based on purpose rationality only. (4) The historically and theoretically based skepticism regarding the possibilities of directing the process of market coordination in a modern economy in a useful way, and even more so, of putting such a policy into practice. Again, it took mainstream economics much longer to recognize the limitations of rational intervention, both on the micro and on the macro level. (5) The emphasis placed upon the interdependence between the various subsystems of society which must be taken into account when structuring and adapting the corresponding institutions. Regarding the heated public discussion on the future political and economic order of Germany during the first years after the war, Böhm's reasoned denial of the possibility of combining a constitution for a democratic government under the law with a socialist planning system (Böhm, 1950) was one of the important contentions based on Eucken's view of the 'interdependence of systems'.

Later developments
Although the academic and political influence of the Freiburg school faded somewhat after Eucken's death and with the adoption of Anglo-American economics in Germany, the tradition is not something of the past. It is continued in both the disciplines of law and economics and is carried out at various locations with the same individuality which, from the beginning, prevented the emergence of a narrow and monolithic doctrine. The outstanding example of one who combined continuity of the tradition with stimulating changes was Friedrich A. Hayek. The continuity stands out clearly when comparing Böhm's 'Rule of Law in a Market Economy' (1966) with Hayek's

'Order of Law and Order of Actions' (in German, 1967). The latter marks the beginning of a process in which he deepened the analysis of the relationship between a market system as a spontaneous order and its constitutive system of rules, including private law. The analysis culminated in the trilogy 'Law, Legislation and Liberty'.

Stimulating changes resulted from the Austrian subjectivism of Hayek and the related emphasis on the knowledge problem. Whereas Eucken gained distance from the historical school by adopting at least to some extent neo-classical economics and – with it – rationalistic elements, Hayek broke with this approach and found a new theoretical access to competition as well as to the role of institutions. His 'competition as a discovery procedure' has its theoretical and constitutional equivalent in competition policy with the conception of 'freedom to compete'. It implies a breaking away not only from the structure–conduct–performance paradigm of the Harvard school, which comes close to views of Eucken and his scholars, but also from the efficiency orientation of the Chicago school. The conception itself was established in Germany primarily by Erich Hoppmann (for example, 1988, part II) who was the successor of Hayek at Freiburg. As far as jurisprudence is concerned, the continuity and further development of the thinking of the Freiburg school is closely related to Ernst-Joachim Mestmäcker, the most distinguished scholar of Böhm. This holds true for constitutional as well as antitrust considerations (for example, Mestmäcker 1973–4, 1980).

See also:
Chapter 38: Law and economics; Chapter 14: Competition; Chapter 39: Legal philosophy

Bibliography
Böhm, F. (1933), *Wettbewerb und Monopolkampf. Eine Untersuchung zur Frage der rechtlichen Struktur der geltenden Wirtschaftsordnung*, Berlin: Carl Heymanns.
Böhm, F. (1950), 'Wirtschaftsordnung und Staatsverfassung', in E.-J. Mestmäcker (ed.), *Freiheit und Ordnung in der Marktwirtschaft*, Baden-Baden: Nomos, reprinted 1980.
Böhm, F. (1966), 'Rule of Law in a Market Economy', in A. Peacock and H. Willgerodt (eds), *Germany's Social Market Economy: Origins and Evolution*, London: Macmillan, reprinted 1989, pp. 46–67.
Eucken, W. (1940), *The Foundations of Economics – History and Theory in the Analysis of Economic Reality*, translated by T.W. Hutchison, Berlin: Springer, reprinted 1950, 1992.
Eucken, W. (1948), 'On the Theory of the Centrally Administered Economy: An Analysis of the German Experiment', in M. Bornstein (ed.), *Comparative Economic Systems*, Homewood, IL: R.D. Irwin, reprinted 1965, pp. 157–97.
Eucken, W. (1952a), 'A Policy for Establishing a System of Free Enterprise', in *Standard Texts on the Social Market Economy*, ed. Ludwig-Erhard-Stiftung, Stuttgart/New York: Fischer, reprinted 1982, pp. 115–131.
Eucken, W. (1952b), *Grundsätze der Wirtschaftspolitik*, Tübingen: Mohr, reprinted 1990.
Grossekettler, H.G. (1989), 'On Designing an Economic Order – The Contributions of the Freiburg School', in D.A. Walker (ed.), *Twentieth Century Economic Thought*, vol. 2, Aldershot: Edward Elgar, pp. 38–84.

Großmann-Doerth, H. (1933), 'Selbstgeschaffenes Recht der Wirtschaft und staatliches Recht', *Freiburger Universitätsreden*, **10**.

Hayek, F.A. (1967), 'Rechtsordnung und Handelnsordnung', in E. Streissler (ed.), *Zur Einheit der Rechts- und Staatswissenschaften*, Karlsruhe: Müller.

Holzwarth, F. (1985), *Ordnung der Wirtschaft durch Wettbewerb – Entwicklung der Ideen der Freiburger Schule*, Freiburg: Haufe.

Hoppmann, E. (1988), *Wirtschaftsordnung und Wettbewerb*, Baden-Baden: Nomos.

Hutchison, T.W. (1979), 'Notes on the Effects of Economic Ideas on Policy: The Example of the German Social Market Economy', *Zeitschrift für die gesamte Staatswissenschaft*, **135**, 426–41.

Mestmäcker, E.-J. (1973–4), 'Power, Law and Economic Constitution', *Law and State*, **10**, 117–32.

Mestmäcker, E.-J. (1980), 'Competition Policy and Antitrust: Some Comparative Observations', *Zeitschrift für die gesamte Staatswissenschaft*, **136**, 387–407.

Robbins, L. (1952), *The Theory of Economic Policy*, 3rd edn, London: Macmillan, 1961.

Streit, M.E. (1992), 'Economic Order, Private Law and Public Policy – The Freiburg School of Law and Economics in Perspective', *Journal of Institutional and Theoretical Economics*, **148**, 675–704.

74 Marxisms and market processes

David L. Prychitko

Critics of the Austrian school appeared in many forms, from Schmollerian historicists and Veblenian institutionalists to Keynesian interventionists. Compared to their traditional rivals, Austrians seem furthest removed from Marxism on almost any level we wish to compare. For instance, Austrian methodology is deductive, Marxism's is dialectical; the Austrians developed a radically subjective theory of value, while Marxians, with their own unique twists, followed Ricardo's labor theory of value; Austrians champion the capitalist market system and claim the impossibility of socialist planning; Marxians championed socialist planning and claimed the death of capitalism.

The differences between Marxians and Austrians are almost too obvious to list. This essay has a different task: it will explore some of the contemporary Austrian (and non-Austrian) interpretations of Marxian socialism to suggest to younger Austrians that something might be gained by picking through the rubble that characterizes the crisis in contemporary Marxism.

Marx and the utopians

Socialism is by no means a homogeneous movement (see Wright, 1986). There are as many visions of socialism as there are socialists, maybe even more. Marx, in his criticism of Saint-Simon, Fourier, Owen and their disciples, ushered in a self-proclaimed 'scientific' (as opposed to 'utopian') socialism. Rather than design a detailed blueprint of some imaginary socialist community, and try to convince well-meaning bourgeois types that socialism can be the best of all possible worlds (a practice the utopians were inclined to attempt – and fail at), Marx would instead thrust forward a radical criticism of capitalism, and from it demonstrate socialism's inevitability.

Marx focused on the organizational principles that structure capitalist and pre-capitalist societies; in this way he may be interpreted as an originator of comparative economic systems analysis. Marx conceived of three categorically distinct ways to organize society (through tradition, market or plan) and claimed that conflicts of interest and structural contradictions of the modern market system (capitalism) must eventually lead to its demise. An entirely different system – socialist planning – would unfold, ending the class struggle and alienation.

Perhaps the key difference between Marx and the earlier utopian socialists was this: Marx tried to ground his criticism of capitalism in an exhausting analysis of its 'base' – the commodity mode of production and the circulation of capital. Hence, while the utopians attacked the morality of capitalism and offered intricately detailed blueprints of some future socialist alternative, Marx focused on capitalism as an organizational system first, and argued that the moral/legal/religious dimension (what he called the 'superstructure') cannot be understood separately from capitalism's economic base. Thus Marx believed the utopians were wasting their time (and stunting the revolution) by ululating over the immorality of capitalist institutions such as profit seeking, wage labor and private property. Without an adequate (indeed, for Marx, 'scientific') analysis of the structure of capitalist economic organization, the utopians failed to pierce capitalism's ideological veil; rather than exposing the alleged 'Laws of History' (such as the necessity of the class struggle and the revolutionary potential of the proletariat), the utopians dreamed of phalansteries, New Harmonies and brimming oceans of lemonade.

Marx resisted the utopian temptation to write 'recipes for the cookshops of the future'. He meant this literally. After all, Fourier *did* provide details on food preparation and kitchen table management for the future socialist society. Marx also meant it metaphorically. He would rather focus on the contradictions of capitalism and let the implications for socialism speak for themselves. But followers of Marx, and critics alike, have disagreed on just what, or how much, Marx has to say about socialism. We can identify at least three interpretations that may be of interest to Austrian economists: an orthodox interpretation, an organizational–economistic interpretation of Marx (as an advocate of centralized, command planning) and a philosophical–humanistic interpretation of Marx (as an advocate of decentralized, self-managed socialism).

The orthodox interpretation of Marx

The orthodox interpretation suggests that Marx – a furious critic of utopian socialism – was necessarily silent on the topic of socialist economic organization. He instead left it to his followers to decide all the difficult details. In this view, Marx offered a radical criticism of capitalism, but no vision of fully evolved socialism. For instance, the leading Soviet economic historian, Alec Nove, supports the orthodox interpretation when he writes that 'Marx had little to say about the economics of socialism, and ... the little he did say was either irrelevant or directly misleading' (1983, p. 10). Nove applied the orthodox view to interpret the early Soviet experiment with socialism (during the so-called 'War Communism' period of 1918–21) as 'forced reaction to an emergency situation' (Nove, 1969), rather than a revolutionary attempt to plan inspired by Marx's vision of socialism. Contemporary Austrians in general have not subscribed to the orthodox view.

Marx as an organization theorist

A second interpretation of Marx, which claims Marx is an organization theorist who necessarily advocates central planning, stems from a criticism of the orthodox view. Economists Paul Craig Roberts and Matthew Stephenson, and Austrians Don Lavoie and Peter Boettke, argue that Marx's assault on the organizational 'anarchy' of the market process suggests definite, consistent implications for the socialist economy, and thus Marx's overall research program and revolutionary agenda cannot be understood without this organizational interpretation. Boettke claims, for example, that

> viewing Marx as an organization theorist enables the student of Marx to see a tremendous unity in Marx's life-work that is denied by those who wish to split Marx into a young Marx and a mature Marx. The young Marx, just as the mature Marx, was concerned with transcending the organizational form of alienation, that is, the commodity production of capitalist social relations. (1990, p. 44, n. 29)

Lavoie claims that 'Marx's scientific socialism was not merely an excuse for avoiding any examination of socialist society. It was a recommendation of a particular method for the conduct of such an examination – that is, that socialism be described through a systematic critique of capitalism' (1985b, p. 29). He further contends that 'there is implicit throughout Marx's writings a single, coherent, and remarkably consistent view of socialism' (p. 30) – namely, economic planning – which 'Marx consistently foresaw ... as centralized and comprehensive' (1985a, p. 19). Roberts and Stephenson contend that, indeed, central planning constitutes the 'defining characteristic of Marxian socialism' (1973, p. 94).

This theme – that Marxism ultimately strives for centralized economic planning – is common in the Austrian comparative systems literature, whose well-known argument that central planning must fail, because of a severe lack of knowledge confronting the central planners, need not be repeated here (see Lavoie, 1985b). More recently, viewing Marxism as promoting central, command planning has prompted a revisionist account of the War Communism era immediately following the Bolshevik Revolution. Contrary to Nove and other Soviet historians, Roberts (1971) and Boettke (1990) have demonstrated that Lenin and the Bolsheviks tried to plan the fledgling Soviet economy centrally in order to revolutionize Russia and create socialism, and thus the failure of War Communism in 1921 was, in effect, a failure of Marxian socialism.

Marx as a praxis philosopher

A third interpretation of Marx emphasizes his philosophical–humanistic dimension, as opposed to the dialectical materialism of the orthodoxy, or the organizational interpretation of the Austrians. Here the focus is upon Marx's praxis philosophy and his corresponding notion of alienation. Writers in this tradition – most notably the Yugoslav Praxis Group (see Markovic and Petrovic, 1979), fellow travelers Karel Kosik (1976) and Erich Fromm (1961), and contemporary economists such as Branko Horvat (1982) – do agree that Marx's critique of capitalism offers a vision of socialism. But they disagree that his vision must be one of centralized command planning. Contrary to the organization theory interpretation, they argue that central planning does not abolish alienation, but in fact may intensify it.

This is curious because both the organizational interpreters of Marx and the praxis interpreters claim to draw their conclusions from Marx's concept of alienation. Boettke claims, for instance, that 'The transcendence of alienation means to Marx the transcendence of market relations' (1990, p. 44, n. 29); Roberts emphasizes this point: 'in the Marxian scheme, central economic planning eliminates *Marxian* alienation by eliminating the exchange relationships of commodity production' (1971, p. 10). The praxis interpretation claims that abolishing the market system constitutes a necessary, but not sufficient, condition for de-alienation.

In other words, the organization theory interpretation tends to limit alienation to its economic dimension, while the praxis philosophy interpretation focuses on Marx's concept of praxis as a totality: as Kosik writes, 'In the concept of praxis, socio-human reality is discovered as the opposite of giveness, i.e. at once as the process of forming human *being* and as its specific form. *Praxis* is the *sphere of human being*' (1976, p. 136). To say that a human is a praxis being is to say that he or she has the potential to be a free, creative being – to participate democratically with others and rationally design, create and control society. To be alienated, then, means that, for whatever reason, our praxis potential is blocked. By definition, alienation is the gap between human essence and human existence (Horvat, 1982, p. 84). For Marx, people are alienated under the 'anarchy' of the market system. (This is clear in his *The Economic and Philosophic Manuscripts of 1844*, 1964.) But Marx also attacks political alienation that results from bureaucratic hierarchy and control. He writes in the *Critique of Hegel's 'Philosophy of Right'* (1970), for example, that 'in true democracy the *political state disappears*' (p. 118). As long as the modern bureaucratic state exists, it is separated from civil society by a hierarchy of knowledge and control. Under the state 'Man's content is not taken to be his true actuality' (ibid., p. 82).

According to the praxis philosophy interpretation, the implications for socialism are clear: 'Man is not only what he has been; he is in the first place what he can and ought to be,' writes Gajo Petrovic (1967). 'Marx's turn to praxis follows from this in the sense that his conception of man cannot remain a mere conception, but it is also a criticism of alienated man who does not realize his human possibilities and a humanistic program of struggle for humanness.' Hence it necessarily follows that 'Marx's conception of man can thus not be separated from his humanistic theory of alienation and de-alienation' (ibid., pp. 80–81). Full-fledged socialism is supposed to end alienation, whether economic or political; it is supposed to end the contradiction between human existence and essence. As Marx wrote, socialism would inevitably 'return man to himself' (1964, p. 135).

From this purely philosophical analysis, socialism would abolish both the anarchy of the market process and the hierarchy of the political structure. Abolishing the market in favor of despotic, command planning would merely replace many competing capitalist despots with a universal despot (the central planning board) that dictates the plan to the rest of society. Full de-alienation would require abolishing the market in favor of a *comprehensive yet decentralized* plan – a council-based, non-hierarchical planning network – grounded in radical democracy and self-management (see Markovic, 1974).

Which Marx? (and why Austrians might want to care)
It is reasonable to believe, contrary to the orthodoxy, that Marx's scientific socialism offered *some* direction for socialism. Both the organization theory and praxis philosophy interpretations provide scholarly evidence of this, but we run the risk of making an exegetical mistake if we focus on one interpretation while ignoring the other. The organization theory approach, by itself, offers only an 'economistic' understanding of Marxian socialism – it deduces the economic logic of abolishing the market process, but at the cost of ignoring the praxis benchmark. Surely, organizational analysis is fruitful because it suggests that comprehensive planning must collapse into hierarchical centralism in the face of information scarcities and conflicts of interest (see Hayek, 1944; Prychitko, 1988). But that in itself does not mean central planning was an aspiration, let alone a 'defining' characteristic, of full-fledged Marxian socialism. Although the work of Roberts and Stephenson, for example, actually claims to comprehend the meaning of Marxian alienation, it is questionable because they ignore Marx's praxis concept, the fulcrum upon which the entire alienation issue rests. On the other hand, the praxis philosophy interpretation, by itself, is much too 'philosophistic' – from the praxis benchmark it deduces a theory of alienation and de-alienation, which suggests an end to markets and hierarchies. It provides a nice *gedanken experiment* which describes the parameters of a de-alienated, socialist society, but that society is dubious because it ignores organization theory and economic logic; the praxis philosophy interpretation fails to comprehend the unintended consequences of decentralized planning.

Isolated, each interpretation tends to claim that Marx has a consistent, coherent vision of socialism. Yet the visions contradict each other. This is a hermeneutical problem. Organization theory ignores the full implications of

Marx's turn to praxis; praxis philosophy ignores the unintended organizational consequences of abolishing the market process in a world of scarcity. Both the organizational interpretation and the philosophical interpretation might instead shed more light on our understanding of Marx when juxtaposed. Each arguably represents one side of a tension, a conflict or struggle, in Marx's vision of socialism (see Prychitko, 1991). Perhaps Marx's vision of socialism is not nearly as coherent as we once thought.

This may interest more than historians of thought. It may also affect the way Austrians interpret the historical record. For instance, problematizing Marx's vision of socialism suggests three counter-intuitive examples, upon which we shall conclude: (1) if central planning is ultimately inconsistent with Marxian *de*-alienation, then the failure of command planning would not *necessarily* establish a failure to implement Marxian socialism – for that is not its defining characteristic; conversely, (2) any theoretical (or practical) model of socialist planning that *requires* hierarchical centralization to work successfully represents a theoretical (or practical) *failure* to achieve Marx's fully de-alienated utopia (for instance, even if Lenin or Stalin centrally planned the USSR successfully, Marxism would still be a flop); and (3) if the Austrians are correct in arguing that the market process *cannot* be abolished in favor of rational economic planning – that the market system is here to stay – we are not 'stuck' with alienation. If comprehensive planning is humanly impossible, then Marx's claim that we are beings of praxis, whose essence is freely and creatively to design the society we live in, is patently false. If the achievable, as Marx saw it, is epistemologically unachievable, the gap disappears and *Marxian* alienation simply ceases to be.

See also:

Chapter 4: Market process; Chapter 33: Comparative economic systems; Chapter 69: The socialist calculation debate

Bibliography

Boettke, Peter J. (1990), *The Political Economy of Soviet Socialism: The Formative Years, 1918–1928*, Boston: Kluwer Academic.

Fromm, Erich (1961), *Marx's Concept of Man*, New York: Frederick Ungar.

Hayek, F.A. (1944), *The Road to Serfdom*, Chicago: University of Chicago Press.

Horvat, Branko (1982), *The Political Economy of Socialism: A Marxist Social Theory*, Armonk, NY: M.E. Sharpe.

Kosík, Karel (1976), *Dialectics of the Concrete: A Study of Problems of Man and World*, Boston: D. Reidel.

Lavoie, Don (1985a), *National Economic Planning: What is Left?*, Cambridge, Mass.: Ballinger.

Lavoie, Don (1985b), *Rivalry and Central Planning: The Socialist Calculation Debate Reconsidered*, New York: Cambridge University Press.

Marković, Mihailo (1974), *From Affluence to Praxis: Philosophy and Social Criticism*, Ann Arbor: University of Michigan Press.

Marković, Mihailo and Gajo Petrović (eds) (1979), *Praxis: Yugoslav Essays in the Philosophy and Methodology of the Social Sciences*, Boston: D. Reidel.

Marx, Karl (1964), *The Economic and Philosophic Manuscripts of 1844*, New York: International Publishers.

Marx, Karl (1970), *Critique of Hegel's 'Philosophy of Right'*, New York: Cambridge University Press.

Nove, Alec (1969), *An Economic History of the USSR*, reprinted New York: Penguin Books, 1984.

Nove, Alec (1983), *The Economics of Feasible Socialism*, London: George Allen & Unwin.

Petrovic, Gajo (1967), *Marx in the Mid-Twentieth Century: A Yugoslav Philosopher Considers Karl Marx's Writings*, Garden City, NY: Doubleday and Co.

Prychitko, David L. (1988), 'Marxism and Decentralized Socialism', *Critical Review*, **2**, (4), fall.

Prychitko, David L. (1991), *Marxism and Workers' Self-Management: The Essential Tension*, Westport, Conn.: Greenwood Press.

Roberts, Paul Craig (1971), *Alienation and the Soviet Economy: Toward a General Theory of Marxian Alienation, Organizational Principles, and the Soviet Economy*, Albuquerque: University of New Mexico Press.

Roberts, Paul Craig and Matthew A. Stephenson (1973), *Marx's Theory of Exchange, Alienation, and Crisis*, Stanford: Hoover Institution Press.

Wright, Anthony (1986), *Socialisms: Theories and Practices*, Oxford: Oxford University Press.

75 Pre-Keynes macroeconomics

Leland B. Yeager

Keynes characterized the doctrines of his predecessors unfairly, perhaps out of inadequate acquaintance with them. He was by no means the pioneer he claimed to be in developing a theory of output as a whole and in integrating monetary theory with general value theory (Marget, 1938/1942, II, chapter I). Keynes said (*General Theory*, p. 13) that 'all members of the orthodox school' tacitly assumed that all unemployed workers 'though willing to work at the current wage will withdraw the offer of their labour in the event of even a small rise in the cost of living'. Yet he explicitly agreed with the supposedly classical proposition 'that, in general, an increase in employment can only occur to the accompaniment of a decline in the rate of real wages' (p. 17). Ironically, when agreeing with his predecessors, he agreed on an erroneous point.

Keynes quoted (1936, p. 18) from John Stuart Mill's *Principles of Political Economy* to represent Mill as a thoroughgoing adherent of Say's Law: supply of commodities constitutes demand for commodities; sellers are inevitably buyers. Besides committing slight inaccuracies, Keynes ended the quotation just where Mill went on to explain how the use of money requires qualifications to Say's Law. Indications are that Keynes did not bother to consult the *Principles* itself but instead quoted Mill from some secondary source. Keynes also neglected Mill's even crisper discussion in *Essays on Some Unsettled Questions of Political Economy* (1844, Essay II). Mill clearly explains how an excess demand for money holdings can show itself in the short run in a general glut – in modern terms, in a recession or depression.

Say's Law, properly interpreted, expresses a fundamental insight: people (and business firms) produce particular goods and services to exchange them, sooner or later, for the specialized outputs of other people. Since production represents power and desire to acquire other things in exchange, there can be no deep-seated, 'real' inadequacy of demand to absorb the output of a fully employed economy; no inexorable limitation from the demand side impedes long-run economic growth.

Mill's qualification concerning money is also fundamental. People desire cash balances of sizes related, if only loosely, to the volumes of transactions they lubricate. If people want cash balances totaling more than the actual money supply, they try to build up their holdings by showing reduced eagerness to buy and increased eagerness to sell in the markets for goods and services (and securities), where quantities demanded fall short of supplies at previously prevailing prices. In the opposite case of the actual money supply exceeding desired cash balances, excess demands appear on ordinary markets (Wicksell, 1898, pp. 39–41).

Although an excess demand for money can indeed disrupt the operation of Say's Law, automatic market forces work to correct the imbalance. They work through the real-balance effect as excess supplies of goods and labor exert downward pressure on prices. As Don Patinkin has shown, however, most classical and neoclassical theorists, reassured by Say's Law, did not bother to examine the exact nature of the equilibrating forces. They also neglected to consider whether these forces would always work quickly and powerfully enough to avoid painful consequences even from monetary disturbances. Keynes, far from remedying this neglect, confused the issue by attacking even the valid central insight of Say's Law.

What were economists thinking during the depression years just before Keynes published his *General Theory*? Joseph Dorfman's survey (1959, chapters XX–XXV) conveys the impression that no well-worked-out macroeconomic doctrine was generally accepted in the USA. Say's Law did not go unchallenged. Writing in the 1929 edition of *Encyclopaedia Britannica*, Allyn Young recognized that supply of goods would not always constitute adequate demand for goods and that general production might sometimes fall short of and sometimes outrun the expansion of money incomes. In the 1920s most responsible leaders and economists had thought that government could do little to cure a serious depression. When the Great Depression struck, opinion leaders were slow to grasp its nature and extent. By 1933, though, earlier distrust of government action had weakened. Ideas about overproduction, underspending, pump priming and secular stagnation were commanding thoughtful attention. Public works spending and government deficits were widely seen as necessary remedies or at least as palliatives (Dorfman, 1959; compare Davis, 1971).

Still, opinions ranged widely. Some economists used the depression as an opportunity to push ideas for more extensive government controls. R.T. Ely advocated a peacetime industrial army to enlist the unemployed at a soldier's pay for reforestation and other public works. Rexford Guy Tugwell was sympathetic to economic planning. Frank H. Knight exemplified a reluctant pragmatism. He blamed commercial banking as it then existed for intensifying business fluctuations and advocated what amounted to managed money. If gold supplies were inadequate for maintaining the 1929 price level, well, the gold contents of money units were not sacrosanct. Overcoming his natural inclination against 'social control', Knight supported Senator Wagner's proposal for public works financed by a bond issue; government should spend as much and tax as little as possible at such a time (Dorfman, 1959, pp. 767–70).

While some economists advocated reflationary policy, others blamed the monetary authorities for having already done too much. H. Parker Willis said that the cheap money policy to aid European finance had stimulated speculation. Government bond sales to the banks had diverted funds from normal business loans. After England left the gold standard in 1931, Willis warned even more strenuously against an easy money policy and against undermining the gold standard. He advised efforts to cancel what he considered inflated credit. A 'wonderful power of self-healing and recuperation in American industry' promised better results than unwise financial measures (Dorfman, 1959, pp. 698–702). Similarly, A.C. Miller of the Federal Reserve Board counselled the government as late as May 1932 to keep its hands off the sick economy and rely on nature to accomplish the cure (ibid., p. 609).

Fred R. Fairchild of Yale University voiced apparently 'Puritan' thinking: good times had to be paid for by bad times. He deprecated the new theory of spending as opposed to the old-fashioned emphasis on thrift: 'The unhappy experiences of the past three years were a "retribution" for disregard of "natural economic law"' (Dorfman, 1959, p. 734). Not all economists clung to such unanalytical dogma. Some were propounding what Clark Warburton later called monetary-disequilibrium theory and Karl Brunner more recently named monetarism. After the 1929 crash, Irving Fisher developed his debt-deflation theory of depression. He regretted the popular idea that deflation must be allowed to run its course in the interest of natural self-correction. He became the best-known advocate of easy money and credit to cure the depression; he advocated 'reflation' to restore prices to a level that would minimize and equalize injustice to creditors and debtors, after which that level would be stabilized. He saw some merit in various local stamp-scrip schemes to speed up velocity, but he stopped short of advocating fiat money. Yet the gold standard retained such a hold on the thinking of public men and most economists that even Fisher recognized 'complications and disturbances which would be incident to going off the gold standard' (*Booms and Depressions*, 1932, quoted in Dorfman, 1959, pp. 682–3).

James Harvey Rogers saw a shortage and international maldistribution of gold as near the heart of the depression. While attacking rigid adherence to the 'gold standard creed' and favoring stabilization after 'controlled inflation' through heavy public works expenditures, he never actually advocated scrapping the standard (Dorfman, 1959, pp. 688–93). Economists of a 'monetarist' orientation were not offering their diagnoses merely by hindsight. Throughout the 1920s, Ralph Hawtrey of England and Gustav Cassel of Sweden, among others, were warning that restoring currencies to their pre-war parities without international limitations on the demand for gold threatened deflation and depression. They particularly warned, before 1929, about the working of the gold standard in conjunction with what they considered the tight money policies of the USA and France. Cassel actively urged his views in the USA. In Congressional testimony of May 1928, he warned against the potentially deflationary consequences of a Federal Reserve policy oriented towards fighting speculation in Wall Street. In articles of 1930, expressing views similar to Irving Fisher's, he favored easy money (but not expansion of public works) and recommended that central banks try to raise price levels to a point where they would accord with rigid wage levels (Dorfman, 1959, pp. 660–61; Batchelder and Glasner, 1991).

Harry Gunnison Brown had already, claiming no originality, given a clear monetarist explanation of business fluctuations in an elementary textbook. In a remarkable article (1933) written for a fraternity magazine just days before Franklin D. Roosevelt took office as president, Brown forthrightly blamed the deflation of money, credit, property values and economic activity on the Federal Reserve's operation with fallacious theories. He warned against insistence on balancing the government budget even in such exceptional circumstances and urged the new president to compel the Federal Reserve's cooperation in a recovery program. He apparently had no hesitation about dispensing with the gold standard if it interfered with restoring prosperity.

Monetarist macroeconomics has a venerable history. Clark Warburton (1981 and unpublished manuscripts) maintains that monetary-disequilibrium theory was the prevailing explanation of business fluctuations in early twentieth-century America. Elements of it can be traced at least as far back as David Hume (1752) and Pehr Niclas Christiernin (1761), writing in Scotland and Sweden. Even earlier in the same century the theory must have been in the minds of policy makers in several American colonies, where new issues of paper money apparently had their intended effect in relieving a 'decay of trade' (Lester, 1939, chapters 3–5). Henry Thornton made a notable contribution in his book of 1802. Other nineteenth- and early twentieth-century contributors (on whom see Dorn, 1987) include Erick Bollman, Condy Raguet, William M. Gouge, C.F. Adams, George Tucker, Amasa Walker and Joseph French Johnson. Although such classical and neoclassical writers as David Ricardo, John Stuart Mill and Alfred Marshall were usually concerned with long-run microeconomic questions and so legitimately abstracted from short-run monetary disequilibrium, they recognized that such disequilibrium does occur and sometimes paid explicit attention to it. In 1913, both Ralph Hawtrey and Herbert Joseph Davenport published books containing clearly monetarist business cycle theory.

Two developments, apparently, crowded monetarism off the intellectual scene: first, the depth and persistence of the Great Depression, along with the supposed failure – as interpreted with erroneous theory – of easy money policy to remedy it, and, second, the Keynesian revolution. Keynesianism also crowded off various other business cycle theories, including the monetary–malinvestment theory developed from nineteenth-century currency school doctrines by Ludwig von Mises and refined by F.A. Hayek (see Haberler, 1958). The Keynesian revolution, along with the depression to which it itself was a reaction, shook up the complacency about macroeconomic questions into which much of the economics profession had lapsed. Unfortunately, it also diverted professional attention away from promising lines of economic research that would begin to revive and flourish only some two decades later.

See also:
Chapter 63: The Great Depression; Chapter 81: Monetarism

Bibliography

Batchelder, Ronald W. and David Glasner (1991), 'Pre-Keynesian Monetary Theories of the Great Depression: Whatever Happened to Hawtrey and Cassel?', paper presented at the History of Economics Society meetings, College Park, MD, June.

Brown, Harry Gunnison (1931), *Economic Science and the Common Welfare*, 5th edn, Columbia, Mo.: Lucas Brothers.

Brown, Harry Gunnison (1933), 'Nonsense and Sense in Dealing with the Depression', Beta Gamma Sigma *Exchange*, pp. 97–107.

Christiernin, Pehr Niclas (1761), *Summary of Lectures on the High Price of Foreign Exchange in Sweden*, translation by Robert V. Eagly in Eagly, *The Swedish Bullionist Controversy*, Philadelphia: American Philosophical Society, 1971, pp. 41–99.

Davenport, Herbert J. (1913), *The Economics of Enterprise*, New York: Macmillan; reprinted New York: Kelley, 1968.

Davis, J. Ronnie (1971), *The New Economics and the Old Economists*, Ames: Iowa State University Press.

Dorfman, Joseph (1959), *The Economic Mind in American Civilization*, vol. 5, New York: Viking Press.

Dorn, James A. (1987), 'The Search for Stable Money: A Historical Perspective', in James A. Dorn and Anna J. Schwartz (eds), *The Search for Stable Money*, Chicago: University of Chicago Press, pp. 1–28.

Fisher, Irving (1932), *Booms and Depressions*, New York: Adelphi.

Fisher, Irving (1933), 'The Debt-Deflation Theory of Great Depressions', *Econometrica*, 1, October, 337–57.

Haberler, Gottfried (1958), *Prosperity and Depression*, 4th edn, London: Allen & Unwin.

Hawtrey, Ralph (1913), *Good and Bad Trade*, London: Constable; reprinted New York: Kelley, 1970.

Hume, David (1752), 'Of Money', reprinted in Eugene Rotwein (ed.), *Writings on Economics*, Madison: University of Wisconsin Press, 1970, pp. 33–46.

Keynes, John Maynard (1936), *The General Theory of Employment, Interest and Money*, London/New York: Harcourt, Brace.

Lester, Richard A. (1939), *Monetary Experiments: Early American and Recent Scandinavian*, Princeton: Princeton University Press; reprinted Newton Abbot, England: David and Charles Reprints, 1970.

Marget, Arthur W. (1938, 1942), *The Theory of Prices*, two vols; reprinted New York: Kelley, 1966.

Marshall, Alfred (1887), 'Remedies for Fluctuations of General Prices', *Contemporary Review*, 51, January–June, 355–75.

Mill, John Stuart (1844), *Essays on Some Unsettled Questions of Political Economy*, written 1829–30; reprinted Clifton, NJ: Kelley, 1974.

Patinkin, Don (1956, 1965), *Money, Interest, and Prices*, 1st and 2nd edns, New York: Harper & Row.

Thornton, Henry (1802), *An Enquiry into the Nature and Effects of the Paper Credit of Great Britain*; reprinted Fairfield, NJ: Kelley, 1978.

Warburton, Clark (1966), *Depression, Inflation, and Monetary Policy*, Baltimore: Johns Hopkins Press.

Warburton, Clark (1981), 'Monetary Disequilibrium Theory in the First Half of the Twentieth Century', *History of Political Economy*, **13**, summer, 285–99.

Wicksell, Knut (1898), *Interest and Prices*, translated by R.F. Kahn, 1936; reprinted New York: Kelley, 1965.

76 Austrian economics and American (old) institutionalism

Malcolm Rutherford

Ever since Veblen attacked Menger on the grounds that his retention of hedonistic conceptions made his economics less than fully evolutionary (Veblen, 1898), the Austrian and American (old) institutionalist traditions have been at loggerheads. Each has tended to adopt a dismissive attitude towards the other, a viewpoint that has been expressed most forcefully by writers such as Dugger (1989), Gordon (1989) and Stanfield (1989) on the institutionalist side, and by Seckler (1975), Schotter (1981) and Langlois (1989) on the Austrian side. For most institutionalists, Austrian economics disqualifies itself owing to its a priorism, methodological individualism, view of the individual actor as a rational evaluator, emphasis on spontaneous order and rejection of governmental intervention – particularly in the form of economic planning. For most Austrians, institutionalism disqualifies itself for exactly the opposite set of reasons: its empiricism, methodological holism, emphasis on habit and cultural conditioning, tendency to emphasize institutional design (most obvious in the work of J.R. Commons) and positive view of governmental intervention – particularly in the form of economic planning. On a cursory examination it would be easy to conclude that on virtually all important issues Austrian and institutional economics are irreconcilably opposed. Nevertheless, some recent work has attempted both to indicate and assess certain commonalities and complementarities between the two traditions. These points of contact relate to the facts that both Austrians and institutionalists reject orthodox neoclassical full information assumptions, equilibrium theorizing and formal techniques, and focus instead on process, on change and evolution, and on the importance of social rules and institutions (Samuels, 1989; Boettke, 1989; Caldwell, 1989; Rutherford, 1989; Wynarczyk, 1992). The rest of this entry will attempt to outline briefly the nature of the various oppositions, similarities and complementarities that have been identified so far.

A priorism and empiricism
Two main issues arise with respect to the comparison of Austrian and institutionalist methodology. These can be expressed in terms of the traditional oppositions between a priorism and empiricism, and between individualism

and holism. The first issue will be dealt with here, and the second in the next section.

Austrian methodology originally developed in opposition to that of the German historical school, and has always contained an emphasis on the need for a deductive theoretical approach and one focused on the general or universal rather than on the particular or historically relative. This approach differs in obvious ways from the much more empirical orientation of many institutionalists (particularly Commons and Mitchell) that was developed primarily in opposition to neoclassical economics. Nevertheless, institutionalists are not naive inductivists, nor do they reject universal categories or the possibility of cross-cultural generalizations. Veblen criticized German historicism and argued that all systems of thought must be based on metaphysical preconceptions; Ayres clearly regarded his instrumental/ceremonial distinction as of universal applicability; and even Commons and Mitchell conducted their empirical work with theoretical guidance. While undeniably more historical and empirical than Austrians, institutionalists are not the antitheorists they are sometimes portrayed as being.

Furthermore, both Austrians and institutionalists reject the static equilibrium theorizing of neoclassical economics and neither use mathematical formalism, preferring instead a literary style. The reasons given for the rejection of orthodox approaches are remarkably similar, the key points having to do with the importance of change and the factors that give rise to change, and the notion of the *complex* nature of the social system and its evolution, a notion that results in the rejection of the full information and optimizing assumptions that underlie most formal methods. The problem of dealing with a complex evolving system provides an important common thread running through the various methods found in both traditions. These methods may differ, but they represent, in significant part, responses to the same difficulty. It is true that complexity generates barriers in the way of untangling the relationships involved without a great deal of theoretical effort, but it is also the case that complex dynamic systems often exhibit an indeterminacy that indicates the importance of the particularities of time and place. It might be argued that Austrian and institutionalist methods have each concentrated on only one side of this problem, and that while institutionalism needs more theory Austrian economics could do with a good deal more history.

Individualism and holism
Austrian economics is associated with methodological individualism and institutionalism with methodological holism. Individualism focuses on the way individual action gives rise to social institutions, while holism concentrates on the way social institutions define the values, roles and behaviors adopted by individuals. For individualists, the key point is that only individu-

als are actors. They complain that holists often argue in ways that imply that social entities have functions or purposes of their own. For holists, the key point is the social molding of individuals. They complain that individualists often adopt the reductionist view that social institutions can be explained solely in terms of the actions of autonomous individuals, a position that implies that institutions are merely epiphenomenal in nature. The notion of holistic purposes conflicts with the individualistic insistence on only individual agents being actors, while reductionist versions of individualism conflict with the basic holist stress on the social influence on the individual. It is, however, quite possible to argue both that only individuals act and that existing institutions shape individual preferences and goals. This middle position rejects equally the idea of distinct holistic purposes and the reductionist version of individualism, and combines the reasonable elements in each approach.

The opposition of Austrian and institutionalist methodology, then, depends on the holism of institutionalists involving social purposes and/or the individualism of Austrians being of a reductionist nature, but it is not obvious that these characterizations apply. Although one can find examples of reductionist individualism in the writings of Austrians (most obviously Mises), one can also find quite explicit rejections of reductionist approaches (for example in Wieser and, recently, Langlois). Somewhat similarly, institutionalist writings contain language that suggests distinct social purposes, but in many cases these social purposes are intended only to signify the outcome of political and other processes of social choice. For the most part, institutionalists would have no difficulty with the proposition that it is only individuals who can act. What this implies is that the Austrian emphasis on the individual acts that give rise to institutions is not necessarily in conflict with the institutionalist emphasis on the social conditioning of individuals.

Rationality and rule following

A further aspect of the holism/individualism debate is to be found in the distinction between the view of man as rationally evaluating his actions, and the view of man as following rules (habits, routines and norms) and not engaging in case-by-case evaluation. Austrian analysis has traditionally treated man as a subjectively rational evaluator, always attempting to make the best choice but with imperfect knowledge and facing considerable uncertainty. Mises, for example, even treats an individual's 'choice' of ideology as the same as any other self-interested choice (Mises, 1949, p. 46). In contrast, institutionalists have stressed both the psychological and social constraints on subjecting everything to continual rational appraisal. Veblen, for example, argues that individuals form habits and adopt social norms. Habits can be periodically re-evaluated and adjusted by individuals as conditions change, but norms provide the socially accepted ends of action and, in Veblen's view, develop and change as a result of processes that are behavioristic and evolutionary rather than rational and evaluative.

Veblen's behaviorism has often been criticized by Austrians, and not without reason. The links drawn by Veblen between patterns of life and patterns of thought are not always very satisfactory. Nevertheless, largely as a result of Hayek's work, Austrians are placing increasing emphasis on rule following and on the evolutionary selection of rules. They argue that, given ignorance and uncertainty, individuals may do better to follow a rule than to attempt to make decisions on a case-by-case basis. In addition, social rules, including social norms, are seen as functioning to make behavior predictable and to provide for social coordination. Thus, although the rules adopted may be seen as consistent with the outcome of a conscious choice, the actual processes involved are usually presented as involving some type of evolutionary selection mechanism. Unfortunately, whether rules that are individually or collectively rational will be selected depends on the exact nature of the process involved, and it has proved difficult to demonstrate that social norms are, in general, explicable in terms of the individual or group benefits they generate (Elster, 1989). The problem of dealing adequately with the relationship between rationality and norm-guided behavior still faces both traditions of thought.

The invisible hand and collective choice

Austrian economists, especially Menger and Hayek, have placed special emphasis on the spontaneous, invisible hand, processes that produce (beneficial) social rules as the unintended consequences of intentional actions. On these grounds Austrians criticize institutionalists, particularly Commons, for concentrating on processes of collective choice. Recent game-theoretic analyses of invisible hand processes, however, have shown that special circumstances are required for social rules to emerge and remain in force spontaneously. In many cases, the rules necessary for social order, or required to produce a particular social benefit, will have to be implemented and enforced by an organized state apparatus (Vanberg, 1986).

Moreover, the identification of institutionalism with collective choice processes is not entirely accurate. Commons is concerned with the way in which a workable social order can arise out of conflict of interest. Many of the rules that create such an order Commons sees as arising spontaneously as customs and common practices, but Commons is aware that the invisible hand can fail, and that organized political and judicial means for resolving disputes are required to maintain workability. Veblen's work deals very largely with institutional change as an unintended result of intentionally introduced new technology. The difference between Veblen and Austrians is that Veblen does not focus his attention only on consequences that are socially beneficial. In Veblen's work unintended consequences may not only violate the interests of the individuals who (unintentionally) generated the social consequence, but may also be socially dysfunctional.

Markets and government

Institutionalists do not accept that competitive or spontaneous evolutionary forces can be relied upon to produce socially desirable outcomes. They have adopted the view that, through scientifically guided government intervention, social institutions can be reformed and the economy planned for greater social benefit. There are many versions of this basic position to be found within institutionalism, but they all appear to run directly counter to the well-known Austrian arguments concerning the subjective and decentralized character of knowledge, the complex and poorly understood nature of social systems, and the normative appeal of market orders. These points sum to the Austrian aversion to the application of science to social planning.

Despite this apparent opposition, moderate views can be found on both sides. Even the most ardent of modern-day institutionalist planners propose only a Scandinavian system of indicative planning, and many institutionalists have made proposals that go significantly less far. Commons, for example, opposed any extension of direct government involvement, preferring other more flexible devices such as independent agencies and commissions. On the Austrian side, and despite the importance attached to spontaneous processes, it is quite clear that it is not accepted that spontaneously generated rules will always be beneficial, or that needed rules will always emerge by themselves.

This convergence, however, goes only so far and basic differences in values remain. Austrians place a particular stress on the values of individuality and freedom from coercion that they associate with markets, whereas institutionalists stress the invidious and inequitable nature of market competition and adopt the values of community and equity. There is, unfortunately, a tendency in both traditions to seek absolutes and to play down the problem that individuals value many things, not all of which can be increased together. Ignoring the problem of trade-offs between values is something that leads to the type of dogmatism that is too often found among Austrians and institutionalists alike.

Conclusion

From the above it is obvious that the research programs being pursued by Austrians and institutionalists differ in many respects, but these differences should not be seen as necessarily irreconcilable or as involving incommensurabilities. Very often the differences represent differences in approach to the same problem, or differences in the particular aspects of the same totality that are being emphasized. The observed similarities between the programs represent the similarity of the problems being addressed, the differences between the programs represent differences in approach and focus. The deepest divisions between the two, and the cause of much of the antagonism, are the different value premises that are embedded deep within each program. As long as these differences in basic values remain, the opportunities that exist for fruitful communication are likely also to remain unexploited.

See also:
Chapter 2: Methodological individualism; Chapter 5: Aristotelianism, apriorism, essentialism; Chapter 80: Social institutions and game theory; Chapter 77: The 'new' institutional economics

Bibliography

Boettke, Peter J. (1989), 'Evolution and Economics: Austrians as Institutionalists', *Research in the History of Economic Thought and Methodology*, 6, 73–89.

Caldwell, Bruce J. (1989), 'Austrians and Institutionalists: The Historical Origins of their Shared Characteristics', *Research in the History of Economic Thought and Methodology*, 6, 91–100.

Dugger, William M. (1989), 'Austrians vs. Institutionalists: Who are the Real Dissenters?', *Research in the History of Economic Thought and Methodology*, 6, 115–23.

Elster, Jon (1989), 'Social Norms and Economic Theory', *Journal of Economic Perspectives*, 3, fall, 99–117.

Gordon, Wendell C. (1989), 'Comparing Austrian and Institutional Economics', *Research in the History of Economic Thought and Methodology*, 6, 133–41.

Langlois, Richard N. (1989), 'What was Wrong with the Old Institutional Economics (and What is Still Wrong with the New)?', *Review of Political Economy*, 1, November, 270–98.

Mises, Ludwig von (1949), *Human Action*, London: Hodge.

Rutherford, Malcolm (1989), 'Some Issues in the Comparison of Austrian and Institutional Economics', *Research in the History of Economic Thought and Methodology*, 6, 159–72.

Samuels, Warren J. (1989), 'Austrian and Institutional Economics: Some Common Elements', *Research in the History of Economic Thought and Methodology*, 6, 53–71.

Schotter, Andrew (1981), *The Economic Theory of Social Institutions*, Cambridge: Cambridge University Press.

Seckler, David (1975), *Thorstein Veblen and the Institutionalists*, London: Macmillan.

Stanfield, J. Ron (1989), 'Of Paradigms and Discipline', *Research in the History of Economic Thought and Methodology*, 6, 173–9.

Vanberg, Viktor (1986), 'Spontaneous Market Order and Social Rules: A Critical Examination of F.A. Hayek's Theory of Cultural Evolution', *Economics and Philosophy*, 2, April, 75–100.

Veblen, Thorstein B. (1898), 'Why is Economics not an Evolutionary Science?'; reprinted in *The Place of Science in Modern Civilization*, New York: Russell and Russell, 1961, pp. 56–81.

Wynarczyk, Peter (1992), 'Comparing Alleged Incommensurables: Institutional and Austrian Economics as Rivals and Possible Complements?', *Review of Political Economy*, 4, January, 18–36.

77 The 'new' institutional economics

Richard Langlois

Many if not most of the strands that come together in the emerging tapestry of the 'new' institutionalism emerge from Ronald Coase's 'The Problem of Social Cost' (1960). That paper challenged not merely the conclusions but, more fundamentally, the analytical perspective of conventional welfare economics as then practiced (and indeed still practiced) in the tradition of the prewar Cambridge economist A.C. Pigou. Rather than seeing physical externalities as generating divergences between private cost and 'social cost', Coase argued, we ought instead to see the matter in comparative–institutional terms. The real issue is: which competing user of a resource ought to have command of that resource? In the absence of transaction costs, the user who is willing to pay the most for the resource will ultimately possess it. If transaction costs impede such gains from trade, however, the right of use may remain inefficiently in the hands of the party who values it less. Harold Demsetz (1967) quickly extended this insight beyond questions of externality to questions of institutional change more broadly. If any institutional change – like the creation of a system of property rights where none had existed – would yield net benefits, that change will take place unless transaction costs prevent it. For example, when the demand for animal pelts increased after European traders arrived in North America, the aboriginal Montagnais of Québec began experiencing common-pool problems in trapping. This created net benefits for the creation of a system of property rights, which the Montagnais promptly adopted.

By the 1970s, a number of writers had begun applying these ideas to the explanation of a variety of social institutions, including legal doctrines (Posner, 1972) and business firms (Williamson, 1975). Perhaps the most thoroughgoing application came in the area of economic history, where Douglass North and his collaborators (for example, North and Thomas, 1973) set out to explain the pattern of past institutional development as a series of responses to gains from trade created by population growth and other quasi-exogenous forces. In this enterprise, the Coasean theory of institutional change (if it may be called that) merged with a theory of transaction costs borrowed from the field of public choice. Coase's theorem is in its way an affirmation of the universality of the rent-seeking impulse. And, as the theory of rent-seeking behavior tells us, changes promising net increases in social wealth are easily blocked when those who stand to lose from the change are small in number and easily organized but those who stand to gain are numerous and costly to organize. To pick an example from North and Thomas (1973), manorial lords of the thirteenth century blocked changes in property rights that might have led to increased agricultural productivity because such innovations would also have tipped the share of rents from agriculture towards the peasants.

This growing focus on institutions fed, and was in turn fed by, the much-noted penchant for neoclassical economics to engage in cross-disciplinary imperialism. Put another way, the development of the 'new' institutional economics – a phrase almost certainly dating from the 1970s, and most often traced to Williamson (1975) – was at the core of a general broadening of the interests of more or less mainstream economists beyond the traditional concerns of price-and-allocation theory. Neoclassical economics had (re)discovered institutions, the ignoring of which had been at the center of criticism from 'old' institutionalists. Yet there were problems. For reasons that will be expanded upon below, the inherently dynamic nature of institutional evolution strained at the static confines of neoclassical theory. It is here that the Austrian tradition enters the picture. For in the Austrian leg of the marginalist tripod, the economist could find, ready-made as it were, a dynamic theory of social institutions to complement the static Coasean approach.

Austrian economics and the new institutionalism
Following the lead of Carl Menger, a modern Austrian theory of social institutions would necessarily be a causal-genetic or process theory. By that is meant a theory in which explanation involves tracing out a sequence of events rather than merely constructing the conditions for an equilibrium. The exemplar of this approach is Carl Menger's theory of the institution of money. To put it another way, Austrian theories of social institutions rely on invisible hand explanations. Such explanations describe the development of institutions as a sequence of the actions of individuals aggregated by some compositional principle (Langlois, 1986, chapter 10). The compositional principle need not be merely 'adding up' the behavior of the individuals (whatever that means), but would typically involve filtering or selection mechanisms. There is in my view no fundamental distinction between invisible hand explanations and evolutionary explanations, except to the extent that one takes the biological analogy to restrict the latter to particular types of selection principles. Indeed, it is now well understood that Menger's approach to social institutions and Darwin's theory of biological evolution have a common ancestor in the writings of the Scottish Enlightenment.

At the base of virtually all formulations of the concept of a social institution lies the notion of rule-following behavior. Institutions reflect behavior that is highly organized, in the sense that the behavior represents a relatively predictable or non-random pattern. And such patterns emerge as the result of the following of rules: they are, as Hayek (1967) puts it, systems of rules of conduct. This characterization applies to the sorts of political and economic institutions implied in the foregoing discussion: systems of property rights or of agricultural organization are sets of rules that constrain the behavior of the human agent. But the notion of rule following also applies to more funda- mental kinds of institutions, like language, morals and culture. Indeed, we might say that there are two (overlapping) branches of the new institutional economics: the branch concerned with basic and abstract social institution (like morals and culture) and the branch concerned with legal and political institutions.

Norms and conventions

The neoclassical economic theory of abstract social institutions can easily be recast in the terms of Carl Menger. A number of philosophers and economists have looked at social institutions instructively from within the framework of game theory. (For surveys, see Langlois, 1986, 1993). Although game theory as practiced by neoclassical theorists is most often a formal equilibrium technique, a game-theoretic approach to social institutions need not therefore be incompatible with a causal-genetic approach.

Although this theory is complex and rather subtle, one can get some feel for it by considering the two most important canonical games that appear in this work. The first of these is the *coordination game*. Think of the problem of choosing which side of the road to drive on in a world with no established convention. If I choose to drive on the left-hand side of the road and an oncoming motorist chooses the right (or vice versa), the 'pay-offs' to both of us in this 'game' will likely be negative. If, however, we both choose the same side of the road – either side – we will not incur these penalties. With repeated play of this game, one would expect drivers to keep to one particular side as a matter of *convention*. Notice that such a convention is self-enforc- ing: anyone who consistently drives on the left in the USA will be punished by negative pay-offs quite apart from any penalties invoked by the courts. Notice also that, while far superior to discoordination, a convention solution need not be optimal. (Suppose, for example, that driving on the right some- how resulted in cheaper cars. A convention to drive on the left is preferable to no convention, but not preferable to having chosen the right-hand side.) Conventions of this sort are thus path-dependent processes. Moreover, it is typically costly to alter a convention once established, and it may take some kind of centralized coordination to do so, as when Sweden and Okinawa changed their side-of-the-road driving conventions.

In a coordination game, the incentives of both players are aligned; their common objective is facilitated by the reduction in information costs a convention achieves. By contrast, what characterizes a *prisoners' dilemma* is a divergence of incentives. The parable commonly attached to the game is as follows. Two suspects are hauled in by the police for a bank robbery. Without a confession, the authorities have insufficient evidence to convict the two, although they could convict them of a lesser crime. The police interrogate the criminals in separate rooms and propose a deal to each: if you turn state's evidence and testify against your cohort, you go free, and we throw the book at him. In this case, each prisoner has a private incentive to confess, whereas the 'social optimum' is for both to hold firm, in the sense that such steadfast-ness minimizes the total number of years in prison. Because of the private incentive to confess – both to lower one's own sentence and to insure against confession by one's compatriot – the solution of such a game played once is for both to confess, a result that maximizes total years in prison. If, however, the game is played repeatedly, and neither of the players knows when the game will end, there may emerge a *norm* of reciprocity, according to which the players refrain from confessing despite the private incentive to do so. If we generalize the prisoners' situation to the sort of situation one faces every day with respect, say, to honesty in business dealings, then we see how a very basic sort of social institution might emerge as the unintended result of individual action.

Like a convention, a prisoners' dilemma norm is an institution with an information function. It substitutes for the costly direct communication and negotiation between the players that might otherwise facilitate agreement on the joint-maximizing solution. Unlike a coordination convention, however, a norm of this sort is not completely self-enforcing. Whenever the players face an end-game, the discipline of repeated play evaporates and the private incentives loom large. Thus prisoners' dilemma situations often call for some sort of external policing mechanism. For example, businesses can usually be expected to adhere to their contracts out of fear of harming their reputations and losing future business; but if the private incentive for breach of contract becomes great enough, the contract leaves the 'self-enforcing range', and the parties may find themselves in court. We should distinguish, however, be-tween privately rational reciprocity enforced by repeated play and the idea of a norm proper. In many situations, people follow norms of behavior – like honesty – even in end-game situations. One often tells the truth even when lying would be costless and privately beneficial. The reason is that norms of this sort are often internalized to form a part of culture. After repeated play of a prisoners' dilemma game by many different individuals, the original game situation and the sanctions of repeated play are forgotten. Only the norm remains. In this sense, the norm is *itself* an enforcement mechanism. This is not to say that a norm must always emerge or that the mechanism of repeated play must always solve the prisoners' dilemma in happy fashion. There are far too many examples of social situations in which norms have collapsed or failed to emerge and in which the dilemma of this game is all too real. It is a major task of research in this area to understand the circumstances under which efficiency-enhancing norms will in fact emerge.

Legal and political institutions

With the exception of the economics of the Common Law (Rizzo, 1980), Austrian influence has not penetrated far beyond the theory of abstract social institutions into the realm of economic and political institutions. This deficiency is especially glaring in the area of business institutions, an oversight only now being rectified (Langlois, 1993). Nonetheless, writers starting from the Coasean base have begun to raise issues of knowledge and economic process with which Austrians would be sympathetic.

In most cases, this indirect injection of Austrian concerns arises from the difficulties inherent in attempting to jam a theory of institutional change into the confines of static neoclassical theory. Although the Coasean approach is in some sense a theory of change, it presents change in a static framework. That is to say, it recasts the problem of institutional evolution as a problem of choice among discrete institutional alternatives with varying costs and benefits. Although this is certainly an improvement over institution-free neoclassicism, and although there is undeniably much wisdom in this approach, it does not see institutional change as an unfolding process over time. Moreover, the unvarnished Coasean approach does not concern itself with the role of knowledge in institutional change, except perhaps to the extent that 'imperfections' in knowledge are rolled into the concept of the transaction cost.

Recently, however, Douglass North (1990) and others have begun to recognize some of these difficulties. The first difficulty – the problem of conceiving of change in static terms – raises its head in the context of 'path dependence'. Both the set of available institutional alternatives and the costs and benefits of those alternatives may depend not only on factors active today but on the institutional choices of the past. As Hayek (1967, p. 75) remarks, the existence of an evolved structure 'may in fact depend not only on [the] environment, but also on the existence in the past of many other environments, indeed on a definite sequence of such environments'. In present-day parlance, this is the problem of path dependency. The literature recognizes one principal source of path dependency in the analysis of institutions: the phenomenon of 'lock in'. And here we see a connection with the theory of conventions. As in the case of a convention, an institutional structure can be 'locked in' by past events whenever there are increasing returns or 'network effects' to the adoption of an institution. The choice of institutions today – whether it be side-of-the-road driving conventions; choice of *lingua franca*; technological standards for typewriters, electricity, broadcasting, software and so on; or systems of legal rules generally – may depend on chance events or powerful individuals in the past that nudged the system onto a path from which it has become costly to deviate, even in the face of superior alternatives.

The problem of knowledge has entered the economics of institutions, at least in the work of North, under the guise of the problem of ideology. For North, 'the subjective and incomplete processing of information plays a critical role in decision making. It accounts for ideology, based upon subjective perceptions of reality, playing a major role in human beings' choices' (1990, p. 23). Ideology is important in explaining institutional change in two ways: ideas may shape political and economic preferences in the aggregate (as in the cases of, say, the Medieval Church or the nineteenth-century abolitionist movement), which in turn affects the costs and benefits of alternative institutions; or ideas may enter through the beliefs of a crucial individual or small group (like the US Supreme Court) who are insulated from competitive pressures and whose choices can be decisive. In all events, however, the theory of ideology and knowledge in institutional change is not well developed, and it calls out for further application of Austrian insights.

See also:
Chapter 9: Causation and genetic causation in economic theory; Chapter 78: Evolutionary economics; Chapter 28: Self-organizing systems; Chapter 80: Social institutions and game theory

Bibliography
Coase, Ronald H. (1960), 'The Problem of Social Cost', *Journal of Law and Economics*, 1, 3.
Demsetz, Harold (1967), 'Toward a Theory of Property Rights', *American Economic Review*, 57, 347–59.
Hayek, F.A. (1967), *Studies in Philosophy, Politics and Economics*, Chicago: University of Chicago Press.
Langlois, Richard N. (ed.) (1986), *Economics as a Process: Essays in the New Institutional Economics*, New York: Cambridge University Press.
Langlois, Richard N. (1993), 'Orders and Organizations: Toward an Austrian Theory of Social Institutions', in Bruce Caldwell and Stephan Böhm (eds), *Austrian Economics: Tensions and New Directions*, Dordrecht: Kluwer Academic
North, Douglass C. (1990), *Institutions, Institutional Change and Economic Performance*, New York: Cambridge University Press.
North, Douglass C. and Robert Paul Thomas (1973), *The Rise of the Western World*, New York: Cambridge University Press.
Posner, Richard (1972), *Economic Analysis of Law*, 1st edn, Boston: Little, Brown.
Rizzo, Mario J. (1980), 'Law Amid Flux: The Economics of Negligence and Strict Liability in Tort', *Journal of Legal Studies*, 9, (2), 291–318.
Williamson, Oliver E. (1975), *Markets and Hierarchies*, New York: Free Press.

78 Evolutionary economics
Ulrich Witt

Although the contributions to evolutionary economics have a rather heterodox lineage they all seem to agree on one point: the interest in, and the focus
on, endogenously generated economic change, its causes and its consequences.
As endogenously caused change appears on many different levels, research
into evolutionary economics has been done in quite diverse fields. Pre-emi-
nent topics of research have been : (1) the changes of aggregate economic
activity under the influence of an incessant, yet possibly discontinuous, flow
of innovations in the Schumpeterian tradition (Schumpeter, 1934); (2) the
performance of industries and firms in the competitive innovative struggle
and the relevance of Darwinian concepts to understanding this problem (Nelson and Winter, 1982); (3) the functioning of markets as perceived in an
evolutionary perspective (Hayek, 1978); (4) the 'path dependency' of historical economic developments (Arthur, 1988); (5) the emergence and variation
of societal rules and institutions that form the changing framework of economic interactions (Hayek, 1988); and (6) the individual background of the
striving for change (Loasby, 1983).

Schumpeterian themes

It was Schumpeter (1934) who, for the first time, provided a consistent
evolutionary interpretation of economic change. He developed a theory of
entrepreneurship and submitted that cyclical patterns in aggregate economic
activity can be derived from the particular time patterns of entrepreneurial
activities. Being an entrepreneur is, according to Schumpeter, not an occupation or a profession, but rather a unique, and rarely found, capacity to carry
out new combinations of resources; that is, innovations. The basis of this
capacity is held to be a peculiar personality and motivation (Schumpeter
1934, pp. 74–94), an interpretation with obvious elitist connotations. In this
respect, Schumpeter clearly contrasts with Mises and Kirzner who interpret
the entrepreneurial element as a basic human capacity, an alertness that
everyone possesses more or less. Likewise, Schumpeter's view of entrepreneurial activities as a disruption of a stationary state ('circular flow') of the
economy contrasts with the Austro-American position that attributes an equilibrating effect to entrepreneurial alertness.

It is important to note that, for Schumpeter, the information on the underlying inventions and discoveries is readily available. It is not the creation of

novel ideas as such but their carrying out, their translation into concrete innovative ventures, that is interpreted as what entrepreneurs achieve. Given this orientation, it is no wonder that Schumpeter tends to overemphasize the role of spectacular innovations and, by the same token, underrates small-scale innovative activities. It is often argued, however, that major innovations and small-scale innovative improvements of technologies and products systematically alternate (see, for example, Nelson and Winter, 1982, chapter 11). When Schumpeter stresses entrepreneurial will and the capacity required to turn into reality that which he assumes readily available – new knowledge – he obviously plays down the role of novelty and its creation. This does not fit well with the emphasis on the endogenous causation of economic change since, in effect, an explanation for the ultimate source of change is thus circumvented.

Later on Schumpeter (1942, pp. 132–3) himself changed his assessment of the role of the entrepreneur. He argued explicitly that the pioneering promoter loses out against the teams and trained specialists of the large corporations and trusts and becomes increasingly obsolete. Instead of being an heroic leader's achievement, innovative activities become the form of bureau and committee work. However, Schumpeter remained reluctant to address the problem of how novelty emerges in the economy. After abandoning the psychologically backed theory of the entrepreneur, his approach had therefore arrived at a point where it was open to invasion by neoclassical reinterpretations. Indeed, this was what happened in the 1970s and 1980s. Neoclassical writers were attracted by Schumpeter's provocative vision of an incessant, routine-like, industrial innovativeness which revolutionizes the economy but also embraces monopolistic practices as a necessary concomitant (Schumpeter, 1942, chapter 8). Such a view grossly deviated from the assessment derived from the static model of perfect competition. Little of Schumpeter's work has attracted as much attention as the rather isolated conjecture about the relationships between market structure and innovativeness, today discussed in innumerable contributions under the heading of 'Schumpeterian competition'. Much of that work, empirical as well as theoretical, is totally unrelated to evolutionary economics. In fact, major efforts have been made to recast the notion in the neoclassical terms of optimal innovation race strategies and equilibrium investments into innovative activities.

Economic 'natural selection' and the firm
Analogies to Darwinian concepts have always attracted economists. The economic 'natural selection' argument refers to biological analogies in the theory of the firm that were discussed at the beginning of the 1950s. It is obviously inspired by Darwinian thought. The question raised was to what extent diversity in the firms' goals and performances would be eliminated by

competition which may be supposed to drive all those forms out of the market that are not able to operate sufficiently profitably. As it turned out in the debate, the argument tacitly presupposes much more than its advocates seem to have been aware of. In order to judge to what extent all the preconditions on which the argument depends are fulfilled, various possible behavioral patterns must be carefully explored under diverse possible environmental conditions. This is, of course, exactly what the argument hoped to avoid.

The influential contribution to evolutionary economics made by Nelson and Winter (for example, 1982) is strongly informed by the debate on economic natural selection. These authors try to synthesize ideas from organizational and behavioral theories of the firm, in particular as suggested by the Carnegie school, on the one hand, and a loose analogy to the model of natural selection, on the other. On the basis of this synthesis, Nelson and Winter are able to carry further an idea suggested by Schumpeter (1942), who claimed that the role of the entrepreneur as an innovator was taken over by teams and departments in corporate organizations. Where Schumpeter had no detailed conceptions as to how those corporate divisions operate, Nelson and Winter try to provide a theoretical basis. Following notions developed by the Carnegie school, they argue that organizations are based in their internal interactions on behavioral routines, rules of thumb and regular interaction patterns. Production planning, calculation, price setting and even the allocation of R&D funds thus follow rule-bound behavior.

Since there is little in the realm of the theory of firm that corresponds to the structure of reproductive processes in biology, Nelson and Winter interpret routines in only loose analogy to the theory of natural selection as 'genotypes'. The firm's specific decisions thus derived, the 'phenotypes', may be more or less favorable for the firm's overall performance as measured in terms of profitable growth. Assuming that routines which successfully contribute to growth will not be changed, the actual expansion can be understood as an increase in relative frequency of those 'genes', while routines affecting deteriorations in the firm's performance are unlikely to expand. Indeed, drawing on the satisficing hypothesis it can be argued that those deteriorations trigger a search for improved routines – a kind of intentionally produced mutation. Among the results which Nelson and Winter obtain from extensive simulation experiments conducted on this basis is the conclusion that their approach supports the inverse rather than the original Schumpeter hypothesis concerning the relationship between market structure and innovativeness. According to the inverse hypothesis, the degree of concentration within an industry, pointing to a potential for monopolistic practices, is a consequence of, rather than a prerequisite for, a high rate of innovativeness in the industry.

New developments in biology, such as the controversy about gradualism v. punctualism, have recently revived the interest in analogies to biological concepts. Yet, given the rather loose character of possible analogies, their pay-off for the development of evolutionary economics should not be over-rated. If key elements of evolutionary thought in biology are expressed in terms of the triple notion of variation, selection and replication, it seems that only the concept of selection is of direct relevance in the domain of economics. However, this concept is a very powerful tool indeed. It may help to respond to valid subjectivist reservations concerning the theoretical treatment of individual expectations and desires. Likewise, it may help to overcome the problem that, once elements of bounded rationality are admitted, this usually implies an inherent dependence of all theoretical predictions on initial conditions. If, because of limited cognitive capacities and an only subjectively rational use of information, general predictions about individual behavior can no longer be derived, competitive selection may be the only systematic influence which still produces regularities. Where this is the case, evolutionary economics can have recourse to a theory of competitive selection (Metcalfe, 1989).

The evolutionary approach to the market process
In the perspective of evolutionary economics, market processes may be theoretically approached from different angles. If, to start on the individualistic level, imperfect knowledge and uncertainty are the conditions under which economic agents act, then the question emerges as to how this state changes under the human capacity to learn. More precisely, it seems crucial to ask of what nature learning is. Consider Bayesian learning, which is assumed to start from a nucleus of truth (the prior knowledge of the true probability distribution) and implies a convergence of subjective beliefs to the true conditions. If this were the only kind of learning, all agents in the economy could well be imagined to end up in a state of general (market) equilibrium in which all their knowledge-based expectations are confirmed. This is, of course, the neoclassical, general equilibrium version of the coordination story. Its disadvantage is that further change cannot be explained by this theory. After all adaptations have been made, further change cannot come but from outside.

If focus is on endogenously generated change, it must be assumed that there is still another kind of learning, which includes creation of novel ideas and insights, discovery and expansion of knowledge. Indeed, this seems to be a core problem of any individualistic foundation of evolutionary economics. A close relationship to positions held by the Austrian school and subjectivists such as Shackle is obvious. Shackle rejected the standard assumption that the alternatives (more technically, the state space) which decision makers face is always already given, and that the decision makers only 'learn' in an adaptive way about its properties (such as associated probabilities). He held that one of the most remarkable capacities of human decision makers is that they can create and extend what, in their subjective imagination, are the (future) alternatives to choose from. How is the creative task, which is so important to understanding the ultimate source of change, achieved? On an individualistic level this question suggests enquiring, as Loasby (1983) starts to do, into what insights psychology might have to offer.

Even if progress can be made in this way, the subjectivity of knowledge still remains a problem. Whenever the sphere of the creative mind is entered, the subjectivity of newly created ideas has to be respected. Subjectivity is likely to mean diversity of individual purposes and desires out of which novel ideas emerge. The subjective particularities of each individual case are difficult to reconstruct and objectify. This obviously delimits the scope of individualistic explanations, but not necessarily that of evolutionary theorizing. What appears necessary is to extend analysis to the population level. In their interactions the agents, intentionally as well as unintentionally, impose mutually binding constraints on each other. As in a selection process, these constraints determine which actions will turn out to be tolerated or even rewarded and which will not. The constraints and their effects may often be reconstructible without knowledge of the particularities of the subjective motives and views of the involved agents.

Especially powerful forms of interactions that reveal the difference between rewarded and non-rewarded undertakings are those in the marketplace (Hayek, 1978). The competitive market process operates like a selection device, discriminating between innovative individual activities whatever the subjective state of the innovator is. Often the diversity of behavior exposed to the logic of this selection device may even be denoted in terms of observable attributes such as cost differentials, quality features, market penetration measures, and so on. Then the effect of selection can be expressed by a diminishing variance of these attributes in the population (see Metcalfe, 1989). This amounts to a perspective similar to what is called 'population thinking' in biology, which is obviously at odds with the notion of the representative individual. In any case, the emergence of novelty and its diffusion through the markets always has allocative consequences and calls for a reconceptualization of a core element of economics – the theory of coordination. Coordination has come to be identified today almost exclusively (a notable exception being the Austrian interpretation) with the concept of general equilibrium which focuses on a state where the optimal, individual plans happen to be mutually compatible.

In this version of coordination theory there is obviously only room for activities such as arbitrage, adaptive learning and parameter adjustments by which the coordination of individual plans in the economy is increased. Innovative activities which, in the first place, decoordinate and disrupt may occur, but they are 'exogenous' events, that is, events outside what the theory wants to explain. In an evolutionary perspective, by contrast, coordinating and decoordinating activities are usually simultaneously present and jointly form the observable market processes (Witt, 1985). Accordingly, market processes usually perpetuate 'disequilibrium states', as neoclassical theory labels them, without offering an explanation for the regularities governing these states. Learning and adjusting, on the one hand, and the search for, and trying out of, innovations, on the other, coexist. The consequences of other agents' improved knowledge and adjustment may well be imagined to induce dissatisfaction with those who profited from having an edge in information or a possibility of arbitraging. The dissatisfaction may trigger the search for new possibilities of action and, as a consequence, may cause a state 'far from equilibrium' to persist.

The coordination of individual economic activities in the markets may sometimes result in irreversible, self-reinforcing tendencies associated with 'network externalities', 'learning-by-using' and other instances that give rise to increasing returns to the adoption and application of one solution or standard out of several competing ones. The increasing returns may then 'lock in' (Arthur, 1988) the development in such a way that further adoption/ application decisions are bound to favor the same solution or standard, even if it turns out not to be the most effective one. The background of the phenomenon is a multiplicity of possible (technological) solutions, and the increasing returns to adoption/application are thought to induce interdependencies between the agents' decisions. This means that, instead of a unique coordination equilibrium which was supposed to exist under neo-classical assumptions, the technology here implies a multiplicity of mutually exclusive equilibria or, to denote the dynamic nature of the problem, attractors. The phenomenon is rather typical of a class of problems arising from non-linear dynamics. It implies 'path dependency', a significant feature of evolution.

Societal evolution
More global notions of socioeconomic evolution would seem to require some kind of 'grand view'. Unfortunately, this is still lacking, with the exception of the one proposed by Hayek (1988) which, of course, is far from providing any detailed explanation or precise specification of the conjectured processes and their relationships. Hayek assumes three levels of evolution. The first one is that of genetic evolution, in which primitive forms of social behavior, of preferences and attitudes effectuating an order in social interactions have been fixed genetically during man's phylogeny. Second, there is the evolution of the products of human intelligence and knowledge. Freed from the finite existence of each individual brain by efficient forms of coding, storing and

transmitting information, human knowledge has expanded enormously, so that today it allows the mastery of nature to an impressive extent. Third, and this is what Hayek considers the core of his approach, there is another level of evolution: cultural evolution as it operates 'between instinct and reason' (Hayek 1988, chapter 1). Culture, in Hayek's interpretation, is neither genetically conditioned nor rationally designed. It is a tradition of learnt rules of conduct whose role is often not even understood by those who follow the rules. They are passed on through cultural transmission – a 'blind' process, in the sense that it is not consciously planned or controlled.

Hayek's ideas have a certain resemblance to the more recently emerging theory of cultural transmission in sociobiology. How rules come into being, and which ones, is a question of historical accident; not so, according to Hayek, the question of which ones survive. The latter is determined by the selection process that underlies cultural evolution, a selection process operating on groups of humans sharing the same rules of conduct. Those groups succeeding in developing and passing on rules better suited to govern their social interactions are supposed to grow and feed a larger number of people. Their relative superiority may enable them to conquer and/or absorb less well equipped, competing groups and thus, unintentionally, propagate the superior sets of rules. A growing population requires increasing specialization and division of labor which, in turn, presuppose the spontaneous order to increasingly extend. The rules become ever more differentiated, abstract and difficult to understand. Over thousands of years, Hayek thus sees an 'extended order' spontaneously emerging which enabled modern societies to achieve a historically unique level of civilization and productivity. This order, the most important achievement of which, Hayek (1988, chapter 3) submits, is trade and the emergence of a system of markets, embodies an impersonal intelligence as it has been accumulated during the selection processes in the form of surviving impersonal rules of conduct.

Thus Hayek's theory of societal evolution provides a new foundation for the theory of spontaneous order which was first conceived of by the Scottish moral philosophers. The idea that regularities in social interactions may be constituted by the individual choices of all participants without anybody having intended or even understood this effect is, of course, also a core notion in Austrian economics. As Hayek repeatedly points out, it has independently been derived by Menger on the basis of such concrete examples as language, custom, moral, manners and common law. For Menger all individual actions taken together spontaneously establish a mutually coordinated behavior which helps all, and which everybody, by forming a habit, takes for granted and expects as a prevailing regularity or order. It is perhaps only today that, with the tools of game theory, the logic of the conjectured processes can be fully understood. Indeed, recent research on the evolution of economic institutions, informed by game theory, proceeds along these lines (Hirshleifer, 1982). Models developed in this context confirm in a striking way the importance of path dependency. The multiplicity of attractors comes here in the configuration of multiple equilibria of the underlying games. Institutional evolution is accordingly characterized by more or less frequent transitions between different attractors governed once again by a frequency dependency effect which may even take such dramatic forms as revolutions.

See also:
Chapter 9: Causation and genetic causation in economic theory; Chapter 77: The 'new' institutional economics; Chapter 4: Market process; Chapter 15: Entrepreneurship; Chapter 28: Self-organizing systems

Bibliography
Arthur, W.B. (1988), 'Self-Reinforcing Mechanisms in Economics', in P.W. Anderson, K.J. Arrow and D. Pines (eds), *The Economy as an Evolving Complex System*, Redwood City: Addison-Wesley.
Hayek, F.A. (1978), 'Competition as a Discovery Procedure', in *New Studies in Philosophy, Politics, Economics, and the History of Ideas*, Chicago: Chicago University Press.
Hayek, F.A. (1988), *The Fatal Conceit*, London: Routledge.
Hirshleifer, J. (1982), 'Evolutionary Models in Economics and Law', *Research in Law and Economics*, **4**, 1–60.
Loasby, B.J. (1983), 'Knowledge, Learning, and Enterprise', in J. Wiseman (ed.), *Beyond Positive Economics?*, London: Macmillan.
Metcalfe, S. (1989), 'Evolution and Economic Change', in A. Silberston (ed.), *Technology and Economic Progress*, London: Macmillan.
Nelson, R.R. and S.G. Winter (1982), *An Evolutionary Theory of Economic Change*, Cambridge, Mass.: Harvard University Press.
Schumpeter, J.A. (1934), *The Theory of Economic Development*, Cambridge, Mass.: Harvard University Press (first German edition 1912).
Schumpeter, J.A. (1942), *Capitalism, Socialism, and Democracy*, New York: Harper.
Witt, U. (1985), 'Coordination of Individual Economic Activities as an Evolving Process of Self-Organization', *Economie Appliquée*, **37**, 569–95.

79 Austrian models? Possibilities of evolutionary computation

Don Lavoie

The question most commonly asked by neoclassical economists of Austrian school economists is, 'Where is your model?' The question causes some irritation to Austrians, and the most common answer they give, which is a methodological one along the lines of 'Models aren't everything', causes at least as much irritation back. This essay will not provide a much more satisfactory answer, but it will at least avoid that methodological detour.

Austrians, like any theorists, use verbal models, or as they call them, 'imaginary constructions', all the time. There is no reason why Austrians should feel compelled to come up with a non-verbal model, in order to 'mature' as a science or something. At the same time, there is no reason why we should not experiment with various kinds of modeling. The Austrian school is critical of *formalism*, the preoccupation with model building for its own sake, to the exclusion of other legitimate scholarly activities, but it has no objection to the use of formal models as imaginary constructions. Ludwig von Mises argued that imaginary constructions aimed at clarifying our theory do not need to justify themselves abstractly, by building philosophical foundations that prove in general that they give us Truth. Rather, they justify themselves pragmatically, by showing that they work. Imaginary constructions that usefully provoke our imaginations in a way that improves our understanding of economic processes should be used. Those that do not should not.

Although Austrians are surely right to say formal models are not everything, it must be admitted that they are *something*. At the very least, they are fun to play with, and anyone who knows much about cognitive development knows that playing with educational toys can be one of the most effective ways to learn. Access to the school's insights is made possible only by reading several large books, which are straight text all the way, lacking even the simple illustrative graphical aids neoclassical texts use. Austrian economics is already great fun for some of us, of course, even without any high-tech toys, but the school could definitely use a wider set of expositional tools.

The fact that there has not yet been much in the way of formal modeling by members of the school has been attributed by critics to the school's own limitations, but it may be due to limitations of the traditional modeling technologies. The equilibrium and game-theoretic modeling tools popular in neoclassical economics, because of the way they depict action as strictly maximizing and interaction processes as equilibrating, are not apt to be very useful to Austrians. There are, however, other modeling technologies that are now becoming available. Computational modeling, the use of computer programs to create artificial, complex evolutionary systems, is an approach to modeling that a Hayekian would find interesting. In evolutionary biology, and in the machine learning branch of the artificial intelligence literature, for example, considerable thought has been given to the modeling of dynamic processes which cannot be said to equilibrate, even though they clearly exhibit order (Allen, 1988). One of the most interesting approaches to computational modeling is the work of John Holland and his associates on Genetic Algorithms and Classifier Systems. This research explores with computational models some of the same features of social learning which Austrians have explored conceptually, especially the experimental and evolutionary aspects. (For interesting applications of Holland's work to economics, see John Miller, 1989; Marimon, McGratten and Sargent, 1989). In principle there is no reason why Austrian economists could not try their hand at adapting such evolutionary models to their own purposes.

A group of graduate students and faculty at the Program on Social and Organizational Learning at George Mason University have been doing just that. Inspired by a couple of pathbreaking articles by Mark S. Miller and Eric Drexler (1988a, 1988b), they have been investigating the use of such computational modeling tools for conveying and advancing Austrian economic theory, for conducting computer-assisted mental experiments. Hugo de Garis, Pawel Stefanski and Hadon Nash of the School of Information Technology and Engineering have worked with Howard Baetjer, Bill Tulloh, Kevin Lacobie and Dave Burns from the economics department on trying to simulate market processes in computational systems. It is too early to tell whether this type of model has the potential to enhance our understanding of anything important in Austrian economics, but the prototype models that have been developed so far, aimed at illuminating the Mengerian process by which money evolves, have been promising (see Lavoie, Baetjer and Tulloh, 1990).

Neoclassicism in words?
But hold on. Is not the very idea of an Austrian model self-contradictory? In a recent paper, Tyler Cowen (1991) argues that what is called the 'Austrian school' is really the verbal part of neoclassical economics. Thus, if an Austrian-oriented economist turns to model-building, he or she is, by definition, not doing Austrian economics. Indeed, on many issues economists who would call themselves Austrian hold positions that are indistinguishable – except in style of exposition – from what can be called mainstream neoclassicism.

Cowen's argument is not to be taken lightly. He is not making the familiar but ungrounded charge that Austrianism is a school that is dogmatically opposed to all formal modeling. He is saying that Austrian economics is not a *school* of thought at all, it is a mode of expression of neoclassical economics. It is, by definition, verbal neoclassical economics. To Cowen this is no condemnation. One could argue that mainstream economists ought to 'speak Austrian' more often. Verbal reasoning can do some things non-verbal models cannot. But, he argues, if people who otherwise do Austrian economics start working on formal models, their work becomes indistinguishable from neoclassical economics.

If one likes, of course, one can define 'Austrian' to mean verbal economics, and it is true that there is considerable overlap between the Marshallian, applied price theory and the Mengerian branch of neoclassical economics. But the conventional meaning of the term identifies a recognizable collection of scholars who picked up one another's questions, and formed a common discourse. It seems to go much too far to say that the Austrian tradition has no other recognizable characteristics than the fact that its contributors did *not* happen to build any formal models. Many Austrians are convinced that, on the contrary, they have a distinct perspective, a substantively different understanding of the way markets work in many important respects. Their view of human action does not reduce it to maximizing. Prior to a constrained optimization problem, whereby the best among given means is chosen to achieve given ends, comes the issue of what actors are paying attention to in the first place, how they make choices under conditions of Knightian uncertainty, how habits might shape the process of decision making, how tacit knowledge is involved, how certain sorts of institutions such as money, property rights and organized markets orient the agent, and how disruptions of such institutions might disorient him, and so forth. Their theory of capital is not duplicated anywhere in mainstream literature; their monetary theory contrasts strikingly with quantity theory and neo-Keynesian approaches; their most elaborate substantive theory, the business cycle theory, involves a complex combination of the monetary and capital theory (and is particularly in need of better forms of exposition such as might be available with visual computer modeling). Their famous confrontation with the 'market-socialists' in the 1930s amounted to a challenge to certain widely held neoclassical views about the nature of competition. Recent contributors to the school are increasingly critical of the whole approach of treating markets as in some meaningful sense 'tending towards equilibrium'.

Some of the points the Austrians are making are neither conveniently rendered in existing neoclassical models nor as sharply rendered in the Austrians' own verbal expositions as they might be were the school to deploy an appropriate sort of modeling. It is widely agreed that the appropriate standard for assessing a model is not whether it is realistic, since no model is, but whether it captures the aspect of reality it aims at capturing. And the issue must be judged comparatively. No model 'captures' perfectly. It can only be assessed by comparison with other available ways of making something understood. The aspects of reality stressed in Austrian theorizing have not been illuminated very well in the models used by neoclassical economics, and might be rendered more satisfactorily in Austrian-oriented models. In short, Austrians should try their hand at a bit of modeling of their own.

Modeling spontaneous orders

The substantive questions the Austrians raise suggest that a rather different approach to modeling from the neoclassical norm is called for. Austrian theorizing diverges from mainstream economics over fundamental issues: the nature of *action* (it is not just maximizing) and of *interaction* (it is not just general equilibrium). The point is not that the neoclassical approach to action and interaction is wrong, but only that it tends to divert attention from the issues to which Austrians want to draw our attention.

On the issue of interaction, mainstream economics likes to view interactive market processes in terms of the theory of equilibrium. Even where 'evolutionary' ideas are mentioned, they are generally conceived of as nothing but paths toward equilibrium. Austrian-oriented economists have increasingly come to question whether it is helpful to depict entrepreneurial processes as equilibrating. Critics have routinely asserted that rejecting equilibrium implies that market processes are completely random or chaotic. Here, it appears, our ability to show an orderly, yet non-equilibrating, evolutionary process in a computational model might contribute to our case.

We might take a cue here from computer science and the modeling literature that tries to simulate other complex evolving systems, such as biological and cognitive processes. The Austrians describe market processes as 'spontaneous orders' that are in some ways similar to genetic and cognitive evolutionary processes. Spontaneous order phenomena can be artificially generated on a computer and, as general as some economic principles are, many of them certainly must apply to such artificial economies (Forrest, 1990). Some sort of computational model might represent, in a more useful way than neoclassical models have, exactly what spontaneous order processes are and why markets are usefully interpreted in this way.

What, then, might distinctively Austrian models of (non-equilibrating) market processes look like? Dynamic interaction might be orderly enough to be represented by a visualizable pattern on a computer screen without being so orderly as to be equilibrating. The theorist might use visualizations of dynamic market processes to help think through the logic of the dynamic. A computational model can be thought of as a general framework for mental experimentation of the following sort. Suppose we were to ask this question about the evolution of money: in the dynamics of the Mengerian process, what difference would it make, if any, whether agents paid more attention to the question of which *goods* have sold well, or to which *agents* bought them? One way to help us to think about this question might be to set up alternative scenarios where the virtual agents pay attention either to goods or to other agents, and see what happens. If, in modeling scenarios where more of the agent strategies attend to goods, money tends to emerge faster than in those scenarios where more agents attend to buyers, then this would illuminate something about the Mengerian process.

But no matter how evolutionary one makes the artificial economy, Austrians will be impatient with it unless it is populated with artificial agents who can learn.

Modeling non-atomistic agents capable of learning

Individual actors are for Austrians the crucial building-block of economic theory. While Austrians endorse a kind of 'methodological individualism', they do not necessarily stand for the atomistic individualism implicit in much mainstream neoclassicism. Agents are not 'atoms', in either of two senses that word may connote: they are not *indivisible* entities that constitute the irreducibly basic building-blocks of all analysis; nor are they radically *independent* from one another. They are composed of habitual ways of understanding and behaving, patterns of action they get from the larger culture in which they participate (Hayek, 1962). They are not distinct bundles of preferences but linked participants in cultural processes. They are shaped and adjusted to one another by the unintended evolution of institutions by which they orient themselves, such as money. And agents are not merely maximizing machines. Although there is a constrained maximization aspect to purposeful action, the Austrian view stresses other aspects which neoclassicism systematically ignores. Agents do not only maximize under given constraints, they learn about new opportunities, they discover unnoticed costs, they create new possibilities.

How much of all this can be usefully represented in a computer model? Only some, to be sure. The virtual agents that have been developed so far in the machine learning literature are not the kind of folks you would invite to dinner. But the machine learning literature shows that artificial agents can be modeled that are capable of interesting achievements of experimental learning. Artificially intelligent agents may have some advantages over atomistic maximizers for Austrians. They need not be indivisible, but can be constructed as composites of mini-agents, that is, habitual modes of behavior. And they need not be independent, since they can get these patterns of behavior from the larger community. In Hayek's terms, we are trying to depict the mind of the virtual agent as a 'sensory order' (1952), a product of the rivalrous contention of divergent predispositions to act. Each agent can be equipped with the capacity to engage in an evolutionary learning process. The market would thus be depicted in Hayekian fashion as a spontaneous order of spontaneous orders, whereby both the agent and the overall order are conceived as dynamic processes. On both levels we are not interested in any equilibria the system or the individual might be tending towards, but in observing the dynamics of the process itself.

The creator's and the creature's points of view
We can build 'virtual economies' into the construction of which we can put Austrian ideas. We can populate these economies with agents who embody elements of action, such as attention, uncertainty and habits, which we think the mainstream framework underemphasizes. The complexity of the 'virtual economy' is of course nowhere near that of real economies, just as the intelligence of the 'virtual agent' is nowhere near that of real human agents. But the *relative* ability of virtual agents to comprehend their world might be comparable. The question is whether we can develop virtual agents and economies which are interesting to Austrian economists, given the questions they are trying to ask.

The objection might be raised that it is logically impossible to model true uncertainty. Since the 'gods' of the virtual economy, its programmers, know how they built the system, we are still dealing with a perfect knowledge system, and the programmers could not possibly learn anything from it. Of course, even if the programmers knew what was going to happen, so that we did not really learn anything from *running* the model, we might well learn a great deal from *building* it and, in any case, it could still be useful for educational purposes. But the thing is, even the gods do not know what is going to happen. When one devises a sufficiently complex computational framework, it can be quite impossible for the designer to know what results are built into it, except by running it. These kinds of models are really much more experimental than equilibrium modeling, not only in substance, but also in spirit. Running the model is itself an interesting learning experience.

The agents in a computational model need not be given much knowledge of one another, or of the model's working. They lack, just as we in our world lack, any direct lines to the gods. They do not 'know the model' they are in, and need to struggle to learn what is going on. Agents like this might strike Austrian economists as somewhat interesting. We would not expect the virtual agents of such computational models ever to be terribly creative creatures, by our standards. They could be interpreted as creative *for their world*, however, in the sense that they will experiment with modes of behavior they stumble upon, learn from their experience and adopt the ones that seem to work. The set of all possible modes of behavior that are there to stumble into will be available only to the gods. This seems similar, in the relevant respects, to the circumstance in which we mortals find ourselves within our world.

See also:
Chapter 7: Formalism in twentieth-century economics; Chapter 80: Social institutions and game theory; Chapter 78: Evolutionary economics; Chapter 30: Spontaneous order

Bibliography
Allen, Peter M. (1988), 'Evolution, Innovation, and Economics', in G. Dosi *et al.* (eds), *Economic Theory and Technical Change*, New York: Printers Publishers.
Cowen, Tyler (1991), 'What is Austrian Economics?', unpublished manuscript, George Mason University.
Forrest, Stephanie (1990), 'Emergent Computation: Self-organizing, Collective, and Cooperative Phenomena in Natural and Artificial Computing Networks', introduction to the *Proceedings of the Ninth Annual CNLS Conference*, Center for Non-linear Studies and Computing Division, Los Alamos National Laboratory, MS-B258.
Hayek, F.A. (1952), *The Sensory Order*, Chicago: University of Chicago Press.
Hayek, F.A. (1962), 'Rules, Perception and Intelligibility', reprinted in *Studies in Philosophy, Politics, and Economics*, Chicago: University of Chicago Press, 1967.
Lavoie, D., H. Baetjer and W. Tulloh (1990), 'High Tech Hayekians: Some Possible Research Topics in the Economics of Computation', *Market Process*, 8.
Marimon, Ramon, E. McGratten and T. Sargent (1989), 'Money as a Medium of Exchange in an Economy with Artificially Intelligent Agents', unpublished manuscript, Sante Fe Institute.
Miller, John H. (1989), 'Coevolution of Automata in the Repeated Prisoners' Dilemma', unpublished manuscript, Sante Fe Institute.
Miller, Mark S. and K. Eric Drexler (1988a), 'Comparative Ecology: A Computational Perspective', in B.A. Huberman (ed.), *The Ecology of Computation*, Amsterdam: North-Holland.
Miller, Mark S and K. Eric Drexler (1988b), 'Markets and Computation: Agoric Open Systems', in B.A. Huberman (ed.), *The Ecology of Computation*, Amsterdam: North-Holland.

80 Social institutions and game theory

Andrew Schotter

Introduction

The theory of games and the theory of social institutions have been intimately linked since John von Neumann and Oskar Morgenstern wrote *The Theory of Games and Economic Behavior* (*The Theory*) some 45 years ago. As I have argued elsewhere (see Schotter, 1981), the theory of games must be considered first and foremost a formal theory of social institutions. Even a casual reading of the introduction to their book indicates that von Neumann and Morgenstern viewed game theory as a unifying theory for the social sciences and not as a narrow replacement for neoclassical economic theory. In this new theory the object to be explained was what type of alternative stable institutional arrangements could emerge from a given societal problem. To demonstrate that this was their intent we have only to look at the introduction to *The Theory* and replace the words 'orders of society' and 'standards of behavior' with the words 'institutional relationships' in the following passage:

> The question whether several stable 'orders of society' or 'standards of behavior' based on the same physical background are possible or not, is highly controversial. There is little hope that it will be settled by the usual methods because of the enormous complexity of this problem, among other reasons. But we shall give specific examples of games of three or four persons, where one game possesses several solutions in the sense of 4.5.3 [the stable set solution]. And some of these examples will be seen to be the models of certain simple economic problems. (Von Neumann and Morgenstern, 1947, p. 43).

The original intention of game theory (or at least cooperative game theory) was to explain how it comes to be that one fixed societal problem can be solved by the emergence of a variety of different and alternative stable economic institutions. Hence, when game theory is to be applied to economics, it is not price that is the key variable whose value is to be determined but rather the set of price–institution pairs that, taken together, form the stable set of societal arrangements for the economy.

Since these standards of behavior or societal arrangements are not planned but rather emerge in an unintended manner from the individual strivings of agents in the society, the program set out by von Neumann and Morgenstern can be considered the mathematical extension of the program enunciated earlier by Menger (1883) where he wrote: 'the most noteworthy problem of the social sciences [is] how ... institutions which serve the common welfare and are extremely significant for its development came into being without a common will directed toward establishing them' (Menger, 1883, p. 147). He then went on to say, 'The solution to the most important problems of theoretical social sciences in general and of theoretical economics in particular is thus closely connected with the question of theoretically understanding the origin and change of "organically" created social institutions' (ibid.). The similarity between the goals of Menger and von Neumann and Morgenstern is not coincidental since Morgenstern, at least, was a student of the Austrian school and well versed in all of Menger's ideas. Still, game theory was to be the tool with which to realize Menger's program.

The success of the von Neumann–Morgenstern program
There can be no doubt that, to a large extent, game theory has become the analytical tool of institutional economic analysis. We can say this because almost all serious attempts at institutional analysis are either formally game-theoretical or at least implicitly so. However, as time has gone on, four distinct approaches to the study of institutions have developed which have gone beyond the original intentions of von Neumann and Morgenstern but are still consistent with their broad agenda. For lack of better terms we will call these the positive, the normative, the explanatory (or evolutionary) and the experimental approaches to economic institutions. Since these different approaches are responses to different notions of what exactly social institutions are, let us first pause and discuss these different definitions so that the raison d'être of our four approaches becomes clear.

Definitions of social institutions and institutional approaches
The term *economic institution* might have many different meanings. An institution might be a convention of behavior that is created by society to help it solve a recurrent problem that it has. For example, when we go to a restaurant we leave a tip because it is the conventional thing to do. Under this definition, institutional behavior is conventional behavior and institutions are conventions.[1] This definition is the inspiration for what we have called the explanatory or evolutionary approach to social institutions since this approach tries to explain why we have the set of social institutions we have, how they emerged and what purpose they are serving in society.

Alternatively, institutions can be viewed as sets of rules which constrain behavior of social agents in particular situations.[2] For example, the US Congress is called an institution, but it is really a collection of abstract rules defining how governmental decisions will be made. Presidential vetoes need a two-thirds majority to be overridden, bills need a simple majority, and seniority is important in committee appointments. When one concentrates on institutions as rules, one is led to look at the normative question of how best to choose these rules so that the outcomes that result from our institutions are optimal. This definition leads us to investigate what I have called the normative approach since it asks how the rules of economic behavior ought to be set so as to implement or achieve a particular outcome or set of outcomes at the equilibrium of the game defined by the rules we design. In other words, the normative approach looks at the study of social institutions as one of social engineering or game design and sees the analyst as an institutional architect.

The positive approach to social institutions, as well as the experimental approach, also sees social institutions as sets of rules and not as conventions of behavior given exogenously determined rules. In this sense both of these approaches are like the normative approach. However, both the positive and experimental approach attempt to investigate the allocative properties of economic and social institutions and do not attempt any normative analysis. The positive and experimental approaches must therefore be considered as complementary to the normative approach since, once the normative institutional analysts have designed their optimal institution, the question remains as to whether the set of rules designated will lead to the type of behavior posited by the designers of the institution.

Finally, many times people use the word 'institution' in a loose and non-technical manner. In this context an institution is any pre-existing organization. A bank is called a financial institution, universities are called 'institutions of higher learning', and many of us engage in the hallowed 'institution of marriage'. While this use of the term 'institution' can be fitted into our other meanings, this third meaning is left intentionally vague and we will not pursue it here.

The positive approach

The primary figure adhering to a positive approach to social and economic institutions is Martin Shubik. Starting with his close association with Morgenstern at Princeton, Shubik early on became dissatisfied with the institutionally naked theory of value as portrayed in Debreu's *Theory of Value* and the cooperative game-theoretical work on the core. Shubik's interest was in creating an institutionally realistic theory of value in which the non-cooperative Cournot–Nash equilibrium concept was to replace the cooperative core solution concept as the central analytical device. To do this it was necessary to introduce money as the strategic variable used by the agents, but the introduction of money led to the further need to specify a wide variety of other institutions in order to close the model and create a well defined game. For instance, if money exists, is it fiat money or commodity money? If it is fiat money then banks are required to issue and lend it, so the model must contain banks. But if people borrow money from banks, what happens to those traders who borrow more than they can pay back? To specify such penalties we must have bankruptcy laws. In addition, once we introduce money, how are the prices of goods and their allocations dependent upon the money bids of traders and the stock of money? To answer these questions a wide variety of market institutions, clearing-houses and warehouses must be specified. Consequently, when one takes even one small step in this non-cooperative game-theoretical direction it is inevitable that one will come away with a variety of very rich institutional models filled with a variety of specific real-world institutions such as money, banks, bankruptcy laws, marketing institutions, clearing-houses, warehouses and so on. The next step is to investigate the impact of these explicitly introduced institutions on the economies studied to see how the resulting allocations and prices associated with each specific set of institutions are related to the neoclassical set of Walrasian prices and allocations (or any other set of outcomes, for that matter).

What has been shown, miraculously, is that for a wide variety of these non-cooperative institutionally rich models the Nash equilibria of the games defined are equivalent to the set of competitive equilibria if the economy is large. Note that, since Shubik's *et al*'s work is solely on the properties of predesignated institutions without any normative judgement about them, we call it a positive approach.

Political scientists also provided a rich tradition of work in the theory of positive institutional analysis using both cooperative and non-cooperative game theory. For example, while the early work in political science was on the application of cooperative solution concepts like the core, the value, the bargaining set and the competitive solution of McKelvey and Ordeshook to study the outcomes of committee voting institutions with agents whose preferences were defined on a spatial issue space, later work has concentrated on the non-cooperative analysis of strategic voting and agenda manipulation. In all of this work, the institutional structure is given exogenously and the analysis looks at the equilibrium outcome of these pre-existing institutions. Hence we categorize this work as positive.

The normative institutional approach
If one views positive economics through the non-cooperative institutional game-theoretical perspective discussed above, one's definition of normative or welfare economics must be changed. This change would involve a shift away from viewing welfare economics as a discipline whose job it was to investigate the properties of various states of the economy (that is, various allocations of resources) and towards one that investigated the properties of various economic institutions. Hence, instead of ranking social allocations in

terms of their social welfare properties, welfare economics would rank various abstract sets of rules or social institutions according to some relevant social welfare criteria. However, since games are nothing more than abstract sets of rules and game forms, combined with a set of utility functions, welfare economics becomes the study of the welfare properties of n-person games analysed by comparing the social states defined at their equilibria (where the equilibrium concept can be either Nash, strong Nash, Bayesian, Minimax or the dominant strategy equilibrium). The problem in this context then becomes one of studying various allocation or voting institutions (or mechanisms) to see if they implement some preassigned set of social outcomes.

To be more precise, consider a society with $n(\geq 3)$ agents who must choose some alternative a from a set A. Each agent has preferences over A. Now assume that, while each agent knows his own preferences, he does not know anyone else's and, more importantly, the social planner, whose job it is to choose some alternative, does not know the preferences of any agent at all. Hence, the planner, in order to make the 'proper' choice for society, must rely on messages sent by agents to him in order to make his choice. Hence, let M be the space of all messages that can be sent from any agent to the planner. Finally let $O(m)$ be an outcome function mapping each n-tuple of messages, $m \in M$, into a social alternative. An institution or mechanism can be defined as a pair $I = [M; O(m)]$. Such an institution or mechanism is a game form and can be analysed as an n-person game by specifying a preference, ρ, of the agents. Let us call this game $G(I;\rho)$.

Now given the game $G(I;\rho)$ defined by the preferences of agents and an institution, we can define an equilibrium rule for this game as a mapping of each game into an equilibrium n-tuple of messages. It describes the behavior we can expect to observe at the equilibrium of the institutional game. Obviously this expected behavior will depend on the equilibrium concept we use for the game; that is, the dominant strategy equilibrium, the Nash, the strong Nash, the Bayesian, the minimax and so on.

The normative approach to institutional analysis concerns itself with the following question: can the planner design a game (or institution) for the agents to play which will have as its equilibrium outcome that same outcome that would be chosen by an all-knowing planner with perfect information about people's preferences who was trying to maximize some given social decision or welfare function? It is a question of institutional design, the design of a social planner. (See Hurwicz, 1973, 1989.) As such, this view of social institutions is quite different from that of the explanatory approach which is more consistent with the views of Menger and von Neumann and Morgenstern and their emphasis on the unplanned or 'organic' development of social institutions. Still, the point that needs emphasis is that all of this work, whether in economics or political science, uses game theory as its unifying tool.

The explanatory evolutionary approach

The explanatory/evolutionary approach to social institutions does not concentrate on the rules of the game defined by a particular institution but rather on the regularities in behavior or social conventions that the agents create when they repeatedly or recurrently interact in a particular social situation or game form given to them exogenously. In this view it is not the rules of the game that are of importance but rather the equilibrium behavior that emerges endogenously or organically, given the rules. Also, in this view the rules themselves may be endogenous, so that the institutions are not fixed exogenously but rather emerge in an unplanned evolutionary manner.

Let us examine this idea more closely by examining what David Lewis (1969) has called the 'telephone game'. The story behind this game is as follows. In Oberlin, Ohio there was a private telephone company that did not have enough telephone lines to service the entire town. Consequently, whenever one person in the town called another he would be given three minutes in which to talk and then the company would disconnect the line. The problem created was: if the conversation was not completed, who would call whom back? This problem can be portrayed by the following game matrix:

		Callee	
		call back	wait
Caller	call back	0,0	2,2
	wait	2,2	0,0

Here we see that each player, the caller and the callee, has to decide whether they should call the other back or wait. If they both wait, neither phone rings and they are standing there waiting next to silent phones. If they both try to call the other, they both get busy signals and still cannot continue their conversation. Obviously, they will only be able to continue if one calls back and the other waits. The question is, which one will call back and which one will wait?

Since the problem was a recurrent one in Oberlin, Lewis argues that eventually some convention of behavior will be established that will define who calls back and who waits. Hence it may be established and become generally known that the caller is the one who always calls back or always waits and this rule or convention will become regularized and learned by the town's citizens. Such a regularity in behavior which is created or evolves to solve a recurrent social or economic problem is what Lewis (1969) calls a convention, what Schotter (1981) calls a social institution, and what Ullman-Margalit (1978) has called a norm. Consequently, in this view of social institutions, institutions are unplanned evolutionary regularities in behavior that are created by the agents themselves to solve a series of recurrent problems that they face.

In formal terms, social institutions in this view can be thought of as the non-cooperative Nash equilibria to a variety of supergames that economic and social agents face. The problem that must be solved by the analyst then is to specify which equilibrium is likely to be settled upon by the players in the game as the equilibrium convention of behavior to adhere to. It should be emphasized that the evolutionary approach to social institutions should not be viewed as merely a theory of equilibrium selection for n-person games with multiple equilibria since, using some notions of bounded rationality, it is quite possible that a non-Nash outcome may be settled upon.

In this connection a number of evolutionary approaches (see Witt, 1989; Wärnereyd, 1990; Boyer and Orlean, 1991) concentrate on the dynamic process which selects a particular evolutionary stable convention of behavior for agents to use. For example, Witt uses a dynamic imitation process in which successful strategies or conventions with good fitness properties are imitated over time and gain adherents. Since evolutionary stable equilibria are very often the fixed points of this dynamic process, Witt looks to see if any conventions are such stable points. Boyer and Orlean look at the evolution of conventions as a process containing local externalities. Under this approach, the conventional rule you use affects the pay-offs of those close to you but not of those far away. Hence we see the emergence of local conventions which eventually sweep through the population and become global conventions. In some sense this application of evolutionary biological game theory is natural for a theory whose aim is to explain the emergence and growth of institutions defined as conventions.

The experimental approach
Space constraints prevent talking at any length about the experimental school and its relationship to institutional economics and game theory. (A complete description of this connection can be found in Vernon Smith's well known article, 'Microeconomic Systems as an Experimental Science', 1982.) However, the connection should be clear. The experimental school should be considered as the empirical adjunct to the positive and normative schools. The connection is simple. Both of those schools investigate the performance of hypothesized social institutions. However, these institutions exist only in the mind of the theorist and before a real world planner or corporate CEO would ever implement one of them in the real world, he might like to get an idea of how these hypothesized institutions may actually function when they

are put into action. It is therefore the role of experimental economics to provide a cheap pre-test for these hypothetical institutions. If they perform well in the lab, one may give more weight to actually implementing them in the real world. It is also interesting that, in attempting to test the properties of an institution in the lab, one sees clearly the connection between institutions and games. For instance, running an experiment requires that subjects be given a complete set of rules which will govern their behavior during the experiment and which will determine pay-offs for them as a function of the strategies they and their counterparts choose. These rules are nothing more than the game form of the institution under investigation, so that in order to test an economic or social institution one must first turn it into a playable game and play it in the lab.

Conclusions

There is much more that can be said about social institutions and their game-theoretical analysis. The main point, however, is that game theory is, in some sense, the natural tool to use for the study of social institutions and, as has been argued above, such a study was probably the original intent of von Neumann and Morgenstern. As time goes on the emphasis will probably shift away from a repeated game analysis and onto a more evolutionary dynamic analysis, but that development is still in its infancy.

Notes

1. For a fuller exposition of this view of institutions, see Andrew Schotter (1981), David Lewis (1969), Edna Ullman-Margalit (1978).
2. For a summary of this view, see Leonid Hurwicz (1989).

See also:

Chapter 76: Austrian economics and American (old) institutionalism; Chapter 77: The 'new' institutional economics; Chapter 10: Ideal type methodology in economics; Chapter 79: Austrian models? Possibilities of evolutionary computation

Bibliography

Boyer, R. and A. Orlean (1991), 'How Do Conventions Evolve?', mimeo, CERPREMAP, Paris.
Hurwicz, L. (1973), 'The Design of Mechanisms for Resource Allocation', *American Economic Review*, 63, 1–30.
Hurwicz, L. (1989), 'Mechanisms and Institutions', in Takashi Shiraishi and Shigeto Tsuru (eds), *Economic Institutions in a Dynamic Society*, London: Macmillan.
Lewis, D. (1969), *Convention: A Philosophical Study*, Cambridge, Mass.: Harvard University Press.
Menger, K. (1981), *Untersuchungen über die Methode der Sozialwissenschaften und der politischen Ökonomie insbesondere* (1883), translated by Francis J. Nock as *Problems in Economics and Sociology*, Urbana, IL: University of Illinois Press, 1947.
Schotter, A. (1981), *The Economic Theory of Social Institutions*, Cambridge: Cambridge University Press.
Smith, V. (1982), 'Microeconomic Systems as an Experimental Science', *American Economic Review*, December, 72, 923–55.

Ullman-Margalit, E. (1978), *The Emergence of Norms*, New York: Oxford University Press.
von Neumann, J. and O. Morgenstern (1947), *The Theory of Games and Economic Behavior*, Princeton: Princeton University Press.
Wärnereyd, K. (1990), 'Conventions: An Evolutionary Approach', *Constitutional Political Economy*, **1**, (3), fall, 83–109.
Witt, U. (1989), 'The Evolution of Economic Institutions as a Propagation Process', *Public Choice*, **62**, 155–73.

81 Monetarism

John B. Egger

Monetarism is a study of money that uses the Quantity Equation as its theoretical structure and the search for empirical relationships among aggregates as its method. Like all economics, monetarism is a process of reasoning from basic premises to implications for policy. Its empirical focus has led some economists to identify it by listing its empirical findings and policy conclusions, which include the following: changes in the nominal money stock are the main factor explaining changes in nominal income; inflation is always a monetary phenomenon; monetary policy cannot permanently reduce the rate of unemployment; and discretionary macroeconomic policy should be foresworn for a constant rate of growth of the nominal money supply. To understand monetarism, though, we must trace these conclusions to their underlying premises, particularly about the nature and method of economics.

History

Monetarism rescued the Quantity Theory from a world of Keynesian income-expenditure analysis, so one might be tempted to identify it with the long Quantity Theory tradition. It could be traced from Milton Friedman back through Clark Warburton and Carl Snyder to Fisher, Wicksell, Mill, Hume, Locke and perhaps even Aristophanes and the Chinese of 500BC. Those who, further, agree with Marget (1938) that the quantity framework was universal before Keynes will identify all non-Keynesian monetary theorists as (at least nascent) monetarists. The popular expression of this view is that a monetarist is anyone who believes that 'money matters'. Friedman himself does "'not like the term 'monetarism' ... [and] would prefer to talk simply about the quantity theory of money...'" (quoted in Macesich, 1983, p. 16nl).

Such a history is wrong. When Mises called 'the modern theory of money an improved variety of the quantity theory' (1966, p. 405) and Marget (1938) praised the quantity framework for accommodating the individualistic analysis of sequential monetary processes, they referred not merely to attributes of the quantity tradition that are outside monetarism, but to attributes the significance of which it denies. Monetarism cannot be considered identical to the quantity tradition. It is a narrow but significant subset of the quantity approach to money.

What differentiates monetarism, and must be a defining property, is its embracing of Friedman's method. Earlier writers (Warburton, Snyder, Currie) had sought statistical relationships among aggregates, but they lacked the conscious methodological support that Friedman offered. We may date monetarism from the mid-1950s because it can be considered an application to 'The Quantity Theory of Money – a Restatement' (1956) of 'The Methodology of Positive Economics' (1953). Friedman's demonstrations of his approach were powerful and articulate, reflecting his great personal energy, quick mind and skilful use of language. Important contributions include 'The Demand for Money: Some Theoretical and Empirical Results' (1959), 'Money and Business Cycles' (1963) and 'The Relative Stability of Monetary Velocity and the Investment Multiplier in the United States, 1897–1958' (with David Meiselman, 1963). The most lasting of them may well be Friedman and Anna Jacobsen Schwartz's magnificent *A Monetary History of the United States, 1867–1960* (1963). Later works include 'The Role of Monetary Policy' (1967), 'The Optimum Quantity of Money' (1969), 'A Theoretical Framework for Monetary Analysis' (1970) and 'Inflation and Unemployment: Nobel Lecture' (1977). This 1977 Nobel Lecture offers a convenient close to our monetarist period. Of course the important work inspired by the tradition continues, but by the mid-1970s theoretical interest was shifting to microfoundations and rational expectations.

Method

The profound differences between a monetarist and an Austrian analysis of money follow from different conceptions of the nature and purpose of economics. Starkly put, the monetarist research program emphasizes prediction, while the Austrian focuses on understanding.

In his influential 1953 essay on methodology, Friedman explains: 'The ultimate goal of a positive science is the development of a "theory" or "hypothesis" that yields valid and meaningful (i.e., not truistic) predictions about phenomena not yet observed' (1953, p. 7). Important themes are that 'the only relevant test of the *validity* of a hypothesis is comparison of its predictions with experience' and that 'to be important ... a hypothesis must be descriptively false in its assumptions' (1953, pp. 8–9, 14). A good theory results from an optimum trade-off between two goals: better prediction and simpler assumptions.

Reinforcing this positivist method was a set of beliefs about the functioning of markets that Reder (1982) explains had long characterized the Chicago school. Reder calls them 'Tight Prior Equilibrium' and 'the good-approximation assumption' and they amount to the conviction that – in the absence of solid evidence to the contrary – the prices and quantities of particular goods are at their long-run perfectly competitive equilibria. This assumption (the realism of which is considered irrelevant) provides the best predictions with the simplest models.

This method gives monetarism the flavor of a physical science. It investigates relationships among statistical time series that, according to the Quantity Theory, have something to do with money. The fact that the data originate in human behavior is insignificant to method (Friedman, 1953, pp. 4–5); statistics are statistics, whatever their source. This position would be hard to defend if it were necessary to examine the processes by which individuals in particular markets respond to disequilibria, but such a study has a high cost in complexity, with little or no benefit in improved prediction. The positivist rejects 'methodological dualism' (the belief that the method of the social sciences is importantly different from that of the physical sciences); the monetarist also rejects methodological individualism.

The contrast between the monetarist and the Austrian method is sharp and dramatic. The Austrians have always considered the purpose of economics to be the understanding of an observable event as the outcome of the choices of the individuals who caused it. Its method is to identify a causal process that links the event to the prior perceptions and actions of individuals. The school's statistical aggregates (such as 'the price level') are unintended consequences of individual choices. They are fabricated ex post from the quantities and prices of particular goods, and play little or no role in the causal sequences. Lecturing in 1930–1 at the London School of Economics (LSE) on the proper nature of monetary theory, Hayek boldly expressed the principle: 'neither averages nor aggregates do act upon one another, and it will never be possible to establish necessary connections of cause and effect between them as we can between individual phenomena' (Hayek, 1967, pp. 4–5).

The Austrians embrace introspection because the subject of their study is the same process of purposive human action in which the economist himself engages. (The monetarist rejects it because his subject is not that process, but relationships among statistical series. These data result from individual choices, but the analysis of those choices has little to contribute to the statistics.) The subjectivism of both value and expectations makes quantitative prediction difficult. While the Austrian is not averse to tentative predictions about patterns (for example, 'resources are likely to be shifted from this sector to that'), he accepts the quantitative imprecision as inherent in the nature of human action.

This conception of economics and its proper method are nearly polar opposites of those of monetarism. Indeed, the monetarist method is an ideal example of the 'scientism' of which Hayek has so often warned. From his 1930 lecture at LSE to his sharply worded Nobel Lecture of 1974 ('The Pretence of Knowledge') – which is at least as much a criticism of monetarism as of Keynesianism – Hayek has supported the Austrian method of the individualistic tracing of causal processes. For this reason it is astonishing to find the chairperson of an American Economic Association session on Hayek referring to 'the 1920's and 1930's when he was laying the foundations of monetarism' (Carrington, 1992).

Theory
Its method explains monetarism's focus on measurable aggregates, its small models and even its preference for a Quantity Equation rather than the Keynesian income expenditure 'language' (whatever influence the 'Chicago oral tradition' may have been). Whether the differences between monetarism and Keynesianism are theoretical or empirical (Friedman has generally claimed the latter) depends on the meaning of 'theory'. In 1953 Friedman considered theory to be a combination of a 'language' and a set of falsifiable empirical hypotheses, so empirical disagreements would necessarily be theoretical. Later, he used 'theory' to refer only to his language. His famous statement that 'We are all Keynesians now' acknowledged that a proper 'language' is sufficiently general to express either monetarist or Keynesian empirical propositions. Leijonhufvud (1981), Hahn (1980) and the Austrians have disagreed, arguing that certain of Friedman's empirical beliefs led him to adopt a language (theory?) of limited vocabulary, attaining conceptual economy by excluding a means for expressing a class of ideas that he considers insignificant but which have been important to Keynesian, pre-Keynesian and Austrian monetary theorists.

This significant theoretical shortcoming, arising from the positivist method of monetarism, is its dismissal of distributional ('first-round' or 'allocational') effects. Empirical studies had convinced Friedman that the *path* of monetary change – the way in which the money supply is changed and the sequence in which particular sectors are affected – had no significant quantitative impact on aggregate income or the price level (Gordon, 1974, pp. 146–8). This view is consistent with the position that an excess supply of money affects all markets simultaneously, and explains the antipathy to the large econometric models that the Keynesian sectoral approach requires: complexity without superior prediction spells bad theory.

In the Austrian method, casting out first-round effects denies methodological individualism and that simply eliminates economic theory from the endeavor. Nobody would be surprised if available data revealed no difference between monetary expansions of equal size effected by open-market purchase, on the one hand, and by reduction of reserve requirements, on the other. But discovering that is not the point, not the goal and purpose of economics. To understand why the data were indifferent, the possibility of effects that they conceal and, above all, the processes that created them, the Austrian insists on a study of the sequence of individual actions. Do these two methods initially affect different types of financial institution? Does one type of loan expand relative to others? How, then, are demands and supplies, prices and quantities, and sectoral resource allocation likely to differ? Expectations (and the modern technology of communication) may speed these processes to conclusions for which aggregate data are indistinguishable. Austrians consider this outcome either irrelevant or an interesting curiosity to be explained by an individualistic comparison of the two causal processes; the monetarist concludes that the process is theoretically irrelevant.

If 'the theory of money' is a study of the causes and effects of individual choices involving money, as the Austrian would insist, then the monetarist's rejection of methodological individualism – if taken seriously – makes the formation of monetary theory impossible. (This is why Frank Hahn, who should not be identified with the Austrian School, noted (1971, p. 61) that 'Friedman neither has nor claims to have a monetary theory'; it also explains why those who write about monetarism have trouble pinning down its theory and tend to describe monetarism as a collection of empirical propositions.) The theoretical attributes that the consistent monetarist considers to be irrelevant and superfluous and that, therefore, good theory must exclude, constitute precisely what the Austrian considers to be the *essence* of monetary theory.

It is hardly surprising that 'monetarist theory' has taken a puzzling, and in some cases bizarre, form. First, in Friedman's major theoretical works (for example, 1956, 1969, 1970) a facade of individualism appears in the analysis of the utility-maximizing individual, but it evaporates (taking with it the crucial Hayekian distinction between economy and catallaxy) when he dismisses distributional effects (for example, 1969, p. 61) so that he can attribute his conclusions to the aggregate. Second, the attempt to develop a monetary theory in which distributional effects are insignificant accounts for the strangest passages in monetarist literature. The most extreme is Friedman's explanation that, even when individuals pick up random amounts of money dropped by a helicopter, 'the ultimate position will be the same, *not only for the aggregate, but for each individual separately...* Nothing has occurred to change the ultimate alternatives open to him. Hence he will eventually return to his former position' (1969, p. 6, original emphasis). While he notes that there will be winners and losers of wealth 'during the period of adjustment', he implies that this period is not likely to be of aggregate significance (and 'eventually' is not even important to any individual). Third, it is not surprising that – from an Austrian perspective – Friedman produces his best theory when he is trying not to be theoretical: in his oral addresses. To explain some of the short- and longer-run effects of monetary change on nominal interest rates and unemployment, for example, he relies on a Wicksell-inspired discussion of causal processes that Austrians applaud but which is quite out of keeping with the rest of his Walrasian theorizing.

Theory, in the sense of causal explanation, simply has an exceedingly uneasy role in monetarism. Friedman recognizes its usefulness, but, despite his famous political and philosophical individualism, his methodological beliefs promote a monetary theory of causal relationships among aggregates. This is the kind of economics that Hayek identified as primitive in 1930, and it explains why many Austrians feel more theoretical kinship with Keynes than with monetarism.

Policy

In spite of these sharp differences in purpose, and therefore in method and theory, the Austrian accepts the general policy recommendation – that neither discretionary monetary nor fiscal policy is helpful – emerging from the monetarist approach. Paradoxically, the latter's scientism produces a case against policy that is theoretically less strong than the Austrians' (lacking their causal-process explanation, imperfect markets, first-round distortions and permanent capital destruction), but more convincing (partly because of the monetarists' emphasis on and impressive presentation of historical facts, and partly catering to and reinforcing widespread scientistic error about the nature and method of social science). The Austrian may, therefore, express a certain ambivalence: gratitude for Friedman's effective role in debunking Keynesian fine-tuning, but regret that his very success lent credence to a method that they believe is considerably worse, not merely than their own, but even than that of Keynes and his disciples.

The goal of the monetarist's monetary policy is the socially optimum conduct of a monopolistic central bank. (The modern free banking, competing currency literature began to emerge near the end of my monetarist period.) Because Austrians emphasize the harmful allocational effects of the injection of the new money that would be needed to maintain price level stability in a growing economy, and generally perceive neither economic nor ethical problems in a slowly falling price level, they are likely to accept only a nominal-money growth rate of *zero* as 'optimum central bank policy'. In a fully Austrian approach, however, monetary policy as such would not exist. The 'quantity of money' would be an unintended outcome of a catallactic process involving individual demanders and suppliers of differentiated monies.

Conclusions

The well-known preference of economists of each school for 'free markets' conceals fundamental disagreement, at the deepest level, between monetarists and Austrians. Each grudgingly accepts the other's support for their common policy prescriptions, and many members of each school have the highest personal respect for leading figures of the other. The schools' primary concerns are – in principle – complementary, but each has strongly identified itself with opposition to important features of the other. Their contrary beliefs about the very nature and method of economics are long-standing and appear to be permanent.

See also:
Chapter 9: Causation and genetic causation in economic theory; Chapter 32: Austrian business cycle theory; Chapter 2: Methodological individualism

Bibliography
Carrington, S. (1992), 'Note Added in Proof: Friedrich August von Hayek, 1899–1992', *American Economic Review*, **82**, (2), May, 36.
Friedman, M. (1953), *Essays in Positive Economics*, Chicago: University of Chicago Press.
Friedman, Milton (1956), 'The Quantity Theory of Money – A Restatement', in Milton Friedman (ed.), *Studies in the Quantity Theory of Money*, Chicago: University of Chicago Press.
Friedman, M. (1969), *The Optimum Quantity of Money and Other Essays*, Chicago: Aldine.
Friedman, Milton (1970), 'A Theoretical Framework for Monetary Analysis', in Robert J. Gordon (ed.), *Milton Friedman's Monetary Framework*, Chicago: University of Chicago Press, 1974.
Friedman, M. (1974), 'Comment on the Critics', in R.J. Gordon (ed.), *Milton Friedman's Monetary Framework*, Chicago: University of Chicago Press.
Friedman, Milton and Anna Jacobson Schwarz (1963), *A Monetary History of the United States, 1867–1960*, Princeton: Princeton University Press.
Gordon, R.J. (ed.) (1974), *Milton Friedman's Monetary Framework*, Chicago: University of Chicago Press.
Hahn, F. (1971), 'Professor Friedman's Views on Money', *Economica*, February, 61–80.
Hahn, F. (1980), 'Monetarism and Economic Theory', *Economica*, **47**, February, 1–17.
Hayek, F.A. (1967), *Prices and Production*, New York: Kelley.
Hayek, F.A. (1974), 'The Pretence of Knowledge' in F.A. Hayek, *New Studies in Philosophy, Politics, Economics and the History of Ideas*, Chicago: University of Chicago Press, pp. 23–34.
Hayek, F.A. (1978), *New Studies in Philosophy, Politics, Economics and the History of Ideas*, Chicago: University of Chicago Press.
Leijonhufvud, A. (1981), *Information and Coordination*, New York: Oxford University Press, pp. 131–202.
Macesich, G. (1983), *Monetarism: Theory and Policy*, New York: Praeger.
Marget, A.W. (1938, 1942), *The Theory of Prices*, New York: Prentice-Hall.
Mises, L. (1966), *Human Action*, Chicago: Henry Regnery.
Reder, M.W. (1982), 'Chicago Economics: Permanence and Change', *Journal of Economic Literature*, **XX**, (1), March, 1–38.

82 Supply-side economics
Roy E. Cordato

What constitutes supply-side analysis can differ a great deal from analyst to analyst and from topic to topic. For example, in the area of monetary policy one can find those generally described as supply-side economists advocating free banking, monetary growth rules, the gold standard and Keynesian style activist policies. Another part of the problem in assessing supply-side economics comes in trying to sift through the misrepresentations of supply-side views that are presented both in the media and, on occasion, by antagonistic non-supply-side economists. In this regard, it is both unfair and wrong to characterize supply-side economics as 'trickle down' economics (whatever that means), or the view that tax policy should attempt to maximize government revenues *à la* Laffer curve, or the even more naive view that tax rate cuts will always bring forth tax revenue increases.

The unifying themes in supply-side economics are not antagonistic to Austrian analysis. Furthermore, the area of broadest agreement among supply siders, that is, tax analysis and policy, is an area in which Austrians can learn a great deal from supply-side economists. There are two principal underpinnings of supply-side analysis. First is the strong belief in Say's Law or, more specifically, the view that the exchange of productive endeavors is what generates the capacity for consumption. Second is the view that fiscal policy should be assessed using the tools of neoclassical microeconomics and not Keynesian demand-side macroeconomics. As one prominent supply sider has described it, 'Supply side economics is merely the application of price theory – so called "microeconomics" – in the analysis of problems concerning economic aggregates – so called "macroeconomics". Its conceptual antecedents are to be found in the work of the classical economists ... Adam Smith and J.B. Say' (Turé, 1982, p. 11).

As noted, the specific area of most wide-ranging agreement among supply siders is tax analysis and policy and that is the area that this discussion will focus on. Reflecting the underlying microeconomics of supply-side tax analysis is a statement often used by supply siders that truly captures the supply-side approach to the subject – that for purposes of economic analysis, 'people aren't taxed, activities are'. On a purely positive level, supply-side economics examines the kinds of activities that different taxes tax or, in other words, penalize. Another way of looking at this is to recognize that all taxes have an excise effect; that is, they penalize some activities relative to others. Positive supply-side economics focuses on the excise effects of different kinds of taxes.

The best known and now most widely recognized of these excise effects is the bias that an income tax creates against all income-generating, that is, productive, activity. Certainly the income tax bias against work effort relative to leisure is now recognized by even those who, generally speaking, are quite antagonistic to supply-side analysis. Less accepted, but equally valid, is the notion that income tax is biased against saving and investment of all kinds. The reason for this lack of recognition is probably twofold. First, the arguments with regard to this issue are slightly more complicated and therefore less easily understood by politicians and media pundits. Second, since saving is done most prominently by businesses and middle- and upper-income individuals, moves to reduce the bias against saving generally have the superficial appearance of being regressive and therefore politically unacceptable. Debates concerning the taxation of capital gains are a continuing example of this.

Normatively, supply-side economists take the position that, to the extent possible, the excise effect of taxes should be minimized; that is, taxation should be neutral with respect to relative prices. But supply-side policy proposals in this regard do not reflect a naive search for *the* neutral tax. The general approach is to identify specific biases, or non-neutralities, and put forward tax proposals that would eliminate those biases. As examples that have particular relevance to Austrian economics, it is instructive to focus on the supply-side justification of consumption-based taxes, in particular the consumed income tax, and by extension their support for expensing, as opposed to depreciating, investment expenditures in determining the more neutral tax base.[1]

These policy prescriptions hinge on the fact that broad-based income taxes inherently bias decision making in favor of consumption and away from saving. It is argued that such taxes 'double tax' saving relative to consumption. More strictly speaking, while an income tax reduces the returns to consumption once, it reduces the returns to saving twice. A simple example can illustrate this. Imagine an individual with $100 in pre-tax income. In the absence of taxation this means that he has $100 available for either saving or consumption. With a simple 10 per cent per annum interest rate, the individual can decide whether he prefers to spend $100 now or $110 a year from now. Austrians would argue that this decision would flow directly from the individual's subjectively determined time preference. If the individual faces a 10 per cent-tax on his initial $100 in income, not only is his return to consumption reduced by 10 per cent, from the utility that he could receive from $100 to the utility that can be gained from $90, but the tax also reduces his potential returns to saving by 10 per cent, from $10 to $9. But a broad-based income tax will reduce his returns to saving a second time because the interest on that saving will also be taxed. Instead of falling to $9, the after-tax return to that saving will fall to $8.10 at the end of the time period. Hence the income tax is non-neutral with respect to the consumption–saving trade-off, institutionalizing a bias against saving.

The supply-side solution to this problem is to exempt either the returns to saving or the amount saved from the tax base. The latter case is known as a consumed income tax (see Schuyler, 1984). In this case, the income is taxed only when it is withdrawn from saving and used for consumption. Analytically the two approaches are equivalent: the returns to both consumption and saving are reduced only by the initial 10 per cent. This is obvious when the returns to saving are exempt outright from the base. In the consumed income tax case, if the $100 were saved it would not be part of the tax base. At the end of the year, $10 in pre-tax interest would have been earned, which would be subject to a 10 per cent tax, assuming it is not reinvested. Hence both approaches to neutralizing this tax bias yield a $9 after-tax return at the end of the year.

It has been argued that, because supply siders advocate tax breaks for all forms of saving, they are attempting to subsidize saving and therefore are engaging in a form of industrial policy. This is an uninformed view. Clearly, the goal of such policies is to eliminate a penalty, not to institute a subsidy.

An interesting corollary to this analysis which dovetails with and enhances Austrian structure of production theory is the supply-side view with respect to the tax treatment of business expenses. It is argued that all business costs should be expensed; that is, they should be deductible in the year that they are incurred, not amortized or depreciated over an extended period of time. Amortization causes a tax bias against 'longer-lived' goods, that is, equipment that wears out over a longer period of time.

Supply siders, sounding very much like Austrians, argue that the standard view, which claims that the cost of assets should be deducted from the tax base only as those assets generate income, ignores the role of time in business decision making. Consistent with the analysis of a consumed income tax, since business expenditures are a form of saving they should not be included in the tax base and the full cost of all productive inputs, including real estate, should be exempt from taxation. If the tax code forces the purchaser of an asset to delay the deduction, the real value of the deduction will be for less than its full cost in present-value terms. Given positive time preferences, a dollar is worth less in the future than it is now. If a construction company purchases a bulldozer for $60 000 this year, immediate expensing will ensure that the full cost is being deducted. If that deduction cannot be taken for five or ten years, then it will be worth less than its full value when it is realized. The longer the depreciation period the greater the difference between the asset's actual value and the value of the tax deduction. Under a depreciation system, an incentive is created to substitute, where possible, the use of shorter-lived assets for longer-lived assets. In other words, given longer- and shorter-lived capital assets with equal pre-tax present values, under a depreciation system the after-tax present value will be greater for the shorter-lived assets. Full expensing eliminates this tax distortion.

Conclusion

The theories reviewed here form the core of supply-side tax analysis and represent the theoretical touchstones for nearly all supply-side tax policy proposals for tax reform, particularly in the areas of saving and investment. This analysis is completely consistent with Austrian methodology and can be invoked by Austrians to enhance their criticisms of the tax system and in formulating their own proposals in the area of tax policy.[2] Supply siders take a more neoclassical approach to capital, with little or no attention to the effects of taxation on the overall time structure of production. It is clear, though, that the supply-side analysis presented here does have implications for the time structure of production and Austrians can clearly enhance and enrich the supply-side analysis by fleshing out these implications.

Notes

1. For a mathematical exposition of these arguments see Ture (1983).
2. It should be pointed out that Austrian critics of supply-side economics have not typically taken the time to understand the arguments presented here. For example Fink (1982, p. 380), in assessing supply-side economics from an Austrian perspective, agrees that there should be tax breaks for saving but on the grounds that, after paying all of their taxes, federal, state and local, people have little left for saving. But in order to support special tax treatment for saving, it must be shown that taxation penalizes saving relative to consumption.

See also:

Chapter 75: Pre-Keynes macroeconomics; Chapter 54: Taxation

Bibliography

Fink, Richard H. (1982), 'Economic Growth and Market Processes', in Fink (ed.), *Supply Side Economics: A Critical Appraisal*, Frederick, Md.: University Publications of America.

Schuyler, Michael A. (1984), *Consumption Taxes: Problems and Promises*, Washington, DC: Institute for Research on the Economics of Taxation.

Turé, Norman B. (1982), 'Supply Side Analysis and Public Policy', in David G. Raboy, (ed.), *Essays in Supply Side Economics*, Washington, DC: Institute for Research on the Economics of Taxation.

Turé, Norman B. (1983), 'The Accelerated Cost Recovery System: An Evaluation of the 1981 and 1982 Cost Recovery Provisions', in Charles E. Walker and Mark A. Bloomfield (eds), *New Directions in Federal Tax Policies for the 1980s*, Cambridge, Mass.: Ballinger.

83 The New Classical economics

Kevin D. Hoover

A clearly discernible school of economic thought since the early 1970s, the new classical macroeconomics, is the product of a twofold reaction to the then reigning 'Keynesian' orthodoxy. On the one hand, it was the culmination of the drive to provide microfoundations for macroeconomics that began shortly after the publication of Keynes's *General Theory*; on the other hand, it was an answer to the perceived failure of econometric macro models and the demand management policies based upon them to cure the ills of stagflation. The essence of the new classical macroeconomics is the belief that the Walrasian general equilibrium model closely approximates the actual behavior of the economy. The new classical assumptions that economic actors are fully rational and that economic information is efficiently processed rule out money illusion; the assumption that prices move rapidly to clear all markets rules out disequilibrium. The real allocation of goods and services depends only on real endowments, real production possibilities and the tastes of consumers for real goods. Without money illusion, the New Classical model-established monetary and fiscal policies that act on nominal income do not possess the control over economic performance that was traditionally assumed in the Keynesian model. Monetary policy can affect inflation, market interest rates and exchange rates, but cannot affect relative prices, real interest rates, real exchange rates, employment or real output.

The stark assertion of the 'classical dichotomy' between the real and monetary economies suggested to some that the new classical macroeconomics was a species of, or perhaps successor to, monetarism. That the earliest new classical articles used the monetarist Milton Friedman's expectations-augmented Phillips curve together with the rational expectations hypothesis to analyse monetary and fiscal policy suggested a close kinship between the two schools. Monetarism, however, shares an aggregative, Marshallian approach to the macroeconomy with Keynesian economics. The 'new' element in the new classical economics is the insistence that only a disaggregative, Walrasian approach will do.

Even today the new classical economics is sometimes identified as the rational expectations school. The rational expectations hypothesis claims that economic agents should not be modeled as making systematic errors in forming expectations. Put differently, agents should be modeled as forming expectations consistent with the forecasts of the maintained model. Although the rational expectations hypothesis, borrowed from the econometrician John Muth (1961), is perhaps the new classical school's only novel addition to the macroeconomists' toolkit, it is nonetheless a subsidiary doctrine. Most new classicals mistakenly regard it as a necessary implication of the general assumption of rationality. Furthermore, the hypothesis is readily detachable, and has been incorporated into Keynesian and other competing models.

From the mid-1970s to the mid-1980s, the new classical macroeconomics intellectually dominated mainstream macroeconomics. Since the mid-1980s, however, it has been challenged by a resurgent new Keynesian macroeconomics that stresses imperfect competition, (rational) failures of markets to clear and coordination failures.

Characteristic doctrines
As already noted, the first substantial achievement of the new classical macroeconomics was to incorporate the rational expectations hypothesis into the expectations-augmented Phillips curve. Friedman and Edmund Phelps had independently argued that output and unemployment would deviate from their natural rates only to the degree that workers mistook inflation for changing relative prices. Robert Lucas argued that the rational expectations hypothesis and flexible prices implied that such mistakes were unsystematic and fleeting.

The new classical analysis of the Phillips curve led immediately to Thomas Sargent and Neil Wallace's (1975) celebrated 'policy-ineffectiveness proposition': aggregate monetary policy could not *systematically* alter real outcomes. At the same time, Robert Barro (1974) argued that deficit finance of government expenditure could not provide real stimulus. Known as 'Ricardian equivalence', Barro's ineffectiveness proposition relied on general equilibrium to ensure that taxpayers faced well-defined intertemporal budget constraints and rational expectations to ensure that they understood the consequences of policy actions. Increased debt, financing a tax cut today, must be paid off with interest tomorrow. Foreseeing this increase in their liabilities, taxpayers will save the extra income from a tax cut to pay future taxes. A tax cut, therefore, does not alter their discretionary income or their expenditure patterns, and so has no real effects.

The Phillips curve represents an inverse relationship between inflation and unemployment. The rational expectations-augmented Phillips curve suggests that this relationship will shift as expectations change in the face of rationally perceived changes in monetary policy. Lucas generalized this insight with his famous 'Lucas critique' (1976). He argued that econometrically estimated relationships between aggregate economic data would not remain stable in the face of changing policies because rational expectations introduce an unaccounted for interdependence between policy rules and underlying behavioral relations. The Lucas critique was at once an explanation of the inability of Keynesian macroeconometric models to predict the effects of changing policy and the foundation for a new classical research agenda. Henceforth, models would be acceptable only if they were grounded in the bedrock of tastes, endowments and technology, so that the microeconomics of general equilibrium and the interdependencies introduced by rational expectations could be accounted for.

Business cycles pose a problem for the new classical economics. Fluctuating output is compatible with continuous equilibrium and the rational expectations-augmented Phillips curve only if the natural rate of output (employment) itself fluctuates. The new classicals universally turn to Robert Solow's neoclassical growth model to provide a propagation mechanism for business cycles. Such a model is always in equilibrium; but, if the capital stock is away from its steady-state growth path, then the optimal path back to the steady state is the slow raising or lowering of the capital stock. Output and employment fluctuate along with capital. Where new classical economists differ amongst themselves is over the source of the initial impulses that drive the capital stock away from its steady-state growth path.

Following on from their work on the Phillips curve, new classical economists (for example, Lucas, 1975) initially looked to monetary fluctuations as the source of business cycles. Observed prices reflect both inflation and relative prices. An increase in the supply of money raises inflation. Under rational expectations, workers and producers with limited information may mistake such inflation temporarily for a favorable increase in their real wages or product prices, and supply more labor and more output, and add to the capital stock. Because capital is long-lived, such unsystematic errors are transformed through the neoclassical growth model into systematic fluctuations of employment and output typical of the business cycle.

Accumulated failures of attempts to verify the 'monetary surprise' hypothesis empirically led to the dominance of 'real business cycle' models. In Finn Kydland and Edward Prescott's (1982) paradigm, real business cycle model, technology shocks replace monetary shocks as the original source of cyclical fluctuations. Systematic fluctuations are amplified in this model through the incorporation of the fact that there is some construction time involved before capital becomes productive and the assumption that labor possesses a high degree of intertemporal substitutability.

The new classical economics and the Austrian school: common themes and radical differences

Lucas (1977) sees new-classical business cycle theory as a successor to Austrian theories of the cycle of the 1930s. In particular, he argues that the monetary version of the new-classical business cycle model is what Friedrich

Hayek (1933, 1935) might have constructed had he had the sophisticated modern tools of mathematical economics. Lucas is surely right to see similarities: both Lucas and Hayek implicate monetary policy as the source of fluctuations, and changing capital structure as their mode of propagation; and both insist on the importance of a microeconomic account in which expectations play a decisive role. Aside from business cycles, common themes recur in both the Austrian and new classical schools: methodological individualism, rationality, the importance of information, the importance of expectations and hostility to aggregative analysis. These similarities are genuine but, nonetheless, superficial. The differences between the schools are fundamental.

First, the new classicals view the economic problem narrowly: how does a Walrasian economy adapt to exogenous or policy-generated fluctuations when tastes, endowments and production possibilities are given? The Austrians conceive of the economic problem more broadly: the economic considerations behind the evolution of technology and social institutions, and the processes through which tastes and expectations are formed, are central to Austrian analysis.

Second, the new classicals take the economist's problem to be to predict or, at least, to emulate the performance of the economy, using precisely defined, quantifiable models. They stress the development of mathematical and statistical technique and emphasize closed, determinate models. The central appeal of the Walrasian general equilibrium framework is that it fosters closure and technical development. In contrast, the Austrians take the economist's problem to be one of understanding (*verstehen*) in which the economist attempts to transfer himself imaginatively into the situation of the economic agent in order to understand the agent's rational action from the inside. The new classical models also claim to take the agent's point of view. In new-classical models, however, agents are represented by their (stable) utility functions and rational choice is reduced to maximization of utility given constraints. Austrians reject such an eviscerated rationality as misplaced scientism. The mechanization of choice is a denial of human action and predictive closure is a denial of human history.

Third, the new classicals treat information as dispersed to just the degree necessary to generate business cycles or induce risk premia or to emulate some other feature of the economy in their models. The Austrians, in contrast, treat the dispersal of information as the fundamental basis of a capitalist economy. The price system can be thought of as a natural adaptation to the complexity of dispersed local information. While the new classicals would agree that prices convey information, the general equilibrium model, upon which they so heavily rely, is highly centralized. The auctioneer (or his mathematical analogue) must know all the relevant quantity information in order to find a market-clearing set of prices. Real economies do not possess such an efficient auctioneer. Command economies do not function efficiently, because centralized processing loses too much of the information necessary to move the right amount of goods to the right places at the right times. The new classicals offer no alternative theory of price formation that would replace the implicit auctioneer in their models.

Fourth, while actively appealing for the reduction of aggregate macroeconomics to disaggregated microeconomics (Lucas, 1987), new-classical economists employ representative-agent models in which one agent (or a few types of agents) stands in for all the agents in the economy, and the aggregate accounting identities are treated as his budget constraint. Such modeling is sham microeconomics, because the representative agent really represents no one. His utility function does not represent average preferences or society's preferences, and taking the aggregate accounting identities as his budget constraint solves the intractable aggregation problem only by ignoring it. In contrast, the Austrians accept the intractable complexity of the economy and eschew prediction. Instead, they seek to understand (*verstehen*) typical economic behavior through the medium of the ideal type. The ideal type differs from the representative agent, because the Austrian economist would never find an ideal type suitable as an element of a determinate, quantified economic model.

Fifth, and finally, for the new classicals, equilibrium is a matter of all prices clearing all markets. For the Austrians, equilibrium is the coincidence of plans and realizations. Both definitions are compatible for an individual. For the Austrians the substance of economics is the account of the way incompatible plans of individuals become coordinated. For Hayek (1937) the issues are to explain, on the one hand, how individuals come to hold the expectations that would have to be confirmed in social equilibrium and, on the other hand, what processes direct the economy towards equilibrium. For Lachmann (1956), the issue is how market institutions evolve to bring about consistency in plans. In either case, equilibrium is an end state and not a thing continuously achieved. In contrast, equilibrium for the new classicals is tautological: an economic explanation *is* an equilibrium explanation; economic actors are *always* doing the best that they can, given the constraints that they face, and the price system *always* coordinates their plans. Again, the Walrasian general equilibrium model allows them to short-circuit the issues central to the Austrians; tâtonnement and the auctioneer (or their functional equivalents) are always assumed to be in place; people are always assumed to have rational expectations; but the mechanisms that ensure the functioning of the one or the possession of the other remain mysterious.

See also:
Chapter 81: Monetarism; Chapter 53: The Phillips curve; Chapter 11: Praxeology; Chapter 4: Market process

Bibliography

Barro, Robert J. (1974), 'Are government bonds net wealth?', *Journal of Political Economy*, **59**, (2), 93–116.

Hayek, Friedrich A. (1933), *Monetary Theory and the Trade Cycle*, translated by Nicholas Kaldor and H.M. Croome, London: Jonathan Cape.

Hayek, Friedrich A. (1935), *Prices and Production*, 2nd edn, London: Routledge & Kegan Paul.

Hayek, Friedrich A. (1937), 'Economics and knowledge', *Economica*, NS, **4**, (1), 33–54.

Hoover, Kevin D. (1988), *The New Classical Macroeconomics: A Sceptical Inquiry*, Oxford: Basil Blackwell.

Kydland, Finn E. and Edward C. Prescott (1982), 'Time to build and aggregate fluctuations', *Econometrica*, **50**, (6), 1345–69.

Lachmann, Ludwig A. (1956), *Capital and Its Structure*, London: Bell.

Lucas, Robert E., Jr. (1972), 'Econometric testing of the natural rate hypothesis', in Otto Eckstein (ed.), *The Econometrics of Price Determination*, Washington, DC: Board of Governors of the Federal Reserve System; reprinted in R.E. Lucas, *Studies in Business Cycle Theory*, Oxford: Basil Blackwell, 1981.

Lucas, Robert E., Jr. (1975), 'An equilibrium model of the business cycle', *Journal of Political Economy*, **83**, (6), 1113–44.

Lucas, Robert E., Jr. (1976), 'Econometric policy evaluation: A critique', in Karl Brunner and Allan H. Meltzer (eds), *The Phillips Curve and Labor Markets*, Carnegie-Rochester Conference Series on Public Policy, vol. 1, Amsterdam: North-Holland.

Lucas, Robert E., Jr. (1977), 'Understanding business cycles', in Karl Brunner and Allan H. Meltzer (eds), *Stabilization of the Domestic and International Economy*, Carnegie-Rochester Conference Series on Public Policy, vol. 5, Amsterdam: North-Holland.

Lucas, Robert E., Jr. (1987), *Models of Business Cycles*, Oxford: Basil Blackwell.

Muth, John F. (1961), 'Rational expectations and the theory of price movements', *Econometrica*, **29**, (6).

Sargent, Thomas J. and Neil Wallace (1975), 'Rational expectations, the optimal monetary instrument and the optimal money supply rule', *Journal of Political Economy*, **83**, (2), 241–54.

84 The new Keynesian economics
Sean Keenan

Theoretical and historical overview

What is new Keynesianism? It is essentially an approach, or the result of that approach, to macroeconomics. That is to say, it is a set of economic theories and observations produced by directing attention towards a few particular analytical themes. Although the arguments which have been developed around these themes are diverse, they give rise to a set of related conclusions about the efficiency of markets. The leading figures include N.G. Mankiw, L.H. Summers and R.J. Gordon. Many economists not generally associated with new Keynesianism have had elements of their work adopted into the framework. Indeed, some of the most important papers have been written by economists who would be unlikely to term themselves 'new Keynesians'.

New Keynesianism has in common with its predecessor, 'Keynesianism', a perspective on market economies as being fraught with rigidities which frustrate the purposes of economic agents and reduce welfare. Nominal supply and demand shocks are seen as having significant and persistent real output effects. The observation that goods and labor markets do not always clear, and the recurrent business cycles experienced by industrialized economies, combine to form a view of the economy as being unable to adjust in order to attain a latent equilibrium. Mankiw (1990) summarizes, 'If there is a single theme that unites Keynesian economics it is the belief that economic fluctuations reflect not the Pareto-efficient response of the economy to changes in tastes and technology, but rather to some sort of market failure on a grand scale.' Although new Keynesianism tends to focus on disequilibrium or non-market-clearing phenomena, analysis is conducted within the standard neoclassical equilibrium framework.

Old Keynesianism was, of course, a complete theory, embodied in Keynes's *General Theory* which posited a specific type of market failure and drew out the implications thereof. The 'belief', then, of the old Keynesians was a belief in the soundness of the theoretical construct as a whole. In the case of new Keynesianism, on the other hand, the unifying belief is plainly prior to the heterogeneous theoretical tissue on which it is based. Its newness is in the first place an historical fact. Without explicitly dating its birth, the 1977 paper of Stanley Fisher on staggered wage contracts is certainly among the early works.

In the second place, the term new reflects the discontinuity which resulted from the complete displacement of Keynesian theory, first by monetarism, and then more completely by new classical theory and the 'rational expectations revolution' of the early 1970s. As a leading new classical economist remarked in an article entitled 'The Death of Keynesianism', 'One cannot find good, under-forty economists who identify themselves or their work as "Keynesian". Indeed, people even take offense if referred to as "Keynesians". At research seminars people don't take Keynesian theorizing seriously, anymore; the audience starts to whisper and giggle to one another", (Lucas, 1983).

The dominance of this new paradigm, with its emphasis on microeconomic foundations, was a problem for Keynesian 'believers', not because it required them to adopt a new theoretical approach, but because it arrived at opposite conclusions, such as the inability of monetary policy to stabilize output. It was against the backdrop of this successful attack on old Keynesianism that new Keynesianism developed. The movement has been called a reincarnation, as opposed to a resurrection: the 'rebirth of Keynesianism into another body' (Mankiw, 1991). This characterization reflects the fact that new Keynesians have not challenged the theoretical advances of new classical macroeconomics in the 1970s. Rather, their program has been to attempt to use the new and accepted insights in constructing arguments in support of the old 'belief'.

These arguments, or 'theories', are grouped around several main themes: (1) price 'stickiness' in goods and factor markets, (2) labor market inefficiencies, and (3) coordination failures. Around each particular theme, these arguments are able to achieve the limited objective of supporting the Keynesian perspective while making use of rational expectations based microfoundations. As a whole, however, the arguments are disintegrated and sometimes inconsistent. In presenting a wide variety of independent theories of market failure, little effort is directed towards quantifying their relative importance.

Menu costs

While a multiplicity of theories of gradual or non-price adjustment have been advanced, a central theme of goods price stickiness is the 'menu cost' argument. This argument recognizes the fact that firms are able to set prices; that is, they are not 'perfect competitors'. However, changing prices is costly to the firm, as a restaurant would be forced to print new menus to display its new prices. If a firm does not adjust its price downward, given a negative demand shock, there will be lower final output than at equilibrium. It is argued (Mankiw, 1985) that, even if such costs are small, the aggregate effect of such rigidities may be to propagate small aggregate demand shocks into large output fluctuations. Under this scenario, since firms are exhibiting profit-maximizing behavior, the menu cost can be seen as a component in the variable cost component of the firm's objective function. As such, it should be expected that firms would choose a technology which minimizes this cost. The empirical fact that, across countries and over time, inflation rates do not correlate well with output reflects, in part, the ability of firms to adapt to environments in which prices must be changed frequently, even daily. These inefficiencies which result from rigid prices have been referred to (Carlton, 1986) as 'costs of using the price system', although they cannot be opportunity costs without a well specified alternative.

The assumption that all firms are monopolistic competitors creates serious problems of aggregation. Demand for individual firms' products fluctuates daily and does not cause recessions. We are here required to conceive of a truly 'aggregate' demand shock for menu costs to play their asserted role in business cycles. Such a shock would have to be distributed broadly over firms in the economy, which precludes the possibility of a purely nominal shock, unless a helicopter drop monetary disturbance is being considered. If these primitive forces are viewed as distributed shocks to real GNP, the theory may shed light on the propagation of shocks, but it certainly cannot claim to be explaining business cycles. Empirical analysis has been offered in support of this theory: work which attempts to measure menu cost effects through the correlation between output fluctuations and price variations. Much of this work has the theoretical bias that absence of price changes are defined as rigidities so that '[prices will be rigid] if supply and demand are unchanging' (Carlton, 1986).

Wage rigidities
New Keynesians, like their predecessors, have directed a good deal of attention to the causes of persistent unemployment, and their explanations focus on the rigidity of nominal wages. Theories of wage rigidity fall into two classes: long-term contract theories and efficiency wage theories. The long-term contract argument simply states that renegotiation costs are sufficiently high to cause rational workers and employees to contract over long periods. Employers of non-contracted workers, admittedly four-fifths of all wage earners (Gordon, 1990), are seen as being bound by 'implicit' contracts defined by the contracts of the outstanding fifth. This leaves open the possibility of an effective monetary policy, in spite of rational expectations, as, at any point in time, only the renegotiating segment of the workforce can act to offset changes in expected inflation.

The efficiency wage theory attempts to provide a microfoundation for involuntary unemployment. Critics of the old Keynesianism 'nominal wage rigidity theory' have focused on the rationality of workers, charging that unemployed workers ought to bid nominal wages down during recessions. The efficiency wage theory focuses on the rationality of employers. It holds that productivity of workers is a function of the wage rate, and that there exists a unique productivity and thus profit-maximizing wage. Wages are therefore sticky, while output and employment are more sensitive to demand shocks, since employers have a disincentive to vary the wage from this optimal level. Although both the wage rigidity and efficiency wage theories are new Keynesian, they are contradictory or, at least, mutually exclusive, since the former assumes wages are set through a negotiation process and the latter holds that they are set by employers.

Coordination failure

The assumption of coordination failure plays a crucial role in new Keynesian economics. A recurrent problem in macroeconomics generally, and new Keynesian economics in particular, is aggregation. As we have seen, the program of new Keynesian economics has been to develop rational micro explanations for rigidities of various kinds. Reassembling these as macroeconomic stories while preserving their logical consistency has been a challenge, frequently met by invoking the coordination failure assumption.

The price rigidities arguments, for example, suggest that nominal demand shocks will have their output effects amplified by sticky prices. If, however, marginal costs fall simultaneously, these output losses could be avoided, menu costs notwithstanding. In particular, there is a specific amount by which the marginal cost curve for any one firm must shift down in order to offset any specific demand shock and leave output unchanged. This has been termed the 'required MC curve' (Gordon, 1990, p. 219). The amplified aggregate output reduction argument, then, rests on the assertion that marginal cost curves generally do not shift sufficiently in the face of these aggregate demand shocks.

This assertion is held to provide an example of the game-theoretic notion of coordination failure, in which agents achieve a suboptimal outcome even though a superior outcome exists, because no mechanism exists through which they can mutually organize their choices of action. Firms, it is claimed, will not adjust prices down because they 'have no reason to believe that their multiplicity of suppliers will adjust the prices of intermediate goods instantly in response to demand shocks' (Gordon, 1981).

Use of the static game theory example as an analogy requires us to believe that aggregate demand shocks occur instantaneously, requiring all firms either to lower prices or not, together. Further, it requires us to believe that firms would rather go out of business than lower their prices, while at the same time believing that the reason they do not adjust their prices is to avoid instantaneous bankruptcy. Otherwise prices generally, and therefore marginal costs, would tend to move lower as soon as aggregate demand began to shift. This could serve as a signal providing a coordinating device for price setters. The fact that economic activity generates prices which *do* provide such signals and are the *principal vehicle* by which firms and agents obtain information about the conditions of supply and demand, is neglected in this approach.

There is certainly a sense in which coordination failure can affect macroeconomic outcomes: dynamic Hayekian coordination failure. The extent to which individuals cannot systematically acquire information which would improve their choice of actions, either because of institutional barriers or simply because such information is dispersed, is a macro- as well as a microeconomic problem. However, the new Keynesians have not relied on such an explanation, nor have they offered any reason why such coordination failure should be affected by aggregate demand shocks.

Conclusions and policy implications
Throughout new Keynesian literature, and in keeping with traditional Keynesianism, is the emphasis on the importance of aggregate nominal demand shocks. The genetic cause of these shocks is not explored rigorously, yet it is easy to understand in an intuitive heuristic sense that demand is unlikely to be stable over time. On the other hand, the characterization of any such fluctuation as a 'shock' raises questions about the relative magnitude of such disturbances. In particular, a possible internal inconsistency of the general new Keynesian perspective turns on this issue. If, as has been argued, prices are highly resistant to change, and if, in addition, workers are explicitly or implicitly locked into nominal wages, what is the source of shifts in consumer behavior of such magnitude and suddenness as to be considered 'shocks'? It would seem on the basis of the underlying economic characteristics stressed by the new Keynesians that stability ought to be the rule, and that 'shocks' ought to have readily identifiable causes.

The general policy implications of new Keynesianism following from their consistent assertion of market failures naturally suggest an active role for government in managing the macroeconomy. More specific policy conclusions are difficult to derive as the various new Keynesian theories imply different and even contradictory policy recommendations. For example, the staggered wage contract theory suggests that, in spite of rational expectations, expansionary monetary policy can be effective in reducing unemployment. Since the efficiency wage theory implies that demand shocks can cause amplified unemployment effects which may propagate into a recession, we seem to have matched a policy tool with a welfare need. On the other hand, the welfare loss attributable to menu costs is alleged to be substantial. These costs tend towards zero, however, as the general price level is stabilized, since that would eliminate the need for firms to engage in costly price adjustments. Thus we have a strong argument against the use of expansionary monetary policy, with its consequent pressure on prices, as a method of stimulating the economy.

Management through an active fiscal policy is equally problematic in an environment with wage and price rigidities. Some new Keynesians advocate both monetary and fiscal stability in spite of perceived market failures. L.H. Summers (1989), writing about the unemployment problem, says, 'expansionary aggregate demand policies are unlikely to be able to reduce it to the levels of the 1950s and 1960s without creating excessive inflationary pressures'.

Thus new Keynesianism does not offer much in the way of alternative arrangements for economic interaction. Nor does it provide a clear set of policy recommendations. What can be said about the substantial body of work which falls under the umbrella of new Keynesianism is that it investigates macroeconomic market failure and seeks to establish microeconomic foundations for it. Perhaps because of the difficulties inherent in aggregation, or because of the difficulties of research which attempts to utilize heterogeneous and competing theories to support an *a priori* belief, the new Keynesian paradigm seems to have lost in the early 1990s the momentum it gained in the early 1980s.

See also:
Chapter 75: Pre-Keynesian macroeconomics; Chapter 68: The Hayek–Keynes macro debate

Bibliography
Carlton, D.W. (1986), 'The Rigidity of Prices', *American Economic Review*, September, 113.
Fisher, S. (1977), 'Long-term Contracts, Rational Expectations, and the Optimal Money Supply Rule', *Journal of Political Economy*, 85.
Gordon, R.J. (1981), 'Output-Fluctuations and Gradual Price Adjustment', *Journal of Economic Literature*, **XIX**, June, 526.
Gordon, R.J. (1990), *Macroeconomics*, 5th edn, Glenview, IL.: Scott, Foresman.
Lucas, Robert E. Jr. (1983), 'The Death of Keynesian Economics'.
Mankiw, N.G. (1985), 'Small Menu Costs and Large Business Cycles: A Macroeconomic Model of Monopoly', *Quarterly Journal of Economics*, May, 529–39.
Mankiw, N.G. (1990), 'A Quick Refresher Course in Macroeconomics', *Journal of Economic Literature*, **XXVIII**, December, 1654.
Mankiw, N.G. (1991), 'The Reincarnation of Keynesian Economics', National Bureau of Economic Research Working Paper 3885, p. 5.
Summers, L.H. (1989), 'Why is the Unemployment Rate So Very High, Near Full Employment?', *Brookings Papers on Economic Activity*, vol. 2, p. 359.

85 The neo-Ricardians

Fiona C. Maclachlan

The neo-Ricardians share with the Austrian school a dissatisfaction with contemporary mainstream economics and, as with the Austrians, the reaction is to go back in the history of economic thought and pick up the neglected trails of earlier economists. But while the Austrians go back only as far as Menger, the neo-Ricardians go back beyond the marginalist revolution to the era of classical economics. The trail they wish to pick up can be traced back to Sir William Petty and Richard Cantillon and runs through Quesnay, Adam Smith, Ricardo and Marx. The central notion of this classical approach is that of a '"social surplus" or "net product" which is defined as the total produce of the economy minus the requirements of productive consumption (i.e. the material requirements of production and for the sustenance of labour)' (Bharadwaj, 1988, p. 80).

Since Marx there has been a continued interest in the surplus approach. The publication in 1960 of Piero Sraffa's *Production of Commodities by Means of Commodities* (PCBMC), however, gave the approach new momentum and generated a discernible school. Sraffa's other accomplishments include collecting and editing Ricardo's writings and providing a new interpretation of the Ricardian theory of profits. The strong association between Sraffa's name and that of Ricardo is, no doubt, the reason the school inspired by the PCBMC has been dubbed neo-Ricardian. Sraffa, however, objected to the label on the grounds that it plays down the role of Marx and others besides Ricardo in the development of the surplus approach (Eatwell and Panico, 1987, p. 451). The core of PCBMC had been sketched out by Sraffa by the late 1920s (Sraffa, 1960, p. vi) before he had begun work on Ricardo, with the inspiration appearing to derive from Marx's schemes of reproduction from volume 2 of *Capital* (Potier, 1991, p. 60).

Sraffa's model consists of a system of simultaneous equations. Each equation has, on the left-hand side, the sum of the values of the inputs required to produce a given amount of output of a commodity and, on the right-hand side, the value of that amount of output. The inputs consist of homogeneous labor and commodities. The value of the commodity inputs enters each equation multiplied by one plus the rate of profit. The given variables in the system are the levels of outputs, the technical coefficients indicating how much of each input is required to produce the given output, and one of the two distributive variables, either the rate of profit or the wage. Sraffa shows how the system can be solved to determine the prices of the commodities and the remaining distributive variable.

When Sraffa's slim volume was published, it received mixed reviews. Many economists believed that he had merely rediscovered the Non-Substitution Theorem, which says that if (1) labor is the only primary factor, (2) there are no joint products and (3) constant returns to scale prevail, then for any given rate of profit the prices of goods will be independent of demand conditions. Economists with an interest in the surplus approach, however, believed Sraffa accomplished much more. Meek (1961), for instance, argues that Sraffa provides Marx's theory of the origin of profits as the extraction of surplus labor, a more rigorous presentation. Under this view Sraffa's important innovation was the construction of a standard system and its associated standard composite commodity.

The standard system is derived from the actual system of input–output equations by (1) eliminating all the equations for non-basic goods (that is, goods that do not enter, either directly or indirectly, into the production of all other goods); (2) finding a set of multipliers, such that, by multiplying each input–output equation by one of these multipliers, one creates a system in which the ratio of the aggregate amount of a commodity used in production to the aggregate amount of that commodity produced, is constant across all goods; and (3) multiplying the whole new system by a scalar so that the aggregate labor inputs sum to one. The standard composite commodity is a commodity bundle made up of goods in the same ratio to one another as is the total output of the standard system. The standard ratio (R) is the ratio of the difference between the value of total output in the standard system and the value of the commodities used in its production, to the value of the commodities used in production.

Sraffa finds that if the wage (w) is measured in terms of the standard commodity, then the rate of profit (r) of the actual system will be given by $r = R(1 - w)$. A feature of this expression that the surplus theorists find appealing is that it shows that distribution can be determined without reference to any marginal productivity principle. Moreover, it shows that the change in the rate of profit associated with a change in the wage rate is independent of any change in price. Since neo-Ricardians often take wages to be determined outside the model by institutional factors, they assert, on the basis of Sraffa's expression, that distribution is 'logically prior' to pricing. One should note, however, that the wage in Sraffa's expression is measured in terms of the standard commodity and it is not usually reasonable to assume that the wage will be given by institutional factors measured in such terms. For this reason, Sraffa (1960, p. 33) himself took the standard commodity wage to be an endogenous variable and instead took the rate of profit as given from the outside, by the banking system.

Besides providing a rigorous alternative to the neoclassical theory of value and distribution, Sraffa is also credited by his followers with isolating a fatal flaw in the neoclassical theory of the rate of profit (or interest). In particular, Sraffa attacks Böhm-Bawerk's notion that interest is related to the period of production, or the degree of 'roundaboutness' of the production process. Sraffa demonstrates the possibility of double-switching within the Böhm-Bawerkian scheme. He considers two techniques with different degrees of 'roundaboutness' and shows how it is possible that one of the techniques will be optimal at two different rates of profit, while the other will be optimal at an intermediate rate. The possibility of double-switching means that one cannot assert, as Böhm-Bawerk does, that the rate of profit is determined by the period of production.

For Austrians who adhere to Böhm-Bawerk's theory of capital and interest, Sraffa's critique represents a serious challenge. Many Austrians, however, do not subscribe to the theory. Schumpeter (1954, p. 847, fn.8) reports how Menger told him once that 'the time will come when people will realize that Böhm-Bawerk's theory is one of the greatest errors ever committed'. Similarly, the Austrian pure time preference theorists maintain that, after his effective refutation of capital productivity explanations of interest, Böhm-Bawerk's own theory constitutes a surprising reversion.

The ground on which the neo-Ricardians and the Austrians have a much clearer disagreement is at the level of methodology. The basic questions of theory construction, such as what abstractions are useful, what questions a theory should address, and even what sort of statements constitute a theory, cannot be resolved through appeal to facts or logic. But on these questions the gulf between the neo-Ricardians and the Austrians is so wide that there appears little hope of any communication on more substantive issues in economics.

Probably the most striking difference between the neo-Ricardians and the Austrians is on the role of subjective factors. Both schools perceive an inconsistency in Marshall's synthesis of the subjectivist demand theory of Jevons and Menger with the objective cost of production theory of the classical economists. But while the Austrian answer is to make costs subjective, the neo-Ricardian chooses to remedy the inconsistency by amputating the demand side and ridding value theory of any appeal to subjective factors. The neo-Ricardian objection to including subjective factors in economic theory is that they are unobservable (Eatwell and Panico, 1987, p. 445) and that a better theory can be constructed employing only the observable or objective economic factors. While it is true that a theory which has resort only to observable phenomena would be easier to test and would give economics a closer alliance to the more respected physical sciences, it is not clear that neo-Ricardian theory always achieves its ideal. Sraffa's model, for instance, does not claim to explain actual observable prices but rather only their long-period or 'center of gravity' values. Neo-Ricardians allow that, in the short period, prices may be bid away from their center of gravity values by subjective and other factors, so that what we observe may differ from what the theory predicts. Either the neo-Ricardian must admit that his theory does not explain observable phenomena or he must append to the long-period theory a theory that incorporates unobservable factors like preferences and expectations. If he chooses the latter tack, he cannot so readily reproach the subjectivist economist. Moreover, he must convince the subjectivist economist that the two neo-Ricardian theories – one for the short period and one for the long period – are preferable to one, more encompassing, subjectivist theory.

If the key concept in Austrian economics is subjectivism, the key concept in neo-Ricardian economics is the idea of a social surplus. And just as neo-Ricardians are committed to a theory free of subjectivism, Austrians are determined to theorize without resort to concepts like the social surplus. The idea of a social surplus rubs against the Austrian tenet of methodological individualism. Explanations are supposed to be conducted in terms of individual actions and decisions; but the social surplus is an aggregate that does not enter into any individual's preferences or constraints. Thus for an Austrian it is irrelevant. A related reason that an Austrian might be uncomfortable with the concept is that it is based on the idea of the economy 'reproducing' itself. By definition, the social surplus is the difference between the output of an economy and the requirements for its reproduction, be it simple (stationary) or expanded (growing). From an Austrian perspective, the question is why we should be interested in the features of an economy that reproduces itself if, in reality, the economy is constantly evolving and responding to change. The neo-Ricardian models appear more fitting for primitive agricultural economies in which outputs and methods of production change only slowly. The difference between the two schools on this issue involves a difference in the level of abstraction that is judged appropriate.

The role played by gravitation in the neo-Ricardian theory is another methodological issue on which the two schools diverge. For the neo-Ricardian, gravitation is an axiom of the theory, not a result (Schefold, 1988, p. 111). In Austrian theory, however, the emphasis is on the process though which something like the neo-Ricardian notion of gravitation plays itself out. The Austrian will often specify an equilibrium position, but the focus of the theory is not so much in characterizing the equilibrium as in demonstrating that a market process exists through which it is approached. In Austrian theory, the market process through which the gravitating forces operate is central; whereas, in neo-Ricardian theory, the operation of the gravitating forces is kept in the background and the focus of the theory is on specifying the final position.

Further differences in basic theory construction arise in the treatment of distribution. As we discussed earlier, the neo-Ricardian regards distribution as logically prior to the pricing of the final output; that is, distribution can be explained, in neo-Ricardian theory, without resort to the theory of the determination of prices of commodities. For the Austrian, in contrast, distribution concerns the question of the pricing of the factors of production and the factors of production are thought to derive their value from the value of the output that they cooperate to produce. Thus the Austrian would regard as inadmissible any theory in which distribution is logically prior to pricing.

Finally, there is a significant rift between the two schools on what sort of statements are thought to constitute a theory. For an Austrian, economic theory elucidates the connection between the actions of individuals and the economic phenomena to which they give rise. The method is one of setting out causal stories in which economic phenomena are traced to their roots in individual action. The neo-Ricardian, on the other hand, looks at the system as a whole and then draws conclusions about the way the various phenomena fit together. The method, like that of neoclassical general equilibrium theorists, is the construction of a mathematical model. While Austrian theory generates statements of a causal nature, the neo-Ricardian theory generates mathematical relations.

Given the radically different approaches of the neo-Ricardians and the Austrians, there appears little hope for communication between the schools, or for much profit from looking at one another's work. Some awareness of one another, however, does serve the purpose of making us sensitive to the importance of methodological judgement in conditioning our theories and allows us to fully appreciate the vast difference of opinion on fundamental issues of theory that still exists within the economics profession.

See also:
Chapter 67: The debate between Böhm-Bawerk and Hilferding; Chapter 31: Capital theory; Chapter 3: Subjectivism; Chapter 9: Causation and genetic causation in economic theory

Bibliography

Bharadwaj, K. (1988), 'Sraffa's Ricardo', *Cambridge Journal of Economics*, **12**, 67–84.
Eatwell, J. and C. Panico (1987), 'Sraffa, Piero', in J. Eatwell, M. Milgate and P. Newman (eds), *The New Palgrave: A Dictionary of Economics*, volume 4, London: Macmillan.
Meek, R.L. (1961), 'Mr Sraffa's rehabilitation of classical economics', reprinted in *Economics and Ideology and other Essays: Studies in the Development of Economic Thought*, London: Chapman Hall, 1967.
Potier, J. (1991), *Piero Sraffa, Unorthodox Economist (1898–1983): A Biographical Essay*, London: Routledge.
Schefold, B. (1988), 'The dominant technique in joint production systems', *Cambridge Journal of Economics*, **12**, 97–123.
Schumpeter, J.A. (1954), *History of Economic Analysis*, edited from manuscript by E.B. Schumpeter, New York: Oxford University Press.
Sraffa, P. (1960), *Production of Commodities by Means of Commodities. Prelude to a Critique of Economic Theory*, Cambridge: Cambridge University Press.

86 The new monetary economics

Tyler Cowen and Randall S. Kroszner

The 'new monetary economics' (Hall, 1982a) refers to a broad set of writings that examine alternative or 'innovated' models for providing financial services, without recourse to traditional concepts of money, within an unregulated economy. Different strands of this view have also been labeled 'legal restrictions theory of money' (Wallace, 1983, 1988) and the 'BFH system' (Greenfield and Yeager, 1983; Yeager and Greenfield, 1989), where the letters BFH refer to Black, Fama and Hall. The new monetary economics (NME) is best understood as a series of questions rather than a definite set of answers. Writings in the new monetary economics consider various aspects of the following propositions:

1. The provision of monetary services is conceptually distinct from the provision of money (a unified medium of account and exchange). Provision of monetary services through laissez-faire is a useful analytical benchmark for monetary theory.
2. Two of the traditional functions of money (medium of account and medium of exchange) need not be united in a single asset called 'money'. The medium of account could be a commodity basket, may coincide with only a small percentage of circulating exchange media or may be abstract in nature. In these economies traders use media of exchange that do not have predefined nominal values in terms of the economy's media of account. Marketable financial assets serve as exchange media and are explicitly priced with advanced transactions technologies and electronic transfer systems.
3. The removal of legal restrictions on private financial intermediation would alter the properties of a financial system. Fischer Black (1970, p. 9) has asserted that alternative institutional frameworks 'would make current monetary theory almost completely invalid', and that, in a laissez-faire economy, 'money in the usual sense would not exist'. Both the quantity theory of money and the Keynesian liquidity preference theory hold only under a regime based on specific sets of legal restrictions. The emphasis on legal restrictions leads many NME theorists to the view that 'money is exactly a creature of regulation' (Hall, 1982a, p. 1554).
4. The separation of medium of account and exchange under laissez-faire mitigates macroeconomic disturbances by integrating the monetary and

real sectors of the economy. NME systems could also lead to a competitive choice of accounting media.

5. Financial intermediation will evolve away from traditional shareholder banks and towards mutual fund banks and commercial credit lending. The rise of liquid financial markets and securitization allows liquidity transformation and monitoring functions to be performed outside traditional banking institutions. In mutual fund banks, depositors possess legal title to financial assets that are traded through a clearing-house system and depositors are residual claimants on the value of assets held. Bank runs are impossible because the value of bank liabilities fluctuates in step with the value of bank assets. Mutual fund banking proposals of this nature have been examined by Fama (1980), Goodhart (1987), Glasner (1989) and Cowen and Kroszner (1990, 1993).

A brief history of the new monetary economics

The modern form of the new monetary economics originates in Fischer Black's seminal article, 'Banking and Interest Rates in a World Without Money' (1970). In this essay, Black considered the use of a sophisticated barter system, based on transactions technologies that dispense with cash. Black believes that the American economy is heading towards such a state of affairs, as a result of the rapid growth of electronic funds transfers, interest-bearing checking accounts, checkable money-market fund accounts, and other cash-economizing devices. In another paper, Black (1981) examined another innovated system, one which uses a commodity bundle medium of account to stabilize the price level.

Although initially neglected, Black's analyses were developed later by Fama (1980), Hall (1982b), Greenfield and Yeager (1983) and Yeager and Greenfield (1989) with their BFH system. Hall, Greenfield and Yeager focus on monetary reform and examine it using a commodity basket medium of account as a means of increasing price level stability. Greenfield and Yeager's commodity basket medium of account would be comprised of many different commodities, insulating the price level from supply and demand shocks to any particular commodity, such as gold. Merchants would post prices in terms of this commodity bundle medium and private banks would issue accounts denominated in terms of this bundle. Most likely, these claims would not be directly redeemable in terms of the bundle but rather in value-equivalent terms of some other asset which is easier to handle and store ('indirect convertibility'). Governmental 'compensated dollar' plans (following Irving Fisher) and smaller, less comprehensive commodity bundles with direct convertibility represent other policy options related to the BFH system.

The BFH system has come under criticism from several quarters. McCallum (1985), in a general survey critical of the new monetary economics, questions whether the plan provides price level determinacy, although he does not consider indirect convertibility systematically. White (1984, 1986, 1989) argues that the BFH system requires government intervention because individuals are unlikely to switch voluntarily to a commodity bundle medium of account, away from a dollar or gold-based medium; Greenfield and Yeager (1986) respond by arguing that government intervention is in any case necessary to dismantle current institutions. Schnadt and Whittaker (1993) and Cowen and Kroszner (1993) analyse whether attempts to stabilize the price of a commodity bundle are vulnerable to speculation and arbitrage opportunities. If commodity prices are sticky, bank commitments to stabilize the price level may require them to sell redemption media at below the open market price. Furthermore, Cowen and Kroszner (1993) argue that price stabilization breaks down if market participants prefer regional and sector-specific media of account and exchange rather than convergence on a single common bundle. The above arguments suggest that restrictions on monetary competition may be needed to implement a stable BFH system.

The legal restrictions theory
In a series of separate developments, Neil Wallace and several colleagues (including John Bryant, John Kareken and Thomas Sargent) constructed a legal restrictions theory of money at the University of Minnesota and the Federal Reserve Bank of Minneapolis. The legal restrictions theory asks why interest-bearing assets do not displace non-interest-bearing currency completely. Under laissez-faire, either all exchange media bear interest or the nominal rate of interest is bounded by the costs of breaking down large-denomination bonds into smaller-denomination monetary claims. These results follow from the imposition of a zero-profit condition on private financial intermediaries. In several articles (see Wallace, 1983, 1988, for surveys) these authors construct models where large-denomination bonds can be broken down into smaller monetary denominations. Incorporating the costs of money/bonds arbitrage in this fashion modifies traditional results of monetary theory. A money growth rule, for instance, must involve restrictions on private credit creation and is not consistent with a Pareto optimum. In other cases, open market operations may be neutral (a result drawn from Modigliani–Miller reasoning) or may even cause the price level to fall (if the government can break down bonds into money more cheaply than the private sector can and thus save on intermediation costs).

Extending Wallace's work, Cowen and Kroszner (1993) consider the macroeconomic properties that arise when all exchange media bear pecuniary returns. The money/bonds distinction disappears and the monetary and real sectors become one and the same, bringing about an optimum quantity of money. A version of Say's Law holds and Keynesian monetary theory is no longer valid because liquid assets also earn pecuniary returns (see Burstein, 1991). The interest rate no longer expresses the opportunity cost of holding money and the IS and LM curves cannot be defined independently. These same macroeconomic properties cannot be achieved through implementing Friedman's optimum quantity of money rule with government currency. The governmental recipe for the optimum quantity of money also integrates the monetary and real sectors but implies that the currency issuer, government, must own society's capital goods.

Critics of the legal restrictions theory include White (1984, 1987, 1989) and O'Driscoll (1985). These authors question whether interest payments on small-denomination claims are worth the transactional costs and whether non-interest-bearing currency will ever disappear. Furthermore, if the costs of money/bonds intermediation are sufficiently high, intermediation costs, while placing a maximum value on the nominal interest rate, do not provide the binding maximum constraint, as the models of Wallace and his co-authors suggest. McCallum (1983) also criticizes the overlapping generations models used by Wallace and others, claiming that these models ignore money's medium of exchange role.

An evolutionary approach to the NME
Cowen and Kroszner (1987, 1993) attempt to synthesize Black, Menger and Wallace with an evolutionary approach to monetary theory, emphasizing the market development of the separation of monetary functions. In their *Explorations in the New Monetary Economics*, Cowen and Kroszner examine how money and finance are likely to evolve in a pure market context. With their evolutionary approach, Cowen and Kroszner offer the most 'Austrian' version of the new monetary economics among extant writings.

Cowen and Kroszner (1993) build on Carl Menger's (1892) theory of the origins of money by considering what might evolve from current monetary and financial institutions. Menger's theory explains how monetary economies originated from barter through an invisible hand process, but stops there. Monetary history illustrates that the marketability of various assets continually changes. Assets that were once suitable for use as liquid media of exchange are superseded eventually by competing assets. Similarly, today's exchange media may someday be displaced as well. The evolution of money and finance is a continuing process that does not stop with the development of a generally accepted medium of exchange from barter. Drawing on Benjamin Anderson's (1917) criticism of Austrian monetary theory, Cowen and Kroszner (1993) argue that the growth of a monetary economy itself enables the development of alternative monetary institutions. Advanced transactions technologies, liquid spot and futures markets, and the development of financial intermediaries all contribute to the replacement of one set of exchange media by another. Through evolution, each set of financial and monetary institutions contains the seeds of its own destruction.

In this synthesis of Black, Menger and Wallace, pecuniary returns motivate the displacement of current exchange media in a deregulated environment. The superior pecuniary returns of financial assets give market participants an incentive to increase their marketability and convenience. Financial assets become convenient for transactional use and replace current exchange media. The use of currency as a physically traded medium of exchange will dwindle and may eventually disappear, even if the dollar remains as an abstract or 'ghost' medium of account.

In lieu of a single dominant medium of exchange, Cowen and Kroszner (1993) argue that unregulated markets will offer a variety of liquid financial assets with different risk–return properties and convenience services. Individuals will construct their preferred portfolios by choosing from a menu of competitively supplied exchange media, and use risk-hedging devices as desired. Firms that issue exchange media compete against each other to supply media that command high marketability premia. At the same time, transactions technologies eliminate the inconveniences of multiple media of exchange. Similarly, multiple media of account will coexist under a regime of monetary competition. Market participants choose media of account for informational reasons, to minimize the costs of price stickiness and to achieve desired risk-sharing arrangements. Multiple media of account are also used in credit relationships to construct desirable risk–return positions at low cost. Optimum medium of account areas, analogous to Robert Mundell's optimum currency areas, evolve to serve efficiency. In this regard, Cowen and Kroszner (1993) synthesize the new monetary economics with the Hayekian idea of currency competition.

Drawing on a series of earlier articles (1987, 1992), Cowen and Kroszner (1993) also trace the antecedents of the new monetary economics through the history of economic thought. A number of earlier writers, including Henry Meulen, Arthur Kitson, Benjamin Anderson, Knut Wicksell, Robert Liefmann and Heinrich Rittershausen, anticipated many later developments and added innovative twists of their own. Earlier writers from classical economics with affinities to the new monetary economics include James Steuart, Jeremy Bentham and some writers in the real bills doctrine tradition. The new monetary economics offers a promising future for analysing financial institutions and a lengthy and illustrious past in the history of economic thought.

See also:
Chapter 59: Free banking; Chapter 61: Financial regulation; Chapter 34: Financial economics

Bibliography
Anderson, Benjamin M. (1917), *The Value of Money*, New York: Macmillan.

Black, Fischer (1970), 'Banking and Interest Rates in a World Without Money', *Journal of Bank Research*, autumn, 9–20.

Black, Fischer (1981), 'A Gold Standard with Double Feedback and Near-Zero Reserves', reprinted in *Business Cycles and Equilibrium*, New York: Basil Blackwell.

Burstein, Meyer Louis (1991), *The New Art of Central Banking*, New York: New York University Press.

Cowen, Tyler and Randall Kroszner (1987), 'The Development of the New Monetary Economics', *Journal of Political Economy*, June, **95**, 567–90.

Cowen, Tyler and Randall Kroszner (1990), 'Mutual Fund Banking: A Market Approach', *Cato Journal*, Spring/Summer, **10**, 223–37.

Cowen, Tyler and Randall Kroszner (1992), 'German-Language Precursors of the New Monetary Economics', *Journal of Institutional and Theoretical Economics*, September, **145**, 387–410.

Cowen, Tyler and Randall Kroszner (1993), *Explorations in the New Monetary Economics*, Boston: Basil Blackwell.

Fama, Eugene F. (1980), 'Banking in the Theory of Finance', *Journal of Monetary Economics*, January, **6**, 39–57.

Glasner, David (1989), *Free Banking and Monetary Reform*, Cambridge: Cambridge University Press.

Goodhart, Charles (1987), 'Why Do Banks Need a Central Bank?', *Oxford Economic Papers*, March, **39**, 75–89.

Greenfield, Robert and Leland Yeager (1983), 'A Laissez-Faire Approach to Monetary Stability', *Journal of Money, Credit and Banking*, August, **15**, 302–15.

Greenfield, Robert and Leland Yeager (1986), 'Competitive Payments Systems: Comment', *American Economic Review*, September, **76**, 848–9.

Hall, Robert (1982a), 'Monetary Trends in the United States and the United Kingdom: A Review from the Perspective of New Developments in Monetary Economics', *Journal of Economic Literature*, December, **20**, 1552–6.

Hall, Robert (1982b), 'Explorations in the Gold Standard and Related Policies for Stabilizing the Dollar', in Robert Hall (ed.), *Inflation: Causes and Effects*, Chicago: University of Chicago Press.

McCallum, Bennett T. (1983), 'The Role of Overlapping Generations Models in Monetary Economics', *Carnegie-Rochester Conference Series on Public Policy*, spring, **18**, 9–44.

McCallum, Bennett T. (1985), 'Bank Deregulation, Accounting Systems of Exchange, and the Unit of Account: A Critical Review', *The New Monetary Economics, Fiscal Issues and Unemployment*, Carnegie-Rochester Series on Public Policy, autumn, **23**, 13–45.

Menger, Carl (1892), 'On the Origin of Money', *Economic Journal*, June, **2**, 239–55.

O'Driscoll, Gerald P., Jr. (1985), 'Money in a Deregulated Financial System', *Economic Review*, Federal Reserve Bank of Dallas, May, 1–12.

Schnadt, Norbert and John Whittaker (1993), 'Inflation-Proof Currency? The Feasibility of Variable Commodity Standards', *Journal of Money, Credit, and Banking*, **25**, (2), 214–21.

Wallace, Neil (1983), 'A Legal Restrictions Theory of the Demand for "Money" and the Role of Monetary Policy', *Federal Reserve Bank of Minneapolis Quarterly Review*, Winter, 1–7.

Wallace, Neil (1988), 'A Suggestion for Oversimplifying the Theory of Money', *Economic Journal*, conference volume, 25–36.

White, Lawrence H. (1984), 'Competitive Payments Systems and the Unit of Account', *American Economic Review*, September, **74**, 699–712.

White, Lawrence H. (1986), 'Competitive Payments Systems: Reply', *American Economic Review*, September, **76**, 850–53.

White, Lawrence H. (1987), 'Accounting for Non-Interest-Bearing Currency', *Journal of Money, Credit, and Banking*, November, **19**, 448–56.

White, Lawrence H. (1989), 'What Kinds of Monetary Institutions Would a Free Market Deliver?', *Cato Journal*, fall, **9**, 367–91.

Yeager, Leland B. and Robert L. Greenfield (1989), 'Can Monetary Disequilibrium Be Eliminated?', *Cato Journal*, fall, **9**, 405–21.

PART V

CONCLUSION

87 Alternative paths forward for Austrian economics

Peter J. Boettke

The *Foundations of Modern Austrian Economics*, published in 1976, was the defining work in the resurgence of the Austrian school in the 1970s. The hundredth anniversary of Menger's *Principles* in 1971, Mises's death in 1973, and Hayek's Nobel Prize in 1974 focused attention on the contributions of this school of thought in the history of the discipline, but it was *The Foundations* which served as the focal point for renewed interest among younger scholars. The book was comprised of the lectures given by Israel Kirzner, Ludwig Lachmann and Murray Rothbard at a conference organized in 1974 to introduce a new generation of scholars to the basic teachings of the Austrian tradition. An essay by Gerald O'Driscoll and Shuda Shenoy on the macroeconomic events of the mid-1970s was added to the published collection to demonstrate the strength of the Austrian approach in comparison with the Keynesian model of the then dominant neoclassical synthesis. The Keynesian model had been repeatedly called into question in the face of the stagflation of that period. In addition, Edwin Dolan, the book's editor, provided an introductory essay which attempted to place the Austrian school within the Kuhnian characterization of scientific revolutions.

In Thomas Kuhn's classic work on progress in the natural sciences, *The Structure of Scientific Revolutions* (1962), scientific work is divided into *normal* and *extraordinary* science. Most practicing scientists uncritically accept the basic premises of the dominant paradigm. Their attention is focused on working out solutions to the problems which the received wisdom throws up at them. Normal science consists of this routine behavior and, during periods of normal science, progress takes place in small incremental steps of improved explanations of the problems which the paradigm allows the scientist to pursue. But an essential tension in scientific progress exists between the necessity to train young scientists in the standard practices and basic principles of the discipline, and the desire to innovate and overturn existing practice and principles.

New ways of looking at phenomena or new questions to be raised demand paradigmatic shifts. Extraordinary science is the attempt by some within the community of science to work within an alternative paradigm to the mainstream. Scientific revolutions occur when the dominant paradigm is confronted by troublesome anomalies which an alternative paradigm is better suited to explain. The displacement of one paradigm by another reflects the revolutionary moment and the process by which leaps in the progress of knowledge occur.

Kuhn's account of scientific revolutions has been the subject of debate for over three decades. Some have discounted his story of progress in the natural sciences, others have questioned the applicability of Kuhn's theory to the history of the social sciences. Nevertheless, it is useful to reconsider what Dolan was attempting in his introduction. His conjecture was that Austrian economics was extraordinary science – an alternative paradigm that could displace the dominant paradigm of neoclassical economics circa 1970. In the Kuhnian story, normal science takes place in scientific journals; extraordinary science is conducted largely outside the mainstream journals and predominantly in books. The displacement of one paradigm by another is the result of a lingering anomaly which the current mainstream simply cannot explain. Looking at this simple story it is easy to see the logic behind Dolan's argument.

Austrian economics was predominantly a *book culture*, and not journal-oriented. By the 1950s and 1960s, the mainstream journals were simply no longer as receptive to Austrian-style arguments as they may have been in the period from the 1880s to the 1940s. In the post-Second World War era, most of the best work in the Austrian tradition was in books, such as Ludwig von Mises's *Human Action*. This was especially true among the latest generation of Austrian economists. Murray Rothbard's *Man, Economy and State*, *America's Great Depression* and *Power and Market*, and Israel Kirzner's *The Economic Point of View, An Essay on Capital* and *Competition and Entrepreneurship* reflected this general point about books rather than journals. Moreover, the stagflation of the 1970s could not be explained by the neo-Keynesian model and the received wisdom concerning a stable trade-off between inflation and unemployment. Socialist countries suffered economic inefficiencies and political repression, which the neoclassical model of market socialism did not predict and could not explain. The conditions were ripe for a Kuhnian revolution in economics, and Austrians seemed as likely as anyone else to offer the alternative paradigm. Dolan's essay possessed a certain argumentative weight which one would be hard pressed to deny.

This Kuhnian story, however, breaks down at precisely this juncture, as neoclassical economics proved to be unbelievably elastic in the coming years. The neoclassical approach came to be defined as a set of technical assumptions and not predictions or conclusions derived from those assumptions. The neoclassical approach employed unflinchingly three assumptions: (1) maximizing behavior, (2) stable preferences, and (3) equilibrium. The macroeconomic anomalies of the 1970s were explained by working out the implications of models built on these assumptions. Keynesianism was overturned, but that was because it was not neoclassical enough. New Classic Economics was born as the traditional assumptions of neoclassical microeconomics were consistently applied to macroeconomic phenomena. What took place in the 1970s was not a paradigm replacement as much as a paradigmatic completion – the expansion of the basic paradigm of mainstream microeconomic thought until the entire discipline of economics was subsumed. Despite the blip of interest, and the growing number of younger scholars attracted to the school, Austrian economics did not replace neoclassical economics – it stayed on the periphery of the profession throughout the 1980s.

Many of the same conditions exist today, in the 1990s, as existed 20 years ago. Mainstream economics cannot explain satisfactorily the dynamics of market activity, let alone the recurrence of macroeconomic crises, the problems of interventionism and regulation, the fiscal crises of democratic welfare states, the failure of development planning and the collapse of socialist regimes in the late 1980s. These anomalies, however, are not treated as a serious threat to the dominant approach to economics analysis. Austrian economists seem to be well situated to offer an alternative, but unable to crack the formidable edifice of the academic establishment in economics.

Despite the shock wave of external events of the mid- to late 1980s, mainstream economics remains undaunted. In fact, neoclassical economics is in the process of going through a new transformation. A fashionable contemporary research strategy is to build models employing the standard assumptions of maximizing behavior and stable preferences, but to introduce some selective realism (such as strategic behavior, imperfections in knowledge and imperfect competition). Economists following this research program are able to generate different equilibrium states than the ones traditionally derived – with the corresponding differences in the welfare implications implied (the Folk theorem from game theory, in fact, states in essence that any equilibrium outcome is possible to derive). The most obvious of these current developments are the challenge to New Classic Economics offered by new Keynesianism (for example, Joseph Stiglitz and Lawrence Summers) and the challenge to the doctrine of free trade offered by the new international trade theory (for example, Paul Krugman). Both new Keynesianism and new trade theory, however, are neoclassical developments; as such they do not replace the dominant paradigm, but revise it slightly. The techniques and basic questions are the same, but the subsidiary assumptions and the conclusions are different.

Like these modern developments in thought, the Austrian school could also be seen as a slight variant on the mainstream. Despite Austrian criticisms of neoclassical models for lack of realism, and so on, Austrians are firmly within the rational choice camp of social science (a theme we will return to later). Rather than maximizing behavior, stable preferences and equilibrium, the core assumptions of Austrian economics are (1) purposive behavior, (2) demonstrated preference, and (3) process analysis. Austrian economists could rework the mainstream results under this alternative set of assumptions (and all that they imply concerning subjectivism, knowledge, expectations and the passage of real time) and derive different conclusions about market behavior and public policy. As economists *qua* economists, in fact, that is much of what Austrians do. There is, though, something troublesome with limiting one's view of Austrian economics to such a description, not the least of which is the fact that, if mainstream economics is found seriously wanting in its portrayal of human behavior, and an alternative paradigm for the social sciences is sought, then Austrian economics will be thrown out along with the mainstream of economics.

In addition, mainstream economists do not seem that interested in the alternative results Austrians can derive – at least as reflected in what articles one can get accepted in the prestigious journals, such as the *American Economic Review* or the *Journal of Political Economy*. New Keynesian and new trade theorists do not have trouble getting into the leading journals, but there simply have not been many articles in these journals for the past 40 years which one could describe as contributions to the development of Austrian insights. Most of the articles by the younger generation of Austrians that have appeared in the top professional journals are *strategic* articles. These articles take the form of either 'tenure articles' (that is, articles which do not even pretend to advance Austrian ideas but rather pass the professional test needed to earn tenure) or 'synthesis articles' (articles which find a sympathetic trend within the mainstream and then try to build a bridge to Austrian ideas – which are usually hidden in the footnotes). Both of these activities are respectable scientific endeavors and, given the modern academic environment, they are not just respectable but essential for maintaining the institutional base of the school within the research community. Despite their strategic importance, however, these articles in themselves do not represent the kind of scientific work required to advance an Austrian understanding of the economic and social world.

Uniquely Austrian arguments do have outlets in the scholarly book market. University presses and independent scholarly publishing houses find that a market exists for Austrian work. Libraries, historians of ideas, interdisciplinary scholars, other non-mainstream economists, public policy intellectuals and an interested lay audience provide enough of a market to support the continued publishing of Austrian books. Explicit Austrian works have been published by Cambridge University Press, University of Chicago Press, Oxford University Press, New York University Press, Basil Blackwell, John Wiley, Kluwer Academic, Westview Press, Greenwood Press, Routledge and Edward Elgar within the past two decades.

These books must meet an external referee process, just as articles in the journals do. The difference is that the 'language barrier' in the academic book market is not as imposing as that which exists in the journals. Austrian economics is 'verbal' and not mathematical. That should not be taken to imply non-formal, for the arguments presented in Austrian works can be quite formal, but they are not mathematical. The leading journals in the profession seem to have adopted mathematical reasoning as the universal language of economic science. Since the questions Austrian economists desire to ask for the most part do not lend themselves to mathematical formulation, their work is systematically eliminated from the top journals. As a result, Austrian economics remains a book culture, rather than a journal-oriented school of thought. It is still in books that progress in Austrian economics is made and conveyed to others.

This prognosis does not mean that there do not exist opportunities for scholars to do innovative work in economics and the social sciences, and to improve the insights of the Austrian school within the journals. My own assessment, however, is that in the near term the most significant work in Austrian economics will continue to be conveyed through books or in field journals and non-mainstream general journals. The *Review of Political Economy* is one of the most important new outlets for subjectivist work. *The Review of Austrian Economics* represents a forum for Austrian scholarship in the tradition of Murray Rothbard. *Advances in Austrian Economics*, a research annual edited by Israel Kirzner, Mario Rizzo and myself, also promises to be an important outlet for Austrian-oriented research and other subjectivist schools of thought. Opportunities exist in more traditional outlets as well, and there is hope that even more will appear in the future as Austrians continue to advance their understanding of economic and social organization and present their arguments more persuasively. One of the goals of scientific endeavors is continually to expand readership and, thus, increase influence within the community of scholars. That can only occur by addressing one's arguments to the general community of scholars and not insulating oneself from the criticisms or rejection of the profession. It would be a scientific disaster if Austrian economists tried to shelter themselves from the theoretical and empirical arguments of mainstream and other non-mainstream economists.

As I mentioned in the introductory essay to this volume, Austrian economics is really just a set of questions and a basic attitude about the best way to attempt to answer those questions. This *Companion* provides the reader with a sampling of the basic theoretical arguments and conceptualizations developed by scholars working in the Austrian tradition to address the scientific concerns of the school. But, unless Austrians can change the basic questions which other economists consider worth asking, then the mainstream of economics will remain impervious to the Austrian message. Many of the philosophical beliefs that crowded out Austrian economics in the past have been demonstrated to be flawed views of scientific progress and the growth of knowledge. In the wake of post-positivist philosophy of science, Austrian economists should be able to get a better hearing for their views on the economy and society.

In my introduction, three distinct research stratagems within Austrian economics were identified: (1) technical economics, (2) philosophical radicalism, and (3) interdisciplinary social theory. I argued that within the finest contributions in the history of the Austrian school one often finds these three stratagems woven together. Nevertheless, it is useful to separate them and see where opportunities for further development of Austrian insights may lie in the future. The contemporary trend in mainstream economics mentioned above seems to me to offer a tremendous opportunity for comment from Austrian scholars. In fact, I am working on a book manuscript which critically surveys these developments from an Austrian perspective, tentatively titled, 'The Trend in Economic Thinking and Public Policy' (1993b). The focus of attention on theoretical work in new Keynesianism and new international trade theory is predicated on the belief that what we are currently witnessing is a 'revolution' in economic thought not unlike the one pioneered by Paul Samuelson in the late 1940s. I do not mean here a Kuhnian paradigmatic revolution, but rather the passing of the mantle of 'expert' and 'standard bearer' of good science from one set of scholars to another who practice within the same basic paradigm. In the 1980s, Robert Lucas, Thomas Sargent and Robert Barro were the 'experts'; in the 1990s expert status has shifted to Joseph Stiglitz, Lawrence Summers and Paul Krugman.

What does it take to generate a 'revolution'? First, the individual scientist must demonstrate brilliance and, second, he must be quite strategic. In the late 1940s, Samuelson rewrote economic theory employing mathematical techniques. He saturated the journals with his articles, he soon captured graduate education with his *Foundations*, and then he captured undergraduate education with his *Principles*. Samuelson's name became synonymous with American economics, and he was accordingly the first American to win the Nobel Prize in economics, in 1970. Milton Friedman would arguably displace Samuelson in the 1970s and 1980s as the most recognizable public persona in economics, but he did not have in place the 'weapons' in terms of textbooks to really challenge Samuelson on the educational front. Friedman's monetarist views (which he always claimed merely represented an empirical difference of opinion with Keynesianism and *not* theoretical differences) became part of the basic education in economics, and certainly his 'Essay on Positive Economics' was on the reading lists of all first-year graduate students. But Friedman did not displace Samuelson as the guiding light in economic technique and research strategy. Robert Lucas, for example, argued as much when he stated that what he represented was basically a combination of Friedman's *Capitalism and Freedom* – which gave him his political perspective – and Samuelson's *Foundations* – which taught him how to do economic science – in his interview with Arjo Klamer (see Klamer, 1983).

Starting in the 1970s and continuing in the 1980s, Joseph Stiglitz captured the top professional journals. It is probably safe to say that no other individual has contributed to as many fields within modern economics as Stiglitz. Accordingly, Stiglitz was the John Bates Clark Award winner in 1979 – recognition by the American Economic Association of the economist under 40 years of age who has made the most significant contributions. Graduate training in economics is mainly done through familiarity with the formal techniques and the relevant journal literature; books have little or nothing to do with the formal education of economists any more, except for those books which teach technique. Stiglitz is clearly the dominant figure in the journals, having contributed seminal articles in pure theory, as well as in the various subfields from market structure theory to macroeconomics to public economics to development economics. In the mid-1980s, he became the editor of the *Journal of Economic Perspectives*, one of the three journals of the American Economic Association and the one professional journal charged with conveying the cutting edge of research to an audience beyond the academic community – to journalists, government officials and students of economics. In 1993, Stiglitz published his *Economics*, which summarizes the developments in economic theory he has pioneered over the past two decades, and which he terms the 'new economics'. If I am correct in my assessment, then the period from the 1990s on will be the Stiglitz era. Microfoundations of macroeconomics based on imperfect information and imperfect markets will define the dominant research program in the coming years.

In that case, those working within the Austrian tradition need to direct their attention towards this work. The Stiglitz revolution is based on building economic models using the standard techniques but with the assumptions of imperfect information, strategic interaction and imperfect market structure. Austrians find themselves in a peculiar situation since they are largely in agreement with Stiglitz's criticism of the 'unrealism' and inadequacy of the perfect competition core of traditional neoclassical economics, but do not find the theoretical implications of the Stiglitzian alternative promising. Imperfect market structure theory and its implications for antitrust policy, the new trade theory and its arguments for strategic trade policy, New Keynesianism and the efficiency wage theorem, and the new theory of market socialism all find antecedents in Stiglitz's work in pure theory. Moreover, Stiglitz has made fundamental contributions to all these developments. If Austrians want to be 'players' in the modern debates, they must address the theoretical and public policy arguments that follow from this variant of neoclassical economics. Esteban Thomsen's *Prices and Knowledge* (1992), which contrasts the developments in information economics pioneered by Stiglitz and Sanford Grossman with the Austrian contribution, is an excellent start to addressing the contemporary trend in economic thought.

Besides commenting on these modern developments within the economics profession, Austrians have ample opportunity to improve their own technical arguments in several important areas of theoretical economics. Perhaps the unique core of Austrian market process theory is its understanding of the capital-using economy. Hayek's *The Pure Theory of Capital* was only supposed to be a first volume of a promised two-volume work. *The Pure Theory* was the static volume, volume two was to provide a dynamic theory of the capital structure – one not so wedded to equilibrium theorizing. This project remains incomplete.

There are certain substantive propositions from Austrian capital theory that can be usefully employed to make points within the mainstream literature. Capital is not homogeneous, as assumed in standard growth theory, but rather heterogeneous and possesses specific uses. Unique combinations of capital goods form the capital structure in any economy. Modern technical issues of complementarity and fit worked on by Paul Milgrom, along with the work on technological lock-in and increasing returns associated with Brian Arthur, can all be addressed and redressed from an Austrian capital theory perspective.

A more dynamic Austrian theory of the capital-using economy, combined with the theoretical propositions that (1) a large portion of the relevant knowledge for economic decision making within an economic system is conveyed through relative price movements, and (2) money is inherently non-neutral, would also set the stage for a modern reconstruction of Austrian trade cycle theory that can be offered as a viable alternative to contemporary theories of the business cycle, including real business cycle analysis. Not only would real business cycle analysis be challenged, but Austrians would also be able to offer an empirically meaningful discussion of unemployment that differed from the one provided by new Keynesianism.

A reconstructed Austrian capital theory would also serve as the basis for an alternative perspective on development economics (see, for example, Boettke, 1994). With the collapse of communism, questions of development and the transition to capitalism have moved to the center stage of applied economics and public policy. Austrian economists should take full advantage of the opportunity to push their own unique perspective on these pressing issues of the day (see, for example, Boettke, 1993a). Moreover, Austrian economics possesses a certain comparative advantage in these discussions. Throughout the history of the school it has always paid significant attention to the political and legal infrastructure of social organization. Economic development is primarily a question of political and legal institutions, and cultural practices, not foreign aid or government planning. Journals such as *The Journal of Comparative Economics* and *Economic Development and Cultural Change* are important research outlets that may be receptive to tightly reasoned arguments that convey an Austrian perspective on these issues.

The traditional Austrian concern with the institutional environment suggests that the work of new institutionalism should be particularly relevant to scholars seeking to further develop Austrian economics (see, for example, Eggertsson, 1990). Journals such as the *Journal of Institutional and Theoretical Economics, Journal of Law, Economics and Organization* and *Journal of Economic Behavior and Organization* represent important outlets for research. The new economic history of Douglass North (1981, 1990), the new political economy associated with public choice scholars such as James Buchanan and Gordon Tullock, and the literature on organization and management that follows the work of Oliver Williamson (1985) and Paul Milgrom and John Roberts (1992) all represent current research trends to which Austrians can make significant contributions.

Law and economics is another field in which Austrians have a natural affinity. In the Viennese educational system, economics was not a separate degree from law. Both Mises and Hayek, for example, possessed doctorates in law, though they specialized in economics. Hayek's *The Constitution of Liberty* and *Law, Legislation and Liberty* offer important insights into the structure of law and legal institutions, and their impact on economic performance. Hayek's argument for the necessity of rules over discretion in a complex world has influenced legal scholars such as Richard Epstein. Moreover, Hayek's arguments about the common law – much different from the efficiency arguments made by neoclassical law and economics scholars – could be clarified and stressed within the literature (see, for example, Aranson, 1992). *The Journal of Legal Studies* and *The Journal of Law and Economics* should be receptive to an Austrian approach to law and economics, as the work of Mario Rizzo has proved (see, for example, Rizzo, 1980).

Industrial organization and money and banking represent the two mainstream fields where Austrian economists have made significant contributions in the past two decades. Modern industrial organization, however, has come to be dominated by game theorists (see, for example, Fisher, 1991). The kind of industrial organization that Austrian economists could contribute to has now been subsumed under the heading of 'new institutionalism', which has already been mentioned. On the other hand, money and banking still seems open to Austrian contributions. The whole development of the literature on free banking was spawned by Lawrence White's economic history research on the Scottish banking system and his theoretical argument concerning the feasibility of the system based on earlier monetary theories of Menger, Mises and Hayek (see White, 1984, 1989). Much work still needs to be done in this area, but White's research has opened up the field so that research on alternative monetary regimes can find an outlet in mainstream journals such as *The Journal of Money, Credit and Banking*.

The problem with these inroads into the mainstream journals is that they will be short-lived unless the basic methodological biases of the profession are changed. Israel Kirzner, for example, could produce seminal work on the nature of market processes, but, unless it is mathematically represented, most economists will still not consider it a contribution to economic *theory*. The same is true for the various contributions in specific fields such as money and banking, industrial organization and comparative economic systems. An interesting idea, unless captured in mathematical form, will simply remain an interesting idea and not a contribution to scientific economics according to most economists. But what if the interesting idea defies mathematical formulation? Unfortunately, despite abundant evidence to the contrary, many economists still do not believe that this is possible.

That is why methodology and the history of thought is vitally important. The contributions to technical economics will not get their proper hearing unless the philosophical position of the Austrians with regard to the human sciences is respected. Thus the second stratagem within Austrian economics of philosophical radicalism is necessary. Staking a philosophical claim against mainstream economics helps build bridges and improve one's argument in ways that otherwise would be overlooked. First, Austrians are not the only economists disillusioned with mainstream economics. Second, even among those not disillusioned there are some who find the philosophy of economics to be an interesting vocation. Both of these groups are potential allies in an intellectual battle to make economics a more philosophically aware discipline.

Economic methodology has become a subfield within the economics profession. Those attracted are often historians of economic thought, but that does not have to be true. Methodologists can stand on their own. Bruce Caldwell, Lawrence Boland, Wade Hands, Arjo Klamer, Don McCloskey and Daniel Hausman are just a few of the names associated with modern research in economic methodology. Historians of economics such as Mark Blaug, Warren Samuels and A.W. Coats have also made important contributions to methodology, and are often able to place modern economics within a broader perspective than is generally appreciated by modern practitioners. *Economics and Philosophy, History of Political Economy*, the *Journal of the History of Economic Thought, Methodus* and *Research in the History of Economic Thought and Methodology* represent the major outlets through which research in this field is conveyed to other scholars. Scholars can spend a fruitful lifetime of research engaged in economic methodology nowadays, but this research, despite its extremely high quality of argumentation, has to date had very little impact on the economics profession at large.

Part of the philosophical radicalism strategy is coalition building with other heterodox schools of economics. Post Keynesians, institutionalists, neo-Ricardians and Marxists can agree with Austrians that neoclassical economics must be replaced by a more philosophically sophisticated and realistic economics. The *Review of Political Economy*, mentioned above, is such an effort at coalition building among the various schools of subjectivist economic thought. *The Cambridge Journal of Economics* is another outlet which is open to the various heterodox schools. Building an effective coalition to challenge the hegemony of neoclassicism, however, is only the first stage, for once the neoclassical paradigm is deconstructed the question will then be which alternative paradigm will replace it.

The technical economics and the philosophical radicalism strategy are related to each other in a symbiotic manner and are not in conflict. The technical Austrian economist needs the Austrian philosopher of science to legitimize the questions he wants to ask about the economic and social order. The Austrian philosopher of science, on the other hand, needs the Austrian technical economist to provide him with the theoretical system he intends to offer as an alternative to competing paradigms.

The interdisciplinary social theory strategy combines the first two strategies and seeks to bring Austrian insights to additional disciplinary audiences. Mises, for example, saw his contribution to the development of Austrian economics as an extension (and correction) of the social theory project of Max Weber. Praxeology, according to Mises, was a general theory of human action; economics was simply the most developed branch of the discipline. In this sense, Mises represents one of the pioneers of modern rational choice theory. The point was to develop a unified theory of the social sciences with the purpose of doing history. This aspect of Mises's thought has usually been overlooked in the current generation of both neo-Weberians and rational choice theorists (see, however, Holton and Turner, 1989, pp. 30–67). This ignorance of Mises's connection to these research programs provides a great opportunity for young scholars. The whole movement to develop stronger connections between economics and sociology represents one of the more interesting areas of research in contemporary social science (see, for example, Swedberg, 1990). Moreover, the field of comparative historical sociology may actually be the most appropriate avenue for Austrians to present their views on social development and change.

Peter Berger's Institute for the Study of Economic Culture (ISEC) at Boston University, for example, supports detailed historical and ethnographic research on the pattern of economic development throughout the less developed world. ISEC's scholars examine the political, legal and cultural infrastructure that leads to economic progress in some regions, while deterring progress in others. Berger has described this endeavor as a search for a theory of 'comparative cultural advantage' (see Berger, 1986). Austrian economics possesses several substantive propositions concerning the effect of alternative social institutions on human behavior that could form the core of the theory Berger is looking for.

In this regard, the interdisciplinary social science journal, *Critical Review*, edited by Jeffrey Friedman, represents an important outlet for Austrian economists as they develop their unique theoretical arguments concerning the nature of economic, political and social processes and apply these theoretical structures in empirical investigations of the social world and move their research agenda into the area of comparative historical political-sociology.

The return of 'grand theory' in sociology, as represented in James Coleman's *The Foundations of Social Theory* (1990), provides an additional opportunity for Austrians to further develop praxeology along the lines laid out by Mises. Coleman's rational choice sociology possesses all the strengths and weaknesses that standard neoclassical economics possesses. This is natural, given the strong mutual influence that exists between Coleman and Gary Becker. From an Austrian perspective, the basic problem with the Coleman project – despite his claims to the contrary – is that he relies on an undersocialized view of the individual (atomistic maximizing) to construct an oversocialized view of the system (functionalism). Praxeology, on the other hand, provides an evolutionary social theory alternative to functionalist theories of society. Carl Menger's theory of the origin of money provides, as Mises put it, 'the elucidation of fundamental principles of praxeology and its methods of research' (1966, p. 405).

Coleman also edits the journal, *Rationality and Society*, which is an interesting publication. Historical, political, sociological and methodological articles have appeared in its pages. The first two issues in 1993, for example, contain a symposium on Alfred Schütz (the Austrian economist–sociologist) and a symposium on the role of emotions. Rational choice theory has opened the door for innovative theorists such as Robert Frank (economics) and Jon Elster (political science) to discuss broad conceptual issues in the social sciences within a systematic structure of argumentation. These scholars are talking about the same problems that interest Austrian economists, but from a different perspective. An Austrian twist should find a hearing. It remains up to Austrians to involve themselves in the conversation.

Not only rational choice sociology, but also rational choice political science can be reconstructed along praxeological lines. The new political economy associated with scholars such as William Riker, Kenneth Shepsle, Robert Bates, Peter Ordeshook, Barry Weingast and others provides important insights into the nature of political processes and organizations. This school of thought, however, is too closely wedded to the core assumptions which define the neoclassical paradigm for modeling human behavior. Basic results of this line of research in political science must be rethought under the alternative perspective of the Austrians. Weingast's research, for example, has already broken out of the neoclassical mold to a considerable degree and is more consistent with a new institutionalist perspective, especially his political economy history work with Douglass North (see, for example, North and Weingast, 1989) and his recent work on the economic role of political institutions (see, for example, Weingast, 1993). The further development of praxeology requires that a theory of political and social processes be developed and fully incorporated into the Austrian theory of market processes.

The interdisciplinary social theory strategy may also entail developing a unique Austrian twist on moral and political philosophy. One of the most egregious errors committed in the various obituaries of F.A. Hayek was the lack of attention paid to the economic roots of his political philosophy. Hayek's political philosophy was grounded in his understanding of the basic teachings of Austrian economics. Without our understanding these Austrian roots, his political philosophy seems to degenerate into some form of Burkean conservativism. But Hayek was predominantly *not* a Burkean. He was in this respect, as in so many others which have been misunderstood, a Misesian (see, for example, Boettke, 1990).

Mises's commitment to liberalism also followed directly from his understanding of the nature of economic processes and the problems inherent within socialism and interventionism. 'Liberalism, in its 19th century sense,' Mises wrote, 'is a political doctrine. It is not a theory, but an application of the theories developed by praxeology and especially by economics to define problems of human action within society' (1966, pp. 153–4). The moral foundations of the liberal society were to be found, according to Mises, in the generalization of the basic principles governing the division of labor and social cooperation. Henry Hazlitt's *The Foundations of Morality* was built upon Mises's, and other liberal thinkers', utilitarian arguments concerning social order. Hayek gave his own non-rationalist twist to the argument in *The Constitution of Liberty, Law, Legislation, and Liberty* and *The Fatal Conceit*.

Some modern Austrian writers, particularly Murray Rothbard, have argued that the utilitarian foundation of political and moral philosophy in these other Austrian works was seriously flawed. Instead, natural rights theory is offered as an alternative. Other writers have suggested that social contractarianism provides the most solid grounds from which to study the moral and political foundations of liberalism. The contractarian approach to moral and political philosophy is another example of the further development of rational choice theory.

The Social Philosophy and Policy Center at Bowling Green State University, with its journal, *Social Philosophy and Policy*, has emerged as one of the leading forums for research along these various lines of a reconstructed liberalism. Other journals are also open to these styles of argument. *Ethics, Economics and Philosophy* and *Constitutional Political Economy* are just a few of the journals where the kind of discussion alluded to above can be found.

There is quite a bit of work that Austrian economists can occupy themselves with as we approach and enter the twenty-first century. Challenges abound in the realm of pure theory, applied theory and historical interpretation and public policy. It is certainly not a dearth of new ideas nor a lack of new directions for scholars to pursue that represents a deterrent to the advancement of Austrian-oriented research in the social sciences. The fate of Austrian economics lies in the hands of its practitioners. It is up to those of us who find this approach persuasive to produce the high quality scholarship that will in turn persuade other scholars. Our research will be judged by others within the general intellectual community on how robust Austrian theory is in meeting the challenges thrown at it by events in the world and the theories of other social scientists. The coming fin de siècle offers nothing but great promise for the further development and acceptance of the Austrian school of economics.

Bibliography

Aranson, Peter (1992), 'The Common Law as Central Economic Planning', *Constitutional Political Economy*, **3**, fall, 289–319.
Berger, Peter (1986), *The Capitalist Revolution*, New York: Basic Books.
Boettke, Peter (1990), 'The Theory of Spontaneous Order and Cultural Evolution in the Social Theory of F.A. Hayek', *Cultural Dynamics*, **3**, 61–83.
Boettke, Peter (1993a), *Why Perestroika Failed: The Politics and Economics of Socialist Transformation*, London: Routledge.
Boettke, Peter (1993b), 'The Trend in Economic Thinking and Public Policy', unpublished manuscript, New York University.
Boettke, Peter (ed.) (1994), *The Collapse of Development Planning*, New York: New York University Press.
Coleman, James S. (1990), *The Foundations of Social Theory*, Cambridge, Mass.: Harvard University Press.
Dolan, Edwin (ed.) (1976), *The Foundations of Modern Austrian Economics*, Kansas City: Sheed & McMeel.
Eggertsson, Thrainn (1990), *Economic Behavior and Institutions*, New York: Cambridge University Press.
Fisher, Franklin (1991), 'Organizing Industrial Organization: Reflections on the *Handbook of Industrial Organization*', *Brookings Papers: Microeconomics*, 201–25.
Holton, Robert and Bryan Turner (1989), *Max Weber on Economy and Society*, London: Routledge.
Klamer, Arjo (1983), *Conversations with Economists*, Totowa, NJ: Rowman and Allanheld.
Kuhn, Thomas (1962), *The Structure of Scientific Revolutions*, Chicago: University of Chicago Press.

Milgrom, Paul and John Roberts (1992), *Economics. Organization and Management*, Englewood Cliffs, NJ: Prentice-Hall.

Mises, Ludwig von (1966), *Human Action: A Treatise on Economics*, 3rd rev. edn, Chicago: Henry Regnery.

North, Douglass (1981), *Structure and Change in Economic History*, New York: Norton Publishing.

North, Douglass (1990), *Institutions, Institutional Change and Economic Performance*, New York: Cambridge University Press.

North, Douglass and Barry Weingast (1989), 'The Evolution of Institutions Governing Public Choice in 17th Century England', *Journal of Economic History*, **49**, 803–32.

Rizzo, Mario (1980), 'Law Amid Flux: The Economics of Negligence and Strict Liability', *Journal of Legal Studies*, **9**, 291–318.

Stiglitz, Joseph (1993), *Economics*, New York: W.W. Norton.

Swedberg, Richard (1990), *Economics and Sociology*, Princeton: Princeton University Press.

Thomsen, Esteban (1992), *Prices and Knowledge*, London: Routledge.

Weingast, Barry (1993), 'The Economic Role of Political Institutions', unpublished manuscript, Hoover Institution on War, Revolution and Peace, Stanford University.

White, Lawrence H. (1984), *Free Banking in Britain: Theory, Experience and Debate, 1800–1845*, New York: Cambridge University Press.

White, Lawrence H. (1989), *Competition and Currency*, New York: New York University Press.

Williamson, Oliver (1985), *The Economic Institutions of Capitalism*, New York: Free Press.

Index

action (praxeology), science of 15,
    77–82, 216, 289
action theory 66–7
Addleson, M. 100
Adler, Mortimer 331
advertising 156–7, 158–9, 383–4,
    389–93
affirmative action 362–70
Alchian, Armen A. 152
Allen, Peter M. 550
Allen, R.G.D. 90
Alsop, Stewart 332
Althusius, Johannes 337, 339–40
Andersen, P.W. 188
Anderson, Benjamin 596
anti-discrimination measures 362–70
apriorism 33–7, 529–30
Aquinas, Thomas 487, 489
arbitrage 149, 201
Arbitrage Price Theory 236
Aristotelian methodology 33–7, 462,
    463
Aristotle 34, 36, 44, 489, 491
Armentano, Dominick T. 97, 131, 135,
    244, 246, 247, 382
Arndt, Helmut 500, 501, 506
Arrow, Kenneth 48, 49, 52, 119, 152,
    188, 291
Arthur, Brian 608
asset specificity 174
atomism 56–8
Auspitz, J. Lee 91
Austrian economics
    development of 1–4
    future directions for 601–14
    see also individual topics
autopoiesia 190
Axelrod, Robert 270, 278
axiomatic models 52
Azpilcueta, Martin de 488, 490

Bachelier, Louis 231
balance of payments 249–53
Ballestrem, K. 338

banks 403, 434–5, 609–10
    free 406, 408–13, 414–18, 609–10
    regulation of 419–23
bargaining 262
    costs of 182–6
Barro, Robert 577
Barzel, Yoram 140
Bastiat, F. 354
Batemarco, R. 219, 221
Baumol, W.J. 106, 277
Beck, Lewis White 41
Becker, Gary S. 264, 296–7, 298
Bellante, D. 259, 261, 262, 369, 375
Benson, Bruce L. 270, 272, 274, 275
Berger, Peter 611–12
Bergner, Jeffrey T. 51
Bergson, Henri 70, 111, 112, 113, 115
Berle, Adolph A. 397, 422
Bernardino of Siena, St. 488
Bernouilli, Daniel 52
Bernstein, Peter L. 231
Bernstein, Richard J. 81
beta risk measurement 236
Bharadwaj, K. 588
Black, Duncan 285, 291
Black, Fischer 231, 593, 594
Błaszczyk, Barbara 453
Block, Walter 123
Bode, K. 69
Boettke, Peter J. 54, 228, 518, 519,
    529
Böhm, Franz 509, 512–13
Böhm-Bawerk, Eugen von 1, 43, 64,
    65, 69, 89, 90, 104, 129, 209, 210–
    13, 214, 216, 226, 324, 325, 465–9,
    590
Bork, Robert 244, 246, 382, 399
Bostaph, Samuel 460
Boudreaux, Donald J. 181
boundaries of the firm, theory of 173–
    8
Boyer, R. 562
Bratman, M. 67
Brentano, Fritz 35, 36

617